HISTORIA
de la
NUEVA MÉXICO

Pasó Por Aquí
Series on the Nuevomexicano Literary Heritage
Edited by Genaro M. Padilla and
Erlinda Gonzales-Berry

Title page to 1610 edition of *Historia de la Nueva México*.

Courtesy of the University of New Mexico General Library, Center for Southwest Research.

Historia de la Nueva México, 1610

Gaspar Pérez de Villagrá

A Critical and Annotated Spanish/English Edition
Translated and Edited by Miguel Encinias,
Alfred Rodríguez, and Joseph P. Sánchez
University of New Mexico Press
Albuquerque

Map pages xii and xiii designed by Deborah Reade with draft map
by Joseph M. Sánchez and Denise R. Bleakly.

Library of Congress Cataloging-in-Publication Data
Villagrá, Gaspar Pérez de, d. 1620.
[Historia de la Nueva México.   English & Spanish]
Historia de la Nueva México, 1610 / Gaspar Pérez de Villagrá; a critical and annotated
Spanish/English edition, translated and edited by Miguel Encinias, Alfred Rodríguez, and
Joseph P. Sánchez.—1st ed.
p.   cm. — (Pasó por aquí)
Includes bibliographical references and index.
ISBN 0-8263-1392-2
1. Oñate, Juan de, 1549?–1624—Poetry.   2. New Mexico—History–To 1848–Poetry.
I. Encinias, Miguel. II. Rodríguez, Alfred. III. Sánchez, Joseph P. IV. Title.
V. Series.
PQ7296.V54H5713   1992
861—dc20   92-28780
                                                                                                          CIP

For four great sons of modern New Mexico

MANUEL LUJAN, JR.

TOM BENAVIDES

LOU GALLEGOS

ARTURO ORTEGA

Contents

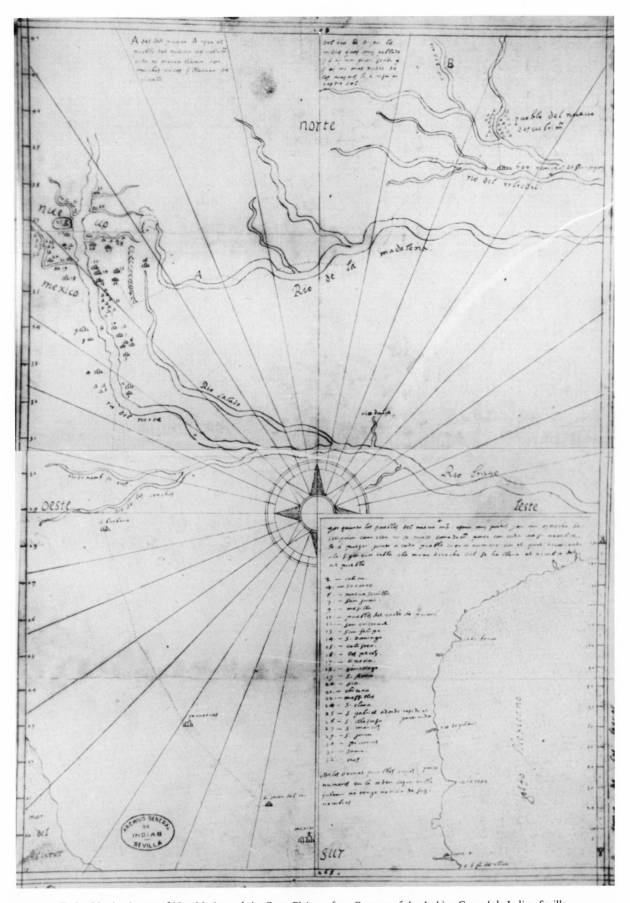

Enrico Martinez's map of New Mexico and the Great Plains, 1601. Courtesy of the Archivo General de Indias, Sevilla.

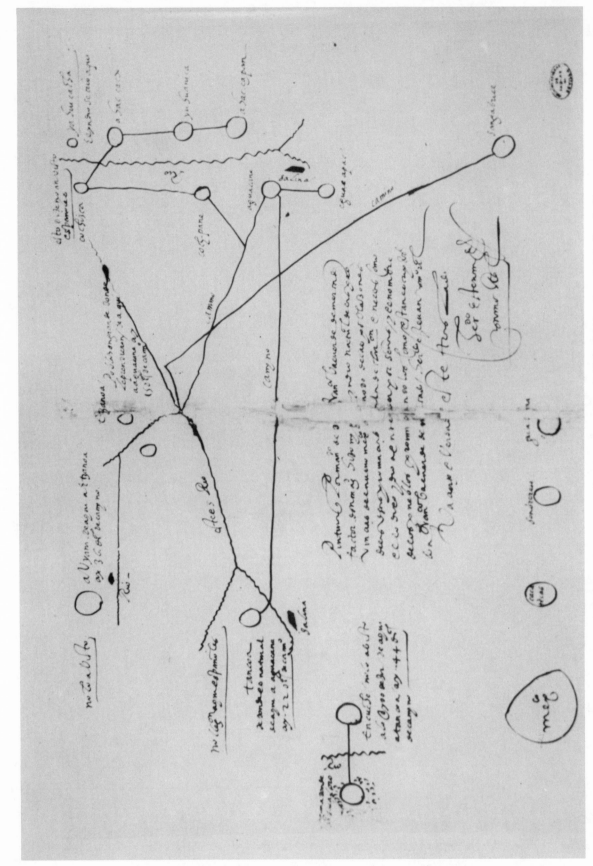

Map of the Great Plains, featuring San Gabriel, ca. 1599. Courtesy of the Archivo General de Indias, Sevilla.

Sketch of a buffalo, ca. 1599. Courtesy of the Archivo General de Indias, Sevilla.

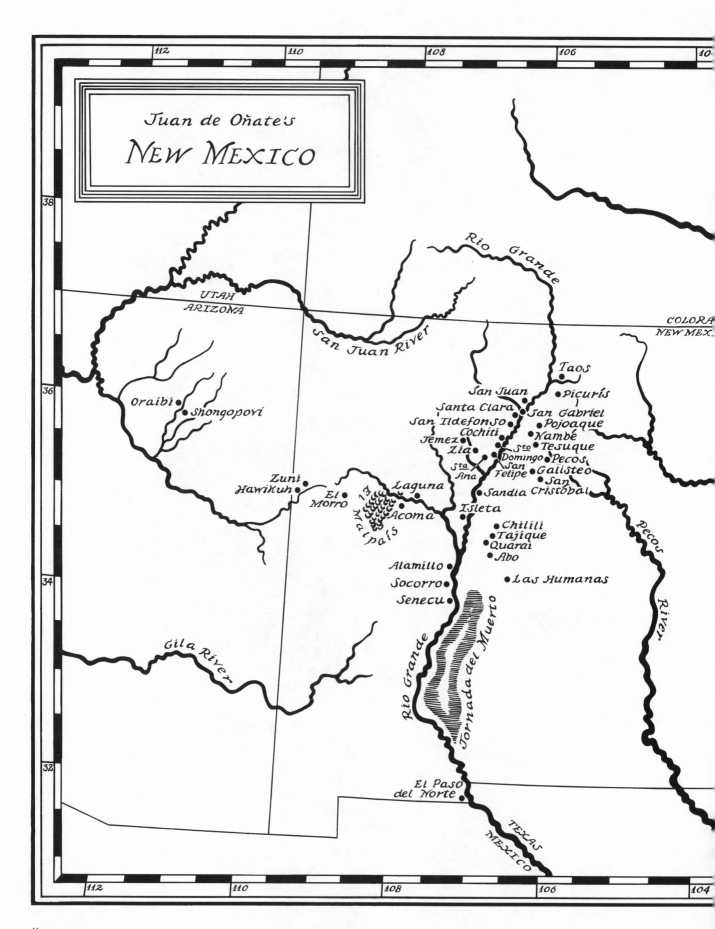

Juan de Oñate's
NEW MEXICO

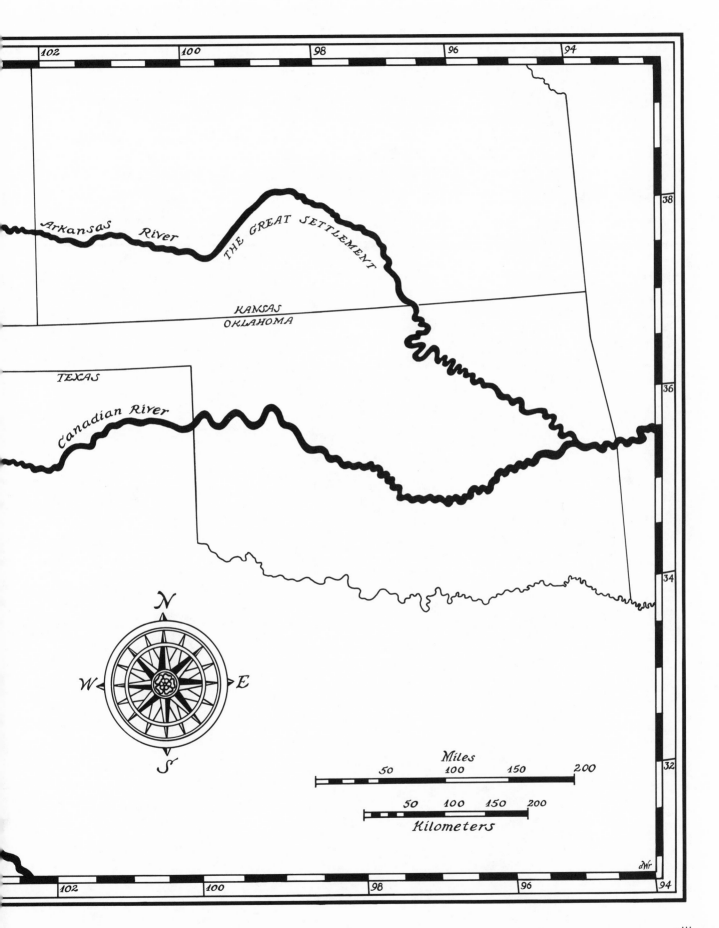

Arkansas River

THE GREAT SETTLEMENT

KANSAS
OKLAHOMA

TEXAS

Canadian River

N

W   E

S

Miles

50   100   150   200

50   100   150   200

Kilometers

102   100   98   96   94

38

36

34

32

102   100   98   96   94

dWr

NOTE FROM THE SERIES EDITORS

W E are pleased to present a groundbreaking linear edition of Gaspar Pérez de Villagrá's *Historia de la Nueva México* retranslated, edited, annotated, and introduced by Miguel Encinias, Alfred Rodríguez, and Joseph P. Sánchez, as the first volume in the Pasó Por Aquí Series. Villagrá's *Historia de la Nueva México* launches this series dedicated to the restoration of New Mexico's Hispano, Mexican American, Chicano literary tradition, a tradition spanning four centuries and including one of the major literary documents of the new world: Villagrá's epic poem of 1610. The revised translation, with a historical overview, copious reference notes, and textual annotation is the product of diligent textual scholarship and substantive historiographic research. It is presented as what must certainly become the standard edition of Villagrá's epic poem well into the next century. We believe the scholarly apparatus will stimulate an entirely new interest in Spanish colonial literature of the Southwest and will reinvigorate historical and cultural scholarship on the colonial period in New Mexico. Moreover, the publication of *Historia de la Nueva México* will reestablish Villagrá as a central figure in the literary history of the Southwest and will install his epic poem as one of the central literary documents of the Americas.

Beginning with Villagrá, therefore, we hope to participate in the reconstruction of our literary heritage. In our estimation, New Mexico possesses one of the oldest and richest literary traditions of any region in the United States and the Americas. The literary production of Nuevomexicanos can be traced to the Spanish colonial mid-sixteenth century. Through the intervening four centuries this literary production has been sustained through the Mexican (1821), U.S. Territorial (1848–1912), and recent Hispano-Chicano periods with remarkable aesthetic force and duration. As more and more recent scholarship is indicating, although the Nuevomexicano cultural legacy is moored in the strong verbal and performative tradition of the *cuento* (folktale), seasonal dramatic productions like "Los Pastores" and the oral poetic tradition of the *romance* (ballad narrative) and *alabados* (sacred ballads), there has long been a sustained textual presence in the form of dramatic and personalized exploration narratives and colonial chronicles, lyric and sacramental poetry, dramatic scripts such as "Los Tejanos" (a play celebrating the defeat of Texas Filibusters in 1841), and since 1848 a vast body of personal narrative, poetry, and prose fiction, much of it contained in Spanish-language newspapers of the territorial period. This literary tradition notwithstanding, *Nuevomexicano* literature has been virtually ignored in mainstream literary histories of the United States and the Southwest.

We believe that by offering a broad revisitation of New Mexico's Hispano literary heritage, the Pasó Por Aquí Series will offer profound recognition of the Nuevo-mexicanos' contribution to the arts and letters of the Southwest.

Among the volumes we hope to publish in the next few years will be a collection of Juan de Oñate's letters and *relaciones* (ca. 1598), Fray Alonso de Benavidez's "Memorial" of 1630, Padre Antonio José Martínez's essays, letters and autobiographic "Relación de méritos," a volume of such folkdrama as "Los moros y Cristianos," "Los Comanches," and "Los Tejanos," Cleofas Jaramillo's *Romance of a Little Village Girl* (1955) and a collection of Sabine Ulibarrí's short stories. By presenting a rich cross section of the New Mexico cultural landscape we expect to provide a shelf of Hispano literary production from its earliest inception during the sixteenth century through the contemporary Chicano period. It is thus in the spirit of acknowledging the contributions of *Nuevomexicano* writers and their forebearers to the composite literary histories and identities of the United States and of the Americas that we offer this series.

Genaro M. Padilla, University of California-Berkeley
Erlinda Gonzales-Berry, University of New Mexico
Pasó Por Aquí Series, General Editors

INTRODUCTION

RELATIVELY little is known about Gaspar Pérez de Villagrá. His father, Hernan Pérez de Villagrá, was from Campos de Villagrán, in Spain,[1] but the son's birth at Puebla de Los Angeles, in New Spain, probably in 1555,[2] classifies the younger Villagrá as a creole. His generation of Spaniards born in the New World does not appear to have felt any less Spanish.[3] Although the date of his departure from the New World has not been established, he was one of the relatively few creoles privileged to study in Europe, obtaining his degree from the University of Salamanca.[4]

It is not known when he returned to New Spain,[5] but it had to have been before 1596, the year in which he became associated with Don Juan de Oñate's New Mexican enterprise.[6] Following what appears to have been the vocation of his *hidalgo* family (possibly related to the Villagráns who participated in the conquest of Chile and were immortalized in the epic poems of Ercilla and Oña), Villagrá enlisted in Oñate's *entrada*, one of the last territorial expansions of the Spanish Empire and the basis of his epic poem. He was made captain and legal officer of the New Mexican expedition in 1596, and ecclesiastical counsel in 1598.[7] The physical descriptions we have of Captain Villagrá are from this period. He was short, well-muscled, with a graying beard, bald, and with deep furrows beneath his eyebrows.[8]

Villagrá's poetic recreation of that colonizing expedition, discounting the author's prescribed humility, includes him among those captains (Márquez, Espinosa, Farfán) who, only exceeded in authority and responsibility by the Zaldívar brothers, Juan and Vicente, field commander and sargeant-major, respectively, were most efficacious in both the pacification and the political and social organization of the new territory. A short time after the victory at Acoma, with which the poem ends, Villagrá was chosen by Oñate to lead an expedition back to New Spain to seek reinforcements. When the viceroy, the Count of Monte Rey, removed him as head of that expedition for its return trip to New Mexico, Villagrá hid away in order not to return, under the expedition's new leadership, to the scene of his epic exploits.[9]

Little is known about Villagrá's existence in the years immediately following, except that he served, 1601–1603, as *alcalde mayor* at the mines of Guanacevi and Nuestra Señora de Alancón in Nueva Vizcaya, and was instructed, in 1602, to recruit six soldiers and establish a *presidio* among the Tepehuanes, then being evangelized by the Jesuits.[10] The official audit, *residencia,* of Villagrá's tenure as *alcalde mayor* took place between December 30, 1602 and January 13, 1603.[11] Two years later he appeared before the *audiencia* of Guadalajara to validate official information regarding his merits and services.[12]

Since no documents have appeared placing Villagrá in New Spain after 1605, it is likely that he returned to Spain at that time. Documentary evidence exists that he returned at least once, in 1608, to New Spain, from whence he voyaged back to Spain in 1609.[13] Details concerning his life in Spain during the first and second decades of the seventeenth century are speculative. He may have followed the court from Valladolid to Madrid (1605), petitioning for a new position in recompense for services rendered the crown; or he may have resided in Alcalá de Henares, where his poem was published in 1610.

The poem, directed to the king, Philip III, apparently had little effect in bringing his services to the court's attention, since written petitions for a hearing by the king have survived from 1613 and 1615.[14] This royal deaf ear to Villagrá's petitions may be in part due to the fact that in 1612, in New Spain, serious charges had been leveled at Oñate and his officers for actions taken during the New Mexican expedition. After a prolonged trial (1612–1614), Villagrá was found guilty, in absentia, of the deaths of two deserters from the expedition, an episode narrated in the poem.[15]

Villagrá was sentenced to a six-year banishment from New Mexico, a two-year banishment from the vice-regal court of New Spain, a two-year ban on the holding of any office, and court costs.[16] This probably had little effect upon him, then most likely living in Spain, except, perhaps, for the regal silence to his petitions for a new position. It is doubtful, given the sentence received, that Villagrá would have returned to New Spain between 1615 and 1620, the year of his death.[17] Ironically, once his petitions had been heeded, he died en route to the New World to occupy the position of *alcalde mayor* of Zapotitlán in Guatemala.[18]

We know next to nothing of Villagrá's stay in Spain before he embarked on his fateful trip. Some information may be gleaned from *Canciones lúgubres y tristes a la muerte de don Cristóbal de Oñate,* an elegy for Cristóbal de Oñate, Don Juan de Oñate's son, who died in New Mexico, compiled by Murcia de la Llana and published in Madrid in 1622.[19] We also know next to nothing concerning the creative process that produced *Historia de la Nueva México.* If, once in Spain, Villagrá moved in literary circles, whether in Valladolid, Madrid, or the university town of Alcalá de Henares, we have found no evidence of it. Neither Cervantes, in his *Viaje del Parnaso,* nor Lope de Vega, in his *Laurel de Apolo,* make mention of him among the poets of the day. This omission, however, is not significantly damning, since few of the epic singers of New World conquests found a place in the cited compilations.

Historia de la Nueva México by Captain Gaspar de Pérez Villagrá, Alcalá de Henares, 1610, is the first published history of New Mexico. Although written accounts by participants in other Spanish explorations of North America had appeared earlier—Alvar Núñez de Vaca (1542), Caballero de Elvas (1577), Antonio de Espejo (1586), Juan Martínez de Montoya (1602), among others—only Villagrá's epic poem recounts the actual establishment of New Mexico by Juan de Oñate between 1595 and 1601.[20] As a history of European colonization in what is today the United States, Villagrá's poem precedes Captain John Smith's *General History of Virginia* by at least fourteen years.[21] As a participant in the founding of New Mexico, Villagrá perceived events through a Spanish colonist's eyes, at times embellishing his own role in the endeavor.

Nevertheless, John Gilmary Shea, one of Villagrá's earliest critics, noted in 1887 that "as an historical work it possesses remarkable value."[22]

Henry R. Wagner described the first, 1610 edition as follows: "8, title, leaf with portrait of Villagrá, 22 unnumbered leaves of preliminaries, 287 numbered leaves, and 1 leaf with the colophon. Folios 34 and 152 misnumbered for 74 and 162, while folios 18 and 38 lack numbers."[23] The preliminaries include the portrait, the *tasa*, indicating the date of publication, April 27, 1610, followed by a one-page errata, two pages of censor approvals, three pages of licensures dated March 7, 1610, a five-page dedication to the king, three pages of prologue, twenty-two pages of poetry, and a nine-page listing of the canto captions.[24]

Two other editions of the work have been published:[25] a reprinting in two volumes done in Mexico in 1900, of which volume two contains documents related to the life of Villagrá gathered by José Fernando Ramírez;[26] and a recent Spanish edition.[27] Although excerpts of the poem have on occasion been published, only one other edition was ever planned. In 1892, for the fourth centennial of the discovery of the New World, the editor of *Libros raros o curiosos que tratan de América* in Madrid announced a new edition that was never published.[28]

Prior to the present edition the only published English translation of Villagrá's poem was that, cited earlier, by Gilberto Espinosa.[29] Espinosa's translation, rendered in prose, was based on the 1900 Mexican reprint and includes twenty documents translated into English from the latter's second volume. An earlier, unpublished English translation of Villagrá's *Historia* was completed in the 1920s, in verse, by Fayette S. Curtis, Jr. A Yale graduate, Curtis arrived in New Mexico at the end of World War I, assuming the headmastership of Los Alamos Ranch School.[30] An expert on Spanish colonial weaponry in the Southwest,[31] Curtis appears to have initiated his extraordinary translation as early as 1923,[32] completing a first draft four years later. His untimely death at age 30, in 1927, precluded its publication. The present edition in English is a revised and corrected version of Curtis's translation.[33]

Historia de la Nueva México, its title so directly expressive of the author's historical proclivity,[34] may well suffer in its literary quality. Such, in any case, would be the judgment of the many scholars who agree with George Ticknor's general evaluation of the epic genre in *Siglo de Oro* Spain:

> . . . [they] belong oftener to patriotism than to poetry; the best of them being so closely confined to matters of fact, that they come with nearly equal pretentions into the province of History, while the rest fall into a dull, chronicling style, which makes it of little consequence under what class they may chance to be arranged.[35]

This broad assessment, insofar as it may refer to patriotism and religious fervor (difficult to separate in the Spanish literature of the period), touches very especially on epic literature concerned with the American conquest.[36]

We will not attempt, in these few pages, the solution to a problematic fusion of history and poetry that has troubled serious thinkers since Aristotle's day. On the one hand, we are not convinced that historical matter, when charged with patriotic emotion and poetized as such, is, *ipso facto,* unpoetic. Nevertheless, and therein lies the great controversy surrounding the subject, there may be some substance to the long-standing radical separation of history and poetry.

With regard to Villagrá, it may well be pointed out that in certain parts of his poem a patent desire to sequentially present historical detail produces the kind of chronicle style, of measured prose, that Ticknor so laments. But it is no less true that in many other passages the poet who presents the emotionally charged encounters of men and a harsh and menacing nature, of men facing the adversity that other men foment, of men against other men in combat, needing to kill in order to survive, makes us forget that he is describing historical actions and men.

In the aesthetic conflict between the historical and the poetic, Villagrá's poem attains both positive and negative results. As a literary effort that uses historical material, *Historia de la Nueva México* must be considered "verist" rather than merely "verisimilist."[37] That is to say, it is a literary recreation that not only holds strictly to the historical events and their chronology, but that introduces a very bare minimum of fictional material, however verisimilar the latter may be. In effect, Villagrá's poem contains practically nothing that may be considered novelistic or fantastic and makes only a minimal concession (unlike Ercilla, for example) to the interpolation of a subjectively lyrical poetic vein. If one discounts the almost necessary fictionalization of the Acoman world, to which the narrator had little access, *Historia de la Nueva México* interpolates no fictional passages other than the long retelling of the legendary coming of the primitive Mexicans (Aztecs) and the relatively short interlude of the enamoured Indian woman, Pilca, a fixed *topos* of the New World epic.

On the other hand, the creole Villagrá, just as the European Ercilla, had participated in the actions he recounts. The former's autobiographic stance, if not as pronounced as that of the poet of the Araucanian struggle,[38] often envelopes narrations and descriptions, notwithstanding the historian's rigorous standards, in a perceptible sheen of recollected passion. To what degree this occurs, and how often, is very much open to the reader's sensitivity and interpretation. In the final analysis, then, it is the individual reader who must determine that which achieves poetic heights in Villagrá's work and that which clearly prioritizes the chronicled preservation of a segment of his people's history.

Villagrá was one of the few Spanish epic poets who, breaking with the Renaissance epic verse tradition of the *octava real,* attempted his narration in blank (only the final two verses of each canto rhyme, couplet-like) hendecasyllabic lines. It is difficult to say whether he so proceeded upon finding the standard verse form too difficult or did so out of a desire to more closely imitate the heroic hexameter of the classics.[39] Francis William Pierce feels that "it is doubtful that such a verse form, as yet little rooted in Castilian, could be sustained for very long, even in the hands of great poets, without degenerating into mere prose."[40]

Again, we must summarize Villagrá's poetic attempt with pluses and minuses. It would be impossible to deny long passages of prosaic degeneration; but there are others, not a few, in which the blank hendecasyllabic verse may attain, for the attentive ear, the echo of the poet's classical models. Villagrá generally maintains the accentuated tone of heroic hendecasyllabic verse; but, again, he deviates from that tonal pattern often enough so that the rigorous critic, assuming the heroic pattern as Villagrá's set goal, may judge him a weak poet. Written in the baroque ambience of seventeenth-century Spain, Villagrá's work offers some syntactical complications. In most cases, however, this may be attributed more to the difficult reduction of often emotionally charged descriptions to the demands of hendecasyllabic verse than to any special artistic pursuit of hyperbaton.

Villagrá's poem is one of the longest of the many epic works that appeared in Spain's *Siglo de Oro*.[41] The longer epic poems of that period dealt, as a rule, with historical or religious subjects, as does *Historia de la Nueva México*. Regarding the latter, its thirty-four canto length—a number that does not coincide with any of Villagrá's models, classical or renaissance—appears to have been determined by both biographical/historical and artistic factors. As a factual witness to the events he narrates, Villagrá reasonably ends the poem close to the point at which he left the Oñate expedition. It would be difficult to argue, on the other hand, against the artistic appropriateness of concluding the epic immediately after the fall of Acoma.

The creole poet's work, although reflecting, as do all Spanish *Siglo de Oro* epics, the overwhelming presence of Virgil and, to some lesser degree, of Lucan, also clearly reflects, as does the Spanish epic generally, the Christian demystification that the Italian Renaissance epic, Ariosto and Tasso in particular (along with their sixteenth-century Spanish imitators), had imposed upon those classical models. *Historia de la Nueva México* is an epic of Christian inspiration, and as such closely follows the direction established by Tasso, although it concerns events from the narrator's life. This explicit primacy of the religious, christianizing mission, if not as central in the epics of Ercilla, Oña, or Barco Centenera, is already the moving impulse in those of Lasso de la Vega and Saavedra Guzmán, singers of the Cortesian exploits and Villagrá's most immediate Spanish models.[42]

Like *La araucana* and the many New World epics that modeled themselves upon it, Villagrá, following Ariosto, offers summarized ethical conclusions in his canto introductions that anticipate the lessons to be drawn from the episode to follow. This does not deter the poet from further ethical observations, within the narrated episode, that stress the presence of God in the lives of his Christian protagonists. Even when somewhat removed from the sensibilities of the modern reader, these observations, charged as they often are with the true believer's passion, genuinely project the poet's feelings.

Villagrá's work is filled, perhaps overly filled, with poetic comparisons, a literary characteristic of the genre. Following the norms of his predecessors and models, the poet abundantly employs all of nature's kingdoms, the type of animal, vegetable or mineral imagery that has been classified, for the Spanish epic, by Rudolfo Oroz.[43] Mercedes Junquera has classified this imagery in *Historia de la Nueva México,* with the highest incidence, fifty-eight, pertaining to the animal world.[44] On occasion, Villagrá, perhaps reflecting the baroque tastes of his day, will double or even triple these comparative images; but, if the reader moves beyond the inherent linguistic difficulty involved, many of these comparisons, especially those drawn from the animal world (some of which, like that of the rampant lion, echo Lucan; many others, like those of the stallion or the boar, reveal their Virgilian origins), are meaningful and interesting. Less in tune with the modern reader, and with their now archaic vocabulary offering special problems, are the many nautical comparisons that Villagrá employs.

Villagrá's poetic language, almost bereft of Americanisms, is hardly distinguishable from that being used at the time by his Spanish contemporaries. Perhaps a soldier first despite his university studies, Villagrá's language is somewhat more popular than that employed, for example, by Ercilla, Lasso de la Vega or Saavedra Guzmán. This may also be the result, at least in part, of the creole poet's precise fidelity in describing the minute details of military life, as well as of the physical, zoological, and floral world that he encountered. It could never be said of Villagrá, as it has been said of the great Ercilla,[45] that his descriptions of nature are too literary, too pastoral. Although presenting, as one might expect of a poet, an occasional *locus amenus,* Villagrá's descriptions of the physical world of New Mexico do not give the impression of having been written under the influence of pastoral models.

Perhaps the greatest linguistic difficulty encountered in the poetic text is directly related to the special attraction that the nautical world had for Villagrá, a characteristic that he shares, according to José Toribio Medina,[46] with the New World epic in general. If this special attraction may be explained by the fact that the American adventure was naval in its origins and that sea voyages, so lengthy and protracted, made up an important source of human experience in those times, it should be borne in mind, as well, that Virgil's *Aeneid,* the bible of the renaissance epic, is also very much nautically centered. The linguistic problem arises, as indicated earlier, from the fact that great changes in seafaring have made most of its seventeenth-century vocabulary obsolete or archaic.

We have used the 1900 Mexican reprinting of Villagrá's poem as the working basis for this edition, indicating in our notes its occasional deviations from the rare Alcalá de Henares, 1610 *princeps.* Our main task, beyond clarifying a text filled with archaic terms, personal usages, and many syntactic convolutions, was the rationalization of Villagrá's anarchic punctuation. In terms of modern readership, the poet uses the comma to burdensome excess while refusing to use the period. The reduction of Villagrá's poem to a rational punctuation has at the very least rendered a poetic text with adequate and logical pauses.

We have exercised great restraint, on the other hand, in altering Villagrá's spelling. We have only altered those letters in the text that, having disappeared from modern Spanish usage, might cause the contemporary reader problems: the 'ç,' for which we consistently substitute the modern 'z,' and the 'u' with a 'v-b' phonetic value, which is consistently rendered by its modern equivalent of either 'v' or 'b.' All other archaic spelling forms, those that do not phonetically force a change in the modern pronunciation of Spanish (the doubled 's,' the random interchange of 'v' and 'b,' of 'v' for 'u') have been kept. We have added modern accents to Villagrá's words, hopefully facilitating the contemporary reader's phonetic appreciation of the poetic text. This created a problem in only one word, 'vltima/vltimo,' in which we opted for leaving out the accent in order to retain the original's 'v' for 'u' usage. Numerous words are spelled differently in different parts of the text. We decided against regularizing what so clearly conveys the language's meandering road toward its fixed modern form.

As regards the English translation offered here, we must assume that Curtis used the 1900 Mexican reprinting of the poem, for his translation often coincides with that Mexican text in its errata *vis à vis* the 1610 edition. Curtis, in translating the Villagrá poem, rationalized, as we have done in our Spanish edition, the original's anarchic punctuation and run-on lack of periods. We have altered Curtis's punctuation on those occasions in which our reading of the Spanish text indicated a different periodicity, and, necessarily, on those many others in which we have corrected the translator's English rendition of the original Spanish.

Curtis—wisely, in terms of rendering the Spanish blank hendecasyllable—opted for a poetic translation centered, for the most part, on blank iambic parameter, but allowing himself much leeway (with about half the verses breaking that pattern) both in terms of the number of metrical feet, with many hexameters and trimeters, and of tonal beat, with other than iambic combinations.[47] In effect, the modern reader may wish to read Curtis's poetic rendition of Villagrá as if it were in free blank verse.

Annotations in this edition, when not directed to clarifying lexical matters, are most often intended to point out the poet's possible sources. They are, for the most part, literary, and they cumulatively underscore the humanistic wealth behind the pen of an author who wielded so well the sword. Those annotations that deal with historical matters seek to clarify the textual narration, and offer the historically inclined reader a basic bibliography. The "Historical Overview" that follows is intended to clarify for the layman a historically documented outline of the background to and the general progression of the Oñate expedition.

This edition offers a side-by-side presentation of the original Spanish text and its English translation. For a contemporary New Mexico, in which those two languages and cultures—together with those of the Indian peoples that are the heroic co-protagonists of the epic narration—have become fused, this facilitates the most general access to a text that constitutes, both in literary and historical terms, the very cornerstone of our common edifice.

Finally, a special note of gratitude is owed to several of our colleagues for their assistance in the typographical presentation of our manuscript: Camille Martínez, Angelica Sánchez, Gerry Gurulé, Eva Gallegos, Rosalind Rock, Ph.D., Ximena Sosa, William Broughton, and Ursula Roberts.

NOTES

1. F. W. Hodge, Foreword to G. Espinosa, ed. and trans., *History of New Mexico by Gaspar Pérez de Villagrá* (Los Angeles: The Quivira Society, 1933), 18.

2. The most recent study on the poet, that of L. Leal, "The First American Epic: Villagrá's *History of New Mexico*," *Pasó por aquí: Critical Essays on the New Mexican Literary Tradition, 1542—1988*, ed. E. Gonzales-Berry (Albuquerque: Univ. of New Mexico Press, 1989), contains what little bibliography there is. For some discrepancy involving the date of Villagrá's birth, see, G. de Villagrá, *Historia de Nuevo México*, ed. M. Junquera (Madrid: Historia 16, 1989), 25.

3. For the "criollismo" of New World writers in that period, consult J. de Castellanos, *Elogios de varones ilustres de Indias*, ed. I. J. Pardo (Caracas: Academia Nacional de Historia, 1962), LXXXIX–XCIV.

4. See G. de Villagrá, *Historia de la Nueva México*, ed. L. González Obregón (México: Imprenta del Museo Nacional, 1900), II: 24; and E. Mejía Sánchez, "Gaspar Pérez de Villagrá en la Nueva España," *Cuadernos del Centro de Estudios Literarios* 1 (1970):6.

5. Villagrá's recent editor, Junquera (25), suggests 1580 as the date. Villagrá himself indicates in the poem, however, that he spent seven years in the court of Philip II, which, when added to his years of university study in Salamanca, would appear to make 1580 too early a date for his return home.

6. González Obregón, II:5.

7. Ibid., 14, 24. For honors garnered by Villagrá during the expedition, see ibid., 28, 31, 35.

8. Hodge, 17.

9. For the Viceroy's motivation in removing Villagrá, Oñate's appointee, as head of the returning expedition, see G. F. Hammond and A. Rey, *Don Juan de Oñate, Colonizer of New Mexico, 1595–1628* (Albuquerque: Univ. of New Mexico Press, 1953), 70, 73.

10. González Obregón, II:67, 59.

11. Ibid., 75.

12. Ibid., 77.

13. Ibid., 9. For his return to New Spain between 1608 and 1609, also see Junquera, 26.

14. *Servicios que a su Magestad ha hecho el Capitán Gaspar de Villagrá, para que V. M. le haga merced* (Madrid, 1615). Also see Junquera, 26.

15. For the full charges leveled at Villagrá, see Hammond and Rey, 1116.

16. Ibid.

17. For documentary discrepancies regarding the date of Villagrá's death, see Junquera, 27.

18. For information on Villagrá's family in New Spain, subsequent to his death, see González Obregón, II:9, 86.

19. E. Beerman, "Death of an Old Conquistador: New Light on Juan de Oñate," *New Mexico Historical Review* 54 (1979):305–19.

20. Leal, 47.

21. Hodge, 17.

22. John G. Shea, "The First Epic of Our Country by the Poet Conquistador, Captain Gaspar de Villagrá," *United States Catholic Historical Magazine*, New York, April, 1887, 4.

23. H. B. Wagner, *The Spanish Southwest, 1542–1794* (Albuquerque: The Quivira Society, 1937), 195.

24. Ibid.

25. When already in press, a very recent new Spanish edition of the *Historia* has come to our attention: edited by Augusto Quintana Prieto, Victorino Madrid Rubio, Elsia Armesto Rodríguez, and Manuel Gullón y de Oñate (León, Biblioteca de Autores Astorganos, 1991).

26. See note 4 above.

27. See note 2 above.

28. Leal, 50.

29. See note 1 above. Espinosa's translation has been reprinted: New York: Arno Press, 1967.

30. "Necrology," *The New Mexico Historical Review* 2 (1927):98–99.

31. For a listing of his scholarly articles see *New Mexico Historical Review* 2 (1927):198.

32. R. E. Twitchell, "Captain Don Gaspar de Villagrá," *New Mexico Historical Society Publications* 28 (1924):1–2.

33. Curtis's original lines, those altered and corrected for this edition, are retained in an appendix.

34. The catalogue of epic poems compiled in F. Pierce, *La poesía épica del Siglo de Oro* (Madrid: Editorial Gredos, 1968), 328–62, contains, for the sixteenth and seventeenth centuries, only three other titles as explicitly historical.

35. Cited by Pierce, 155.

36. For bibliography concerning this matter, see, for example, Gabriel Lasso de la Vega, *Mexicana*, ed. J. Amor y Vázquez (Madrid: Biblioteca de Autores Españoles, 1970), LIII.

37. For a technical distinction between the two approaches in the epic, and the pertinent bibliography, see Amor y Vázquez, XXII; and M. A. Vega, *La araucana de Ercilla* (Santiago: Editorial Orbe, 1970), 132.

38. For Ercilla's autobiographism, see A. de Ercilla, *La araucana*, ed. M. A. Morínigo and I. Lerner (Madrid: Castalia, 1979), I:42–43.

39. For the few other attempts along these lines, see Pierce, 223–25.

40. Ibid., 225.

41. Ibid., 226–28.

42. Amor y Vázquez, XXXVIII.

43. Pedro de Oña, *El Vasauro*, ed. R. Oroz (Santiago: Universidad de Chile, 1941), XLIII–XLIX.

44. Junquera, 64–67.

45. Vega, 53.

46. Pedro de Oña, *El auraco domado*, ed. J. T. Medina (Santiago: Imprenta Universitaria, 1917), 124.

47. We are much indebted to professors James Thorson and Mary Beth Whidden of the University of New Mexico English department for a metrical analysis of Curtis's translation.

HISTORICAL OVERVIEW

THE background of Villagrá's epic poem is documented in thousands of pages housed in Spanish and Mexican archives. The salient themes and facts regarding the founding of New Mexico in 1598, an event tantamount to the founding of Jamestown, Virginia, in 1607, is as much a part of the United States' national story as it is that of Mexico's. Against the broad theme of the Age of Discovery, New Mexico became the focal point of Spanish exploration in North America. In 1540, within 48 years of Christopher Columbus's landing on San Salvador in 1492, Spanish explorers camped on the banks of the Rio Grande, which traversed through a large Indian province called Tiguex, in the valley of present-day Albuquerque, New Mexico. The expeditionary force of Francisco Vázquez de Coronado (1540–1542)[1] had already visited Zuni and Acoma as well as many of the pueblos stretching from Taos to Senecu near present-day Socorro. By 1542 the Spanish claim to New Mexico ran from the Hopi villages in northeastern Arizona to the Rio Grande pueblos, eastward to the pueblos of Galisteo and Pecos, and beyond to the Great Plains as far as the Plains Indian settlements near present-day Great Bend on the Arkansas River in central Kansas. Vázquez de Coronado not only established the Spanish claim to New Mexico—he also came away with the first European view of the interior of North America and its people and its resources. The encounter left the Pueblo Indians with a distrust of anything European.

Nearly forty years passed before another Spanish expedition entered New Mexico. In 1581 Francisco Sánchez Chamuscado[2] led a reconnaissance party into New Mexico to explore for mineral wealth and to allow the Franciscan missionaries traveling with him to evaluate the area for possible missionization. Both objectives met with little success. Sánchez returned to Mexico, dying en route to Santa Barbara in Nueva Vizcaya, present-day Chihuahua. The few Franciscans on the expedition remained in New Mexico with the hope of converting the natives.

A second expedition led by Antonio de Espejo[3] crossed the Río del Norte into New Mexico in 1582. Other missionaries accompanied Espejo, since the Franciscans from the Sánchez Chamuscado expedition may have been in need of rescue. Having arrived in New Mexico and having determined that the missionaries from the Sánchez Chamuscado expedition had been killed, Friar Bernardino Beltrán and Espejo had a falling out about their objectives. Beltrán preferred to stay on the Rio Grande to attempt his missionization of the natives. Concerned with reconnoitering for mineral wealth, Espejo soon separated from the missionaries and explored as far west as the Verde River in Arizona. Meanwhile the missionaries, faced with the hostility of the Rio Grande Pueblo Indians, returned to Santa Barbara in Nueva Vizcaya. Upon learning that the Pueblos had prepared a war against them, Espejo decided to return by a safer route and headed east to the Pecos River, then south to Santa Barbara. The reports from his and Sánchez Chamuscado's expeditions significantly influenced the future of New Mexico as a Spanish province.

In March 1583, King Felipe II issued a royal decree approving Viceroy Lorenzo Suárez de Mendoza y Figueroa's recommendation to authorize the settlement of the *tierra adentro,*[4] the land north of the Rio Grande. Indeed, the reports of the expeditions led by Francisco Sánchez Chamuscado and Antonio de Espejo to New Mexico had inspired the viceroy's request to the king. Espejo's report stirred up considerable interest among prominent investors in Spain and New Spain who vied for the privilege of leading the colonization expedition. Antonio de Espejo and Hernán Gallegos, who had been with Sánchez Chamuscado, were among the prospective applicants. Gallegos quickly fell out of the competition since he lacked the necessary wealth to support the expedition. Espejo, on his way to the court in Spain, fell ill and died unexpectedly in Havana, Cuba. Meanwhile, the viceroy searched for a leader with wealth as well as experience in such matters.

Twelve years passed before the viceroy and the Council of the Indies finally selected Juan Pérez de Oñate of Zacatecas.[5] Viceroy Luis de Velasco knew the Oñate family well and appreciated its willingness to underwrite the cost of the expedition. But there were other factors which prompted the selection of Oñate: too much time had elapsed since the authorization to settle New Mexico had been announced and there were others already on the restless frontier of northern Mexico who would dare to strike out on their own and possibly ruin conditions for the royal enterprise.

The illegal expedition of Gaspar Castaño de Sosa from 1590 to 1592 had alerted Spanish officials to the possibility of an uncontrolled rush to New Mexico.[6] Although Castaño de Sosa was finally stopped by royal authorities, his arrest occurred after he had taken several hundred settlers to New Mexico. On the heels of Castaño de Sosa's ill-fated attempt, Captain Francisco Leyva de Bonilla also went beyond the bounds of legality. The outcome of his story, however, was not known until 1598. As part of his contract to settle New Mexico, Oñate had been ordered by the viceroy to investigate the whereabouts of Leyva and his men and to arrest them for illegal entry into New Mexico.

In 1593 Captain Leyva led a company of soldiers out of southern Chihuahua on a punitive expedition against marauding Indians who had fled northward. Somewhere in the northern Chihuahua desert, after the soldiers had completed their mission, Leyva told his men of his desire to penetrate the *tierra adentro.* Six soldiers refused to join the party, but the rest of them were intrigued about what lay ahead. The horsemen led by Leyva and Antonio Gutiérrez de Humaña crossed the Rio Grande and followed the trail to the pueblos of the Rio Abajo (the lower Rio Grande between El Paso and Cochiti Pueblo near La Bajada, the descent from the higher elevations of the Rio Arriba, or the upper Rio Grande). After having spent some months among the pueblos, they traveled to the northernmost Indian village, probably Taos, and made another decision.[7]

Perhaps it was at Taos or Pecos where they learned about the Great Plains, or maybe the Spaniards had arrived in time for the annual trading fairs attended by Plains Indians. In any event, Leyva and Gutiérrez learned about the plains and were determined to go there in the hope that some great civilization similar to the Aztecs existed. After all, they may have reasoned, Vázquez de Coronado, Sánchez Chamuscado, and Espejo probably did not go far enough in the correct direction to find it. Leyva and Gutiérrez headed northeastward into what is now Kansas. They may have reached as far as the Nebraska plains—farther than any European had heretofore gone into the North American heartland. Somewhere in the lonely expanse of that region, Leyva and Gutiérrez had a falling out. Gutiérrez killed his captain in the fight that followed.[8] Antonio Gutiérrez de Humaña now found himself in command of the troops in hostile territory.

Not long after Leyva's death, presumably in Kansas, Gutiérrez and his men were ambushed by Plains Indians. The attack began at daybreak under cover of a grass fire. All of the Spaniards and their Indian guides were slain except for a Mexican Indian named Jusepe. Five years later, in 1598, Juan de Oñate met Jusepe at San Juan Pueblo.[9] Oñate at last learned the sad fate of those Spaniards who had dared to defy the crown and venture beyond the authorized frontier. Still others for whom no record exists, save for vague references, had ventured into the *tierra adentro* and had returned to spin tales about what they had seen beyond the Rio Grande. Despite royal orders which prohibited exploration, conquest, and colonization without official sanction, Spanish frontiersmen often ventured beyond the limits of their authority.

In 1595 Viceroy Velasco and Juan de Oñate agreed on a formal contract for the settlement of New Mexico.[10] Under the terms of the contract, Oñate would pay all expenses for the expeditionary force, except for the Franciscan missionaries who were subsidized by the *Patronato Real,* or royal patronage, a special fund for missionaries. In return for underwriting the cost of the expedition, Oñate would receive a salary of six thousand ducats a year and would have almost unlimited power answerable only to the Council of the Indies. He would also hold the title of *adelantado,* the only person in New Mexico's colonial history to receive the privilege of advancing the frontier's range of settlement. Additionally, he would serve as governor and captain general in command of all troops within his jurisdiction, and he would administer the *encomienda,* a feudal collection of tribute from the Indians under Spanish control. Generally, if Indians could not pay the tribute, the amount due was converted to a payment in servitude. There were other provisions which the contract stipulated.[11]

Before the contract could be executed, however, Viceroy Velasco was replaced by a new viceroy, Gaspar de Zúñiga y Acevedo, the count of Monterrey. While Velasco became viceroy of Peru, Viceroy Zúñiga asked to review Oñate's contract. For three years, the viceroy scrupulously reviewed all provisions of the contract and had it investigated for its legal and practical merit. In order to ensure that all elements of the contract were observed by the contractor, Oñate's expeditionary force was inspected, as were its provisions of food, supplies, and military equipment.[12] Finally, after much consideration, Viceroy Zúñiga issued a new and greatly modified contract, giving himself greater control over the expedition than Velasco had enjoyed in the previous contract. Presumably, Oñate was not happy with the new contract but because he had invested so much in the expedition, he agreed to the new terms. He hoped to recover his losses in New Mexico.

On 26 January 1598, after much delay, and great expense to Oñate, the expedition was permitted to leave for New Mexico. In a great cloud of dust, the slow moving, oxen-drawn caravan creaked out of the Valley of San Bartolomé in the Bolsón de Mapimí. Driving thousands of sheep, pigs, goats, cattle, mules, and horses, the soldiers and settlers began the trek to their new homeland far to the north. Scouts, led by Sergeant Major Vicente de Zaldívar, nephew of Oñate, wandered far ahead of the wagon train to find a route with water and pasturage.[13] Light snow had fallen as they approached the Rio Grande, and a cold wind swept the desert of northern Chihuahua.

For three months, the air of northern Chihuahua resounded with the sharp cracks of the teamsters' whips as the caravan pushed farther into the *tierra adentro*. They reached the Rio Grande by the end of April 1598. One settler wrote about the occasion of their thanksgiving festival in the wilderness:

On 30 April 1598, day of the Ascension of our Lord, at this Río del Norte, Governor Don Juan de Oñate took possession of all the kingdoms and provinces of New Mexico, in the name of King Felipe [II], our lord, in the presence of Juan Pérez de Donis, royal notary and secretary of the jurisdiction and expedition. There was a sermon, a great ecclesiastical and secular celebration, a great salute and rejoicing, and in the afternoon, a comedy. The royal standard was blessed and placed in charge of Francisco de Sosa Peñalosa, the royal ensign.[14]

They followed the river to a point where the mountains came down to form "the pass of the river and the ford." The crossing was named "Los Puertos,"[15] although later it would be known as El Paso. The warm spring sun of May the 4th witnessed Oñate's army and forty Indians on that desolate spot on the earth, as they moved their cargo, carts, and livestock across the river. It was near here that they met the first Indians from New Mexico.

The well-armed and European-attired Spaniards contrasted with the almost nude natives, who came to make peace. "They had Turkish bows, long hair cut to resemble little Milan caps, head gear made to hold down the hair and colored with blood or paint. Their first words were *manxo, manxo, micos, micos,* by which they meant 'peaceful ones' and 'friends.' They make signs of the cross by raising their fingers."[16]

Looking northward into the *tierra adentro* beyond the river crossing at El Paso, Oñate realized "there [was] no other road for carts for many leagues."[17] The Spaniards would have to blaze their own road. He asked the Indians about Cibola, and they responded "very clearly by signs that the settlements were six days distant, or eight days along the route of travel" for the carts. But Oñate's opinion about there being "no other road"[18] was soon contradicted. Before the day was over, "we passed the ruts made by ten carts that Castaño and Morlete took out from New Mexico"[19] almost a decade earlier. Indeed, some of Oñate's men had been with Morlete.

Ten days later, they moved up the desolate trail, stopping to repair their carts, to observe a holy day of obligation, and to wonder about the place "where it is said that Captain Morlete hanged four Indians because they had stolen some horses."[20] The summer rains and heat alternated as often as the thirst and hunger which afflicted the slow-moving wagon train, passing beneath the Sierra del Olvido, with its craggy spirals, a short distance to the east of the Río del Norte. The range (which today is called the Organ Mountains) was so named because Oñate's soldiers who had been with Morlete could not remember ever having seen them. Eight decades later, the Sierra del Olvido, named for the forgetfulness of Oñate's men upon entering New Mexico, would be renamed "Los Organos" by Spaniards fleeing the province in the Pueblo Revolt of 1680.

At this point, in the vicinity of present-day Las Cruces, at Ensign Robledo's gravesite, Oñate, the Father Commissary Friar Cristóbal de Salazar, Juan de Zaldívar, Vicente de Zaldívar, and a complement of sixty horsemen set out for the Indian settlements far to the north. They rode ahead of the caravan to prepare the pueblos for their coming, to calm the Indians "at the appearance of such an array."[21] As the expedition was in need of provisions, Oñate hoped to replenish the supplies.

Beyond the Sierra del Olvido to the east lay a plain that would be easier for the carts to travel despite its lack of water. "We all fared badly on account of the lack of water, because we were traveling five or six leagues to the right of the river, toward the east. On this day, when a dog appeared with muddy paws and hind feet, we searched for some water holes. At a place commemorated as El Perrillo [the little dog], Captain Gaspar de Villagrá found one and Cristóbal Sánchez another, not far from where we were toward the river."[22]

The trail, away from the river, was overcome after much hardship to man and beast. "We were exploring and feeling our way along this entire route for the first time, and we suffered a great deal because of not knowing it,"[23] wrote one of the priests. The 65-mile trail, known as the Jornada del Muerto, took approximately six days to cross. Somewhere on the *jornada* they left their carts behind because the terrain was too difficult. Finally, they came out of the plain and arrived at a marsh below a plateau of black rock near present-day San Marcial. There, near the San Felipe Pueblo named by Sánchez Chamuscado, they said Mass and took Holy Communion as they prayed for better luck. After one more day of travel, they camped at a pueblo called Qualacú, in the direction of the river where they were headed. Suspicious and fearful after previous encounters with the white man, the Indians of Qualacú abandoned their pueblo.[24] Qualacú was twelve miles beyond the northern end of the *jornada* and at the southern end of the Rio Abajo.

The Spaniards, to reassure the natives that they intended no harm, gave them trinkets, then moved near the river to camp for a month and await the return of Governor Oñate.[25] Within a fortnight, the governor and his small escort had returned from their advance trip to the carts to the south. By this time dissension among the settlers had grown. Hardship—spawned by lack of water and provisions, the rough terrain, the heat, and the cumulative effect of the lengthy, wearisome journey which resulted in some deaths—was causing considerable discouragement among the settlers. Seeing the discord, Governor Oñate spoke to them and assured them their journey was almost over. "He smoothed everything by his act. . . . His visit gave us new life,"[26] wrote one of the settlers.

The cart train moved out along the west bank of the Rio Abajo and by mid-June reached the pueblo of Teypana, which the settlers called Socorro (help, relief) because the people there "furnished us with much maize." One of the Teypana leaders, Letoc, spoke Piro and communicated to the Spaniards about the other pueblos they would pass on their trek northward. Most of them, however, were found abandoned out of fear of the Spaniards and their terrible weapons and horses. The caravan passed by the abandoned pueblos north of Socorro and left them undisturbed. Somewhere north of Socorro, the Spaniards recrossed the river and traveled along the east bank on the slightly flatter terrain. Shortly they reached an abandoned pueblo they called Nueva Sevilla which later maps would show as Sevilleta. There, in the abandoned pueblo, the settlers camped for a week.[27]

Meanwhile, Oñate's nephews, the *Maese de Campo* Juan de Zaldívar and the *Sargento Mayor* Vicente de Zaldívar, explored the nearby pueblos northeast of the camp. Although some of the pueblos they visited were on the Rio Grande, the Zaldívar brothers were attracted to those east of the large Sierra Morena. Where present-day Abo Pass—which the Spaniards later called *el portuelo* (the little gateway)—comes into view from the river, the small scouting party turned east. At the southern end of the Manzano Mountains, they visited other pueblos, doubtless seen by Antonio de Espejo in 1582 and probably Sánchez Chamuscado the previous year. Upon their return to Nueva Sevilla, the Zaldívars reported having seen many pueblos on the other side of the mountain. One of them they identified by the fascinating name of "Aboó,"[28] doubtless the site of the present day ruins at Abo. The drama of the discovery was not lost on Gaspar de Villagrá, for he had been a member of the scouting party.

From their camp at Nueva Sevilla, Oñate led his detachment of some sixty horsemen northward once again. Passing through the valley of Puaray, they saw many pueblos and planted fields on both sides of the river, in the area of present-day Albuquerque. Most of the pueblos of Puaray, located along the river, had been abandoned, for the Indians lived in fear of a returning Spanish army. Their lore constantly reminded them of the war of "fire and sword" waged against them by Francisco Vázquez de Coronado almost six decades earlier. In 1598, their fear, caused by having killed Friar Agustín Rodríguez and his missionary companions (members of the Sánchez Chamuscado expedition of 1581), seemed to loom over Puaray like a curse. Almost every time a Spanish expedition passed by, the people fled to the Sandia Mountains or to nearby pueblos. Although Oñate had no such intentions, the people of Puaray and those of other pueblos believed that the Spaniards would seek revenge for the deaths of the missionaries.

The detachment of horsemen rode past abandoned Puaray to the Keres pueblo known as Santo Domingo.[29] They knew of the pueblo because of the eventful arrest of Castaño de Sosa by Juan de Morlete in 1592. There the Spaniards sought out two of the Mexican Indians, Tomás and Cristóbal, who had been with Castaño and had decided to remain at Santo Domingo. Oñate needed them as translators. Although Spanish activities along the Rio Abajo between Nueva Sevilla and Santo Domingo had been peaceful, Tomás and Cristóbal were taken by surprise[30] and quickly enlisted as interpreters.

Although the Santo Domingo Indians looked on with guarded displeasure, they soon realized that Oñate intended them no harm. Oñate, through his Mexican Indian interpreters, called a general council at Santo Domingo and invited the seven nearby pueblos to send representatives. Once the council was assembled, Governor Oñate, speaking through Tomás and Cristóbal, explained the purpose of the new Spanish presence among them and asked each leader to pledge obedience to the Spanish crown, an act which he believed they comprehended.[31] Then he announced that Santo Domingo would be the site of a Franciscan convent dedicated to Nuestra Señora de la Asunción and that the pueblo's patron saints would be Peter and Paul.[32] Saint Anthony of Padua, on the other hand, was then dedicated as the patron saint of the large valley of Puaray. Convinced that peace had been established between the pueblos of the Rio Abajo and the Spaniards, Oñate departed from Santo Domingo in a northerly direction.

Seeking a place to settle, Oñate and his men pushed their horses along the Rio Arriba portion of the Rio Grande where Castaño de Sosa and his men had been eight years before. En route, Oñate passed the pueblo called Bove, which they named San Ildefonso in honor of the expedition's father commissary, Fray Alonso Martínez.[33] Having passed much of the land Castaño had described, they reached the confluence of the Rio Grande and the Rio Chama. There, on 4 July 1598, at a small pueblo called Okhe, Oñate set up camp. He renamed the pueblo San Juan de los Caballeros and ordered the *Maese de Campo* Juan de Zaldívar and a small contingent of soldiers to return to Nueva Sevilla and bring up the settlers.[34] By mid-August the settlers and sixty-one carts had arrived at San Juan de los Caballeros. Of the eighty-three wagons that had begun the expedition, twenty-two had been left along the trail from El Paso, through the Jornada del Muerto, to Nueva Sevilla. Because of their value to colonial transportation, they would be retrieved at a later date.[35]

While the settlers were moving forward to San Juan, the governor busied himself with the reconnaissance of the Rio Arriba and the eastern pueblos near the Great Plains. While at Taos Pueblo, which the Spaniards knew as Braba, Tayberón, and San Miguel,[36] and at Picuris Pueblo, Oñate got his first glimpse of the Plains Indians, who had come to trade there. Wending its way southward through the mountains, the party traveled to Galisteo, where the plains were quite visible to the east of the mountain range which the Spaniards later called the Sierra de San Lázaro, today's Ortiz Mountains.[37] At a pueblo called San Cristóbal, Oñate released a young Indian woman named Doña Inés to her pueblo friends and relatives.[38] Doña Inés, born at San Cristóbal, as a child had been taken by Castaño de Sosa to be trained as an interpreter. "Her parents and almost all of her relatives were already dead, and there was hardly anyone who remembered how Castaño had taken her away,"[39] wrote a colonist. She, however, had resisted her role as interpreter for the Spaniards and refused to become a "second Malinche, but she does not know the language or any other spoken in New Mexico, nor is she learning them,"[40] lamented a Spaniard. Doña Inés had craftily won her freedom from the Spaniards. Curious about the Pueblo Indians's relationship with the Plains Indians, the *adelantado* left Galisteo, bound for the great pueblo of Pecos.

At Pecos the Spaniards had better luck with another of their Indian interpreters, Juan de Dios, who had learned to speak their tongue from Pedro Oróz, a captive from Pecos who had spent many years living in Mexico. Like Castaño de Sosa, early explorers in New Mexico followed the practice, common throughout the colonial period in the New World, of taking natives such as Doña Inés and Pedro Oróz and teaching them Spanish, so that they could teach others their native languages. That way, reasoned the practical colonists, they would have translators whenever they returned to a given area.

In 1582, Antonio de Espejo, hoping to return and conquer New Mexico, abducted two men from Pecos. One of them managed to escape, but the other, closely guarded, was taken southward to Santa Barbara. Espejo, meanwhile, convinced authorities there to place the native under the tutelage of Fray Pedro Oróz. At baptism, the native took the name of his tutor and was known as Pedro Oróz, indio (Indian). Before the New Mexico expedition got underway, Pedro died at Tanepantla without ever again seeing his homeland.[41] Prior to his death, however, Pedro taught the Pecos language to a Mexican Indian, Juan de Dios, who served as a Franciscan lay brother on the Oñate expedition. Once at Pecos, Juan tested his linguistic skill and learned valuable information, which Oñate later found useful, about Pecos and the Great Plains. After four days at the fortress pueblo, Oñate returned to the Rio Grande to explore the pueblos west of the river. What he had learned about the plains after his visits to Taos, Picuris, Pecos, and Galisteo piqued his curiosity, and he soon made plans to go out to the Great Plains and see that wilderness for himself.

As the summer of exploration came to a close, the settlers at San Juan organized their village and prepared for winter. By the end of August, they had commenced work on the *acequia madre,* the main irrigation ditch, and had planned their fields for the following spring. Assisted by some fifteen hundred Indians, the church at San Juan was constructed in three weeks, between 23 August and 7 September. "It was large enough to accommodate all of the people in the camp,"[42] wrote one settler. The church, San Juan Bautista, was dedicated on 8 September. The priests blessed the church and consecrated the altar and the chalices. Father Salazar delivered the homily before a packed congregation. Amidst great rejoicing after Mass, the village celebrated in the wilderness of North America with music, food, drink, loud voices, and laughter. In the afternoon, the pageantry of the sham battle, *moros y cristianos* (Moors and Christians), was acted out for the entertainment of all.[43] To the natives looking on, the scenario appeared somewhat perplexing, yet familiar. It may have disturbed them to remember what they had retained in their lore about the Europeans, who had come to their land in the past with terrible weapons and horses. Whatever the prophecies may have been concerning the coming of the white man, the natives now stood witness to the fact that the Pueblo world, indeed, the Indian world, would never again be the same.

The next day a general assembly of the village was convened. Indian leaders of the pueblos of the Rio Arriba and the Rio Abajo were also in attendance. Governor Oñate addressed the assembly. With the aid of interpreters, the governor gave an account of the country he had explored and announced that the pueblos of New Mexico would be divided among the eight Franciscan friars in the expedition. The divisions would be called *conversiones evangélicos,* and the entire evangelic conversion of New Mexico would be called the *Conversión de San Pablo de la Provincia de Nuevo México.* One priest wrote: "Just as the Spaniards venerate him as their patron saint, so the Indians in their chapel revere Saint Paul on the feast day of his conversion, and thus Saint Paul is considered the patron saint of all New Mexico, as Saint Joseph is of New Spain."[44]

Before the assignments of the priests were announced, Fray Alonso Martínez and Governor Juan de Oñate addressed the pueblo leaders. With the aid of interpreters, Don Juan explained that he had come to this land to bring them the knowledge of God, on which depended the "salvation of their souls, and to live peaceably and safely in their countries, governed justly, safe in their possessions, protected from their enemies."[45] He told them that he had come in peace. It was fitting, he told them, that they should "render obedience and vassalage to God and king, and in their stead, to the most reverend father commissary in spiritual matters, and to the governor in temporal matters and those relating to the government of their public affairs."[46]

After Oñate had thus explained himself through his interpreters, the leaders acknowledged that they understood what he had said. The governor repeated his message and the Indians, wise in the ways of survival, stated that they wished to render obedience to God and king and that they did so voluntarily in the names of their respective nations.[47] At least, this is what Oñate assumed they said.

Then the meeting took on the character of ritual. Accepting their pledge, Don Juan asked them to stand up, for they had been seated on the ground for quite some time. He bade the Indians to approach him, to kneel before him and Father Martínez, and to kiss their hands as a sign of submission. One by one the pueblo leaders did so as the two Spaniards, representing the duality of church and state, received their homage as a sign of obedience and vassalage.[48] The pomp and circumstance of Spanish colonialism was played out under a canopy of cottonwoods at San Juan.

As planned beforehand, the governor and the commissary assigned the friars to the *conversiones evangélicos* of the pueblos. "Take the priests and ministers of God," Oñate told them, "so that they might learn their languages and so that the natives may be instructed about God's law." He told them that they "should be baptized so that they might go to heaven and escape going to hell." Somewhat confused, the pueblo leaders replied that they would accede, based on what Oñate said next. "Look after the padres," he said, "treat them well, and support and obey them in every respect." This he repeated three times with the admonition that if they failed to do so, they and their pueblos would "be put to the sword and destroyed by fire."[49] This they understood. Although they must have had second thoughts about their agreement, they also realized they were powerless to resist.

The leaders of the pueblos of the Rio Abajo sat courteously and patiently as the assignments for the Franciscan ministers were read aloud and the friars were presented.

The list was long and detailed, indicating the exactness of Oñate's intelligence gathering. Then their attention was focused on two Franciscans who stood before them as the assignments regarding the Rio Abajo were read.

"To Father Fray Juan de Rosas, the province of the Cheres, with the pueblos of Castixe called San Felipe, and Comitze and the pueblo of Santo Domingo, and Olipoti, Cochiti, and the pueblos of the Ciénega of Carabajal and San Marcos, San Cristóbal, Santa Ana, Ojana, Quipacha, and El Puerto, the burned pueblo [*pueblo quemado*]. . . . Father Fray Juan Claros, the province of the Chiguas, or Tiguas and the pueblos of Napeya and Tuchiamas, Pura, together with the four next in order down the river, Popen, Puarai, Tziymatzi, Guayotzi, Acacagui, Henicoho and Viareato, with all those subject to Puarai, both up and down the Rio del Norte; and the province of Xala, the province of Atzigues down the river, with all its pueblos, which include Puguey, Tuzahe, Aponitze, Vumaheyn, Quiapo, Cunguili, Pinoe, Calziati, Aguiabo, Emxa, Quiaguacalca, Tzelaqui, Puquias, Ayqui, Yanamo, Teyaxa, Qualacu, Texa, Amo, on this side of the river and on the opposite side, the pueblos of Pencoana, Quiomagui, Peixole, Cumaque, Telytzaan, Puguey, Canocan, Geydol, Quiubaco, Tohol, Cantemachul, Tercao, Poloaca, Tzexey, Quelquelu, Ategua, Tzula, Tzeygual, Tdcahan, Qualahamo, Piloqte, Penjeacu, Teypama, and lastly Tzenaqual de la Mesilla, which is the first settlement in this kingdom toward the south of New Spain."[50]

The list went on. It also included the pueblos of Las Salinas east of the Manzano mountain range and the desert pueblos of Zuñi and Hopi to the west. Oñate left no question that he had knowledge of every pueblo by its Indian name in the entire province of New Mexico. After hearing the list of assignments, the pueblo leaders present were instructed to kiss the hand of the friar chosen for them. The Indians rose and "kissed his habit and embraced him."[51] The missionization of New Mexico's pueblos had begun, albeit on a very small scale, for the friars were too few and the distance between many of the pueblos too great to administer their assignments.

The men of Oñate were indefatigable explorers. Even before San Juan had been firmly established, they had made their reconnaissance of the pueblo world along the Rio Grande and had probed the edge of the Great Plains. The pueblos to the west of San Juan intrigued them as well.

In early August of 1598, after exploring the Rio Abajo, they passed by Zía on their way to Jémez. Pulling their horses over a most difficult hill to get to "the great pueblo of the Emmes," they lost two of their mounts which rolled down shortly before getting to the top.[52] Jémez impressed them. Ever diligent, the observant Spaniards took note of everything they saw. At Jémez they saw a "petty chieftain" wearing around his neck a paten with a hole drilled through its center. Oñate's men discerned that it had belonged to one of the priests who had been martyred seventeen years earlier at Puaray on the Rio Abajo. Now they sought to retrieve it. "He traded it for hawks' bells," wrote one Spaniard, "but even if he had not accepted them, he would not have been allowed to take it away."[53] It was August 3rd, they noted, the feast day of San Estevan when they recovered the paten. Later, it was kept in the ciborium of the convent at San Juan. Doubtless, too, when the Spaniards moved their headquarters to San Gabriel, the paten was moved there along with the ciborium.

Jémez and environs were explored at this time. The "other Emmes pueblos" numbered eleven, but the Spaniards only saw eight of them, reported Oñate. The terrain was exceedingly rough and the descent to the other pueblos was so steep that two horses were killed when they tumbled down a precipice. On the way to one pueblo, they saw the "marvelous hot baths,"[54] with their cold and hot waters and many deposits of sulfur and alum. The hot springs at Jémez were frequented many times by Spaniards throughout the colonial period. Jémez was the last of the summer explorations in 1598. They returned to San Juan by way of Santo Domingo and San Ildefonso.

By the fall of 1598, the Oñate explorers were out on the trail again. Once established, the trail to the Great Plains ran from San Juan (later from San Gabriel) to Santo Domingo, thence to San Cristóbal at Galisteo, where provisions were taken. San Cristóbal formed a sort of crossroads, for the route divided there, leading to Pecos in the north, to the Salinas pueblos in the south, and to the Great Plains in the direction of the rising sun.

In September of 1598, the *Sargento Mayor* Vicente de Zaldívar and a contingent of soldiers marched past San Cristóbal to the buffalo plains. His route to Galisteo, via the Rio Abajo pueblos, was uneventful.

Once out on the plains, somewhere near the Canadian River beyond the Texas Panhandle, the Spaniards found plenty of buffalo. Hoping to capture some of these "monstrous cows," they spent several days constructing a large corral from the cottonwoods growing along the river. Then they tried to herd the buffalo into it, but the wild animals could not be penned. In the attempted roundup the Spaniards lost three horses that were gored by the buffalo. When the Spaniards roped some calves, the animals were severely injured in their attempts to break loose. Finally, Zaldívar decided that the buffalo could not be captured and had some killed for their meat. After nearly two months on the trail, Zaldívar, the consummate explorer of the Great Plains, returned to San Juan.[55]

Sad news awaited Vicente de Zaldívar, for on his return he learned that his brother, Juan de Zaldívar, had been slain in an ambush at Acoma.[56] The Acomans, a proud warrior culture, had challenged the Spanish right to rule over them. Using threats, coercion, and persuasion, the warriors from Acoma urged other pueblos to join them in their defiance, but the others, who had witnessed Spanish military power at Pecos and at the Rio Abajo pueblos of Moho and Arenal decades before, were too wary and instead adopted a wait-and-see attitude.

While Vicente de Zaldívar was out on the Great Plains, Oñate had planned to explore westward to the Pacific Ocean to find a harbor from which to better supply New Mexico. Following the Rio Grande southward, the Spaniards, in order to supply themselves, demanded that the pueblos along the route trade their food for Spanish goods. On this journey, Oñate took a roundabout route to Galisteo and then southward to Salinas. It was mid-October when Oñate and his men left the Manzano pueblos through the pass he called El Ortuelo, near present-day Abo Pass. They recrossed the Rio Grande at Isleta and traveled north to Puaray, thence west to Acoma[57] after they had supplied themselves at the Rio Abajo pueblos. At Acoma they traded for food with the resentful natives who watched their food supply dwindle as winter approached.

In a plot which failed, according to Villagrá, the Acomans invited Oñate to their pueblo atop a *peñol,* or mesa, some 220 feet high. Climbing the footholds carved into the rock, Oñate and some of his men made the precarious ascent. The Acoman plan, against the better judgement of some among them, was to isolate Oñate from his men and kill him.[58] When they invited the Spanish governor into one of their kivas, he declined. Again they tried to persuade him to enter another one, telling him that he would see something wondrous inside. Peering into the entryway of the kiva, the wary Oñate sensed a trap. According to Villagrá, his men urged him to decline, which he politely did. Unknown to him at the time, a dozen or so armed warriors were apparently inside ready to dispatch him the moment he entered. The Acomans would have to wait for another opportunity.

Before he had departed Puaray for Acoma and the far west, Oñate sent a message to his nephew, *Maese de Campo* Juan de Zaldívar, to join him. From Acoma Oñate proceeded to the Zuñi region. From Hawikuh he sent Captain Marcos Farfán to inspect a salt lake about forty miles to the southeast. While Farfán was gone Captain Villagrá showed up after returning from his pursuit of the four soldiers who had deserted earlier. On November 8 the entire expedition set out for Hopi, or Moqui Land, probably arriving at Awatobi from where Farfán was sent to look at some mines reported by the Indian guides. He went as far as the modern mining ghost town of Jerome, Arizona.

Meanwhile Juan de Oñate started back to Hawikuh on November 18 where he waited for Farfán. On December 12 they all started back to San Juan with the exception of seven soldiers who had been left among the Hopis with exhausted horses.[59]

Later, after leaving Zuñi, Oñate and his men were overtaken by a heavy snowstorm in which they lost many horses. While they were camped near El Morro, which the Spaniards called El Estanque del Peñol, a messenger from Zaldívar's command rode in from Acoma to tell the governor of the deaths of his nephew and of others in an ambush. It was mid-December when a grieving Oñate rode back to San Juan. There he would learn more of the details regarding the fight at Acoma and would make a momentous decision which would affect Spanish-Indian relations in New Mexico for the rest of the colonial period.[60]

Oñate learned that while Juan de Zaldívar and his troop of soldiers were camped near the bottom of the *peñol de Acoma,* some Indians had come down and invited a few of the Spaniards to ascend and visit their pueblo.[61] Leaving part of his troop below to guard the camp and horses, Zaldívar and the rest of his men climbed the stone ladders to the top. The Spaniards began to trade for food, as usual. This time, however, the Indians led them about so that the Spaniards were divided.[62] The Indians rapidly fell on them, killing the *maese de campo* and twelve others and throwing their bodies from the cliffs. The guard at the bottom of the *peñol* was helpless to come to their aid. In desperation, three men survived by leaping from the escarpment; one other was killed as he plummeted down from the pueblo's edge.[63]

After the wounded were attended to, the detachment divided into three squads of less than a dozen men each. One group retreated to San Juan to warn the settlers, a second party was sent to warn the friars at the various pueblos, and the third squad hastened to report the attack to Oñate.[64]

While the Indians at Acoma gloried in their victory over the *Castillas,* the settlers at San Juan tried to come to terms with an uncertain future. Fear gripped the settlement, for the Spaniards believed that the successful revolt at Acoma could signal a rebellion of all the pueblos. When Oñate and his men arrived at San Juan, they found the settlement heavily guarded.[65] Amidst the mourning for the dead soldiers, Oñate called a council of war and heard testimony from those who had been with Juan de Zaldívar at Acoma. Prompt action would be necessary to show Acoma and the rest of the pueblos that defiance against Spanish authority would not be tolerated. From a military point of view, the Spaniards knew they could not permit Acoma to get away with the attack, lest the other pueblos interpret Spanish inaction as a sign of weakness. At the council of war, Oñate consulted his captains and the friars about their course of action.[66] All agreed that Acoma should be made an object lesson, if the Spanish settlement were to survive. One priest wrote that "peace was the principal end for which war was ordained." In order to re-establish peace and control, they believed, Oñate had to attack Acoma.[67]

Although Oñate had planned to command the seventy troops selected for the mission, the *Sargento Mayor* Vicente de Zaldívar, whose brother had been slain at Acoma, claimed the right to lead the punitive expedition. Some Spaniards believed he had the right to avenge his loss.[68] Oñate gave him instructions to proceed to Acoma,[69] "plant [his] artillery and musketry," and deploy the troops in "battle formation." That done, Zaldívar, with the aid of Mexican Indians, particularly the interpreters Tomás and Cristóbal, or other suitable interpreters, was to "summon the Indians of Acoma to accept peace, once, twice and thrice, and urge them to abandon their resistance, lay down their arms, and submit to the authority of the king, our lord, since they [had] already rendered obedience to him as his vassals."[70]

Zaldívar was to ask the people of Acoma "to surrender the leaders responsible for the uprisings, and the murders, assuring them that they [would] be justly dealt with." The bodies of the dead Spaniards, along with their accoutrements, were to be returned. If the Acomans should resist, then Zaldívar was authorized either to attack or to postpone the fight, depending on his judgment. The attack should be called off, warned Oñate, if the Indian strength was too great, "for there would be less harm in postponing the punishment for the time being than in risking the people with you."[71] If the Acomans wanted a fight, then the Spaniards were ready. Oñate's instructions to Zaldívar were clear. "Inasmuch," he ordered, "as we have declared war on them without quarter, you will punish all those of fighting age as you deem best, as a warning to everyone in this kingdom." The orders which covered the possibility that the Indians would surrender those responsible for the attack called for a restrained effort in the punishment of Acoma, but left open the possibility of war of "fire and sword" if they refused to meet the Spaniards' demands. Dipping a quill in ink, Oñate signed the instructions to Zaldívar before his secretary, who notarized the document.[72]

When Zaldívar and his troops arrived at Acoma on 21 January 1599, they were greeted by taunts, jeers, insults, and obscene gestures from the defiant warriors of the mighty pueblo. Undaunted, Vicente de Zaldívar deployed his men and artillery with an odd calm. Experienced in siege warfare, his scouts collectively ascertained the best point for the assault on the *peñol*. Standing around a campfire, the members of the war council formulated a plan: They would feign an assault on the pueblo by climbing up the main stone ladders while a detail of men pulled up an artillery piece at the rear of the pueblo, catching the Indians in a cross fire.

Meanwhile, as the Spaniards planned their attack, Zaldívar and his interpreters offered the prescribed peace gestures,[73] "once, twice and thrice." Despite warnings from some of their leaders, the Acomans rejected Zaldívar's peace offerings. Jeering, shooting arrows, hurling wooden spears,[74] and throwing rocks at the Spaniards, the Acomans made clear their intention to fight. That night the Spaniards camped below the pueblo and rested; the Indians spent the night "in huge dances and carousals, shouting, hissing . . . and challenging the army to fight."[75] Zaldívar reported that "the Indians all shouted loudly, raised their swords on high, and presented themselves in the coats of mail and other pieces of equipment they had taken from the dead Spaniards, boasting that they had killed ten Spaniards and two Mexicans, and that we were a pack of mongrels and whoremongers."[76] Throughout the entire encounter, reported the Spaniards, the Indians kept shouting they wanted to fight. The Indians, Zaldívar said, asked "why were we waiting, and why we did not fight, since they were ready for battle and were waiting for nothing but to kill us and then kill the Queres and the Tiguas and everyone at Zía because they failed to kill the Spaniards."[77]

The attack began at three o'clock in the afternoon of 22 January. Under cover of the previous night's darkness, twelve Spaniards had hauled a small cannon to the top of the mesa at the rear of the pueblo and hid themselves. The next day, when the attack began, the main body of troops feigned an attack on the main entrance. The Acomans engaged the intruders, leaving the rear of the pueblo unprotected. Soon the twelve Spaniards had reached the top and fired their cannon into the pueblo. Meanwhile, Zaldívar, seeing a warrior wearing his brother's uniform, slashed his way toward him, and finally killed him with his sword. Night ended the first day's battle. Many Indians had surrendered, but a large body of warriors had secreted themselves in the chasms in the rock.

The next day the battle continued from early morning until five o'clock that afternoon. Zaldívar again asked them to surrender the instigators. They refused, and the battle resumed. Zaldívar ordered that "all Indian women and children who could be found should be taken prisoners to save them from being killed by the Indian warriors."[78] About five hundred of them were taken for that purpose. The *sargento mayor* ordered the soldiers to proceed without quarter, setting fire to all of the houses and even the provisions. Spanish arms and assault tactics were too much for the courageous Acoman warriors. The fall of Acoma shook its inhabitants, but it did not break them; most of them would escape to rebuild their pueblo, and they would continue to defy the Spaniards and challenge other pueblos to resist the *Castillas*.

The defenders of Acoma had been subdued for the moment and they were taken to the pueblo of Santo Domingo for trial. There, Captain Alonso Gómez Montesinos was appointed as their attorney and guardian. On 9 February 1599, Spaniards and Indians gathered to hear the testimony of those who had taken part in the battle of Acoma. Statements were taken from Acoman warriors named Caoma, Taxio, Catticati, Xunusta, Excasi, Caucachi[79] and others. The next day, Captain Gómez Montesinos presented a petition to Oñate on behalf of the Acomans. He declared:

I, Captain Alonso Gómez Montesinos, defense attorney for the Indians, state that I have frequently explained to them through the interpreter that if they have any pleas to offer or any witnesses to present in their defense, they should have them appear so that the appropriate inquiries may be made. They replied that they had no witnesses or defense pleas to offer for having killed the Spaniards. This being the case, their only defense was that many of them were not guilty as they were absent when the Spaniards were killed, and they were unaware of the crime the others had committed. For this reason and from what was learned in the testimony that your lordship took from some of the Indians, you should acquit them, set them free, allow them to go wherever they wish, and order that they be compensated for the expenses resulting from their arrest.

Wherefore, I beseech your lordship to grant this petition and show clemency to the Indians in view of the fact that they are uncivilized.[80]

Gómez Montesinos pleaded the case in colonial terms, expressing his compassion for the Acomans and revealing his Eurocentric view of the natives under his charge.

After other pleas for clemency, the three-day trial at Santo Domingo came to an end. On 12 February, Oñate read out the sentence which would harshly punish the Acomans for having "wantonly killed Don Juan de Zaldívar Oñate" and twelve others and for having refused the peace offered them by Vicente de Zaldívar. "I must and do sentence all of the Indian men and women from the said pueblo under arrest,"[81] he began. Boys and girls under twelve years of age whose parents were involved in fighting against the Spaniards were placed under the guardianship of the missionaries.[82] Those between twelve and twenty-five years of age were sentenced to twenty years of servitude. The elderly men and women were freed but entrusted to the Querechos, Indians from the Great Plains, who "may not allow them to leave their pueblos."[83] Then Oñate read the sentence which brought protests from the colonists themselves. "The males," ordered Oñate, "who are over twenty-five years of age, I sentence to have one foot cut off and to twenty years of personal servitude."[84] The sentence was carried out on twenty-four Acoman males at Santo Domingo and at other nearby pueblos on separate days. Some colonials helped Indian captives escape.

Shocked by the severe sentences, the anti-Oñate faction brought charges against Oñate and Zaldívar in 1612 and 1613 for their excesses. Oñate and Zaldívar were found guilty, heavily fined and banished from New Mexico.[85] They lost all of their landholdings and investments in the conquest and settlement of New Mexico, a heavy price for a colonial to pay. To Oñate and Zaldívar however, the swift and severe punishment of Acoma had evidently served its purpose.

The anti-Oñate faction was equally outraged at Oñate's excesses against them. When four soldiers deserted Oñate's force, he sent two captains, Gaspar de Villagrá and Gerónimo Márquez, to track them down as they fled along the Rio Abajo. Someplace in Chihuahua the deserters were surprised, captured, and executed. Their right hands were amputated, preserved in salt, and presented to Oñate as proof that they were dead.[86] Two of the men were apparently beheaded.[87]

Other Indians continued to defy Spanish rule in New Mexico, but Oñate's force was sufficient to quiet them. About this period, from 1600 to 1604, other explorations took place from the new capital at San Gabriel. In the early part of that phase of exploration, the Spaniards explored the Great Plains as far as the great bend of the Arkansas River. In the second phase, they went westward. In October 1604, Oñate took up his old dream, interrupted earlier by the death of his nephew at Acoma, of exploring to the Pacific Ocean. On this expedition, Oñate found no mines, saw no gold or silver and, once on the Colorado River in western Arizona, located no pearl fisheries. At that point, without ever reaching the Pacific coastline, the expedition turned back.[88]

Disappointed in his final hope for mineral wealth, Oñate pointed his men toward the rising sun and began the long, toilsome journey back to San Gabriel. On passing El Morro (Inscription Rock), Oñate paused long enough to leave a message for posterity.

> *Pasó por aquí el Adelantado don Juan de Oñate del descubrimiento de la mar del sur a 16 día de abril año 1605.*
>
> Through here passed the Adelantado Don Juan de Oñate from the discovery of the South Sea on the 16th day of April, year 1605.

Oñate's inscription is the oldest Spanish inscription on the rock; only the Indian petroglyphs are older.

The New Mexico settlement was in trouble. Dissension over Oñate's leadership and his handling of Indian affairs had split the settlers into pro- and anti-Oñate factions. Many had deserted the settlement and returned to New Spain. They made reports to authorities against Oñate and his loyal followers. The accusations were investigated by Spanish officials who commenced proceedings against Oñate and some of his captains. In the end, Oñate lost all he had worked to secure for himself in New Mexico. He was found guilty of some charges and absolved of others.[89]

Exiled from New Mexico, he returned to Spain and became an inspector of mines. He died in Guadalcanal, Spain, in the first week of June, probably 3 June 1626. He was about seventy-four years old. On the day of his death, he had entered an inundated mine to try to pump out the water when he collapsed and expired soon after.[90] His nephew, Vicente de Zaldívar, about sixty-four years of age, died in Zacatecas, New Spain, in the third week of February 1636. A wealthy *hacendado* (landowner) he was a knight of the Order of Santiago.[91] On 21 February 1636, Agustín Barroso, a royal scribe, rode his horse to the hacienda of the *Maese de Campo* Vicente Zaldívar y Mendoza near Ciudad Nuestra Señora de los Zacatecas. Greeted by servants, Barroso was led to the Zaldívar family chapel, where he witnessed the body of Don Vicente lying in state. The deceased, wrote Barroso, had been laid in a coffin dressed in the uniform of the *Orden de los Caballeros de Santiago*. Later that day, Vicente de Zaldívar, conqueror of Acoma in the Province of New Mexico, was buried.[92] With the deaths of Villagrá (1620), Oñate (1626), and Zaldívar (1636), a chapter in New Mexico's early stormy history had come to an end.

The Oñate period in New Mexico (1598–1609) set the pattern for the settlement of the province and established the long trail from Mexico City to San Gabriel which increasingly became important as the Camino Real de Tierra Adentro, the Royal Road of the Interior, especially after Santa Fe was established in 1610. Like their counterparts in northern New Mexico, the pueblos of the Rio Abajo supplied travelers on the Camino Real as they had the early explorers who came by them. Missionization, which began on the upper Rio Abajo at Santo Domingo during the late Oñate period, would soon spread in the seventeenth century to all the other pueblos. For that reason, Santo Domingo would become the ecclesiastical headquarters of the province of New Mexico. Church-state issues, which went unresolved during the strongman rule of Juan Pérez de Oñate, would prove volatile throughout the decades preceding the Pueblo Revolt of 1680. The friars, some of them related to members of the Oñate faction, supported Oñate's actions, but others sided with the settlers and Indians. The Franciscans hoped to reserve New Mexico as a mission field, even during Oñate's day, and strived for the civilian abandonment of the province. Nevertheless, the founding of Santa Fe in 1610 by Pedro de Peralta began a new era for New Mexico.

NOTES

1. For English translations of documentary accounts of the Francisco Vázquez de Coronado expedition, see George P. Hammond and Agapito Rey, eds. and trans., *Narratives of the Coronado Expedition, 1540–1542* (Albuquerque: University of New Mexico Press, 1940).

2. For English translations of documentary accounts of the Francisco Sánchez Chamuscado expedition, see George P. Hammond and Agapito Rey, eds. and trans., *The Rediscovery of New Mexico, 1580–1594* (Albuquerque: University of New Mexico Press, 1966).

3. See Hammond and Rey, *Rediscovery.*

4. Joseph P. Sanchez, *The Rio Abajo Frontier, 1540–1692: A History of Early Colonial New Mexico* (Albuquerque: Museum of Albuquerque History Monograph Series, 1987), 51. The author gratefully acknowledges the permission of the Albuquerque Museum to reprint portions of the monograph in this introduction.

5. For comprehensive English translations of documentary sources related to the Oñate period, see George P. Hammond and Agapito Rey, eds. and trans., *Don Juan de Oñate, Colonizer of New Mexico, 1595–1628*, 2 vols. (Albuquerque: University of New Mexico Press, 1940).

6. Memoria del Descubrimiento que Gaspar Castaño de Sosa hizo en el Nuevo México, siendo teniente de Gobernador y Capitán General del Nuevo Reino de Leon. Copy of vol. 70, expediente 1543, Real Academia de la Historia, Madrid. In the Spanish Colonial Research Center, National Park Service-University of New Mexico Collection. For an English translation see Albert H. Shroeder and Dan S. Matson, eds., *A Colony on the Move: Gaspar Castaño de Sosa's Journal, 1590–1591* (Santa Fe: School of American Research, 1965).

7. Alfred Barnaby Thomas, *After Coronado, Spanish Exploration Northeast of New Mexico, 1696–1727* (Norman, Oklahoma: University of Oklahoma Press, 1935), 5; and Herbert E. Bolton, *Spanish Exploration of the Southwest, 1542–1706* (New York: Charles Scribner and Sons, 1908), 224.

8. Bolton, *Spanish Exploration,* 201.

9. Francisco de Thoma, *Historia Popular de Nuevo México* (New York, 1896), 49; and Bolton, *Spanish Exploration,* 201.

10. Bolton, *Spanish Exploration,* 201.

11. Ibid.

12. H. H. Bancroft, *History of Arizona and New Mexico* (San Francisco, 1889), XVII:119.

13. Joseph P. Sanchez, "Vicente de Zaldívar and the Jumano War, 1599–1601." Unpublished manuscript, in files of the Spanish Colonial Research Center, University of New Mexico, Albuquerque.

14. "Itinerario," in Joaquin F. Pacheco, Francisco de Cardenas, Luis Torres de Mendoza, eds., *Colección de Documentos Ineditos Relativos al Descubrimiento, Conquista y Organizacion de las Antiguas Posesiones Españoles de America y Oceania.* 42 vols (Madrid, 1864–1884), XVI:228–76.

15. Ibid., 244.

16. Ibid., 243–44.

17. Ibid., 244.

18. Ibid., 244.

19. Ibid., 243.

20. Ibid., 245.

21. Ibid., 247.

22. Ibid., 248.

23. Ibid., 248.

24. Ibid., 250.

25. Ibid., 251.

26. Ibid., 251.

27. Ibid., 252.

28. Ibid., 252.

29. Ibid., 253.

30. Ibid., 253.

31. Ibid., 254.

32. Ibid., 254.

33. Ibid., 256.

34. Ibid., 254.

35. Ibid., 255.

36. Ibid., 257.

37. Ibid., 257.

38. Ibid., 258.

39. Ibid., 258.

40. Ibid., 258.

41. Ibid., 258.

42. Ibid., 264.

43. Ibid., 264.

44. Ibid., 264.

45. "Act of Obedience and Vassalage by the Indians of San Juan Bautista," Hammond and Rey, *Don Juan Oñate*, I:342–47.

46. Ibid., 343.

47. Ibid., 342–43.

48. Ibid., 343–44.

49. Ibid., 344.

50. Ibid., 345–46.

51. Ibid., 346.

52. Pacheco, Cardenas y Torres, *Colección de Documentos Ineditos*, XVI:260.

53. Ibid., 260.

54. Ibid., 261.

55. Bolton, *Spanish Exploration*, 228.

56. Ibid., 237.

57. Ibid., 233–34.

58. Espinosa, *History*, 167; and Miguel Encinias, Alfredo Rodriguez, and Joseph P. Sanchez, eds. and trans., *Gaspar de Villagrá's Historia de la Nueva México, 1610: A Critical and Annotated English/Spanish Edition* (Albuquerque: University of New Mexico Press, 1992), canto XVIII.

59. Hammond and Rey, *Don Juan de Oñate*, I:393–97, 409–15.

60. Ibid.

61. Espinosa, *History*, 190.

62. Ibid., 189–95.

63. Ibid., 189–95.

64. Bancroft, *History*, 142.

65. Ibid., 142.

66. Ibid., 142.

67. Espinosa, *History*, 208.

68. Testimony of Alonso Sanchez, 28 February 1599, Hammond and Rey, *Don Juan de Oñate*, I:427.

69. Instructions to the *sargento mayor* for the punishment of Acoma, Hammond and Rey, *Don Juan de Oñate*, I:456–59.

70. Ibid., 458.

71. Ibid., 458.

72. Ibid., 459.

73. Proceedings at Acoma, Hammond and Rey, *Don Juan de Oñate*, I:460–63.

74. Ibid., 460.

75. Ibid., 461.

76. Ibid., 460.

77. Ibid., 461.

78. Ibid., 462.

79. Ibid., 464–68. Indian testimony and other accounts given passim.

80. Ibid., 469.

81. Ibid., 477–79. See also Hammond and Rey, *Don Juan de Oñate*, II:889 and II:1127.

82. Ibid., 477.

83. Ibid., 477–78.

84. Ibid., 615. Captain Luis Gasco de Velasco stated "Twenty-four Indians had their feet cut off as punishment."

85. Ibid., 1114, 1127–28.

86. Ibid., 1136–37.

87. El Capitán Gaspar de Villagrá para justificación de las muertes, justicias, y castigos que el Adelantado don Juan de Oñate dizen que hizo en la Nueva Mexico, 1612? in Wagner, *Spanish Southwest*, 199, indicates that "he [Villagrá] only cut off the hands of some deserters, but in his Relación de servicios of 1615 he says that he pursued the deserters two hundred leagues, captured them, and cut their throats."

88. Ibid., 616.

89. Ibid., 1109.

90. The death of Juan de Oñate is referenced in a series of documents beginning with: Poder que dio Juan de Oñate Adelantado de las provincias de Nuevo México, visitador General de Minas de España, a Andres de Carrasquilla, su secretario para que tomase el asiento del rendimiento, trabajas y administracion de todas las minas del Reino descubierto y por descubrir, 1625–1627. Archivo General de Simancas, Spain, Contadurias Generales 852.

91. Información de la Geneología y Limpieza de el Maese de Campo Vicente de Zaldívar, Vecino de Zacatecas. Archivo Histórico Nacional, Madrid, Sección Inquisición, legajo 1367 (old number Legajo 1, número 8). See also, Arbol de la Generación de el Capitán General de la Nueva Galicia de esta Nueva España en que con toda claridad se vee el grado de parentesco, en que se halla cada uno de los que litigan este vinculo formal. Archivo General de la Nación, Mexico City, Sección Vinculos 110. See also, Joseph P. Sanchez, "Vicente de Zaldívar and the Jumano War, 1599–1601." Unpublished manuscript, in the files of the Spanish Colonial Research Center, University of New Mexico, Albuquerque.

92. Información de la Geneología y Limpieza de el Maese de Campo Vicente de Zaldívar. Archivo Histórico Nacional, Sección Inquisición, legajo 1367.

HISTORIA
de la
NUEVA MÉXICO

CANTO PRIMERO

QUE DECLARA EL ARGUMENTO DE LA HISTORIA
y sitio de la nueva México[1] *y noticia que della se tuvo en*
quanto la antigualla[2] *de los Indios, y de la salida y*
decendencia de los verdaderos Mexicanos.

L AS armas y el varón heroico canto,[3]
El ser, valor, prudencia y alto esfuerzo
De aquel cuya paciencia no rendida,
Por vn mar de disgustos arrojada,
A pesar de la envidia ponzoñosa
Los hechos y prohezas va encumbrando
De aquellos españoles valerosos
Que en la Occidental India remontados,[4]
Descubriendo del mundo lo que esconde,
'Puls ultra'[5] con braveza van diziendo
A fuerza de valor y brazos fuertes,
En armas y quebrantos tan sufridos
Quanto de tosca pluma celebrados.
Suplicoos, Christianísimo Filipo,[6]
Que, pues de nueva México soys fénix,[7]

1. Esta designación topinímica, que la zona ha retenido hasta
nuestros días, no procede, como podría parecerle al lector moderno, de
lo que hoy es conocido como México, nombre que sólo adquiere Nueva
España a raíz de su independencia en el siglo pasado. Nueva México,
tal y como se usaba en el siglo XVI, procedía de la esperanzada
asociación que llegaron a hacer los españoles (tras las imaginativas
descripciones del sudoeste americano que hicieron Cabeza de Vaca y el
padre Marcos de Niza) de las tierras desconocidas del norte con el
fabuloso imperio azteca que había hallado Cortés. Que hayamos podido
comprobar, la designación de Nueva México para esas tierras al norte
fue primero usado por Francisco de Ibarra, gobernador de Nueva
Vizcaya, tras su entrada por las mismas en 1563. (H. H. Bancroft,
History of Arizona and New Mexico: 1533–1588. Albuquerque: Horn and
Wallace Publishers, 1962. 72
  2. Antigualla = Noticia o relación de sucesos muy antiguos.
  3. Imitación del comienzo de *la Eneida* de Virgilio, modelo
primario de la épica renacentista. No se trata sólo del primer verso, ya
que la presentación del héroe, Oñate, con su sufrida resistencia frente a
múltiples adversidades, es todo eco del comienzo virgiliano.
  4. Remontados = alejados.
  5. Patente errata de la reproducción mexicana que trae *Puls ultra.* Es
el *más allá* que fue lema, épico, del descubrimiento y la conquista
americana, formando parte del escudo de Castilla.
  6. El poema va dedicado y dirigido a Felipe III.
  7. Desde Plinio, *Historia Naturalis,* el ave fénix se decía renacer de
las cenizas de sí mismo. Villagrá hace un interesante símil entre el
ardor de la fe católica y el auto-enardecedor fuego de esa ave mítica.

CANTO I

Which sets forth the outline of the history and the location of
New Mexico,[1] *and the reports had of it in the traditions of the*
Indians, and of the true origin and descent of the Mexicans.[2]

I sing of arms and the heroic man,[3]
The being, courage, care, and high emprise
Of him whose unconquered patience,
Though cast upon a sea of cares,[4]
5   In spite of envy slanderous,
Is raising to new heights the feats,
The deeds, of those brave Spaniards who,
In the far India of the West,[5]
Discovering in the world that which was hid,
10   'Plus ultra'[6] go bravely saying
By force of valor and strong arms,
In war and suffering as experienced
As celebrated now by pen unskilled.
I beg of thee, most Christian Philip,[7]
15   Being the Phoenix[8] of New Mexico

1. This geographic identification, that the area has retained into our
own day, does not proceed, as a modern reader might surmise, from
what is today known as Mexico, a name that New Spain only acquired
after its independence in the nineteenth century. Nueva México, as it
was called in the sixteenth century, stems from the Spaniards's hopeful
association (after the glowing reports made by Cabeza de Vaca and
Father Marcos de Niza of the American southwest) between the
unknown lands to the north and the fabulous Aztec Empire found by
Cortez. To our knowledge, the term "Nuevo México," used to identify
those unknown northern lands, was first employed by Francisco de
Ibarra, viceroy of Nueva Vizcaya, after his exploration of the same in
1563 (H. H. Bancroft, *History of Arizona and New Mexico: 1530–1588.*
Albuquerque: Horn and Wallace Publishers, 1962).
  2. The reference is to the Aztecs, whose historical-legendary origin
in the north, in the general area of the new lands being explored and
settled, intrigued the Spaniards, always hopeful of encountering similar
societies in that area.
  3. This is a very direct imitation of the first line of Virgil's *Aeneid,*
the primary model of the Renaissance epic. Although less direct, this
entire presentation of the hero, Oñate, patiently suffering a multitude
of adversities, echoes Virgil's poetic opening.
  4. Villagrá's nautical imagery initiates a pattern of usage that,
perhaps stemming from the primary Virgilian model but more likely
reflecting the novel and extreme experience of New World writers, is
an essential characteristic of the New World epic.
  5. Villagrá refers to the New World land mass as India of the West.
  6. This "further on" became the watchword and motto of those who
had broken the geographical limits of the ancient world, forming part
of the Castilian coat of arms.
  7. The poem is dedicated to Philip III, son of Philip II, still king
when Oñate negotiated and started his expedition.
  8. The phoenix's rebirth from its own ashes was common to most
medieval and Renaissance bestiaries, with their common origin in
Pliny's *Historia naturalis.* Villagrá parallels that rebirth from fire with
the renewed faith of Philip II's Counter-Reformation Catholicism.

Nuevamente salido y producido
De aquellas vivas llamas y cenizas
De ardentísima fee, en cuyas brasas
A vuestro sacro Padre y señor nuestro
Todo deshecho y abrasado vimos,
Suspendáis algún tanto de los hombres[8]
El grande y grave peso que os impide
De aquese inmenso globo que en justicia
Por sólo vuestro brazo se sustenta
Y, prestando, gran Rey, atento oído,
Veréis aquí la fuerza de trabajos,
Calumnias y aflicciones con que planta
El evangelio santo y Fee de Christo
Aquel Christiano Achiles[9] que quisistes
Que en obra tan heroica se ocupase.
Y si por qual que[10] buena suerte alcanzo
A teneros, Monarca, por oiente,
Quién duda que con admirable espanto
La redondez del mundo todo escuche
Lo que a tan alto Rey atento tiene.
Pues siendo assí de vos favorecido,
No siendo menos escrevir los hechos
Dignos de que la pluma los levante
Que emprender los que no son menos dignos
De que la misma pluma los escriba,
Sólo resta que aquellos valerosos
Por quien este cuydado yo he tomado
Alienten con su gran valor heroico
el atrevido buelo de mi pluma,
Porque desta vez pienso que veremos
Yguales las palabras con las obras.
Escuchadme, gran Rey, que soi testigo
De todo quanto aquí, señor, os digo.[11]
Debajo el polo Artico en altura
De los treinta y tres grados que a la santa
Ierusalem sabemos que responden,[12]
No sin grande misterio y maravilla,

Now newly brought forth from the flames
Of fire and new produced from ashes
Of the most ardent faith, in whose hot coals
Sublime your sainted Father and our lord
20 We saw all burned and quite undone,
Suspend a moment from your back
The great and heavy weight which bears you down
Of this enormous globe which, in all right,
Is by your arm alone upheld,
25 And, lending, O great King, attentive ear,
Thou here shalt see the load of toil,
Of calumny, affliction, under which
Did plant the evangel holy and the Faith of Christ
That Christian Achilles[9] whom you wished
30 To be employed in such heroic work.
And if in fortune good I may succeed
In having you, my Monarch, listener,
Who doubts that, with a wondering fear,
The whole round world shall listen too
35 To that which holds so high a King intent.
For, being favored thus by you,
It being no less to write of deeds worthy
Of being elevated by the pen
Than to undertake those which are no less
40 Worthy of being written by this same pen,[10]
'Tis only needed that those same brave men
For whom this task I undertook
Should nourish with their great, heroic valor
The daring flight of this my pen,
45 Because I think that this time we shall see
The words well equaled by the deeds.
Hear me, great King, for I am witness
Of all that here, my Lord, I say to you.[11]
Beneath the Arctic Pole, in height
50 Some thirty-three degrees, which the same
Are, we know, of sainted Jerùsalem,[12]
Not without mystery and marvel great,

8. Patente errata del original por "hombros."

9. Como "Cristiano Achiles," cristiano Aquiles, identifica Villagrá a Juan de Oñate. La identificación entre el caudillo épico y su finalidad religiosa, de agrandar el reino de Cristo, es especialmente notable en la epopeya relacionada con la Nueva España, en las obras de Lobo Lasso de la Vega, *Mexicana,* y Saavedra Guzmán, *El peregrino indiano.* Para el estudio de este aspecto y sus orígenes en Tasso, véase la edición de *Mexicana* a cargo del profesor Amor y Vázquez, Biblioteca de Autores Espanoles, 232, xxxviii–xlix.

10. Qual que = cual que, cualquier.

11. Aquí acaba la invocación para dar comienzo al canto propiamente.

12. La referencia es a la latitud. La subrayada coincidencia latitudinal entre Jersualén y las nuevas tierras refleja la noción prevalente de la finalidad religiosa de la empresa española.

9. The identification of the epic hero's Christian mission with the Homeric hero, Achilles, is characteristic of the New World epic. It is highlighted, especially, in the epics narrating the conquest of Mexico: Lobo Lasso de la Vega's *Mexicana* and Saavedra Guzmán's *El peregrino indiano.* For the study of the procedure and its origin in Tasso's Christian epic, see Professor Amor y Vázquez's edition of *Mexicana,* BAE, 232, xxxviii–xlix.

10. Villagrá, like Ercilla (*La araucana*) and several other poets of the conquest of the New World, was an active participant in the events he narrates.

11. The epic evocation (introduction) ends here.

12. This stressed coincidence of latitude between the new land and holy Jerusalem is meant to underscore the then widely held idea that the former, with great significance for Spain's missionary goals, had been especially preserved by God.

Se esparcen, tienden,[13] siembran y derraman
Unas naciones bárbaras, remotas
Del gremio de la Iglesia, donde el día
Mayor de todo el año abraza y tiene
Catorze horas y media quando llega
Al principio de Cancro[14] el Sol furioso,
Por cuyo Zenith passa de ordinario
De Andrómeda la imagen y Perseo,[15]
Cuya constelación influye siempre
La calidad de Venus y Mercurio.
Y en longitud nos muestra su districto,
Según que nos enseña y nos pratica
El meridiano fixo más moderno,[16]
Dozientos y setenta grados justos
En la templada zona y quarto clima;[17]
Dozientas leguas[18] largas por la parte
Que el mar del Norte[19] y golfo Mexicano
Acerca y avecina más la costa
Por el viento sueste;[20] y por la parte
Del bravo Californio[21] y mar de perlas[22]
Casi otro tanto dista por el rumbo
Que sopla el sudueste la marina;[23]
Y de la zona elada dista y tiene
Quinientas leguas largas bien tendidas;
Y en círculo redondo vemos ciñe
Debajo el paralelo, si tomamos
Los treinta y siete grados lebantados,
Cinco mil leguas buenas Españolas,
Cuya grandeza es lástima la ocupen
Tanta suma de gentes ignorantes
De la sangre de Christo, cuya alteza
Causa dolor la ignoren tantas almas.
Destas nuevas Regiones es notorio,
Pública voz y fama que decienden
Aquellos más antiguos Mexicanos
Que a la Ciudad de México famosa
El nombre le pussieron porque fuesse

55

60

65

70

75

80

85

Are spread, extended, sown, and overflow
Some nations barbarous, remote
From the bosom of the Church, where
The longest day of all the year contains and has
Some fourteen hours and a half when it arrives,
The furious sun, at the rising of Cancer,[13]
Through whose zenith he doth usually pass
The image of Andromeda and Perseus,[14]
Whose constellation always influences
The quality of Venus and Mercury.
And shows to us its location in longitude,
According as most modern fixed meridian
Doth teach us and we practice,[15]
Two hundred just degrees and seventy
Into the temperate zone and the fourth clime,[16]
Two hundred long leagues[17] from the place
Where the Sea of the North[18] and Gulf of Mexico
Approach the most and nearest to the coast
On the southeast; and to the side
Toward the rough Californio[19] and Sea of the Pearls[20]
The distance in that direction is about the same
Toward where the southwest wind strikes the coast[21]
And from the frozen zone its distance is
About five hundred full long leagues;
And in a circle round we see it hold,
Beneath the parallel, if we should take
The height of thirty-seven degrees,
Five thousand goodly Spanish leagues,
Whose greatness it is a shame it should be held
By so great sum of people ignorant
About the blood of Christ, whose holiness
It causes pain to think so many souls know not.
From these new regions 'tis notorious,
Of public voice and fame, that there descended
Those oldest folk of Mexico
Who to the famous city, Mexico,
Did give their name, that it might be

---

13. Tienden = extienden.
14. Cancro = Trópico de Cáncer, el septentrional.
15. Andrómeda y Perseo son constelaciones septentrionales.
16. En aquella época no se había aún convenido sobre meridianos de uso internacional para las medidas de longitud. Cada país solía usar el de su propia capital. El descubrimiento del Nuevo Mundo supuso la creación de nuevos meridianos.
17. Clima = espacio geográfico entre paralelos o líneas latitudinales. Los antiguos dividían en siete los climas del mundo.
18. La legua, según Covarrubias, contenía tres millas.
19. Mar del Norte = Océano Atlántico.
20. El uso de los vientos para designar direcciones es de usanza marinera.
21. Californio = el Río Colorado.
22. Mar de Perlas = Golfo de California.
23. Marina = costa.

13. The Tropic of Cancer, the northern latitudinal division.
14. Andromeda and Perseus are northern constellations.
15. At that time there was as yet no agreed upon keying meridian (Greenwich), and nations used instead the meridian of their own capital city. The discovery of the New World implied the creation of many new meridians.
16. At that time a "clime" was defined as the geographic area between latitudinal lines. The ancients divided the world into seven climes.
17. The Spanish league, at that time, according to Covarrubias, contained some three miles.
18. The Atlantic Ocean.
19. The Colorado River.
20. The Gulf of California.
21. The use of winds to designate cardinal points was common nautical usage of those times.

Eterna su memoria perdurable,
Imitando aquel Rómulo prudente
Que a los Romanos muros puso tassa,[24]
Cuya verdad se saca y verifica
Por aquella antiquísima pintura
y modo hieroglíphico que tienen,[25]
Por el qual tratan, hablan y se entienden,
Aunque no con la perfección insigne
Del gracioso coloquio que se ofrece
Quando al amigo ausente conversamos
Mediante la grandeza y excelencia
Del escrebir illustre que tenemos.[26]
Y fuerza y corrobora esta antigualla
Aquel prodigio inmenso que hallamos
Quando el camino incierto no sabido
De aquella nueva México tomamos.
Y fue que en las postreras poblaciones
De todo lo que llaman nueva España,
Y a los fines del Reyno de Vizcaia,[27]
Estando todo el campo levantado
Para romper marchando la derrota[28]
Bronca, áspera, difícil y encubierta,
Supimos una cosa por muy cierta
Y de inmortal memoria platicada
Y que de mano en mano abía venido,
Qual por nosotros la venida a España
De aquellos valerosos que primero
Vinieron a poblarla y conquistarla.[29]
Dixeron, pues, aquellos naturales,
Vnánimes, conformes y de vn voto,
Que de la tierra adentro, señalando
Aquella parte donde el norte esconde
Del presuroso Boreas[30] esforzado
La cóncava caverna desabrida,[31]
Salieron dos briosíssimos hermanos[32]

90 Memorial eternal of their name, and lasting,
In imitation of wise Romulus
Who put a measure to the walls of Rome,[22]
Whose truth is drawn from and is proved by
That extremely ancient painting
95 And hieroglyphic method which they have,[23]
By which they deal and speak and are well understood,
Though not with the same excellent perfection
Of graceful conversation which is offered
When we converse with absent friends
100 By means of the excellence and greatness
Of the noble writing which we have.[24]
And there reconfirms and corroborates this tradition
That prodigy immense which we did find
When taking road, uncertain and unknown,
105 For that New Mexico. It happened that
In the last towns of what is called New Spain,
And on the border of the Kingdom of Vizcaya,[25]
The whole camp having risen
To make a start upon the route,
110 Wild, rough, and difficult and hidden yet,
One thing we learned for very certain
And talked of through immortal memory
And which had come from hand to hand,
Just as midst us the coming here to Spain
115 Of those brave hearts who at the first
Came here to populate and conquer it.[26]
They told us then, those native folk,
Unanimous, agreed, and with one voice,
That from that land beyond, and pointing out
120 That section where the North doth hide
The hollow cavern, craggy,
Of vigorous and hasty Boreas,[27]
There came two most courageous brethren,[28]
Of high and noble Kings descended,

24. Rómulo, con su hermano Remo, son los fundadores legendarios de Roma. Narrado en Ovidio, *Metamorfosis* XIV.

25. No extraña que Villagrá tuviera, por experiencia propia, algún conocimiento de la escritura de los aztecas.

26. Este elogio del castellano, especialmente como lengua escrita, es indicio de la educación humanística del escritor.

27. El Reyno de Vizcaia, Reino de Nueva Vizcaya, es hoy la zona de México inmediatamente al sur del Río Grande.

28. Derrota = camino.

29. Se refiere a la prehistoria, no menos legendaria, de la península ibérica.

30. Boreas, nombre mitológico del viento norte, estaba encerrado en una cueva.

31. Desabrida = áspera.

32. Las leyendas que han llegado hasta nosotros acerca de la venida de los mexicanos (aztecas) hasta donde los hallaron los españoles hablan de dos figuras principales (Huitzíton y Tecpátzin), pero sin sugerir que fuesen hermanos (F. J. Clavijero, *Historia antigua de México*. México: Editorial Porrúa, 1976. 66). Es posible que lo que aquí cuenta Villagrá

22. Romulus and his brother Remus, legendary founders of Rome. Their feat is narrated by Ovid, *Metamorphoses* XIV.

23. Villagrá may possibly have had some knowledge of Aztec glyph writing. Father Bernardino de Sahagún's *Historia antigua de México* would have been accessible to him.

24. This praise of Castilian, especially as a written language, is a clear indication of Villagrá's humanistic education.

25. Nueva Vizcaya is today the area of Mexico bordering on the Rio Grande.

26. Villagrá refers to the no less legendary prehistory of Iberia.

27. Boreas, the mythological name for the north wind, was held in a cave.

28. The legends that have come down to us regarding the origins of the Aztecs refer to two principal figures, not necessarily brothers, Huitzíton and Tecpátzin. See F. J. Clavijero, *Historia antigua de México* (Mexico: Editorial Porrúa, 1975), 76. Villagrá may offer here a legend not known to earlier or later historians. But his making the two figures brothers and the manner in which they divide jurisdictions may possibly reflect other influences; on the one hand, Statius's *Thebaid*,

De altos y nobles Reyes decendientes,
Hijos de Rey, y Rey de suma alteza,
Ganosos de estimarse y levantarse
Descubriendo del mundo la excelencia
Y a sus illustres Reyes y señores
Con triunpho noble y célebre trofeo,
Por viva fuerza de armas, o sin ellas,
Quales corderos simples al aprisco,
Reduzirlos, sugetos y obedientes
Al duro yugo de su inmenso imperio,
Soberbio señorío y bravo estado;
Y que llegando allí con grande fuerza
De mucha soldadesca bien armada,
En dos grandiosos campos divididos
De gruessos esquadrones bien formados,
El maior de los dos venía cerrando
Con gran suma de esquadras la banguardia,
Y de otras tantas brabas reforzaba
La retaguardia, en orden bien compuesta,
El menor con grandíssima destreza,
Y por el medio cuerpo de batalla[33]
Gran suma de bagage y aparato,
Tiendas y pabellones bien luzidos
Con que sus Reales fuertes assentaban,
Y como sueltos tiernos cervatillos[34]
Infinidad de niños y muchachos
Por vna y otra parte retozando,
Embueltos en juguetes muy donosos[35]
De simples infanticos inocentes,
Sin género de traza[36] ni concierto.
Y también por aquel soberbio campo
Entre las fieras armas se mostraban,
Así como entre espinas bellas flores,
Vizarras[37] damas, dueñas y donzellas,
Tan compuestas, discretas y gallardas
Quanto nobles, hermosas y avisadas;
Y en fresca flor de jubentud, mancebos,
Gentiles hombres, todos bien compuestos,
Compitiendo los vnos con los otros

125 Sons of a King, and king of highest lineage,
Desirous of esteem and elevation
By discovering the marvels of the world,
And all its kings illustrious and all its lords,
With noble triumph and with famous trophies,
130 By active force of arms, perhaps without them,
Like gentle lamblings to the fold,
Reduce, subject, and obedient
To the harsh yoke of their immense empire,
Proud lordship, great estate;
135 And that, arriving there with a great force
Of many soldiers and well armed,
Divided in two camps most large
Of mighty squadrons and well formed,
The elder of the two did lead the van
140 With number great of squadrons,
And the younger brother reinforced
The rear guard with a number just as great
And led it with great skill,
And in the middle of the force
145 Great sum of baggage and of apparatus,
Tents and pavilions shining bright
With which their Highnesses did make their camp,
And like to free and tender fawns
Infinity of children and of babes
150 Here, there, and elsewhere frolicking,
Surrounded by most pretty toys
Of simple, innocent infancy,
And with no sort of plan or concert.
And also in that proud camp
155 There showed themselves among the deadly arms,
As flowers beautiful are seen 'mid thorns,
Fair dames and ladies and bright damsels,
As dainty, lovely, and discreet
As noble, beautiful, and well-advised;
160 And, in the very flower of youth, young men,
And gentlemen and well dressed, all,
Each one competing with the rest
Such sum of finery and of livery

sea una leyenda más, no recogida por los historiadores, contemporáneos o posteriores; pero el hermanar a los dos jefes y su reparto de jurisdicciones quizás refleje otras influencias: por una parte, de *La Tebaida* de Estacio, posiblemente en su traducción española de Juan de Arjona; y, por otra, de *Argentina y conquista del Río de Plata* de Martín del Barco Centenera, publicado en Lisboa en 1602, en que los hermanos Tupi y Guarani se dividen los reinos.

33. Este medio cuerpo de batalla representaría el centro, entre vanguardia y retaguardia.

34. Cervatillos = ciervos pequeños; crias de rumiantes.

35. Donosos = graciosos.

36. Traza = plan.

37. Vizarras = bizarras, gallardas.

much read in its sixteenth-century Spanish translation by Juan de Arjona; on the other, Martín del Barco Centenera's *Argentina y conquista del Río de Plata*, published in Lisbon in 1602, in which the brothers Tupi and Guarani divide up the lands of that region.

Tanta suma de galas y libreas[38]
Quanto en la más pintada y alta Corte
En grandes fiestas suelen señalarse
Los que son más curiosos cortesanos.
Y assí mismo los gruesos esquadrones
Mostraban entre tanta vizarría
Vn número terrible y espantoso
De notables transformaciones fieras:
Qual piel de vedegoso[39] León cubría,
Con que el feroz semblante y la figura
Del soberbio animal representaba;

Qual la manchada fiera tigre hircana,[40]
Presta onza, astuto gimio[41] y suelto pardo;[42]
Qual el hambriento lobo carnicero,
Raposo,[43] liebre y tímido conejo;
Los grandes pezes y águilas caudales,[44]
Con todo el resto de animales brutos
Que el aire y tierra y ancho mar ocupan
Allí muy naturales parecían,
Invención propia, antigua, y que es vsada
Entre todas las gentes y naciones
Que vemos descubiertas de las Indias.[45]
Abía de armas fuertes, belicosas,
Vna luzida, bella y grande copia:[46]
Turquescos[47] arcos, corbos, bien fornidos,
Anchos carcages, gruessos y espaciosos,
De muy livianas flechas atestados,
Ligeras picas y pesadas mazas,
Fuertes rodelas con sus fuertes petos
De apretado nudillo[48] bien obrados,
Rebueltas hondas, prestas por el aire,
Gruessos bastones con pesados cantos
En sus fuertes bejucos[49] engastados,
Y, sembradas de agudos pedernales,[50]
Fortísimas macanas[51] bien labradas,
Y tendidas al aire tremolaban
Con vizarro donaire y gallardía

165 As in the finest and most lofty courts
Are customed to be worn on festal days
By the most conspicuous courtiers.
And then, also, the mighty squadrons
Showed in the midst of such gallantry
170 A number terrible, and fearful, too,
Of notable animal disguises:
One wore the hide of a manéd lion
With which he represented well
The face ferocious and the appearance of the proud
animal;
175 Some the striped hide of fierce Hircanian tiger,
Of speedy ounce, astute monkey, and leopard,
There were the hungry wolf carnivorous,
The fox, the hare and the rabbit shy,[29]
The fishes huge and lordly eagles, too,
180 With all the rest of the brute beasts
Which occupy the earth and sky and the broad seas.
There they appeared all, most natural,
A native, old invention, one that's used
Among all peoples and all nations
185 Which we have yet discovered in the Indies.[30]
There were of arms, warlike and strong,
A shining, great, and goodly sum:
Bent Turkish bows, well strung,
Broad quivers, broad and of a capacious size,
190 Well stuffed with arrows light,
Light javelins and maces heavy,
Strong bucklers and cuirasses strong,
Well made, of knotted, woven work,
Mischievous slings, swung in the air,
195 Thick clubs with heavy stones
Imbedded in their strong wood,
And, lined with sharp flints,
Strong, well-wrought, wooden swords;
And lofted in air there fluttered,
200 With gallantry and grace bizarre,

---

38. Libreas = vestimentas distintivas.
39. Vedegoso = vedijoso, lanudo, hirsuto.
40. Hircana = de Hircania, Caspio.
41. Gimio = simio.
42. Pardo = leopardo.
43. Raposo = zorro.
44. Aguilas caudales = águilas reales.
45. La generalización de Villagrá sugiere algún conocimiento que hoy llamaríamos antropológico del Nuevo Mundo.
46. Copia = cantidad.
47. Turquescos = turcos.
48. Nudillo = material reforzado mediante nudos.
49. Bejucos = nombre de varias plantas y maderas tropicales.
50. Pedernales = piedras.
51. Macanas = machetes de madera con filo de piedra.

29. Curtis added an "elk" to the Villagrá text.
30. Villagrá's statement suggests some anthropological knowledge of the New World.

Cantidad de vanderas y estandartes
De colores diversos matizados.
Y las diestras hileras de soldados,
Cada qual empuñando bien sus armas,
Con gran descuydo y con vizarros passos
Por el tendido⁵² campo yban marchando,
Y, de las muchas plantas azotado,
El duro suelo, en alto levantaban
Vna tiniebla densa tan cerrada
Que resolverse el mundo parecía
En cegajoso⁵³ polvo arrebatado
De vn ligero y presto terremoto
Que por el ancho cóncavo⁵⁴ del aire
En altos remolinos va esparciendo.
Pues yendo assí, marchando con descuido,
Delante se les puso con cuydado,
En figura de vieja desembuelta,
Vn valiente demonio resabido
Cuyo feroz semblante no me atrevo,
Si con algún cuydado he de pintarlo,
Sin otro nuevo aliento a retratarlo.

52. Tendido = extenso.
53. Cegajoso = que hace lagrimear.
54. Cóncavo = concavidad.

A quantity of banners and of standards
Of different colors, many hued.
And the well-serried ranks of troops,
Each gripping fast his arms,
205 Kept marching over the great field
With greatest ease and gallant tread,
And, lashed by tread of many men,
The hard-baked earth sent high into the air
A cloud of dust so thick and dense
210 It seemed that the whole earth was there dissolved
In blinding dust, whirled on
By swift and sudden earthquake,
Which through the broad dome of the air
Spreads out in lofty whirlwinds.
215 Well, going thus and traveling carelessly,
There placed himself before them by intent,
In form of an old and haglike woman,
A valiant and cunning demon
Whose face ferocious dare I not,
220 If I must with some care depict it,
Set out to paint without new strength.

CANTO SEGVNDO

COMO SE APARECIO EL DEMONIO A TODO EL CAMPO en figura de vieja y de la traza que tuvo en dividir los dos hermanos, y del gran mojón de hierro que assentó para que cada qual conociesse sus estados.

QVANDO la Magestad de Dios aparta
Del cathólico vando algún rebaño
Señal es evidente y nadie ignora

Que aquello lo permite su justicia
Por ser aquel camino el menos malo
Que pudieron llevar sus almas tristes.
Y assí, como a perdidos miserables
Y de la santa Iglesia divididos,
Marchando assí estos pobres reprobados,
Delante se les puso aquel maldito[1]
En figura de vieja rebozado,[2]
Cuya espantosa y gran desemboltura
Daba pavor y miedo imaginarla.
Truxo el cabello cano mal compuesto
Y, qual horrenda y fiera notomía,[3]
El rostro descarnado, macilento,
De fiera y espantosa catadura;
Desmesurados pechos, largas tetas,
Hambrientas, flacas, secas y fruncidas,
Nerbudos pechos, anchos y espaciosos,
Con terribles espaldas bien trabadas;
Sumidos ojos de color de fuego,
Disforme boca desde oreja a oreja,
Por cuyos labios secos, desmedidos,
Quatro sólos colmillos hazia fuera
De vn largo palmo,[4] corbos, se mostraban;
Los brazos, temerarios, pies y piernas
Por cuyas espantosas coiunturas
Vna ossamenta gruessa rechinaba,
De poderosos nerbios bien assida.
Y assí como nos pintan y nos muestran
Del bravo Atlante[5] la feroz persona,
Sobre cuyas robustas y altas fuerzas
El grave, incomparable, assiento y peso

---

1. Se refiere a un demonio.
2. Rebozado = disfrazado.
3. Notomía = esqueleto.
4. Palmo = medida, vertical casi siempre, de la extensión de la mano.
5. Atlante es el titán sostenedor del globo terráqueo en la mitología. Llevan tal nombre las figuras de piedra labrada utilizadas como pilares para sostener edificios. Quizás Villagrá se refiera más bien a éstas, a menudo de catadura grotesca.

CANTO II

How the devil appeared to the whole camp in the shape of an old woman, and of the scheme he had to separate the two brothers, and of the great heap of iron that he left so that everyone might know his true estate.

WHEN the majesty of God removeth
Some flock from out the Catholic fold,
It is a sign most evident, ignored by none,
That this His justice doth permit

5 Because this road least evil is
Of those that their sad souls could take.
And thus, as though to miserable lost souls
Divided from the holy Church,
These poor reprobates marching forward thus,
10 That accursed one placed himself before them
In form of an old woman well disguised,
Whose great and fearful cleverness
Doth cause both fear and terror to imagine.
He had his gray hair badly dressed,
15 And like a horrible, fierce skeleton
His fleshless and emaciated face,
Of an expression wild and fearsome,
Misshapen breasts and dangling teats,
Starved, flaccid, dry, and wrinkled,
20 Great chest, both wide and spacious,
With shoulders terrible, well set,
Eyes sunk and colored as of fire,
A mouth malformed, from ear to ear,
Through whose dry and distorted lips
25 Of fangs just four protruded
And, curving, showed themselves a good palm's length;
His arms were fearful, feet and legs,
In whose fearsome joints
The bones creaked loud,
30 Well set, with muscles powerful.
Just as they picture for us and do show
The ferocious person of brave Atlas,[1]
Upon whose great and robust strength
The great, incomparable weight and thrust

---

1. In mythology, Atlas, a Titan, holds the world on his shoulders. Villagrá, given the grotesqueness of the figure described, was perhaps plastically recalling the often grotesquely topped columns of buildings, which, understandably, also went by that name in Spanish.

De los más lebantados cielos cargan,
Por lo mucho que dellos alcanzaba
En la curiosa y docta Astrología,[6]
Assí esta feroz vieja judiciaria[7]
Afirman por certísimo que truxo
Encima de la fuerte y gran cabeza
Vn grave, inorme, passo[8] casi en forma
De concha de tortuga lebantada,
Que ochocientos quintales excedía,
De hierro bien mazizo y amasado.
Y luego que llegó al forastero
Campo y le tuvo atento y bien suspenso,
Con lebantada voz desenfadada,
Herguida la cerviz, assí les dijo:
"No me pesa, esforzados Mexicanos,
Que como bravo fuego no domado
Que para su alta cumbre se lebanta
No menos seáys movidos y llamados
De aquella brava alteza y gallardía
De vuestra insigne, ilustre y noble sangre,[9]
A cuya heroica, Real, naturaleza
Le es propio y natural el gran desseo
Con que alargando os vais del patrio nido
Para sólo buscar remotas tierras,
Nuevos mundos, también nuevas estrellas,
Donde pueda mostrarse la grandeza
De vuestros fuertes brazos belicosos,
Ensanchando por vna y otra parte,
Assí como el soberbio mar ensancha
Las hondas poderosas y las tiende
Por sus tendidas Plaias y Riberas,
Que assí se esparza, tienda y se publique
Por todo lo criado y descubierto
La justa adoración que se le debe
Al príncipe supremo y poderoso
Del tenebroso albergue que buscamos.[10]
Y para que toméis mejor el punto,
Qual presurosa jara[11] que se arranca

35 Of highest-lifted heavens doth rest,
    Of which he partook to some degree
    In curious and learned Astrology,[2]
    Thus of this fierce old woman and astrologer[3]
    They say most certainly she bore
40 Upon her head, so great and strong,
    A huge, enormous weight, almost in form
    A tortoise-shell set upright,
    Exceeding some eight hundred quintal weight,
    Of iron, massive and well molded.
45 And when he came upon the foreign camp,
    Holding it attentive and in suspense,
    With a loud voice and unembarrassed,
    His head erect, he then addressed them thus:
    "I am not pained, O valiant Mexicans,
50 Because, as raging fire never quenched
    Which rises to its summit high,[4]
    You are in no way less moved or beckoned
    By the rude haughtiness and gallantry
    Of your illustrious, grand, and noble blood,
55 To whose heroic, royal, character
    'Tis natural, inborn, this great desire
    With which you go from the paternal nest
    Only to seek for lands remote,
    New worlds, new stars, as well,
60 In which the greatness can be shown
    Of these, your strong and warlike arms,
    Extending out to either side
    As the proud sea extends itself
    In powerful waves and stretches them
65 Out to its far-flung shores and banks,
    That thus be spread, extend, and be made known
    O'er all created and discovered
    The fitting adoration which is due
    Unto that prince supreme and powerful
70 Of that dark shelter which we seek.[5]
    And so that you may better take the point,
    As a most rapid arrow which flies fast

6. Parece que Villagrá debiera referirse a la mitología, que sí recoge el intento de los titanes contra el Olimpo.

7. Judiciaria = agorera. Recuerda esta descripción a la maga de Lucano, *La Farsalia* VI. Las escenas de agueros, tan prominentes en la épica clásica, abundan asimismo en la épica renacentista. En la épica americana, aunque no de manera absoluta, tales hechicerías se las atribuían a los pueblos primitivos.

8. Passo = efigie o grupo sacado en procesión, a cuestas, en Semana Santa. Si no es errata del original, por peso, Villagrá lo ofrece como ejemplo del tamaño de lo que llevaba en la cabeza.

9. La imagen del natural impulso del fuego por subir, aplicada al alma en su búsqueda natural de Dios, está en Dante, *Paraíso* I.

10. Se refiere a Satanás, con quien se identificaban los dioses sangrientos de los aztecas, y al infierno.

11. Jara = saeta de punta aguda y quemada.

2. It would seem that Villagrá would mean "mythology," which does indicate the Titans' attempt to storm the heavens.

3. The description of the witch-seer appears to echo that of Lucan, *Pharsalia* VI.

4. The comparison with the natural impulse of fire to rise, although applied to the soul's search for God, is found in Dante, *Paradiso* I.

5. The reference is to Satan and his dominion, Hell, toward which the evil are headed. The Aztec gods were considered by the Spaniards as manifestations of Satan.

Para el opuesto blanco que se opone,
Notad la voluntad, que es bien se cumpla,
De aqueste gran señor que acá me embía.
Ya veis que la molesta edad cansada
De vuestro noble padre, caro, amado,
Tiene su Real persona tan opresa,
Desgraciada, cuitada y afligida,
Que más no puede ser en este siglo,[12]
Y que ya su vegez enferma y cana
A la débil decrépita[13] ha venido,
Bolviéndose a la tierna edad primera.
Y para que los más de sus estados,
Qual un veloz cometa que traspone,
No queden por su fin y triste muerte
Sin natural señor que los ampare,
Es forzoso que luego el vno buelva
Y el otro siga de su estrella noble
El próspero distino y haga assiento
No donde vieron fuera de los hombros
Los antiguos Romanos destroncada
La cabeza de quel[14] varón difunto,[15]
Ni donde la gran piel del buei hermoso
Tan gran tierra ocupó que fue bastante
A encerrar dentro de sus largas tiras
Los levantados muros de Cartago,[16]
Mas donde en duro y sólido peñasco,
De christalinas aguas bien cercado,
Viéredeis vna Tuna estar plantada,
Y sobre cuias gruessas y anchas hojas
Vna Aguila caudal bella, disforme,
Con braveza cebando se estuviere
En vna gran culebra que a sus garras
Veréys que está rebuelta y bien assida,
Que allí quiere se funde y se lebante
La metropolí alta y generosa
Del poderoso estado señalado,
Al qual expresamente manda
Que México Tenuchtitlán se ponga.[17]
Y con aquesta insignia memorable

	Into the target waiting it,
	Hear ye the will which 'tis best to obey
75	Of the great lord who sent me here.
	You know already that tired, weary age
	Keepeth the royal person of your noble father,
	Well-beloved, so painfully oppressed,
	Downcast, afflicted, miserable,
80	That more could not well be within this life,
	And that his old age, sick and gray,
	has come to weak decrepitude,
	Returning now to childhood once again.
	And so that most of his estates,
85	Like a swift comet which doth set,
	May not remain, by his end and sad death,
	Without a natural lord to care for them,
	'Tis necessary now that one of you return
	And that the other still pursue his noble star,
90	Its prosperous destiny, and make his place,
	Not where the ancient Romans saw the head
	Of that huge dead man struck from off his shoulders[6]
	Nor where the great hide of the beauteous bull
	Took up so much land that it was enough
95	To close within its mighty strips
	The lofty walls of Carthage,[7]
	But where on a hard and solid rock
	Girded by waters crystalline
	A cactus planted you shall see
100	Upon whose thick and spreading leaves
	A beautiful red-tailed eagle sits, quite enormous,
	And it be eating greedily
	On a great snake that in his claws,
	As you shall see, is twisting, but well gripped.
105	Here it is willed that you shall found and raise
	The lofty, generous, metropolis
	Of the strong state indicated,
	For which 'tis ordered most express
	It Mexico Tenochtitlán be named.
110	And with that memorable sign
	You shall make, afterward, new arms

12. Este siglo = esta vida.

13. Decrépita = decrepitud.

14. Parece errata en el original por "aquel."

15. Puede referirse, aunque algo remoto parezca, a la vista que tuvieron los troyanos (antiguos romanos) que huían de la pérdida de Troya del cuerpo sin cabeza de su rey, Priamo. Virgilio, *Eneida* II, 749–50.

16. En la leyenda de la fundación de Cartago, se le concedió a Dido el terreno que cubriese una piel de buey, y que ella, haciéndola tirajas llegó a cubrir una gran extensión. Lo indica Virgilio (*Eneida* I, 520–22) y, más extensamente, Ercilla (*La araucana* III, 33).

17. Resume la conocida leyenda azteca del hallazgo y fundación de la Ciudad de México.

6. The reference may possibly be to the sight the Trojans (ancient Romans) had of the headless body of King Priam when they fled from the burning Troy. It is narrated in Virgil, *Aeneid* II, 749–50.

7. In the legend of the founding of Carthage, Queen Dido was conceded all the land that could be covered by the skin of an ox. By making it into thin strips, she was able to claim an extensive area. Narrated by Virgil, *Aeneid* I, 520–22 and more extensively by Ercilla, *La araucana* III, 33.

Levantaréis después de nuevas armas
Y de nuevos blasones los escudos.
Y porque la cobdicia, torpe vicio
Del mísero adquirir, suele ser causa
De grandes disensiones y renzillas,
Por quitaros de pleytos y debates
Será bien señalaros los linderos,
Términos y mojones[18] de las tierras
Que cada qual por sólo su gobierno
Ha de reconocer, sin que pretenda
Ninguno otro dominio más ni menos
De lo que aquí quedare señalado."
Y lebantando en alto los talones,
Sobre las fuertes puntas afirmada,
Alzó los flacos brazos poderosos
Y, dando a la monstruosa carga buelo,
Assí como si fuera fiero rayo
Que con grande pavor y pasmo assombra
A muchos y los dexa sin sentido,
Siendo pocos aquellos que lastima,
Assí, con súbito rumor y estruendo
La portentosa carga soltó en vago,[19]
Y apenas ocupó la dura tierra
Quando temblando y toda estremecida
Quedó por todas partes quebrantada.
Y assí como acabó, qual diestra Circe,[20]
Allí desvaneció sin que la viesen,
Señalando del vno al otro polo
Las dos altas coronas lebantadas.
Y como aquellos Griegos y Romanos
Quando el famoso Imperio dividieron,[21]
Cuio hecho grandioso y admirable
El Aguila imperial de dos cabezas
La división inmensa representa,[22]
De aquesta misma suerte, traza y modo
La poderosa tierra dividieron.
Y assí como pelota que con fuerza
Del poderoso brazo y ancha pala[23]
Resurte[24] para atrás y en vn instante

And, for the shields, new blazons.
And because greed, a wicked vice
Of sinful acquiring, is often cause
115 Of great dissensions and of grudge,
To free yourselves from lawsuits and debates
It will be well to mark the limits down,
The borders and the boundaries of the lands
That each for his sole governance
120 Will accept, nor pretend
To any other rule, nor more nor less
Than that which shall be there assigned to him."[8]
And raising from the ground his heels,
Set firm upon his mighty toes,
125 He raised his powerful, mighty arms
And giving to his monstrous load a push,
As though it were a mighty thunderbolt
That 'stonishes with fear and terror great
The many, and does leave them without sense,
130 There being few it hurts,
So with a sudden and horrendous noise
He threw aside the mighty load,
And hardly did it strike the flinty earth
When, trembling and shaking all,
135 That earth was broken everywhere.
And when 'twas done, like Circe skilled,[9]
He vanished thence without their seeing him,
Pointing to one and to the other Pole
The two crowns raised on high.
140 Just as the Romans and the Greeks
When they divided the empire famed,[10]
Which great and wonderful action
The imperial Eagle, double-headed,[11] in symbol
That immense division represents,
145 In this same manner, way and sort
They did the powerful earth divide.
And, as the pelota ball, sent forth with strength
Of mighty arm and stick so broad,
Flies back and in an instant,
150 Quick as we saw it come, returns,[12]

18. Mojones = señales de límites o lindes.
19. Vago = vacío.
20. Circe, maga de la mitología. Virgilio (*Eneida* VII, 22–25) y Ovidio (*Metamorfosis* XIV) narran sus hechos.
21. Se refiere a la división del Imperio Romano en oriental y occidental.
22. El águila imperial de dos cabezas es, en la casa de Hapsburgo, escudo del Sacro Imperio Romano, sucesor del Imperio Romano de occidente.
23. Parece referencia al juego de pelota vasca. El juego de pelota debió ser muy popular entre descubridores y conquistadores, pues la imagen de la pelota y su movimiento aparece desde Ercilla en adelante.
24. Resurte = rebota.

8. This summarizes the well-known legend of the founding of Mexico City.
9. Circe is the mythological witch, described by Virgil, *Aeneid* VII, 22–25 and Ovid, *Metamorphoses* XIV.
10. The reference is to the division of the Roman Empire into its eastern and western parts.
11. The two-headed eagle symbolizes the Holy Roman Empire, successor to the Western Roman Empire.
12. The description is of some form of Basque ball, very popular with the Spanish conquerors in the New World. References to it abound in the New World epic, beginning with Ercilla.

Tan presto como viene vemos buelve,
Assí, con fuerte bote²⁵ el campo herido²⁶
Con lo que assí la vieja les propuso,
La retaguardia toda dio la buelta
Para la dulze patria que dexaban
Por la parte del Norte riguroso,
Y para el Sur fue luego prosiguiendo
La banguardia, contenta, le da,²⁷ vfana,
Abiéndose los vnos y los otros
Tiernamente abrazado y despedido.
Y como aquella aguja²⁸ memorable
Que por grande grandeza y maravilla
Oy permanece puesta y assentada
En la bella Ciudad santa de Roma
A la vista de quantos verla quieren,
No de otra suerte assiste y permanece
El gran mojón que allí quedó plantado
En altura de veinte y siete grados
Con otro medio. Y no vbo ningún hombre
De todo vuestro campo que atajado,²⁹
Pasmado y sin sentido no parase
Considerando aquesta misma historia
Y por sus mismos proprios ojos viendo
La grandeza del monstruo que allí estaba.³⁰
Al qual no se acercaban los caballos
Por más que los hijares les rompían,
Porque vnos se empinaban y arbolaban³¹
Con notables bufidos y ronquidos,
Y otros, más espantados, resurtían
Por vno y otro lado rezelosos
De aquel inorme peso nunca visto,
Hasta que cierto Religioso un día
Celebró el gran misterio sacrosanto
De aquella Redención del vniverso
Tomando por Altar al mismo hierro,
Y dende entonces vemos que se llegan
Sin ningún pavor, miedo ni rezelo
A su estalage³² aquestos animales,
Como a lugar que libertado ha sido
De qual que infernal furia desatada.
Y como quien de vista es buen testigo,
Digo que es vn metal tan puro y liso
Y tan limpio de orín como si fuera

155 Thus, in a bound, the stricken camp became
From what the woman had proposed to them,
All the rear guard did turn again
Toward that sweet fatherland they'd left
In regions of the hardy North,
And toward the South there still kept on
The vanguard, marching proudly and content,
First having each embraced the other
Most tenderly and taken leave.
160 And like that memorable needle
Which, as a great wonder and marvel,
Still stands upright in place
In the beautiful and holy city, Rome,¹³
Plain to be seen by all who wish to see it,
165 There still remains, in the same way,
The mighty mass which there was placed,
In height some twenty-seven degrees
And a half more.¹⁴ And there was no man
Of all your camp who did not stop
170 Astonished, stunned, and almost senseless,
Considering that same story
And seeing with his own two eyes
The greatness of the monstrous mass was there.
And of the horses not one would approach it
175 Unless one tore their flanks,
For some stood on their hind legs, rebellious,
With whistlings and snorts,
And others, frightened more, did shy,
Suspicious, to one side or to the other,
180 From that enormous mass, such as was never seen,
Until one day a certain priest
Did celebrate the great, most holy mystery
Of that redemption of the universe,
Taking for altar that same mass of iron,
185 And ever since we noticed that those beasts
Came, without fear or trembling or suspicion,
Right to its foot
As to a place which has been freed
From some unloosed infernal fury.
190 And I, as one who is good witness of that sight,
Say that it is as pure and smooth a metal,
And free of rust, as if it were
Silver refined of Copella.¹⁵

25. Bote = salto.
26. Herido = dividido, separado.
27. Probable errata del original por "leda."
28. Aguja = obelisco egipcio.
29. Atajado = parado.
30. No tenemos noticia de este monte de metal, y puede muy bien ser fantasía de Villagrá.
31. Arbolaban = encabritaban.
32. Estalage = estalaje, estancia o asiento.

13. The reference here is to the Egyptian obelisk in Rome.
14. Despite Villagrá's fairly precise latitudinal reference, we have found no reference to such a metal mountain in the historical accounts of the expedition.
15. The reference is to a procedure, using calcined bones, for the melting of precious metals.

Vna refina plata de Copella.³³

Y lo que más admira nuestro caso
Es que no vemos género de veta,
Horrumbre,³⁴ quemazón³⁵ o alguna piedra
Con cuia fuerza muestre y nos paresca
Aberse el gran mojón allí criado,
Porque no muestra más señal de aquesto
Que el rastro que las prestas Aves dejan
Rompiendo por el aire sus caminos
O por el ancho mar los sueltos pezes
Quando las aguas claras van cruzando.
Y aquesta misma historia que he contado
Sabemos, gran señor, que se pratica³⁶
En lo que nueva México llamamos,
Donde assí mismo fuimos informados
Ser todos forasteros, y apuntando
De aquestos dos hermanos la salida
Al passar dan indicio se quedaron
Sus padres y mayores, y señalan
Al lebantado norte, donde dizen
Y afirman ser de allá su decendencia.
Y dizen que contienen sus mojones
Gran suma de naciones diferentes,
En lenguas, leies, ritos y costumbres
Los vnos muy distintos de los otros,
Entre los quales cuentan Mexicanos
Y Tarascos,³⁷ con gente de Guinea.³⁸
Y no parando aquí también afirman
Aber, como en Castilla, gente blanca,
Que todas son grandezas que nos fuerzan
A derribar por tierra las columnas
Del *non Plus Vltra*³⁹ infame que lebantan
Gentes más para rueca y el estrado,
Para tocas, vainicas y labores,⁴⁰
Que para gobernar la gruessa pica,
Generoso bastón y honrrada espada.
Y aber salido destas nuevas tierras⁴¹

And what our people wondered most
195 Is that we saw no sort of vein,
Nor scoria, trace, nor any rock
By means of which we might be shown or see
How the great mass could be created there,
Because there's no more trace of that
200 Than the swift birds leave traces in the air
Through which they make their road,
Or, in the sea, the swimming fish
When they go plying through the waters clean.
And this same story which I here have told
205 We know, great lord, is oft related
In that same place we call New Mexico,
Where, we ourselves were told,
They all were strangers, and in so narrating
The long journey of those two brethren,
210 In passing, they do say, their forefathers and ancestors
Remained, and they point out
The far off Northland, whence they say
And do affirm themselves to be descended.
And they do say their boundaries do contain
215 Great sum of nations, different,
In language, laws, rites, and customs,
Each very different from the rest,
Among which they do count the Mexicans,
Tarascans and the folk of Guinea.¹⁶
220 Nor stopping here, they do affirm
That they have people white, as in Castile.
All these are grandeurs which do lead us on
To throw to earth the columns
Of that same Non Plus Ultra¹⁷ which they raise,
225 Folk more for distaff and for parlor fit,
For coifs, for sewing and such labor,
Than for the wielding of the mighty pike,
The generous scepter, and the honored sword.
And having come from these new lands,
230 The fine Mexicans, is proved to us by

---

33. Copella = copela, crisol de huesos calcinados para fundición de metales preciosos.
34. Horrumbre = horrura, escoria de primera fundación de un metal.
35. Quemazón = espuma de metal, señales de la veta.
36. Pratica = plática, habla o comenta.
37. Los tarascos era tribu indígena de México, radicada al norte del antiguo imperio azteca.
38. Como "gente de Guinea" se designaba, generalmente, a los negros. La "gente blanca" que se menciona poco después ha de ser referencia a albinos.
39. Legendaria inscipción en las Columnas de Hércules, Estrecho de Gibraltar, indicando los límites del mundo.
40. Todos los lugares, artefactos y oficios indicados son femeninos, con lo cual queda clara la intención del poeta.
41. La reproducción mexicana trae "trierras."

16. The Tarascans were an indigenous Indian tribe located in the northern part of the ancient Aztec empire. "People of Guinea" refers to blacks. The whites mentioned below almost certainly refers to albinos.
17. *Non plus ultra* was the classical signal, on the columns of Hercules, Straits of Gibraltar, to go no further.

Los finos Mexicanos nos lo muestra
Aquella gran Ciudad desbaratada
Que en la nueva Galicia todos vemos,[42]
De gruessos edificios derribados
Donde los naturales de la tierra
Dizen que la plantaron y fundaron
Los nuevos Mexicanos que salieron
De aquesta nueva tierra que buscamos.
Desde Cuios assientos y altos muros,
Con todo lo que boja[43] nueva España,
Hasta dar en las mismas poblaciones
De lo que nueva México dezimos,
Quales van los solícitos rastreros,[44]
Que por no más que el viento van sacando
La remontada caza que se esconde,
Assí la cuidadosa soldadesca
A más andar[45] sacaba y descubría,
Desde los anchos límites que digo,
Patentes rastros, huellas y señales
Desta verdad que vamos inquiriendo,
A causa de que en todo el despoblado
Siempre fuimos hallando sin buscarla
Mucha suma de loza, mala y buena,
A vezes en montones recogida,
Y otras toda esparcida y derramada.
Que esto tuvieron siempre por grandeza
Los Reyes Mexicanos que dezimos,
Porque la más vagilla que tuvieron
Fue de barro cozido, y luego al punto
Que del primer servicio se quitaba
Todo lo destrozaban y quebraban.[46]
Y dentro de las mismas poblaciones
Todos los más de vuestro campo vimos
Algunos edificios y pinturas
De antiguos Mexicanos bien sacadas.[47]
Y assí como por brújula descubre
El buen tahur la carta desseada,
Assegurando el resto[48] que ha metido,
Assí, con estas pintas y señales
Seguros, assentamos todo el campo

The ruins of that city great
Which we all see in New Galicia,[18]
Of mighty buildings, all laid waste,
Where they, the natives of the land,
235 Say it was made and founded there
By those New Mexicans who came
Out of the new land that we seek.
From whose foundations and high walls,
With all the area that New Spain contains
240 Until reaching the very towns
Of what we call New Mexico,
Just like the solicitous scouts,
Who from no more than the wind can detect
The remotest game in hiding,
245 Thus did the careful soldiery
Constantly find and discover,
In the broad boundaries I said,
Clear traces, signs, and indications
Of this truth we are referring,
250 Because in all the desert land
Always we found, and without seeking it,
Great store of pottery, both good and bad,
Sometimes heaped up in mounds
And others spread about and broke.
255 For this they always took for grandeur,
Those rulers Mexican we named,
Because most of the service that they had
Was of baked mud, and just as soon
As it was taken out from its first use
260 They broke it and destroyed it.[19]
And in those selfsame towns
Most of your people saw
Some edifices, aye, and pictures
Of ancient Mexicans well depicted.[20]
265 And thus, just as the skillful gambler discovers
The much desired card as with compass,
Saving the money he has bet,
E'en so, by these same traces and these signs
Assured, we set up the whole camp
270 Within this pleasing refuge we'd discovered,

---

42. Se refiere a las ruinas precolombinas de Casas Grandes, en Nueva Galicia, hoy el estado mexicano de Chihuahua.

43. Boja = mide.

44. Rastreros = rastreadores.

45. A más andar = muy de prisa.

46. Para este uso entre los incas y otras tribus mexicanas, véase G. de Villagrá, *Historia de Nuevo México,* ed. M. Junquera (Madrid: Historia 16, 1989), 87.

47. Respecto a las ruinas indias que la expedición de Oñate pudo haber hallado, véase A. V. Kidder, *Southwestern Archeology* (New Haven: Yale Univ. Press, 1962).

48. Resto = apuesta constituyendo lo que le queda a un jugador.

18. The reference is to the pre-Columbian ruins of Casas Grandes, in the present state of Chihuahua, then called Nueva Galicia.

19. For this practice among the Aztecs and other Mexican indians, See G. de Villagrá, *Historia de Nuevo México,* ed. M. Junquera (Madrid: Historia 16, 1989), 87.

20. For the many abandoned native ruins that the Oñate expedition may have encountered, see A. V. Kidder, *Southwestern Archeology* (New Haven: Yale Univ. Press, 1962).

En el gustoso albergue descubierto,
Tomando algún descanso que pudiesse
Esforzar y alentar alguna cosa
Los fatigados cuerpos quebrantados
Del peso de las armas trabajosas.
Por manera, señor, que aquí sacamos
Que ésta es la noble tierra que pisaron
Aquellos brabos viejos que salieron
De la gran nueva México famosa,
Por quien *El peregrino Indiano*[49] dize
Que muy pocos la quieren ver ganada
Y con mucha razón nos desengaña
De verdad tan patente y conocida.
Porque para ensanchar los altos muros
De nuestra santa Iglesia y lebantarlos
Son muchos los llamados y muy pocos
Aquéllos a quien vemos escogidos
Para cosa tan alta y lebantada.
Mas dexemos aquesta causa en vanda,[50]
Que pide larga historia lo que encubre,
Cerrando nuestro canto mal cantado
Con aber entonado todo aquello
Que de los más antiguos naturales
Ha podido alcanzarse y descubrirse
Acerca de la antigua decendencia,
Venida y población de Mexicanos,
Que para mí yo tengo que salieron
De la gran China todos los que habitan
Lo que llamamos Indias.[51] Mas no importa
Que aquesto por agora aquí dexemos.
Y porque vuestra gente Castellana,
A quien parece corta la grandeza
De todo el vniverso que gozamos
Para pisarla toda y descubrirla,
Por sí misma alcanzó vna grande parte
De aqueste nuevo Mundo que inquirimos,
Adelante diremos quáles fueron
Y quiénes pretendieron la jornada
Sin verla en punto puesta y acabada.

275 And so, my lord, this was the way we knew
That this is the noble land they trod,
Those brave old ones who came
From New Mexico, great and famous,
Of whom *El Peregrino Indiano*[21] says
280 That very few desired to see it won
And very rightly doth it set us right
In truth so evident and well known.
Because in order to extend the lofty walls
Of this our Holy Church, and raise them higher still,
285 Many are called, but very few
Are those whom we see chosen
For such high and lofty work.
But let us lay this thing aside,
Which needs a story long to tell it all,
290 Closing our canto, badly sung,
By having sung quite all of what
By the most ancient natives here
Could be remembered and discovered
About the ancient descent,
295 The coming and the settlement of Mexicans,
Who, for myself, I think that they did come
From the great China, all who live
In what we call the Indies.[22] But it matters not,
That here, for now, we leave the matter.
300 And because your Castilian folk,
To whom the grandeur of the Universe entire
That we enjoy, to tread and to discover
Seems small,
Did for themselves grasp a great part
305 Of this new world which we explore,
I shall say later who they were,
Those who the journey undertook
Not seeing it done and ended in a moment.

Taking such rest as might
Somewhat refresh and comfort us,
Our tired bodies broken down
By weight of heavy arms.

49. Se refiere a la obra de Saavedra Guzmán, poetización de la conquista de México, canto XI.

50. En vanda = en banda, a un lado.

51. Curiosa esta corazonada acerca de la procedencia asiática de los aborígenes americanos.

21. The reference is to Saavedra Guzman's epic of the conquest of Mexico, Canto XI.

22. Note Villagrá's insight into the Asian origin of the New World peoples.

Canto Tercero

*COMO POR SI SOLOS LOS ESPAÑOLES TUVIERON
principio para descubrir la nueva México y cómo entraron
y quiénes fueron los que primero pretendieron y pusieron
por obra la jornada.*

BLASON gallardo y alto es el trabajo,
De aquella illustre fama memorable,
Que en la triunfante Corte soberana

Y militante albergue que vivimos[1]

Sabemos que se anida y se atesora
Mediante aquellos héroes valerosos
Que su inmortal vandera[2] professaron.
Cuya alta zima y cumbre poderosa
Podéis notar, señor incomparable,
Que por escudo heroico y sublimado
Quiso aquel poderoso Dios eterno
Que, por alteza grande y triunfo, el hombre,
Que en Trinidad y essencia representa
Su beldad propia y alta semejanza,
Sacada de su mismo ser al vivo,
Le guardase y dél mucho se estimase
Si todas las más cosas desta vida
Seguras en buen puerto ver quisiesse.[3]
Y assí no se verá ningún trabajo,
Si con heroico pecho es recebido,
Que en él el mismo Dios no resplandezca,
Mostrándonos patente la belleza
De sus notables hechos y prohezas.
Y esto, quales resplandecientes soles,
Allá en el quarto cielo[4] lebantados,
Con no pequeño assombro nos mostraron,
Después que en la Florida se perdieron
Por aquel largo tiempo prolongado,
El grande negro Esteban valeroso
Y Cabeza de Vaca memorable,
Castillo, Maldonado, sin segundo,

---

1. Se refiere al cielo, "triunfante Corte soberana," y la tierra, "militante albergue que vivimos," pues la Iglesia se divide en triunfante o celestial y militante o terrenal.
2. La inmortal bandera es la de Dios, de la Iglesia.
3. Dios quiso que el hombre, hecho a semejanza suya, guardase y respetase, como escudo de armas, esa bandera (cruz) si en esta vida quisiera triunfar.
4. Parece que Villagrá se equivoca al recordar a Dante, puesto que el cuarto cielo es el de los teólogos. El quinto es al que se refiere, el de ls capitanes y mártires: Dante, *Paraíso* XIV. Sí recuerda bien, no obstante, que el cuarto cielo es el del sol.

Canto III

How, by themselves, the Spaniards began the discovery of New Mexico, and how they entered, and who were those who first began and undertook the journey.

A glory high and gallant is the work,
Of memorable, illustrious fame,
Which in the sovereign, triumphant Court
And in the most militant[1] shelter where we live
5   We know is cherished and is treasured
By virtue of those heroes valorous
Who followed His immortal flag.[2]
Whose lofty peak and summit powerful
You well may note, incomparable lord,
10   In that, as scutcheon heroic and sublime,
That powerful, eternal God did wish
That man, as lofty height and triumph great,
Who represents in Trinity and in essence
His own beauty and high resemblance,
15   Taken from His own living being,
Should venerate it and esteem it much
If he should wish to see most things
Of this our life safe in fair harbor.
And thus no work shall there be seen,
20   If truly by heroic breasts t'would be received,
That God Himself in it does not shine,
Showing us clearly the beauty
Of their notable deeds and prowess.
And this, like to resplendent suns,
25   Raised there unto fourth heaven,[3]
They show us, with no small astonishment,
After in Florida they were lost
For that prolonged time,
The great and valorous negro Esteban
30   And memorable Cabeza de Vaca,
Castillo, Maldonado, without peer,

---

1. Villagrá's reference is to the church triumphant, in heaven, and the church militant, still here on earth.
2. The reference is to God's standard.
3. In recalling Dante (*Paradiso* XIV), Villagrá appears to confuse heavenly circles: the fourth is identified with theologians and the fifth with captains and martyrs. He is, however, correct in identifying the fourth with the sun.

Y Andrés Dorantes, más aventajado,
Todos singularísimos varones.[5]
Pues en la tempestad más fiera y brava
De todas sus miserias y trabajos
Por ellos quiso obrar la suma alteza
Vna suma grandiosa de milagros.
Y como su Deidad con sólo aliento
Infundió espíritu de vida al hombre
Y a otros sanó, venditos, de su mano,
Assí passando aquestos valerosos
Por entre aquestas bárbaras naciones
No sólo a sus enfermos los sanaban,
Lisiados, paralíticos y ciegos,
Mas daban también vida a sus difuntos
Con sólo vendición y aliento santo
Que por sus santas bocas respiraban,

Pítima[6] viva, atriaca[7] y medicina
Que sólo en la botica milagrosa
Del poderoso Dios pudo hallarse.
Por cuya virtud alta y soberana,
Suspensos los Alárabes[8] incultos,
Assí como si fuesen dioses todos
Vna vez por tributo y vassallaje
Les consagraron, dieron y ofrecieron
Passados de seyscientos corazones
De muchos animales que mataron.[9]
Que no es pequeño pasmo y maravilla
Que gente bruta, bárbara, grossera,
De todo punto viesse y alcanzase
Que con razón no más que corazones
Deben sacrificarse y ofrecerse
A los que semejantes obras hazen,
Porque no obstante que es porción pequeña
Para satisfacer la débil hambre
De un milano flaco, acobardado,
Nadie ignora el gran ser de su nobleza,
Pues siendo en sí tan corto y encogido[10]
Sabemos que no cabe en todo el mundo.
Y en el abreviado[11] que es el hombre

And Andrés Dorantes, most remarkable,
All being men most singular.[4]
In the most fierce and raging storm
35 Of all their miseries and trials sharp,
Through them the Highest Power chose to work
Great store of miracles.
And as his Deity with just his breath
Infused the living spirit into men
40 And others He made well, blessed by his hand,
So these brave men thus passing on
Among those nations barbarous
Not only healed for them their sick,
Their lame, the paralytic, and the blind,
45 But also gave life to their dead
Merely through blessing and their holy breath
That through their sainted mouths they did breathe
forth,
Poultices, treacle, medicine
Which only in the miraculous pharmacy
50 Of God all-powerful could well be found.
Through whose high and sovereign virtue,
The unlearned Arabs[5] in suspense,
As though they all were gods,
One time, as tribute and sign of vassalage
55 Did consecrate and give and offer them
More than six hundred hearts
Of many animals they'd killed.[6]
Which is no small astonishment, and wonder,
That people stupid, barbarous, and gross
60 Should see and comprehend in every way
That, in all reason, nothing else but hearts
Ought to be sacrificed and offered
To those who did such works,
For, notwithstanding that it is scarcely enough
65 To satisfy the feeble hunger
Of a weak and fearful bird of prey,
No one denies the great fact of its nobleness,
For being in itself so small and timid
We know that the whole world will not contain it.
70 And in the little world that's man

---

5. En su resumen cronológico de exploradores anteriores de las tierras nuevo mexicanas, Villagrá comienza apropiadamente con Cabeza de Vaca, cuyas experiencias fueron narradas en *Relación de naufragios y comentarios,* publicado muchas décadas antes de la expedición de Oñate.

6. Pítima = emplaste medicinal.

7. Atriaca = triaca, contraveneno.

8. Alárabes = árabes, por extensión todo enemigo no europeo.

9. Se halla el pasaje en el capítulo 32 de la *Relación de naufragios y comentarios* de Nuñez Cabeza de Vaca.

10. Encogido = reducido.

11. Mundo es aquí el antecedente: el abreviado mundo que es el hombre. El concepto se halla, por ejemplo, en Cervantes, *La Galatea* IV.

4. In his chronological presentation of previous explorers of those lands, Villagrá begins, properly, with Cabeza de Vaca and his small group of survivors from a Spanish expedition which shipwrecked in Florida. Cabeza de Vaca gave an account of his travels through the southern United States in *Relación de naufragios y comentarios,* published long before the Oñate expedition to New Mexico.

5. Villagrá will frequently use *Alarabe,* arab, as generic for enemy, probably a linguistic identification derived from Spain's long history of reconquering the Iberian Peninsula from the Moors.

6. The event is narrated by Cabeza de Vaca, *Naufragios,* chapter 32.

El es la primer vasa[12] y fundamento
Que da calor de vida al artificio
De todo el edificio milagroso;
Y es en sí tan heroica su grandeza
Que, como es fuerza passe y se registre
Por vna de las salas del juzgado,[13]
En cuio puesto assisten los sentidos,
Lo que a la suma alteza y excelencia
Del bello entendimiento se propone,
Assí, no puede ser que llegue cosa
Que le hiera y de muerte le lastime
Sin que primero acabe y se destruia
El mundo breve y toda su grandeza,
Porque él es el postrero que fenece
Y el que postrero pierde el movimiento.
Y assí en él, como en hermoso templo,
La magestad del alma se aposenta,
De donde al poderoso Dios embía
Sus santas y devotas oraciones,
Sus obras, pensamientos y alegría,
Su verdadero amor y su tristeza,
Sus lágrimas, suspiros y gemidos.
Y assí, como abundante fuente viva
De donde manan cosas tan grandiosas,
A sólo Dios el corazón se debe
Sacrificar en todas ocasiones
Y a todos los demás varones fuertes
Que sus venditos passos van siguiendo,
Notando el sacrificio inestimable
Destos rústicos, bárbaros, salbajes
Que tantos corazones ofrecieron
A estos quatro famosos que en sus tierras
Por tiempo de nueve años trabajados
Vn millón de miserias padecieron.
Al cabo de los quales aportaron[14]
A la provincia cálida, famosa,
De Culiacán, que en otros tiempos nobles
Muy nobles caballeros la poblaron.
En cuyo puesto y siglo de oro illustre[15]
Aquel humilde Provincial[16] celoso
De la orden del Seráfico Francisco

It is the base and primary fundament
That gives the heat of life unto the whole device
Of all the edifice miraculous;
And so heroic is its greatness in itself
75 That, since all must pass and be registered
In one of the halls of judgment,
in which place the senses all preside,
All that which to the greatest height and excellence
Of the great understanding is proposed,[7]
80 Thus comes it nothing can approach
To wound it and to hurt it unto death
Unless it first do end and quite destroy
The little world[8] and all its greatness,
For it is the last thing to die
85 And is the last to lose its movement.
And so, in it, as in a lovely temple,
The soul's own majesty doth have its seat,
From whence to God all-powerful it sends
Its prayers so holy and devout,
90 Its works, its thoughts, its joy,
Its true love, and its sadness,
Its tears and sighs and groans.
And thus, as the abundant fount of life
From which such mighty things do spring,
95 To God alone the heart should be
On all occasions sacrificed
And to all other men of strength
Who follow in His blessed steps,
Noting the sacrifice inestimable
100 Of these barbarian rustic savages,
Who offered there so many hearts
To these four famous men who in their lands
Throughout the time of nine laborious years
Suffered a million miseries.
105 At the end of which they came at last
Unto the hot and famous province
Of Culiacán, which in other times
Most noble gentlemen had populated.
And in whose famous century of gold
110 That humble, zealous, Provincial,[9]
He of Seraphic Francis's order

12. Vasa = basa, fundamento de un edificio y, por extensión, de cualquier cosa.

13. Salas del juzgado = centros del juicio. La filosofía expresada (que nada hay en el intelecto que no hubiera estado primero en los sentidos) es la aristotélico-escolástica que se enseñaba en la Universidad de Salamanca.

14. Aportaron = llegaron.

15. En cuyo lugar y en su período de grandeza.

16. El provincial era el encargado de los monasterios de una provincia.

7. The philosophy somewhat confusedly expressed here (that there is nothing in the intellect that has not first been in the senses) is Aristotelian-Scholasticism, taught at the University of Salamanca which Villagrá attended.

8. The reference is to an earlier identification of man as a microcosm or "little world." The idea was commonplace and is expressed, for example, by Cervantes: La Galatea IV.

9. The provincial was the religious head of the monasteries in a given province.

Que fray Marcos de Niza[17] se llamaba,
Abiéndose bien dellos informado
Por aber descubierto cierta parte
Destas nuevas Regiones escondidas,
Y como ya alcanzaba de los Indios
La razón que atrás queda referida,
Que salieron de[18] aquí los Mexicanos,
Qual famoso Colón, que nuevo Mundo
Dio a vuestra Real corona de Castilla,
Assí determinó luego de entrarse
Por cosa de dozientas leguas largas
Con sólo vn compañero, confiado
En aquel sumo bien que nos gobierna.
Y por enfermedad que a el compañero
Sobrebino fue fuerza se quedase,
Y él se entró con divino y alto esfuerzo,
Con cantidad de bárbaros amigos,
La tierra adentro; y como aquél que halla
Vn rico y preciosíssimo tesoro
Cuya abundancia fuerza y le combida
Que buelva con presteza por socorro,
Assí el gran Capitán de pobre gente
Con grande priessa rebolvió diziendo
Notables excelencias de la tierra
Que abía visto, notado y descubierto.
Y como no ay en todo el vniverso
Cosa que más parezca y represente
La magestad de Dios como es el hombre,
Como si fuera Dios emprende cosas
Que a sólo Dios parecen se reservan.
Y assí podéis notar, Rey poderoso,
Que teniendo de aquesta nueva tierra
Copiosa relación de aqueste santo
Y heroico Religioso de Franciscos,
Aquel grande Cortés, Marqués del Valle,
Después de aber sulcado la brabeza
Del ancho bravo mar y echado a fondo
Las poderosas naves de su flota,[19]
Hecho de tanto esfuerzo y ossadía
Tal qual nunca abrazó varón famoso,
Llevado del valor illustre y alto
De sola su persona no domada,

Who was called Fray Marcos de Niza,[10]
He having well-informed himself
From those who had discovered certain parts
115 Of these new, hidden, regions,
And as he knew already from the Indians
The story that I told you above,
That hence the Mexicans had come,
Like famed Columbus, he who gave a world
120 All new unto your royal Kingdom of Castile,
E'en so he then determined he would enter
A matter of two hundred leagues or more
With one companion only, trusting well
Unto that Highest Good which governs us.
125 And by the sickness which then came upon
His comrade, 'twas necessary to remain,
And he went on with effort high, divine,
With numerous barbarian friends,
Into the land; and, like to one who finds
130 A rich, most precious, treasure,
Whose great abundance forces and invites him
To quickly come again for aid,
E'en so the mighty captain of poor folk
With swiftness great returned
135 And saying most notable good things about the land
Which he had seen and noted and discovered.
And as there is not in the universe
A thing which is more like and represents
The majesty of God than man himself,
140 As if he were God's Self he undertakes
Things which it seems must be reserved to God.
And thus, O powerful King, you here can note
That, having now of this new land
A copious tale got from this man,
145 This holy and heroic monk of Francis,
That great Cortez, the Marquis of the Valley,
Having endured the fury great
Of furious sea, having sunk
The powerful vessels of his fleet,
150 Deed of such effort and such daring
As never famous man had done,[11]
Borne on by the illustrious and lofty valor
Of his person, never o'ercome,

---

17. Fray Marcos de Niza fue de los primeros en investigar las noticias de Cabeza de Vaca acerca de las tierras hacia el norte. Sus exageradas descripciones de grandezas incitaron a la exploración de las mismas. Para un resumen de sus exploraciones, véase H. E. Bolton, *Coronado, Knight of Pueblos and Plains* (Albuquerque: The Univ. of New Mexico Press, 1964), 23–39.

18. La reproducción mexicana trae "que."

19. La hazaña de Cortés era ya muy popular y está poetizada en las obras épicas que, como se ha visto, Villagrá conocía.

10. Fray Marcos de Niza was the first to follow up on the news of the new lands to the north given by the members of the Cabeza de Vaca party. His glowing and mostly imaginary descriptions of great cities to the north was paramount in encouraging further explorations. For a summary of his explorations, see H. E. Bolton, *Coronado, Knight of Pueblos and Plains* (Albuquerque: The Univ. of New Mexico Press, 1964), 23–39.

11. Cortez's deeds were already legendary and had been written about in at least two epics with which Villagrá was familiar, *Mexicana* and *El peregrino indiano*.

Que ya por todo el Orbe no cabía,
No porque no está bien desengañado 155
Que sólo siete pies de tierra sobran,[20]
Mas descubrir por cada pie pretende
Vn nuevo Mundo y ciento si pudiesse
Para mejor subir el edificio
De nuestra santa Iglesia y lebantarle 160
Por estas tierras bárbaras perdidas,
Pues poniendo la proa de su intento
Para largar al viento todo el trapo
Siguiendo desta impressa la demanda,
Como amar y Reynar jamás permiten 165
Ninguna competencia que les hagan,
Sucedió lo que al muy famoso César
Con el brabo Pompeio sobre el mando
Que cada qual por fuerza apetecía,[21]
Porque le contradijo don Antonio, 170
Primero Visorrey de nueva España,[22]
Diziéndole que a él sólo la jornada,
Como a tal Visorrey, le competía,
Cortando el apretado y ciego[23] nudo
Que de amistad antigua y verdadera 175
El vno con el otro professaban.
Mas Dios nos libre quando quiebra y rompe
Interés, y que puede atrabesarse
Porque al punto que quiere embravecerse
No hay Rey, razón, ni ley ni fuerza tanta 180
Que a su furor diábolico resista.
Y assí dize muy bien el Mantuano:[24]
"¡O sacra hambre de riquezas vanas,
Qué desbenturas hay a que no fuerces
Los tristes corazones de mortales!" 185
Y pónele este nombre sacrosanto,
Grandioso, soberano y lebantado
Porque ningún mortal jamás se atreva[25]
Emprenderla jamás contra justicia.
Mas, como nos advierte la Escritura, 190
Quién será aquéste y alabarle hemos
Por aber hecho en vida maravillas.[26]

Which ne'er could be contained by all the world,
Not because he did not know well 155
But seven feet of earth more than sufficed,[12]
But trying to discover at each step
A newer world, a hundred if he could,
In order to better raise up the edifice
Of our Holy Church and lift it high 160
In these lost lands barbaric;
Well, setting the prow of his intent
To set all sails before the wind
Following the demand of this emprise,
Since loving and ruling never bear 165
Competition to be offered them,
The same occurred to him as to the famous Caesar
With the brave Pompey over the command
Which each one necessarily desired,[13]
For Don Antonio refused him, 170
The first Vice-regent of New Spain,[14]
Telling him that to him alone the emprise,
as Viceroy, belonged,
Cutting the firm and cunning knot
Of true and ancient friendship 175
Which they had unto each other.
Now God deliver us from interest
When it breaks and shatters, and can cut deep,
For at the time that it becomes furious
There is no King nor reason, law, nor force so great 180
As to resist its diabolical impulse.
And thus the Mantuan[15] well says:
"O sacred hunger of vain wealth,
What misfortunes are there to which you do not force
The sad hearts of mortals!" 185
And he gives to it this title sacrosanct,
Sovereign, lofty, grandiose,
So that no mortal ever dare
To undertake it ever against justice.
But as the Scripture warns us: 190
Who can this be that we may praise him
For having performed marvels while alive.

---

20. La referencia a los siete pies que señalan toda la tierra que, a la larga, necesita el hombre se halla, por ejemplo, al principio mismo de Ercilla (*La araucana* I, 1.)

21. Referencia al material épico recogido en *La Farsalia* de Lucano, uno de los modelos de la épica renacentista.

22. Antonio de Mendoza, nombrado primer Virrey de Nueva España por Carlos V el año 1535. Véase C. Pérez Bustamante, *Don Antonio de Mendoza* (Santiago de Chile, 1928).

23. Ciego = aplicado a nudo, uno muy difícil de desatar.

24. Se refiere Villagrá a Virgilio. Los versos citados seguidamente son los 73–74 del canto III de la *Eneida*.

25. Villagrá, con licencia poética, omite la "a" que seguiría.

26. Tan difícil es que el hombre se resista al interés que un tal habría que alabarle por milagroso.

12. The reminder, especially to New World conquerors of great empires, that seven feet of earth suffice one in the end, may be found as well, in Ercilla: *La araucana* I, 1.

13. The Caesar-Pompey conflict is the subject matter of Lucan's epic, one of the primary models of the Renaissance epic.

14. Antonio de Mendoza, the first viceroy of New Spain, was appointed by Charles V in 1535. See C. Pérez Bustamante, *Don Antonio de Mendoza* (Santiago de Chile, 1928).

15. Virgil is often referred to as the Mantuan. The quote that follows is from the *Aeneid* III, 73–74.

Pues porfiando los dos sobre esta causa
Como si fueran dioses poderosos,
Cada qual pretendía y procuraba
Rendir a todo el mundo si pudiese.
Y vista aquesta causa mal parada,
Al punto procuró²⁷ el Marqués heroico,
Por ser del mar del Sur Adelantado,²⁸
Que por este derecho pretendía
Y alegaba ser suya la jornada,
Y assí por no perderla ni dexarla
Vino a tomar de España la derrota
Para tratar con la imperial persona
De vuestro bien aventurado Abuelo,
Carlos Quinto, de toda aquesta causa,
Cuio alto y prudentísimo gobierno
Tuvo de los imperios más notables,
Reynos y señoríos desta vida
La suprema y más alta primacia,
Siendo amado, acatado y estimado
De todo lo que ciñe el vniverso.
Pues luego que dio fin a su carrera
Y recogió las velas destrozadas
De aquel largo viage trabajoso,
Qual nave poderosa que da fondo
En desseado puerto y al instante
La vemos yr a pique y sin remedio,
Assí llegó la cruda y feroz muerte,
Diziendo en altas vozes lebantadas,
"A ninguno perdonó",²⁹ y puso pazes
Quitándole de vista la jornada.
Y con horrible imperio poderoso
Al punto le mandó se derrotase,³⁰
Tomando, sin escusa y sin remedio,
Aquel mortal y fúnebre camino
Tan trillado y seguido de los muertos
(Quanto jamás handado de los vivos),
Y más de aquellos tristes, miserables,
Que vida prolongada se prometen.
Y como muchas vezes acontece
Que con descuido suele deslizarse
Vn regalado vaso de las manos
Dexándonos muy tristes y suspensos
Y casi sin aliento boqui abiertos
De verle por el suelo destrozado,

195	Well, these two quarreling upon this cause
	As if they were two powerful gods,
	Each one intended and did try
	To subject all the world, if well he might.
	And, deciding the matter would end ill,
	Immediately the heroic Marquis claimed,
	As Adelantado¹⁶ of the South Sea,
200	This right he claimed and alleged
	To make the voyage was his in fact.
	And so he might not lose or let it lapse
	He took at once the way to Spain
	To treat with the imperial person
205	Of your most fortunate grandfather,
	Carlos the Fifth, on all that case,
	Whose lofty and most prudent government
	Did have of empires the most notable,
	Of kingdoms and of lordships in this life
210	The highest and most lofty primacy,
	Being beloved, respected, and esteemed
	By all the universe girds round.
	As soon as he had ended his long voyage
	And furled the tattered sails
215	Of that long toilsome trip,
	Like powerful ship that does safely anchor
	Right in the longed-for port and in an instant
	We see it sink and without hope,
	So came death, rude, ferocious,
220	Saying in loud and upraised voice,
	"I pardon no one!",¹⁷ and made peace,
	Taking the emprise from before his gaze.
	And with horrible and powerful command
	Ordered him instantly to change his route,
225	Taking without excuse or remedy
	That mournful, mortal road
	So frequented and followed by the dead
	(As it is never trod by those alive)
	And more by those sad, miserable, ones
230	Who promise to themselves a life prolonged.
	And as it many times doth hap,
	A precious glass from out our hands
	Doth slip, from carelessness,
	Leaving us sad and in suspense
235	And almost breathless, open-mouthed,
	To see it broken on the floor,

27. Procuró = solicitó.
28. El adelantado estaba encargado de defender y ampliar unas fronteras.
29. Villagrá pone en boca de la Muerte las palabras, *concedo nulli*, que en la literatura emblemática de la época se le atribuyen a Cronos, dios pagano del tiempo.
30. Se derrotase = se saliera del camino que se había trazado.

16. Coming from the military-political tradition of the Spanish reconquest, the 'Adelantado' was charged with protecting and expanding a specific frontier area.
17. Villagrá attributes to Death the words *concedo nulli*, usually attributed in the emblematic literature of his day to Cronus, the pagan god of time.

Assí causó grandísima tristeza,
Assombro, pasmo, miedo y sobresalto
El ver aquel varón tendido en tierra,
Resuelto todo en polvo y vil ceniza,
Siendo el que aventajó tanto su espada
Que sujetó con ella al nuevo mundo.
Mas quién será, señor, aquél tan fuerte
Que a la furiosa fuerza de la parca[31]
Pueda su gran braveza resistirla,
Si a[32] Reyes, Papas y altos potentados
Por fúnebres despojos y trofeos
Debajo de sus pies están postrados.
Mas qué mucho si al hijo de Dios vivo
Sabemos todos le quitó la vida,
Por cuya causa cada qual se apreste,
Pues sin remedio es fuerza que se rinda
Y sin vital espíritu se postre
Debajo de su pala y fuerte azada.
Con esto, Don Antonio de Mendoza
Tomó y quedó por suyo todo el campo,
Qual aquél que a su gran contrario dexa
En él tendido, pálido y el alma
Del miserable cuerpo desasida.
Y para descubrir mejor el blanco
Valiose del tercero don divino,[33]
Que es quien más bien nos lleva y encamina,
Qual refulgente luz que nos alumbra,
Con cuia claridad tomó consejo
Con aquel gran varón, noble, famoso,
Que Christóbal de Oñate[34] se dezía,
Persona de buen seso y gran gobierno
Y vno de los de más valor y prendas
Que, de capa y espada,[35] en nueva España
Y reynos del Pirú abemos visto.
Al qual pidió su parecer y voto
Acerca del soldado más gallardo,
Sufrido, astuto, fuerte y más discreto
Que le fuesse possible que escogiese
Para sólo ocuparle y encargarle
Que por explorador de aquesta entrada
Con treinta buenos hombres se aprestase
Antes que todo el campo se partiese.
Y como el buen fin tanto se adelanta
Quanto el principio es más bien acertado,

240

245

250

255

260

265

270

275

280

So it caused very great distress,
Astonishment and wonder, fear and dread,
To see that man fallen upon the earth,
All turned to dust and ashes vile,
This being he who won such vantage with his sword,
Who with it conquered a new world.
But who shall be so strong, O lord,
That his great strength may still resist
The furious force of death
If Kings and Popes and lofty potentates
Lie prostrate beneath its feet
As funeral spoils and trophies;
No feat, since we know it took the life
Of the live Son of living God,
For which cause let each one prepare,
For, without remedy, needs be we must surrender
And lie prone, without the vital spirit,
Beneath his hoe and mighty spade.
With this, Don Antonio de Mendoza
Took and kept all the field for his,
Like one who leaves his adversary great
Lying all pale in the arena and his soul
Gone from the miserable corpse.
And better to find out his goal
He made use of the third of divine gifts,[18]
The one which best doth guide and carry us,
Like a refulgent light that shows the way,
By whose clear ray he counsel took
With that great, noble, famous man
Who was called Cristóbal de Oñate,[19]
Person of great good sense and self-control,
One of the most virtuous and valorous
'Mong those of cape and sword[20] that we have seen
In all of New Spain and Kingdoms of Peru.
Him he did ask opinions and advice
As to the soldier most resourceful,
Experienced, astute, and strong, and most discreet
That it was possible for him to choose
That he might use him and employ him
Simply as scout for this ingress,
To go ahead with thirty chosen men
Before the camp entire should sally forth.
And as a good end is hastened on
In measure as beginning is well made,

---

31. Parca = muerte.

32. Esta "a" sobra para la mejor lectura.

33. El "tercero don divino," el entendimiento o razón es una de las tres potencias del alma.

34. El padre de Juan de Oñate, héroe del poema.

35. La expresión "de capa y espada" sugiere la feliz combinación en una persona de buen trato y eficaz acción.

18. The reference is to intelligence, one of the three powers (intelligence, will, and memory) associated with the soul.

19. The father of Juan de Oñate.

20. The phrase *de capa y espada* suggested the ideal of a man socially and militarily adept.

Qual vn agudo lince que traciende	As a shrewd lynx doth sharply see
O Aguila Real que sin empacho[36]	Or royal eagle that without timidity
El más bravo rigor del Sol penetra,	Doth look into the brightness of the sun,
Assí, con gran presteza luego dixo,	Thus, with great quickness he spoke then,
Poniéndole delante la persona,	285 Placing before him the person
De aquel Iuan de Zaldíbar, su sobrino,[37]	Of that Juan de Zaldívar, his nephew,[21]
Soldado de vergüenza[38] y tan sufrido	A valiant soldier and as much long-suffering
Quanto para vna afrenta bien probado,	As he was well-prepared for all affronts.
Al qual sin más acuerdo le encargaron	They gave to him without discussion
Vna gallarda esquadra de Españoles	290 A gallant squadron of Spaniards
Que treinta brabas lanzas gobernaban.	Who numbered thirty lances stout.
Con éstos se metió la tierra adentro,	With these he pierced deep into the land,
Por donde les corrió muy gran fortuna[39]	Where troubles very great came to them
Y tempestad deshecha de trabajos	And also a very tempest fierce of labors
Tan esforzados, vivos y alentados	295 So vigorous and vivid, spirited,
Que sólo su valor pudo sufrirlos.	Naught but his valor could have borne them.
Y en el inter,[40] el diestro Mendocino[41]	Meanwhile the insightful Mendoza
Previno, como astuto, gran socorro,	Quickly prepared great aid, being a man astute,
Formando un gruesso campo reforzado	Forming a camp supplied right well
De bella soldadesca, tan vizarra	300 With sturdy soldiers, as excellent
Quanto más no pudieron esmerarse	As could possibly be achieved
Aquéllos que llegaron y pusieron	By those who arrived and imparted
El bélico primor en su fineza.[42]	The art of war in all its finest points.
Pues viendo esta belleza lebantada,	Now, seeing this brave levy raised,
Con ellos se bolvió el santo Niza,	305 There would return with them the holy Niza,
Provincial de pobríssimos[43] Franciscos,	Provincial of the poor Franciscans,
Por sólo que tuviesse franca entrada	Only that the voice of doctrine Evangelical
La voz de la Evangélica doctrina	Might have free entry
Entre estos pobres bárbaros perdidos.	Among those poor and lost barbarians.
Y porque el cuerpo humano destroncado	310 And since it is quite impossible
Y puesto sin cabeza es impossible	That headless human body be, without a head,
Que pueda bien mandarse y gobernarse,	Able to govern and command itself,
Nombraron por gobierno deste campo	They named as Governor of this camp
A vn grande caballero que Francisco	A mighty knight whom they did call
Vázquez de Coronado se dezía,	315 Francisco Vázquez de Coronado,
Persona de valor y grande esfuerzo	A man of valor and of great emprise
Para cosas de punto y grave peso.	In things of substance and of serious weight.
Y porque reberencia le tuviessen	And that they have reverence for him
Con título de General illustre	They wished to single out his person
Quisieron illustrar a su persona,	320 By honorable title, that of general.
Y honrrándole el Virrey en quanto pudo,	The Viceroy, honoring him in every way he could,

---

36. Empacho = perturbación, vergüenza.

37. Parece ser el padre del Juan de Zaldívar que acompañó a Juan de Oñate, pero Villagrá, *Historia*, edición de Junquera, 97, niega que lo fuera.

38. Vergüenza = virtud.

39. Fortuna = sucesos fortuitos; en el léxico marino, tiempo adverso, acepción que cobra muchas veces.

40. Inter = entretanto.

41. Se refiere a don Antonio de Mendoza.

42. En su fineza = en su punto más logrado.

43. La reproducción mexicana trae "pobíssimos."

21. He appears to have been the father of Juan and Vicente Zaldívar, who accompanied Oñate as his top military officers. But Villagrá, *Historia*, Junquera edition, 97, denies this family tie.

Para más alentar aquesta entrada,
En persona salió haziendo escolta
Hasta poner el campo en Compostela,
De la Ciudad de México apartada
Largas dozientas millas⁴⁴ bien tendidas,
Donde vino a salirles al encuentro
El Capitán Zaldíbar, quebrantado
Del áspero camino trabajoso,
Que vino de explorarle y descubrirle
A fuerza de armas, hambre y sed notable,
Y otros muchos trabajos que no cuento
Que por inormes páramos sufrieron.
Y diziendo al Virrey que aquella tierra
Que abía visto, notado y descubierto
No le parecía nada aventajada,
Respecto de ser pobre y miserable
Y de rústicos bárbaros poblada,
Mas que no fuesse parte todo aquesto
Para que vn solo passo atrás bolviesse,
Porque donde se pierde la esperanza
Allí los más solícitos monteros⁴⁵
Suelen con mucho gusto y passatiempo

Lebantar, sin pensar, muy grande caza.
Y como para el bien jamás le falta
Quien lo impugne, resista y contradiga,
No faltó quien dixese y atizase
Ser pobríssima tierra y que, por serlo,
Era terrible caso que aquel campo
En cosa tan perdida se ocupase.
Al alma le llegó al Virrey la nueva,
Mas como muy prudente y recatado,
Considerando que de vn grande hierro⁴⁶
Suele salir vn grande acertamiento,
Desimulose todo lo que pudo,
Y assí como en súbito peligro
Se debe aconsejar con gran presteza
Aquél que vive dél más descuidado,
Sin dilación mandó que se pusiese
Grandíssimo silencio y se callase
Todo lo referido, sin que cosa
Quedase para nadie descubierta.
Pues con esto era fuerza que el peligro
De deshazerse el campo se venciese,
Cuia prevención hizo porque el gasto
Estaba ya perdido y consumido,

44. Millas = medida, entonces, de mil pasos.
45. Monteros = cazadores.
46. Hierro = yerro.

The better to inspire that party of explorers,
Came on in person to give escort
Until they pitched their camp at Compostela,
325 A distance from the City of Mexico
Of good two hundred miles,²² long ones,
Where there came on to meet them on the way
Our Captain Zaldívar, all broken down
By the harsh and laborious trail
330 He, for him, had just then explored and discovered
By force of arms, of hunger and great thirst
And many other labors that I do not tell
That through great deserts they suffered.
And saying to the Viceroy that the land
335 He had seen, noted, and discovered
To him appeared as of no advantage
Because it was so poor and miserable
And peopled by barbarians rude;
But all this still was not a reason
340 For any to turn back a single pace,
Since just when hope is lost
Right there 'tis that most skillful hunters
Make it their custom, with great pleasure,
        entertainment,
To raise great game quite without thinking to.
345 And, as there never lacks to good
Someone to contradict, resist, deny it,
Here, too, there was not lacking one to say and to affirm
It was a miserable land, and for this cause
It were a terrible thing for that great camp
350 To occupy itself in things so ruinous.
The bad news touched the Viceroy to the quick,
But, like a prudent and cautious man,
Considering that great good luck
Doth often come from grave error,
355 He did dissimulate as best he might
And, just as in a sudden danger
'Tis best to quickly counsel with
A man who lives quite far from it,
Without delay he ordered that
360 They should keep silence and be quiet
In all such matter, so no thing
Should be by anyone found out.
Because 'twas necessary that this way
The peril of a dissolution of the camp be met,
365 Decision made because the expense
Was by then lost and all consumed,

22. The mile, as its name suggests, was measured at a thousand paces.

Con cincuenta mil pesos de buen oro
Que Christóbal de Oñate quiso darle,
Prestándolos con pecho generoso
Por sólo que esta entrada se hiziesse,
Y que sería possible, si se entrase
Segunda vez, que fuesse de provecho.
Y como siempre suele aventajarse⁴⁷
Al cansado montero la porfía,
Porfiando mandó que luego al punto
El nuevo General diesse principio
A lebantar el campo, y que marchase.
Y abiéndose de todos despedido,
Tomó el Virrey de México la buelta
Y el Real⁴⁸ fue tomando su derrota
Con grande furia y fuerza de trabajos,
Los quales los llevaron y aportaron
A los pueblos de Cíbola, llegados
A otros circunvecinos comarcanos,
Donde el gran padre Niza y los Floridos⁴⁹
Y el capitán Zaldíbar con su esquadra
Llegaron y bolvieron con la nueva.
En cuio puesto, el general, gustoso
De ver aquella tierra, mandó luego
Que grandes fiestas todos ordenasen;
Y haziéndose assí, salió en persona
En vn brabo caballo poderoso
Y en vna escaramuza⁵⁰ que tuvieron,
Batiendo el duro suelo desembuelto,
Desocupó la silla de manera
Que del terrible golpe atormentado
Quedó de todo punto sin juizio.
Y assí como los miembros adolecen
Luego que en la cabeza sienten falta,
Y cada qual dispara y no gobierna,
Assí la soldadesca, viendo estaba
La fuerza del gobierno zozobrada,
Destroncada y enferma, luego quiso,
Teniendo tanta tierra en que estenderse,
Parar con el trabajo y cercenarle.
Y assí, juntos a vna y en vn cuerpo,
Qual aquél que de hecho desespera,
Assí dieron de mano a la esperanza,
Verdadero remedio de los fines
Que con grandes cuidados pretendemos.
Y sin ver que mejor le hubiera sido

With fifty thousand dollars²³ of good gold
That Cristóbal de Oñate gave him gladly,
Lending them from his generous heart
370   With the sole purpose that this journey might be made,
For it was possible that a second
Exploration be of advantage.
And as the tired hunter is often
Restored by stoic persistence,
375   Persisting, then, he ordered on the spot
That the new General should make a start
To breaking camp, and march.
And, having taken leave of all,
The Viceroy then returned to Mexico;
380   The encampment took to its route
With fury great and force of effort,
Which did carry them and bring them to
The Cities of Cibola and
To other places neighboring,
385   Where great Father Niza and the Floridians²⁴
And Captain Zaldívar with his squadron
Had come and returned with the news.
In this place, the General, well pleased
To see that land, did order then
390   That all should make great holiday;
And, doing this, he came in person
On a great, powerful horse,
And, in a skirmish²⁵ which they had,
He fell from out his saddle,
395   Striking the hard ground forcibly,
So that, tormented by the fearful blow,
He was and did remain all senseless.
And as the separate members suffer pain
When they do feel the head is failing them,
400   And each does writhe and is not governed,
Just so the soldiery, seeing
The strength of government stricken,
Maimed, and sick, they then did wish,
Having so much land over which to extend,
405   To stop and curtail further work.
So, joined together in a body,
Like one who quite despairs of all,
So they despised all hope,
The one true remedy for the ends
410   Which we attempt, with such great care, to reach.
And, without seeing that 'twould have been best

---

47. Aventajarse = mejorar.
48. Real = campamento.
49. Llama Floridos a los del grupo de Cabeza de Vaca, que habían partida de Florida.
50. Escaramuza = pelea simulada de jinetes.

23. Curtis translates Villagrá's *pesos* with the modern equivalent of "dollars"; but the latter did not exist then as a monetary unit.
24. Floridians is a reference to the Cabeza de Vaca party.
25. These "skirmishes" were not with any enemy, but jousting games simulating war.

A todo aqueste campo disgustoso
No aber dado principio⁵¹ aquella impressa
Que bolver las espaldas vergonzosas
Abiéndose vna vez metido dentro
De la difícil prueba y estacada,
Con toda aquesta lástima furioso
Rebolvió con grandíssima presteza
Las presurosas plantas desembueltas.
Y aunque muchos quisieron como buenos
Resistirlos a todos con razones
Y fuerza de palabras eficaces,
Del santo Provincial faborecidas
Y amparadas también por don Francisco
De Peralta, grandíssimo guerrero,
Y del gallardo pecho de Zaldíbar,
Y de aquel caballero insigne y raro,
Don Pedro de Tobar, Padre de aquella
Illustre, bella y generosa dama,
Tan cortés como grande cortesana,
Doña Ysabel, en cuyo ser se encierra
Vna virtud profunda, lebantada
Al soberano amor en que se enciende
Valiéndose del mártir abrasado⁵²
En cuio templo vemos que se abrasa
Y como viva brasa se consume
En amoroso fuego del esposo
Que es vida de su vida y alma vella,⁵³
Todas illustres prendas heredadas
De su esforzado padre valeroso,
El qual con otros muchos caballeros
Instaban porque el campo no bolviese.
Y como siempre el bulgo y chusma torpe
No admiten lo que es fuera de su gusto,
Sin hazer de ninguno cuenta alguna,
Fue tanta su dureza y pertinacia
Que con muy grande pérdida notable
Bolvieron las espaldas al trabajo.
Porque como no entraron tropezando
Con muchas barras de oro y fina plata,
Y como vieron que las claras fuentes,
Arroyos y lagunas no vertían
Doradas sopas, tortas y rellenos,
Dieron todos en maldezir la tierra

For all that downcast camp
Not to have made beginning of the enterprise
Rather than turn their backs in shame
415 Once having put themselves into
The demanding test and challenge,
With all their furious grief
They turned, in greatest haste, to rear
Their hasty and impudent steps.
420 Although a many tried, like worthy men,
To stop them all with reasoning
And force of efficacious words,
Favored by the holy Provincial,
Protected, too, by Don Francisco
425 De Peralta, warrior extremely great,
And by the gallant heart of Zaldívar,
And by that gentleman most rarely famed,
Don Pedro de Tovar, father of that
Illustrious, beautiful, and generous dame,
430 As courteous as she was great in court,
That Doña Isabel who did incorporate
A virtue deep, lifted
To Sovereign love, with which she glows,
Having recourse to the roasted²⁶ martyr
435 In whose temple we do see she burns
And is consumed like glowing coals
In amorous passion for her Spouse,
Who is the life of both her life and soul,
All illustrious gifts inherited
440 From her father valiant and vigorous,
Who, with many other gentlemen,
Insisted that the camp should not return.
As always, the base rabble and the crowd
Would not permit what was outside their wish,
445 Nor gave to anyone the slightest heed;
Such was their harshness and obduracy
That, with a loss both great and notable,
They turned their backs upon the work.
Because they had not traveled stumbling
450 O'er many bars of gold and silver fine,
And since they saw the fountains clear,
Brooklets, and lakes did not pour out
Gilded soups, cakes, and sausages,
They set themselves to curse the land

---

51. Falta en el original la "a" que mejora la lectura.

52. San Lorenzo.

53. Aunque no ha de faltar en ésta, como se verá, la india
enamorada que es tópico en la épica americana, a diferencia de Ercilla,
que inserta una autobiográfica referencia a su propia vida amorosa, la
única referencia laudatoria a mujer española que hace Villagrá es a una
monja. Es un dato más que diferencia la intensidad religiosa de un
poema y otro.

26. The reference appears to be to Saint Lawrence, usually
associated with a roasted martyrdom.

Y a quien en semejantes ocassiones

Quiso que se metiesen y enrredasen.

Y assí, todos cuitados y llorosos,

Como si fueran hembras se afligían,

Cuia vageza, digna de deshonra,

Con que éstos sus personas infamaron

Lebantando las manos del trabajo

Que es fuerza que en la guerra se padezca,

Será bien se suspenda a nuevo canto

Si abemos de escrebir su triste llanto.[54]

455

460

And everyone who wished them to be put

And snared into such a place.

And so, all miserable and weeping,

They wailed their fate as though they had been women,

A meanness, worthy of dishonor,

With which they made themselves right infamous,

Withdrawing their hands from the labors

That must be suffered in war.

It would be well to wait for a new canto

If we must write about their dolorous weeping.[27]

54. Aunque la caída del caballo de Coronado esté documentada (Bolton, *Coronado,* 300), ocurrió hacia el final de la expedición; y la supuesta deserción de sus hombres, que Villagrá criticará acerbamente a través de varios cantos, no tiene base histórica. El poeta pudo haber extraído semejante impresión de la lectura de la descripción de la disolución del ejército de Coronado, cuando habían alcanzado Culiacán en viaje de vuelta, que ofrece Pedro de Castañeda. Véase Bolton, *Coronado,* 347.

27. Although there is historical documentation for Coronado's fall from horseback, (Bolton, *Coronado, Knight of Pueblos and Plains,* 330), it occurred very near the end of the expedition, and the supposed desertion of his men, a diatribe that Villagrá carries over into Canto IV, is not historically accurate. The poet may have gotten such an impression, possibly, from reading Pedro de Castañeda's account of the disbanding of the army (Bolton, *Coronado,* 347) after it had reached Culiacán on the return trip.

CANTO QVARTO

DE LA INFAMIA Y BAGEZA QUE COMETEN LOS
Generales, oficiales y soldados que salen a nuevos
descubrimientos y se buelven sin perseverar y ver el fin
de sus impresas.

QUIEN muy bastantes prendas no sintiere
De los quilates y valor que alcanza[1]

Para seguir con valeroso esfuerzo
Del iracundo Marte[2] el duro oficio,

Si no quiere vivir vida afrentosa,
Infame, miserable y abatida,
Huiga[3] de todo punto y no se empache
En el subido son de sus clarines,
Roncas cajas[4] y pífanos[5] templados,
Que presta[6] que en la quieta paz se arrastren.
¿Con muy vizarros passos, gruessas picas,
Y que con esmeriles[7] y mosquetes
Arrojen por el aire prestas valas,
De qué sirve, el benablo más tendido,
Las plumas lebantadas y las galas,
Gineta[8] honrrosa y gran bastón fornido,
Los pomposos entonos y palabras,
Promesas y brabeza, que nos muestran
Los que al furor indómito se ofrecen,
Si en llegando que llegan a las veras
Su ánimo se rinde y acobarda
Qual aquél que de ver los filos tiernos
De vna débil lanzeta[9] desfallece?
No hay visoño[10] soldado que no sepa,
Ni corto cortesano que no alcance,
Que no hay palabras viles más infames
Ni execución de manos más perdida
Que pretender por la nobleza de armas
Honor aquél que no es para alcanzarle.
Y assí no puede ser desemboltura[11]
Ni soberbia que pueda compararse

1. Alcanza = se necesita.
2. Dios romano de la guerra.
3. Huiga = huya.
4. Cajas = tambores.
5. Pífanos = flautas.
6. Presta = conviene.
7. Esmeriles = piezas pequeñas de artillería.
8. Gineta = lanza corta.
9. Lanzeta = lanceta, pequeño instrumento para sangrar o abrir tumores.
10. Visoño = bisoño, nuevo.
11. Desemboltura = desenvoltura, desvergüenza.

CANTO IV

Of the infamy and baseness committed by the generals, officers,
and soldiers who go out to new discoveries and return without
persevering, and seeing the end of their enterprises.

E who does not feel sufficient virtue
In the degree of perfectness and
distinction required
To follow with an effort valiant
The rigorous duties of the wrathful
Mars,[1]

5   If he wish not to lead an ignominious life,
Infamous, miserable, and dejected,
Then let him flee at once, nor be embarrassed
By sudden sound of trumpets of the war,
Of sounding drums and shrilling fifes,
10   For 'tis convenient that in peace he lurk.
With very martial steps, with heavy pikes,
And the light field guns and the muskets, too,
Throwing in air their swiftly flying balls,
Of what use are they, the longest lance,
15   The flying plumes and finery,
Honorable spear and powerful truncheon,
More so the pompous haughtiness, the words,
The promises and the bragging that they show,
Those who partake of war's fury,
20   If coming, as they do come, to the truth,
Their souls surrender and show cowardly,
Like those who, seeing the small edge
Of a mere lancet, faint?
There's not a novice soldier does not know,
25   Nor timid courtier doesn't understand,
That there are no vile words more infamous
Nor deed of hand more villainous
Than to seek by nobility in arms
Honor who cannot by arms achieve it.
30   And thus there can be no such brazenness, vainglory
Or vanity can be compared

1. Roman god of war.

Al que ocupa en el bélico exercicio
Qualquiera de sus plazas lebantadas,
No me da más[12] la que es de pobre infante
Que la del mismo General famoso,
O qualquiera otro prático guerrero,
Si puesto en la ocasión a campo abierto
Rebuelve las espaldas, sin empacho
De aquéllos que de afuera los señalan
Y por sus mismos nombres los conocen,
Cuio grave descuido[13] descuidado
Es mucho más dañoso y afrentoso
Que si en pública plaza las bolviese
Al brazo de vn verdugo, despojadas,[14]
Con voz de pregonero levantada
Y pública trompeta conocida.
¿Quién vio a los que hemos dicho yr marchando
La vuelta[15] desta impresa señalada,
De la Audiencia y Virrey acompañados,
Con tanto parabién de caballeros
Y aplauso de las damas más gallardas
De todas las que ciñe nueva España,
Y qual otro Nembrot,[16] que pretendía
Subir y conquistar el alto cielo,
Assí nos dio a entender todo este campo
Ser poco todo el mundo y su grandeza
Para sólo cebar su fiera diestra
En cosas de importancia que ygualasen
Al subido valor de sus personas,
Y quién los ve bolver a rienda suelta
Con lenguas tan discordes y diversas,
Las vnas con las otras encontradas,
Assí como sabemos se encontraron
Aquellos palabreros que olvidados
De sus vanos intentos se bolvieron
Confusos del trabajo comenzado
En la gran Babilonia celebrada
De las divinas letras consagradas?[17]
Assí los afligidos coronados,[18]
Viendo a su General de todo punto
Privado de memoria y de sentido,
Confusos se bolvieron de la tierra,
Vnos doliéndose de aber dejado

To that of one who in a warlike force
Doth occupy any important post,
It matters not to me whether it be
35 Poor soldier of the infantry or famous general,
Or any other soldier tried,
If, tried upon the battlefield,
He turns his back, quite without shame
Of those about who point him out
40 And know him by his very name,
Whose grave delinquency and negligence
Thus is more damaging and more outrageous
Than if they showed their backs in public squares,
Stripped, to the hangman's arm,
45 Announced by voice of common crier,
Known by trumpet's publication.
Whoever saw those we have mentioned march
At the outset of this famed enterprise,
Accompanied by the Viceroy and the Council,
50 With such good wishes of the gentlemen,
Applause from the most beauteous dames
Of all New Spain contains,
And like another Nimrod who doth hope
To conquer and subdue the lofty Heavens,[2]
55 This whole camp would have us know
That the whole world was small and all its greatness
But a thing to feed their fierce right arms
In matters of importance and deserving of
The swelling valor of their persons,
60 And then did see them at full speed return
With words discordant and diverse,
Each talking 'gainst the rest,
Just as we know there found themselves
Those talkers who, forgetting,
65 Turned from their vain intent
Confused, and left the work commenced,
In Babylonia great and celebrated
By holy, sacred writ?[3]
So, the afflicted soldiers,
70 Seeing their General quite hopelessly
Deprived of memory and consciousness,
These, all confused did turn back from the land,
Some wailing out that they had left

---

12. No me da más = me da igual.
13. Descuido = incumplimiento, negligencia.
14. Despojadas = desnudas.
15. La vuelta de = camino de.
16. Nembrot, Nemrod, rey de Caldea, gran cazador. Algunas interpretaciones de *Génesis* (10:8–12) le dan como rebelde contra Dios.
17. Se refiere a la torre de Babel.
18. Se refiere a los hombres de Coronado.

2. Nimrod, king of Chaldea, great hunter. Some interpretations of *Genesis* (10:8–12) would have him rebelling against God.
3. The reference is to the Tower of Babel.

Sus fuerzas a la orilla zozobradas,[19]
Otros que sus trabajos fueron vanos,
Pues en vano llegaron y bolvieron
Sin ver de aquel estado la grandeza,
Negando, con gran fuerza de razones,
Ser para sólo heriazo allí criada,
Pues la divina mano poderosa,
Siendo en pequeñas cosas admirable,
En las que eran tan grandes y espaciosas
Era caso forzoso aventajarse.[20]
Otros, por el contrario, se afligían,
Llorando hambre, desnudez, cansancio,
Terribles yelos, nieves y ventiscos,
Pesados soles, aguas y granizo,
Gran pobreza y trabajos de la tierra,
Miserias del camino trabajoso,
Postas[21] y centinelas peligrosas,
El peso de las armas desabridas,
Inclemencia del Cielo riguroso,
Y riesgos de la vida no pensados,
Enfermedades y otros disparates,
Como si el duro oficio de la guerra,
Bolviendo atrás su natural vertiente
Y el poderoso ímpetu furioso
Con que su brabo curso va vertiendo,
Acaso les hubiese prometido,
No lo que el muy sangriento Marte ofrece,
Sino aquello más puro y regalado
Que de fértil razimo beneficia[22]
El gran nieto de Cadmo y de Saturno,[23]
O lo que aquel profeta prodigioso
Que en la casa de Meca reberencia
La gente Sarracena porque aguarda
Gran fuerza y opulencia de manjares
En el futuro siglo que pretende,[24]
Sin advertir los pobres miserables
Que tocar un clarín alto, gallardo,
Y ronca caja y pífano templado,
Y arbolar[25] a su tiempo un estandarte
Y tremolar en campo vna vandera,

Their efforts beached on the shore,[4]
75 Others that all their work was vain,
Since they in vain had come and gone
Without a sight of that state's greatness,
Denying, with great show of thought,
That it was good for naught but desert,
80 For the divine and powerful hand,
Being admirable in small things,
In those that were so spacious, great,
'Twas necessary to improve.[5]
Others, in contrary, were much cast down,
85 And wept their hunger, nakedness, fatigue,
The fearful cold, the snow, blizzards,
The burning sun, the rain, the hail,
Great poverty, the labors of the land,
The miseries of toilsome road,
90 Watches and sentry posts most perilous,
The overwhelming weight of arms,
Inclemency of rigorous skies,
Most unconsidered risks of life,
Sickness and other bits of nonsense,
95 As if the duties of harsh war,
Turning their natural current back
And checking the furious, powerful impetus
With which their rushing course goes on,
Perhaps to them had promised,
100 Not what bloody Mars doth offer,
But that, most pure and delicate,
Which the great heir of Cadmus and Saturn[6]
Extracted from the fertile grape,
Or what that prophet prodigious
105 Who's reverenced in the house of Mecca[7]
By Saracens because he keeps
Great stock of opulence and entertainment
There in the future life they all hope for,
These miserable creatures noting not
110 That sounding out the trumpet high and clear,
The harsh drum and the sounding fife,
Waving a standard in their turn
And carrying a banner on the field

19. Estos serían los que lamentaron la decisión de Coronado de acabar la expedición después de sólo dos años. Véase Bolton, *Coronado*, 333.
20. Pues si Dios hace maravillas en cosas pequeñas qué no haría en aquella tierra tan extensa.
21. Postas = puestos señalados al soldado.
22. Beneficia = extrae. Se refiere al vino.
23. El dios Fauno, Pan romano, dios de los campos fértiles y pacíficos.
24. Mahoma, cuyo paraíso ("futuro siglo") promete bienestar físico.
25. Arbolar = enarbolar.

4. This nautical imagery is meant to express that their hopes had been dashed. It no doubt reflects the feelings of those who would have stayed, objecting to Coronado's decision to return to Mexico after but two years. See Bolton, *Coronado*, 333.
5. The meaning here is that if God wrought such wonders with small things he would have surely outdone himself with such a vast land.
6. The god Faunus, the Roman Pan.
7. The reference is to the prophet Mohammed, whose revelation of paradise included worldly comforts.

Que no es para gustosos passatiempos,
Contentos ni regalos delicados,
Florestas ni vanquetes muy solenes,
Mas para professar con brabo esfuerzo
Aquel blasón Romano belicoso
Que dize en altas bozes lebantadas:
"Nos, por vivir en paz queremos guerra."
¡O miserables tristes, abatidos
Tristes, que sin valor queréis poneros,
Assi como Faetón ponerse quiso
A gobernar el carro poderoso
Allá en la quarta Esfera lebantado,²⁶
Tomando tanta altura porque fuesse
Su ambiciosa soberbia más sabida
De todos los mortales que notaron
Su mísera desgracia, triste, infame!
Y para no venir en tanta afrenta,
Advierta aquél que quiere someterse
Al bélico furor y professarle
Que, como firme harpón o gallardete²⁷
Que en altíssima cumbre está assentado,
De poderosos vientos combatido,
Que mientras más le afligen y combaten
Más firme muestra el rostro a la braveza
De aquél que más se esfuerza en contrastarle,²⁸
Que assí, firme, esforzado y valeroso
Ha de poner el rostro a los trabajos,
Miserias y fatigas que vinieren.
Y, fuera de perder el alma, entienda
Que no puede aber cosa que no aguarde
Y espere en todo trance el buen guerrero,
Si ya no es que las leyes militares
Otra cosa dispensen y permitan,
Porque esto significan los escudos
Con que, muy alto Rey, queréis honrrarlos,
De fresca y roja sangre matizados,
Con tantas barras, fuegos y leones,
Castillos, lobos, tigres y serpientes,
Con otros muchos fieros animales,
Insignias y divisas que nos muestran
La torpeza de aquéllos que pretenden
Entre tantos disgustos tener gusto.
Y a estos tales mejor les estuviera
Serbir a los que tienen gruessas tiendas
De aquel licor sabroso que adormece
O a los que son más práticos y diestros

Are not done for mere pleasing pastimes,
For mere amusement or for idle pleasure,
For woodland trips or solemn feasts,
But to affirm with valiant toil
That ancient, warlike Roman badge
Which says in no soft voice,
"That we may live in peace we now wish war."
O miserable sad, and downcast ones,
Sad since you wish to win a place, though courageless,
As Phaeton⁸ wished to set himself
To rule the powerful car
There in the Fourth Sphere lofty,
Taking such height so that his soaring pride
Be even better known
Of all the mortals who did see
His miserable misfortune, sad and vile!
And that he may not come to like disgrace
Now let him note who thinks to give himself
To all war's fury and enlist himself:
Firm as a lance or flagstaff high
That on a lofty summit placed
and swept by powerful winds
Yet, while they strike it most and most afflict,
Doth show a firmer face to the fury
Of that which most embattles it;
That even so, firm in effort and in courage,
He must set his face to tasks,
To miseries and fatigues that come,
And short of losing one's soul, let him understand
There's nothing that a good warrior
Must not expect, await, in all events,
Lest the military laws, in truth,
Permit or sanction something else,
For this do signify the shields
With which, O highest King, you honor them,
All many hued with fresh, red blood,
With bars so many, lions, fires,
Castles, tigers, wolves, and serpents,
With many other furious beasts,
The ensigns and devices which do show
To us the foolishness of those who hope,
Amid such displeasures, to find pleasure.
For them 'twere better if they were
A'serving them who keep great stores
Of that sweet liquor which brings sleep
Or those who are more practiced and more skilled

Line numbers: 115, 120, 125, 130, 135, 140, 145, 150, 155

26. Faetón, hijo de Helios, quiso gobernar el carro del sol, pero fracasó. La quarta esfera o cielo es, en Dante, la del sol.

27. Gallardete = banderín rematado en puntas.

28. Contrastarle = combatirle.

8. Phaeton, son of Helios, failed in his attempt to drive his father's chariot, the sun.

En saber sazonar dulzes manjares
Que no serbir con tanto sobresalto,
Peligro, riesgo y costa de la vida
A vuestra Magestad, pues que no puede
Abilitar[29] con otra[30] a quien le falta.
Y si por más valer y ser pretenden
Yr contra la corriente y agua arriba,
Sigan aquellos hechos hazañosos
De aquel grande varón, alto famoso,
Del Imperio Romano gran monarca,
Y sobre cuios hombros descargaban
Negocios de grandíssima importancia,
Que por más lebantar su brabo imperio
Todo lo más del tiempo se ocupaba
En sólo matar moscas, sin cuidado
Del poderoso ceptro que tenía,[31]
Bageza, cierto, de varón indigno
De tal imperio, y digno de soldados
Tales quales aquí se van mostrando.
Mal professaran éstos las vanderas
De aquel muy esforzado Macedonio,[32]
Pues para no dormirse en la milicia
Estaba de continuo tan alerta
Qual nos pintan aquella centinela
En un pie puesta y toda lebantada,
Con cuidado la piedra bien assida.
No de otra suerte siempre le pussieron
A este varón notable vna gran bola,
De fina plata gruessa bien fornida,
Sobre la diestra mano porque fuesse
Parte para que luego despertase
Dando sobre otra güeca que tenía
Debajo de la mano poderosa.[33]
Y si haziendo aquesto es fuerza viertan
Aquestos pobres lágrimas amargas,
Molestados de tantas desventuras,
Viertan aquellas lágrimas famosas
Deste mismo varón a quien abraza
Por vno de los nueve la gran fama,[34]
Cuia grandeza es cierto que lloraba
Porque otros nuevos mundos le dixeron

In knowing how to season victuals sweet,
And not in serving, with such sudden fear
And danger, risk, and cost of life,
Your Majesty, for one cannot
Supply another life when this is lost.
And if to seem worth more, they do attempt
To go against the current and upstream,
Now let them follow the heroic deeds
Of that great monarch of the Roman Empire,[9]
That great, that lofty, famous man
Upon whose shoulders they did place
Affairs of the most high import,
Who, so to higher raise his empire great,
Mostly spent all his time
Merely in killing flies and gave no care
Unto the powerful scepter that he held,
Surely a baseness quite unworthy of a man
Of such great power, but worthy quite
Of soldiers such as these did show themselves.
Poorly would these have followed the banners
Of that most valiant Macedonian,[10]
Who, not to fall asleep on watch
Was always so alert
As they depict that sentinel
Standing on one foot, straight, erect,
A stone, well-held with care.
Not otherwise they always gave
This man so notable a goodly sphere
Of refined silver, stout enough,
In his right hand, to be a means
Of waking him immediately
By falling on a hollow ball he had
Beneath his mighty hand.[11]
Were't necessary this to do
What bitter tears those poor things there would shed,
Greatly afflicted by such misadventures,
Let them shed those famed tears
Of that same man whom fame
Embraces as one of the nine,[12]
Whose greatness wept, 'tis sure,
Because they told him there were yet new worlds

29. Abilitar = habilitar, proveer.

30. Otra vida.

31. Se refiere al emperador romano, Domiciano. Está relatado en Suetonio, *Vida de los doce césares* XII, 3.

32. Se refiere a Alejandro Magno.

33. Lo relata Quinto C. Rufus, *Historia de la vida y reino de Alejandro Magno* I, 2.

34. Los Nueve de la Fama eran: Josué, David y Judas Macabeo; Alejandro, Héctor y César; Arturo, Carlomagno y Godofredo de Boullón.

9. The reference is to the Roman emperor Domician. The matter is narrated in Suetonius, *Lives of the Twelve Caesars* XII, 3.

10. The reference is to Alexander the Great of Macedonia.

11. This practice is related by Quintus C. Rufus, *History of the Life and Reign of Alexander the Great* I, 2.

12. The reference is to Joshua, David, and Judas Maccabee; Alexander, Hector, and Caesar; and King Arthur, Charlemagne, and Godfrey of Bouillon.

Tenía la magestad de Dios criados
Y que era fuerza tiempo le faltase
Para poder mostrar su brabo esfuerzo
En la grande conquista que pensaba
Hazer de todos ellos si la vida
Se dilatara tanto y se alargara
Quanto su brabo pecho se estendía.
Y si algún gentil ombre que me escucha
Hubiere retirado su persona,
Desamparando el puesto que pudiera
Ocupar otro más aventajado
En propagar la sangre derramada
Por aquel soberano Dios que quiso
Que todos los del mundo se salvasen,
Haga muy grande cargo de conciencia
En aber despreciado el santo riesgo
Que pudo derramarse por aquéllos
A quien desamparó sin ver que estaban
A pique de perderse y condenarse.³⁵
Y para confusión de aquestos tristes
Quiero traer, señor, a la memoria
Vn caso digno de que no le cubran
Las poderosas aguas del olvido.
Y es que cierto Virrey de nueva España
Escribió a vuestro gran señor y Padre
A cerca de las rentas Filipinas,
Diziendo que por cierta y buena cuenta,
Sacada con grandíssimo cuidado,
Abía notado, visto y descubierto
Ser muchos más los gastos que el provecho
Que de las Islas resultaba,
Por cuia suficiente y justa causa
Era de parecer se despoblasen.
Y qual vemos aquél a quien lastiman
Con qual que fiera llaga penetrante,
Assí muy mal herido y lastimado
Del consejo que sin pensar le vino,
Al punto respondió sin detenerse
El santo Rey Cathólico, diziendo:
"En lo que me advertís que con cuidado
Abéis hechado cuenta de las rentas
Que Dios quiso serbirse de encargarnos
Y darnos en las Islas de Poniente,
Que sois de parecer que se despueblen
Porque son más los gastos que el provecho,
Digo que si es possible sustentarse
Vna muy pobre hermita lebantada
En toda aquella tierra y sus contornos,

Created by the majesty of God
And time would lack, of need,
For him to show his great essay
In the great conquest that he planned
205 To make of all of them if life
Would wait so long and stretch
As far as his brave heart did reach.
And if a gentleman who hears me now
Had then withdrawn himself,
210 Leaving his post, which better might
By another been occupied, more able
To propagate the blood was shed
By that same sovereign God who wished
That all in the world might be saved,
215 Let him feel a heavy conscience
To have laid aside the holy risk
Which could be run for those
Whom he abandoned, not seeing that they were
At point of being ruined and condemned.¹³
220 For the confusion of these sorry ones,
I wish to bring, lord, to your memory
A thing too worthy to be covered up
By powerful waters of oblivion.
And 'tis that certain Viceroy of New Spain
225 Wrote to your great lord and father
About the income from the Philippines,
Saying for certainty, by skilled account,
Taken with greatest care,
He had found out, seen, and discovered
230 The expense was far more than the revenue
That came from all the Isles;
Wherefore, for this sufficient and just cause,
It seemed to him they must depopulate them.
As we see one who's wounded sore
235 By deep and penetrating wound,
So he was wounded and was hurt
By that advice which came to him unthought of.
Immediately, without delay, the holy
Catholic King replied and said:
240 "Since you advise me that with care
You made accounting of the revenue
That God has been so gracious as to give
And render us from Islands of the West,
And that to you depopulation seems of need
245 Since the expenses are above the revenue,
I say that if 'tis possible to keep
One poor sanctuary upraised
In all that land and its surrounding lands,

---

35. Se refiere a los indios que no habrían de quedar evangelizados.

13. The reference is to the Indians, the goal of the missionary effort.

Mediante la qual venga a presumirse
Que se puede salvar vn alma sola,
Que si para este fin sin otro alguno
Las rentas y tesoros que tenemos
En todos essos Reynos no bastaren,
Que luego me aviséis porque con tiempo
Con las que acá alcanzamos os socorra,
Que en esto quiere Dios que se consuman,
Dispensen, gasten, pierdan y derramen."
¡O gentes que tomáis tan alto buelo,
Quales ormigas tristes, cuyas alas
Tan por su mal sabemos que les nacen,
Frenad el passo y advertid que os notan
Que de la quieta paz queréis saliros
Sin suficientes fuerzas que os sustenten
Las cortas prendas de los flacos brazos,
Que sin discreción vemos que se arrojan
Tras del sangriento Marte belicoso
Para sólo bolberos con las manos
En las cabezas, tristes y llorosos,
Infames, abatidos y afrentados,
Llenos de desonor y de vergüenza!
Dexad, dexad aquesta noble impressa
Para aquéllos, heroicos, que assistiendo
Enmienden vuestras faltas miserables
Y con illustre esfuerzo las fenezcan.
Y buelva cada qual a sus madejas[36]
Y dentro en su rincón passe su vida
Notando el gran tesoro que se ofrece
Por vna alma de aquéllas que dexastes
Pobre, desamparada y sin remedio;
Y ponderad con esto que los vienes
De todo el vniverso que gozamos
No es precio sufficiente ni bastante
Para rescate de una sola gota
De la sangre vertida y derramada
Por el gran Dios que quiso redimirla,
Y que si toda fuera necessaria
Para faborecerla y rescatarla
Sin duda que la vieramos vertida
Qual por todos la vemos derramada,
Con cuio inmenso precio soberano
Podéis sacar el gran valor y estima
De lo que por tal precio se rescata.
Pues siendo esto verdad como dezimos,
Quando no lebantéis en nuevas tierras
Templo ni pobre hermita donde pueda
La magestad de Dios reberenciarse

By which it well may be supposed
250 That just one soul yet can be saved,
And if for this and for no other end
The income and the treasures which we have
In all those Kingdoms still were not enough,
Then you shall let me know, so that in time
255 I may send aid to you from those that we have here,
For 'tis in this God wills they be consumed,
Doled out, spent, used, and lavished."
Ye folk who'd take so high a flight,
Like sorry ants whose wings
260 We know do grow to their own dole,
Restrain your steps and see that you are watched
When you do wish to leave your quiet peace
Without sufficient strength well to maintain
The scanty strength of your weak arms,
265 With which we see you indiscreetly rush
After the warlike, bloody Mars,
Only to turn again, your hands
Upon your sad and weeping heads,
Base, downcast, infamous,
270 Filled with dishonor and with shame!
Leave, leave that noble enterprise
For those heroic ones who, attending,
Will remedy your miserable lacks
And wipe them out with deeds illustrious.
275 And let each one of you back to his skein
And pass his life in his own lurking place,
Noting how great the treasure offered
For one soul of the ones you left
Poor, unprotected, and beyond all help;
280 And think, with this, that all the goods
Of all the world that we enjoy
Is not a price sufficient or enough
For ransom of a single drop
Of that blood shed and spilled
285 By that great God who wished to redeem it,
And that if all were necessary
To help and redeem it,
There is no doubt that we would see it shed
Just as for all we see it spent,
290 From whose immense and sovereign price
You can deduce the esteem and the value great
Of what is ransomed at so great a price.
Well, this that we were saying being true,
Though you did not erect in these new lands
295 A temple nor poor hermitage in which
The Majesty of God may reverenced be

36. Madejas = hilo aspado formado en círculos; por extensión,
tarea femenina.

Y sólo consumáis vuestros trabajos
En baptizar, limpiando de la culpa
A vn sólo parbulito[37] quando parte
De esta penosa vida donde estuvo
Privado y condenado para siempre,
A perpetuo destierro desterrado
De la divina essencia soberana,
Dezid, ¿dónde pondremos el esfuerzo
De vn hecho tan heroico y lebantado?
Y es cosa muy donosa, Rey sublime,
Que para más cubrir su gran vageza
Quieren hazerse grandes mayordomos
De vuestras Reales rentas, porque dizen
Fueron en estas cosas mal gastadas,
Sin mirar que si fueran despenseros
Y ellos las manijaran y trataran,
Que por menos del número de treinta,
Porque[38] aquel triste quiso suspenderse,[39]
A ellos también los viéramos colgados.[40]
Sabe Dios que he notado muchas vezes
Que no ha cien años que el horrible infierno
Tuvo todos los años de tributo
De más de cien mil almas para arriba
Que en sólos sacrificios bomitaba
La gran Ciudad de México perdida.
Y qual del erizado invierno escapan
Todas las mieses, árboles y plantas,
Y en primavera vemos que se visten
De infinidad de flores con que olvidan
El riguroso tiempo ya passado,
Assí, olvidada tanta desventura,
Tanta efusión de sangre derramada
Y tanto sacrificio desdichado,
Podemos dezir cierto en nuestros tiempos
Que está todo lo bueno de la Iglesia
Dentro desta metrópoli famosa
Que fue en tan corto tiempo[41] tan perdida.
Porque no sé que tenga parte el mundo
Donde el culto divino más se estime
Ni más se reverencie ni se acate,
Ni donde sus ministros más se teman,
Honrren, amen, respeten y lebanten.
Y assí parece que permite el Cielo,
En pago de respectos tan gloriosos,
Que pinten y florescan maravillas

300

305

310

315

320

325

330

335

340

And consumed all your works
Baptizing, making free from sin,
One poor wee one who leaves
This painful world in which he was
Greatly deprived, condemned forever
To a perpetual exile thus sentenced
From essence, sovereign, divine,
Say, how shall we measure the effort
Of such heroic, lofty deed?
And 'tis a truly comic thing, O King sublime,
That, so to cover more their baseness great,
They wish to make themselves great managers
Of these your royal revenues, for they say
That they were badly spent in these affairs,
Not seeing that, were they the stewards there
And tried to manage them,
We'd see them also hanged
For less than thirty pieces, sum for which
That sorry creature wished to hang himself.[14]
God knows that I have noted many times
That it is not a hundred years since horrid hell
Took as its tribute every year
The more than hundred thousand souls
That the great City of Mexico, the lost,
Did vomit forth in sacrifice alone.
And just as there escape the winter's frost
The grain and trees and plants,
And in the spring we see them clothe themselves
With countless flowers with which they do forget
The rigorous time now past,
E'en so, forgotten so great misery,
So great effusion of the blood poured out,
So great, unhappy, sacrifice,
We can say truly in our times
That all the goodness of the Church is found
Within that famous capital
That was so short a time ago so lost to God.
For I know not what place the world doth hold
Where divine worship can be more esteemed,
Or is more worshipped or more revered,
Nor where its ministers are feared more,
More honored, loved, respected, held more high.
And thus it seems that Heaven permits
In payment of such glorious respect
That there be shown and flourish marvels great

37. Parbulito = niño.
38. Porque = por las que (monedas).
39. Suspenderse = colgarse, ahorcarse.
40. Se refiere a Judas.
41. Que fue hace tan poco tiempo.

14. The reference is to Judas, the betraying disciple of Jesus.

De Mártires y Confessores santos
Que han sido luz de toda aquesta tierra,
Donde, por la bondad de Dios inmenso,
Hay tanta suma de famosos templos,
Hermitas, monasterios y hospitales,
Colegios y combentos muy poblados,
De las grandes primicias que dexaron
Nuestros primeros Padres que vinieron
A reduzir en bien tan tristes males,
Y todos, a vna mano, de admirables,
Bellos y felicíssimos ingenios
En todas ciencias y artes liberales.
Y lo que más se muestra y se señala
Es la caridad santa, generosa,
Que, como Sol enmedio de su curso,
Assí, con bello resplandor, descubre
Muchos grandes varones y mugeres
Que a manos llenas vierten y derraman
Limosnas tan grandiosas y admirables
Que sólo Reyes pueden competirlas,
Con cuia alteza vemos lebantados
Gran suma de hospitales generosos,
Nobles templos, de bellos edificios,
Gallardos monasterios sumptuosos,
Peregrinos conventos memorables,
Y vna muy gran belleza⁴² de donzellas,
Sin otro grande número de pobres,
Por sus limosnas santas socorridos.⁴³
Y todo aquesto por el alto esfuerzo
De aquel varón famoso que se puso
A descubrir aqueste nuevo mundo,
Cuios illustres hechos hazañosos,
Después de aber passado algunos años,
No han de ser menos grandes y admirables
Que los de aquel gran César y Pompeio,
Artus⁴⁴ y Carlo Magno y otros brabos
A quien el tiempo tiene lebantados
Con su larga memoria prolongada,
Cuia antigualla es cierto que ennoblece
Los illustres sucessos ya passados.
Y si los deste campo no bolvieran
Las espaldas tan presto como vimos,
Fuera possible aberse descubierto
Otro mundo tan grande y poderoso

Of Martyrs and Confessors blest,
Those who have been the light of all this land,
Where, by the immense goodness of God,
There is such sum of temples famed,   345
Of hermitages, monasteries, hospitals,
Of colleges and convents, peopled well,
The great, first fruits that were left
By our first fathers who did come
To turn such sorry evils into good.   350
All these, a band of admirable men,
Were minds both skilled and fortunate
In all the sciences and liberal arts.
And what shows forth and is most pointed out
Is holy, generous charity,   355
Which, like the sun at middle of its course,
Discovers with its beauteous splendor
Many men and women great
Who give and scatter with full hands
Such great and admirable alms   360
That only Kings can vie with them,
By whose nobility we see set up
Great sum of generous hospitals,
Of noble temples, buildings beautiful
And graceful, sumptuous monasteries,   365
And convents rare, memorable,
A great beauty of maids,¹⁵
Not mentioning another number great of poor,
All aided by their holy alms.¹⁶
And all this through the effort high   370
Of that right famous man who set himself
To discovering this new world,
Whose famed adventurous deeds
After some years have passed
Will be no less admirable and great   375
Than those of that great Caesar and Pompey,
Artus and Charles the great and other greats¹⁷
Whom time keeps lifted high
Through their great memory, long preserved,
Whose tradition certainly ennobles   380
Illustrious events now long gone by.
And if those of the camp had not turned round
Their backs so quickly as we saw them do,
'Twere possible then to have found
Another world as great and powerful   385

---

42. Aquí, poética si dificultosamente, Villagrá utiliza el adjetivo descriptivo por cuantitativo.

43. Hay, en todo este elogio de la Ciudad de México, ecos de *Siglo de oro y grandeza mejicana*, capítulos VII y VIII, de Bernardo de Valbuena.

44. Se refiere al legendario rey Arturo.

15. Villagrá uses the descriptive *bellezas* in an unusual quantitative sense.

16. This praise of Mexico City echoes that of Bernardo de Balbuena's *Siglo de Oro y grandeza mejicana*, chapters VII and VIII.

17. The references are to the legendary King Arthur and the historical Charlemagne.

Qual éste que tenemos y gozamos.
Sóla vna terrible falta hallo,
Christianíssimo Rey, en vuestras Indias,
Y es que están muy pobladas y ocupadas
De gente vil, manchada y sospechosa.[45]
Y no siendo en España permitido
Que passen estos tales a estas partes,[46]
No sé qué causa pueda aber bastante
Para que no los hechen de la tierra
Que les es por justicia prohibida;
Pues la oveja roñosa es cosa llana
Que suele inficionar[47] todo vn rebaño.
Quanto más, gran señor, que no sabemos
Lo que puede venir por vuestra España,
Y si abréis menester aquestas tierras
Para faboreceros y ampararos
De alguna miserable desventura
De las que Dios permite que sucedan
Por poderosos Reynos lebantados.
Por cuia justa causa es bien se arranque
Aquesta mala hierba y se trasponga,
Sin que se dexe cosa que no sea
De buen sabor, color, olor y gusto
En jardín que es tan nuevo, tierno y bello,
Principalmente con tan buena ayuda
Qual la del tribunal santo[48] famoso
Que gobiernan aquellos eminentes,
Insignes y doctíssimos varones,
Don Alonso, gran gloria, lustre y triunfo
De la muy noble casa de Peralta,
Y Gutierre Bernardo, que lebanta
La más antigua, de Quirós nombrada,
Y aquel prudente Martos, que a Bohorques
Con singular valor subió de punto,
Todos vigilantíssimos guerreros
Contra la peste y cáncer contagioso
Que, por algunos miembros de la Iglesia,
Los del vil campo herético de Raman,[49]
En cuia siembra vemos que descubren
Pestilenciales nidos y veneros
De perbersos errores contagiosos,
Como más largamente lo refiere
Aquel Ribera illustre que compuso

As this we have here and enjoy.
I find one fault, and that one terrible,
O King most Christian, in this your Indies,
And it is that they are too much filled and settled

390 By a people base, corrupted, untrustworthy.
And since it's not allowed in Spain
That such do come into these parts,[18]
I know not what cause could suffice
To keep us from ejecting them

395 From out this land that justice would deny them,
Since it is evident the scabby sheep
Infecteth all the flock,
So much the more, great lord, that as we know not
What may befall your Spain

400 Or if you may require these lands
As refuge and to save yourself
From many a miserable misfortune
That God permit to happen can
To powerful and haughty crowns.

405 'Tis well, for this just cause, to root
Out this bad weed and quite remove it,
And leave no thing which shall not be
Of goodly savor, color, odor, taste,
In such new garden, tender, beautiful,

410 And do it chiefly with such goodly aid
As of that holy, famous tribunal[19]
That those most eminent and famed
And learned men do rule,
That Don Alonso, glory great and light and triumph

415 Of that most noble house of Peralta,
And Gutierre Bernardo, who lifts
The even older house of Quirós,
And that same prudent Martos who
The house of Bohorques greatly raised,

420 All warriors most watchful
'Gainst cancer and contagious plague
That, through some members of the Church,
Those of the vile heretic camp propagate,
In whose vile seed we see discovered

425 Most pestilential nests and source
Of errors contagious and perverse,
As more at length are told
By that famous Ribera[20] who composed

45. Se refiere a los conversos, recientemente convertidos del judaismo, y, posiblemente, también, a los recientemente convertidos del islam.
46. Se refiere a la legislación prohibiendo la inmigración de los antedichos al Nuevo Mundo.
47. Inficionar = infectar.
48. Tribunal de la Santa Inquisición.
49. Patente errata del original por "derraman."

18. Villagrá refers to the legislation prohibiting the emigration to the New World of newly converted Jews and Muslims, always suspect of retaining their old religion.
19. The reference is to the Tribunal of the Holy Inquisition.
20. The reference is to Juan de Ribera, 1532–1611, Archbishop of Valencia.

De vuestro santo Padre las obsequias,[50]
En cuia docta y funeral historia
Me acuerdo que refiere vn caso estraño
De vn Iosepho, lumbroso[51] relaxado,[52]
Que dixo en altas vozes que le oyeron,
Con vna no pensada desbergüenza:
"¡Mal aya el tribunal del santo Oficio!,"
Que si él[53] no vbiera estado de por medio
Por estos sólos dedos yo contara
Los Christianos de toda aquesta tierra.
Cuia gran desbergüenza, temeraria,
Por sólo aberse dicho en nueva tierra
Y que es de nuestra Fe tan nueva planta,
Parece que insta, fuerza y os combida
A que pongáis el hombro de manera
Que todas vuestras Indias se despojen
Desta bestial canalla y que se pueblen
De sólos Hijosdalgo y Caballeros
Y de Christianos Viejos muy ranciosos,[54]
Que con éstos y no con otra gente
Podéis bien descubrir el vniverso
Y conquistarlo todo y reduzirlo
Al suabe jugo[55] de la Iglesia santa.
Y esto, sin la tormenta de gemidos,
Ansias, sollozos y lamentos tristes
Que aquestos miserables derramaron.[56]
Y porque derrotado del camino
Estoi muy largo trecho remontado,
Bolviendo por el rumbo que llebaba,
Dándoos razón de las demás noticias
Y de aquellos gallardos pretensores
Y altos descubridores desta tierra,
Destrozado[57] de gente tan cansada,[58]
Tan desdichada, vil y poco firme,
Quiero al siguiente canto remitirme.

Eulogies for your sainted Father,
Within whose learned funeral history   430
I do recall he tells a wondrous case
Of one hardened heretic,[21] Joseph,
Who said aloud for all to hear,
With shamelessness quite unconsidered:
"Evil should fall on the tribunal of the Holy Office!"   435
For had it not been in our midst,
I'd count upon these fingers all
The Christians throughout all these lands.
Whose great and daring shamelessness,
Only for having been spoken in new lands   440
And where our faith is plant so new,
It seems it urges and invites you
To lend your shoulder in such wise
That all your Indies be quite freed
Of that evil crew, and populated   445
Only by knights and noblemen
And very strong old Christians,
For with them, not with other folk,
You well can all the universe discover
And conquer and reduce it all   450
To gentle yoke of Holy Church.
And that, without the torment of the groans,
The sighs and sobs and laments
Those miserable creatures loosed.
And since, way off course, from the road   455
I am removed a goodly way,
Returning to the route I started on,
Giving you news of other things
And of those brave pretenders
And haughty discoverers of this land,   460
Much depressed by such weary folk,[22]
So vile, unfortunate and so infirm,
I would break off until the canto following.

---

50. Se refiere a Juan de Ribera, 1532–1611, después arzobispo de Valencia.

51. Lumbroso = alumbrado, miembro de la secta herética española del siglo XVI.

52. Relajado = vicioso.

53. Se refiere al Tribunal de la Inquisición.

54. Se refiere a cristianos desde muchas generaciones ("ranciosos" = rancios), a diferencia de judios y musulmanes mucho más recientemente convertidos.

55. Parece errata del original por "iugo," yugo.

56. Se vuelve a referir a los desertores de la expedición de Coronado.

57. Destrozado = aniquilado moralmente.

58. Cansada = de antecedentes hebraicos.

21. In Villagrá's text, *lumbroso* refers to a specific Spanish heretical sect of the sixteenth century.

22. The term *cansado* "tired" (the old law) was used at the time for those with Hebraic antecedents.

CANTO QVINTO

*DE OTRAS NOTICIAS QVE VBO DE LA NUEVA
MÉXICO y de otros que assí mismo pretendieron la jornada.*

QVANDO con pertinacia el hombre sigue
A sólo su apetito y dél se ceba,[1]

Cosa difícil es que tal dolencia
Pueda ser de ninguno socorrida.
Abiendo, pues, señor, los coronados
Visto en aquesta tierra que dezimos
Vnos bellos y grandes alcatrazes[2]
De fina plata y oro, lebantados
En las agudas proas y altas popas
De ciertas gruessas naves que toparon
A caso y sin pensar, por la marina,[3]
Sin procurar saber qué vasos[4] fuessen,
De dónde y para adónde navegaban,
De su mismo apetito ya vencidos,
Según que tengo dicho, luego al punto
Bolvieron todos juntos, sin empacho
De aquellos caballeros esforzados
Que vageza tan grande abominaron.
Viendo, pues, tan gran daño sin remedio
El santo Provincial de san Francisco,[5]
Qual suelen los que a Dios se sacrifican,
Que todo lo posponen y lo dexan,
Dexándolos a todos quiso solo
Quedarse a merecer en aquel puesto
La palma[6] illustre y alta del martirio,
Que allí los bravos bárbaros le dieron.
Viendo, pues, don Francisco de Peralta
En militar oficio tanta mengua
Y que vuestro Virrey sintió en el alma,
Con toda nueva España, tal vageza,
Ocupado de empacho y corrimiento
La buelta para Italia tomó luego,

1. Se ceba = se alimenta, se engorda.
2. Alcatraces = pelícanos.
3. No hay referencia de que unos desertores de la expedición de Coronado hubiesen encontrado barcos como los aquí descritos. Villagrá probablemente confunde, o inserta poéticamente, las referencias que hizo el indio llamado el turco a Coronado acerca de Quivira, un eco, lo más probable, de antiguas descripciones de Tenochtitlán. Véase, Bolton, *Coronado*, 198, 231.
4. Vasos = naves, ya que vaso representa la capacidad de una nave, según Covarrubias.
5. Probable referencia a Fray Juan de Padilla, que, mucho más tarde en la relación de los hechos de Coronado, volvió a Quivira, donde fue martirizado. Véase Bolton, *Coronado*, 339–41.
6. Palma = victoria; se utiliza tradicionalmente para el martirio.

CANTO V

*Of what other news there was of New Mexico and of others
who attempted the journey.*

WHEN man with pertinacity follows
His appetite alone and on't is
firmly bent,
'Tis difficult for such disease
To be by anyone relieved.
5 So, lord, these men of Coronado having seen
Within that land of which we speak
Some large and beauteous pelicans
Of gold and silver fine set up
On the sharp prows and lofty sterns
10 Of certain mighty ships they saw by chance,[1]
Nor seeking them, upon the shore,
Without discovering what ships they were
Or whence or where they sailed,
Quite conquered, then, by their own appetites,
15 As I have told already, and at once
They all turned back and took no shame
From those brave cavaliers
Who did detest such baseness vile.
Seeing a harm so great and without remedy,
20 The holy Provincial of Good Saint Francis,
Like those who sacrifice themselves to God
Put all behind them, brave it all;
He, leaving all behind, did wish
There to remain and win, there at his post,
25 The high and famous palm of martyrdom,
Which there the rude barbarians did give.[2]
Now, Don Francisco de Peralta, having seen
Such a disgrace in military things,
And that your Viceroy and all New Spain
30 felt to their very souls such base conduct,
All overwhelmed with shame and all abashed
Straightway for Italy set out,

1. There is no historical record of deserters from Coronado's expedition encountering such ships. Villagrá possibly confuses, or poetically inserts, the things told Coronado about mythical Quivira by the Indian called the Turk, which themselves appear to be echoes of secondhand descriptions of Tenochtitlán. See Bolton, *Coronado*, 198, 231.
2. A probable reference to Fray Juan de Padilla, who much later during the Coronado expedition returned to Quivira and was martyred. See Bolton, *Coronado*, 339–41.

Y siguiendo la corte dentro en Roma
Vio por vista de ojos que tenía
El Duque de Saxonia retratada
Aquesta nueva tierra en sus tapizes
Y en muchos reposteros[7] muy curiosos.
Y estando embebecido assí mirando
La peregrina tierra tan al vivo,
Ayudado de cierto caballero
Por vista de ojos vio también que el Duque
Tenía vna gran piel bella, disforme,
De aquellas vacas sueltas que se crian
En los llanos de Cíbola tendidos;
De donde resultó que supo cierto
Que no de sóla gente Castellana
Ha sido aquesta tierra pretendida,
Mas también de remotos estrangeros.[8]
Demás de todo aquesto, es ya notorio
Que saliendo de Francia vna gran nave
Fue con tormenta brava derrotada
A dar en estas tierras peregrinas,
Y andando alguna gente en el esquife
Por sólo ver la tierra y demarcarla
Vieron vna ensenada de dos puntas
Y en cada vna dellas lebantada
Vna grande Ciudad de gruessos muros,
De donde les salieron al encuentro
Vn número grandioso de vecinos
En prolongados varcos o canoas,
Las popas y las proas aforradas,[9]
Al parecer, en planchas de oro bajo.
Y siendo dellos presos los llevaron
Al palacio de vn Rey de noble estado
Cuia frente ceñía y rodeaba
De aquel mismo metal vna corona
Con singular destreza bien sacada.
Este gran Rey mandó que con cuidado
A todos los llevasen y les diesen
Su casa de aposento y regalasen.
Y cumpliendo el mandato con presteza
Fueron de frutas, carnes y pescado,
Con muy grandes caricias, bien serbidos.
Estando, pues, assí todos contentos,
Como la carne en todos tiempos muestra
Su mísera flaqueza y desbentura,
Parece que vno dellos, olvidado

And entering the court of Rome
He saw with his own eyes
35 The Duke of Saxony had pictured
On his tapestries that same new land,
And pictured, too, on many coats of arms most curious.
And standing there amazed and gazing on
The wondrous land so strikingly portrayed,
40 Being aided thereto by a certain gentleman,
He also saw with his own eyes the Duke did have
A beautiful, great hide of those wild,
Deformed cows that breed
Upon the wide plains of Cibola;
45 Whence it resulted that he surely knew
That land had been attempted
Not alone by our Castilian folk,
But also by foreigners remote.[3]
Beside all this, it is well known
50 That a great ship from France
Was sent astray by tempest rude
To come upon these wondrous lands,
And some folk, landing in a boat
Merely to see the land and survey it,
55 Did see an inlet with two capes
And raised upon each one of these
A city great with mighty walls,
From which, to meet them, there came out
A mighty crowd of dwellers there
60 In long, slim vessels or canoes,
The prows and sterns all sheathed,
Or so it seemed, with sheets of low-grade gold.
And, being by them made prisoners, they took them
Into the palace of a King of noble state,
65 Whose brow a crown of that same metal ringed
And bound, well-made, with special skill.
This great King ordered that these men
Be treated with all care and shown
To lodgings that he gave them.
70 And, these orders being with speed fulfilled,
They were well served with fruits and meats
And fish, and all with signs of friendship.
Thus, being all content,
As human flesh at all times shows
75 Its terrible weakness and mischance,
It seems that one of them, oblivious
Of the good conduct that he owed

---

7. reposteros = paños con emblemas heráldicos.
8. Curiosamente, un deudo o pariente del tal duque, nombrado en el canto III del *Arauco domado* de Pedro de Oña, anduvo, efectivamente, por tierras del Nuevo Mundo.
9. Aforradas = cubiertas.

3. Curiously enough, a relative of the said duke, named in the third canto of Pedro de Oña's *Arauco domado*, did visit the New World.

Del buen comedimiento que debía
Al beneficio noble recebido,
Llegose a pellizcar con mal respecto
A vna hermosa bárbara que estaba
Mirándolos a todos descuidada.
De aquesto el Rey tomó tan grande enfado
Que si la misma bárbara ofendida
Por ellos con gran fuerza no intercede,
Murieran sin remedio por el caso.
Y assí mandó que luego los hechasen
De toda aquella tierra y que les diesen
Su mismo esquife bien abastecido.
Y assí salieron éstos desterrados,
Y cobrando la nave dieron buelta
A los Reynos de Francia, y desta historia
Tenéis, excelso Rey incomparable,
Información muy cierta y verdadera
En vuestro Real Consejo de las Indias.[10]
Con estas relaciones y otras muchas
(Que éstas son las que suben y lebantan
Los nobles corazones de mortales),
Es cierto que en el año que contamos,
Mil y quinientos sobre ochenta y vno,
Por orden del gran Conde de Coruña,[11]
Fray Agustín, fray Iuan y fray Francisco,
Vnos devotos Padres Religiosos
De aquel que representa al mismo Christo,[12]
En pies, costado y manos lastimadas,
Con valeroso esfuerzo se metieron
Por todas estas tierras, y con ellos
Aquel Francisco Sánchez Chamuscado,[13]
Con quien entró Felipe de Escalante,
Pedro Sánchez de Chaves y Gallegos,
Herrera y Fuensalida, con Barrado,
También entró Iuan Sánchez, por ser todos
Valientes y boníssimos guerreros.
Estos corrieron parte desta tierra,
Y dejándose allá los Religiosos
Salieron todos juntos y contentos

The noble kindness there received,
Did pinch, in evil way,
A beautiful barbarian who was
Observing them all thoughtlessly.
At that the King so greatly was enraged
That, had not the offended girl
Most strongly pleaded for them all,
They would have died then, without hope.
And so he ordered they should be expelled
From all that land and that they be given
Their own ship, very well provisioned.
And so, exiled, they left.
And having gained the ship, returned
Unto the realms of France; and of the tale
You have, incomparable, highest King,
Most true and certain information
Within your Royal Council of the Indies.[4]
Now, with these tales and many more
(For these are such as do excite
And spur the noble hearts of men)
'Tis certain in this year of which we write,
One thousand five hundred and eighty-one,
By order of the great Count of Coruña,[5]
Fray Agustín, Fray Juan, and Fray Francisco,
All most devout and holy fathers
Of him who represents Christ's self
In wounded feet and hands and side,[6]
With valiant effort did set out
For all these lands, and with these came
Francisco Sánchez Chamuscado,[7]
With whom there went Felipe de Escalante,
Pedro Sánchez de Cháves and Gallegos,
Herrera, Fuensalida, and Barrado.
And with them went Juan Sánchez, being all
Brave men, most excellent warriors.
These did explore part of this land
And, leaving there the three friars,
They, all together, left content
At having seen, discovered, wandered over it.

---

10. No existe, que sepamos, comprobación documental de lo que aquí afirma Villagrá. Pudiera ser eco de los muchos escritos y narraciones de aquella época acerca de naufragios y viajes de hallazgos misteriosos.

11. El Conde de Coruña fue Virrey de Nueva España entre 1581 y 1582, muriendo en ese año.

12. Se refiere a San Francisco de Asis y, por lo tanto, a los franciscanos.

13. La expedición de Francisco Sánchez Chamuscado, con los tres frailes indicados anteriormente, representa el primer intento misional en tierras de Nuevo México. Produjo, asimismo, los primeros mártires a manos de los indios Pueblo. Véase H. E. Bolton, *Spanish Exploration in the Southwest* (New York: Charles Scribner's Sons, 1916), 150–51.

4. We have been able to find no historical record of this trip from France to the New World.

5. The Conde de Coruña was viceroy of New Spain between 1581 and 1582, the date of his death.

6. The reference is to Saint Francis of Assisi.

7. The Chamuscado (Francisco Sánchez Chamuscado) expedition, with the three friars mentioned earlier, was the first prepared attempt at missionary work among the Indians of New Mexico. It produced the first martyrs at the hands of the Pueblo Indians. See H. E. Bolton, *Spanish Exploration in the Southwest, 1542–1706* (New York: Charles Scribner's Sons, 1916), 150–51.

De aberla andado, visto y descubierto.
Y assí, luego, por orden de Ontiberos,[14]
Que vuestra autoridad, señor, tenía,
Entró Antón de Espejo,[15] por el año
De los ochenta y dos, dexando en vanda
A los mil y quinientos que contamos.
Y no vbo bien llegado quando supo
Que, con un gran martirio que les dieron,
A los venditos Padres que quedaron
Aquestos mismos bárbaros perdidos
Las vidas todos juntos les quitaron.
Y después de aber visto aquella tierra
Salió también diziendo maravillas,
Loándola de muchas poblaciones
Y minas caudalosas de metales
Y gente buena toda y que tenía
Bezotes,[16] brazeletes y oregeras
De aquel rubio metal, dulze, goloso,
Tras que todos andamos desbalidos.
De aquesto todo luego se hizieron
Grandes informaciones que llevaron
A vuestra insigne Corte lebantada,
Por las quales constaba aberle dado
Casi quarenta mil mantas bien hechas
A este Capitán noble esforzado
Los Indios naturales de presente.
De más de todo aquesto, bien sabemos
De aquel fray Diego Márquez,[17] perseguido
De gente luterana en mar y tierra,
Que por la Reyna Inglesa se hizieron
Sobre esta nueva tierra que tratamos
Muy grandes diligencias y pesquisas,
Por cuia causa dentro de su Corte,
Estando este varón allí cautibo
Por ser de Iesu Christo gran soldado,
Mandaron que jurase y declarase,
Pues que era natural de nueva España,
Qué tierra fuesse aquesta y qué sentía
De las cosas que allí le preguntaron.

And soon, by order of Ontiberos,[8]
Who, lord, had your authority,
Antón de Espejo[9] entered, in the year
120 Of eighty-two, included with
The fifteen hundred we did count.
And hardly had he come when he did learn
How, with great torture being given
Unto the blessed fathers who remained,
125 Those same barbarians lost
Had taken all their lives.
And, after having seen that land,
He did return telling of marvels,
Praising it for many towns
130 And mines of precious ores
And all good people who did have
Lip rings and bracelets and earrings
Of that gold metal, toothsome sweet,
For which we all go wandering destitute.
135 Then they did make of all these things
Reports right great, which same were borne
Unto your famous, most high Court,
From which 'tis evident that there were given
Some forty thousand well-made robes
140 Unto this noble, stalwart Captain by
The Indians, natives of this place.
And more than all, we well know this
From that Friar Diego Márquez,[10] persecuted
By Lutheran folk by land and sea,
145 That by the queen of England were made
For this new land we speak about
Researches and investigations great,
Because of which within her court
This man being captive there
150 Through being a soldier great of Jesus Christ;
They ordered he should take oath and declare
Since he was native of New Spain,
What land that was and what he thought
On things there which they questioned him about.
155 And when he had replied to all

14. Este Ontiberos, Juan, capitán y alcalde mayor de Cuatro Ciénagas es difícil que tuviera la autoridad real que indica Villagrá. Puede consultarse G. P. Hammond y A. Rey, *Rediscovery of New Mexico* (Albuquerque: University of New Mexico Press, 1966), 18.

15. La expedición de Espejo, organizada para confirmar los rumores del martirio de los antedichos frailes, se recuerda por sus descubrimientos mineros. Hallaron algunas minas de cobre, como indicará Villagrá más adelante. Véase Diego Pérez de Luxán, *Expedition into New Mexico made by Antonio de Espejo, 1582–83*. Trad. por G. P. Hammond y A. Rey (Los Angeles: The Quivira Society, 1929).

16. Bezotes = adornos de labio de los indios americanos.

17. Este mismo Fray Diego Márquez reaparecerá en la narración de Villagrá; pero no hemos hallado documentación acerca de su cautiverio en Inglaterra.

8. This Ontiberos, mayor of the town of Cuatro Ciénagas, would not appear to have had such authority. See G. P. Hammond and A. Rey, *Rediscovery of New Mexico* (Albuquerque: Univ. of New Mexico Press, 1966), 18. This more modern text covers the same period dealt with in Bolton's book, and does so more extensively.

9. The Espejo expedition, sent to investigate rumors of the martyrdom of the previously mentioned friars, is mainly remembered for its mineral assaying efforts. Some copper mines were located, as Villagrá will later indicate. See Diego Pérez de Luxán, *Expedition into New Mexico made by Antonio de Espejo, 1582–83*, trans. G. P. Hammond and A. Rey (Los Angeles: The Quivira Society, 1929).

10. This same Fray Diego Márquez will reappear in Villagrá's narrative, but we have found no historical documentation relative to his English captivity.

Y luego que vbo en todo respondido
Y fue de cautiberio libertado,
Acudiendo a el oficio que debía,
Porque de luteranos nunca fuesse
Aquesta noble tierra descubierta,
Dando larga razón de todo aquesto
A vuestro insigne Padre, luego al punto
Mandó que la jornada se assentase.
Esta, sin detenerse, emprendió luego
Iuan Bautista de Lomas,[18] hombre rico,
Antiguo en esta tierra acreditado.
Este assentó su causa, y no vbo efecto,
Por el año de ochenta y nueve al justo.[19]
Y por el de noventa entró Castaño,[20]
Por ser allá teniente más antiguo
Del Reyno de León, a quien siguieron
Muchos nobles soldados valerosos,
Cuio Maese de campo[21] se llamaba
Christobal de Heredia, bien probado
En cosas de la guerra y de buen tino
Para correr muy grandes despoblados.
A los quales mandó el Virrey prendiese
El Capitán Morlete, y sin tardarse,
Socorrido de mucha soldadesca
Braba, dispuesta y bien exercitada,
A todos los prendió y bolvió del puesto.
Después de todo aquesto que he contado,
Siguiendo el Capitán Leiva Bonilla,[22]
Por orden de don Diego de Velasco,
Gobernador del Reyno de Vizcaia,
Los Indios salteadores rebelados,
Precipitado de soberbia altiva,
Determinó de entrarse en esta tierra
Con todos los soldados que tenía,
No obstante que don Pedro de Cazorla,
Vn noble Capitán, salió a intimarle,
De parte de don Diego, vn mandamiento

And from captivity was freed,
Complying with his natural duty,
That never be that noble land
By Lutherans discovered,
160 Giving long statements of all this
Unto your famous Father, he at once
Did order an expedition be sent.
This, without hesitating, instantly commenced
Juan Bautista de Lomas,[11] a rich man,
165 Well-known of old within this land.
He made his effort and without effect
Exactly in the year of eighty-nine.
And in the year ninety came Castaño,[12]
Being there the ranking lieutenant
170 Of the Kingdom of León, who was followed
By many noble soldiers valorous,
Whose Master-of-the-Camp[13] was named
Cristóbal de Heredia, one well-proved
In things of war and of great skill
175 In crossing desert lands.
These the Viceroy ordered taken by
Captain Morlete, and without delay,
Aided by good supply of soldiery,
Brave, well-disposed, well-disciplined,
180 He took them all and came back from that place.
After all this I have related,
Following, Captain Leyba Bonilla,[14]
By order of Don Diego de Velasco,[15]
Governor of the Kingdom of Vizcaya,
185 The rebel Indian revolutionists,
Tempted by his unreasoning pride
Determined he would go into that land
With all the soldiers that he had;
This notwithstanding that Don Pedro de Cazorla,
190 A noble Captain, came out to deliver him
An order from Don Diego saying that
On pain of treason he was not to dare

18. Juan Bautista de Lomas y Colmenares, cuya expedición, al no ser aprobada por el rey, nunca tuvo lugar. Véase Bolton, *Spanish Exploration,* 200.

19. Al justo = justamente.

20. Gaspar Castaño de Sosa, teniente gobernador de Nuevo León, entró sin permiso en Nuevo México. Fue por ello detenido por el capitán Morlete, mencionado unos versos más abajo. Véase Bolton, *Spanish Exploration,* 200.

21. El maese de campo era oficial con mando de ejércitos.

22. Francisco Leyva de Bonilla, junto con Antonio Gutiérrez de Humaña, entraron sin autorización en Nuevo México. Juan de Oñate, como indicará el poema, quedó encargado de apresarlos. Véase Bolton, *Spanish Exploration,* 200. Lo que le sucedió a esta expedición queda en parte narrado en el poema de Villagrá.

11. Juan Bautista de Lomas y Colmenares, whose expedition, not approved by the king, never took place. See Bolton, *Spanish Exploration,* 200.

12. Gaspar Castaño de Sosa, lieutenant governor of Nuevo León, moved without permission into New Mexico. He was arrested by Captain Juan Morlete, mentioned below, who was sent by the viceroy to that end. See Bolton, *Spanish Exploration,* 200.

13. Curtis here translates literally, but his later rendition of the term *army master* comes closer to what the title meant.

14. Francisco Leyva de Bonilla, together with Antonio Gutiérrez de Humaña, led an unauthorized expedition into New Mexico. Juan de Oñate was charged with taking them and returning them to New Spain. See Bolton, *Spanish Exploration,* 200. References to what befell this group are contained in Villagrá's poem.

15. Luis de Velasco, the viceroy who granted Oñate's original patent to go into New Mexico.

Que pena de traidor no se atrebiese
A entrar la tierra adentro. Y sin embargo,
Perdiendo la vergüenza y el respecto
A vuestra Real persona, dio en entrarse.
Y como la traición tanto es más grave
Quanto es la calidad del ofendido,
Como rayos del sol que se dividen
De la tiniebla triste, amodorrida,
Assí se dividieron y apartaron
Del Capitán Bonilla Juan de Salas,
Iuan Pérez y Cabrera y Simón Pasqua
Y Diego de Esquibel y también Soto,
Diziendo a vozes altas con enojo,
Las lanzas empuñando y las adargas,
Que más querían morir como leales
Que cobrar como viles alevosos
Aquel infame nombre de traidores
Con que todos entraban ya manchados,
Y bolviendo las riendas los dexaron.
Y ellos, como milanos que a la parva
De míseros polluelos se abalanzan,
Assí, desatinados y perdidos,
Pensando que los bárbaros cubiertos
Estaban de oro fino y perlas gruessas,
Tomaron, sin respecto ni vergüenza,
Para la nueva México el camino.
Y apenas el Virrey[23] la nueva supo
Quando sin detenerse ni tardarse
Aquesta entrada quiso la hiziesse
Aquel gran Capitán, noble, afamado,
Y que oy gobierna el Reyno de Galicia,
Francisco de Vrdinola,[24] a quien se debe
La paz vniversal y gran sossiego
Que aquesta nueva España toda alcanza
De aquellos bravos bárbaros gallardos
Que por tan largos años sustentaron
Contra vuestro valor y brazo fuerte
Las poderosas armas no vencidas,
Hasta que ya cansados y afligidos,
Corridos, destrozados y oprimidos
Deste varón prudente, se rindieron
Y a su pesar las treguas assentaron.
Pues como muchas gentes entendiessen
Que a tan bravo soldado se le daba
Aquesta grande impressa, alborotados
De gozo y alegría no cabían,

To go into the land. Nevertheless,
Losing all shame and all respect
195 For this, your Royal Person, he went on.
And, just as treason is more great
According to the rank of the offended,
As the rays of the sun which are divided
From the sad sleepy shadows,
200 E'en so there were divided, set aside
From Captain Bonilla, Juan de Salas,
Juan Pérez and Cabrera, and Simón Pascua,
And Diego de Esquibel, also Soto,
Saying aloud and angrily,
205 And gripping hard their lances and their shields,
That they would rather die as loyal men
Than gain, as vile and treacherous ones,
That name of traitor, infamous,
By which they all were being stained,
210 And reining round, they left him.
And they, like birds of prey who swoop
Upon the humble young of barnyard fowl,
Thus, wild and lost,
Thinking the barbarians were covered
215 With finest gold and monstrous pearls,
Took, shameless and respecting none,
The road into New Mexico.
And hardly did the Viceroy know the news
Before, not waiting and without delay,
220 He willed the entry should be made at once
By that great, famous, noble captain who
Now rules the Kingdom of Galicia,
Francisco de Urdinola,[16] whom we owe
The universal peace and great tranquility
225 That all New Spain has won
From those brave, gallant barbarians
Who for so many years maintained
Against your brave and valorous arm
Their powerful, unconquered arms,
230 Until, now tired and downcast,
Pursued, destroyed, and all oppressed
By this prudent man, they surrendered
And much against their wishes made a truce.
Now, since a many people understood
235 That to so brave a soldier there was given
This enterprise so great, they, all excited,
Could not contain themselves for joy and happiness,
Content that so illustrious a thing

---

23. Se refiere a don Luis de Velasco, el virrey que primero expidió
patente a Juan de Oñate.
24. Francisco de Urdinola, como indica Villagrá, nunca aprovechó
el permiso dado por el virrey. Véase Bolton, *Spanish Exploration*, 200.

16. Francisco de Urdinola, who, as Villagrá indicates, never
implemented the permission granted him by Viceroy Velasco. See
Bolton, *Spanish Exploration*, 200.

Contentos de que cosa tan illustre
A sola su persona se encargase.
Y como la invidia miserable
Es mortífero cáncer que en el alma
Arraiga su dolencia y la consume,
Aquesta sóla bestia fue bastante
Para desbaratar y echar por tierra
Cosa tan importante y desseada
De toda nueva España y sus contornos.
¡O beneno mortal, o invidia triste,
Gota coral,²⁵ furioso, derramado
Por lo íntimo del alma desdichada
De aquél que semejante mal padece!
Dios nos libre, señor, de su beneno
Y por su passión santa no permita
Que semejante hidra ponzoñosa
A ninguno persiga, qual veremos
Por toda aquesta historia que escrebimos.
Mas es caso impossible que ninguno
Pueda della evadirse y escaparse,
Que esto tienen los hombres valerosos
Que es fuerza que los ladre y les persiga,
Muerda y los lastime con gran rabia
Aquesta brava perra venenosa.
Bien fuera menester vn gran volumen
Para dezir las cosas que sufrieron
Por no más que serbiros y agradaros
Todos estos varones que hemos dicho;
Mas porque me es ya fuerza que dé salto,
Venga al punto y persona de aquel bravo
Que sin pensar fue electo y escogido
Para poner encima de sus hombros
Cosa de tanto peso y tanta estima,
Con vuestra Real licencia tomo esfuerzo
Para cortar la pluma disgustosa²⁶
Y en cosas de importancia trabajosa.

25. Gota coral = epilepsia.
26. Disgustosa = enfadosa.

240 Should be entrusted to this man alone.
And just as miserable envy is
An eating cancer which within the soul
Roots deep its pain and quite consumes it all,
So this one beast was quite enough
245 To undo all and bring to earth
A matter so important, so desired
By all New Spain and its environs.
O mortal poison, miserable envy,
Epilepsy, furiously spread
Within the inmost of the unhappy soul
250 Of him who suffers such disease!
Free us, O God, our Lord, from such a poison,
And by Thy Holy Passion yet forbid
That such a poisonous hydra
Should attack any, as we see
255 In all this history that we write.
But 'tis a thing impossible that anyone
Should quite escape it and avoid,
And valorous men share this affliction
That necessary 'tis it bark at them, pursue
260 And bite and wound them with great rage,
That rude and venomous dog.
'Twould truly need a volume huge
To tell the things suffered by them
And for no more than serving, pleasing you,
265 All these great men that we have spoken of;
But since 'tis necessary for me at a leap
To come down to the point, the person of that good man
Who unsuspecting, yet was chosen and elect
That on his shoulders might be placed
270 A matter of such weight and such esteem,
I, with your Royal license, now shall try
To trim this my unpleasing pen,
So laborious for things of importance.

CANTO SEXTO

COMO SE ELIGIO PARA ESTA JORNADA A LA
PERSONA de don Iuan de Oñate y del fabor que para ello dio
don Luys de Velasco, y de los estorbos que después tuvo para
impedir sus buenos pensamientos, los quales tuvieron después
consuelo por ser faborecidos del Conde de Monte Rey, Virrey
de nueva España.

LLEGADO abemos, gran señor, al punto
Y engolfados en alta mar estamos.
La tierra se ha perdido y sólo resta
El buen gobierno y cuenta de la nave.
Y porque nada quede en el viaje
Que no se mida bien, ajuste y pese,
Poned en lo más alto bien tendida
La cuidadosa vista atenta, y pare
En aquella pureza y gran grandeza
De la divina essencia soberana.
Y allí echaréis de ver patentemente
Las sendas descubiertas y caminos
Por donde su deidad alta, encumbrada,
Nos haze manifiestas y visibles
Las poderosas obras de sus manos.
Y más, quando su grande alteza quiere
Que alguna dellas suba y se lebante
Con qué facilidad allí notamos
Que los medios que pone simbolizan[1]
Con los mismos principios y los fines
Que quiere que sus santas obras tengan.
De aquesto, gran señor, bien claro exemplo
Tenemos entre manos, porque abiendo
Su grande Magestad por tantos siglos
Tenido aquestas tierras tan ocultas
Que a ninguno ha querido permitirle
Que sus secretos senos le descubra,
Abiéndose de abrir, notad el cómo,
Y quiénes son aquellos valerosos
Por cuyos medios viene a desatarse
Aqueste ñudo ciego que tenemos.
Y estando bien atento y con cuidado,
Aquí echaréis de ver, con evidencia
Que fuerza,[2] de[3] los Reyes ya passados

---

1. Simbolizan = concuerdan, de símbolo en su acepción de contraseña concordante (Covarrubias).
2. Fuerza = convence.
3. De la estirpe de.

CANTO VI

How there was chosen for this journey the person of Don Juan
de Oñate, and of how Don Luis de Velasco favored him in it,
and of the hindrances there were to impede his good intentions,
which later were offset when favored by the count of Monte Rey,
Viceroy of New Spain.

NOW, O great lord, we have come to the
point
And are alone upon the mighty sea.
The land is lost to sight and there remains
Only good management and ruling of the
ship.
5   So in the voyage there be nothing left
That is not measured well, adjusted, weighed,
Do thou fix aloft and carefully
Thy searching gaze intent, and seek
Therein that purity and greatness great
10 Of the essence sovereign, divine.
And there thou shalt see openly
The well-known paths and roads
By which its high and lofty deity
To us makes manifest and visible
15 The powerful works of its own hands.
And this is more when its great Highness wills
That one of them go up, be raised,
With what facility we there do note
That those means which it uses do agree
20 With those same endings and beginnings
Which it wills its holy works to have.
Of this, great Lord, we have example clear
Within our hands, because His mighty Majesty,
So many centuries having had
25 Those lands hidden so utterly
That it had wished to allow no one
Its secret bosom to spy out,
It having to be discovered, note ye how
and who they were, those valiant men
30 By means of whom that obscure knot
We had did come to be untied.
Now being all attentive, listening,
Here ye shall see, with evidence
Sure, that from Kings now dead

Y de aquellos varones que hemos dicho
Que aquellas nuevas tierras descubrieron,
Son los que agora buelven al trabajo;
Cuia verdad nos muestra su grandeza
Por los antiguos Reyes Mexicanos,
Destos nuevos estados decendientes,
En cuia hija, de vnas tres infantas
Que el postrero de todos ellos⁴ tuvo,
Tuvo otra aquel Marqués noble del Valle,
Desta causa primero pretendiente
Y solo domador del nuevo mundo,
Cuios beneros ricos, poderosos,
De poderosa plata, descubiertos
Fueron por aquel Iuanes de Tolosa,
A quien este Marqués quiso por hierno,⁵
Dándole por esposa regalada
A su querida hija y cara prenda,
Estando en aquel Reyno de Galicia
Que conquistó con singular esfuerzo
Y gobernó assimismo con prudencia
Aquel gran General, noble, famoso,
Que Christóbal de Oñate⁶ abemos dicho
Que fue su claro nombre, y también tío
De Juan y de Vicente de Zaldíbar,
El vno General de Chichimecas⁷
Y el otro Explorador de aquesta entrada,⁸
Y padre de don Juan, que fue casado
Con viznieta del Rey, hija que he dicho
Del buen Marqués,⁹ de cuio tronco nace
Don Christóbal de Oñate,¹⁰ decendiente
De todos estos Reyes y no Reyes,
Cuia persona, sin tener cabales
Diez años bien cumplidos, va saliendo,
Assí como Anibal,¹¹ varón heroico,
A serbiros, señor, en la conquista
De aquestos nuevos Reynos que escribimos,

35 And from those men we've spoken of,
    Those who discovered those new lands,
    Come those who now take up the work again;
    Whose truth its greatness shows
    Through those old Kings of Mexico,
40 Who came down from these new lands, by
    Whose daughter, one of those three Princesses
    The last of them begot,¹
    The noble Marquis of the valley had a girl,
    The first pretender to this cause
45 And only conqueror of the New World,
    Whose rich and mighty stores
    of massy silver were discovered
    By that same Juanes de Tolosa²
    The Marquis chose for son-in-law,
50 Giving him for well-dowried spouse
    His daughter loved, his dearest pledge,
    Being in that Kingdom of Galicia
    Conquered all with such singular effort,
    And which likewise was ruled with wisdom great,
55 By that great General, noble, famed,
    Of whom we spoke: Cristóbal de Oñate,³
    That was his famous name, and uncle, too,
    Of Juan Zaldívar and Vicente,
    One General of Chichimecs,⁴
60 The other scout of that exploring band,⁵
    And father of Don Juan, he who was wed
    To the King's great-granddaughter, the cited daughter⁶
    Of the good Marquis, from whose stock was born
    Don Cristóbal de Oñate,⁷ a descendant
65 Of all these Kings and non-Kings,
    Who, although not yet quite ten
    Years old, came forth with us
    Like Hannibal,⁸ heroic man,
    To serve you, lord, in the conquest
70 Of these new realms we write about,

---

4. Se refiere a Moctezuma.

5. La hija de Hernán Cortés, Leonor, habida en una hija de Moctezuma, se casó con Tolosa, fundador de Zacatecas y descubridor de sus ricas minas de plata.

6. El padre de Juan de Oñate, mencionado antes.

7. Chichimecas = indios mexicanos no apaciguados.

8. El Zaldívar mencionado antes como explorador de la expedición de Coronado.

9. El pasaje es algo confuso porque la biznieta del rey (Moctezuma) era nieta, no hija, del Marqués (Hernán Cortés). En todo caso, era el propio Juan de Oñate, nombrado para capitanear la entrada que narra el poema, el que se casó con la que sería biznieta de Moctezuma.

10. Cristóbal de Oñate, el hijo de Juan de Oñate, que acompañó a su padre en la expedición que narra el poema.

11. General cartaginés en las últimas guerras púnicas, que fue adiestrado por su padre en la guerra desde niño. Lo relata Livio, *Anales* XXI.

1. The reference is to Moctezuma.

2. Leonor, Cortez's daughter by Moctezuma's daughter, married Juanes de Tolosa, founder of Zacatecas and discoverer of the rich silver mines that Juan de Oñate would later inherit.

3. The father of Juan de Oñate, mentioned earlier in connection with the Coronado expedition.

4. The term, from the Nahuatl, was used for still unpacified Mexican Indians.

5. The Zaldívar earlier referred to as the scout for the Coronado expedition.

6. Villagrá mistakes "daughter" for "granddaughter," which is what she must have been to Cortez.

7. The son of Juan de Oñate, who accompanied his father to New Mexico and died there on the return trip.

8. Carthaginian leader and general in the last two Punic Wars, prepared for war by his father from childhood. Narrated by Livy, *Annals* XXI.

En quien veréis al vivo aquí cifrados
Todos los nobles Reyes que salieron
Destas nuevas regiones y plantaron
La gran ciudad de México, y con ellos
Veréis también aquellos valerosos
Que a fuerza de valor y de trabajos
Estas remotas tierras pretendieron.
Por cuia justa causa, sin tardanza,
Assí como las aguas christalinas
Suelen sin detenerse ni tardarse
Yrse todas vertiendo y derramando
Llamadas de su curso poderoso,
Assí don Iuan, sin aguardar más plazo,
Llamado de la fuerza y voz de Marte
Y de la illustre sangre generosa
De todos sus maiores y passados
Y destos grandes Reyes que dezimos,
Como el prudente Griego que las armas
Del valeroso Aquiles pretendía
Por debida justicia que alegaba,[12]
Assí dio en pretender aquesta impresa
Por el derecho grande que tenía
A serbiros en ella sin que alguno
Otro mejor derecho le mostrase.
Y assí escribió el[13] Virrey que se sirviese,
Que pues aquesta impressa no se daba
Al Capitán Francisco de Vrdinola,
Que a sóla su persona se fiase,
Pues que della sabía y conocía
Tener aquellas prendas que bastaban
Para cosa tan grave y tan pesada
Como allí le pedía y suplicaba.
Y como el buen señor no satisfaze
Al buen comedimiento que le ofrece
Aquél que a bien serbirle se adelanta
Si no es (a falta de obras) con palabras,
Razones y caricias muy corteses,
Assí el Virrey, que bien le conocía,
Luego le respondió cómo quisiera
Hazer lo que pedía y suplicaba,
Mas que estaban las cosas de manera
Que no le era possible se entablasen[14]
De suerte que pudiesse bien mostrarle
La fuerza del buen pecho con que estaba
De darle en todo gusto y buen despacho.

In whom you may see, fully incarnate,
All of those noble Kings who came
From out these regions new and did set up
The mighty city Mexico. With them
75 You may see, too, those valiant ones
Who, by the force of valor and of work,
Put forth claim to these distant lands.
For which just cause, without delay,
Just as the waters crystalline
80 Do use, all without lingering or delay,
To sweep ahead and flow,
Called to their rushing course,
So did Don Juan, not waiting longer time,
Called by the power and voice of Mars
85 And of the famous, generous blood
Of all his ancestors, forbearers,
And of those great Kings we have spoken of,
Like that judicious Greek who claimed
The arms of valorous Achilles,[9]
90 By justice due, as he alleged,
So he did claim this enterprise
By that great right he had
To serve you in it and since no one else
Could demonstrate a better right.
95 And so he wrote the Viceroy to be kind
Enough, since that emprise had not been given
To Captain Francisco de Urdinola,
To entrust it to himself alone,
Since he did know about him, knew that he
100 Had just those strengths which would suffice
For such grave matter, of such import,
As that he asked and begged of him.
As a good lord does not reward
The one who doth advance to serve him well
105 For service that he offered him
Unless (for lack of deeds) it is with words,
With reasons and most courteous favors,
So the Viceroy, who did know him well,
Replied at once that he did wish
110 To do that which he asked and begged,
But that affairs were in such sort
That 'twas impossible to organize
In a manner that would clearly show
The strength of the good will he had to grant
115 It with all pleasure and at once.

12. Se refiere a Ulises, que disputó, alegando su derecho, por las armas del difunto Aquiles. Ello lo narra Ovidio, *Metamorfosis* XIII.

13. Probable errata del original por "al," que da mejor sentido al texto.

14. Se entablasen = se dispusiesen.

9. The reference is to Ulysses, who claimed the arms of the dead Achilles. It is narrated by Ovid, *Metamorphoses* XIII.

Mas que él ternía[15] siempre gran memoria
De aquélla que a sus Padres se debía
Y de la que a sus deudos y persona
Era también razón que se tuviesse,
Para todo lo qual ayudaría
El crecido desseo con que estaba
De mostrar con las obras la limpieza,
Llaneza y voluntad de sus palabras.
Pues abiendo don Iuan agradecido
Tan singular merced por muchas cartas,
Como la gratitud continuo engendra
Más voluntad y amor en los illustres,
Altos y nobles pechos generosos
De quien largas mercedes esperamos,
Fue el tiempo yrrebocable discurriendo
Y, qual veloz correo, fue llegando
A las cerradas puertas descuidadas
Y batiendo a gran priessa fue rompiendo
El secreto silencio y trujo luego
Oportuna sazón y coiuntura
En que el Virrey resuelto, sin estorbo,
Tuvo por bien de darle y encargarle
Aquesta impressa en veinte y quatro días
Del mes de Agosto y año que contamos,
Mil y quinientos y noventa y cinco.
Y porque aquesta entrada se hiziesse
Con la decencía y orden que pedía
Cosa tan importante y tan pesada,
Determinó escribirle y animarle
En el intento y causa comenzada.
Y porque en cosas graves es muy justo,
Si la ocasión lo pide y lo requiere,
Hazer vuestros Virreyes más de aquello
Que Vuestra larga mano les permite,
Avisole assimismo con cuidado
Que aunque era cosa cierta no tenía
Mano para gastar vuestro tesoro
Ni para dispensar en cosa alguna
Mas de lo que la cédula dezía
En razón de aquéllos que apetecen
A[16] descubrir la tierra y conquistarla,
Que estuviesse certíssimo haría,
En todas ocasiones, tanto efecto,[17]
Por sólo darle gusto y agradarle,
Quanto[18] si de su hijo don Francisco[19]

120

125

130

135

140

145

150

155

160

Yet he had always a full memory
Of that[10] was owed to his forbearers
And that his person and his kin
Were also, in good reason, due,
All of which would be aided by,
As well, the increasing longing that he had
To show in deeds the purity,
The frankness, and the good will of his words.
Now Don Juan, having given thanks
In many letters for so singular a mercy,
As a continual gratitude does breed
More good will and more love in the illustrious,
And high and noble, generous breasts
From whom we hope great mercies,
Time went on, irrevocable, swift,
And, like swift courier, did come
To the closed, neglected doors
And beating hard in haste, it broke
The secret silence and drew forth
A moment opportune and a conjuncture
In which the Viceroy, free from hindrance,
Found it good to give him and deliver him
That enterprise. 'Twas four-and-twenty days
Into the month of August, and the year we count
One thousand and five hundred ninety-five.
And that the entry might be made
With all the decency and order that a thing
So weighty, so important, did require,
He thought to write him and encourage him
In the attempt and cause begun.
And since in matters grave 'tis very just,
If the occasion so require it,
Your Viceroy should do somewhat more than that
Your generous commands permit;
He told him also, though with care,
That though it was a certain thing that he
Had no free hand to spend your treasure there
Nor to disburse for anything
More than the decrees did state
With respect to those who did desire
To explore the land and conquer it,
That he most certainly would do,
To give him pleasure, gratify him,
As much, on all occasions, as he would
If they concerned his son Don Francisco,[11]

15. Ternía = tendría
16. Apetecen a = aspiran a.
17. Que estuviera seguro que le favorecería en todas ocasiones.
18. Quanto = cuanto, como.
19. El virrey se refiere a un hijo suyo.

10. The antecedent here is "good will."
11. The viceroy refers to his own son, thus indicating the strength of his good will toward Don Juan.

Todas fuessen y mucho le importasen.
Y esto porque sabía y alcanzaba
Lo abían de merecer sus buenas obras,
A las quales también aplicaría
Todas aquellas armas y pertrechos
De aquéllos que se entraron contra vando,²⁰
Para cuyo socorro²¹ le daría
La pólvora y el plomo necessario
Y más quatro mil pesos con que luego
Pudiesse socorrer a los soldados,
Pidiéndole con esto diesse cuenta
De todo lo que assí quiso escrebirle
A Rodrigo del Río, caballero
Del hábito del gran patrón de España,²²
Y que junto con él lo confiriese
Con don Diego Fernández de Velasco,
Gobernador del Reyno de Vizcaia,
A los quales mandó que diesse parte
Por las illustres prendas que alcanzaban
Assí en cosas de paz como de guerra,
Para que con prudencia le advirtiesen
Cosas que por ventura no alcanzase.
Y porque tanto pierde y se desdora
La que es buena y cortés correspondencia
Quanto vemos que tiene de tardanza,
Don Iuan sin detenerse ni tardarse
Obedeció la carta, y esto hizo
Ante escribano público, rindiendo
Su vida, su persona y su hazienda
A vuestro Real servicio, sin que cosa
Quedase reservada que no fuesse
En sóla aquesta causa dispensada.
Y luego embió poder a don Fernando,
A don Christóbal y a Luys Nuñez Pérez,
También a don Alonso, sus hermanos,²³
Todos varones ricos y, con esto,
Gallardos cortesanos y muy diestros
Para éstas y otras cosas señaladas.
Estos capitularon²⁴ la jornada,
Faborecidos siempre y amparados
De aquellos dos doctíssimos varones,
Santiago del Riego y Maldonado,
Columnas del Audiencia y del derecho

These things, and to him all of much import.
And this because he knew and fully grasped
The fact that his good works would merit it,
To which, he said, he would adjudge
165 All of those arms and furnishings
Of those who entered there against command,¹²
And for their aid would give to them
The powder and the necessary lead
Beside four thousand dollars with which he
170 Could then assist the troops,
And asking him, with this, to give account
Of all that he then had written
To Rodrigo del Río, a knight
Of the Order of the patron saint of Spain,¹³
175 And that with him he should confer and with
Don Diego Fernández de Velasco,
The Governor of the Kingdom of Vizcaya,
Whom he did order that he keep advised
Because of the illustrious virtues they had
180 As well for things of peace as those of war,
That with their judgement good they might advise
In things that he, perhaps, might not observe.
And as we see that correspondence courteous and good
Doth lose, diminish, in proportion as
185 It is delayed in transit, so
Don Juan, without delay or lingering,
Obeyed the order and did this
Before notary public, there surrendering
His life, his person, and his whole estate
190 Unto your Royal Service, and nothing
Remained reserved or was not there
Resigned to this sole cause alone.
And then he sent proxies to Don Fernando,
To Don Cristóbal and to Luis Nuñez Pérez,
195 Also to Don Alonso, these his brethren,¹⁴
All wealthy men and thus, as such,
All gallant courtiers, skillful too,
For these and other signal things.
These wrote a contract for the emprise,
200 Always with the help and aid
From those two most learned men,
Santiago del Riego and Maldonado,
Columns of the Audiencia¹⁵ and of civil law

---

20. Se refiere a lo confiscado de los que entraban en Nuevo México ilegalmente (contra vando); concretamente, al grupo, antes mencionado, que había entrado con Bonilla.

21. El de la expedición de Oñate.

22. Caballero de la Orden de Santiago.

23. Sus hermanos eran don Cristóbal y don Alonso.

24. Capitularon = concertaron.

12. The reference is to the arms confiscated from those who entered unexplored territory without official permission (*contra vando*) and specifically to the arms confiscated from the Bonilla group mentioned earlier.

13. A Knight of the Order of Santiago.

14. Don Juan's brothers were Cristóbal and Alonso.

15. The *Audiencia*, which Curtis keeps in Spanish, was the highest advisory board to the viceroy of New Spain.

Cibil muy grandes y altos observantes.
También los fuertes hombros arrimaron,
Con todas sus haziendas y personas,
Christóbal de Zaldíbar y Francisco
De Zaldíbar, Lequeitio y don Antonio
De Figueroa, a quien también siguieron
Vicente de Zaldíbar y Bañuelos,
Ruidíaz de Mendoza y, con éste,
Don Iuan Cortés, del gran Cortés viznieto,
Y don Iuan de Guevara, a quien seguía
También Iuan de Zaldíbar, hijo illustre
De aquel varón famoso que primero
Entró por estas tierras que buscamos,
Al fin, prendas, los más de aquestos Héroes,
De Iuanes de Tolosa, cuios brazos
Fundaron con esfuerzo y lebantaron
La famosa Ciudad de Zacatecas,
Y aquel insigne Salas memorable,
Primero Alcalde desta Ciudad rica,
Rica digo, señor, pues cien millones
Sabemos ya por cuenta se han quintado²⁵
Dentro de sus goteras²⁶ no cansadas
De abrir sus ricas venas por serviros.
Y qual feroz León que la braveza
Rinde al que ve rendido sin soberbia,
Assí don Iuan pidió que sólo vn punto
Pidiesen de su parte y no otra cosa,
Y fue que se le diese mano abierta
Para poder hazer castigo entero
O para perdonar si conviniese
Aquéllos que se fueron contra vando,
Porque sería possible aber tenido
Tan noble proceder que fuesse justo
Que a todos con las vidas los dexassen.
Pues como sus agentes con acuerdo
Hubiessen esta entrada ya assentado,
Sin perder tiempo el General prudente,
Cuyo título grave acompañaba
El de Gobernador y adelantado,
Hizo Maese de Campo sin tardanza
A don Iuan de Zaldíbar y a Iuan Guerra
Nombró por su teniente, y luego puso
Sobre sus bravos hombros el gran peso,
Gobierno y magestad de todo el campo.
Y porque en todo vbiesse buen despacho²⁷

As well, exceeding great and deep observers.

205 Then, too, there lent their shoulders strong,
With all their persons and estates,
Cristóbal de Zaldívar and Francisco
De Zaldívar, Lequeitio and Don Antonio
De Figueroa, whom there followed, too,
210 Vicente de Zaldívar and Bañuelos,
Ruidíaz de Mendoza and, with him,
Don Juan Cortés, great-grandson of the great Cortés,
And Don Juan de Guevara, who was followed by
Juan de Zaldívar, the illustrious son
215 Of that right famous man who first
Did come into these lands we sought;
Descendants, most of them, of these heroes,
Of Juanes de Tolosa, he whose arms
Did found with effort and raise up
220 The famous Ciudad de Zacatecas,
And that memorable, famous, Salas,
First *Alcalde* of that city rich.
I say rich, lord, since we do know
A hundred millions were yours¹⁶
225 From its environs, never tired
Of opening its rich veins to serve you.
Like lion ferocious, whose stark bravery
Bows to the one it sees surrendered without pride,
So Don Juan asked that but one point
230 be for himself demanded and no other thing,
And 'twas that he be given a free hand
And power to give the whole of punishment
Or pardon, if it should seem best,
To those who had entered 'gainst command;
235 For it were possible that they'd acted
So nobly that it would be just
To let all these go with their lives.
Now, as his agents, all with one accord,
Already had arranged this expedition,
240 Without the loss of time, the General, prudent man,
Whose weighty title did accompany
That, too, of Governor and *Adelantado*,
Immediately made his Army Master¹⁷
Don Juan de Zaldívar and named
245 Juan Guerra his lieutenant, and did place
Upon their stalwart shoulders the great weight
Of governing and ruling all the force.
And so there be in all most prompt dispatch,

25. Quintado = apartado para la corona.
26. Goteras = alrededores.
27. Buen despacho = cumplimiento rápido.

16. The word used by Villagrá, *quintado,* refers to the fifth part set aside for the crown.

17. Curtis has earlier translated this as "master of the camp," but Army Master gives a better idea of the rank of overall military command of an expedition.

También quiso nombrar por su teniente
A don Christóbal[28] para todo aquello
Que fuesse necessario se hiziesse
En la illustre Corte Mexicana,
Y al Capitán Vicente de Zaldíbar
Por sargento mayor[29] nombró, y por cabo,[30]
Y qual suelen las Aguilas Reales,
Que a los tiernos polluelos de su nido
Largo trecho los sacan y remontan
Para que con esfuerzo cobren fuerzas
En el libiano buelo y dél se balgan
En provechosa y diestra altenería,[31]
Assí determinó don Iuan saliese
Su hijo don Christóbal, niño tierno,
Para que con él fuesse y se adestrase,
Sirbiéndoos, gran señor, en el oficio
De la importante guerra trabajosa,
Siendo testigo fiel de sus palabras,
Para que con las obras que allí viese
Le tuviesse después en bien serbiros
Por único dechado y claro ejemplo,
Imitando en aquesto al diestro Vlixes
Quando del regalado y blando trato
Que tuvo entre las damas y donzellas
En el Real palacio el bravo Achiles,
Que dél quiso sacarle porque supo
Lo mucho que importaba a toda Grecia.[32]
Assí quiso que del regalo dulze
De su querida patria y deudos caros
Saliese para impressa en sí tan alta.
Y como en grandes justas y torneos
Todo se enciende, alegra y alborota,
Triunfa, gasta, derrama y se dispende,
Assí muchos gustosos y contentos
Con toda priesa juntos se aprestaron.
Y no con más presteza las abejas
Al sol en sus labores suelen verse
En la sazón que sacan sus enjambres
Por los floridos campos quando empieza
El nuevo Abril su fuerza o quando hinchen
De aquel licor sabroso y regalado
Los bien compuestos vassos que ordenados

250 He also chose to name his lieutenant
Don Cristóbal[18] for all those things
It might be necessary to have done
Within the illustrious Court of Mexico,
And Captain Vicente de Zaldívar
He did make Sergeant Major;[19] and to end,
255 Just as the royal eagles are accustomed
To drive the tender fledglings from their nests
And make them soar a goodly flight
That they, by effort, may gain strength
In soaring flight and make good use
260 In skillful and in gainful hunting,
So Don Juan determined there should go
His son, Don Cristóbal, a tender child,
So that he might be with him and gain skill
In serving you, great lord, in all the art
265 Of war important, toilsome,
Being a faithful witness of his words;
So that in all those works he then should see
He might, in serving you in after times,
Have them his only standard, clear example,
270 Imitating thus the shrewd Ulysses
When he wished to lure
The brave Achilles from the soft, luxurious stay
That he was making 'mid the dames and damsels
About the royal palace,[20] since he knew
275 How much it meant to all of Greece.
So he wished that the sweet pleasures
Of his dear Fatherland and loving kin
He should leave for so great an enterprise.
And, as in tourneys great and jousts
280 All is alive, made happy, agitated,
Triumphs, spends, pours out, exerts itself;
So, many, happy and well-pleased,
Sped on to join with all the haste they could.
And with no more haste do the bees[21]
285 Bestir, all at their labors in the sun,
At the time when their swarms appear
Among the flowery fields, when April new puts forth
His strength and when the cunningly wrought buds
Do swell with the sweet liquor, odorous,
290 Life-giving, and ordained unto that end,

28. El hermano antes mencionado.
29. El sargento mayor era jefe superior a los capitanes.
30. Por cabo = finalmente.
31. Altenería = altanería, caza con pájaros de presa.
32. Se refiere al viaje que hizo Ulises a la corte de Licómedes, donde Aquiles se hallaba vestido de mujer y entre ellas por orden de su madre, que quería evitar que fuera a la guerra de Troya.

18. This is a reference to Don Juan's brother, his agent at the viceregal court, mentioned earlier.
19. The Sergeant Major was the highest ranking combat officer, just below the Army Master.
20. The reference is to Ulysses's trip to the court of Licomedes, where Achilles was dressed as a woman and living with these by order of his mother, who wished to avoid his going to the Trojan war.
21. This bee simile, already in Virgil (*Aeneid* I, 611–20), was widely used in the Renaissance epic.

Están para el efecto, y assí, juntas,
Las vnas a las otras se socorren[33]
Qual vimos los soldados socorrerse
Los vnos a los otros y aprestarse.
Y hervorosos todos y alentados,
Gastando sus haziendas, se assentaron
A professar el vso y exercicio
Del gallardo estandarte que arbolaron.
Echaron luego vandos y contentos
Por las calles más públicas y plazas
Pregonaron aquellas libertades[34]
Que concedéis, señor, a los que os sirven
En el oficio duro de las armas.
Tocáronse clarines lebantados,
Los pífanos y cajas, con vizarro
Estrépito y ruido de soldados
Bravos, dispuestos, nobles y animosos
Y en pruebas de la guerra bien cursados.[35]
Pues estando ya todos prevenidos
Y con maduro acuerdo[36] pertrechados,
Rabiando por salir y despacharse,[37]
Como a los gustos siempre se les sigue
Vn millón de disgustos y tormentos,
Llegó, señor, la flota y como en ella
Mandó vuestro gran Padre y señor nuestro

Que don Luys de Velasco se partiese
Y que al Pirú se fuesse y que quedase
Gobernando el señor de Vlloa y Bietma,
Conde de Monte Rey, a nueva España.
Como la torpe invidia siempre busca
Veredas y ocasiones donde pueda
Bomitar su mortífera ponzoña,
Con sóla esta mudanza fue rompiendo[38]
Y al nuevo Visorrey se fue acercando,
Y qual el tentador[39] que con cubierta
De grande santidad sólo atendía
A salir con su causa y con su hecho,
Assí se fue llegando aquesta bestia,
Haziendo relación de nuestra entrada
Y como toda estaba encomendada,

	And together give a mutual aid,
	Than we did see the soldiers help
	Each other and do make ready.
	Impatient all, all encouraged,
295	Pledging their properties, they enlisted
	To swear the proper use and exercise
	Of that brave standard they set up.
	They then read proclamations and gaily
	Through all the plazas and the public streets
300	Heralded well the liberties
	That you, O lord, concede to those who serve you in
	The hard employ of arms.[22]
	The stirring trumpet called,
	The fifes and drums, with uproar brave
305	And gallant shouts of soldiers
	Brave, well-disposed, noble and eager, too,
	Schooled well by tests of actual war.
	Well, now being all prepared
	And furnished well by skill mature,
310	Raving to leave and do the work,
	As it falls always that on pleasure's heels
	A thousand torments and misfortunes come,
	The fleet arrived and how in it
	Your mighty Father and our lord
315	Had given command Don Luis de Velasco should set forth
	And go into Peru and there should here remain,
	As Governor of New Spain, the lord
	Of Ulloa and Biedma, Count of Monterey.
	Since always wicked envy seeks
320	Paths and occasions by which it may
	Throw out its deadly poison,
	By this mere change it broke its bounds
	And to the new Viceroy it made approach,
	And, like the tempter[23] who beneath the cloak
325	Of special sanctity alone doth try
	To win his cause and so his ends,
	So that beast made advance,
	Commenting upon our *entrada*,[24]
	And how all things had been entrusted,
330	High and excellent as they were,

33. La comparación con las abejas, ya en Virgilio (*Eneida* I, 611–20), se halla en casi toda la épica renacentista.

34. Se refiere Villagrá a los privilegios y exenciones que solían concedérseles a los que se alistaban a tales empresas: privilegios de rango social y de posesión de tierras y exenciones de impuestos.

35. cursados = entendidos.

36. Acuerdo = razón, juicio.

37. Despacharse = ponerse en funciones.

38. Rompiendo = empezando.

39. Tentador = demonio.

22. Villagrá refers to the privileges often granted those who settled new lands: titles granting social rank, proprietorship of lands, and exemption from taxes.

23. The reference is to the devil.

24. Curtis keeps the Spanish word, which roughly means exploratory expedition.

Siendo de tanta alteza y excelencia,
A quien era impossible la hiziesse.
Y súpole intimar también[40] el caso
Que le dexó suspenso y con cuidado;
Y como el pecho noble tanto es fácil,
Quanto es más rebozado el trato doble,[41]
Desseoso el Virrey de bien serviros
A don Luys de Velasco escribió luego
Una carta cortés sobre este caso,
Pidiendo que con pies de plomo[42] fuesse
Y que esta nueva entrada dilatase
En el inter que a México viniesse,
Y con esto escribió también a España,
Con notable secreto y gran recato,
A vuestro Real Consejo, que si fuessen
De parte de[43] don Iuan a que aprobasen
Aqueste asiento y causa ya tratada,
Se suspendiese todo y dilatase
Hasta que él de otra cosa diesse aviso,
Porque por no tener tomado el pulso
Ni tentado los vados[44] desta tierra,
De presente juzgaba convenía
Que aquello se hiziesse y no otra cosa.
Y como no nos basta tener limpia
El alma y la conciencia si con esto
Con toda diligencia no se quitan
Indicios y sospechas que lebantan
Escándalos y culpas en aquéllos
Que libres desde afuera nos imputan,[45]
Assí, qual Julio César, que no quiso
Sufrir tuviesse culpa su consorte,
Mas libre de sospecha quiso fuesse,[46]
Assí el Virrey[47] discreto, tracendiendo,[48]
Como prudente, sabio y recatado,[49]
Alguna gran calumnia por la carta
Que recibió del Conde,[50] luego hizo,
Qual práctico piloto recatado
Que las tendidas velas assegura

To one who 'twas impossible could do them,
And managed so well to make his case
It left him in suspense and in much doubt.
And since treachery enters the noble heart

335   In that proportion in which 'tis concealed,
The Viceroy, wishing most to serve you well,
Then wrote Don Luis de Velasco
A courteous letter dealing with the case,
Asking that he go forth with measured steps

340   And put off this new exploration 'till
He should arrive in Mexico,
And at the same time he wrote, too, to Spain,
With marked secretiveness and caution great,
Unto your Royal Council, that if they received

345   From Don Juan requests for approval
Of this affair and cause already dealt with,
It be suspended and put off
Until he should give orders otherwise;
For he, not having felt the pulse

350   Nor tried the depths of fords[25] in the new land,
Did for the present deem it best
That this and nothing else be done.
And because it is not enough to have
Clean souls and consciences, if thus

355   We can not, with all diligence, keep down
The rumors and suspicions that do raise
Up scandals, accusations, from the ones
Who freely, from without, lay them on us
Like Julius Caesar, who'd not bear

360   Any guilt falling on his wife,
But would that she be free of suspicion;[26]
The Viceroy, a prudent, wise, and modest man,
Scenting out cleverly some calumny as cause
Of that epistle from the Count received,

365   Like a skilled, practical mariner,
Who maketh fast the bellying sails
Before the storm attacks them,
Drew up immediately strong, sufficient evidence

40. También = tan bien.
41. El pecho noble es tanto más fácil al engaño cuanto más disfrazado viene éste (trato doble).
42. Con pies de plomo = con cautela y cuidado.
43. De parte de = en nombre de. Se refiere a cartas.
44. Tentado los vados = comprobado las condiciones.
45. Imputan = acusan.
46. César rechazó a Pompeya, su mujer, en las condiciones que indica el texto, por un escándalo que hubo en su casa con Clodio. Plutarco, *Vidas,* narra el hecho en su biografía de César.
47. Luis de Velasco, aún virrey de Nueva España en funciones.
48. Tracendiendo = trascendiendo, viendo perspicazmente.
49. Recatado = cauto.
50. Conde de Monterrey, el nuevo Virrey, aún no en funciones.

25. The image, as Curtis translates it, literally, means to "test the waters."
26. Caesar rejected his wife, Pompeya, in the condition indicated by Villagrá, over a scandal in his home concerning Clodius. Plutarch, *Parallel Lives,* narrates the matter in his biography of Caesar.

Antes que los assalte gran borrasca,
Vna fuerte probanza, tan bastante,
Acerca de los Padres y los deudos,
Persona, discreción, prendas y partes
Del don Iuan que ninguno en nueva España
Pudo con más justicia competirle
Aquesta noble impressa que le dieron.
Pues en el inter que los dos Virreyes
Pudieron ventilar aqueste hecho,
Qual fresca flor que luego se marchita
Sin el debido riego que la enciende,
Assí se fue secando y marchitando
Todo el luzido campo lebantado,
Caiendo del buen nombre que tenía.
Y como el vulgo es siempre tan amigo
De novedad confussa y alboroto,
Alborotados juntos en corrillos
Dezían y afirmaban sin vergüenza
Aquello que la invidia vil, infame,
A todos publicaba y les dezía.
Dios nos libre, señor, de aquesta sierpe
Cuia fiera braveza es cosa cierta.
No tiene rayo el Cielo que assí rompa,
Destruya, desbarate ni destroze
La fuerza de virtud qual es su lengua.
Esta causó la muerte al que primero
Partió de aquesta vida trabajosa;⁵¹
Esta hizo que el hombre no tuviesse
Segura su conciencia y se salvase;
Esta pobló el infierno y fue primera
En despoblar el Cielo, y tuvo aliento
Para atreverse a Dios, ¡mirad qué tiro
Y a quántos derribó que ya los vimos
Sobre el impíreo Cielo colocados!⁵²
Viendo, pues, los soldados que arrastraban
Tan altos pensamientos por el suelo
Por sólo deshazer aquesta entrada,
Y que estaban ya todos tan gastados,
Deshechas sus haziendas y negocios
En que estaban de assiento entretenidos,
Afligidos los vnos y los otros,
Qual vemos a los flacos navichuelos
De gran fuerza de vientos combatidos
Cortar apriesa rizas⁵³ y rendirse
A la inclemencia brava poderosa,

370 About the ancestors and relatives,
The person, wisdom, strengths, and parts,
Of our Don Juan, to prove that no one in New Spain
Could, with a better right, compete with him
That noble enterprise they'd given him.
During the interim while this affair
375 Could be cleared up between the Viceroys,
Like a fresh flower that withers fast
Without the watering that inspires it,
Thusly did dry up and wither
The whole high-spirited and glittering camp,
380 Falling from the good name it had.
And as the common herd is always friend
To news confused and tumult,
Gathered in noisy groups
They said and without shame affirmed
385 That which vile envy, infamous,
To all did publish and did say.
May God deliver us, O lord, from that serpent
Whose wrathful impudence is a certain thing.
Heaven has no lightnings which can so much break,
390 Destroy, cast down, and ruin quite
The force of virtue as its tongue.
This caused the death of him who first
Departed from this toilsome life.²⁷
This makes no man feel that
395 His conscience is safe or can be saved.
This peopled Hell and was the first
To break the ranks of Heaven, and had the strength
To dare to rival God; look thou what impudence,
And how many it threw down that we saw
400 Within the Sky empyrean placed!²⁸
The soldiers, seeing that such high intents
Were leveled to the ground
Only to break up that expedition,
And that they all had spent their all,
405 Their business and estates broke up
While they were occupied in camp,
And one and all afflicted, as we see
Small boats attacked by mighty winds
Quickly make rippling waves²⁹ and quite surrender to
410 The powerful, rude, inclement storm,
So they were all upset and lost,
And quite surrendered without recourse.
But he, the Governor and his lieutenant,

---

51. Se refiere a Abel, víctima de la envidia de Caín.
52. Se refiere a los ángeles, Lúcifer a la cabeza, envidiosamente sublevados contra Dios.
53. Rizas = olas pequeñas; pero la imagen, especialmente con cortar puede referirse al corte de la cebada (Covarrubias) cerca de la raíz, es decir, al corte de los palos en las naves.

27. The reference is to Abel, victim of Cain's envy.
28. The reference is to Lucifer's rebellion against God.
29. The words employed by Villagrá, *cortando rizas,* could possibly refer to the cutting of grain near the root, thus suggesting, in the storm described, the cutting of the masts.

Assí, todos perdidos, zozobrados,
Estaban sin consuelo ya rendidos.
Mas el Gobernador y su teniente,
Como esforzados, viendo la tormenta
Y deshecha borrasca que cargaba
Con tantos desatinos y juicios
Como la gente toda concebía,
Diziendo que no abiendo de hazerse
Aquella entrada, que porqué respecto⁵⁴
A todos los abían engañado,
Otros a grandes bozes publicaban
Que assolados a todos los tenían,
Sin poder lebantar jamás cabeza,
Y como aquesto mucho lastimaba,
Quales diestros bridones⁵⁵ desembueltos,
Que a fuerza de la espuela y duro freno
En manijos⁵⁶ ligeros la braveza
Del caballo animoso desembuelven,
Assí el Gobernador y su teniente,
Cuias suabes lenguas parecían
Que las mismas abejas endulzaban,
Según que con Platón y el sabio Omero
Es público y notorio lo hizieron,⁵⁷
Assí, con mucha fuerza de razones,
Dulzes palabras y sentencias vivas,
Los fueron gobernando y sossegando
Hasta que vino nueva que se abían
Visto los dos Virreyes en Oculma,⁵⁸
En cuyo puesto fue informando luego
Don Luys de Velasco, con aviso,⁵⁹
De la buena elección que abía hecho.
Y viendo manifiesto el desengaño,⁶⁰
Qual suelen apagarse y deshazerse
Los lebantados astros que bañados
Se ven, del sol heridos quando viene
Rasgando la mañana alegre y clara,⁶¹
Assí el de Monte Rey quedó suspenso,⁶²
Del todo satisfecho y agradado.

Viewing like brave men all the storm
415 And all the shattered wreck it bore,
With all the foolishness and judgment wild
The people did conceive,
Saying if the entry would not be made
For what conceivable reason
420 They all had been deceived in that respect?
And others were crying aloud
That all were quite destroyed,
And never could make good again;
And as all this did damage great,
425 Like skillful, easy horsemen, who by dint
Of prodding spur, controlling rein,
And skillful handling quite control
The spirit of the mettled horse,
E'en so the Governor and his lieutenant,
430 Whose tongues, it seemed, the very
Honey bees sweetened themselves,
As it is public knowledge and well known
To Plato and wise Homer did,³⁰
Did keep on ruling and appeasing them
435 By dint of reasoning, good words, and pointed speech,
Until the news came that there'd been
A meeting of the Viceroys at Oculma,³¹
At which meeting Don Luis de Velasco
Had carefully bestowed much information
440 Concerning the good choice that he had made.
And seeing the truth so manifest,
Just as the lofty stars are seen
To vanish quite away and disappear
Both bathed and wounded by the sun who comes
445 Cleaving the morning,³² cheerful, clear,
So he of Monterey was both surprised
And in all points was satisfied and pleased.
The more as Don Juan prudently
Had written him a courteous letter there,
450 Congratulating him on his arrival
And how the mighty haste that he was in

54. Respecto = causa o razón.
55. Bridones = jinetes.
56. Manijos = manejos.
57. Era muy generalizada en el mundo clásico, y aplicado a muchos otros, esta noción.
58. Lugar, cerca de la Ciudad de México, del primer encuentro entre el virrey saliente, Velasco, y el entrante, el conde de Monterrey.
59. Aviso = discreción.
60. Desengaño = verdad.
61. La imagen del amanecer, aunque de empleo universal, es especialmente repetida en la épica del Nuevo Mundo. Los descubridores y conquistadores españoles, tantos de ellos criados en zonas montañosas del interior, hubieron de haber sido muy afectados por los esplendorosos amaneceres de la travesía y de las costas americanas.
62. suspenso = admirado.

30. We have not found the source of this notion, applied as well to other eloquent figures from antiquity.
31. Located near Mexico City, site of the first meeting between the outgoing viceroy, Velasco, and the incoming viceroy, the count of Monterrey.
32. The morning breaking image, present throughout all of literature, was among the most favored by the New World epic. The Spanish poets, often raised in landlocked and mountainous areas of Spain, may well have been amazed by the oceanic and coastal sunrises they experienced.

Al qual, don Iuan abía con prudencia
Escrítole vna carta cortesana
Dándole el para bien de su venida
Y cómo la gran priesa que tenía   455
En el despacho desta nueva entrada
Cerraba los caminos que era justo
Estuviessen abiertos y trillados
Para sólo ofrecerse en su servicio,[63]
Partiendo sin tardanza, y luego fuera   460
sino[64] dejara sin remedio aquello
Que con tan viva fuerza le pedía.
Suplicole assimismo que, si fuesse
Su persona de efecto para el caso
Que le tenían dado y encargado,   465
Que sin su bendición no permitiese
Que cosa se hiziesse ni acabase.
Con esto y con la fuerza que pusieron
Aquellos dos Iuezes que hemos dicho
Y todos los agentes cuidadosos,   470
Con notable contento luego el Conde
A don Iuan respondió con vn correo
Mostrándosele grato y obligado
Al parabién que dio de su venida
Y voluntad sencilla que mostraba   475
Tener a su persona y a sus cosas,
Y que en lo que tocaba a sus despachos[65]
Abía ya mostrado sentimiento
De que no los tuviesse despachados
Don Luys de Velasco, pues podía,   480
Como ministro de tan gran prudencia
Y también acertado en cosas graves.
Por cuia justa causa le era fuerza
Aprobar todo aquello que estuviesse
Tratado y assentado, sin que cosa   485
en ninguna manera se alterase,
Y assí determinaba y le ordenaba
Que con la vendición de Dios y suia
Saliesse sin estorbo y se partiesse,
Ofreciendo con veras de assistirle,   490
Sin faltarle jamás, en todo aquello
Que para proseguir tan justo intento
La experiencia y el tiempo le enseñasen.
Y porque pueda yo dezir las cosas
Que a tan buenos principios sucedieron,   495
Quiero con atención buscar vereda
Por do mi tosca pluma, por atajo,
Pueda salir a luz de tal trabajo.

For the dispatch of the new expedition
Had closed to him the road that it was just
Should have been open and well trod
Only to offer himself to his sole service,
Going without delay, as he would have
But for leaving unattended
What he'd begged for with such vehemence.
He asked him also if his person were
One proper for the thing
That they had given and entrusted him,
He should permit, without his blessing and approval,
Ought to be done or carried out.
With this and with the force that those two Judges
Whom we have mentioned and all the agents
Carefully applied,
The Count did then with notable content
Reply unto Don Juan in a message,
Showing himself much pleased and obliged
For the congratulations he had given on his arrival
And for the great goodwill he showed
He had unto his person and affairs,
And that with reference to his business
He had shown much unhappiness
That Don Luis Velasco had not proceeded
To its completion, since he could,
He being a minister of such great prudence
And also shrewd in weighty things.
For which just cause 'twas necessary he
Approve all that had been agreed
And set on foot, without a thing
Being altered there in any way,
So he decided and he ordered him
That, with God's blessing and his care,
He go without a hindrance and set out,
Offering most truly to assist him
And fail him never in all that
Experience and time should teach
To forward such a just intent.
And that I may well tell things
That followed on such favorable beginnings,
I wish to seek attentively a path
By which my rude pen, through shortcut,
May succeed in so great a work.

63. Oñate indica que no va a recibirlo, ofreciéndose directamente en
su servicio, por no atrasar la expedición.
64. Sino = si no. Villagrá suele escribirlo como una palabra.
65. Despachos = comisiones, cédulas.

Canto Septimo

DE ALGVNOS SVCESSOS BVENOS Y MALOS DE LA
jornada y de vna cédula Real y mandamiento del Virrey que
se intimó[1] a don Iuan para que hiziesse alto y no prosiguiesse
la jornada.[2]

QVESTA vida triste miserable
Sólo vemos, señor, que se sustenta
De mezquinas y vanas esperanzas,
Cuia corta substancia apenas llega
A entrar por nuestras puertas quando
    luego
De súbito se hunde y desvanece
Tan sin rastro de aber allí llegado
Qual si nunca jamás ubiera sido.
Cuia verdad vissible bien nos muestra
Aquesta pobre historia que escrebimos,
Donde vereys, gran Rey, que estando el campo
Alegre con la carta regalada[3]
Que el Conde despachó con tanto gusto
Y, sin esto, animado y alentado
Con la mucha presteza y diligencia
Con que los estandartes despachaba
Al bravo Californio descuidado[4]
Del Cántabro gallardo[5] que nombraron
Por General del campo poderoso
Que para aquella entrada fue criando[6]
De bella soldadesca y oficiales
En armas y quebrantos bien curtidos
Para llevar trabajos tan pesados
Quanto jamás ningunos padecieron
Sulcando el bravo mar con gran tormenta
Y la tendida tierra con deshechas
Fortunas y miserias nunca vistas.
Y assí, por no poder ya ser sufridos,[7]
Entrando por sus tierras estos bravos,
Viendo el heroico esfuerzo que mostraban,
Poderoso señor, en bien serviros,

1. Se intimó = notificó oficialmente.
2. Las discrepancias entre rey y virrey, aunque históricas, no dejan de recordar las disputas entre dioses, a la merced de las cuales se hallaba, con resignada fortaleza, Eneas en el texto de Virgilio.
3. Regalada = placentera.
4. Descuidado = abandonado.
5. Se refiere a los estandartes de Juan de Oñate.
6. Criando = creando.
7. Sufridos = pacientes. Se refiere Villagrá a la paciencia de los que habiendo hecho la campaña, hallaron poca o ninguna recompensa después. Hasta el verso 45 el poeta se adelanta a los hechos que narra para quejarse, por él y otros, del abandono en que los tiene la corte.

Canto VII

Of some events, both good and bad, of the journey, and of the
Royal decree and order of the Viceroy which was given to Don
Juan to make a halt and not pursue the journey.[1]

HIS sad and miserable life, O lord,
We see to be sustained by naught
But trifling, vain hopes,
Whose little substance hardly comes
And enters in our gates before
              5
It suddenly sinks down and vanishes
So without trace of its arrival that
It seems as if it had not been.
The truth of which, so evident, is shown
By this poor history we write,   10
Wherein you see, great King, the army being
Overjoyed at the pleasing letter
That the Count dispatched with so much pleasure,
Moreover by the exceeding haste and diligence
With which he sent the standards,[2] to   15
The wild and unsettled Californio,[3]
Of the valiant Cantabrian[4] whom they named
As General of the powerful force
That was being gathered for that exploration,
Of excellent soldiery and officers,   20
Experienced in arms and hardships too
To bear such heavy labors as
No man had ever suffered
Plowing the brawling sea with great distress
And traveling the land with much misfortune,   25
Ill-luck and miseries such as never seen.
And now, our patience being exhausted,[5]
These brave men entering your lands,
Seeing the heroic effort that they showed,
Powerful lord, to serve you well,   30
Rejected by the land and by the sea,

1. The discrepancies between the king and the viceroy, although historically accurate, echo the disputes between the gods which Aeneas, as does Oñate, suffered patiently in Virgil's text.
2. The reference is to Oñate's banners.
3. Probably taking its name from the Colorado River, and referring, generally, to the American southwest.
4. Juan de Oñate's Spanish stock originated in Cantabria, the area in Spain bordering the Bay of Biscay.
5. Beginning at this point and through verse 45, Villagrá breaks off his narrative to anticipate the plight of those who went on the expedition and returned and were still awaiting some royal recompense for their efforts.

Bomitados del mar y de la tierra
Al fin bolvieron estos esforzados
A vuestra nueva España, donde muchos
Famosos Españoles que quisieron
Armar aquesta entrada y lebantarla
Quedaron assolados y perdidos
Mas no cansados, Rey, de las fatigas,
Miserias y trabajos ya passados,
Cuia grandeza es lástima deshecha
Se quede para siempre, sepultada
En materia tan llena y tan honrrosa,
De hechos hazañosos rebocando,[8]
En campo tan vizarro y tan tendido
Quanto no fue possible más tenderse.
Pues dexando, señor, aquesto en vanda,
Que pide muy gran pluma lo que encubre,
Como el despacho bueno de vna cosa
Promete a la que viene buen sucesso,
Y más quando convienen en los fines
Para que son las dos faborecidas,
Viendo quan bien el Conde despachaba
Aquesta brava entrada que hemos dicho,
Todos más alentados y esforzados
Vn próspero sucesso conozido
De todas nuestras causas esperamos.
Y assí el Gobernador sólo aguardaba
No más que a sus despachos confirmados,
Y como aquel primero Padre[9] a solas
No pudo ser Iglesia lebantada,
Más que principio della conocido,
Porque ninguna cosa le faltase
Pidió le diessen Religiosos graves,
De buena vida y fama, pues con ellos,
Más que con fuerza de armas, pretendía
Serviros, gran señor, en esta entrada
Y alibiaros la carga de los hombros
Que es fuerza sustentéis mientras el mundo
Nuestra ley sacrosanta no guardare,
Estando todo vnido y congregado[10]
Debajo de vn Pastor y de vn rebaño.
Por cuia justa causa fue nombrado
Por Comisario y Delegado illustre,
Con plena potestad de aquel monarca,
Iuez vniversal de todo el mundo,[11]
Fray Rodrigo Durán, varón prudente

At last these daring ones returned
To your New Spain, where many men,
And famous Spaniards, who had wished
35 To arm and aid the expedition
Were devastated, ruined quite,
But still untired, lord, by the fatigues
And miseries and labors experienced,
Whose greatness 'tis a shame it should be lost
40 And so remain forever thus interred
Material so full and honorable,
Fair bursting with extraordinary deeds,
In a field so resplendent and so large
That 'twere impossible to increase it more.
45 But leaving, lord, all this aside,
That needs a mighty pen to cover it,
As the timely handling of a thing
Doth promise good success to what ensues,
And more when the ends fully coincide
50 For which both have been inaugurated,
Seeing how well the Count sent off
That expedition brave, as we have said,
All most encouraged and inspired
We hoped to have for this our cause
55 A known and prosperous success.
And so the Governor did only await
For confirmation of his grant,
And as that Father first[6] alone
Could not be a whole Church established,
60 But known beginning of it,
So that there might be nothing lacking,
He asked that serious monks be sent,
Men of good life and fame, because with them,
More than by force of arms, he might
65 Attempt to serve you, lord, upon this expedition
And ease from off your shoulder that burden
Which needs must be you bear while this our world
Still doth not keep our law most sacrosanct,
Being all united, congregated,
70 'Neath one Shepherd, of one flock.
For which proper cause was named
As Commissary and illustrious Delegate,
With the full powers of that monarch,
Universal Judge of all the world,[7]
75 Fray Rodrigo Durán, a prudent man
And greatly learned in things of government;

8. Probable errata del original por "rebosando."
9. Se refiere, probablemente, al Padre Niza, aunque podría pensarse también en San Pedro.
10. La reproducción mexicana trae "congredado."
11. El papa.

6. The reference appears to be to Saint Peter, but it might also apply, if only New Mexico is considered, to Fray Marcos de Niza.
7. The reference is to the Pope.

Y en cosas de gobierno gran supuesto;[12]
Y por el tribunal del santo Oficio
Entró con santo esfuerzo trabajando
El buen fray Diego Márquez, perseguido
De aquellos luteranos, por quien vino
A ser primero movedor y el todo
De todo aqueste campo lebantado.
Vino fray Baltasar y fray Christóbal
De Salazar, en letras eminente,
Y con ellos vinieron otros Padres
De singular virtud y claro exemplo.
Y como apenas llega el bien que viene
Quando cien mil disgustos nos fatigan,
Resuelto ya el Virrey en despacharnos,
Vbo de reformar algunas cosas,
Por parecerle justo se alterasen,
Que estaban ya tratadas y assentadas
En razón de franquezas y essenciones[13]
A nuevos pobladores concedidas.
Y como la estrecheza y escaseza
De libre libertad y nobles fueros
Es la que más aflige y más lastima
A los hidalgos pechos que se meten
Por medio de las picas enemigas
De vuestra Real corona y allí rinden
Las vidas y las almas por serviros,
Llevaron con grandíssimo disgusto
Todos los más del campo trabajado
Esta reformación que el Conde hizo,
Diziendo en los corrillos y en la plaza
Que lo vna vez tratado y assentado
No era ley ni justicia se alterase,
Principalmente abiendo sido el pacto
Con ligítima parte celebrado,
Por cuia causa todos sus haziendas
Abían ya deshecho y consumido
Por cumplir sus assientos ya assentados[14]
Con su Rey natural, cuia palabra
Era fuerza sin quiebra se cumpliese
Y que imbiolablemente se guardase,
Pues que, en bajo lugar constituido
El hombre o en el más alto lebantado,
Tener de Rey palabra y mantenerla
Era lo que illustraba y lebantaba

And for the tribunal of the Holy Office
There came with holy effort laboring
The good Fray Diego Márquez, persecuted
80 By those same Lutherans,[8] for which he came
To be the one prime mover and the soul
Of all that lofty camp.
There came Fray Baltazar, Fray Cristóbal
De Salazar, the eminent in letters,
85 And with them came other Fathers
Of singular virtue and high example.
And as the good that comes hardly arrives
Before a hundred thousand evils wear us out,
The Viceroy, now resolved to send us off,
90 Had to reform some things,
For it seemed just to him to alter them,
That were now settled and agreed upon
In matters of exemption and of freedom
Conceded to new settlers.
95 And as the narrow bounds and scarcity
Of real free liberty and noble privilege
Is that which most afflicts and injures most
The noble hearts who place themselves
Within the stroke of pikes of enemies
100 Unto your Royal crown and there give up
Their lives and souls to serve you,
The most of that laborious camp
Received with most profound distaste
This reformation that the Count did make,
105 Saying in groups and in the marketplace
That what was once set down, agreed upon,
'Twas neither law nor justice that it change,
The agreement in the first place being made,
Agreed upon, by parties authorized,
110 Because of which they'd broken up
And spent all their estates
To fulfill their agreements previously made
With him, their natural King, whose word
'Twas necessary be fulfilled, and with no breaking,
115 And thusly should be inviolably kept,
Since, were a man placed in a lowly state
Or to the very highest raised,
To keep and to maintain his word, as he were King,
Was that which made him famous and did elevate
120 The clear resplendence of his person.

12. Supuesto = autoridad.

13. Franquezas y essenciones = franquicias y exenciones, derechos y libertades.

14. El gusto estilístico de la época por la aliteración barroco-conceptista explica el uso, aunque no excesivamente frecuente, de este tipo de expresión, en que "assientos" vale por contratos y "assentados" viene a significar acordados.

8. This Márquez was the priest referred to earlier as having been a prisoner in the English court.

El claro resplandor de su persona.
Y assí, todos rebueltos y alterados,
Maldiciendo la entrada se quejaban,
Diziendo los abían engañado
Y echádolos por puertas[15] ya perdidos.
Y como por ley justa en la milicia
Las armas se suspenden quando tocan
A retirar, assí fue retirando
Don Iuan y su teniente a los soldados,
Frenando sus disgustos de manera
Que todos sossegados concedieron
Con lo que el Conde hizo, por dezirles
El pobre caballero lastimado
Que con acuerdo santo y con justicia
Fue todo aquello hecho y ordenado.
Y como en el inchado mar soberbio
Sobre vna gran resaca otra rebienta
Y en la tendida plaia se deshace
En blanca espuma toda conbertida,
No de otra suerte vino rebentando
Con deshecha tormenta y terremoto
Vna gran sierra de agua lebantada
Imputando a don Iuan a grandes vozes
No menos que de aleve a la corona
Con que ceñís, señor, las altas sienes.
Mas apenas llegó quando la vimos
Toda deshecha, llana y quebrantada
En la inocente roca donde quiso
Quedar en blanca espuma conbertida,
Color de la inocencia que tenía
Aquél que pretendió manchar sin culpa.
Y como siempre arrima algún consuelo
La magestad inmensa al afligido,
Y más si con esfuerzo sufre y passa
El peso del trabajo que descarga,
Assí vimos que vino gran consuelo
Por todo vuestro campo, ya rendido
Con vn turbión de cosas que la invidia
Y fuerza de mentira a boca llena,
Sin género de rienda, publicaban
Por sólo deshazerlo y destruyrlo.
Mas poco les valió, porque tras desto
Quiso vuestro Virrey hazer despacho,
Mandando que don Lope[16] se partiese
Y como su teniente despachase
A todo aqueste campo, y que hiziesse
Visita general de gente y armas

And so, all angered, upset,
Cursing the expedition, they complained,
Saying that they had been deceived
And, ruined now, been abandoned.
And as by proper law in military use   125
Fighting's suspended when retreat doth sound,
Don Juan and his lieutenant did begin
To draw away the soldiers,
Curbing their ill-humor in such a sort
That, all appeased, they did admit   130
What the Count did to them,
The poor, grieved gentleman saying to them
That with holy accord and justice
All this was done and ordered.
And as the proud and swelling sea   135
Breaks, one great surge upon another,
And on the beach disintegrates,
Converted into snowy foam,
Not otherwise there came and broke,
With earthquake and with broken torment,   140
A watery mountain huge and high,
Imputing to Don Juan with mighty voice
No less than treachery against the crown
With which you gird, O lord, your lofty brows.
But hardly had it come when we did see   145
It all dashed flat and broken up
Upon the rock of innocence where it chose to
Remain, converted into snowy foam,
Color of the innocence that he
It tried to blame, though stainless, had.   150
And as the Divine Majesty doth ever grant
Some need of consolation to the afflicted one,
And more if he with strength doth bear, endure,
The weight of burden that he carries,
So we saw a great consolation come   155
To all your camp, already broken down
By force of lies by mouthfuls
Spread with no sort of restraint
Only to break it up, destroy it.
But little they availed, for after this   160
Your Viceroy deemed it proper to make haste,
Ordering Don Lope[9] to set forth
And haste, as his lieutenant, unto all the camp
And, coming there, that he should make
A general inspection, both of folk and arms,   165
And also test the quality and quantity
Of all equipment furnished by

15. Echádolos por puertas = abandonádoles.
16. Don Lope de Ulloa. Sobre su inspección, véase Villagrá, *Historia*, edición de Junquera, 140.

9. Don Lope de Ulloa. For documentary evidence of his visit of inspection, see Villagrá, *Historia*, Junquera edition, 140.

Y que también hiziesse cala y cata[17]
De todos los pertrechos ofrecidos
De parte de don Iuan y sus agentes;
Y que si lleno todo lo hallasse,
Que libremente luego permitiesse
Hiziesse su jornada y la acabasse;
Y que Antonio Negrete, secretario,
Hiziesse aquel despacho por la pluma.[18]
Para todo lo qual mandó viniesse
Francisco de Esquibel por comisario,
Con cuios oficiales quiso el Conde,
Para más animar aquesta entrada,
Escrebir a don Iuan con gran regalo,
Iuzgándole por prático en las cosas
De aquella grande impressa que llevava,
Suplicándole, con esto, a Dios le diesse
Tan próspero sucesso y buen viage,
Qual siempre desseaba que viniessen
Por las illustres prendas y las partes
Que su persona y deudos merecían.
Y qual aquél que con señales claras
La fuerza de su intento nos descubre,
Assi vuestro Virrey quiso advertirle
Que más por cumplimiento del oficio
Que por sospecha alguna que tuviesse
Del pleno cumplimiento de su assiento
Mandaba que don Lope le tomase
Visita general, y que esperaba
Que todo lo tenía tan cumplido
Que assí para el[19] don Iuan la diligencia
Vendría tan colmada y tan honrrosa
Como[20] para el descargo del oficio
Que de vuestro Virrey exercitaba.
Y con esto también le fue diziendo
Otras muchas caricias regaladas
Con que contentos todos estimaron
Su próspera fortuna y buena andanza,
Cuio sabor gallardo bien mostraron,
Solenizando fiestas y torneos
Quinientos buenos hombres esforzados
Que para aquesta entrada se juntaron,
Todos soldados viejos conocidos
Y entre bárbaras armas señalados.
Mas como siempre el tiempo faborable
Desaparece y queda surto[21] en calma

Don Juan or by his agency;
And, if he should find all quite correct,
170 He then should freely give him leave
To make his journey and to finish it;
And that Antonio Negrete, the secretary,
Should write down that permit in pen and ink.
For all which things he ordered there should come
175 Francisco de Esquibel as deputy.
With these officers the Count did choose
To write unto Don Juan with great politeness,
Saying he judged him skillful in the things
Of that great enterprise he led,
180 And, with this, praying God give
Such prosperous success and journey good
As he had always wished might come
To the illustrious virtues and standing
That his own person and his kinfolk merited.
185 And as one who shows in clear terms
The great strength of his intentions,
Your Viceroy thus wished to inform him
That, more in fulfillment of duty
Than for any suspicion that he had
190 As to the full compliance with the contract,
He was ordering Don Lope to perform
A general inspection, and he hoped
That he would find all things so well fulfilled
That the act would be for Don Juan
195 As fulfilling and honorable
As was the discharge of the duty
That as your Viceroy he exercised.
And, too, with this he also said
Many more things, polite, affectionate,
200 From which all men, contented, did esteem
Their fortunes prosperous and prospects good.
This splendid feeling they showed well,
By celebrating feasts and tournaments
Five hundred good, able men
205 Who had gathered for this expedition,
All well-known old soldiers
And signalized by feats of arms 'gainst barbarians.
But, as always, favorable winds
Do disappear and in calm peace is left
210 Who always, durable, remains;
After all this that we have said,
Much time now having passed,

---

17. Cala y cata = inspección.
18. Tomara por escrito lo negociado.
19. Probable errata del original al incluir este "el" que hace largo el verso y complica indebidamente el sentido.
20. Se ha de entender un implícito "requerido."
21. Surto = tranquilo.

Aquél que permanece siempre estable,
Después de todo aquesto que hemos dicho
Abiendo mucho tiempo ya passado,   215
Llegó luego vn correo con gran priessa
Pidiendo albricias[22] por el buen despacho
De las nuevas alegres que traía
De vuestro Visorrey, en que mandaba
Que luego todo el campo se aprestase   220
Y que la noble entrada prosiguiesse.
Y como está más cerca del engaño
Aquél que está más fuera de sospecha,
Assi fue que el correo, assegurado,[23]
Con gran contento entró y dio su pliego,   225
El qual se abrió en secreto y con recato
Que ninguno supiesse ni entendiesse
Lo que el cerrado pliego allí traía.
Y como no ay secreto tan oculto
Que al fin no se revele y se nos muestre,   230
El que en aqueste pliego se encerraba,
Contra las buenas nuevas que el correo
Con inociencia a todos quiso darnos,
Sin quitar vna letra ni añidirla,
Quiero con atención aquí escribirla.   235

There then arrived a courier in hot haste,
Seeking reward for the great speed he'd made
With the good news he brought
From your Viceroy, in which he ordered
The whole camp should immediately set out
And should pursue the noble exploration.
And as deceit is always nearest him
Who is the furthest from suspicion,
So it was the reassuring messenger,
All being content, did enter and give o'er his letter,
Which was opened in secret and with caution
So that none might know or understand
What that closed sheet brought there.
And as there is no secret so well hid
That at the end 'tis not revealed and shown to us,
I wish to write here with all care,
Taking away no letter, adding none,
What was enclosed in that packet,
Contrary to the good news that the messenger
Most innocently wished to give us.

EL REY

ONDE de Monte Rey, pariente, mi Virrey Gobernador y Capitán General de la nueva España, o a la persona, o personas, a cuyo cargo fuere el gobierno della: abiendo visto la carta que me escribistes, en veynte de diziembre del año passado, en que tratáys del assiento que el Virrey don Luys de Velasco, vuestro antecessor, abía tomado con don Iuan de Oñate sobre el descubrimiento del nuevo México, y las causas porqué dezís os deteniades en la resolución, advirtiendo que convenía no aprobar el concierto, si acá se acudiesse a pedirlo por parte del dicho don Iuan de Oñate, hasta que me bolviessedes a escrebir, y consultándome por los de mi Real Consejo de las Indias, con ocasión de aberse ofrecido don Pedro Ponce de León, señor que disque es de la villa de Bailén, a hazer el dicho descubrimiento, e determinado que se suspenda la execución de lo capitulado con el dicho don Iuan de Oñate. Y assí os mando no permitáis que haga la entrada ni la prosiga si la obiere comenzado, sino que se entretenga, hasta que yo provea y mande lo que me pareciere convenir, de que se os

THE KING

THE Count of Monte Rey, my relative, my Viceroy, Governor and Captain General of New Spain, or to the person or persons in whose charge the government of it may be: having seen the letter which you wrote me on the twentieth of December of the past year, in which you deal with the contract which the Viceroy Don Luis de Velasco, your predecessor, had made with Don Juan de Oñate concerning the discovery of New Mexico, and the reasons for which you say you delayed in carrying it out, noting that it did not suit you to approve the agreement, if any should come here to ask it on behalf of the said Don Juan de Oñate, until you had written to me, and consulted me through my Royal Council of the Indies, because Don Pedro Ponce de León, a gentleman whom they say is from the town of Bailén, had offered to make the said discovery, I have determined to suspend what had been agreed upon with the said Don Juan de Oñate. And so I command you not to permit him to make entry, nor to pursue it if he shall have commenced it, but that he wait until I may

---

22. Albricias = recompensa al portador de noticias.
23. Assegurado = asegurado, tranquilo.

avisará con brevedad. Fecha en Azeca, a ocho de Mayo de mil quinientos y noventa y seys años. Yo el Rey, por mandado del Rey nuestro señor, Iuan de Ibarra.

Tras cuia cédula, para más fuerza embió el mandamiento que se sigue:

Mandamiento del Virrey

DON Gaspar de Zúñiga y Azevedo, Conde de Monte Rey, señor de las casas y estado de Biedma y Vlloa, Virrey, lugar teniente y Capitán General de su Magestad en esta nueva España, y Presidente de la Real Audiencia y Chancillería que en ella reside: A vos don Lope de Vlloa, Capitán de mi guarda, a quien cometí la vista tocante a la muestra y averiguación del cumplimiento del assiento que con don Iuan de Oñate está tomado acerca la jornada del descubrimiento, pacificación, y conversión de las Provincias del nuevo México, con nombramiento de mi Lugar teniente, para prevenir, oviar, y castigar las desórdenes y excesos que los soldados y gente de la dicha jornada hiziere en el tránsito e camino deste viage: Sabed que por cédula del Rey nuestro señor, a mí dirigida, dada en Azeca a ocho de Mayo deste año de mil y quinientos e noventa y seys, se me manda y ordena no permita que el dicho don Iuan de Oñate haga la entrada del dicho nuevo México, ni la prosiga si la vbiere comenzado, sino que se entretenga hasta que su Magestad provea y mande lo que le pareciere convenir, y que desto me embiará aviso con brevedad, porque entre tanto su Magestad a determinado se suspenda la execución de lo capitulado con el dicho don Iuan de Oñate, según todo consta de la dicha Real cédula original que con este mi mandamiento vos embío. Y porque conviene que conste al dicho don Iuan de Oñate lo que su Magestad manda, para que lo guarde y cumpla, os mandamos notifiquéis y hagáis notificar al dicho don Iuan de Oñate la dicha Real cédula original y ansí mismo esta mi orden y mandamiento, para que lo guarde y cumpla como en él se contiene. Para lo qual, en nombre de su Magestad y mío, como Virrey, lugar teniente suyo, y Capitán general supremo desta nueva España y de las Provincias y jornada del nuevo México, mando al dicho don Iuan de Oñate que, guardándola y cumpliéndola, luego que este mi mandamiento por vos le sea notificado y hecho notificar haga alto y no passe de la parte y lugar donde se le notificare, ni consienta passar la gente que tiene lebantada, ni los bastimientos, municiones, y bagajes, ni otra cosa alguna, ni prosiga la dicha jornada, antes la sobresea y entretenga hasta ver nueva orden de su

provide and order what may seem to me to be suitable, of which I shall briefly advise. Done at Azeca, the eighth of May, one thousand five hundred and ninety-six. The King. By order of the King, our lord: Juan de Ybarra.

After which decree, for greater effect, he sent the order which follows:

Order of the Viceroy

DON Gaspar de Zúñiga y Acevedo, Count of Monte Rey, lord of the houses and estates of Biedma and Ulloa, Viceroy, Lieutenant and Captain General of His Majesty in this New Spain and President of the Royal Audience and Chancellory which are therein: to you Don Lope de Ulloa, Captain of my guard to whom I committed the opinion concerning the investigation and verification of the fulfillment of the contract made with Don Juan de Oñate concerning the journey made for the discovery, pacification, and conversion of the province of New Mexico, with designation as my lieutenant to prevent, obviate, and punish the disorders and excesses which the soldiers and people of the aforesaid exploring party might commit in transit and on the road of this journey, know that by decree of the King, our lord, directed to me, given at Azeca, the eighth of May of this year one thousand five hundred and ninety-six, I am commanded and ordered not to permit that the said Don Juan de Oñate make entry into the said New Mexico, nor pursue it if he shall already have commenced it, until His Majesty may provide and order what may seem best to him, and that he will send me that news shortly, because meanwhile His Majesty has determined that there be suspended the execution of the agreement with the aforesaid Don Juan de Oñate, according to the contents of the original Royal Decree which I send you with this my order. And because it is proper that the said Don Juan de Oñate should know what His Majesty commands, that he may keep and fulfill it, I order that you notify and cause to be notified the said Don Juan de Oñate of the original Royal Decree and likewise of this my order and command, that he may keep and fulfill it according to its contents. For which, in the name of His Majesty and my own, as Viceroy, His Lieutenant and Captain General supreme of this New Spain and of the Provinces and expedition to New Mexico, I order the said Don Juan de Oñate that, keeping it and fulfilling it, as soon as this my order shall be transmitted to him by you and he be caused to know it, he shall halt and not go from the region and place where he shall be notified of it, nor permit the people he has raised to go,

Magestad y mía, en su Real nombre; y en defecto de no lo cumplir, en caso que passe adelante contra lo proveído en la dicha Real cédula, y por mi mandado, en este mi mandamiento, sino fuere algunas pocas leguas, y con expreso permiso vuestro, por escrito, para mejor entretener la dicha gente, desde luego en el dicho Real nombre, reboco y anulo los títulos, patentes y condutas, provisiones, comissiones y otros recaudos que en nombre de su Magestad se han dado al dicho don Iuan de Oñate y a los Capitanes y oficiales que él nombró para la dicha jornada y para el efeto della, para que en manera alguna no vsen ni puedan vsar dellos, con apercibimiento que lo contrario haziendo, no se le cumplirá cosa que en su fabor esté otorgada en el dicho assiento y capitulaciones, y se procederá contra sus personas y vienes, como contra transgressores de las órdenes e mandatos de su Rey e señor natural, y como contra vassallos rebeldes y desleales, vsurpadores del derecho de los descubimientos, entradas y conquistas de Provincias a su Magestad pertenecientes; que para los processos que en razón desta inobidiencia, rebeldía y delito tan grave se ovieren de hazer, desde luego los llamo, cito y emplazo para que dentro de sesenta días de la notificación deste mandamiento parescan personalmente en esta Ciudad de México en las casas Reales della, donde es mi morada, ante mi persona, y las de los Iueces que para el conocimiento de las dichas causas yo nombrare, donde pareciendo serán oydos y se les hará justicia, y no pareciendo, en ausencia suya, y por su rebeldía se procederá y se les notificaran los autos en estrados[24] y les pararán tanto perjuizio como si en sus propias personas se les notificasen. Lo qual mando como dicho es, no sólo al dicho don Iuan, sino a los Capitanes, soldados, oficiales y gente que va a la dicha jornada en qualquier manera, y a cada vno dellos, con los dichos apercibimientos y penas, citaciones y señalamiento de estrados: y que éste mi mandamiento, si os pareciere, se notifique a los Capitanes y oficiales del dicho campo que están prestos para la dicha jornada, y luego que os paresca, para que venga a noticia dellos y de los demás soldados y gente dicha, y hagáis echar vando público para que se publique, declarando a todos los dichos oficiales, soldados y gente que en qualquier manera van a la jornada que so pena de la vida y perdimiento de vienes y de ser, como dicho es, abidos por vassallos rebeldes y desleales a su Magestad, no passen adelante su viage, y en razón dello, no sigan ni obedescan al dicho don Iuan. Y assí lo proveio e mando que este mi mandamiento vaya refrendado de Iuan Martínez de Guillestigui, mi Secretario, y haga tanta fee como si por gobernación fuesse despachado, por quanto en virtud de la Real cédula particular que yo tengo para despachar en los casos que me pareciere con Secretarios míos mando, por justos respectos, que el dicho

nor the provisions, munitions, and baggage, nor any other thing, nor pursue the aforesaid journey, but rather delay and restrain it until seeing a new order of His Majesty and of myself, in his Royal name. And in case he may not comply, in case he may go forward against what is provided in the aforesaid Royal Decree and what I have commanded in this my order, unless it be but a few leagues and with your express permission, in writing, to better maintain the aforesaid people, from thence forward, in the aforesaid Royal name, I do revoke and annul the titles, patents and conducts, provisions, commissions and other gifts which have, in the name of His Majesty, been given to the aforesaid Don Juan de Oñate and to the Captains and officers whom he has named for the aforesaid journey and for the purpose of it, so that they shall not in any way use, nor be able to use them, observing that by doing the contrary there will not be fulfilled toward them anything which has been granted in their favor in the aforesaid contract and capitulations, and that proceedings will be drawn up against their persons and their property as against transgressors of the orders and mandates of their King and natural overlord and as against rebel and disloyal vassals, usurpers of the rights of discovery, entry, and conquest of Provinces belonging to His Majesty; that for the processes of law which by reason of this disobedience, rebellion, and so grave crime, may have to be instituted, I immediately summon, cite, and call upon them that within sixty days after the notification of this order they appear personally in the City of Mexico, in the Royal buildings therein where my residence is, before my person and those of the judges that for the recognition of the aforesaid cases I shall appoint, where appearing they shall be heard and justice shall be done them, and not appearing, in their absence, they will be proceeded against because of their rebellion, and the decrees will be announced to them in the courtroom and they shall carry as much force as though they had been notified of them in their proper persons. The which I command not only the aforesaid Don Juan but also the Captains, soldiers, officers, and people who go on the aforesaid journey in any way, and each of them, with the aforesaid warnings and penalties, citations, and indications of courts; and that this my order, if you wish, be shown the Captains and officers of the aforesaid camp who are bent on the aforesaid journey as soon as you wish, that it may come to the notice of the rest of the soldiers and aforesaid people; you shall have a proclamation made, that it be made public, declaring to all the aforesaid officers, soldiers, and people who in any capacity go on the expedition that under penalty of death and loss of property, and being, as is said, considered as rebellious vassals and disloyal to His Majesty, they shall not continue their journey

mi Secretario lo refrende. Fecho en México, a doze de Agosto de mil quinientos e noventa y seys años. El Conde de Monte Rey. Por mandado de su señoría, Iuan Martínez Guillestigui.

Con estas notificaciones, el Gobernador quedó suspenso:
y porque yo lo estoy, quiero al siguiente canto remitirme.

further, and because of it they shall not follow nor obey the said Don Juan. And I provide and order that this my command be countersigned by Juan Martínez Guillestegui, my Secretary, and be obeyed as done by government, wherefore in virtue of the special Royal Decree which I have to dispatch in such cases as may seem proper to me by my Secretaries I order for good reason that my aforesaid Secretary countersign this. Done in Mexico, the twelfth of August of the year one thousand five hundred and ninety-six. The Count of Monte Rey. By command of his lordship, Juan Martínez de Guillestegui.

At this news the Governor was amazed, and because I am also,
I wish to slacken until the next canto.

Canto Octavo

*DE LA RESPVESTA QUE DIO DON IVAN OÑATE a la
notificación que se le hizo y de la prudencia y discreción con que
habló a todo el campo, y fiestas que se hizieron de contento, y
del generoso ofrecimiento de Iuan Guerra su teniente, y de otros
trabajos que a estas fingidas alegrías sucedieron.*

¿QVIEN vio jamás, señor, en este mundo
Caduco, fragil, débil, movedizo,
Sin notable discordia paz alegre,
Gustoso rato sin tristeza amarga,
Manso sossiego sin pavor terrible,
Y, en fin, noble bonanza y tiempo bueno
Sin áspera tormenta y gran borrasca?
¡O triste condición de mundo breve,
Y corto entendimiento de mortales
Si ciegos no conocen sus mudanzas,
Sus Lunas, sus enrredos, sus traiciones,
Sus trazas, sus palabras, sus rebozos,
Tanto más encubiertos quanto sienten
Los pechos de los nobles más cenzillos!¹
Abiendo, pues, la invidia con sus redes
Persuadido al Virrey porque alcanzase²
La cédula Real que abemos dicho,
El pobre caballero lastimado
De aquel nuevo accidente, y ofendido,
Qual suele con fortuna serle fuerza
Sufrir al que navega golfos bravos,
Assí, con grande esfuerzo y con paciencia,
Vn ancho y venenoso mar bebiendo
De mil amargas hieles enojosas,
Temeroso que todo se esparciese
Con novedad tan grande, y se acabase,
Por atajar el pasmo, que costaba
Más de quinientos mil ducados largos,
Con toda diligencia quiso luego
Acabar con³ don Lope le intimase,
Con el mayor secreto que pudiesse,
La voluntad Real y el mandamiento
Que por vuestro Virrey le fue embiado.
Pues haziéndose assí, sin más acuerdo,
Qual suele responder con grato fruto
La fértil sementera bien labrada,
Aquellos dos escritos fue tomando
Y, con grande respecto, qual si fueran

---

1. Cuanto más sencillos perciben ser los pechos de los nobles.
2. Alcanzase = llegase.
3. Acabar con = conseguir de.

Canto VIII

*Of the reply Don Juan de Oñate gave to the notification made to
him and of the prudence and discretion with which he spoke to
all the camp, and the fiestas of satisfaction that were held, and
of the generous offer of Juan Guerra, his lieutenant, and of
other labors which followed these feigned celebrations.*

WHO ever saw, O lord, within this world
Enfeebled, fragile, weak, inconstant,
Joyous peace without marked discord,
Happy times without as bitter sorrow,
5   Pleasant calm without terrible fear,
Or, finally, noble prosperity and weather good
Without rough storms and great disturbances?
Oh, sad condition of this little world
And comprehension small of mortal folk
10 If, blind, they do not know its changes,
Its moons, its tricks, its betrayals,
Its schemes, its words, its pretexts,
The more concealed the more they feel
That noblest breasts are those most simple!
15 Well, envy with its snares having persuaded
The Viceroy to make applicable
The Royal Decree, just as we have said,
The poor knight being wounded sore
By this new accident, offended,
20 As fortune makes it necessary for
The man to suffer who would sail rude gulfs,
So with great effort and with patience,
Drinking a wide and poisonous sea
Of thousand bitter annoyances,
25 Fearful that all would be dispersed
By so grave news, and all would be ended,
To avoid the panic, that would cost
More than five hundred thousand ducats broad,
He then tried with all diligence
30 To induce Don Lope to impart to him
As secretly as he possibly could,
The Royal will and also the commands
Sent to him by your Viceroy.
So, doing this, without further agreement,
35 As the sown field's accustomed to respond,
When worked well, with grateful fruits,
He soon took those two writings
And with great respect, as if they were

Coronas principales de dos Reynos,
Fueron en su cabeza lebantados.⁴

Y buelto en vn gran monte de paciencia,
Tocándoles los labios, fue diziendo
Que aunque por justas causas y razones
Pudiera suplicar⁵ de aquel mandato
Por los daños y grande inconveniente
Que de perderse el campo se seguía,
Con todos sus pertrechos y bagajes,
Que tanta hazienda y sangre le costaban,
Que no quería hazerlo ni pensarlo,
Mas antes, como leal vassallo vuestro,
Con suma reverencia obedecía
La cédula Real y mandamiento
Según que en ella y él se contenían,
Y que inviolablemente guardaría
Todo quanto allí se le ordenaba,
Sin que vna sola letra quebrantase.

Y como todas estas diligencias
Con gran silencio fuessen acabadas,
Estaba todo el campo tan suspenso
Quanto ansioso por ver qué contenía
El buen despacho y pliego que el correo
Con tan grande alegría abía traído.
Y para quitar dudas y sospechas,
Qual suelen las castíssimas abejas
Que en sabroso licor vemos convierten
Aquello que es amargo y desabrido,
Assí salió don Iuan, la boca dulze,
Diziendo a grandes voces con contento:
"Señores compañeros, ¿qué hacemos?
Entremos, y a la entrada no durmamos,⁶
Que a pesar de fortuna estamos todos
Con notables ventajas despachados."
Oyendo los soldados esta nueva,
Qual suelen con aplauso dar gran grita
Los verdes años, todos rebozando
Aquel sumo contento que nos muestran
Al pretender de Cáthedras honrrosas,⁷
Assí la soldadesca toda junta
Vn alarido fuerte fue subiendo,
Y a fuer de caballeros hijos dalgo,

The chief crowns of the two Kingdoms,
40 He touched them to his forehead.¹
And, turned to a mountain of great patience,
Touching them to his lips, went on to say
That though for just causes and reasons just
He might appeal from that mandate,
45 Because of damages and inconveniences great
That sure would follow ruin of the camp
With all its munitions and its baggage,
Which had cost him so much of blood and of estate,
That he wished not to do it or to think of it,
50 But rather, as your loyal vassal, he
With the highest reverence would obey
The Royal order and command
According to their contents, and he would
Inviolably keep all that
55 In them was ordered to be done,
Nor break a single letter of them all.
And as these things were done
And finished with great discretion,
The whole camp was in great suspense
60 And anxious to behold what was contained
In the dispatch and packet good the messenger
Had brought with so much joy.
And so, to quiet doubts, suspicions,
As the very chaste bees do make their custom
65 To convert into liquor savory
That which is bitter, disagreeable,
Don Juan came forward with sweet lips,
Saying aloud, with much content:
"Gentlemen, companions, what shall we do?
70 Let's proceed and, proceeding, not relax,
For, spite of bad luck, we are all
Sent forward with most notable advantages."²
The soldiers, hearing then this news,
As all the undergraduates, enthusiastic,
75 Use to applaud, with great shout
Showing to us their great content,
During the contests for professorships,³
So the soldiery all together
Set up a lusty shout,
80 And as knights and noblemen,

4. Fórmula de acatamiento a una orden real.
5. Suplicar = recurrir, apelar.
6. Parece indicar que una vez en funciones no se dejen relajar; pero si se tiene en cuenta el frecuente uso de terminología marinera en toda la épica americana, puede pensarse que les pide que no dejen estropearse, malograrse, la expedición.
7. Recuerdo de la vida universitaria, del proceso de oposiciones a cátedra.

1. The lifting of the royal decree above one's head was a formula of submission to its dictates.
2. Don Juan's words here, suggesting they continue, when he had agreed he would not defy the king's order, were clearly intended only to maintain the morale of the camp
3. This appears to refer to the public contests, *oposiciones*, in which the students participated in the selection of university professors. It is a recollection, probably, of Villagrá's days at the University of Salamanca.

Vizarros y galanes, se juntaron
En gallardos caballos animosos
Y después de vna gran carrera alegre
Vna vistosa escaramuza hizieron
Los más famosos hombres de a caballo
Por el maese de campo y gran sargento
Los dos valientes cuernos[8] gobernados,
Entre los quales, no con poco orgullo,
Vizarro, el General aquella fiesta
En vn bravo caballo celebraba.
Y luego que cansados suspendieron
El regozijo y gusto, con descuido,
Qual aquel discretíssimo Zineas,
Que por su gran prudencia valió tanto
Como el valiente Pirro por la espada,[9]
Assí don Iuan, con rostro reportado,[10]
Alegre, prevenido y recatado,
Para mejor cubrir aquella herida
Que tanto le afligía y lastimaba,
El caballo enjaezado y enfrenado,
Luego que se apeó le dio en albricias,
Pagándole, al correo el buen despacho
Y presta diligencia con que vino.
Por cuio hecho, y otros, me parece
Los Fabios, Cipiones y Metellos,
Pompeio, Cilla, Mario ni Locullos,[11]
Y entre ellos Iulio César, no mostraron
En su tanto[12] más pecho a los trabajos,
Ni en ellos más discretos anduvieron,
Que aqueste illustre y alto caballero.
¡O discreción sagaz, qué bien pareces
Quando con buen aviso assí deslumbras
La vista más aguda y tracendida,[13]
Cerrando los caminos a las lenguas
En cosas de importancia mal sufridas!
No de otra suerte aquellos bravos Griegos
A los diestros Troianos engañaron
Quando el vello caballo dentro en Troia

Spirited, gallant, they assembled
On eager, pawing mounts
And, after a great, joyous race,
They had a showy skirmish
85   The most famous cavaliers,
The two valiant flanks being captained
The one by the Army Master and
The other by the Sergeant Major,
And 'mid them all the gallant General,
90   With great pride, brave and arresting,
Upon a fiery horse, did join the celebration.
And when they, tired, did suspend
Rejoicing and their pleasures, untroubled,
Like Zineas most discrete,
95   Who for his prudence great was worth as much
As Pyrrhus for his sword,[4]
Even so Don Juan, his visage well controlled,
Happy, cautious, and concealing much,
Better to cover up the wound
100   That so afflicted and so injured him,
His horse in fancy trappings and well reined,
As soon as he alighted, he presented a reward
Unto the messenger to pay his goodly haste
And the quick diligence with which he came.
105   For which deed, and for more, it seems to me
Not all the Favii, Scipii and Metelli,
Pompey, Sulla, Marius and Lucullus,[5]
And Julius Caesar, too, did show
Such heart as he to difficulties,
110   Nor in them more discretely acted
Than did this famous, lofty knight.
Oh, wise discretion, how good dost thou seem
When thou with good visage dost so deceive
The keenest and most piercing gaze,
115   Closing the way to babbling tongues,
In matters of importance hardly borne!
Not otherwise did the bold Greeks
Deceive the crafty Trojans on that day

8. Cuernos = alas de los cuerpos que simulaban la batalla.
9. Zineas, Cíneas, fue ministro de Pirro, rey de Epiro.
10. Reportado = comedido, controlado.
11. Fabios, familia romana que combatió sola a los veyanos; Cipiones, Escipiones, familia romana que produjo varios importantes generales; Metellos, Metelos, familia romana que produjo varios importantes cónsules y generales; Pompeio, Pompeyo, valiente jefe y general romano, principal rival de César; Cilla, Sila, general y dictador romano; Mario, rival principal del anterior; Locullos, Luculo, general romano a quien Pompeyo sucedió. Las vidas, para los que no formaran parte de la historia de España, se hallan en Livio, Plutarco y otros historiadores romanos que Villagrá conocería.
12. En su tanto = en su favor.
13. Tracendida = trascendida, perspicaz.

4. Zineas was minister to Pyrrhus, king of Epirus.
5. The Fabius family of Rome had at one time defended the city by itself; the Scipios, a Roman family that produced many important generals, consuls, and senators; the Metellus family of Rome did likewise; Pompey, a Roman general and Caesar's chief rival; Sulla and Marius, were Roman generals and rivals; Lucullus was a Roman general succeeded by Pompey. The biographies of all are found in Plutarch's *Parallel Lives* and Livy's *Annals,* in all probability read by the university educated Villagrá.

Fue dellos todos juntos recibido.[14]
Sabida, pues, la detención del campo
Por Iuan Guerra de Ressa,[15] su teniente,
A quien con diligencia y gran secreto
El mismo General quiso avisarle
Por ser su deudo y assí mismo dueño
De toda aquesta causa lebantada
Y vno de los vassallos importantes
Que ciñen noble espada en vuestras Indias,
Cuios agudos filos, a su costa,
Muchas fronteras grandes han guardado
Que gran suma de plata os han valido,
Sin el colmo excessivo que os ofrecen
De quintos sus haziendas cada vn año,
Pues como en gastar exercitado
Estaba ya, y curtido en bien serbiros
Aqueste franco y bravo caballero,
Qual illustre Iacob por la belleza
De la linda Rachel de nuevo quiso
Assentar con Labán[16] y darle gusto,
Sin mirar los serbicios ya passados,
Assí escibió a don Iuan con nuevos bríos
Que cien mil pesos largos le ofrecían
De fruto cada vn año sus haziendas,
Ganados y adqueridos por su lanza,
Que todos los gastase y consumiesse,
Mostrándose qual ámbar oloroso,
Que quanto más le afligen y deshazen
Más es su viva fuerza y gran flagrancia,
Y que en manera alguna no mostrase
La fuerza de su pecho vil flaqueza,
Porque él estaba allí que provehería
A todos los del campo de las cosas
Para poder valerse necessarias.
Y como el gran Ioseph quando previno
La gran fuerza de hambre que esperaba,[17]
Prevínole con tiempo que guardase
Todos los vastimientos que tuviesse
Y que en manera alguna los gastasen.
Por cuia justa causa agradecido,
Don Iuan le replicó con gran contento,
Haziendo mucha estima de su carta,
Respecto de ser hombre cuias obras

The beauteous horse was in Troy
120 By all, in crowds, received.[6]
The halting of the march being known
To Juan Guerra de Resa,[7] his lieutenant,
To whom with care and with great secrecy
The General himself imparted it,
125 As being kin to him as well as master, too,
Of all the goods that had been raised
And one among the vassals most important
Who wear a noble sword within your Indies,
The whetted edge of which, at his own cost,
130 Has guarded many great frontiers
That have to you been worth great sums of silver,
Beside the great wealth you receive,
Each year a fifth of his estates,
That frank and gallant gentleman,
135 Being practiced in wise spending and
Apt at serving you well,
As famous Jacob for the beauty great
Of beauteous Rachel would again
Agree with Laban, do his bidding, not
140 Regarding all he served him in the past,[8]
So he, with vigor new, did write Don Juan
To offer him a hundred thousand dollars,
A year's income from his estate,
Gained and acquired by his lance,
145 That he might spend, consume them all,
Showing himself like amber odorous,
Which, in proportion as it is destroyed,
Its living force and fragrance great is more,
And not to show within his forceful heart
150 Vile weakness, not in any way,
For he was there who would provide
For all the camp the many things
That might prove necessary.
Like Joseph great when he foresaw
155 The mighty threat of hunger yet to come,[9]
He advised him that there should be kept
All the supplies he had,
Not wasted be in any way.
Thankful for this just cause,
160 Don Juan replied to him with great content,
Holding his letter there in great esteem,

---

14. Virgilio, *Eneida* II, narra el incidente largamente.

15. Juan Guerra de Ressa, pariente de Oñate, organizador económico de la expedición, de la que nunca formó parte.

16. Labán, tras haber tenido sujeto a Jacob durante años, le ofreció la mano de Lía y no Raquel, con lo cual éste hubo de continuar su servicio durante más años (*Génesis* 29).

17. Ioseph, el José del Antiguo Testamento, que pronosticó las malas cosechas con lo que el faraón pudo prevenirse (*Génesis* 45).

6. Virgil (*Aeneid* II) narrates the incident with some detail.

7. Juan Guerra de Ressa, a relative of Oñate, was, although he never actually took part in it, the main economic backer of the expedition.

8. The story of Jacob, Laban, and Rachel is found in *Genesis* 29.

9. The story of Joseph and the Egyptian famines are found in *Genesis* 45.

Hizieron gran ventaja a sus palabras
En cosas de importancia y de vergüenza.
Y assi luego por orden de don Lope
Hizo alto con el campo en vnas minas,
De bastimentos faltas, montes y aguas,
Que llaman las del Casco, donde el Conde,
Despés de aber gran tiempo ya passado,
Mando segunda vez que le intimasen
La cédula Real y mandamiento
Para que con más fuerza se abstuviesse
Y aquella noble entrada no intentase,
De que podía estar bien descuidado
Por el grande respecto y reverencia
Con que don Iuan guardaba y acataba
Las cosas de justicia y sus ministros.
Y como suelen darse a los enfermos
Algunas medizinas con que alibian
La fuerza del dolor que los lastima,
Assi siempre el Virrey quiso escribirle
Que no llevase a mal lo que ordenaba,
Porque aunque estaba cierto no haría
Cosa con que manchase su persona,
Que, sin mirar aquesto, que entendiesse
Que por sola observancia de justicia,
Más que por otra cosa, se mandaba
Que aquellas diligencias se hiziessen,
Y que estuviesse cierto se dolía
De todos sus trabajos y disgustos.
Y assí, cual los arroyos que de passo
Refrescan sus Riberas y lebantan
Graciosas arboledas y las visten
De tembladoras hojas y entretejen
Diversidad de flores olorosas,
Amenos prados, frescos, deleitosos,
Y sombras apazibles, agradables,
No de otra suerte el Conde de contino
A nuestro General le entretenía.
Y qual si vn diamante fino fuera,
Cuia brava dureza empedernida
No ay riguroso golpe desmandado[18]
Que sin violencia alguna no resista,
Assi fue resistiendo y contrastando
Las poderosas hondas lebantadas,
Contra cuia braveza siempre vimos
Que regaladas cartas le embiaba,
Pidiéndole con veras se animase
En esforzar la gente ya cansada
Y del mucho esperar desesperada,

Because he was a man whose deeds
Would usually, by much, surpass his words
In matters important and of honor.
165 And so at once, by orders of Don Lope,
He made a halt with all the camp at mines,
Lacking in supplies, in water and wood,
Called of Casco, where the Count
After a long time had been passed,
170 Ordered a second time he be informed
About the Royal order and command
So that he might abstain more certainly
And not attempt the noble expedition,
Though he might well be free from care
175 Because of the respect and reverence
With which Don Juan kept and observed
The things of justice and its ministers.
And as 'tis use to give the sick
Some medicines that may alleviate
180 The strength of pain that tortures them,
The Viceroy, as always, chose to write
That he should not take what was ordered ill,
Because, though he was certain not to do
A thing by which his person might be stained,
185 That, despite all, he must understand
That this was ordered only to observe
The forms of justice and for nothing else,[10]
And that he should be certain he was pained
By all his disappointments and troubles.
190 As little brooks in passing do refresh
Their banks and make to grow
Whole graceful groves and clothe the same
With trembling leaves and interweave
Diversity of sweet-smelling flowers,
195 Pleasant meadows, and retreats
And pleasant, comfortable shades,
Not otherwise the Count, most continually,
Eased our General's pain.
And, as he were a diamond fine,
200 Whose strength and stony hardness doth resist
All blows, however hard they be,
And yet employs no violence,
So he resisted and withstood
The powerful, compelling waves,
205 Against whose fierceness we did see
That he remit good letters always,
Asking him sincerely to will himself
To hold the people, tired now
And desperate from waiting so long,

---

18. Desmandado = excesivo.

10. Curtis reduces his translation of four verses to three, which, nothing substantial being omitted, we let stand.

Si quería gozar del buen sucesso
Y dichoso remate de las cosas
Que tan grandes trabajos le costaban,
Y que aunque no podía dar seguro
Ni esperanzas calientes de remedio,
Que él esperaba en Dios con gran firmeza
Que vuestra Magestad[19] sería serbido
De tener en memoria sus trabajos
Y que sería possible enderezarse
La mal torzida suerte desgraciada.
Y con razón, señor, dixo torzida,
Porque como al principio, con cuidado,
Con zelo de serviros, fue estorbando,
Quando quiso después faborecernos
Fue fuerza obedecer vuestro mandato.[20]
Y assí viendo don Iuan que le era fuerza
Aber de padecer aquel trabajo,
Qual terníssimo Padre, lastimado,
Que a fuerza de dolor y de quebranto
Passa la furia del trabajo amargo
Que con violencia y fuerza le lastima
De ver sus caros hijos afligidos,
Por vna y otra parte destrozados,
No de otra suerte el noble caballero
Miraba todo el campo destruido,
También a su perlado[21] ya cansado,
Los pobres Religiosos mal parados,
La flaca soldadesca entretenida
Con vno y otro engaño dilatado
Y fuerza de palabras mal cumplidas,
La gente de servicio y oficiales,
Los niños inocentes y a sus madres,
Sugetos a vivir a campo abierto
Como si fueran vestias sin abrigo
Por los tendidos prados despoblados.
Miraba a su teniente,[22] cuio pecho,
Después de todo aquesto que hemos dicho,
Abiendo con valor y grande esfuerzo
Por tiempo de año y medio sustentado
A todo aqueste campo por disiertos
Y Páramos que anduvo entretenido,
Cómo la grosedad de sus haziendas
Estaba por mil partes derramada,
Viendo que se gastaba a manos llenas

210 If he would see the good outcome
And happy end to his affairs,
Which cost him so much labor.
And, though he could not give surety
Nor warm hope of a remedy,
215 That he trusted in God with firmness great
Your Majesty[11] would be so kind as hold
In memory his labors and that 'twould
Be possible to set once more aright
Our badly twisted, ill-set fate.
220 And, lord, he rightly called it twisted, for
Since at first he most carefully
Disturbed us in his zeal to serve you,
When afterward he wished to favor us
'Twas necessary we obey your[12] mandate.
225 So, Don Juan seeing that he must
Endure that suffering as well,
As a most tender father hurt,
By force of sorrow and of ruin, too,
Endures the fury of the bitter blow,
230 Although he's hurt by violence and force,
Seeing his children dear beset,
Destroyed on either hand,
Not otherwise the noble gentleman
Looked over all the camp, destroyed,
235 And also at its Prelate, tired now,
The poor monks, now in sorry state,
The soldiery, weak, only held
By trick on trick, now long drawn out,
And force of words but ill fulfilled,
240 The serving folk and officers,
The children innocent, their mothers,
Forced now to live in open camp,
As though they were but beasts without a home
Upon the spreading desert plains.
245 He looked at his lieutenant, whose brave heart,
After all this that we have told
Having, with valor and with effort great,
Maintained that whole camp for a year
And a half more through desert plains
250 Through which it had uselessly wandered, how
The greatness of his estates was now dispersed
Into a thousand parts,
Seeing 'twas spent by handfuls through

---

19. Villagrá parece olvidar, momentáneamente, que se refiere a
Felipe II, y no a su hijo, Felipe III, a quien está dedicado el poema.

20. Villagrá olvida otra vez era Felipe II, y no su hijo, el rey que
entonces funcionaba.

21. Perlado = prelado. Se refiere al comisario religioso.

22. Se refiere a Ressa.

11. Villagrá momentarily forgets that it was then the reign of
Philip II, not his son, Philip III, to whom he dedicated the poem and
to whom he directs himself.

12. Villagrá again mistakes Philip II for Philip III.

Por todo aqueste tiempo que hemos dicho.

Aqueste excesso vino a tanto extremo
Que no se vio soldado conocido
Que viendo hacienda suya²³ no dixesse
Esta hazienda es mía, y quando mucho,
Dezía nuestra, si eran dos aquéllos
Que dispensar querían de sus vienes.
Y como el tiempo todo lo deshaze,
Consume, desbarata y lo destruye,
Assi todos se fueron deshaziendo,
Por vna y otra parte derramando.
Viendo, pues, doña Eufemia, vna señora
De singular valor y grande esfuerzo,
Muger del Real Alférez²⁴ Peñalosa,
Hermosa por extremo y por extremo
De bello, lindo y claro entendimiento,
Que todos los del campo, ya cansados
Con tanta dilación, se despedían
Y que otros assimismo se ausentaban
Por no poder sufrir tan gran trabajo,
Qual aquella gallarda y noble dama
Que en medio de la cuesta memorable
De aquel soberbio Arauco no domado
El poco esfuerzo y triste cobardía
De toda vna Ciudad avergonzaba,²⁵
Assí esta gran matrona a grandes vozes
Dentro de la plaza de armas fue diziendo:
"Nobleza de soldados descuidados,
Dezidme, ¿en qué estimáis el noble punto
De aquellos corazones que mostrastes
Quando a tan dura guerra os ofrecistes
Dándonos a entender ser todo poco
Para harta²⁶ la fuerza y excelencia
De vuestros bravos ánimos gallardos,
Si agora sin empacho y sin vergüenza,
Qual si fuéradeis hembras, vais bolviendo
A cosa tan honrrosa las espaldas?
¿Qué cuenta es la que dais, siendo varones,
Desto que a vuestro cargo abéis tomado,
Si todo lo dexáis en estas tocas,
Que de ver tal vageza y tal afrenta
Afrentadas las siento ya caídas,
Llenas de deshonor y corrimiento
De ver en Españoles tal intento?

The whole of that time we have spoken of.

255 This excess went to such extremes
That there is not a soldier known
Who, seeing his property, would not have said
"This property is mine", or, at the most,
Others said "ours", if they were two
260 Who wished to spend his goods.
And just as everything by time
Is wrecked, consumed, undone, destroyed,
So all was being undone,
Being squandered at every turn.
265 Doña Eufemia, a dame of courage singular
And spirit great, the wife of the Royal Alferez,
Peñalosa, extremely beautiful and, too, unusual
For splendid, quick and clear mentality,
Seeing that all the camp, now quite worn out
270 By such delay, were leaving fast,
And others, likewise, were deserting us,
Being unable to endure such trials,
Like that gallant and noble dame
Who, on the summit of the memorable ridge¹³
275 Of that unconquered, proud Arauco,
Brought into shame the little strength
And sorry cowardice of all the city,
So this great matron in loud voice,
Within the drilling field, stated:
280 "Most noble misguided soldiers,
Tell me, of what good, the noble worth
Of those hearts that you showed
When offering yourselves for doughty war,
Having us understand all was a trifle to
285 The mighty force and excellence
Of your brave, gallant souls,
If now, without embarrassment or shame,
As you were women, you do turn
Your backs on work so honorable?
290 What reckoning will you give, being men,
Of what you took under your charge
If you leave all to these my coifs,¹⁴
Which, seeing such baseness, such insult,
I feel, insulted, falling down,
295 Full of dishonor and of shame
To see in Spaniards such intent?
When all be lost and we lack all,

---

23. Hacienda de Ressa.
24. El Real Alférez estaba oficialmente encargado de los reales estandartes.
25. Se refiere a doña Mencia del canto VII de *La Araucana*. Hay semejanza entre las palabras de la figura de Ercilla y las que dirá doña Eufemia.
26. Harta = mucha.

13. The reference is to Doña Mencia, sung by Ercilla, *La araucana* VII.
14. The coif, feminine wear, is used to designate femininity.

Quando todo se pierda y todo falte,
¿Ha de faltarnos tierra bien tendida
Y vn apazible río caudaloso
Donde vna gran Ciudad edifiquemos
A imitación y ejemplo de otros muchos
¿Que assí su fama y nombre eternizaron?
¿Dónde podemos yr que más valgamos?
Frenad el passo, no queráis mancharos
Con mancha tan infame qual es fuerza
Que sobre todos vuestros hijos venga."
Algo importó aquesto que les dixo
Aquesta noble dama generosa,
Mas como pocas vezes el esfuerzo
En flacos corazones se detiene,
Qual flaco gusanillo que royendo
Vn poderoso, gruesso y alto pino,
Que al suelo le derriba y hecho astillas
En mil pedazos roto allí le dexa,
Assí, faltos de fuerzas, ya rendidos,
Todos el noble campo despoblaron.
Mas qual aquella nave poderosa
Que fue del gran dilubio combatida,[27]
Que tanto más fue siempre lebantada
Quanto más vivas aguas la embistieron,
Al fin como primera que en el mundo
Se vido navegar por aguas bravas,
Assí el Gobernador mostraba siempre
A todos sus quebrantos tanto pecho
Quanto más los trabajos se esforzaban.
Estando, pues, el campo ya deshecho,
Fue fuerza que don Lope le tomase
Visita general, en cuio tiempo
El General se supo dar tal maña,
Y Iuan Guerra de Ressa, su teniente,
Que hechando de sus fuerzas todo el resto
Sobraron diez mil pesos de buen oro
De sólos los pertrechos ofrecidos,
Con más siete soldados de los hombres
Que por concierto y pacto estaba puesto
Que abía de poner en campo armados.
Cuia grandeza y sobra puso espanto
A toda nueva España, porque abiendo
Detenídose el campo tanto tiempo
Era cossa difícil tal excesso.
Y assí Luys Nuñez Pérez, ayudado
De don Fernando y don Christóbal luego,[28]
Suplicaron al Conde despachase

Will we lack widely stretching land,
A peaceful river of much water,
300 Where we may build a noble city
In imitation and example of many more
Who thus made everlasting name and fame?
Where can we go to better purpose?
Hold your steps, nor think to stain yourselves
305 With stain so infamous as surely will
Descend upon your children, everyone!"
That which that noble, generous dame
Did say to them had some effect,
But since weak hearts do seldom hold
310 An inspiration long,
Just as the feeble worm that gnaws
The stalwart, thick, and lofty pine
And throws it to the ground, and, splintered,
Leaves it there, in thousand pieces split,
315 So, lacking strength, surrendered now,
All left the noble camp.
But like that powerful ship
That was tossed on the mighty flood
And floated higher yet
320 The more the waters beat on it,
Like that first ship of all the world,[15]
That navigated the rude waves,
So did the Governor always show
More heart in all misfortunes
325 As his trials were increased.
The camp being now broken up
'Twas necessary that Don Lope make
A general inspection, at which time
The General and his lieutenant,
330 Juan Guerra de Ressa, planned so well
That, using their remaining energies,
Ten thousand dollars of good gold were left
Beyond the offered stores
And seven more soldiers than what men
335 The contract and the pact demanded
He should have armed in camp.
This greatness and the excess did amaze
All New Spain, since, the camp
Having delayed so long,
340 Such excess was a thing most difficult.
And so Luis Nuñez Pérez, aided by
Don Cristóbal and Don Fernando, too,[16]
Immediately begged the Count to send
That expedition forth, since Don Juan had

---

27. Se refiere al arca de Noé.
28. Se refiere a los hermanos y agentes de Oñate en la corte virreinal.

15. The reference is to Noah's ark.
16. Oñate's brothers and agents at Mexico City.

Aquesta entrada, pues don Iuan abía
Con colmo tan grandioso y lebantado
La fuerza de su assiento ya cumplido.
Y como con cuidado el Conde estaba
Aguardando el orden que de España
Mandaban que tuviesse en esta entrada,
No pudo ser possible que hiziesse
Cosa que allí nos fuesse de importancia.
Y assí se fue segunda vez perdiendo
El puesto de este campo reformado,
Por cuia causa el Conde siempre quiso
Animarle con cartas y esforzarle,
Pidiendo siempre no desfalleciesse
Porque sería possible que las cosas
Se fuessen entablando de manera
Que fin dichoso en todo se alcanzase.
Y porque los cansados Religiosos
De nuevo nuevas cosas nos ofrecen,
Será bien nueva pluma aquí cortemos
Y en nuevo canto todo lo cantemos.

345 With so great over-measure, heaping high,
Fulfilled his contract to the uttermost.
And, as the Count was waiting cautiously
The order they should send from Spain
To tell him what to do about the affair,
350 It was impossible that he should do
What might have import to us.
And so a second time was being lost
The advantage of the camp reorganized,
Wherefore the Count did always wish
355 To keep our spirits up, inspiring us
By letters begging we should not lose heart,
Because it might be possible that things
Would in such manner rearrange themselves
That happy end in all might be secured.
360 And as the tired monks again
Did offer us new things,
It will be well we here cut a new pen
And in new canto sing it all.

Canto Nveve

COMO SE BOLVIO CON ALGUNOS RELIGIOSOS FRAY
Rodrigo Durán, Comisario Apostólico de la jornada, y de otros
trabajos que fueron sucediendo, y como el Virrey mandó a don
Iuan se sugetase a segunda visita o que mandaría derramar la
gente, y venida del visitador al despacho de la jornada y
contento que con él se tuvo, y del orden que tuvo en hazer su
visita y cosas que en ella sucedieron.

How Fray Rodrigo Durán, the Apostolic Commissary of the
expedition, returned with some monks, and of other trials that
followed, and how the Viceroy ordered Don Juan to submit to a
second inspection or he'd order the people to disperse, and of the
coming of the inspector to hasten the journey, and the
satisfaction at it, and the method he used in making his
inspection, and things that happened in it.

SI con fuerza de brazos y del tiempo
  Han de quedar perfectos y acabados
  Los memorables hechos que emprendemos,
  La cosa más gallarda y lebantada
  Que en ellos luze siempre y resplandece,
Después que están, en puesto, bien obrados,[1]
Es la importante ayuda de assistencia,[2]
Sin cuia grande alteza, la esperanza,
Queda en sí toda muerta y zozobrada.
Esta, con dilación tan triste y larga,
Vino a desfallezer y destroncarse
En el cansado hijo de Francisco,
Fray Rodrigo Durán, cuia grandeza
De ánimo notable, ya rendida,
Vino a dexar la plaza, sin embargo
de un gran requerimiento que le hizo,
Pidiéndole, don Iuan, que pues estaba
Sobre sus graves hombros sustentado,
Como en coluna fuerte, todo el campo,
Pues en ninguna manera permitiesse,
Pues era cosa llana, que en bolviendo
La fuerza de la Iglesia la cabeza,
Que todo se assolase y destruiesse.
Mas como ya la suerte echada estaba,
Respecto de dar cuenta a su Perlado
De algunas cosas graves y secretas,[3]
Sin réplica salió, por cuia causa
Fray Baltasar y algunos otros Padres
De notable importancia nos dexaron,
Siguiendo sus pisadas disgustosos.
Y como a Río buelto siempre vemos
Sobre las turbias aguas muchas cosas
Que nueva novedad a todos causan,
Tras desto luego vimos que quisieron

IF by the force of arms and time
  The memorable deeds we undertake
  Shall ended and perfected be,
  The most gallant and lofty thing
5 That always shines and glows in them
After they are completely done
Is the important supporting presence[1]
Without whose lofty height all hope
Becomes dead and exhausted in itself.
10 This, with such sad and long delay,
Began to die and be destroyed
Within the weary son of Francisco,
Fray Rodrigo Durán, the greatness of whose
Noble soul, now all cast down,
15 Did come to leave the place despite the fact
Of the great supplication made by
Don Juan, requesting him that, since,
As on a column strong, all of the camp
Was borne on his grave shoulders,
20 He should in no way go,
For 'twas too evident that if the Church's strength
Should turn away,
That all would go to ruin, be destroyed.
But as the die had now been cast,
25 Having made his own priest privy
To certain serious and secret things,[2]
He went without reply, and for this cause
Fray Baltasar and certain other friars
Of notable importance left us, too,
30 Trailing his footsteps in displeasure.
And as upon the turbid waters of a stream
We always see a many things
That do bring novelties to all,
So after this we quickly learned

---

1. Una vez que están (los memorables hechos) bien llevados en el lugar (puesto) que se requiere para efectuarlos.

2. Assistencia = asistencia, presencia.

3. Oñate le había dicho a su comisario religioso la verdad acerca del mandato del virrey.

---

1. It is difficult to conclude here whether Villagrá is referring to God's presence (as reflected in the presence of his priests, which are about to leave the expedition) or to the act of presence itself, of stick-to-itiveness.

2. It is clear that Oñate had confided in his head priest the pessimistic contents of the last dispatch received from the viceroy.

Ciertos soldados, algo lebantados,[4]
Hazer aquesta entrada y proseguirla,
Amotinando el campo, cuio cáncer
Fue con suma presteza y diligencia
Del hastuto sargento remediado
Cortando la cabeza al que quería
Serlo de aquesta causa perseguida.
En este medio tiempo, proveieron
A don Lope de Vlloa, que era amparo
De todas nuestras causas malparadas,
Por General de China, y luego en esto,
Dexándonos a todos, vino nueva
Como en España estaba proveído
Don Pedro Ponce, un grande caballero
De singular prudencia y alto esfuerzo,
Por General de toda aquesta entrada.
Y temiendo el Virrey se deshiziesse
Toda la soldadesca alborotada
Con aquesta mudanza y nuevo acuerdo,
Mandó hechar luego vando que la gente
A sus vanderas toda se juntase
Y aquesta entrada luego prosiguiesse.
Tras cuio vando, sin tardanza alguna,
A don Iuan avisó como tenía
Del Presidente,[5] Pablo de Laguna,
Orden en que avisaba y ordenaba
Que si entendiesse que el don Iuan tenía
Todo lo necessario prevenido
Para hazer la entrada y proseguirla
Que luego libremente permitiesse
Que él solo la hiziesse y acabase;
Y si cumplido todo no estuviesse,
Que sin tardanza alguna diesse aviso
Porque esta causa luego remediasse.
Por cuias ocasiones le ordenaba
Que luego respondiesse si tenía
Expuesto[6] todo aquello que importaba,
Porque sin más acuerdo provehería
Persona tal qual fuesse conveniente
Y general visita le tomase,
A la qual era fuerza sugetarse;
Y que si no, que luego mandaría
Despedir a la gente y derramarla;
Y que le parecía, si no abía
De cumplir por entero, que hiziesse
Gentileza y servicio illustre y alto
A vuestra Magestad en desistirse

35 That certain soldiers, somewhat disobedient, wished
To make this entry and continue it,
So raising mutiny in the camp, a cancer which
Was with the highest speed and diligence
Of that astute Sergeant remedied,
40 Cutting the head from him who wished
To be the head of that lost cause.
In the meantime they had provided
That Don Lope de Ulloa, the protector
Of all our ill-fated cause,
45 Should go as General to China, and, after
He had left all of us, came news
How it had been arranged in Spain
Don Pedro Ponce, a great gentleman,
Of singular discretion, spirit great,
50 Should be the General of all this exploration.
The Viceroy, fearing that the soldiery,
All agitated, would disperse
Upon this change and new accord,
Ordered a proclamation to be made
55 That all the folk should join their colors
And this expedition then set forth.
After which word, with no delay,
He notified Don Juan he had
From Pedro de Laguna, President,[3]
60 An order in which he urged and ordered him
That if he learned that Don Juan had
Provided what was necessary
To make the journey and pursue it through,
He then should freely give permission
65 That he alone should make and finish it,
And if all things were not complete
He should warn him without delay
That such things quickly be set right.
Because of which he ordered him
70 To say immediately if he had
All that he needed ready then,
Because he would at once provide
Such person as might well be fit
And have him make a general inspection,
75 To which he must subject himself.
But if not, that he would at once send word
To let the forces go and disperse them;
And that it seemed to him if he could not
Complete the matter quite, he then would do
80 A favor and a service high, illustrious,
Unto your Majesty by breaking off

4. Lebantados = levantados, rebeldes.
5. Presidente de la Audiencia, cuerpo que aconsejaba al virrey.
6. Expuesto = preparado para la inspección.

3. President of the Audiencia; as noted earlier the key advisory body to the viceroy.

De aquesta noble impressa comenzada
Sin gastar más hazienda ni más vida
Que la que abía gastado y consumido,
Advirtiendo con esto que si estaba
De gusto y parecer que le tomasen
Segunda vez visita, que sería
El Comisario dentro de dos meses
De toda aquella Corte despachado.
A cuia carta el General, contento,
Al Conde replicó que aunque él abía
Cumplido enteramente sus assientos,
Que sin embargo desto, que él gustaba
Rendirse sin tardanza y sugetarse
A segunda visita y a otras muchas
Si fuesse necessario se hiziessen.
Y como en los dos Polos permanecen
Los dos exes tan fijos y clavados
Que esperanza ninguna no tenemos
De verlos de sus puestos apartados,
Assí, sin movimiento, estables, firmes,
Don Iuan y su teniente se mostraron,
Respondiendo que aquella gentileza
Era la que era fuerza se hiziesse
De vuestro Real servicio y se acabase.
Pues, como expuesto todo lo tuviessen
Para el tiempo aplazado que les dieron,
Según que lo demás passose en flores[7]
Porque no fue possible despacharse
A tiempo el Comisario de la Corte
Que pudiesse venir sin detenerse,
Por cuia causa todos se quejaban
Bien apretadamente y con enojo,
Trayendo a la memoria las palabras,
Los plazos y los tiempos mal cumplidos
Que siempre el General les daba a todos,
Afirmando y jurando que eran trazas,
Engaños y cautelas que tenía
Para sólo assolarlos y abrasarlos,
Y que no era possible que las cartas
Fuessen ciertas del Conde, sino embustes
Para el fin que dezían y afirmaban.
Y assí se fueron muchos y dexaron
Aquesta illustre entrada disgustosos,
Mas el Sol de justicia, condolido,
Sus mansos ojos luego fue bolviendo
A su afligido pueblo lastimado,
Haziéndole muy cierto que venía

That noble enterprise he had commenced
Without expending more in treasure or in life
Than he already had consumed and spent,
85 Though at the same time noting that if he
Should be pleased and see fit to undergo
This second visit of inspection, there would be,
Within two months, a Commissary sent
From all that Court.
90 The General, content, unto this letter from the Count
Replied that although he
Had met in full his contract's terms
He, none the less, would well be pleased
To give himself, subject himself,
95 To second visit, or to many more
If it were necessary they be made.
And, as in the two Poles the axes twain
Remain so fixed and firm that we
Do have no expectation in the least
100 Of seeing them removed from their position,
So, without movement, stable, firm,
Don Juan and his lieutenant showed themselves,
Replying that such nobleness of port
Was necessary in your Royal service and no more.
105 And when they had all ready then
For that set time was given them,
Like all the rest it passed unheeded
Since 'twas not possible to send
The Commissary from the Court in time,
110 To come without being detained,
For which cause all the men complained
Most furiously and angrily,
Bringing to memory the words,
The times and dates all unfulfilled
115 The General had given to all,
Affirming, swearing they were tricks,
Deceits, and stratagems he used
Only to ruin and destroy them all,
And that it was not possible the notes
120 From the Count were real, but tricks
To gain the end they spoke of and affirmed.
And many men thought thus and left
This famous expedition all disgusted,
But the Sun of justice, pitying,
125 Turned once more His kind eyes
Upon his suffering, afflicted folk,
Making most certain that there would come
A new inspector so that then

7. Como la fecha pasó (lo demás) sin hacer nada (en flores).

Nuevo visitador[8] para que luego
La jornada de hecho despachase,
A quien se hizo vn gran recebimiento,
De mucha gente de armas bien luzida,
Con su Maese de campo y Real Alférez,
Su Sargento mayor y Capitanes,
Y el General famoso y oficiales,
Que en orden todos fueron, y en llegando
Vna gran salva, alegre, de arcabuzes
Con destreza gallarda fue rompiendo
El secreto silencio y fue turando[9]
Hasta que juntos saludarse vimos
Los dos nobles varones y abrazarse.
Y luego, en orden todos bien compuestos,
A su posada juntos le llevamos,
Donde segunda salva le hizieron
Con notable contento y alegría,
Porque entendieron dél que grande Padre
Abía de mostrarse en nuestras causas.
Y assí, como tal Padre y tal amparo,
Pidió al Gobernador que no le fuesse
Contrario en cosa alguna si quería
Ver de todas sus causas buen despacho,
Con cuias buenas muestras y señales,
Como pavones todos en sus ruedas,
Vfanos y gallardos se mostraban.
Pues como assí estuviessen ya contentos,
Mandó el visitador se echase vando
Para que todo el campo luego fuesse
Siguiendo su derrota y que marchase,
Y viendo el General que aquel mandato
Era ruina total de nuestra entrada,
Porque eran necessarios muchos días
Para apretar[10] los carros y carretas,
En cuio tiempo toda la visita,
Haziendo de vna vía dos mandados,[11]
Podía fenecerse y acabarse,
Y que si aquesto assí no se hiziesse
Era perderse todo. A cuia causa
Pidió con grande instancia que mirase
Que, fuera deste grande inconveniente,
Perdía otra gran suerte y coiuntura
En aprestar la gente y el bagaje
De vn tan largo tiempo entretenida,

130

135

140

145

150

155

160

165

170

The expedition be sent off in fact.[4]
For him they made a great reception
Of many men of arms right justly famed,
The Master of the Camp, the Royal Alférez,
The Sergeant Major and the Captains,
The famous General and his officers,
Did all in order go, and as he came
A great and joyous salvo of the harquebuses
With gallant skill kept breaking on
The secret silence and kept up
Until we saw them meet and greet,
The noble pair of men, and each embrace the other.
And then, all drawn up well, in order,
We escorted them, together, to their lodgings,
Where they fired a second salvo to them,
This with notable content and joy
Because they knew that he a mighty father
Would show himself upon our side.
And, as such father and protector,
He asked the Governor not to be
In anything contrary if he wished
To see a quick dispatch of his affairs,
With which good signs and portents, all,
Like peacocks in their proud parade,
Did show themselves gallant and spirited.
Well, as they thus were so content,
The Inspector ordered proclamation made
That all the camp should start at once,
Continuing its route and march.
The General, seeing that mandate
Was total ruin of our expedition,
Since many days were needed yet
To load the wagons and the carts,
In which time all the inspection,
If carried out as they loaded,
Could finish and be closed,
And that if that were not done thus
It were to ruin all. Because of this
He asked with great insistence he observe
That, beside this great inconvenience,
He would miss that great opportunity
Of gathering the baggage and the folk
That were so long time kept waiting.
'Twere necessary, too, in the taking

---

8. El nuevo inspector, a quien Villagrá no nombra, fue don Juan de
Frías. Véase Villagrá, *Historia*, edición de Junquera, 158.

9. Turando = durando.

10. Apretar = errata por aprestar, preparar.

11. Es decir, haciendo la inspección a la vez que se preparaba la
salida.

---

4. The new inspector, whom Villagrá does not name, was Don Juan
de Frías. See Villagrá, *Historia*, Junquera edition, 158.

De más de que era fuerza que sacando
De sus querencias[12] todos los ganados
Que todos se perdiessen y ahuientasen,
Y que para escusar tan grandes daños
Hiziesse su visita en aquel puesto
Y dél saliessen todos de arrancada
Sin detenerse en parte que pudiessen
Perderse aquellas cosas que llevaban.
Y viendo los soldados lastimados
El tiempo que perdían con enojo,
A vozes y sin rienda, desembueltos,
Dezían que eran trazas porque el campo
Gastase el bastimiento que tenía
Y assí se deshiciesse y acabase.
Y fuera assí, sin duda, si el gran colmo
No fuera, tal qual vimos, bien colmado.[13]
Y viendo el General que no podía
Hazer que le tomasen la visita,
Con pérdida del tiempo irrebocable
Salió con todo el campo sin consuelo,
A fuerza de sudor y de trabajos
Que en aprestarlo todo padecieron.
Y apenas fue marchando cinco leguas
Quando en un puesto pobre de agua y monte
Mandó hiziessen alto y descargasen.
Allí bolvieron todos al trabajo,
Haziendo sus assientos, temerosos
De que era fuerza que agua les faltase.
Mas Dios, que a todos siempre nos socorre,
Hizo que vnos charquillos bien pequeños
Que cerca de nosotros se mostraban
Agua en abundancia derramasen
Y que a vista de todos las vertiessen,
Teniéndolas de antes represadas
Y en sus secretas venas escondidas.[14]
Aquí el Visitador mandó echar vando
Que, pena de la vida, nadie ossase
Salir del quartel de armas sin embargo
Que del mismo don Iuan mandato fuesse,
Con cuio vando luego los soldados,
Desamparando todos los ganados,
Se fueron a gran priessa recogiendo,
Dexándolos perdidos sin sus guardas.
Y aquesta desventura fue tan grande
Que andaban a millares los corderos

Of all the livestock from their haunts,
Many be lost and stray away,
175 And to prevent such monstrous damages
He make inspection at that point
And then all leave from there at once
Without a halt where they well might
Lose those things that they took along.
180 The soldiers, seeing, much cast down,
The time they lost, with anger great,
Aloud and freely, without rein,
Did say this was a trick so that the camp
Might use up the provisions that they had
185 And so be broken up and put to rout.
And so the outcome would have been
If his great patience had not grown to match.
The General, seeing he could not
Cause an inspection to be made,
190 With loss of time no more to be regained,
Set out with all the camp, perforce,
By dint of mighty work and sweat
That all, in making ready, bore.
And hardly had he marched a good five leagues
195 When, in a place in wood and water poor,
The order came to halt and to unload.
There all turned to the work again,
Making their camping place in fear
That surely water would be lacking here.
200 But God, who always aids us all,
Arranged that certain tiny pools
That showed themselves near to our camp
Should pour out water in great abundance
And should flow out in sight of all,
205 Having before held back their streams
And hid them in their secret veins.[5]
Here the inspector ordered proclamation made
That under pain of death no one should dare
To leave the camp itself e'en though
210 Don Juan himself should order it,
Upon which order, then, the soldiery,
Leaving the livestock all unguarded quite,
Did come together in great haste,
Leaving them lost without their guards.
215 The misadventure was so great
That lambs by thousands wandered there
And bleated for their mothers, who,

---

12. Querencias = lugares a los que los animales están
acostumbrados.

13. Se refiere a la paciencia de Oñate.

14. El agua milagrosamente aparecida recuerda lo narrado en *El
peregrino indiano* XIII.

5. This miraculous flow of water is similar to what is narrated in *El
peregrino indiano* XIII.

Balando por sus madres, que perdidas
Balaban assimismo por hallarlos,
Y atónitas las yeguas, discurriendo
Cruzaban por los campos sin sentido
En busca de sus crías relinchando,
Y assimismo las vacas y terneras
Hundían con bramidos las campañas,
Los tiernos rezentales, assombrados,
Con el ganado prieto[15] yban rebueltos
Por verse de las cabras divididos.[16]
Los bueies, los caballos, los jumentos,[17]
El ganado vacuno y la mulada,
Con todo lo demás que el campo pasta,
Esparramados todos y perdidos
A su albedrío y sin orden alguna
Andaban sin sus guardas descarriados.
Y sin mirar aquesta desventura
Y pérdida, sin traza, desdichada,
Vuestro visitador mandó tras desto
Que todos los soldados y oficiales
O gente de servicio que quisiesse
Dexar de proseguir aquesta entrada
Que todos libremente se quedasen
Aunque alistados todos estuviessen.
Hizo demás de aquesto en su visita
Vna cosa también que fue notable:
Andaban, como digo, los ganados
sin guardas por el campo divididos,
Y de parte de noche[18] nos mandaba
Que de mañana yeguas o caballos,
Ovejas o las cabras o las vacas,
O el género que más apetecía,
A registrar traxesemos; y en esto,
Por ser el tiempo corto y tan tassado,
Salíamos perdidos a buscarle,
Y si, como perdida, se traía
Alguna cantidad pequeña o grande
Aquélla registraba, y si tras della
Venía otra qualquiera, no passaba,
Diziendo no podía recibirla
Porque cerrado ya el registro estaba.
Con esto el General, qual fuerte yunque,
Viendo que lo demás assí corría,
Sufriendo aquellos golpes con paciencia,
Al Cielo suplicaba socorriesse,
Que aquesto es lo que vale quando lejos

220

225

230

235

240

245

250

255

260

Lost, too, were bleating hard to find them,
And mares, bewildered quite, went scurrying
And running through the fields, bemazed,
In neighing search of colts,
And likewise cows and heifers too
Did fill the fields with bellowing,
While tender, frightened calves
Were carried off with porcine herds,
Seeing themselves divided from the goats.[6]
The oxen, the horses, asses,
The cattle, and the herd of mules,
With all the rest that crops the grass,
All widely spread and lost,
At their own will and with no order roamed,
All strayed without their guards.
And, disregarding this calamity
And loss, anarchic, unfortunate,
Your inspector did order after this
That all the soldiers and the officers
Or serving folk who well might wish
To cease continuing with this expedition
Might freely then depart
Although all be enlisted there.
And more than this, on his inspection
He did a thing most noteworthy.
The cattle, as I say, were wandering
Over the land unshepherded,
And with his night command he ordered us
That in the morning horses, mares,
Or sheep or goats or cows,
Or any kind of beast that he saw fit,
Be brought to him to register. At once,
Time being so limited and short,
We hastened forth to seek the lost,
And if, as with things lost, some group
Was brought to him, or large or small,
That put he down; and if then, after it
Some other came he would not pass it,
Saying he could not receive that one
Because the registry had now been closed.
With this, the General, like an anvil strong,
Seeing that all the rest would go the same,
Suffering these blows with patience,
Did beg of Heaven to succor him,
For that is what avails when you,
O mighty King, are far from what occurs.

15. Ganado prieto = moreno, el de cerda.
16. La cabra se usaba para dirigir y tranquilizar las manadas.
17. Jumentos = asnos.
18. Parte = orden.

6. Goats were used to calm the more high-strung species.

Estáis, inmenso Rey, de lo que passa.
Hizo notificar a los vezinos
Que en manera ninguna no vendiessen
Ganados a don Iuan, que fue una cosa
Que a todos causó espanto imaginarla.
Mandó también, con pena de la vida,
Que aquél que en esta entrada se alistase
Que si fuesse mestizo lo dixesse,
Y mulato también si se alistase.
En cuia lista fueron despedidos
Vnos por no querer que se assentasen,
Diziendo no abían de yr a la jornada,
Y por la poca hedad dexaron otros[19]
Que sé que están, señor, allá sirbiendo
Con hartas más ventajas que no aquéllos
Que sé también, gran Rey, que se bolvieron
Sin vergüenza del peine que en la barba
Pudo quedar asido y lebantado.[20]
Que con éstos quisiera que tuviera
Vuestro visitador aquellos bríos
Que con vn soldado vimos tuvo:
Y fue que porque, acaso y con descuido,
Sin quitarle la gorra fue passando
Determinó y mandó, por sólo aquesto,
Que seys tratos de cuerda[21] allí le diessen.
Pues como el General por él rogase
Y con esto también reprehendiesse
El descuido que tuvo aquel soldado,
Diziéndole lo mal que abía hecho,
Respondió al General que más justicia
Y más puesto en razón era que honrrase
Vuestro visitador, y otro qualquiera,
A los que en guerra os sirben con su sangre,
Con vida, con hazienda y con su honrra,
Que no que aquestos tales con infamia
Viniessen, por tan altos pensamientos,
A ser infamemente condenados
Por vn solo descuido que tuvieron
En adorar a quien en paz gustosa
Le sembraban de plata los caminos
Si en vuestro Real servicio su persona
Mandaban se ocupase y que os sirviesse;
Y que otro hombre que él fue Carlos quinto,
Vuestro Agüelo caro y esforzado,
Y mucho más soldado y más guerrero,

He had the neighboring people notified
265 That under no condition should they sell
Livestock unto Don Juan, which was a thing
That frightened all men to imagine it.
He ordered, too, upon the pain of death,
That anyone enlisted for the march
270 Who was a mixed-blood should declare the same,
Mulattoes, too, if such enlisted were.
And from the list many were then discharged,
Some because he did not wish them listed,
Saying they would not make the journey,
275 And others they discharged as under age,
Of whom, O lord, I know that some
Are serving with greater heart there
Than those, I also know, my lord, who fled
With no shame that a comb within their beards
280 Might set right firm and stand out straight.[7]
With such it would behoove your inspector
To fall into such temper as we saw
Him fall into against a good soldier
Because of this: that all by chance and carelessly
285 He passed him by nor doffed to him his cap.
For this and only this he gave command
He should be given six lashes on the spot,
And when the General appealed for him
And at the same time scolded him,
290 Telling him what ill work he did,
He answered to the General that 'twas right,
More reasonable, the inspector,
And all else, should recognize the honor
Of those who serve you with their blood in war,
295 With life, with property, and with their honor, too,
Than that these come, for their altruism,
To be condemned most infamously for
A single act of carelessness in reverencing
One for whom, in most enjoyable peace,
300 They sowed the ways with silver
If only in your Royal service he
Were ordered to employ himself, serve you.
Another man than this was Charles the Fifth,
Your grandfather, beloved and spirited,
305 Much more a soldier and a warrior
And who, he knew for a fact, pardoned
Those who had served him in the wars.
The General, seeing his enormous rage

---

19. Es de suponer, por lo que dice Villagrá seguidamente, que éstos llegarían a ir.

20. Indica que los jóvenes que lograron ir con la expedición sirvieron después muy bien, a diferencia de los adultos ("peine que en la barba pudo quedar asido") que abandonaron la empresa.

21. Tratos de cuerda = latigazos.

7. The image is that of a fully bearded, adult male.

Y que sabía cierto perdonaba
A aquéllos que en las guerras le servían.
Y viendo el General su mucha furia
Y que era fuerza a todos regalarlos,
Con palabras de Padre grave, afable,
Riñiéndole, mandó que más no hablase.
Y él, qual rebuelta piedra de molino,
Que quitándole el agua es fuerza pare,
Assi paró y también paró su causa.
De más de todo aquesto que hemos dicho
Otros que aquesta historia a cargo tienen
Dirán en sus escritos otras cosas
Que acerca destas causas sucedieron,
En las quales jamás tuvieron mano
El buen Jaime Fernández, secretario,
Y el Capitán Guerrero, a quien el Conde
Mandó por Comissario aquí viniesse,
El vno por la illustre y clara pluma
Y el otro por la fuerza de la lanza
Hombres de buena estima y noble punto.
Y por venir al hecho de esta causa,
Al fin hizo visita, cala y cata.
Esta vino a tomar de tal manera
Que no sé yo si ay testigo alguno
Que pueda con verdad dezir que vido
Las cosas que assentaron y escribieron.
Sólo sabré dezir que con instancia
Pidió el Gobernador que se le diesse
De toda su visita un testimonio
Para saber las sobras o las faltas
Y componer la quiebra si la vbiesse,
De manera que cosa no faltase.
Esto le denegó con tanta fuerza
Que no sólo no quiso darle gusto,
Siendo justicia que el deudor que paga
Le den carta de pago por escrito,
Mas hizo confesasse que no abía
Cumplido con su assiento, y esto a escuras,
Sin darle lumbre alguna de lo escrito.
Pidiole, demás desto, que Iuan Guerra
Y su muger, doña Ana, se obligasen
En quanto a los soldados que faltaban,
Por pública escritura en esta forma:
Que abían de poner en campo, armados,
Para cumplir su assiento, ochenta hombres
A su minsión[22] y costa, y que pagasen
Todos los daños que éstos cometiessen,

22. Minsión = pensión. Salvo errata del original; cabe pensar en
una abreviada forma de manutención, es decir, que lo contratado
suponía mantener y pagar a los indicados soldados.

And that 'twas necessary to calm all,
310 With grave and affable, paternal words
He ordered, scolding him, to speak no more.
And he, like turning millstone hard,
Which, draining off the water, must be still,
So he did stop and so ended his cause.
315 And beyond all this we have said,
Others who have this history in hand
Will, in their writings, tell some other things
That happened in concernment of this cause,
In which there never intervened
320 The good Jaime Fernández, secretary,
Nor Captain Guerrero, whom the Count
Had ordered to come here as Commissary,
The one for clear illustrious pen,
The other by the strength of his strong lance,
325 Men of the best esteem and noble sort.
And now, to reach the fact of this affair,
At last he made inspection to the full
And this he did in such a way and sort
I know not if there is a single witness who
330 Can say with truth what he saw there
The things they set down and did write.
I only know, to tell, that most insistently
The Governor asked that he be given
An attestation of all this inspection,
335 To know the overplus or what might lack
And mend the vacancy, should there be such,
So that there might be nothing lacking yet.
This he refused with so much force
That he not only would not favor him,
340 It being justice that what debtor pays
Should have written acknowledgement,
But he made him confess that he had not
Fulfilled his contract, and this blindly, too,
Without a glimmer of what he had writ.
345 He asked him, after this, that Juan Guerra
And his wife Doña Ana be required to pledge
Themselves for soldiers such as lacked
By public document after this form:
That they would furnish, armed and in camp,
350 To fill the contract, eighty men
At their expense and cost, and they would pay
All damages that these men might commit,
And they would pay, also, the salaries
Of any agents that the Viceroy wished
355 To come and start the expedition,

Y que también pagasen los salarios
A los ministros que el Virrey quisiesse
Viniessen al despacho desta entrada,
Y que a su voluntad también pudiesse
Quitar o reformar aquellas cosas
Que en su fabor se vbiessen concedido,
Y que por el permiso que le daba
Para poder hazer aquesta entrada
No fuesse visto adquirir dominio
Ni derecho al gobierno de la tierra,
En propiedad ni possesión alguna.
Y qual si fuera monte o bronce duro,[23]
Con todo concedió, los ojos bueltos
Al soberano Dios, en cuyas manos,
Pidiéndole justicia con paciencia,
Gustoso le dexó todas sus causas.
Y porque su teniente ausente estaba,
Porque acordó con él que se quedase
Para el socorro y cosas de importancia
De aquesta nueva tierra y nuevos Reynos,
Mandó que me aprestase y luego fuesse
Para tratar con él que se obligase,
Con su muger, doña Ana de Mendoza.
Y apenas vido el pliego quando luego,
Como aquellos dos Decios[24] memorables,
Que alegremente juntos se ofrecieron,
Por sola la salud de todo el campo,
En brazos de la muerte rigurosa,
Assí los dos contentos se obligaron
Y juntos las dos vidas ofrecieron
A vuestro Real serbicio, sin que cosa
Quedase para nadie reservada.
Passadas estas cosas y otras muchas,
Después que vbo bien visto los poderes,[25]
Hecha ya su visita y acabada,
Mandó marchar el campo destrozado,
Según vereys, señor, aquí pintado.

And that at his discretion, too, he might
Well deny or alter anything
That in their favor had been granted there,
That from the permission to be given him
To set him free to make this expedition   360
He would not seek to gain dominion
Nor right of government in the land,
Proprietorship nor any possession.
And, as he were a mountain, or hard bronze,
He conceded, his eyes turned up   365
To sovereign God, within whose hands,
Asking Him justice patiently,
He joyfully left all his cause.
And as his lieutenant was absent then,
It being agreed with him he should remain   370
To send on aid and matters of import
To that new land and Kingdoms new,
He ordered I should haste and set out straight
To ask him then to bind himself,
With his wife, Doña Ana de Mendoza,   375
And hardly did he see the packet than at once,
Like those two memorable sons of Decius
Who gladly offered themselves together
To go, for the salvation of the camp,
Into the arms of rigorous death,[8]   380
So these two, quite content, did bind themselves,
Together offered their two lives
Unto your Royal service, and no thing
Remained for anyone reserved.
These things being passed, and many more,   385
After he had well seen the contracts,[9]
Inspection made and finished now,
He ordered the ruined camp to march,
As you, O lord, shall see described.
                                               390

---

23. Difícil saber si la referencia es sencillamente al metal o si sugiere estatua.

24. Fueron en realidad tres miembros de esa familia romana que, en distintas generaciones (padre, hijo, nieto), dedicaron sus vidas a los dioses por garantizar a Roma la victoria. Sus acciones están recogidas por Livio, VIII–IX. Como dos los menciona Virgilio (*Eneida* VI, 1093-95) y también Ercilla (*La araucana* I, 3).

25. Es de suponer que se refiere a los poderes dados por Juan Guerra de Ressa para garantizar las obligaciones económicas impuestas por el inspector.

8. Three generations of that Roman family (father, son, grandson) dedicated their lives to the gods to guarantee Roman victory, according to Livy, VIII-IX. As two they are mentioned by Virgil (*Aeneid* VI, 1093–95) and Ercilla (*La araucana* I, 3).

9. The reference is to the empowerments granted by Juan Guerra de Ressa to guarantee the economic obligations imposed by the inspector.

CANTO DIEZ

COMO SALIO EL CAMPO MARCHANDO PARA EL
RIO de Conchas[1] *y del modo que tuvieron en vadearle y puente*
que en él se hizo y de como se despidió el Visitador, dando sólo
permiso para que el campo entrase.

SSI como en la alteza y excelencia
De la hermosa, bella y blanca Luna

Vnas vezes su noble antorcha vemos
De todo punto ciega y eclipsada
Y otras con corta luz y, tras menguante
Con bellos rayos, dulzes y apacibles,
Salir la vemos llena, de creciente,
No de otra suerte y traza fue saliendo
La fuerza deste campo destrozado,
Tendiendo[2] con disgusto los pertrechos
Que a fuerza de trabajos los soldados
Fueron por muchas partes recogiendo,
Los quales fueron luego lebantando
Más de ochenta carretas bien cargadas,
Que con sus carros y carrozas yban,
Quales van en su esquadra bien compuestas
Las hormigas el trigo acarreando.
Assí, marchando todas prolongadas,
Con vn ronco chirrido y sordo aplauso
Vn camino tendido bien abierto
Dexaban con sus ruedas señalado.
Y assí como del arca contrastada
La fuerza de animales fue saliendo
Por géneros distintos y apartados,
Assí, distintos todos los ganados,
Fueron el nuevo rastro prosiguiendo,
Por sus quarteles[3] todos bien sembrados,
Cuia hermosa vista nos mostraba
Aquí vna gran boiada[4] bien tendida,
Allí las cabras que yban discurriendo
Tras del ganado prieto que seguía
Las simples ovejuelas adestradas
De los mansos cencerros conozidos,
Allí los potros tras las yeguas mansas
Retozaban ligeros y lozanos,
Aquí, tras las cerreras,[5] relinchaban
Gran fuerza de caballos animosos,

---

1. Hoy el Río Conchos.
2. Tendiendo = desplegando.
3. Quarteles = cuarteles, divisones, no necesariamente en cuartos.
4. Boiada = boyada, manada de bueyes.
5. Cerreras = yeguas mansas que andan sueltas.

CANTO X

How the camp marched for the Río de Conchas[1] *and of the*
method they employed to ford it, and the bridge that was built
over it, and of how the inspector took his leave, giving
permission for the camp to enter and no more.

S in the height and in the excellence
Of the bright, beautiful, and silvery
        moon
We sometimes see its noble light
In all points blind and quite eclipsed,
5   At others with but little light, then, after shrinking so,
With beauteous, sweet, and soothing rays,
We see it ride at zenith of the full,
Not otherwise and in no other sort the strength
Of this defeated camp began to appear,
10 Unhappily displaying the muniments
That by dint of much work the troops
From many places were assembling again,
And these, were then conveyed along,
Well loaded into more than eighty carts,
15 Which, with wagons and with coaches, too, went
As ants go in a squadron well drawn up
When carrying home their wheat.
Thus, marching in extended line,
With squeakings hard, like dumb applause,
20 A goodly, wide and open road
Was left well indicated by their wheels.
And as from out the ark, all two by two,
The mass of animals did come
By races separate and set apart,
25 So all the stock in separate groups
Set out upon the new-made trail,
Each set apart to its own kind,
Which showed to us a beauteous sight:
Here a great drove of oxen spreading out,
30 There, goats who scurried rapidly along
Behind the porcine cattle, following
The simple sheep, led on with ease
By gentle bellwethers, well-known to them;
There, following the gentle mares, the colts
35 Did spiritedly gambol, gaily play;
Here, after the tame mares, there neighed
Great stock of horses spirited,

---

1. Today the Conchos River.

Tras cuia obscura y alta polvareda
Otra más tenebrosa y encumbrada
El ganado bacuno y el requaje[6]
Por vna y otra parte lebantaban.
Que por lo que esta machina[7] ocupaba
Se podrá bien sacar lo que sería,
Pues tres tendidas millas por lo largo
Y otras tantas por ancho, bien cumplidas,
Tomaba todo el campo lebantado.[8]
Cuia gruessa grandeza fue marchando
Hasta llegar con bien a las Riberas
Del Río de las Conchas, cuio nombre
Tomó por la belleza que se crían
Quales vistosos nácares graciosos,
A bueltas de gran suma de pescado,
Cuia vertiente vemos que derrama
Por donde el claro sol su luz esconde
Y a la remota parte de Lebante,[9]
Por torzidos caminos y veredas
Va al poderoso mar restituyendo.
En cuio assiento y puesto recogidos
Luego la gran faena comenzaron
Para aber de buscar seguro vado
Por donde todo el campo sin peligro
La fuerza de las aguas contrastase,
Porque hondable todo se mostraba,
Por cuia causa luego con la sonda
Assegurar quisieron el partido.
De donde resultó tentar vn vado
Algo dificultoso y mal seguro,
Por cuia causa muchos temerosos
Assegurar passage no quisieron
Por no ser de sus aguas caudalosas
Sorbidos y tragados sin remedio.
Y assí el Gobernador, qual Caio César,[10]
Que sin freno ni rienda gobernaba
La fuerza de caballos bien soberbios,
Assí saltó en vn caballo bravo,
De terrible corage, desembuelto,
Notando con aviso y con destreza
Que nunca es eloquente en sus razones
Aquél que las propone si admirados
Con proprias obras y valor de brazos

Behind whose high, thick cloud of dust
Another, thicker and much heavier,
The beef herd and the herd of mules
Did cause to rise up on both sides.
As to what space this mighty throng took up
One well can judge what it would be
Since three full miles in all its length
And full as many more in width
Were taken by the moving camp
Whose swarming mass[2] kept up the march
Until, with fortune, it came to the banks
Of Río de Conchas, whose name
Is taken from the beauty of its shells, it creates
Like graceful, sightly pearl-mother,
And, too, its mighty store of fish.
We saw there that its source bursts forth
Toward where the glowing sun doth hide his light,
And in some remote place to the Levant
It goes by winding roads and trails
To give its waters back unto the sea.[3]
Collected at this point and place
They then began the toilsome task
Of seeking out a ford secure
By which the camp in safety might
Oppose the rushing water's force,
Because it all appeared quite deep,
For which reason with the depth probe
They wished to find a crossing safe.
Whence they resolved to try a ford
A trifle difficult and hardly safe,
For which cause many fearful ones
Would not attempt a passage
Lest by its waters copious they might
Be swallowed up and drowned without recourse.
So the Governor, like Caius Caesar,[4]
Who without rein or bridle governed
The spirit of the wildest horse,
Then leaped upon a fearless horse
Of terrible and fearful mettle,
Noting advisedly, with skill,
That he is never eloquent in reasoning
He who proposes things, unless by his own works
And valor of his arms he leaves the ones

40
45
50
55
60
65
70
75
80

---

6. Requaje = recuaje, conjunto de bestias de carga.

7. Machina = máquina, cuerpo de partes señaladas.

8. La expedición consistía de cuatrocientos hombres, 150 de ellos con familia; ochenta y tres carros y unas siete mil cabezas de ganado vario.

9. Indica que el río corre de oeste a este.

10. La acción, paralela por acuática, de César la narra Antonio de Torquemada en su *Jardín de flores curiosas,* Tratado IV.

2. The expedition consisted of four hundred men, 150 with families; eighty-three wagons; and some seven thousand head of cattle of various kinds.

3. A poetic indication that the river runs from east to west.

4. Caesar's parallel action, only so in being aquatic, is narrated by Antonio de Torquemada, *Jardín de flores curiosas* IV.

No dexa los oyentes, y rendidos
A sólo el apetito, blanco y fuerza
Que aspira la corriente de su gusto.
Y con un gran bastón en la derecha,
"Ea, nobles soldados esforzados,
Caballeros de Christo," fue diziendo,
"Este es noble principio conozido
Para que cada qual aquí nos muestre
Si el crédito y valor del importuno
Y pesado trabajo que seguimos
En sí tiene valor y si merecen
Aquéllos que le siguen gran corona."
Y con estas razones fue bolviendo
Las riendas al caballo poderoso
Y assí se abalanzó al bravo Río,
Y rompiendo las aguas fue bufando
El animal gallardo, desembuelto.
Y puesto en la otra vanda hijadeando[11]
Bolvió a cortar las aguas, y en la orilla,
Por los hijares, bajo,[12] y anchos pechos
Resollando, vertía y derramaba
Sobre la enjuta[13] arena guijarrosa
Del húmedo licor vna gran copia.
El General prudente que assí puso
Seguro vado a todos por delante,
El mismo comenzó a picar los bueies,
Animando al ejército suspenso
Con vno y otro grito de manera
Que assí como la chusma[14] sosta y carga[15]
Siguiendo al bogabante[16] con destreza,
O de boga arrancada,[17] o sea picada,[18]
O quiera sea larga o sea chapada,[19]
A todo pone el hombro y con esfuerzo
Los poderosos tercios va cargando
Y apriessa la faena va haziendo,
Assí desta manera, traza y modo,
La soldadesca, toda avergonzada,
Como gente de chusma los más dellos,
Fueron echando y despojando apriessa,

Who hear him all surprised, surrendered quite
Unto the target, appetite, and course
The current of his will would take.
Thus, with a long staff in his hand,
85 "Come noble, gallant troops,
Soldiers of Christ," he called,
"This is the noble, well-known test
In which each one may show us here
If the credit and the value of this,
90 The trying, heavy labor we pursue
Is itself great and we deserve
At last to win a mighty crown."
And with these words he then did loose
The reins unto his powerful horse,
95 And thus did plunge into the rushing stream.
The gallant, raging animal,
Snorting, did breast the waves
And, panting on the other shore,
Again he cut the waters. On the bank,
100 All down his flanks and his broad chest
Did flow and trickle, as he panted there,
Great streams of the moist fluid
To the dry and stony sand.
The prudent General, who thus did show
105 To all a safe ford was there found,
Himself commenced to prod the oxen on
And animate the hesitating troops
By shout on shout, to such effect
That, as the galley slaves do heave and sway,
110 Following the stroke of oar skillfully,
Whether in raising oars or dipping them,
A long stroke or a short,
To all they put their shoulders, and with force
Straining their powerful limbs,
115 And so the task is quickly done,
In this same manner, way and sort
The soldiery, now all ashamed,
The most of them like galley slaves,
Began to strip themselves in haste,

11. Hijadeando = ijadeando, moviendo mucho los ijares por efecto de cansancio.
12. Posible errata del original por "bajos," que modificaría "hijares"; pero es también posible, y así anotamos el texto, que "bajo," aunque alejado hasta el hipérbaton, modifique "resollando."
13. Enjuta = seca.
14. Chusma = tripulación.
15. Sosta y carga = afloja y aprieta, en el manejo de los remos.
16. Bogabante = bogavante, primer remero en cada banco de galera.
17. Boga arrancada = remando con fuerza y hondura.
18. Picada = refiriéndose a remar, apenas tocando el agua.
19. Chapada = corta.

Quedándose en pañetes, ropa fuera,
Para amparar aquello que en el agua
Corriesse algún peligro de perderse.
Otros las aguijadas empuñaban
Y a los anchos costados espaciosos
De los vnzidos bueies[20] se ponían.
Y assí como del puesto abandonaban,
En el olimpo campo, aquellos carros,
De los aurigas[21] diestros impelidos
Que con hirviente priessa a rienda suelta[22]
La fuerza de caballos aguijaban
Con piernas, cuerpo y brazos lebantados,
Moviendo el crudo látigo con priessa,[23]
Assí los nuestros, todos desembueltos
Para passar la fuerza de los carros,
Como diestros aurigas, el azote
Zimbraban, en los pértigos[24] subidos.
Y como gruessas naves cuias proas,
Sulcando el bravo mar, espuma grande
Rebuelven y lebantan, salpicando
Las poderosas cintas[25] que descubren,
Assí, en blanco jabón rebuelto el Río,
Las lebantadas cumbres salpicaban
De los cargados carros poderosos,
Cuias herradas ruedas grandes cercos
Y gruessos remolinos rebolbían
A fuerza de las mazas[26] y los rayos[27]
Que en su bravo raudal yban torciendo.
Y en las ligeras yeguas también otros
Los ganados maiores aventaban,[28]
Y otros a pie corriendo por la orilla
Desnudos y descalzos, rebentando,[29]
La fuerza de los brazos descubrían.
Y cada qual allí se acomodaba
Según que la ocasión se le ofrecía.
¡O discreción sagaz o claro exemplo,
Y como nos lebanta vn buen dechado[30]
Si en vn varón illustre resplandeze,
Con qué facilidad los imitamos
Quando con proprias obras nos adiestran,

120 Remaining in no more than trunks,
     To protect all that in the water might
     Run any risk of being lost.
     Others did seize the pointed goads
     And to the broad and spacious flanks
125 Of the yoked oxen set the same,
     And as they moved from out their place
     In the olympian fields, chariots,
     Impelled by skillful drivers who,
     In boiling haste, with loosened rein,
130 Spurred on the willing horses there
     With heels, body, and upraised arms,
     Wielding their stinging whips with speed,[5]
     So all our men with mighty zeal
     To speed the convoy of the carts
135 Climbing upon the poles did swing
     Their whips like skillful charioteers.
     And like to mighty ships whose prows
     Plowing the roaring sea do raise
     Great clouds of spume and spatter up
140 The towering gunwales that they show,
     So the river, churned into white foam,
     Did splash the lofty, towering tops
     Of wagons powerful, loaded deep,
     Whose mighty wheels, with iron hooped,
145 Did turn up roaring whirlpools
     Because of the strong hubs and spokes
     That turned within its fierce current.
     Others, as well, upon swift mares
     Advanced the heavier cattle,
150 And others on foot, running on the shore,
     Splashing all naked and unbreeched,
     Did show the strength their arms possessed,
     And each one there busied himself
     According as occasion came to him.
155 Oh wise discretion, oh good example,
     And how a good example raises us
     When shining in a famous man,
     How them we easily may imitate
     When they instruct us with appropriate works,

20. La reproducción mexicana trae "bueis."
21. Aurigas = conductores de caballerías.
22. La reproducción mexicana trae "ruelta."
23. La imagen es de las carreras en los antiguos juegos olímpicos.
24. Pértigos = lanzas del carro.
25. Cintas = maderas que van por fuera del costado del buque desde proa a popa.
26. Mazas = cubos de la rueda.
27. Rayos = radios de la rueda.
28. Aventaban = ahuyentaban.
29. Rebentando = reventando, trabajando duramente.
30. Dechado = ejemplo, modelo.

5. The image is of the chariot races in the Olympic games of antiquity.

Y qué flacas hallamos sus razones,	160	Yet how weak we find their reasoning,
Qué muertas, qué sin pulsos, quando vienen		How dead and pulseless, when they come
Sin la grandeza de las obras adornadas!		Without adornment of great works!
Todo aquesto causó el noble exemplo,		All this was caused, then, by noble example,
Aviso y discreción de aquel prudente,		Judgment and discretion of that prudent man
Cuias gallardas fuerzas sustentaban	165	Whose gallant efforts were sustained
Sus dos bravos sobrinos con vizarra		By his two noble nephews with enthusiastic
Destreza y gallardía desembuelta.		Skill and boundless energy.
Y no hizieron mucho en señalarse		And it was not surprising they did shine,
Porque siempre en aquestas ocasiones		For always on such occasions
Bellos trabajadores se mostraban.	170	They showed themselves most splendid workers.
Y assí, los Españoles, presurosos,		And so the Spaniards, hastening,
Para sólo aguijar los tardos bueies,		To prod the sluggish oxen,
Hiriendo a puros gritos las estrellas,		Striking the very stars with yells,
Los duros aguijones les arriman		Did prick them with the pointed goads
Y a la fuerza del Río los impelen.	175	And forced them on into the current there.
Y qual confussa flota combatida		And like a fleet confused and beaten back
De poderosos vientos lebantados,		By mighty, roaring winds,
Cuios pilotos diestros, hervorosos,		Whose skillful, ardent pilots do
A puras vozes hazen sus faenas		Their tasks by words alone,
En confussas zalomas[31] entonados,	180	Intoned in confused chanteys,
Assí por vna y otra parte, apriessa,		So, with haste on one side and the other,
Con vozes, chiflos y altos alaridos		Whistlings, shouts, and screeching yells,
Esforzaban los bueyes fatigados.		They forced the tired oxen then.
Y assí, sugetos todos, mal heridos,		And thus, all harnessed, beaten,
Qual obediente al duro yugo atado,	185	Some, being obedient to the yoke they bore,
Hincando el fuerte morro, arranca y tira		Thrusting with their stout necks, pulled forth and drew
La más pesada carga disgustoso,		The heaviest loads, most burdensome,
Qual ya de todo punto fatigado,		Some, being all tired as they were,
Al aguijón rendido, boqui abierto,		Surrendering to the goad, with open mouths,
Suelta la larga lengua, berreaba,	190	Their long tongues out, bellowed loud,
Por cuia causa allí la soldadesca,		And for this cause the soldiery,
Nadando por el agua, los aguijan.		All swimming in the stream, did goad them on.
Y otros en sus caballos los animan		And others on their horses drove them on,
A fuerza del azote, palo y grito		By means of whips and sticks and yells,
También a los ganados que passaban,	195	The other cattle that they crossed,
Qual entre las ovejas dando vozes,		Some, yelling there among the sheep,
Los tiernos corderitos aiudaba,		Did help the little lambs across,
Qual al ganado prieto y al bacuno,		And some the swine herd and the cows,
A la cabra, al cabrito y al caballo,		The goats, the kids, the horses, too,
Al potro, a la potranca y a la yegua,	200	The colts, the fillies, and the mares,
Y al gruesso y gran requaje que venía.		And all the numerous mules that came.
Y como con el peso de la lana		Since with the weight of all their wool
Muchas de las ovejas zozobraban		Large numbers of the sheep did sink,
Por no poder nadar con tanta carga,		Being unable to swim with such a weight,
Por sólo remediar tan grave daño	205	To remedy so grave a loss
Dio luego el General en vna cosa		The General hit on a thing
Al parecer de todos increible.		Incredible, so all did think,

31. Zalomas = voces cadenciosas del trabajo de los marineros.

Y fue que al bravo Río caudaloso
Vna segura puente se le hiziesse,
Para cuio principio dos dozenas
De ruedas de carretas bien fornidas
Quiso que se quitasen y truxessen.
Y éstas mandó poner de trecho en trecho
Por la grande corriente con amarras,
Como si todas gruessas naves fueran.
Luego, de los más altos y crecidos
Hizo cortar los árboles que estaban
Riberas deste Río caudaloso,
De cuios Ramos todos despojados,
Sobre las lebantadas y altas Ruedas
Mandó que se pusiessen y assentasen.
Y luego con fagina[32] y con cascajo[33]
Y tierra bien pisada quedó hecho
El poderoso puente, y fue passando
El resto del bagaje que faltaba.
Y luego al punto todo se deshizo.
Y el General, por ver se abía mostrado
Bernabé de las Casas, trabajando,
Hombre de noble assiento y de vergüenza,
Con título de Alférez quiso luego
Honrrar a su persona y estimarla.
Aquí con noble esfuerzo se mostraron
El Capitán Marcelo de Espinosa,
César Ortiz Cadimo y Iuan de Salas,
Don Iuan Escarramal y Alonso Lucas,
Bartolomé González y Mallea,
Monzón, Martín Ramírez y Iuan Pérez,
Y también Pedro Sánchez Damiero,
Simón de Paz, Medina con Castillo,
Iuan de Vitoria, Vido y los Varelas,
Alfonso Nuñez, Reyes y Herrera,
Y aquel Antonio Conte y don Luys Gasco
Y el Alférez Gerónimo de Heredia,
El Capitán Ruyz, los Bocanegras,
Robledos y otros muchos valerosos
Que valerosamente bien mostraron
Ser hombres de gran suerte[34] en el trabajo,
Que es verdadero premio de los fines
Que todos pretendemos y buscamos.
Pues como todo el campo ya estuviesse
Puesto de essotra vanda, luego vino
La fuerza de la noche sossegando
Los quebrantados miembros fatigados
Del peso del trabajo padecido.
Y apenas por las cumbres y collados

And 'twas that o'er the roaring, raging stream
A secure bridge be made,
210 For starting which he ordered then removed
And brought to him two dozen pair of wheels
From off the well-made wagons there,
And these he ordered placed at certain distances
Across the mighty current, fixed with cables,
215 As if they all had mighty vessels been.
Then he had cut the tallest and most thick
Of all the trees that might be found upon
The banks of this abundant stream,
Which all, denuded of their boughs,
220 Upon the highest, lofty wheels
He ordered should be placed and there made fast.
And then with faggots and with rubbish and
With earth well tamped was made
A sturdy bridge, and o'er it passed
225 What baggage there yet lacked, and then,
Immediately, all was taken down again.
The General, having seen to show himself
A man of noble energy and self-respect,
There in the work, one Bernabé de Las Casas,
230 Wished immediately to show him his esteem
And honor him with the title of Alférez.
Here there showed most noble effort, too,
The Captain Marcelo de Espinosa,
César Ortiz Cadimo and Juan de Salas,
235 Don Juan Escarramal, Alonso Lucas,
Bartolomé González and Mallea,
Monzón, Martín Ramírez and Juan Pérez,
And moreover Pedro Sánchez Damiero,
Simón de Paz, Medina with Castillo,
240 Juan de Vitoria, Vido, the Barelases,
Alonso Núñez, Reyes and Herrera,
And that Antonio Conte and Don Luis Gasco,
And the Alférez Gerónimo de Heredia,
Captain Ruiz, the Bocanegras, too,
245 Robledos, many other valiant men
Who showed themselves courageously and well
To be men of great strength in work,
Which is the true reward of all those ends
We all pretend to and do seek.
250 Well, now that all the camp already was
Upon that other bank, there then did come
A healing force of night to soothe
The tired, aching limbs
That suffered from the weight of toil.
255 And hardly o'er the ridges and the peaks

32. Fagina = leña menuda.
33. Cascajo = piedras menudas.
34. Suerte = tipo, clase.

La nueva y clara luz entró tendiendo
Sus bellos rayos de oro, quando estaba
La gente toda junta en gran silencio
Esperando por última partida
Ser del visitador allí honrrados
Con algunas palabras y razones
A semejantes campos bien debidas.
Cuio Gobernador también estaba
Aguardando, señor, a las mercedes,
Cédulas y despachos que le daba
Para seguir su entrada con consuelo.
Y como el mismo Dios es el principio
De todas nuestras cosas, aunque vengan
A ser los fines otros que esperamos,
Oyeron todos Missa, y acabada,
Allí el Visitador, con gran tibieza,
Al General le dixo prosiguiesse
Aquesta larga entrada y que marchase.
Y assí se despedió, sin más palabras
Y sin darle papel ni cosa alguna
Que fuesse de importancia ni provecho;
Cuio fin pobre y dexo³⁵ desabrido
Causó suma tristeza y desconsuelo
En los pechos cansados y afligidos
De los pobres soldados lastimados,
Viendo la poca ayuda que les daba
Vuestro Visitador, porque si quiera
Vna buena palabra no les dixo.
Mas como está y asiste dentro el grano,
Por notable potencia, el dulze fruto,
Assí en la fuerza grande de aflicciones,
Por el illustre esfuerzo de paciencia,
Triunfa y está la gloria lebantada
Por la nobleza firme de esperanza,
Mediante cuia alteza todos juntos,
Bajando las cabezas, prosiguieron
Sirbiéndoos, gran señor, en esta entrada.
Y assí el Visitador, sin más respecto,
Las crudas riendas luego fue bolviendo,
Dexándonos a todos bien suspensos
De ver quan sin amor allí hablaba
A todo vn campo que a serviros yba
Con vida, con hazienda y con el alma.
Pues como don Iuan viesse que, de hecho,
Yba el Visitador marchando a priessa,
Por no faltar en cosa, salió luego
Con treinta buenos hombres de acaballo.
Y todos de arrancada, los costados,
Largándoles las riendas con destreza,
Con pies ligeros, juntos, les batieron

Had new and clear light entered, stretching forth
Its beauteous rays of gold, before
The people all assembled in great silence
Hoping they would be there honored
260   By your inspector with a last farewell,
Some words, perhaps, or some address
Well owing unto such a camp.
Their Governor was also there
Awaiting, lord, such acts of grace,
265   Decrees and orders as might well be given him
To continue his entry with relief.
And since that God Himself is the beginning
Of all our acts, although the end may come
To be quite different than we hoped,
270   All there heard Mass, and at the end
The Inspector, with great frigidity,
Did tell the General he might pursue
That mighty entry and might march.
Thus he took leave, without more words,
275   Nor giving him a paper nor no other thing
That might be of importance or of use.
Which sorry end and impolite departure
Caused mighty sadness and affliction
Within the tired and troubled hearts
280   Of those poor, weary soldiers,
Seeing the little help was given them
By your inspector, for he gave them not
Even one kindly word.
But as there is and lives within the seed,
285   By notable power, the sweetest fruit,
So in the great load of afflictions,
By the illustrious power of patience,
Elevated glory triumphs
By firm nobility of hope,
290   Through whose high power all, together,
Lowering their heads, kept on, great lord,
To serve you in this expedition.
And so the inspector, without more ado,
Turned about the reins of his mount
295   And left us all in much wonder
To see how without love he there could speak
To all the camp that went to serve you
With lives, estates, and with their souls.
But when Don Juan saw that in fact
300   The inspector marched away apace,
Not to be lacking in a thing, he went
With thirty goodly mounted men,
And quickly racing, their horses' flanks,
Slacking their reins with goodly skill,
305   Light-footed, all together, spurred

35. Dexo = dejo, fin.

Hasta que juntos todos le alcanzaron.
Y allí el Gobernador, con gran respecto,
Le quiso acompañar algunas leguas,
Pidiéndole con veras se sirviesse
De alguna escolta buena de soldados.
A cuio noble y buen comedimiento,
Con las menos razones que ser pudo,
Allí le despidió sin que quisiesse
Que a su persona un passo acompañase.
Con esto, se bolvió y llegando al campo,
Estando todos juntos, fue diziendo:
"Señores Capitanes y soldados,
Nuestra fuerza mayor es el esfuerzo,
A cuio valor alto y lebantado
Iamás le desayuda la fortuna,
Y assí, no ay para qué desmaie nadie.
Corra el rigor del tiempo trabajoso
Aunque ya no podamos más sufrirle
Ni a contrastar su gran furor bastemos,
Que fin han de tener tantas zozobras,
Tantas calamidades y miserias
Como siempre nos siguen y quebrantan.
Que Dios tendrá el cuidado que es buen padre,
Serenando con próspera bonanza
El añublado Cielo que nos cubre.
Que no es cosa muy nueva ver trabajos
Por hombres de valor y de vergüenza,
Dígalo Hermodoro con Camilo,
Hermocrate, Rutilo, con Metelo,
Temístocles,[36] con otros valerosos
Que fueron por ser buenos perseguidos.
Y bien aventuradas las injurias
Que por causa de aquél que está en el Cielo
Se sufren y padecen en la tierra.
Quanto más, que si bien se considera,
Este es camino cierto y verdadero
De la impressa gallarda que llevamos."
Y con esto cesó y luego quiso
Escrebir al Virrey y darle cuenta
De todos sus trabajos y aflicciones.
Por cuia causa es bien aquí paremos
Y al canto que se sigue diferamos
Sus lastimosas quejas, tan sufridas
Quanto para escrebirlas desabridas.

310
315
320
325
330
335
340
345

Until they caught up to their man.
And there the Governor, with great respect,
Wished to accompany him some leagues,
Asking him honestly that he make use
Of some good escort of the soldiery,
At which noble and goodly courtesy,
And with the fewest words could be,
He took leave there, nor did he wish
That he accompany him a step.
With this, he turned, and coming to the camp,
All being there assembled, he spoke thus:
"Messieurs Captains and soldiers,
Our greatest strength is effort now,
Whose lofty valor raised high
Fortune will never cease to aid,
And so there is no reason to dismay.
Let come the toilsome rigors of bad weather
'Til we can bear them now no more
Nor make a stand against their fury,
For such misfortunes yet must have an end,
So many miseries, calamities,
As always follow us and break us down.
For God will care, for He is a good Father,
Calming with prosperous good weather
The cloudy heaven that covers us.
'Tis no new thing to look on toil
By men of courage and of self-respect,
Let Hermodorus and Camillus say it,
Hermocrates, Rutilus, and Metellus,
Themistocles and other valiant men[6]
Who were, for being good, attacked.
And blessèd are the calumnies
That for the cause of Him who is in Heaven
Are borne and suffered on the earth,
The more so if you consider
This is the certain and true road
Of that brave enterprise we take."
With this he ceased and then did wish
To write the Viceroy and give him account
Of all his trials and afflictions.
For which 'tis well that here we stop
And to the following canto we put off
His sorrowful complaint, as well endured
As here to write them 'tis arduous.

---

36. Hermodoro, filósofo, discípulo de Platón; Camilo, tribuno romano, luchador contra los galos; Hermócrate, Hermócrates, general de Siracusa que luchó contra los atenienses; Rutilo, consul romano, desterrado por Sila; Metelo, consul romano que venció a los cartagineses en Sicilia; Temístocles, mandó la escuadra ateniense en Salamina y fue después desterrado. Las posibles fuentes clásicas de Villagrá para esta lista ocuparían mucho espacio. Pueden verse muchos citados en la obra de Pero Mexía, *Silva de varia lección* II, 21.

6. Hermodorus, philosopher, disciple of Plato; Camilus, Roman tribune, fought the gauls; Hermocrates, Syracusan general who fought the Athenians; Rutilus, Roman consul exiled by Sulla; Metellus, Roman consul who defeated the Carthaginians in Sicily; Themosticles, commanded the Athenian fleet against the Persians and was later exiled. Villagrá's sources were undoubtedly multiple, but many of the above are used as examples by Pero Mexía, *Silva de varia lección* II, 21.

CANTO HONZE

COMO ESCRIVIO DON IVAN AL VIRREY Y COMO
HIZIERON bolver al Padre Fray Diego Márquez, y como fue
marchando el campo al Río de San Pedro, y escolta que se embió
para que los Religiosos le alcanzasen, y salida que hizo el
Sargento mayor a explorar el Río del Norte, y trabajos que
padeció siguiendo su demanda.

OMO quiera que el alma lastimada
Es cierto que descansa quando cuenta
La fuerza del dolor que la fatiga,
Por sólo descansar de sus trabajos,
Cercado de dolor y desconsuelo,
Aqueste molestado caballero
Tomó papel y tinta y vna carta
Despachó luego al Conde, en que dezía
Las grandes aflicciones y congojas,
Las pérdidas, los gastos y trabajos,
Persecuciones, cargas y disgustos
Que esta larga jornada abía tenido,
Y aquel ardiente zelo y buen desseo
Que de servir a Dios y a vuestro Padre
En él estuvo siempre, y aquel ansia
De ver la conversión de tantas gentes
Al gremio de la Iglesia reduzidas,
Y aquella gran paciencia y obediencia
Que a vn millón de disgustos y de agravios
También abía tenido y sustentado,
Y la esperanza firme que tenía
En las promesas, cartas y palabras
Que tantas vezes quiso prometerle,
Y aquella voluntad illustre y santa
De vuestro inmenso Padre en las mercedes
Que siempre fue servido de mostrarle
En todos los despachos que hazía,
Mediante cuia fuerza fue assentada
Con él aquesta entrada con empeño
Que de su fee y palabra le fue dada
De guardarle y cumplirle todo aquello
Que con él se pusiesse y assentase,
Cuia inviolable prenda no sufría,
Por ningún caso, quiebra ni tardanza.
Y viendo como vía tan mal logro
De todos sus servicios y trabajos
De dos años y medio ya passados,
Pensando que adelante muchos passos
Estaba ya y muy cerca de la palma,
Corona, gloria y triunfo que esperaba

CANTO XI

How Don Juan wrote to the Viceroy and how they made Fray
Diego Márquez return, and how the camp marched on to the
Río San Pedro, and of the escort that was sent so that the
Monks might reach it, and of the trip the Sergeant Major
made to explore the River of the North, and the labors he
endured in search of it.

INCE of the suffering and tormented soul
'Tis certain it doth rest when it doth tell
The power of the pain that wearies it,
Only as rest from his labors,
5   Borne down with pain, disconsolate,
That sorely troubled gentleman
Took paper and took ink and sent at once
A letter to the Count in which he told
The great afflictions and anxieties,
10 The losses, the expenses, and the work,
The persecutions, burdens, disappointments
That this long entry had endured,
And, too, that ardent zeal and good desire
Of serving God and your father
15 Which he had always had, and his fervent desire
To see conversion of so many folk
Brought to the bosom of the Church,
And that great patience and obedience
Which through a million disappointments and insults
20 He also had kept and maintained,
And that firm hope that he possessed
In promises, in letters and words
That he so often chose to promise him,
And that most famous, holy will
25 Of your great father in the acts of grace
That he had pleased to show to him
In all the things that he had done for him,
Because of whom he had been named
To this adventure with the mighty pledge
30 Of his good faith and word all given him
To keep and to fulfill those things
That were entrusted and contracted to him;
Which pledge, inviolable, suffered not,
For any cause, a break or a delay.
35 And seeing, as he saw, such ill success
Of all his service and his work
For two years and a half now past,
Thinking that now he had gone many steps
Ahead, and very near the palm,
40 The crown, the glory, and the triumph hoped for by

Quien también[1] merecía ser premiado,
Se vía tan atrás que colegía
Dos cosas por muy ciertas e infalibles:
La vna, que esta entrada trabajosa
Que era cierta[2] de Dios pues que llevaba
El camino derecho de sus obras,
Pues a fuerza de Cruz y de quebrantos
Abía sido siempre sustentada;
Y en quanto a la segunda, no sabía
Porqué razón, camino o por qué causa
O por quál de las muchas obras buenas
Que por esta jornada abía sufrido,
Era tan perseguido y maltratado,
Si por llevar la Iglesia y ensancharla
Por entre aquellos bárbaros perdidos,
Ciegos de lumbre, Fe y de la sangre
Que fue por todo el mundo derramada,
O si[3] poner a riesgo por serviros
Su vida, su persona y su hazienda,
Si el ser tratado siempre como esclavo,
Si el sufrir tan gran tiempo los trabajos
De dilación tan larga y tan costosa;
Pidiéndole perdón si se quejaba,
Porque estaba herido y lastimado
Y jamás de ninguno socorrido,
Mas antes calumniado y probocado,
Con otras muchas cosas lastimosas
Que assí quiso escrebirle y avisarle.
Cerrada, pues, la carta y despachada,
Luego tras desto vino vn grande golpe
Que a todos nos causó vn gran disgusto.
Y fue que ciertos tristes desalmados
Por invención diabólica secreta
Trazaron de manera que no fuesse
El buen fray Diego Márquez la jornada,
Vnico confessor, amparo y fuerza
De todo aqueste campo perseguido,
Que mucho por su ausencia se dolía
Por aber sido la primera vassa[4]
Sobre que fue fundado y lebantado.
Y viendo el General su gran desgracia
Y que era ya forzosa su quedada,
En prendas del amor que le tenía

One who richly deserved reward,
He felt so abandoned, he did infer
Two things as certain and infallible:
The one, this toilsome expedition
45 Was certainly of God, because it took
The straight road to His work,
And since by the aid of the Cross[1] and sufferings
It had been aye sustained;
And, speaking of the second, he knew not
50 By what reason or road or by what cause,
Or for which of the many goodly works
That he had suffered for this expedition,
He was so persecuted and ill-used,
If for thus shouldering the Church, extending it
55 Among those lost barbarians,
Blind to the light, the Faith, and to the blood
That was for all the world poured out,
Or if for risking, but to serve the King,
His life, his person and estates,
60 Or being treated always as a slave,
Or suffering so long the woes
Of such costly and long delay,
Asking his pardon if he there complained,
Because he now was wounded and in pain
65 And never helped by anyone,
But rather slandered and provoked,
With many other sorrowful things
That then he chose to write and let him know.
The letter closed, then, and sent off,
70 There came immediately a great blow
That caused us all a great offense,
And 'twas that certain sorry, soulless ones
By secret, diabolical invention,
Did scheme against the going of
75 The good Fray Diego Márquez on the trip,[2]
The sole confessor, shelter, only strength
Of all that persecuted camp,
Which, for his absence, sorrowed much
As he had been the cornerstone
80 Upon which it was founded and raised up.
The General, seeing his misfortune great
And that 'twas necessary he remain,
As token of the love he had for him,

---

1. También = tan bien.
2. Cierta = ciertamente.
3. Omite, con licencia poética, la preposición "por." En las dos condiciones que siguen (versos 60 y 61), se omite asimismo la disyuntiva "o."
4. Vassa = basa, asiento de columna.

1. Villagrá uses *cruz* (cross), metaphorically, as "endured hardship," but it can also be read, as Curtis does, in its strictly religious connotation.
2. For the reasons behind Fray Diego Márquez, commissary of the Inquisition, being recalled from the expedition, see the letter of the viceroy to Philip II, dated 1 May 1598, published by G. P. Hammond and A. Rey, *Oñate, Colonizer of New Mexico* (Albuquerque: Univ. of New Mexico Press, 1953), 387.

Con mil abrazos tiernos y apretados,
Vna devota Imagen y un Rosario   85
Y, de doña María de Galarza,
Que era su muy amada y cara hermana,⁵
Vn bello niño Jesús quiso darle,
Cuia hechura santa no tenía
Ningún valor ni precio por la alteza   90
Con que el artista quiso figurarlo.
Pues luego que de todos despedido
Salió el vendito Padre sin consuelo,⁶
Mandó el Gobernador se previniesse
Escolta suficiente y se aprestase   95
Para traer los Padres Religiosos
Que con su Comissario ya venían
Marchando bien apriessa en nuestro alcance,
Cuia prevención hizo con aviso
Por dezir que la gente Tepeguana⁷   100
Estaba rebelada y alterada.
Estando, pues, la escolta prevenida,
La qual fue encomendada y encargada
Al Capitán Farfán, salió marchando
Y juntamente el campo fue saliendo   105
La buelta de San Pedro, que es vn Río
De cristalinas aguas y pescado
Por todo extremo lindo y regalado,
A cuio puesto yba enderezando
El pobre General, qual gruessa nave   110
Que sin ningún registro⁸ va sulcando
El poderoso y largo mar tendido.
No de otra suerte, assí, se fue lanzando
Al ancho campo por camino incierto
Hasta llegar al puesto donde luego,   115
Aguardando los Padres, fue assentando
La fuerza del exército en sus tiendas.
Y estando algunos días aguardando,
Llegó toda la escolta con la Iglesia
Vna jornada larga de aquel sitio,   120
Y dando aviso, luego, que venía
Fray Alonso Martínez, Religioso
De singular virtud y nobles prendas,
Por cabeza y patrón de aquella nave,

With many a tender, close embrace,
He gave to him a holy figure and a rosary,
And wished to give a beauteous Infant Jesus
From Doña María de Galarza,³
Who was his dear and well-beloved sister,
One whose holy artifice was quite beyond
All value and all price from the great skill
With which the artist chose to make the same.
Well, when farewell to all was thus said
The blessed Father off disconsolate,
The Governor ordered they provide
Sufficient escort and make haste
To bring the holy Fathers to the camp,
Who now were coming with their commissary,
Marching with speed to reach us, which
Precaution he took, advisedly,
It being said the race of Tepehuán
Were in rebellion, dangerous.⁴
The escort, being thus forewarned,
And being given to the charge
Of Captain Farfán, went on its way,
And at the same time the whole camp set out
For the San Pedro, which same is a stream
With crystal waters and with fish
Well-stored and most extremely beautiful,
Unto which point did guide us well
The worn-out General, like a great ship
That without goal still ploughs along
The mighty and wide-spreading sea.
Not otherwise he thus forced on
The spreading camp over uncertain roads
Until arriving at the place where, then,
He placed, to await the Fathers,
The main force of the army in its tents.
And having waited now some days
The escort, with all of the Church, arrived
A long day's journey from that place
And sent on word that with it came
Fray Alonso Martínez, godly man,
Of virtue singular and noble gifts,
As head and patron of that ship,

5. Se trata de la hermana de Oñate, que le había regalado, al parecer, esa imagen.

6. Para las razones por las cuales fue destituido Fray Diego Márquez, comisario del Santo Oficio, puede verse la carta del virrey a Felipe II, fechada el 1 de mayo de 1598, publicada por G. P. Hammond & A. Rey, *Oñate, Colonizer of New Mexico* (Albuquerque: Univ. of New Mexico Press, 1953), 387.

7. Tribu indígena del norte de México.

8. El registro o padrón del buque indicaba su destino. En sentido figurado, sin el contingente de religiosos, la expedición carecía de dirección en su finalidad primaria.

3. It is understood that Oñate received it as a present from his sister.

4. A tribe indigenous to northern Mexico.

Cuia grave persona acompañaban
El Padre Fray Francisco de Zamora,
El Padre Rozas, San Miguel⁹ y Claros,
El Padre Lugo Y Fray Andrés Corchado
Y aquellos dos venditos Padres legos,¹⁰
Fray Pedro de Vergara con el Padre
Fray Iuan, y tres hermanos que truxeron,
Martín, Francisco y Iuan de Dios, el bueno.
Pues luego que don Iuan la nueva supo
Dos Capitanes despachó a darles,
Con vna noble esquadra de guerreros,
El bien venido a todos con palabras
De gran comedimiento y buen Respecto.
Y tras dellos se fue con todo el campo
En formado esquadrón, y, sin tardanza,
Assí como los vido, seys hileras
Mandó se adelantasen de banguardia
Con segundo recado cortesano,
Y¹¹ abiendo el Comissario de su parte
Despachado a dos nobles Religiosos
Para que de la suya visitasen
A nuestro General. Aquesto hecho,
Los dos illustres brazos poderosos
A más andar se fueron acercando,
Y escupiendo las llaves¹² vivo fuego
Vna gran salva todos le hizieron.
Y abiéndose abrazado y recebido
Con términos discretos y razones
Muy graves y pesadas, rebolvieron.
Y luego que al exército llegaron,
Segunda salva todos le hizieron
Y en vna ancha enrramada se apearon,
Donde estaban las mesas prevenidas.
Y allí, los Capitanes y oficiales
Con ellos, todos juntos, se assentaron
Y vna grande comida les sirvieron,
Con muy cortés crianza, regalada.¹³
Después de todo aquesto, por sus tiendas
Fueron los Religiosos recogidos.
En este medio tiempo, abía salido
El Sargento mayor a toda priessa,

125 Whose holy person was accompanied
By Padre Fray Francisco de Zamora,
By Padre Rozas, San Miguel⁵ and Claros,
Padre Lugo and Fray Andrés Corchado,
And those two blessed lay Fathers,⁶
130 Fray Pedro de Vergara and Father
Fray Juan and, too, three brothers that they brought,
Martín, Francisco and, too, Juan de Dios, the good.
As soon as Don Juan learned the news
He sent two Captains together with
135 A noble squadron of bold warriors
To give them welcome with good words
Of great politeness and of high respect,
And after them he went with all the camp
In squadron formed, without delay.
140 As soon as he saw them, he ordered forth
Six ranks of men from the vanguard
With second courteous greeting,
And the Commissary, on his part,
Having dispatched two noble Monks
145 That they might take his place in visiting
Our General. And, that being done,
The two illustrious, powerful arms,
Proceeding on, approached more close
And, muskets spitting living flame,
150 All made to them a grand salute.
And, having embraced each other there,
With words discrete and greetings interchanged,
Right grave and serious they returned.
And when they to the army came
155 All fired a second salvo to them,
And they dismounted in a bower wide
Where tables had been well set forth.
And there the Captains and the officers,
Together with them all, sat down
160 And there was served to them a goodly meal
Set forth with courtly service.
After all which unto their tents
The Monks betook themselves.
In the meantime, there had set forth
165 The Sergeant Major, in great haste,

9. Fray Francisco de San Miguel se había quedado del grupo original de religiosos. Véase G. P. Hammond, "Oñate and the Founding of New Mexico," *New Mexico Historical Review* 1 (1926): 295–96.

10. Legos = sin órdenes religiosas. Villagrá les llama padres, pero debiera usar hermanos, y a los que después llama hermanos debiera llamar donados. Véase F. Scholes & L. Bloom, "Friar Personnel and Mission Chronology," *New Mexico Historical Review* 19 (1944): 321.

11. Posible errata del original por "ya," que haría mejor lectura.

12. Llaves = mecanismos para disparar las armas de fuego.

13. Regalada = abundante, deleitosa.

5. Fray Francisco San Miguel, of the original group of friars, had remained with the camp. See G. P. Hammond, "Oñate and the Founding of New Mexico," *New Mexico Historical Review* 1 (1926): 295–96.

6. Villagrá uses *padres* with *legos*, the latter meaning unordained. He should have more properly used *hermanos* (brothers) with that term. And for those he later refers to as hermanos, he more properly should have used *donados*. See F. Scholes and L. Bloom, "Friar Personnel and Mission Chronology," *New Mexico Historical Review* 19 (1944): 321.

Con tres Pilotos grandes que dezían
Ser en aquella tierra bien cursados,
Por sólo descubrir las turbias aguas
Del caudaloso Río que del Norte
Deciende manso y tanto se embrabece
Que también Río bravo le llamamos.
Saliendo, pues, las guías descubrieron
De San Martín los llanos más tendidos
Y allí desatinaron de manera
Que, como cazadores que disparan
Otra segunda jara desde el puesto
Para poder tomar mejor la vía
De la primera saeta que perdieron,
Assí determinaron de bolverse
Al puesto de los llanos y otro rumbo
Seguir muy diferente que el primero.
Mas qual veloz cometa, cuio curso
No vemos que jamás atrás rebuelve,
Assí, determinado en su distino,
Disgustoso, el Sargento nunca quiso
Que atrás passo se diesse ni pensase
Y que para adelante, por la parte
Que más gusto les diesse, caminasen.
En cuio pensamiento fue resuelto[14]
Por la gran presunción que abían mostrado
Aquestos tres Pilotos, confiados
En su propria virtud y vana ciencia.
Y assí fueron corriendo grandes tierras,
Mas como ciegos que a los ciegos guían,
Que todos se embarrancan y se pierden,
Assí, perdidos, todos zozobrados,
Acudiendo a la tabla y al madero
Que más a mano pudo ser topasen,[15]
Assí buscaron luego algunos Indios
Que fuessen de la tierra naturales.
Y viendo vn grande humo lebantado,
Las riendas rebolvieron con presteza
Marzelo de Espinosa y Juan Piñero,
Villaviciosa, Olague, y assí, juntos,
Como astutos caudillos de pillage,
Redoblando con fuerza el acicate,[16]
Dieron con quatro bárbaros que andaban
Acaso[17] en el desierto monteando,
Pensando de cazar, y fueron pressos.
Y como al elefante y vnicornio

14. Resuelto = decidido.

15. Tratándose del desierto nuevo mexicano, resultan algo extremas las imagenes marinas, tan del gusto de Virgilio y de la épica americana.

16. Acicate = espuela.

17. Acaso = por casualidad.

With three famed guides who said they were
Well learned in all that land,
With purpose to seek out the turbid flood
Of that wide stream that from the north
Flows calm, yet swells so much
That we call it the Río Bravo, too.
Departing, then, the guides sought out
The mighty plains of San Martín
And there they went astray in such a sort
That, like the hunters who do fire
A second shaft from where they stand
The better to find out the flying path
Of that first arrow which they shot,
So they determined to return
To the edge of the plains, and there pursue
A course exceeding different from the first.
But like the comet swift whose course
We never see returning on itself,
So, fixed upon his own fate,
The Sergeant, much displeased, did never wish
To take a backward step or think of it
And said to go ahead wherever they
Should think it best to go.
In which thought he was well resolved
By the presumption that was shown
By those three pilots, trusting in
Their own virtue and science vain.
And so they passed o'er spreading lands,
But like the blind whom the blind guide,
That all are lost and stranded there,
Thus lost and all dispirited
And clinging to the planks and beams
That chanced into their hands,[7]
They then sought for some Indians
Who might be native to the land.
And, seeing a great smoke rise up,
There turned their reins with mighty haste
Marcelo de Espinosa and Juan Piñero,
Villaviciosa, Olague, and so, together,
Like cunning bandit chiefs,
Plying with force their Moorish spurs,
They came upon four wandering barbarians
Beating the desert woods by chance,
Thinking to hunt, and they were seized.
And as the elephant and unicorn,

7. Villagrá's use of nautical and marine imagery is sometimes, as in this case, a somewhat exaggerated expression of this New World epic feature.

Después de pressos suelen regalarlos,
Assí con blandas muestras y señales
A todos les mostraron noble pecho,
De noble corazón, cenzillo y llano,
Y sólo les pidieron los llevasen
A las aguas del Norte, con promesa
Que assí como las viessen les darían
A todos libertad, sin que quebrasen
La fuerza de palabra que en empeño
A todos ofrecieron y empeñaron.
Y porque el Sol tres días naturales
Abía dado buelta al alto Cielo
Y gota de agua nadie abía bebido,
Llegó Manuel, Francisco, con Munuera,
Iuan de León, Rodríguez y Bustillo
Y Pablo de Aguilar con buenas nuevas
De vna apazible fuente descubierta.
Y juntos todos ya con el Sargento,
Que en busca de agua y gente divididos
Andaban por el campo derramados,
Para la fuente juntos embistieron.
Y puestos en el agua, como pezes,
Assí se abalanzaron sin sentido,
Valiéndose más della que del ayre.
Satisfechos, pues, todos, otro día
Mandó el Sargento que los tres Pilotos,
Con algunos amigos,[18] se bolviessen,
Y por cumplir el orden que tenía
Del noble General, mandó callasen
Y cosa de trabajos no dixessen
A nadie del Real, mas que contasen
Alegres nuevas todos, publicando
Dexaban buen camino descubierto,
De buenos pastos, aguas y buen monte,
Y que si alguno fuesse preguntado
Que a qué se detenía, o por qué causa,
Dixessen que por descubrir más tierra
De aquella que dexaban descubierta.
Y esto determinó porque faltaban
De todo punto ya los bastimentos.
Bueltos, pues, los amigos con las nuevas,
El Sargento mayor con sus soldados,
Rompiendo por cien mil dificultades
De hambre, sed, cansancio y de disgustos,
Encuentros y refriegas que tuvieron,
Guiados de los bárbaros, llegaron,

When captured, they do treat right well,
So with kind gestures and with signs
They showed them all a noble front,
Of noble, simple hearts and plain,
215 And asked them only that they lead
Them to the waters of the North, and promised them
That, when they saw them, they would give them then
Their liberty in full, nor would they break
Their given word, which, as a pledge
220 They offered and did pledge to all.
And as the sun for three full days
Had made his circuit in the lofty sky
And none had drunk a drop of water yet,
There came Manuel, Francisco, Munuera,
225 Juan de León, Rodríguez and Bustillo
And Pablo de Aguilar with glorious news
About discovery of a pleasant spring.
And, all now joined with the Sergeant
Who, divided in search of water and folk,
230 Had wandered scattered o'er the land,
Together for the spring they set out.
And, arriving at the water, like to fish
They there plunged in, half unconscious,
Having more need of it than air.
235 All satisfied, the following day
The Sergeant ordered the three guides
To go back with some friends of his,[8]
And, to fulfill the order that he had
From the noble General, he ordered they be still
240 And say nothing about their sufferings
To any in the camp, but that they say
Nothing but good news unto all,
That they had left a fine road they had found,
With pasture excellent and waters and good woods,
245 And that if anyone should question them
Of why he stayed behind and for what cause,
They should say to discover other lands
Than that they had already found.
And this he did determine since he lacked
250 Provisions now in the extreme.
The friends now having turned back with the news,
The Sergeant Major with his soldiers,
Crushing a hundred thousand hindrances,
Of hunger, thirst, fatigue and disappointments,
255 Encounters and skirmishes that they had,
Guided by the barbarians they came,

18. Está claro que se refiere a algunos españoles, que, por ir faltándole ya bastimentos, decidió volvieran.

8. The Spanish text could read, as Curtis did, that the friends referred to were so to the guides; but this is clarified somewhat a little later when it is noted that Zaldívar, very low on supplies, sent back some of his own men.

Por grandes riscos, sierras y quebradas,	Past mighty crags and mountains and ravines,
Al Río que buscaban, y allí juntos	To that river they sought, where together they
Mataron vn caballo y le comieron.	Did kill a horse and ate the same.
Con esto dieron buelta y despidieron	This done, they did return, and took leave of
Aquellos quatro bárbaros amigos,	Those four barbarians, their friends,
Dándoles de la ropa que llevaban.	Giving them of the clothing that they wore.
Y el General, temiendo su gran falta,	The General, fearing for their needs,
Mandó que el Capitán Landín saliesse	Ordered Captain Landín then to set forth
Y algún socorro luego le llevase.	And carry some help unto him.
También quiso que yo[19] con él me fuesse,	Also he wished that I should go with him,[9]
Y assí, juntos los dos, con seys soldados,	And so we two, together with six men,
Salimos en su busca y le encontramos,	Went out in search of him and found him, too,
Al cabo de diez días ya cumplidos,	Having completed ten full days of search,
El alma entre los dientes,[20] animando,	He helping on, his soul between his teeth,
El y toda su esquadra, a Iuan Rodríguez,	Like all his troops, Juan Rodríguez, whom,
Que en vn flaco caballo atravesado,	Slung loose across a famished horse,
De hambre ya rendido, le traían,	Now overcome with hunger, they did bring,
Esperando su muerte y que acabase.	Awaiting his imminent demise.
En cuio puesto, todos socorridos,	All being aided there, at once
Dexándonos allí, nos encargaron	They left us there and ordered us
Que vn gran trecho fuessemos corriendo	To keep on traveling a long distance
Por las faldas de vn cerro prolongado	Along the skirts of a long ridge
Y viessemos si el campo todo junto	And see if all the camp at once
Por él romper pudiesse algunas leguas.	Could pass through it within some leagues.
Con esto todos luego prosiguieron	With this, they all pursued their way
A dar razón y cuenta del sucesso	To make report and tell of the events
A sólo el General, y con contento	Unto the General alone, and with content
A todos los del campo consolaron	Consoled all the folk about the camp
Con nuevas muy alegres de la tierra.	With very happy news about the land.
Y entre tanto, nosotros descubrimos	And meanwhile we ourselves discovered
Vn buen pedazo de camino llano,	A splendid piece of level road,
De buenos pastos y aguas regaladas.	With pasture good and water plenteous.
Aquí se le ofreció hazer despacho[21]	Here it occurred to our General
A la Ciudad de México nombrada	To send to the City of Mexico renowned,
A nuestro General, y confiado	Dispatches, and, as he well trusted in
Del Capitán Landín mandó bolviesse	Captain Landín, he ordered him to go
Y vn pliego con presteza le llevase.	And take a packet there in haste.
Hecho, pues, el despacho, luego fuimos	The message sent, we then went on,
Marchando con el campo muy gustosos	Marching right gladly with the camp
Hasta llegar al agua que llamaron	Until we came unto the water that they call
Del Santo Sacramento, cuio nombre	The River of the Holy Sacrament, whose name
Los Padres Religiosos le pusieron	The holy Fathers gave to it
Porque allí junto della celebraron	Because close by it they did celebrate
El Iueves Santo de la santa Cena,	The Holy Thursday of the Holy Feast,
Por cuia santa noche y santo día	For which most holy day and holy night

Line numbers: 260, 265, 270, 275, 280, 285, 290, 295, 300

---

19. Esta intervención del narrador en la acción tenía su importante antecedente en Ercilla, aunque Villagrá narre también acciones en las que no intervino.

20. El alma entre los dientes = a punto de expirar.

21. Hacer despacho = mandar carta.

9. This intervention of the author in the action of the poem had an important antecedent in Ercilla (*La araucana*), although Villagrá also narrates actions at which he was not present.

Mandó el Gobernador que se hiziesse
De poderosos árboles y troncos
Vna grande capilla muy bien hecha,
Toda con sus doseles[22] bien colgada,
Y enmedio della vn triste Monumento
Donde la vida vniversal del mundo
En él se sepultase y encerrase[23]
Con mucha escolta y guarda de soldados.
Y siendo el General allí de prima,[24]
Los Religiosos todos de rodillas
La noche entera allí belaron.
Vbo de penitentes muy contritos
Vna sangrienta y grande deziplina,
Pidiendo a Dios con lágrimas y ruegos
Que como su grandeza abrió camino
Por medio de las aguas y a pie enjuto
Los hijos de Isrrael salieron libres,
Que assí nos libertasse y diesse senda
Por aquellos tristíssimos desiertos
Y páramos incultos, desabridos,
Porque con bien la Iglesia se llevase
Hasta la nueva México, remota[25]
De bien tan importante y saludable,
Pues no menos por ellos fue vertida,
Aquella santa noche dolorosa,
Su muy preciosa sangre que por todos
Aquéllos que la alcanzan y la gozan.
Y porque su bondad no se escusase,
A grandes vozes por el campo a solas,
Descalzas, las mujeres y los niños
Misericordia todos le pedían.
Y los soldados, juntos, a dos puños[26]
Abriéndose por vno y otro lado
Con crueles azotes las espaldas,
Socorro con gran priessa le pedían.
Y los humildes hijos de Francisco,
Cubiertos de zilicios y devotos,
Instaban con clamores y plegarias
Porque Dios les oyesse y aiudase.
Y el General, en vn lugar secreto
Que quiso que yo sólo le supiesse,
Hincado de rodillas fue vertiendo
Dos fuentes de sus ojos y tras dellas,
Rasgando sus espaldas, derramaba

The Governor did order there be made,
Of mighty trunks of trees,
A goodly chapel, right well made
305   And all with canopies well hung,
And, in the midst of it, sad monument
Where universal life of all the world
In it be buried and enclosed
With mighty escort and with guard of troops.
310   The General being there at prime,[10]
The Fathers all upon their knees,
They there kept vigil all the night.
There was of penitents contrite
A discipline bloody and great,
315   Asking of God with tears and prayers
That, as his power opened out a road
Amid the waters and with feet all dry
The race of Israel went free,
E'en so he would free us and show a path
320   Amid those deserts most exceeding sad
And freezing waste, unsheltered plains,
So that the Church might well be carried on
Into New Mexico, kept from
A gift so important, so salutary,
325   Since none the less for them was shed
Upon that holy night of agony
His very precious blood, than for all those
Who have obtained and do enjoy it now.
And lest His goodness be unmoved,
330   Through all the camp, alone, aloud,
The women and the children, barefooted,
Did beg of Him His mercy. And
The soldiers, all together, with both hands
Laying their backs all open on one side
335   And on the other with the cruel whips,
Were begging aid of Him and in great haste.[11]
And the most humble sons of Francisco,
Clad all in haircloth and devout,
Did beg with clamor and repeated prayers
340   That God would hear them and would aid.
The General, in a secret place
That he wished only I should know,
Kneeling upon the ground did shed
Two fountains from his eyes and then,
345   Lashing his shoulders, he poured out

---

22. Doseles = cortinas.
23. Siendo Viernes Santo, celebraron el entierro de Jesús.
24. Prima = el primer turno de vela.
25. Remota = apartada.
26. A dos puños = con ambas manos.

10. The first watch. The night was divided into three parts for the purposes of sentinel duty.
11. Although self-flagellation was a common penitence of those times, this scene depicted by Villagrá cannot help but recall the later *penitentes* of New Mexican history. See, for example, T. J. Steele and R. A. Rivera, *Penitente Self-Government* (Santa Fe: Ancient City Press, 1985), and Villagrá, *Historia*, Junquera edition, 22–23.

Vn mar de roja sangre, suplicando
A su gran magestad que se doliesse
De todo aqueste campo que a su cargo
Estaba todo puesto y assentado.
También sus dos sobrinos en sus puestos
Pedazos con azotes se hazían,[27]
Hasta que entró la luz y fue alumbrando
Al noble General en el oficio[28]
Que debía hazer porque acertase.
Y assí advirtió que, pues pilotos diestros
En mar y en tierra no eran de importancia
Para el camino que la Iglesia santa
Abía de llevar por el desierto,
Que aquesta causa luego se encargase
A gentes de ignorancia, porque a vezes
Suele su gran bageza aventajarse
A los que son más sabios y discretos.
Y por notar mejor, señor, aquéllos
Que cosa tan pesada les encargan,
Quiero con atención aquí pararme,
Que no tendría a mucho que yo fuesse,
Por ser tan grande idiota señalado
Y en cosas de ignorancia bien probado.

350

355

360

365

A sea of crimson blood while imploring
His Divine Majesty that he have mercy on
All that great camp that in his charge
Was placed and entrusted.
Also, his two nephews at their posts
Did lacerate themselves with whips,
Until the dawn came, illumined
The noble General as to the commands
He needs must give in order to succeed.
And so he saw that pilots skilled
On land and sea were needed not
For that road which the Holy Church
Was to pursue throughout the desert there,
For that cause should be entrusted
To men of ignorance, because at times
Their lowliness doth outperform
Many who are more learned and discreet.
And, lord, that I may better note
Those upon whom such a heavy load was laid,
I wish, with all civility, to break off here,
For it would not surprise that I be one,
Marked out as such a thorough idiot
And richly proved in things of ignorance.

27. Al conocedor de la historia de Nuevo México, no puede menos
que recordarle esta descripción las prácticas que se identificarían, siglos
después, con los llamados Penitentes. Véanse Villagrá, *Historia,* edición
de Junquera, 22–23, y T. J. Steele y R. A. Rivera, *Penitente Self-
Government* (Santa Fe: Ancient City Press, 1985).
28. Oficio = orden, mandato.

Canto Doze

UIEN jamás, gran señor, imaginara
Ser tan illustres y altos los quilates
De la simple ignorancia que por ella
Vbiesse de dezir aquel gallardo
Pelícano sagrado,[1] cuio pecho
Tan mal herido y lastimado vemos
Del mazizo guijarro[2] lebantado
Del penitente brazo, que rebuelve,
Para más bien subirla y encumbrarla,[3]
Sobre las graves letras memorables
De aquéllos, más famosas, que passaron,
Diziendo desta suerte contra todos:
"¡O ignorancia santa, cuia alteza
Es de tan gran valor y tanta estima
Que basta para assegurar al hombre,
Nacido para míseros trabajos,
Seguro y dulze puerto perdurable
Dentro de aquella bienaventuranza
Donde toda limpieza se atesora!
Nunca por las escuelas Atenienses
Alcanzó el gran Platón su gran grandeza,
Aristóteles menos supo della,
Iamás le dio Anaxógoras[4] alcance,
Ni todos los demás mundanos sabios,
Ni en la Academia Griega ni Romana
Nunca jamás supieron ni alcanzaron
El valor de su gran merecimiento."
Y passando adelante va diziendo:
"Y yo también, Gerónimo abatido,
Que siempre fui imitando a todos éstos,
Sé que también se me passó por alto
Antes que por mi grande bien me dieran

1. Se refiere a San Jerónimo, y la designación de pelicano se debe a que el ave, ya en el Antiguo Testamento, Psalmo 101, se identificaba con la soledad, y, por lo tanto, con la vida monástica.
2. Desde el siglo XV se venía representado a San Jerónimo con la piedra en la mano. Véase E. F. Rice Jr., *Saint Jerome in the Renaissance* (Baltimore: The Johns Hopkins Univ. Press, 1985), 76.
3. El antecedente de subirla y encumbrarla es la ignorancia.
4. Anaxógoras = filósofo griego de la escuela jónica.

Canto XII

HO ever, lord, would have imagined
The perfection of simple ignorance
To be so famed, illustrious, that about it
Would say that magnanimous one,
5   The sacred Pelican,[1] whose breast
We see so badly wounded, hurt,
By massive stone raised upon high
By the repentant arm,[2] that he holds it,
The better to lift and elevate it,
10   Above the grave and memorable works
Of those more famous ones who passed,
Saying in this wise to them all:
"O holy ignorance, whose height
Is of such value, such esteem,
15   It is enough to reassure the man
Born unto miserable toil
Safe, sweet, and all-enduring port
Within that human felicity
Where all integrity is treasured up!
20   Never in the Athenian schools
Did the great Plato reach its mightiness;
Aristotle not even knew of it;
Never did Anaxagoras[3] grasp it,
Nor all the other worldly-wise,
25   Nor the Academy of Greece or Rome
Did ever know or attain to
The valor of its great merit."
And, going on, he continues:
"That I, too, an abject Gerónimo,[4]
30   Who always imitated them,
Know that it passed over my head
Before they gave me, for my highest good,

1. The reference is to Saint Jerome, church father. The pelican designation stems from the fact that the bird, already in the Old Testament (Psalm 101), is identified with solitude, and later, in early Christianity, with a monastic existence, with which Saint Jerome is always associated.
2. From the fifteenth century on Saint Jerome is depicted with a rock in his hand, with which he beat his breast in penance. See E. F. Rice Jr., *Saint Jerome in the Renaissance* (Baltimore: The Johns Hopkins Univ. Press, 1985), 76.
3. Anaxagoras was a Greek philosopher, teacher of Pericles and possibly of Socrates.
4. Curtis kept the saint's name in Spanish.

Los sagrados azotes que me dieron."⁵
¡O soberano santo y santo pecho,
Y cómo esta doctrina nos enseña
Aquello que por vista de ojos vimos!
Abiendo, pues, excelso rey, salido
A sólo descubrir este camino
De tierra y mar destríssimos pilotos,
Tan llenos de altibez y de arrogancia
Que sin ellos jamás imaginaron
Que vn solo passo el campo se moviesse,
Y assí como sus vanos pensamientos,
Como de vanos, vanos les salieron,
Acordó el General se señalasen
Ocho soldados, y que sólo fuessen
En armas y trabajos bien sufridos,
Que aquesto es lo que vale quando falta
Quien nos industrie, enseñe y nos adiestre
En las cosas que todos ignoramos.
Para este efecto fueron escogidos
El provehedor y Sebastián Rodríguez,
Dionisio de Bañuelos y Robledo,
Francisco Sánchez y Christóbal Sánchez,
Carabajal, y yo también con ellos,
Para sólo inchir, sin que ygualase,
Mi pequeño caudal a su alto esfuerzo,
Tan ignorantes todos en alturas,
Rumbos, Estrellas, vientos, medios vientos,⁶
Que después de encerrado el Sol sospecho
Que no yba allí ninguno que dixiesse,
Afirmativamente, sin herrarse,
Aquí es Oriente y veis allí a Occidente.
Mas para esto son buenos los trabajos,
Que en ellos es necessidad maestra;
Esta haze a los hombres avisados,
Sabios, prudentes, práticos y diestros
En todas ciencias y artes liberales,
Sacadas de experiencia, que es la madre
Y fuente principal de donde nacen.
Assí que cada qual con su corteza
Aspera, tosca, bronca, mal labrada,
Rindió la voluntad y fue cumpliendo
Lo que su General allí ordenaba.
Y como ciegos que por sólo el tiento
Aquello que pretenden van tentando,

The sacred lashes that they gave."⁵
O sainted, sovereign, and holy heart,
35 And how this doctrine teaches us
That which we saw with our own eyes!
Having, O highest King, gone out
Only that they might find this road,
Most skillful pilots of the land and sea,
40 So full of haughtiness and arrogance
As to believe without their aid
The camp could move no single step,
And as their vain, presumptuous thoughts,
Being of vain men, resulted vain,
45 The General decided there should go
Eight soldiers, only such as were
Well-tried in arms and sufferings,
For that is what is needed when we lack
Men to instruct and teach and make us skilled
50 In those things that we all know not.
For this purpose were selected
The purveyor and Sebastian Rodríguez,
Dionisio de Bañuelos and Robledo,
Francisco Sánchez and Cristóbal Sánchez,
55 Carabajal and I, also, with them,
But to fill up, not that I equaled
Their high effort with my small gifts.
All were so ignorant of latitudes,
Directions, stars, winds, and middle winds⁶
60 That after the sun was hid, I suspect,
There was not one of us could say
Affirmatively and without mistake
"Here is the East and there you see the West."
But for such things 'tis work is good.
65 In them necessity doth rule,
That maketh men well-learned
And wise and prudent, practical and skilled
In all the sciences and liberal arts,
Drawn from experience, which mother is
70 And chiefest fount whence they are born.
Thusly, each with his crustiness,
Harsh, rough and wild, ill-fashioned,
Gave up his will and did fulfill
That which his General there ordered.
75 And like blind men who by the touch alone
Go groping for the thing they wish,

5. Para los azotes que el padre de la Iglesia recibió en el sueño en que se le advirtió apartarse de su gusto por los escritores paganos, véase Rice Jr., 3, y J. N. D. Kelly, *Jerome, His Life and Writings* (London: The Trinity Press, 1975), 42.

6. Vientos o vientos enteros son los que soplan de las cuatro direcciones cardinales; y medios vientos, que son ocho, los que soplan en las subdirecciones en que se dividen las cardinales.

5. Relative to the lashes that Saint Jerome received in the dream in which he was told to curb his appetite for pagan writers, see Rice Jr., 3, and J. N. D. Kelly, *Jerome, His Life and Writings* (London: The Trinity Press, 1975), 42. Saint Jerome's letters, translated into the vulgar languages during the Renaissance, were much read at the time.

6. There were eight half-winds which blew from the subdivisions of the four cardinal points.

Sujetos a herrar y dar de ojos,[7]
Assí, sujetos, ciegos emprendimos
La difícil carrera peligrosa,
Llevando al gran Sargento por caudillo,
Que fue la maior fuerza que nos dieron.
Pues yendo assí marchando muchos días
Por escabrosos páramos tendidos,
Temerarios trabajos padeciendo,
La difícil impressa proseguimos
A gran fuerza de brazos quebrantados
Hasta que vbimos ya de todo punto
Todos los bastimentos acabado,
Y assí fue pura fuerza vernos todos
Por muy gran hambre y sed en gran aprieto.
Mas con aquel esfuerzo que combino
Al inmenso trabajo riguroso,
Pusimos firme y animoso pecho
Y rompiendo por cuestas pedregosas
Y médanos de arena lebantados,
Después que por tres días no comimos
Y agua por pensamiento no gustamos,
Llegada ya la hora del reposo
Y el sueño amodorrido que al sentido,
Sin ser sentido, va el sentir privando,
Cansados y afligidos, arribamos
A descubrir gran suma de faroles[8]
Que bien dozientos ranchos[9] calentaban.
Luego a gran priessa fuimos recogiendo
Los sedientos caballos, disgustosos,
Porque de la fogosa sed vencidos
Allá no se nos fuessen desmandados.
Repartiose la vela con aviso
Para que alerta todos estuviessen,
Y con esto determinó el Sargento
Que en su lugar el provehedor quedase
En el inter que sólos los dos juntos
Ybamos a espiar aquellos ranchos
Por ver qué cantidad de gente fuesse,
Qué fuerza y en qué sitio se albergase.
Y saliendo no más que a aqueste efecto,
Por no erar la buelta y derezera,[10]
Qual aquél que en el bravo laberinto,
La fuerza del gran monstruo acometiendo,
Fue la entrada y salida assegurando,[11]

Subject to error and to falling down,
So, subject, blind, we undertook
The difficult and dangerous route,
80 Taking the great Sergeant for chief,
Who was the greatest strength we had.
For, going thus, and marching many days
Through rough and widely-spreading plains
And rashly undergoing toil,
85 We followed on the difficult task
By the sheer strength of weary arms
Until we now had quite used up
The whole of our provisions,
And so from pure necessity we saw ourselves
90 In a sad plight from hunger and from thirst.
But with that strength which we did need
For the immense and rigorous task
We showed a firm, spirited front
And forcing on o'er rocky slopes
95 And dunes of high-piled sand,
After we had for three days eaten naught
And did not drink a drop of water,
The hour of repose being come
And being overborne with sleep
100 That, all unnoticed, steals our consciousness,
Tired and all worn out we suddenly
Did come to see great store of lights
That heated some two hundred huts.[7]
Then in great haste we gathered in
105 The thirsty, jaded mounts
So that, conquered by raging thirst,
They might not wander from us there.
The watch was carefully assigned
So that we all might be right vigilant,
110 And then the Sergeant did decide
That in his place the purveyor remain
In the meantime that we two should
Go forth to spy upon those tents
To see what quantity of folk there was,
115 What forces, in what place they were sheltered.
And going out for no more than that end,
In order not to miss direction and return,
Like him who in the deadly labyrinth,
Braving the strength of the great monster there,
120 Had entrance and egress assured,[8]

---

7. Dar de ojos = caer de pechos.
8. Faroles = luz de lumbres.
9. Ranchos = rancherías, viviendas de indios nomádicos.
10. Derezera = dirección.
11. Se refiere a Teseo y el hilo de Ariadne que le permitió salir del laberinto de Creta, vivienda del monstruoso minotauro. Se refiere en Virgilio, *Eneida* VI, 40–45).

7. Villagrá uses *ranchos,* usually used by Spanish explorers for the dwellings of nomadic or seminomadic Indians. We prefer *huts* over *tents,* but the latter would also do.

8. The reference is to the Theseus and Ariadne myth, the latter's thread allowing the former to emerge from the Cretan labyrinth, home of the ferocious Minotaur. The myth is narrated by Virgil, *Aeneid* VI, 40–45.

Assí nosotros, por entrar seguros
Y por assegurar también la buelta,
Marcamos vna Estrella derribada
Al pie del Orizonte, bien opuesta
A los bárbaros ranchos donde fuimos.
Y estando que estuvimos agachados
Tan cerca dellos que muy bien los vimos,
A nosotros vinieron embistiendo
Cosa de siete Alárabes furiosos
Y con las mismas pieles que cubrían
Sobre nosotros fueron descargando
Apriessa grandes golpes. Y assí, juntos,
prestos, ligeros, fueron discurriendo
Todos, con gran tropel amontonados,
Dexándonos allí sin más tocarnos.
Nunca espantó jamás pantasma[12] brava
Al que de verla estuvo más seguro,
Dexándole suspenso y sin sentido,
Estremecido y todo en sí temblando,
Como los dos sufrimos aquel rato.
Y luego que algún tanto nos cobramos,
Venimos a entender, según supimos
Por señas y ademanes que nos hizo
Vno de aquestos bárbaros que digo
Quando después con ellos nos hallamos,
Que viniendo de caza con contento
Aquellos siete Alárabes, nos vieron
Y que, entendiendo que heramos amigos,
Compañeros también y sus vezinos,
Quisieron todos juntos espantarnos.
Y para que otra vez no se burlasen,
Ni nosotros con ellos si bolviesen,
Qual suelen los pilotos gobernarse
Por la Estrella del Norte lebantado
Para llevar sus naves a buen puerto,
Assí tomamos luego nuestra guía
Y presto a los amigos nos bolvimos.
Y dándoles razón de nuestro caso,
También les advertimos y diximos
Que abía dozientos hombres de arco y flecha
Y todos combatientes, sin la chusma,
Que entendimos ser número crecido.
Gran confusión nos puso aquesta causa,
Y assí, dando y tomando en ella todos,
Viendo quan mal parada toda estaba
Y que era fuerza perecer de hambre
Y que con la gran sed que descargaba
Tres caballos aquella misma noche

12. Pantasma = fantasma. Sobre fantasmas y sus efectos tiene Antonio de Torquemada, *Jardín de flores curiosas,* todo un Tratado.

So we, to venture forward safe
And also to ensure return,
Did mark a star sunk low and at
The foot of the horizon, opposite
The barbarous huts toward which we went.
And while we were low-crouched
So near to them we saw them well,
Upon us suddenly there rushed
Some seven Arabs, furious,
And with the very hides they wore
They rained upon us, all in haste,
Most mighty blows. Then, in a group,
Quick, light, they scurried off,
All hurrying in confusion,
Leaving us there, nor touched us more.
Never did fierce phantasm[9] fright
Him who of seeing it felt most safe,
Leaving him in suspense, half-conscious,
Shaking and trembling in all his limbs,
As we two suffered at that time.
And when we had recovered somewhat
We came to understand, as now we know
By signs and gestures that were made
By one of those barbarians mentioned here
When afterward we found ourselves with them,
That, coming gaily from a hunt,
Those seven Arabs noticed us
And, thinking we were friends of theirs,
Companions, their neighbors, too,
They, all together, wished to frighten us.
And that they might not joke with us again
Nor we with them if they came back,
Just as the pilots guide themselves
By the North Star, most lofty one,
To bring their ships safe into port,
So we then searched out our guide
And quickly went back to our friends.
And, telling them the facts of our affair,
We also warned them and did say
There were two hundred men of bow and shaft,
And they all fighting men, without the crowd,
That we believed to be of larger size.
That matter caused us great confusion,
And so, all falling in and debating,
Seeing how ill-prepared all was
And that we were about to die of hunger
And that with the great thirst they suffered
Three horses on that selfsame night

9. On Phantoms and their effects, Villagrá may well have read Antonio de Torquemada's treatise in *Jardín de flores curiosas.*

Se nos caieron muertos, trasijados,[13]
Qual aquel prudentíssimo Saxonio[14]
Que al bravo Emperador venció a su salvo[15]
Con sólo que le dio a entender venía
Con gran fuerza de gente belicosa
Sobre todo su campo descuidado,
Assí determinó que fuesse el hecho,
Dando orden que al romper del Alba alegre
El bagaje[16] sobre ellos embistiesse
Y que al aire los prestos arcabuzes
Las espantosas balas escupiessen,
Lebantando rumor y grande estruendo
De muchas vozes, gritos y alaridos,
Porque dándoles a entender con esto
Que pujanza de gente descargaba,
Sería possible que a vna, todos juntos,
Vencidos del gran sueño y del espanto,
A campo abierto, prestos y ligeros,
Desocupando todos sus albergues,
Con presurosa fuga se escapasen;
Y que si bien del hecho se saliesse,
Que luego el provehedor con el Sargento
Y Sebastián Rodríguez con Bañuelos,
Como Españoles bravos que se arrojan
Por la famosa tierra Berberisca
A cautibar los Moros desmandados,[17]
Que assí de los caballos se apeasen
A prender la más gente que pudiessen;
Y en el inter, los otros discurriendo
Por los pagizos ranchos despoblados
Fuessen quebrando y destrozando apriessa
Los arcos y las flechas que pudiessen,
Y que esto fuesse sin que cosa alguna
Por pensamiento allí se les dexase
Por si a nosotros rebolver quisiessen
Armas de todo punto les faltasen.
Pues sin que en esto cosa se excediesse,[18]
Yba la noche húmeda huiendo
Y a más andar el Sol venía largando
Las riendas a su carro y presurosos
Los cándidos[19] caballos sacudían
Las lebantadas clines y assomaban

170 Did fall down dead among us, stark,
Like the most prudent Saxonius,[10]
Who conquered the brave Emperor with much ease
Only by showing that he came
With mighty force of warlike folk
175 Upon his careless camp,
So we decided it should be,
Ordering that on the breaking of the joyous dawn
We drive the baggage horses down on them
And that the ready harquebuses to the air
Should spit their fearful balls,
180 Raising an uproar and a great tumult
Of many voices, shouts, and yells,
That, making them by this to think
A crowd of men was charging them,
It might be possible that in a group,
185 Conquered by sleep and fear as well,
Into the open, quick and swift,
Evacuating all their homes,
In hasty flight they might escape;
And should we come out well in this attempt
190 The purveyor should with the Sergeant and
Sebastián Rodríguez with Bañuelos,
Like Spaniards brave who hurl themselves
Into the famous land of Barbary
To capture the dispersed Moors,
195 Rapidly dismount from their steeds
To capture all the people that they could;
And in the meanwhile others, scurrying
Among the thatched huts deserted,
Should break up and destroy hastily
200 Such bows and arrows as they could,
And this was so that there might be
Nothing left to them absolutely
In case they wished to turn on us
They might not have weapons of any sort.
205 Thus, then, without further orders,
The misty night did wear away
And later on the sun came, loosening
His chariot's reins, and rapidly
The fiery steeds came flying up
210 The lofty slopes, and there did peep

---

13. Trasijados = los ijares recogidos por hambre o sed.
14. No hallamos citado a tal guerrero, y es posible que Villagrá elevara a nombre propio, alterándolo, el de las varias tribus sajonas.
15. A su salvo = a su satisfacción.
16. Bagaje = tren de bagaje.
17. Desmandados = separados de sus compañeros.
18. No dio más órdenes que éstas el sargento mayor.
19. Cándidos = blancos, como lo eran los del carro del sol en la mitología.

10. We have not been able to identify this barbarian chieftain who defeated a Roman emperor. It is possible that *Saxons*, the reference to the Germanic tribe, may have been personalized.

Por el valcón dorado su luz bella,[20]	O'er gilded balcony its beauteous light,[11]
Quando de todo punto fue bolviendo	When suddenly the Castilians
La gente Castellana, retronando	Began a thundering
Los lebantados Cielos de manera	Against the lofty sky in such a sort
Que los caballos flacos, destroncados,	The weak and tottering mounts,
Huiendo del rumor se dividieron,	Fleeing the noise, did break away,
Rompiendo por los Ranchos tan furiosos	Bursting so furiously among the huts
Que sóla su braveza fue bastante	That their ferocity alone sufficed
Para que todos juntos arrancasen	To drive out all at once,
Y como sueltas liebres se acogiessen,[21]	And like to coursing hares they fled,
Dexando los assientos despoblados.	Leaving their homes deserted.
Con esto, los soldados valerosos	With this, the valorous soldiers
Nuevo furor al punto acrecentaron,	Increased new fury instantly,
Y assí como rabiosos lobos todos	And all, like furious wolves
Quando con hambre turban los ganados	When they in hunger trouble flocks
Y en torno de las redes[22] codiciosos,	And through the snares, all ravenous,
Los perros y pastores despreciando,	Despising dogs and shepherds there,
Por la majada[23] juntos se abalanzan	Into the sheep cotes they do burst
Y en son confusso todos arremeten,	And in a confused uproar attack all,
Assí, envistiendo todos, denodados,	So, all audacious, with a rush,
Cargaron los que estaban escogidos	They charged, those who had been chosen
Para prender la gente mal guardada,	To capture the unguarded folk,
Y a las bueltas andando[24] con algunos,	And, struggling with some certain few,
Assí qual fuertes Aguilas Reales	Like royal eagles in their strength
Las fuertes garras prestos ocuparon.	They quickly used their mighty claws.
El Sargento dos bárbaros gallardos,	The Sergeant had seized fast,
Qual bramadero,[25] tuvo bien assidos;	Like a post[12], two barbarians bold;
Bañuelos otros dos tuvo aferrados;	Bañuelos had captured two more;
Rodríguez ygualó también la parte.	Rodríguez bore an equal share,
Y assí como en turbión horrendo	And, as in a whirlwind fierce
El Zéfiro y el Noto[26] se acometen	Zephyrus and Notus[13] meet
Y en poderosa lucha se combaten,	And fight in mighty strife,
Barriendo y arrastrando todo aquello	Hurling and tearing everything
Que su violencia brava y fuerza alcanza,	Their violence and rude force doth meet,
Assí vn valiente bárbaro se vino	So a valiant barbarian came
A sólo el provehedor desatinado,	Against the purveyor, bewildered,
Y él, los valientes miembros recogiendo,	And he, gathering up his limbs,
Los dientes y los puños apretando,	Clenching his teeth and e'en his fists,
Sin frenar passo, le embistió ligero.	Attacked him straight, unhesitant.
Y como un par de naves aferradas,	And like a pair of grappled ships,
Assí aferró el vno con el otro	So each the other grappled there,

Line numbers: 215, 220, 225, 230, 235, 240, 245, 250

20. Los amaneceres con referencias mitológicas son eco de los virgilianos en la *Eneida*. Abundan sobremanera en toda la épica americana.

21. Se acogiessen = se acogiesen, se retiraran.

22. Redes = barreras que ponían los pastores.

23. Majada = paraje donde se recoge el ganado de noche.

24. A las bueltas andando = andando a las vueltas, luchando.

25. Bramadero = poste al que atan las bestias para herrarlas.

26. Zéfiro (céfiro) y Noto son los nombres mitológicos de los vientos oeste y sur, respectivamente. Para semejante contienda de vientos, véase Virgilio, *Eneida* II, 560.

11. This is one of Villagrá's more elaborate sunrises, which, probably stemming from Virgil, so enthused New World epic poets.

12. The image is of the branding post, where animals were tightly bound.

13. Villagrá, probably following Virgil (*Aeneid* II, 560, for example), uses the mythological names of the west and south winds.

Con apretados ñudos bien ceñidos,
Fuertes lazos y bravas ataduras,
Y en los valientes pechos se afirmaron;
Y qual si dos zelosos toros fueran,
Gimiendo y azezando,²⁷ por buen rato
Las poderosas fuerzas se tentaban,
Y sacudiendo cada qual los tercios,²⁸
En bolteado torno²⁹ al descubierto,³⁰
Con vno y otro buelo lebantado
Rendir el vno al otro pretendía;³¹
Cuia violencia brava resistiendo
En las ligeras plantas que afirmaban,
Mas firmes que castillos se quedaban.
Y viendo el poco jugo que sacaba,
El bárbaro el derecho pie ligero
Sobre el contrario hizquierdo fue cargando
Con vn gran gemido poderoso;
Mas por estar los dos tan bien ceñidos,
Haciéndose crugir los duros güessos,
Rollizos nervios, cuerdas y costados,
Qual si fueran dos muros poderosos
Assí parados juntos se quedaron.
Pues bolviendo segunda vez al torno
El Español, vn buelo arrebatado
Al bárbaro le dio con tanto aliento
Que llevándole todo lebantado
En tierra dio con él por medio muerto.
En el inter, nosotros andubimos
Quebrando y destrozando a grande priessa
Los más arcos y flechas que topamos,
Y el Sargento mayor, estando en esto,³²
Con blandas muestras y caricias nobles,
Ternezas y regalos amorosos,
Agasajó la pressa en quanto pudo,
Dándoles a entender que no venía
A darles pesadumbre ni a enojarlos
Y que su causa sólo se estendía
A que dos o tres dellos nos llevasen
Al Río que buscábamos del Norte.
Y assí, por esta causa, les pedía
Que tuviessen por bien de concertarse
De manera que algunos dellos fuessen
Y aquéllos que escogiessen se quedasen.

Gripped tight in clinging knots,
Strong bonds and binding loops,
And on their valiant breasts they both held firm.
255 And as they had been two fierce bulls,
Roaring and rumbling, for a good while
They tried each other's mighty strength,
And each one, straining with his limbs,
In whirling turns most vigorously,
260 With many mighty leaps, also,
Did try to overcome the other,
Who resisting his violence
Upon quick-moving feet set firm,
They stood more firm than fortresses.
265 And, seeing the slight advantage he thus gained,
The barbarian threw his swift right foot
Behind the left foot of his opponent
With a great, powerful grunt,
But as the two were so close gripped,
270 Though the hard bones did creak,
And robust muscles, cords, and ribs,
As though they were two well-set walls
So they stood moveless there.
Well, going to their spins a second time,
275 The Spaniard, with a violent swing
Lifted the barbarian with such force
That, raising him above his head,
He dashed him to the earth half dead.¹⁴
We, meanwhile, were going about
280 Breaking, destroying in great haste
Such bows and arrows as we came upon;
The Sergeant Major being at that time,
With gentle signs and noble caresses,
With tenderness and loving ways,
285 Calming the prisoners as best he could,
Making them understand that he came not
To bring them sorrow nor to anger them,
And that his cause was only this,
That two or three of them should take us on
290 Unto the River of the North we sought.
And so for this cause he asked them
That they should but decide to agree
So that a few of them might go
While those who chose might stay behind.

---

27. Azezando = acezando, jadeando.
28. tercios = miembros fuertes y robustos del hombre.
29. Bolteado torno = volteado torno, girante torno.
30. Al descubierto = al aire libre.
31. Recordando las competencias descritas por Virgilio, apenas hay épica americana que no incluya estas luchas mano a mano: *La araucana* I, 10, y *Arauco domado* IV.
32. Estando en esto ellos, los antes mencionado.

14. The detailed description of one-on-one competitions, probably from the *Aeneid*, in which they abound, was commonplace in the New World epic. See, for example, *La Araucana* I, 10, and *Arauco domado* IV.

Y advirtiendo quan mal se convenían
Y que todos quisieron escusarse,
Por quitarles de duda y de sospecha
Y parecerle aqueste buen camino,
Vsó de potestad en concertarlos.
Y assí, sin dilatar aquesta causa,
Cargándolos de cuentas y abalorios,[33]
A los cinco soltó con grandes muestras
De amistad llana, buena y muy sincera,
Sin ninguna encubierta y trato doble.
Y con las mismas muestras agradables
A los dos prometió que en viendo el agua
Dos hermosos caballos les daría
En que ambos a dos juntos se bolviessen.
Los cinco con contento se partieron;
Los dos bien afligidos se quedaron
Y como aquéllos que forzados llevan,
Mansos de todo punto, ya rendidos
A la fuerza del remo riguroso
Y encendida braveza de crugía,[34]
Assí, mansos forzados, les llevamos.
Y de los bastimentos que dexaron
De venados, tejones[35] y conejos,
Hierbas, raposos, liebres y raízes,
Nuestra insaziable hambre socorrimos,
Previniendo también para adelante
Lo mejor que pudimos prevenirnos.
Y con esto nos fuimos a el aguage,[36]
Que buena media legua retirado
Estaba de los Ranchos descuidados.
Y sabe, gran señor, el alto Cielo
Que aunque sentí muy bien, y siento agora,
Lo que por vista de ojos vi aquel día,
Que me faltan palabras y razones
Para darme a entender en esta historia.
No más que seys pozuelos se mostraban
Sobre la superficie de la tierra,
Como rodelas[37] todos y de hondo
Vna quarta[38] el que más hondable estaba,
Cubiertos todos de agua, y acabada,
Era fuerza aguardar a que inchesen,
Y llenos, por quedar el agua en peso,[39]
Para ninguna parte derramaban.

295 And, noting how ill they agreed
And that all would excuse themselves,
To take away their doubt and suspicion,
And because he thought it was wise,
He used his power to conciliate.
300 And so, not to delay our cause,
Loading them with glass beads and trinkets,
He let five go with plenteous signs
Of full friendship and most sincere,
Quite without trick or double-dealing.
305 And with the same agreeable signs
He promised to the two that, seeing the water,
He would give them two horses fine,
On which, together, they might return home.
The five, right well content, went off.
310 The two, most afflicted, remained,
And, like those sentenced galley slaves,
In all points meek, surrendered
To toiling at the rigorous oar
And fiery harshness of the galleys,
315 So, meek prisoners, we bore them off.
And of provisions that they left,
Of deer, of badger, and of hares,
Grasses, foxes, rabbits, and roots,
We remedied our insatiable hunger
320 And provided for the future, too,
As best we could provide for it.
And then we went unto water
That was a good half-league away
From those abandoned dwellings.
325 And high Heaven knows, great lord,
That though I felt keenly then, and still feel
What I saw that day with my own sight,
Somehow I do lack words and terms
To make myself plain in this history.
330 No more than six wells there were seen
Upon the surface of the earth,
All like small shields and of a depth
The deepest one of eight inches, perhaps,
All full of water, and when that was drunk
335 'Twas need to wait until they filled.
And, full, the water stood level in them
Nor flowed out anywhere,

33. Abalorios = conjunto de cuentas de vidrio.
34. Crugía = paseo o carrera de la galera. Se viene refiriendo a los
que "forzados llevan . . . a la fuerza del remo," es decir, a galeotes.
35. Tejones = mamíferos carniceros.
36. Aguage = aguaje, aguadero.
37. Rodelas = pequeños escudos.
38. Quarta = cuarta, medida de la mano abierta y extendida.
39. En peso = sin inclinarse a una parte u otra.

Y no podían hazerse más hondables
Porque era casi peña aquel assiento.
Vno se reservó para nosotros,
Y puesto encima dél el gran Sargento,
No podimos con él que se rindiesse
Al sabroso licor que le aguardaba
Para matar el fuego poderoso
Que en general a todos consumía,
Respecto de que quiso que primero
Todos su grande sed satisfiziessen.
En este inter, llegó la caballada
Y luego que reconoció el aguage
Todos juntos no fuimos poderosos
Para que vn solo passo atrás bolviesse.
Y viendo que acababan toda el agua,
Rompiendo por los pies de los caballos,
Dexándose pisar de todos ellos,
Dos compañeros nuestros se arrojaron,
Vencidos de la sed que los mataba,
Y allí, sus mismos rostros apretados
Con los muchos hozicos que cargaban,
Secos los pozos y ellos tambíen secos,
Casi muertos, tendidos se quedaron.
Visto esto, todos fuimos⁴⁰ ayudarlos
Y al fin, juntos, allí los socorrimos,
Bien peligrosos de perder las vidas,
Sólo de la terrible sed rendidos
Y fuerza de caballos quebrantados.
¡Alábente los Angeles, Dios mío,
Que assí abates al hombre que lebantas
Sobre las altas obras de tus manos!
Dexo el alma y su belleza en vanda,
¿Es possible, señor, que no le basta
Al estremado vasso⁴¹ que hiziste
Ser vice Dios illustre acá en la tierra,
Imagen de tu misma semejanza,
Para dexar de estar siempre sugeto
Al mísero sustento de que vive?
Y fuera⁴² desta triste desventura,
¿Cómo, señor, se sufre y se permite
Que abiendo de ser esto,⁴³ que los brutos⁴⁴
Prefieran⁴⁵ a tu Imagen,⁴⁶ de manera
Que no se sienta cosa en esta vida

340 And they could not be made deeper
Because that place was almost all rock.
One was reserved for us,
And, the great Sergeant standing over it,
We could not make him yield himself
Unto the savory liquor that awaited him,
345 To quench the raging fire within
That did consume us all in general,
Because he wished that before him
We all should satisfy our mighty thirst.
In the meanwhile, the horses came,
And when they knew the water there
350 We, all together, had not strength enough
To force them back a single step.
And, seeing that the water was all gone,
Hurling themselves amid the horses's feet
And letting themselves there be trampled on,
355 Two of our companions did throw themselves,
Conquered by that thirst that was killing them,
And there, their very faces pressed among
The many muzzles crowding up,
The wells all dry and they too dry,
360 Almost dead, they lay stretched out.
Seeing this, we all did go to succor them,
And finally, all together, brought them aid,
In serious peril there to lose their lives
From no more then their giving up to thirst
365 And being broken by the press of steeds.
The Angels praise You, O my God,
Since thus you lower man, whom You have raised
Above the other mighty works of Your hands.
Leaving the soul and its beauty aside,
370 Is it possible, Lord, 'tis not enough
For that weak vessel that You made
To be a second God here on the earth,
The image of Your own appearance,
To cease to be always subjected to
375 The miserable sustenance by which he lives?
And apart from this sad misfortune,
How, Lord, is it suffered, allowed,
That, this being true of need, the beasts
Do advantage Your image¹⁵ in such sort
380 That there is not a need within this life

---

40. Posible errata del original omitiendo la "a" que daría mejor lectura.
41. Vasso = vaso, criatura.
42. Fuera de = además de.
43. Que el hombre tenga que depender de su sustento.
44. Brutos = animales.
45. Prefieran = excedan, aventajen.
46. Al hombre.

15. The reference is to man, as God's image.

Que en todo no prefieran con ventaja?
Comer, beber, vestir, calzar, contento,
Que es lo que más los hombres procuramos,
¿Quál bruto en todo aquesto no prefiere?
Estos secretos yo no los alcanzo,
Y assí, muy triste, mi alma te procura
Y tanto más se abrasa y te dessea
Quanto está en tus secretos lebantados
Más ignorante, torpe y más confussa.
Y assí, qual torpe, quiero ya bolverme
A los caballos torpes, fatigados,
Que de la grande sed todos vencidos
Sobre las fuentes juntos se quedaron,
Y de allí no pudimos retirarlos
Hasta que, llenos todos los hijares
Como hinchados odres aventados,⁴⁷
Poco a poco se fueron esparciendo
Y dando de beber a los sedientos
Dos compañeros tristes, lastimados.
Luego fuimos nosotros y, qual ellos,
El insaciable vientre contentamos.
Y luego que estuvimos satisfechos
Y ninguno quedó que no bebiesse,
Vino el Sargento y cerca de la fuente
Llegó, y, haziendo vasso del sombrero,
Allí su mortal sed quedó vencida.
Y con esto salimos a lo llano
Por si acaso los Indios rebolviessen
Pudiessemos, con verlos, ser señores
De aprovecharnos bien de los caballos.
Allí a los prisioneros regalamos,
Dándoles de amistad patentes muestras;
Y de la poca ropa que tuvimos
A entrambos los vestimos porque fuessen
Más sin sospecha y menos rezelosos.
En cuio puesto les pidió el Sargento
Dixessen a qué vanda o a qué parte
Derramaban las aguas de aquel Río
Cuia fuente hazia el Norte rebentaba,
Y vno dellos que Milco⁴⁸ se dezía
Sobre aquesta pregunta referida
Hablaba tantas cosas que con ellas

385

390

395

400

405

410

415

420

That they not exceed in advantage?
In food, drink, being clothed, shod, joy,
This being what we men most seek,
What brute in all this is not advantaged?
These secrets I cannot attain,
And so my soul most sadly seeketh Thee
And all the more doth burn and desire Thee
The more it is in Thy most lofty mysteries
More ignorant, stupid, and more confused.
And as such stupid thing I would return
To stupid, tired horses there,
Who, all conquered by raging thirst,
Remained together by the wells,
And we could not force them away
Until, all with full flanks,
Swollen like to well-filled wineskins,
Little by little they drew back
And gave an opportunity to drink
To our two thirsty, sad, and wounded friends.
Then we approached and, like to them,
Contented our insatiable thirst,
And then, when we were satisfied
And none remained who had not drunk,
There came the Sergeant and, close to the well,
He came and, making of his hat a cup,
His mortal thirst was conquered there.
And after this we went into the plain
In case the Indians had returned
We might, on seeing them, master them
By using well our horses.
There we again regaled the prisoners,
Showing them open signs of friendliness,
And from the few clothes that we had
We clothed them both that they might be
More free from fear and less suspicious.
At which point the Sergeant did ask of them
To say in what direction or what place
The waters of that river flowed
Whose source came from the north,
And one of them, whose name was Milco,¹⁶
Upon the question asked of him
Did speak so many things as to

47. Aventados = llenos de aire.
48. Empezando con este primer nombre indio, Villagrá los creará
sin fidelidad a los que llevaran, efectivamente, los indios que
encontraban. Los estudiosos de la épica de la conquista americana han
señalado este fenómeno desde Ercilla en adelante. Véanse, por ejemplo,
A. Ercilla, *La araucana*, edición de M. A. Morínigo y I. Lerner
(Madrid: Castalia, 1979), I, 94–95; P. de Oña, *Arauco domado*, edición
de J. T. Medina (Santiago de Chile: Imprenta Universitaria, 1917),
395; y G. Lobo Lasso de la Vega, *Mexicana*, edición de J. Amor y
Vázquez, XXXIV–V.

16. Beginning with this first Indian name he uses, Villagrá will
create these without much fidelity to true Indian names. Scholars of
the New World epic point out that, beginning with Ercilla, this was
the norm. See A. Ercilla, *La araucana* I, eds. M. A. Morínigo and I.
Lerner (Madrid: Castalia, 1979), 94–95; P. de Oña, *Arauco domado*, ed.
J. T. Medina (Santiago de Chile: Imprenta Universitaria, 1917), 395;
and G. Lobo Lasso de la Vega, *Mexicana*, ed. J. Amor y Vázquez,
xxxiv–v.

Más confusión a todos nos ponía.
Por cuia causa el otro en pie se puso,
Que Mompil dixo a todos se llamaba,
Y era el que el provehedor abía prendido,
Y barriendo del suelo cierta parte
Que toda a caso deservada⁴⁹ estaba,
Desembolviendo el brazo poderoso
Tomó la punta de vna larga flecha
Y assí, como si bien cursado fuera
En nuestra mathemática más cierta,
Casi que quiso a todos figurarnos
La línea y el Zodíaco y los signos,⁵⁰
En largo cada qual de treinta grados,
Los dos remotos Polos milagrosos,
El Artico y Antártico cumplidos,
Los poderosos círculos⁵¹ y el exe.
Y assí, como cosmógrafo excelente,
Respecto al Cielo quiso dibujarnos
Algunas partes de la baja tierra.
Puso del Sur y Norte los dos mares,
Con Islas, fuentes, montes y lagunas
Y otros assientos, puestos y estalages.
Pintonos la circunvezina tierra
Y el assiento del caudaloso Río
Por quien tantos trabajos se sufrieron,
Y todos los aguages y jornadas
Que era fuerza tener en el camino
Por aber de beber sus turbias aguas.
Pintonos vna boca⁵² muy estrecha
Por la qual era fuerza se passase,
Y fuera della no nos dio vereda
Que por ella pudiesse ser possible
Que saliesse el exército marchando,
Por ser aquella tierra en sí fragosa
Y muy pobre de aguage en todas partes.
Allí pintó también las poblaciones
De nuestra nueva México y sus tierras,
Poniendo y dándose a entender en todo
Como si muy sagaz piloto fuera.
No se movió pestaña, porque juntos,
Todos oyendo al bárbaro gallardo,
De gran contento y gozo no cabían.
Y por la mucha parte que me cupo,
Será bien que celebre la grandeza
De la más alta bárbara, gallarda
De pecho y corazón el más rendido,
Que en bárbara nación se a conocido.

Cause us more confusion with them.
Wherefore the other did stand up,
425 Who said to all that he was called Mompil
And was the one the purveyor had ta'en,
And sweeping on the ground a certain space
That was all free from grass for his purpose,
Extending forth his powerful arm
430 He took the point of a long arrow and,
As though he had been educated
In our mathematics accurate,
As if he wished to draw for us
The line, the Zodiac, and the signs,
435 Each one thirty degrees in length,
The two remote, miraculous, Poles,
The Arctic and the Antarctic entire,
The mighty circles, the axle.
And like an excellent geographer,
440 With reference to the heavens he drew us
Some parts of the low lands.
He put the two Seas of the North and South,
With islands, springs, mountains, and lakes,
And other features, places, parts.
445 He painted us the neighboring lands
And the location of the mighty stream
For which so many toils were borne,
And all the water holes and day's marches
That one must needs make on the way
450 To have their turbid waters to drink in.
He painted for us there a narrow pass
Through which 'twas necessary that we go,
And 'cept for it he gave to us no path
Through which it would be possible
455 The army might march on
Because that country was so broken up,
So very poor in water in all parts.
There he drew, too, the villages
Of our New Mexico, its lands,
460 Making us understand it all
As he were a most learned guide.
Not one eyelash did move, for we,
All listening to the gallant barbarian,
Could not contain ourselves for pleasure and content.
465 And for the great part that I had in it,
'Tis well I celebrate the grandeur
Of that most elevated, spirited barbarian,¹⁷
In spirit and in heart the most obsequious
That in a barbarous nation was ever known.

---

49. Deservada = desyerbada.
50. Signos = constelaciones.
51. Círculos = líneas paralelas al ecuador.
52. Boca = apertura entre montañas.

17. The Spanish makes it clear here that what is upcoming is a female barbarian.

CANTO TREZE

COMO LLEGO POLCA EN BVSCA DE MILCO SU MARIDO y dexándola en prisión se fue huiendo, y de la fuga que hizo Mompil, y de la liberalidad que el Sargento tuvo con la bárbara cautiva.

N O se a visto jamás cosa perfecta,
Puesta en su mismo punto y acabada,[1]
Que amor no sea el autor de su grandeza,

Porque él es quien la illustra y quien la esmalta,
Labra, dibuja, pinta y endereza.[2]
Sin él, todo quebranta y da disgusto,
Todo enfada, atormenta y aborrece,
Y a todo, sin él, vemos dar de mano.[3]
Con él, todo se encumbra y se lebanta,
Todo se emprende, todo se acomete,
Todo se vence, rinde y abasalla,
Y, en fin, él es crisol en cuio vasso
Todo se afina, sube y se quilata.
Desto aquí se nos muestra vn buen dechado,
Cuia labor es digna que se escriba
Si ya la tosca pluma no desdora
Aquella viva Imagen que retrata.
Estando, pues, con Mompil platicando
Y tomando razón de su dibujo,
Vimos todos venir a nuestro puesto
Vna furiosa bárbara gallarda,
Frenética de amor, de amores pressa.
Vnas vezes apriessa caminando,
Otras corriendo, a vezes reparada,[4]
Aderezaba[5] bien lo que traía,
Que era vn hermoso niño, lindo y bello,
Que a la triste chupando le venía
La dulze fértil teta, sin cuidado
De aquello que a la pobre lastimaba,
Con vn corbo caiado puesto al hombro
Y del cuento[6] colgando a las espaldas
Vn gracioso zurrón en que traía
Vna pequeña y tierna zervatica,
Con dos buenos conejos y una liebre,
Todo a su modo bien aderezado.

1. Perfectamente equilibrada y terminada.
2. Endereza = adorna.
3. Dar de mano = cesar.
4. Reparada = parada.
5. Aderezaba = disponía.
6. Cuento = extremo.

CANTO XIII

How Polca came in search of Milco, her husband, and, leaving her in prison, he fled; and of the flight of Mompil, and of the liberality the Sergeant showed to the captive barbarian.

N EVER a perfect thing was seen,
Finished, complete in every point,
That love was not the author of its grandeur,
For this it is that makes it famed, adorned,
5 Shapes, draws, paints, and doth rectify.
Without it, all breaks and bothers,
All vexes, torments, and doth make loathsome,
And, at the end, we see all laid aside.
With it, all doth ascend, is raised,
10 All is begun, all undertaken,
All conquered, won, and made a vassal of,
And, finally, 'tis a crucible in which
All is refined, sublimed, enriched.
Of this a good example was shown us,
15 The working of which deserves being described
If the rough pen may not sully
That living image it would draw.
Being, then, talking with Mompil
And noting well the way of his drawing,
20 We all saw, coming toward our post,
A furious, gallant, barbarian woman,
Frenzied by love, by love driven on.
Sometimes walking in haste,
Others running, at times standing still,
25 She adjusted what she did bring,
Which was a pretty child and beautiful,
That came, nursing the fertile breast
Of its sad mother, unperturbed
By that which saddened that poor thing,
30 A curved pole over her shoulder
From whose end there hung on her back
A graceful shepherd's pouch, in which
She brought a tiny, tender fawn,
With two fine rabbits and a hare,
35 All dressed in their fashion.

Viendo, pues, el Sargento su donaire,
La gracia y desenfado que traía,
A todos mandó darle franca entrada
Por ser muger cuya belleza illustre
A toda cortesía combidaba.
Y con razón el término⁷ se tuvo,
Porque aunque es verdad clara y manifiesta
Que es privilegio breve la hermosura,
Engaño y flor que presto se marchita,
Al fin el corto tiempo que ella dura
Ella es la que es más digna de estimarse
Y a quien mayor respecto se le debe.
Y aunque Alárabe y bárbara en el traje,
En su ademán gallardo, cortesana,
Sagaz, discreta, noble y avisada,
Que más que aquesto puede amor si rompen⁸
Del más bruto animal la vil corteza,
Que allí produze amor también grandezas,
Tanto más dignas todas de notarse
Quanto muy dignas éstas de escribirse.
Y assí, furiosa y fuera de sentido,
Inflamada del lento y dulze fuego
En que toda se estaba consumiendo,
Llegó qual fiel y diestra cachorrilla
Quando, después de qual que larga ausencia,
A caso topa y da con el montero,
Que ligera, amigable y alagüeña,
Mansamente gimiendo y agachada,
Para él se va la triste condolida
De la enfadosa ausencia disgustosa.
Assí la pobre bárbara se vino
Para el cautivo bárbaro, afligida,
Triste, alegre, llorosa, mal contenta.
Y después que le dio grandes abrazos,
Tiernamente apretados y ceñidos,
Notando que no estaban bien sentados,
Para que lo estuviessen, fue arrancando
Gran cantidad de hierba con que hizo
Dos graciosos assientos que les puso.
Después abrió el zurrón y de la caza,
Limpiándoles los rostros con un paño,
Al vno dellos siempre prefiriendo,
Con amoroso rostro vergonzoso,
A los dos les rogaba que comiessen.
Y bolviendo a nosotros, encogida,⁹
Toda turbada, triste y congojosa,
Alegrando su rostro quanto pudo,

The Sergeant, then, seeing her grace,
The ease and freedom that she showed,
Ordered us all to give her free passage
As being a woman whose beauty
40 Invited to all courtesy,
And properly he used that term,
For though 'tis clear, manifest truth
That beauty is brief privilege,
Deception, flower that quickly fades away,
45 E'en so, the short time that it lasts
It is, in fact, more worthy of esteem
A thing to which greatest respect is due.
And, though an Arab and barbarous in dress,
In manner gallant, courteous,
50 Wise, discreet, noble, well-advised,
For love achieves e'en more if it breaks down
The rudeness of the most brute heart,
For there, too, love produces victories,
All the more worthy to be noted down
55 And very worthy to be written here.
And so, all furious, beside herself,
Inflamed by slow, sweet fire
By which she was being all consumed,
She came, like a faithful, skillful pup,
60 When after some long absence
By chance doth meet the huntsman and,
All lively, friendly, and fawning,
Whining with joy and crouching down,
The sad beast goes to him, troubled
65 By the vexatious, sad absence,
So came the poor barbarian girl
To the barbarian captive, in distress,
Sad, happy, weeping, ill-content.
And after giving him a long embrace,
70 Tenderly clasping tight to him,
Seeing that they were not comfortable
Where they were placed, she then pulled up
Great quantity of grass with which she made
Two pleasant seats which she gave them.
75 Then she did open the pouch and, wiping dust
From off their faces with a cloth,
Always preferring one of them,
With loving and yet modest face,
Then she did ask the two to eat.
80 And, turning timidly to us,
All anxious, sad and in distress,
Making her face as cheerful as she could,

---

7. Término = modo, trato.
8. Posible errata del original por "rompe," que hace mejor lectura.
9. Encogida = tímida, miedosa.

A todos combidó con buena gracia.
Y como de amor toda se encendía,
Luego que nos mostró su rostro alegre,
Arrasados los ojos, dio a entendernos
Que Milco, que cautivo le traían,
Era su esposo, alma, vida y padre
Del inocente niño que a sus pechos,
Qual verdadera madre, alimentaba.
Y allí con blandas muestras nos pedía
Que piedad de aquel niño se tuviesse
Y que al padre no diessemos la muerte,
Pues güérfanos los dos sin él quedaban;
Ofreciendo con veras de su parte
Que a doquiera que fuessemos yría
Sirviéndonos a todos como esclava
Con que la vida sóla se otorgase
A aquél por quien la triste intercedía.
Y quando esto la pobre nos rogaba,
Vn vivo fuego en ella conozimos,
Vna agradable llaga no entendida,
Vn sabroso veneno riguroso,
Vna amargura dulze desabrida,
Vn alegre tormento quebrantado,
Vna feroz herida penetrante
Gustosa de sufrir aunque incurable,
Y vna muy blanda muerte sin remedio
A la qual dio a entendernos se ofrecía
Con alma y corazón con que dexasen
A Milco con la vida, pues sin ella
Era fuerza la suya se acabase.
Y qual Triara, de Vitelio esposa,
Que, rompiendo la femenil flaqueza,
Por medio de las armas belicosas
Con quien su caro esposo combatía,
Su persona arrojó con tanto esfuerzo
Quanto su misma historia nos enseña,[10]
Assí la pobre bárbara mostraba
Serle muy fácil cosa el atreverse
A perder cien mil vidas que tuviera
Por sólo libertar a su marido.
Demás desto notamos en la triste
Cien mil grandes opuestos y contrarios,
Los vnos bien distintos de los otros:
Lágrimas con gran sobra de contento,
Tristeza y gran extremo de alegría,
Sudando de cansancio y muy ligera,
Temor y atrevimiento nunca visto,

Invited us with goodly grace.
And as with love she then did blush
85 When showing us her happy face,
Her eyes tearful, she made us understand
That Milco, whom we held captive,
To her was husband, soul and life, and father of
The innocent baby which at her breast
90 She nourished like a true mother.
And there, with gentle gestures, she begged us
That we have pity on that child
And not deal death to its father
Since without him they two would be orphans;
95 Offering us sincerely for her part
That she would go wherever we should go
And serve all of us as a slave
If only we could merely grant his life
To him for whom she sadly intervened.
100 And when the poor thing asked us this,
We saw in her a living fire,
A wound, agreeable though unknown,
A savory yet strong venom,
A sweet and sour bitterness,
105 A happy, crushing torment,
A furious, penetrating wound
Pleasant to suffer though incurable,
And a gentle though inevitable death
To which she made us see she gave herself
110 With heart and soul, so we would loose
Milco alive, for, without that,
Needs must her own life would be done.
And like Triaria, Vitellius's wife,[1]
Who, overcoming feminine weakness,
115 In the very midst of warlike arms
With which her husband was fighting
Did throw herself with such effort
As her own story tells us of,
So this poor barbarian did show
120 That for her 'twere an easy thing to dare
To lose a hundred thousand lives, had she so much,
Only to liberate her spouse.
Beside this, in this sad one we did note
A hundred thousand contraries and opposites,
125 Each one most distinct from others:
Tears with great excess of content,
Sadness and great extremes of joy,
Sweating with weariness yet active, too,
Fear, yet with daring unheard of,

10. Triara, esposa de Lucio Vitelio, hermano del emperador del mismo nombre. Su historia la narra Pero Mexía, *Silva de varia lección* II, 15.

1. Triara, wife of Lucius Vitelius, brother of the Roman emperor of the same name. His story is narrated by Pero Mexía, *Silva de varia lección* II, 15.

Y, al fin, pressa de amor, de amor vencida.[11]
Y como es natural de pechos nobles
Dar vado[12] y no afligir al afligido,
Al mismo punto procuró el Sargento
De consolar y dar algún alibio
A su mortal congoja y ansia fiera
Con manifiestas muestras y señales
De dar luego remedio a su tristeza
Poniendo en libertad a su marido.
Y como la esperanza siempre alienta
Al mísero temor y le sustiene
Porque rabioso no se desespere,
Polca, que assí a la bárbara llamaban,
Faborecida toda de esperanza,
Assi como con gracia y son suabe
Remedan a las lluvias regaladas
Las hojas de los álamos movidas
De un fresquezito viento manso, amable,
No de otra suerte aquesta hembra bella,
Movida del fabor del gran Sargento,
Con gran contento quiso assegurarse.
Y para que los duelos menos fuessen
Comer hizo a los pobres prisioneros,
Regalando a su Milco quanto pudo;
Y luego que los tuvo sossegados,
Después de aber gran rato platicado,
Determinaron que ella se quedase
Y que por dos amigos Milco fuesse.
Y assí como nosotros entendimos
La llaneza y buen gusto que tuvieron,
Luego en el mismo punto fue largado[13]
El oprimido bárbaro afligido
Cuia gran prenda allí se nos quedaba
Con todo el gusto que dessearse pudo.
Y qual feroz caballo bien pensado
Que, rota del pesebre la cadena,
Furioso escapa y sale del establo,
Vna y otra corrida arremetiendo,
Parando y rebolviendo poderoso,
Bufando y relinchando con braveza,
La cola y clin al viento tremolando,
El recogido cuello sacudiendo,
Feroz, gallardo, bravo y animoso,
Los quatro pies ligeros lebantando,

130 And finally, prey of love, by love conquered.[2]
And as 'tis natural for noble hearts
To give right of way and not plague the sad,
The Sergeant instantly set out
To console her and give some ease unto
135 Her mortal suffering and wild distress
By manifest gestures and signs
Of promptly remedying her woes
By setting free her husband.
And as hope always doth cheer up
140 Miserable fear and sustains it
So that it doth not furiously despair,
Polca, for so the barbarian was called,
Put all in countenance by hope,
Just as the leaves of poplars, moved
145 By a fresh, gentle, kindly breeze,
Do imitate the rustling rain
With grace and tempered tones,
Not otherwise that woman beauteous,
Moved by the favor of the great Sergeant,
150 Wished with contentment to assure herself.
And that their sufferings might be less,
She made the poor prisoners to eat
Cheering her Milco all she could;
And when she had them satisfied,
155 After a long period of talk,
They determined that she should stay
And that Milco should go and bring two friends.
And just as soon as we did know
The good will and sincerity they showed
160 At once we set at liberty
The overwhelmed, downcast barbarian,
Whose lovely pledge remained behind with us,
With all the willingness we could desire.
Like a ferocious, well-fed horse,
165 Which, having broken the chain in his manger,
Furious, escapes and from the stable runs,
Racing in one direction and another,
Stopping and turning, powerful,
Snorting and neighing vigorously,
170 His mane and tail both waving in the breeze,
Arching his haughty neck,
Ferocious, spirited, fearless, courageous,
Raising his four feet trippingly,

11. La indígena encendida de amores es una constante de la épica americana. Más frecuentemente la enamorada indígena lamenta la muerte de su amante/esposo en batalla contra españoles, aunque hay variaciones, como ésta de Villagrá, que se ajustan a la peripecia histórica. Véase, por ejemplo, *La araucana* XX.
12. Dar vado = dejar pasar, no molestar.
13. Largado = liberado.

2. The lovely female native anguished by love is a constant of the New World epic. Usually she laments the death of her lover or husband in battle with the Spaniards, but there are numerous variations. See, for example, *La araucana* XX.

No de otra suerte Milco, muy ligero,
Furioso salió, casi sin sentido,
Hasta subir la cumbre lebantada
De vn poderoso cerro peñascoso
Por cuia falda a todos nos dejaba,
De cuia zima, en gritos lebantados
Razonando con Mompil y con Polca,
De súbito cessó y al mismo punto
Por la vertiente del fragoso risco
Traspuso como viento arrebatado,
Dexándola de nuevo más rendida,
Y en el fuego implacable más ardiendo,
De cuia fuerte fuerza quebrantada,
Con suspiros amargos y gemidos,
Deshaziéndose en lágrimas la triste,
Allí nos dio a entender que no vendría
Aquel traidor que assí la abía burlado,
Porque desde la cumbre lebantada
Muy bien desengañado los abía,
Qual hizo aquel cruelíssimo Theseo
Con la noble Ariatna, que burlada
Dexó en pago de aberle libertado
De la fuerza del monstruo embravecido,
En cuio fiero albergue temeroso,
Hecho cien mil pedazos, se quedara,
Y de la misma bestia consumido,
Si no fuera por ella remediado,[14]
Propria paga, cosecha y recompensa
De torpes brutos, ánimos ingratos,
Que tanta es más su vil correspondencia
Quanto por más crecidos beneficios
Se hallan los infames obligados.
¡O verdad, que poquitos son aquéllos
Que siguen tu castíssima pureza,
Y quantos son lo[15] que con ella enrredan,
Marañan, vierten, tienden y derraman
Vn mar de ponzoñosos vasiliscos!
No ay ya segura fee en todo el mundo,
No me da más los padres y los hijos,
Deudos nobles, parientes y maridos,
Hidalgos pobres, ricos poderosos,
Caballeros, villanos, titulados,
Con todo el demás resto miserable
De míseros mortales que se encienden
Los vnos con los otros y se abrasan

Not otherwise strong, swift Milco
175 Dashed furiously away, almost without reason,
Till he had climbed the lofty peak
Of a high, rocky hill,
Along whose slope he went from us,
And from whose summit, with loud shouts,
180 Talking to Mompil and to Polca, too,
He suddenly broke off and instantly
Over the edge of that rough cliff
He flew like an impetuous wind,
Leaving her now more overcome
185 And burning fiercer in the fire implacable
By whose fierce force she was cast down.
With bitter sighs and groanings, too,
The sad girl, bursting into tears,
Then made us understand that traitor vile
190 Would not return and made a jest of her,
And from the lofty peak he had
Quite undeceived the two,
As that most cruel Theseus did
With noble Ariadne, whom, deceived,
195 He left as pay for freeing him
From the jaws of the monster vile
In whose fearful and horrid den
He'd have remained in a thousand pieces
And would by that same beast have been consumed
200 Had he not been aided by her;[3]
A proper payment, harvest, recompense
Of wicked brutes, ungrateful souls,
For their return is the more base
Proportionate to the sum of benefits
205 For which the wretches find themselves obliged.
O truth, how very few are those
That follow your chaste purity;
How many are they who lay snares with it,
Entrap, pour out, extend and shed
210 A sea of poisonous basilisks!
Now there is no sure faith in all the world,
It matters not they be fathers and sons,
Noble relations, relatives, husbands,
Poor nobles, powerful rich men,
215 Knights, villains, titled men,
With all the miserable rest
Of miserable mortals who do strive
One with the other and attack

14. Villagrá utiliza el ejemplo de Teseo, Ariadna y el laberinto de Creta, pero la abandonada Polca no deja de recordar a la Dido abandonada de Virgilio, modelo, desde que Ercilla re-narra todo el incidente, de las enamoradas desgraciadas de la épica americana.

15. Errata del original por "los."

3. Villagrá uses the more appropriate Theseus/Ariadne myth, but there is much of Virgil's Dido, too, in this insistence upon her abandonment. See the *Aeneid* IV.

Con terribles engaños no entendidos,
Assechanzas, doblezes, invenciones,
Culpas, delictos, robos y pecados,
Solapas,[16] con lisonjas y bagezas,
Escándalo, crueldad, crimen, exceso,
Y, en fin, guerra sangrienta y cruel batalla
Que a sangre y fuego siempre la lebantan.
No me da más varones cultivados
Que incultos, broncos, bárbaros, grosseros,
Que basta y sobra conocer ser hombres
Para entender que, fuera del demonio,
Sea la más mala bestia, quando quiere,
De todas quantas Dios tiene criadas.
Exemplo claro aquí, señor, tenemos
En esta pobre bárbara engañada,
Que es fácil de engañar a quien bien ama.
Atónita se muestra, y se consume,
Aflige y se deshaze, rebentando
Con la flecha[17] en el alma soterrada,
Furiosa a todas partes rebolviendo
La vista cuidadosa, sin consuelo.
No cabe en todo el campo la cuitada,
Que todo le es estrecho y apretado;
Y assí de lo más íntimo del alma
Entrañables suspiros redoblaba
En lastimosas lágrimas embueltos.
¡O triste amor humano, a quántas cosas
Tu terrible violencia y furia fuerza
Si, assí, ciegos, seguimos tus pisadas!
Diga el más bien librado de tus manos
Quál fue el passo más libre y más seguro
Que enmedio dél sus ojos miserables
Cien mil vezes quebrados no sintiesse.
¡O traidor, alevoso, fementido,
Cruel, ingrato, vil, desconocido,
Di, quál bruto a su hembra la dexara
Como tú, vil cobarde, la dexaste!
¡O ingratitud infame, o caso triste,
Que por no más de aberlo imaginado
Quedarás para siempre aborrecido!
La sin ventura Polca, desdichada,
Arroios por los ojos derramando,
A su afligida alma yba cubriendo
La obscura noche, con su negra sombra
Cerrando en torno todo el Orizonte.
Que ya las velas todas repartidas

With miserable, obscure deceits,
220 Ambushes, double-dealing schemes,
Offenses, crimes, thieving and deadly sin,
Pretenses, flattery and baseness,
Scandal and cruelty, crime, excess,
Finally, bloody war, battle cruel,
225 That they e'er wage with blood and fire.
It matters not that they be cultivated men
Or rude, wild, barbarous, and gross,
For 'tis enough, and more, to know that they are men
And know that, except for the Fiend himself,
230 They all are the worst beast, when they do wish,
Of all the ones that God created.
A clear example, lord, we have here,
In this poor barbarian deceived,
For it is easy to deceive one who loves well.
235 She shows herself astonished, is consumed,
Afflicted, and is crushed and broken down,
An arrow buried in her soul,[4]
Turning in anguish to all sides
Her anxious gaze without relief.
240 The afflicted girl cannot fit in the camp,
For all, to her, is narrow, pressing down,
And so from out her inmost soul
She doth redouble rending sighs
Accompanied with sorrowing tears.
245 O sorry human love, how many things
Thy terrible violence and fury brings us to
If blindly thus we follow in thy steps!
Let him who's freest from thy hands declare
What was the freest, safest love
250 That in its midst his miserable eyes
He'd not felt break a hundred thousand times.
O traitor, treacherous and false,
Cruel, ungrateful, vile, thankless,
Tell me what beast would leave its mate
255 As you, vile coward, left your own!
O infamous ingratitude, O sorry case,
That, for imagining it, no more,
You shall forever be abhorred!
The unfortunate Polca, unhappy,
260 Weeping out rivers from her eyes,
The obscure night with its dark shades
Covered her poor afflicted soul,
Veiling the horizon all around.
And now, the sentries placed about

---

16. Solapas = disimulos.
17. La flecha de Cupido, símbolo del amor, es un elemento de la mitología clásica del todo asimilado a la cultura de Occidente. Véase, por ejemplo, la *Eneida* IV.

4. The wounding shaft as symbol of unrequited love, which again recalls Virgil's Dido, has been completely assimilated into Western culture. See the *Aeneid* IV.

Estaban a caballo y en sus puestos,
Y por más buen seguro de la pobre
Con más cuidado postas[18] le pusieron
Porque Mompil a caso no rompiesse[19]
Y por descuido nuestro la llevase.
Y luego que en mitad del alto Polo,
Según aquel varón heroico canta,[20]
Los Astros lebantados demediaron[21]
El poderoso curso bien tendido,
En el mayor silencio de la noche,
Quando las bravas bestias en el campo
Y los más razionales en sus lechos
Y los pezes en su alto mar profundo
Y las parleras aves en sus breñas
En agradable sueño amodorrido
Reposan con descuido sus cuidados,[22]
En este mismo instante y punto vino,
De la cansada y débil caballada
Rindiendo a la modorra el quarto triste,[23]
La fatigada prima ya vencida,
Y notando que todos reposaban
Y que el buen Mompil escapado abía,
Dexando allí la bárbara cautiva,
A grandes vozes quiso recordarnos.[24]
Y a penas lo entendimos quando todos
Mudos quedamos, tristes y suspensos,
Elósenos la sangre y el aliento
A vna suspendimos, palpitando
Los flacos corazones dentro el pecho
Viendo a nuestro piloto y guía ausente
Por no más de descuido de la vela
A cuio cargo estuvo aquel cuidado.
Y cada qual, gimiendo, se dolía
De los tristes sucessos que apretaban
Tras tantas desventuras padezidas,
Hasta que entró la aurora refrescando,
Y en pie todos, cansados y afligidos,
Mirándonos los unos a los otros,
Buen rato sin hablar nos estuvimos.
Aquí la pobre Polca, sin consuelo,
Pasmada, boqui abierta, nos miraba
Qual triste miserable que aguardando

265 Were on their horses at their posts,
And for more safety to the piteous girl
We set our posts with greater care
So that Mompil might not break out by chance
And by our carelessness snatch her away.
270 And when in the midst of the lofty Pole,
As that heroic man doth sing,[5]
The lofty stars were 'minishing
Their mighty, wide-extended course,
In the most silence of the night,
275 When the brute beasts throughout the fields
And those more rational in their beds,
The fish in their great, profound deep,
The chattering birds upon their boughs,
All sunk in agreeable sleep
280 Repose in freedom from their cares,[6]
At that same point and instant came,
Upon their so weak, tired steeds
Whose heads were hung in wearied sleep,
The weary first watch, its time up,
285 And noting that all were asleep
And that good Mompil had escaped,
Leaving the captive barbarian there,
With mighty shouts it waked us up.
And hardly did we comprehend when all
290 Were dumb and sad and in suspense,
Our blood did freeze and all our breath
We held as one, our timorous hearts
Were palpitating in our breasts,
Seeing our pilot and our guide was gone
295 Through but the slackness of the watch
Within whose charge the duty was.
And each one, moaning, sorrowed at
The sad events that weighed us down
After so many misfortunes endured.
300 Until dawn came, refreshing us,
And, standing up, all tired and depressed,
Gazing each man upon the rest,
We stood a while, nor spoke at all.
Here the poor Polca, desolate,
305 Astonished, with mouth open, stared at us,
Like a miserable wretch who doth await

18. Postas = guardas.
19. Rompiesse = escapase.
20. Virgilo, *Eneida* IV, 725–26. Toda la descripción de una naturaleza en sueño procede del mismo pasaje virgiliano.
21. Demediaron = recorrieron la mitad de.
22. Este pasaje, descriptivo de la alta noche, es eco de otros de Virgilio, *Eneida* IV, 723–30, VIII, 34–35.
23. Quarto triste = en los cuadrúpedos, la cabeza: "cabizbajos"
24. Recordarnos = despertarnos.

5. Virgil, *Aeneid* IV, 725–26.
6. The nighttime description of nature at sleep echoes that found in several passages of the *Aeneid* (IV, 723–30; VIII, 34–35).

Sentencia está de muerte rigurosa
Por inorme delicto cometido.
Assí la triste mísera, afligida,
Tragada[25] ya la muerte por muy cierta,
De su venida infelix aguardaba
Vn desastrado fin y mal sucesso.
Pues viendo ya el Sargento, reportado,
El caso sucedido sin remedio,
Por no desanimar los compañeros,
Hablando allí con todos fue diziendo:
"Señores, no ay ninguno que no alcance
Que el mismo poderoso Dios eterno
Es el camino cierto y verdadero
De los que su ley santa profesamos.
Y assí tiene cien mil florestas bellas,
Amenos bosques, campos y llanados
Por do los flacos, débiles y tiernos
Van sus cortas jornadas caminando.
Otros tiene quajados de cambrones,[26]
Abrojos, duras puntas y pedriscos,
Cerros, quebradas, breñas y barrancos
Por do los esforzados y alentados
Su lebantado curso van corriendo.
Y assí no ay para qué desmaie nadie,
Y entendamos, señores compañeros,
Que como a illustres, nobles y valientes
Quiere el inmenso Dios aquí probarnos,
Y como tales bien será tomemos
Con buen recato todos el camino.
Y pues que[27] aquesta bárbara merece,
Toda noble, cortés correspondencia,
Pues no está media legua de su tierra,
Démosle libre libertad graciosa
Para que allá se buelva sin zozobra."
Y como el alma de la ley heroica
Es la fuerza de la razón illustre
Y aquesta jamás quiso ser forzada,
Todos juntos, alegres, aprobamos
Del Sargento mayor el buen respecto.
Y partiendo con ella nuestra ropa
Y cargándole el niño de brinquiños,[28]
Dímosle libertad que se bolviesse.
Y entendido por ella bien tan grande,
Como la sobra de contento causa
Tierno semblante y lágrimas gustosas
En que los tristes laban sus cuidados,

Sentence of rigorous death
For some enormous crime imposed.
Thus the sad, miserable she, downcast,
310 Considering now death was very sure,
From her unhappy coming did await
Disastrous end and sad outcome.
But the mild Sergeant, seeing then
The thing was done beyond all help,
315 Not to discourage his companions,
Speaking there to them all, said thus:
"Gentlemen, there is none that does not know
That the eternal, powerful God
Is the true, certain road of us
320 Who do profess his holy law.
And as He has a hundred thousand forests beautiful
And pleasant woods, and fields and spreading plains
Through which the tender, feeble, weak
Go marching on their short journeys,
325 So He has other fields with briars,
Thistles and sharp points and heaps of stones,
Hills and ravines and crags and broken ground
Through which the hardy and the spirited
Go running on their lofty course.
330 And so there is no cause here for weakness;
And thereby know, my gentle companions,
That here the great God doth will to prove us
As famous, noble, valiant men.
And as such it is good we take
335 The road with proper modesty.
And since yon barbarian deserves
All noble, courteous requital,
As she is not a half-league from her land,
Let us give, freely, gracious liberty
340 So that she may return without anxiety."
And as the soul of the heroic law
Is but the force of famous reasoning
And that would never be forced,
We, all together, did approve with joy
345 The good decision of the Sergeant,
And, sharing our clothes with her
And loading down the child with gifts,
We gave her freedom to return.
And, understanding such goodness,
350 Since a great contentment causes
A tender look and happy tears
In which the sad do lave their cares,

---

25. Tragada = aceptada.
26. Cambrones = zarzas.
27. Pues que = puesto que.
28. Brinquiños = joyas pequeñas o juguetes.

Como la lengua muchas vezes miente,
Pensando que más fee debía darse
A sus corrientes lágrimas vertidas
Que a sus muchas palabras y razones,
Quando muy bien supiera proponerlas,
Vertiéndolas assí, con gran contento,
Abiéndonos a todos abrazado,
Por tres vezes salió determinada
De recebir el bien de que dudaba.
Y a cosa de cien passos se bolvía
A mostrársenos siempre más gustosa,
Amorosa y más bien agradezida.
Y como siempre vemos se adelanta
La noble gratitud al beneficio,
Quarta vez fue saliendo, y pareciole
Que quedaba muy corta y no pagaba,
Y porque ingratitud no la rindiesse,
Otra fue rebolviendo y de los pechos
El niño se quitó y dio al Sargento
Y allí le suplicó que le llevase,
Pues todo le faltaba y no tenía
Con que poder servir merced tan grande.
El Sargento le tuvo y dio mil vesos
Entre sus nobles brazos bien ceñidos,
Y dándole más cuentas y abalorios,
Con mil tiernas caricias amorosas
El niño le bolvió y pidió se fuesse.
Con cuio cumplimiento regalado,
Qual suele tras la cierva el ciervo en brama,[29]
Herida de su amor,[30] correr tras della,
Y ansioso de alcanzarla, desembuelto,
De salto y de corrida va siguiendo
El amoroso rastro y dulze huella
Por vna y otra parte, sin que pueda
Pararse o detenerse o alentarse
En parte que el cariño no le assista,
Assí, sin seso, ciega y sin sentido,
Atónita del todo, fue siguiendo
La huella de su amado, desbalida.
Y porque priessa dan que me adereze,[31]
Todo aquello que resta de quebranto
Veremos adelante en nuevo canto.

As tongues do lie so many times,
Thinking more confidence would be shown
355 The shedding of her flowing tears
Than to her many words, reasons,
However well she might say them,
Shedding them, thus, in great content,
Having embraced all of us,
360 Three times she left, determined
She would receive the blessing she did doubt.
And, after some hundred paces, turned
Always to show herself more pleased,
More loving, more grateful to us.
365 And as we always see a noble gratitude
Coming before a benefit,
A fourth time she departed and she thought
That she had been too brusque and had not paid,
And that she might not show ingratitude
370 She came again and from her breast
She took the child and gave him to the Sergeant
And there she begged him that we would take it
Since she did lack all things and did not have
The wherewithal such mercy to reward.
375 The Sergeant took the babe, kissed it a thousand times
Held tight within his noble arms,
And, giving it more trinkets and beads,
With thousand loving, tender caresses,
He gave back the child and asked her to depart.
380 With which winning performance,
As the doe the rutting stag
Does use to follow, smote with love,
And eager to o'ertake her all at once
And in a leaping run goes following
385 The trail of love and her dear track
On every side, unable to
Restrain itself or stop, or even breathe
In any place where love is not present,
So, senseless, blind, without reason,
390 Completely stunned, she followed on
The trail of her beloved, all helpless,
And, as there's need of haste that I go on,
All the remains of the affliction
We shall see later in a new canto.

29. En brama = en celo.
30. Si se coloca esta frase antes de dar comienzo la comparación se aclara su sentido.
31. Adereze = aderece, enderezca, vuelva al hilo de su narración.

CANTO CATORZE

COMO SE DESCVBRIO EL RIO DEL NORTE Y
TRABAJOS que hasta descubrirlo padecieron, y de otras cosas
que fueron sucediendo hasta ponerse en punto de tomar posesión
de la tierra.

TANTO se estima, sube y se lebanta
El valor de la cosa que se emprende
Quanto es más estimado todo aquello
Con que se alcanza, adquiere y se consigue.
Traigo esto, gran señor, porque se entienda
Más bien la gran grandeza y excelencia
Del bélico exercicio que professan
Todos aquellos Héroes valerosos
Que a trueque de trabajos y quebrantos,
Vida y sangre, compraron y adquirieron
Sólo el illustre nombre de soldados,
A cuia alta excelencia le es muy proprio
El ver y tracender, de todo punto,
Que por demás se sufren los trabajos,
Miserias, aflicciones y fatigas
Que la sangrienta guerra trae consigo
Si enmedio de su curso sin remedio
El ánimo se rinde y se acobarda.
Y para no venir en tanta mengua,
Zozobrando las fuerzas fatigadas,
Sin ver vn agradable y dulze puerto,
Luego que la contenta y noble Polca
Despedida salió para su tierra,
Qual suele el cazador quando a perdido
Vn rico gerifalte, alcón o sacre,[1]
Que a vozes por los cerros y vallados
Le va con grandes ansias ahuchando,[2]
Mostrándole el señuelo hasta verlo
Seguro y en la mano, donde alegre,
Sin memoria del susto ya passado,
Le alaga y le regala y le compone
La pluma mal compuesta y le apazigua,
Assí la hermosa bárbara, sospecho,
Que fue desalentada tras su Milco,
Y nosotros, señor, con nuevos bríos,
Más de cincuenta días caminamos,
Pesadas desventuras padeciendo.
Y por abernos sin cessar llovido
Siete largas jornadas trabajosas,

1. Sacre = pájaro de presa utilizado en la cetrería.
2. Ahuchando = en la cetrería, llamando al pájaro desviado.

CANTO XIV

How the River of the North was discovered and the trials that
were borne in discovering it, and of other things that happened
until arriving at the point of taking possession of the land.

THE value of a thing undertaken
Is esteemed and praised and raised aloft
In such proportion as that is esteemed
With which it is accomplished, gained, and
        won.
5   This I do say, great lord, so that I may
Make clearer the great greatness, excellence,
Of warlike exercise practiced
By all those heroes valorous
Who, in exchange for toil and suffering,
10   Life and blood, have bought and won
Only the famous name of soldiers,
To whose high excellence 'tis proper
To see and to observe in every way
That 'tis useless to bear the trials
15   Miseries, afflictions, and fatigues
That bloody war always entails
If in the middle of its course unstoppable
Their spirit breaks and becomes cowardly.
And, not to come to such disgrace,
20   Our tired forces sinking down,
Seeing no port agreeable, sweet,
When the noble Polca, content,
Her farewell said, had gone to her country,
As goes the huntsman who has lost
25   A great gyrfalcon, falcon, or saker,
Shouting among the valleys and hills,
Calling it with anxiety,
Showing the lure until he sees him safe
Perched on his hand, where, happily,
30   Without a memory of his recent fright,
He dandles him and pets him and smooths down
His ruffled plumage, and appeases him,
So went the beautiful barbarian, I think,
She went eagerly after her Milco,
35   And we, lord, resolute anew,
Did journey more than fifty days,
Suffering heavy mischances.
And as it had unceasing rained on us
For seven long, hard days' journeyings,

En las carnes la ropa ya cozida,³
Ninguno de nosotros entendimos
Poder salir con vida de aquel hecho.
Por escabrosas tierras anduvimos
De Alárabes y bárbaros incultos
Y otros, desiertos broncos, peligrosos,
Cuio tendido y espacioso suelo
Nunca jamás Christianos pies pisaron.
En cuio largo tiempo consumimos
Los pobres bastimentos que sacamos,
Y alimentando todos con esfuerzo
Los fatigados cuerpos destroncados,⁴
Con sólas raízes brutas, indigestas.
Contra el rigor del hado prohejando,⁵
Nuestra derrota siempre proseguimos,
Ya por espesas breñas y quebradas,
Por cuios bravos bosques enrredados
Las fuertes escarcelas⁶ se rasgaban,
Ya por ásperas cumbres lebantadas,
Por cuias zimas los caballos lasos⁷
Por delante llevabamos, rendidos,
Hijadeando, cansados y afligidos,
A pie y de todas armas molestados,
Y las hinchadas plantas ya desnudas,
Descalzas, sin calzado, se assentaban
Por riscos y peñascos escabrosos,
Ya por muy altos médanos de arena,
Tan ardiente, encendida y tan fogosa
Que de su fuerte reflexión heridos
Los miserables ojos, abrasados,
Dentro del duro casco se quebraban.
Y como el fin de aquello que se espera
Sólo se alienta, esfuerza y se sustenta
Con el valor y punto de esperanza,
Esperando hizimos los trabajos
Mas lebes, comportables y sufribles.
Y como la que es presta diligencia
Arrimada al solícito trabajo
Es madre de qualquier ventura buena,
Esta se tuvo en descubrir la boca
Que aquel hastuto bárbaro nos dixo,
Marcando la circunvezina tierra,
Assientos y lugares que nos puso
Quando con Milco presso le tuvimos.
Y como Magallanes por su estrecho,

40   Our clothing sticking to our flesh,
       No one of us had any thought
       Of coming out with life from that affair.
       We went through rough and craggy lands
       Of Arabs and of rude barbarians
45   And other deserts, wild and perilous,
       upon whose wide and spacious soil
       No Christian foot had ever trod.
       In which long time we did consume
       The poor provisions we had brought,
50   And all with difficulty fed
       Their tired bodies, all worn out,
       Only with coarse roots indigestible.
       Driving against the hardness of our fate
       We ever held unto our course,
55   Now through thick briars and ravines,
       Entangled in whose harsh forests
       Even our strong cuisses were torn,
       Now over high and rugged peaks,
       Over whose summits we did drive
60   Our tired horses on before,
       Panting and tired and quite worn out,
       On foot and hindered by all our arms,
       Our swollen feet, now quite naked
       And shoeless, without shoes we still did set
65   On cliffs and ragged looming rocks,
       Now over lofty dunes of sand,
       So ardent, burning, and fervent
       That, wounded by their strong reflection,
       Our miserable eyes, burnt up
70   'Neath our hard helmets, failed us quite.
       And as the end of what is hoped
       Alone is nourished, thewed, sustained,
       By valor and the ring of hope,
       Hoping, we did those tasks that were
75   But lighter, more endurable, and easier borne.
       And since a ready diligence
       Lent to a careful toil
       Is mother of all good outcome,
       We had that same, discovering the pass
80   That the astute barbarian told us of,
       Marking the lands all round about
       The sites and places that he showed
       When we with Milco captured him.
       And, like Magellan through his strait,

---

3. Cozida = cocida, del proceso para teñir géneros.
4. Destroncados = descoyuntados.
5. Prohejando = proejando, remando contra corriente, luchando.
6. Escarcelas = armaduras desde la cintura al muslo.
7. Lasos = cansados.

Assí desembocando todos fuimos,
Vencidos del trabajo y ya rendidos
De la fuerza del hado riguroso,
Que con pesada mano bien cargada[8]
Mucho quiso apretarnos y afligirnos.
Quatro días naturales se passaron
Que gota de agua todos no bebimos,
Y tanto, que ya ciegos los caballos
Crueles testaradas y encontrones
Se daban por los árboles sin verlos,
Y nosotros, qual ellos fatigados,
Vivo fuego exalando y escupiendo
Saliva más que liga[9] pegajosa,
Desahuziados[10] ya y ya perdidos,
La muerte casi todos desseamos.
Mas la gran providencia, condolida,
Que tanto es más beloz en socorrernos
Quanto con más firmeza la esperamos,
Al quinto abrió la puerta y fuimos todos,
Alegres, arribando el bravo Río
Del Norte, por quien todos padezimos
Cuidado y trabajos tan pesados.
En cuias aguas los caballos, flacos,
Dando tras pies, se fueron acercando
Y, zabullidas todas las cabezas,
Bebieron de manera los dos dellos
Que allí juntos murieron rebentados,
Y otros dos, ciegos, tanto se metieron
Que de la gran corriente arrebatados
También murieron de agua satisfechos.
Y qual suelen en pública taberna
Tenderse algunos tristes miserables
Embriagados del vino que bebieron,
Assí los compañeros se quedaron
Sobre la fresca arena amollentada,
Tan hinchados, hidrópicos, hipatos,[11]
Assí como si sapos todos fueran,
Pareciéndoles poco todo el Río
Para apagar su sed y contentarla.
Y qual si en los Elíseos campos frescos
Vbiéramos llegado a refrescarnos,
Assi, señor, nos fueron pareciendo
Todas aquellas playas y riberas,
Por cuios bellos pastos los caballos,
Repastándose alegres, descansaban
Los fatigados güessos quebrantados

85 We all did pass through it,
    Worn down with toil, now quite worn out
    By the force of the rigorous fate
    Which with a strong and heavy hand
    So pressed us down, afflicted us.
90 Four complete days did pass away
    In which we drank no drop of water there,
    And now the horses, being blind,
    Did give themselves most cruel blows
    And bumps against the unseen trees,
95 And we, as tired as they,
    Exhaling living fire and spitting forth
    Saliva more viscous than pitch,
    Our hope given up, entirely lost,
    Were almost all wishing for death.
100 But the great Providence, pitying,
    Which is always more quick in helping us
    As we more firmly trust in it,
    The fifth day opened us the door
    And we all, happily, did come upon the roaring River
105 Of the North, for which we all had undergone
    Such care and such enormous toil.
    Unto whose waters the weak horses
    Creeping, staggering much, approached
    And, all there plunging in their heads,
110 Two of them drank to such extent
    They there, together, burst and died,
    And two more, blind, went in so far
    That, by the current snatched away,
    They also died, with water satisfied.
115 And as in public taverns there do use
    To lie upon the floor some wretched ones,
    Drunk from the wine they have imbibed,
    So our companions remained,
    Stretched out upon the watery sand,
120 As swollen, dropsical, gasping,
    As they had all been toads,
    The whole river seeming to them but small
    To extinguish and abate their thirst.
    And as if in the fresh Elysian Fields
125 We had arrived, there to refresh ourselves,
    Such, lord, there did appear to us
    All those beaches and banks,
    Among whose goodly pasture the horses
    Were gladly grazing and resting
130 Their tired and exhausted bones

8. Cargada = fuerte, dura.
9. Liga = materia viscosa.
10. Deshauziados = desahuciados, sin remedio.
11. Hipatos = hinchados.

Del pesado camino trabajoso.
Y, assi, por aquel bosque ameno todos
Fuimos con mucho gusto discurriendo,
Por frescas alamedas muy copadas[12]
Cuias hermosas sombras apazibles
A los cansados miembros conbidaban
Que, cerca de sus troncos recostados,
Allí junto con ellos descansasen,
Por cuios verdes ramos espaciosos,
Qual suelen las castíssimas abejas,
Con vn susurro blando y regalado,
De tomillo en tomillo yr saltando
Gustando lo mejor de varias flores,
Assí por estas altas arboledas,
Con entonado canto regalado,
Cruzaban un millón de pajaricos,
Cuios graciosos picos desembueltos,
Con sus arpadas lenguas, alababan
Al inmenso señor que los compuso.[13]
Y aunque las aguas del gallardo Río,
En raudal[14] muy furiosas y corrientes,[15]
Se yban todas vertiendo y derramando
Tan mansas, suabes, blandas y amorosas,
Como si vn sossegado estanque fueran,
Por anchas tablas,[16] todas bien tendidas,
Y de diversos géneros de pezes
Por excelencia rico y abundoso.
Hallamos, demás desto, gruessa caza,
De muchas grullas, ansares y patos,
Donde cebaron bien sus alcabuzes
Los hastutos monteros diligentes.
Y abiendo hecho grande caza y pesca,
Luego de los fogosos pedernales
El escondido fuego les sacamos,
Haziendo vna gran lumbre poderosa,
Y en grandes assadores y en las brasas,
De carne y de pescado bien abasto[17]
Pusimos a dos manos[18] todo aquello
Que el hambriento apetito nos pedía
Para poder rendir de todo punto
Las buenas ganas al manjar sabroso.
Y como la paloma memorable

From the laborious, weary road.
And in the pleasant wood we all
With much pleasure did roam about
'Mid fresh and well-leaved poplar groves
135 Whose beautiful, agreeable shades
Gave invitation to our weary limbs,
By their own prostrate trunks nearby
To rest together with them there.
Through their green branches, spreading wide,
140 As exceeding chaste bees do go,
With buzzing dull and comforting,
Traveling from one thyme to the next
Tasting the best of many flowers,
Likewise among those lofty trunks,
145 With dainty, sweet-intoned song,
There flew a million little birds,
Whose graceful, unembarrassed throats
And lyric tongues did sing the praise
Of that All-powerful Lord who had made them.
150 And even the waters of the harsh river,
At flood, a furious, roaring stream,
Were all flowing and pouring down
As peaceful, suave, pleasing, and mild
As though they were a quiet pool
155 Over wide flats and well spread out,
And, too, with many kinds of fish
Most excellently rich and abounding.
We found, beside this, much hunting,
Of many cranes and ducks and geese,
160 upon which the astute, prompt hunters there
Made good use of their harquebuses.[1]
And having hunted and fished much,
From out the fire-bearing flints
We struck their hidden fires and made
165 A great and excellent campfire,
And on huge spits and in the coals
We put a huge supply of meat and fish,
Placing with liberal hands all that
Our eager appetites did ask
170 To conquer in completest sort
Their great desire for savory food.
And like that memorable dove

12. Copadas = de árboles de alto follaje.
13. El *locus amoenus,* de larga tradición literaria, suele hallar lugar apropiado en la épica americana. Véase, por ejemplo, *La araucana* II, 17.
14. En raudal = en crecida.
15. Y aunque en raudal muy furiosas y corrientes, las aguas del gallardo ríó . . .
16. Tablas = partes llanas del río.
17. Abasto = abundante.
18. A dos manos = con entusiasmo.

1. The *locus amoenus* of literary tradition is, not surprisingly, given the wonders of the new lands, found frequently in the New World epic. See, for example, *La araucana* II, 17.

Que luego que passó la gran tormenta
El verde ramo trujo de la oliba,
No de otra suerte todos nos bolvimos
Colmados de contento y alegría,
Que es verdadero premio del trabajo.
Y luego que al exército llegamos
Con muchas fiestas fuimos recibidos,
Y porque siempre es fuerza y causa gusto
Traer a la memoria los trabajos,
Miserias y fatigas que se sufren
Quando la dura guerra se milita,
Llamado deste gusto, fue contando
El Sargento mayor a todo el campo,
Presente el General, aquellos passos,
Caminos y sucessos que sufrimos
Hasta que al fin llegamos a las playas,
Riberas y alamedas deste Río
En cuias arboledas espaciosas
Todas nuestras fatigas descansamos.
Y como siempre causa grande alibio
No ser en padezer trabajos solo,
Luego como acabó, tomó la mano
El diestro General por dar consuelo
A los quebrantos tristes ya passados,
Diziendo los trabajos que los suyos
Abían también sufrido y padezido,
Y como vno cargó con tantas veras
Que estuvo a pique el campo de perderse.
Y fue que entrando Marzo caluroso
Con poderosos soles assentados,
Vino a faltar el agua de manera
Que, secas las gargantas miserables,
Los tiernos niños, hombres y mugeres
Traspassados, perdidos y abrassados,
Socorro al soberano Dios pedían,
Por ser aqueste el vltimo remedio
Que pudieron tener en tal conflicto.
Y los tristes, cansados, animales,
Como aquéllos de Ninibe,[19] rendidos,
Del insaziable ayuno fatigados,
Assí cuitados todos se mostraban
Con la fuerza del tiempo que cargaba.[20]
Y como siempre acude y faborece
Su gran bondad, inmensa, soberana,
Al que con veras pide y le suplica,
Estando el Cielo claro y muy sereno

175

180

185

190

195

200

205

210

215

Which, after the great storm had passed,
Returned with the green olive branch,[2]
Not otherwise, we all returned,
Filled wholly with content and joy,
Which is the true reward of work.
And when we came to the army
We were received with much festivity,
And, as 'tis always needed and is pleasant, too,
To bring to memory the toils,
The miseries, fatigues, we have endured
When the fierce war was on,
The Sergeant Major, drawn by this pleasure,
Related unto all the camp,
The General being present, those events,
Journeys, occurrences, endured
until at last we came unto the shores,
The banks and groves of that river,
under whose widely spreading trees
We took our ease after all our fatigues.
And as it always causes great relief
To know one suffers not alone,
When he had done, the skillful General
Took to himself the floor and as a comfort
For our sad trials now gone by,
Told of the trials that his men
Had also borne and undergone,
And how one of them was so hard
That the camp came to the edge of ruin.
And 'twas that, March coming on hot
And settling down with burning suns,
Water began to fail to such extent
That, with their throats all miserably dry,
The tender children, women, and the men,
Afflicted, ruined, quite burnt up,
Did beg for aid from sovereign God,
This being the final remedy
That they could have in such distress.
And the sad, tired animals,
Feeble as those of Nineveh,[3]
Worn down by unchecked fast,
Thus all did show themselves worn out
By the weather that they had borne.[4]
And as He always favors and assists
With His immense sovereign goodness
The ones who truly ask and beg of Him,
The sky, being clear and very calm

19. Villagrá recuerda *Nahum*, 1-3.
20. La descripción de la gran sequía tiene algún eco de Estacio, *La Tebaida* IV.

2. The reference is to Noah's ark, an image that Villagrá repeats.
3. Villagrá recalls the Old Testament, *Nahum* 1-3.
4. This long description of drought echoes that in Statius's *Thebaid* IV.

Por vna y otra parte fue turbado²¹
De gruessas nubes negras bien cargadas,
Y sin ningún relampago ni trueno
Tanta agua derramaron y vertieron
Que los bueyes vnzidos con sus yugos
Su mortífera sed satisficieron.
Y luego que el exército afligido
Quedó por todas partes consolado,
La belleza del Sol quedó con rayos
Por vna y otra parte tan tendidos
Que tan sóla vna nube no impedía
Su claro resplandor en parte alguna.
Y assí, por esta causa, le pusieron
Al parage de aquesta santa lluvia
'El agua del milagro', porque fuesse
Eterna su memoria prolongada
Y nunca para siempre se perdiesse.
¡O soberano bien, con qué presteza
Socorres nuestras faltas si ponemos
Tanta fee quanta ajusta, mide y pesa
No más que vn solo grano de mostaza!
Vendito tal varato²² y tal empleo,
No sólo para que las altas nubes
Fuera de tiempo viertan grandes lluvias,
Mas para que los más pesados montes
Remuevan y lebanten sus assientos
Y la belocidad del Sol repare
Su poderoso curso y le detenga
No más que por mandarlo el hombre noble
A cuios pies se rinden y abassallan
Todas las cosas, grandes y pequeñas,
En fin, como en sujeto lebantado
Por manos tan grandiosas y admirables.
Y assí parece que yba su grandeza
Llevando aqueste campo como a suyo,
Vnas vezes cargados de trabajos
Y otras de mil consuelos socorrido,
Viage derecho, cierto y verdadero
De los obreros grandes que lebantan
Heroicos edificios en su Iglesia.
Pues yendo, assí, marchando muchos días,
Llegaron a las aguas deste Río
Y, qual aquel Troyano memorable
Que fue faborecido y amparado
Del húmedo tridente de Neptuno
Después de la tormenta y gran borrasca,²³
Assí el Gobernador con todo el campo

220
225
230
235
240
245
250
255
260
265

In all directions, was disturbed
By huge black clouds, heavy laden,
And without lightening or thunder
They shed and poured down such water
That oxen laden with their yokes
Did satisfy their killing thirst.
And when the afflicted army
Was quite entirely appeased,
The beauty of the sun's bright rays
Was spread so widely over all
That not a single cloud held back
His bright splendor from any place.
And so, for this cause, they did give
The place that holy water fell
The name of "Water of the Miracle" that it
Might have its memory prolonged eternally
And never throughout all time be forgot.
O sovereign Good, with what swiftness dost Thou
Assist us in our need if we have but
Such faith as but a grain of mustard-seed
May measure, weigh, and balance with!
Blessed be such a gift and its use
Not only that the lofty clouds
Out of their season might pour water down,
But that the most massive mountains
Might move and change their locations
And the swift-flying sun might halt
His powerful course and hold it back
For no more than the order of a noble Man
At whose feet there do yield and crouch
All things, both great and small,
Finally, as a man upheld
By hands so great and wonderful.
It seems his greatness continued
To carry on this camp as His,
Being sometimes burdened with great woes
And others aided with a thousand joys,
A certain, direct, and true voyage
Of those great laborers who raised
Heroic buildings for his Church.
For, marching thus for many days,
They came unto the waters of this river,
And, like the Trojan memorable
Who was favored and protected
By Neptune's water trident
After the whirlwind and great storm,⁵
The Governor with all his camp

21. Turbado = alterado, conmovido.
22. Varato = barato, negocio, rendimiento.
23. Se refiere a Eneas (*Eneida* I, 177).

5. The reference is to Aeneas, the *Aeneid* I, 177.

Seguro y dulze puerto fue tomando,
Y a su más fatigada soldadesca,
Por las frescas orillas y riberas,
Abierta mano dio que descansase.
Y como el buen gobierno no consiste
En la que es buena industria de presente,
Sino en prevenir con sazón aquello
Que puede despúes darnos gran cuidado,
Mandó el Gobernador que sin tardanza
El Sargento saliesse y se aprestase
Con cinco compañeros escogidos
Y diestros en nadar, porque buscasen
Algún seguro vado al bravo Río
Para que por él todo vuestro campo
Seguro y sin zozobra le passase.
Y poniendo por obra aquel mandato
Salió Carabajal y Alonso Sánchez
Y el gran Christóbal Sánchez y Araujo
Y yo también con ellos porque fuesse
El número cumplido de los cinco.
Y andando embebecidos todos juntos
En busca de buen vado, cuidadosos,
De súbito nos fuimos acercando
A vnos pagizos²⁴ ranchos, do salieron
Gran cantidad de bárbaros guerreros.
Y por ser todo aquello pantanoso
Y no poder valernos de las armas,
Assí para los bárbaros nos fuimos
Mostrándonos amigos agradables.
Y como el dar al fin quebranta peñas,
Dándoles de la ropa que tuvimos
Tan mansos los bolvimos y amorosos,
Tanto que quatro dellos se vinieron
Y vn lindo vado a todos nos mostraron.
Por cuia causa el General, prudente,
Mandó que a todos quatro los vistiessen
Y con mucho regalo los tratasen,
Por cuia causa todos se bajaron
Y, dándose de paz, trujeron juntos
Vna gran suma de pescado fresco.
Y mandándoles dar vn buen retorno,²⁵
Luego se procuró que se hiziesse,
En vn copado y apazible bosque,
Vna graciosa Iglesia de vna nave,
Capaz para que todo el campo junto
Pudiesse bien caber sin apretarse.
En cuio albergue santo, Religioso,
Cantaron vna Missa muy solemne,

Came to a safe and pleasant port,
And to his sore-tried soldiery
He gave permission free to rest
upon those cooling banks and shores.
And as good government does not consist
In industry of no more than the present time,
But in a timely foresight of
What afterward may trouble us,
The Governor ordered that without delay
The Sergeant should set out at once
With five chosen companions,
All skillful in swimming, to seek
Some safe ford through the swift river
So that by it all this your camp
Might pass safely and without fear.
And carrying that order out
There went Caravajal, Antonio Sánchez,
The great Cristóbal Sánchez and Araujo,
And I, too, with them, that I might
Complete the number of the five.
And, traveling all together, studiously,
Careful in search for some good ford,
We suddenly did come upon
Some thatched huts from whence there came out
Great numbers of barbarian warriors.
And as that place was all marshy
And we could not well use our arms,
We went ahead toward the barbarians
Showing ourselves agreeable friends.
And as giving even breaks rocks,
Giving them of the clothes we had
We made them so peaceful, friendly, to us
That four of them did come with us
And showed to us a goodly ford.
For which reason the prudent General
Ordered that all the four be clothed
And treated with much regalement,
Wherefore all four went down the stream
And, as a sign of peace, brought back
A great number of fresh caught fish.
And, ordering us to make proper return,
He then did cause to be made there,
Within a pleasant, leafy wood,
A graceful church, one with a nave
Of such a size that all the camp at once
Might be contained in it without crowding.
Within whose shelter, holy and religious,
They sang a very solemn Mass,

270

275

280

285

290

295

300

305

310

24. Pagizos = pajizos, de paja.
25. Retorno = las gracias (materiales) por lo recibido.

Y el docto Comissario, con estudio,
Hizo vn sermón famoso, bien pensado.
Y luego que acabaron los oficios
Representaron vna gran comedia
Que el noble Capitán Farfán compuso,²⁶
Cuio argumento sólo fue mostrarnos
El gran recibimiento que a la Iglesia
Toda la nueva México hazía,
Dándole el parabién de su venida
Con grande reverencia, suplicando,
Las rodillas en tierra, les labase
Aquella culpa con el agua santa
Del precioso Baptismo que traían,
Con cuio saludable sacramento
Muchos Bárbaros vimos ya labados
Luego que por sus tierras anduvimos.
Vbo solemnes fiestas agradables
De gente de acaballo bien luzida,
Y por honrra de aquel illustre día
Vna gallarda esquadra suelta yba
De aquel Capitán Cárdenas famoso,
Soldado de valor y de vergüenza
Y que muy bien, señor, os ha servido.
Este, por entender que la jornada
No abía de ser possible se hiziesse,
Quedose, de manera que no pudo
Dar alcance después a vuestro campo,
Por cuia causa dieron su estandarte
A Diego Nuñez. Y con esto, luego
Se tomó possesión de aquella tierra
En vuestro insigne, heroico y alto nombre,
Haziendo en esta causa cierto escrito
Que aqueste será bien que aquí le ponga
Sin corromper la letra, porque importa
Por ser del mismo General la nota:

315
320
325
330
335
340
345

And the learned Commissary, with wisdom,
Did speak a famous sermon, well thought out.
And when the services were done
They did present a great drama
The noble Captain Farfán had composed,⁶
Whose argument was but to show to us
The great reception of the Church
That all New Mexico did give,
Congratulating it upon its arrival,
Begging, with thorough reverence,
And kneeling on the ground, it would wash out
Its faults with that holy water
Of precious Baptism which they brought,
With which most salutary sacrament
We saw many barbarians cleansed
When we were traveling through their lands.
There were solemn and pleasing festivals
Of splendid men on horseback,
And in honor of that illustrious day
A gallant squadron was released
From that illustrious Captain Cárdenas,
A soldier of courage, modesty
And who, O lord, has served you well.
He, thinking that the expedition
Would be unable to set out,
Remained, so that he never afterward
Could overtake this camp of yours,
Wherefore his standard then was given
To Diego Núñez. And with that we then
Did take possession of that land
In your famous, heroic, lofty name,
Making some record of the case,
Which it is well I give to you,
Nor skip a letter, for it imports much
As being the statement of the General himself.

DE COMO SE TOMO Y APREHENDIO LA POSSESION DE LA NUEVA TIERRA

Of how we took and seized upon possession of the new land.

EN el nombre de la Santíssima Trinidad y de la indevidua vnidad eterna, deidad y magestad, Padre, Hijo y Espíritu Santo, tres personas y vna sola essencia y vn solo Dios verdadero que con su eterno querer, omnipotente poder e infinita sabiduría rige, gobierna y dispone, poderosa y suabemente, de mar a mar, de fin a fin, como principio y fin de todas las cosas, y en cuias manos están el eterno Pontificado y Sacerdocio, los Imperios y los

IN the name of the most Holy Trinity and of the individual eternal unity, deity, and majesty, Father, Son, and Holy Ghost, three persons and one single being and one single true God, who with his eternal will, omnipotent power, and infinite wisdom rules, governs, and disposes, powerfully and gently, from sea to sea, from end to end, as the beginning and end of all things, and in whose hands are the eternal Pontificate and priesthood, the

26. Esta obra teatral del capitán Farfán de los Godos, que no ha llegado a nosotros, es, sin duda, la primera creación literaria en lo que ha venido a ser los Estados Unidos.

6. Farfán's play, now lost, would undoubtedly be the first literary work created in what is today the United States.

Reynos, Principados y Ditados,[27] Repúblicas, mayores y menores, familias y personas, como en eterno Sacerdote, Emperador y Rey de Emperadores y Reyes, señor de señores, criador de Cielos y Tierra, elementos, Aves y pezes, animales, plantas y de toda criatura, espiritual y corporal, razional e irrazional, desde el más supremo Cherubin hasta la más despreciada hormiga y pequeña mariposa; e a honor y gloria suya y de su sacratíssima y venditíssima Madre, la Virgen santa María, nuestra Señora, puerta del Cielo, arca del Testamento, en quien el maná del Cielo, la vara de la divina Iusticia y brazo de Dios y su Ley de gracia y amor estuvo encerrada, como en Madre de Dios, Sol, Luna, Norte y guía y abogada del género humano; y a honrra del Seraphico Padre san Francisco, Imagen de Christo, Dios en cuerpo y alma, Su Real Alférez y Patriarca de pobres, a quienes tomo por mis Patrones y abogados, guía, defensores e intercessores, para que rueguen al mismo Dios que todos mis pensamientos, dichos y hechos vayan encaminados al servicio de su Magestad infinita, aumento de fieles y extensión de su santa Iglesia, y a servicio del Christianíssimo Rey don Felipe, nuestro señor, columna fortíssima de la Fe Católica, que Dios guarde muchos años, y corona de Castilla, y amplificación de sus Reynos y Provincias.

Quiero que sepan los que ahora son o por tiempos fueren como yo don Iuan de Oñate, Gobernador y Capitán General y Adelantado de la nueva México y de sus Reynos y Provincias y las a ella circunvezinas y comarcanas, poblador y descubridor y pazificador dellas e de los dichos Reynos, por el Rey nuestro señor, digo que por quanto en virtud del nombramiento que en mí fue fecho y títulos que su Magestad me da, desde luego, de tal Gobernador, Capitán General y Adelantado de los dichos Reynos y Provincias, sin otros mayores que me promete en virtud de sus Reales ordenanzas y de dos Cédulas Reales y otras dos sobrecédulas y capítulos de cartas del Rey, nuestro señor, su fecha en Valencia a veinte y seis de Enero de mil y quinientos y ochenta y seis años, su fecha en San Lorenzo a diez y nueve de Iulio de mil y quinientos y ochenta y nueve años, su fecha a diez y siete de Enero de mil y quinientos noventa y tres, su fecha a veinte y vno de Iunio de mil y quinientos y noventa y cinco, y por otra vltima cédula Real, su fecha de dos de Abril deste año passado de mil y quinientos y noventa y siete, en que, en contradición de partes,[28] su Magestad aprueba la elección hecha en mi persona e estado, exerciendo y continuando el dicho mi oficio; y aora, venido en demanda de los dichos Reynos y Provincias con mis oficiales maiores, Capitanes, Alférez, soldados y gente de paz y guerra para

empires and the kingdoms, principalities and fiefs, republics, greater and lesser, families and persons, as in the eternal Priest, Emperor and king of emperors and kings, Lord of lords, creator of the heavens and earth, elements, birds and fish, animals, plants and of all creatures, spiritual and corporal, rational and irrational, from the most supreme Cherubim to the most despised ant and little butterfly; and to His honor and glory and of His most sacred and blessed Mother, the Virgin, holy Mary, our Lady, gate of heaven, ark of the Testament, in whom the manna of Heaven, the rod of divine justice and arm of God, and his law of grace and love was enclosed, as in the mother of God, sun, moon, north and guide and advocate of the human race; and to the honor of the seraphic father Saint Francis, image of Christ, God, in body and soul, his royal ensign and patriarch of the poor, whom I take for my patrons and advocates, defenders, and intercessors, that they may pray God himself that all my thoughts, sayings, and deeds may go on the road of the service of his infinite Majesty, increase of the faithful and the extension of his holy Church, and to the service of the most Christian King don Felipe, our lord, most strong pillar of the Catholic Faith, may God keep him many years, and the crown of Castile and the increase of its kingdoms and provinces.

I wish that they may know, those who now are here or in time shall be, how I, don Juan de Oñate, Governor and Captain General and Adelantado of New Mexico and of its kingdoms and provinces, and of those neighboring and adjoining, settler and discoverer and pacificator of them and of the aforesaid kingdoms, for the King, our lord, I say that, inasmuch as in virtue of the nomination which of me was made and titles which his Majesty gives me, undoubtedly, as such Governor, Captain General and Adelantado of the aforesaid kingdoms and provinces, beside other greater which he promises me by virtue of his Royal Ordinances and by two Royal Decrees and two other second Royal orders and chapters of the letters of the King, our lord, its date in Valencia the twenty-sixth of January of the year one thousand five hundred and eighty-six, its date in San Lorenzo on the nineteenth of July of the year one thousand five hundred and eighty-nine, its date the sixteenth of January of the year one thousand five hundred and ninety-three, its date the twenty-first of June of the year one thousand five hundred and ninety-five, and by another final Royal Decree, its date the second of April of this past year of one thousand five hundred and ninety-seven, in which, in opposition to certain opinions, his Majesty approves the choice made of

27. Ditados = dictados, estados de los que toman nombre sus señores.

28. Contradición de partes = contra otras opiniones.

poblar y pazificar, e otra gran machina de pertrechos necessarios, carros, carretas, rosas,[29] caballos, bueyes, ganado menor y otros ganados, y mucha de la dicha mi gente, casada, de suerte que me hallo oy con todo mi campo entero y con más gentes de las que saqué de la Provincia de Santa Bárbola, junto al Río que llaman del Norte y alojado a la Ribera, que es lugar circunvezino y comarcano a las primeras poblaciones de la nueva México y que passa por ellas el dicho Río, y dexo hecho camino abierto de carretas, ancho y llano, para que sin dificultad se pueda yr y venir por él, después de andadas al pie de cien leguas de despoblado, e porque yo quiero tomar la possesión de la tierra, oy, día de la Ascensión del Señor, que se cuentan treinta días del mes de Abril deste presente año de mil y quinientos y noventa y ocho, mediante la persona de Iuan Pérez de Donís, Escribano de su Magestad y Secretario de la jornada y gobernación de los dichos Reynos y Provincias, en voz y nombre del christianíssimo Rey, nuestro señor, don Felipe, Segundo deste nombre, y de sus subcessores, que sean muchos y con suma felicidad, y para la corona de Castilla y Reyes que su gloriosa estirpe Reynaren en ella, e por la dicha y para la dicha mi gobernación, fundándome y estribando en el vnico y absoluto poder e juridición que aquel eterno summo Pontífice y Rey, Iesu Christo, hijo de Dios vivo, cabeza vniversal de la Iglesia y primero y vnico instituidor de sus sacramentos, vassa y piedra angular del viejo y nuevo Testamento, fundamento y perfección dél, tiene en los cielos y en la tierra, no sólo en quanto Dios y consubstancial a su Padre eterno, que como criador de todas las cosas es vnico, absoluto, natural y propietario señor dellas, que como tal puede hazer y deshazer, ordenar y disponer a su voluntad y lo que por bien tuviere, mas también en quanto hombre, a quien su eterno Padre, como a tal, y por ser hijo del hombre y por su dolorosa y penosa muerte y triunfante y gloriosa Resurección y Ascensión y el especial título de vniversal Redentor que con ella ganó, dio omnímoda potestad, juridición y dominio cibil y criminal, alta y baja, horca y cuchillo,[30] mero mixto[31] Imperio en los Reynos de los Cielos y en los Reynos de la tierra, y en cuias manos puso el peso y medida, judicatura, premio y pena, del Orbe vniverso, haziéndole no sólo Rey y Iuez, mas también pastor vniversal de las ovejas, fieles e infieles, de las que oy en su voz le creen y siguen y están dentro de su rebaño y pueblo Christiano y de las que no han oído su voz y Evangélica palabra ni hasta

my person and estate, exercising and continuing my said office and now come in claim of the aforesaid kingdoms and provinces with my chief officers, captains, ensigns, and people of peace and war, to populate and pacify, and other great number of necessary apparatus, carts, wagons, buggies,[7] horses, oxen, major cattle and other cattle, and many of my aforesaid people married, so that I find myself today with all my camp entire and with more people than I took from the province of Santa Bárbola, beside the river that they call of the North and lodged on the bank, which is a place neighboring and adjoining the first towns of New Mexico, and the aforesaid river passes through them, and I have left a road made open for wagons, wide and flat, so that it is possible without difficulty to go and come by it, after having gone on foot through a hundred leagues of uninhabited land; and because I wish to take possession of the land today, the day of the Ascension of our Lord, which is counted thirty days in the month of April of this present year of one thousand five hundred and ninety-eight, through the person of Juan Pérez de Donís, Notary of his Majesty and Secretary of the journey and government of the aforesaid kingdoms and provinces, in the voice and name of the most Christian King, our lord, don Felipe, the Second of this name, and of his successors, may they be many and with the highest felicity, and for the crown of Castile and kings whose glorious stock may reign in it, and by the aforesaid and for the aforesaid my government, basing myself and resting on the unique and absolute power and jurisdiction which the eternal, highest, Pontiff and King, Jesus Christ, son of the living God, universal head of the Church and first and only institutor of its sacraments, base and cornerstone of the Old and New Testaments, foundation and perfection of it, has in heaven and earth, not only as to God and consubstantial with his eternal Father, who as creator of all things is the only absolute, natural, and proprietary lord of them, who as such can make and unmake, order and dispose according to his will and what he may consider good, but also as to man, to whom his eternal Father, as such, and as being the son of man, and for his dolorous and painful death and triumphant and glorious Resurrection and Ascension and the special title of universal Redeemer which he gained thereby, gave omnipotent power, jurisdiction and dominion, civil and criminal, high and low scaffold,[8] and simple mixed empire,[9] in the Kingdom of

---

29. Rosas = no hallando semejante nombre para vehículo pensamos pueda ser corto para carrozas.

30. Horca y cuchillo = jurisdicción para imponer la pena de muerte.

31. Mero mixto = mero y mixto imperio: el primero suponía el derecho del soberano para castigar; el segundo, el mismo derecho en jueces.

---

7. Villagrá has *rosas,* which may be short for *carrozas.*

8. This legal formula indicates the power to impose the death penalty.

9. This refers to the power both to exercise justice and to delegate the same to judges.

el día de oi le conozen, las quales dize le conviene traer a
su divino conocimiento porque son suias y es su ligítimo y
vniversal Pastor, para lo qual abiendo de subir a su eterno
Padre, por presencia corporal, vbo de dexar y dexó por su
Vicario y substituto al Príncipe de los Apóstoles, San Pedro,
y demás subcessores, ligíitimamente electos, a los quales
dio y dexó el Reyno, poder e Imperio y las llaves del Cielo,
según y como el mismo Christo Dios le recibió de su eterno
Padre, en él, como su cabeza y señor vniversal, y en los
demás como en sus subcessores, siervos, ministros y Vica-
rios, y assí no sólo les dexó la juridición Eclesiástica y
Monarchía espiritual, mas tambíen les dexó abitualmente
juridición y monarchía temporal, y el vno y el otro brazo
y cuchillo de dos filos, para que por sí o por medio de sus
hijos, los Emperadores y Reyes, quando y como les pareciesse
convenir por vrgente causa, pudiessen reducir la sobredicha
jurisdición y monarchía temporal al acto y ponerla en ex-
ecución, como luego que la ocasión y necessidad se ofreció
la executaron, vsando de la omnímoda potestad temporal,
del brazo y poder secular, assí por sí como para armadas y
exércitos de mar y tierra, en las proprias y en las distintas
y bárbaras naciones, con los pendones, vanderas y estandarte
Imperial de la Cruz, subgetando las bárbaras naciones, hal-
lanando el passo a los Evangélicos Predicadores, assegurando
sus vidas y personas, vengando las injurias que los vna vez
recebidos recibieren, reprimiendo y refrenando el ímpetu y
bestial y bárbara fiereza de los sobredichos, y en el nombre
del poderoso Christo Dios que mandó predicar su Evangelio
a todo el mundo, y por su autoridad y derecho, ensanchando
los términos de la República Christiana y amplificando su
Imperio por mano también de los sobredichos sus hijos,
Emperadores y Reyes, entre los quales el Rey don Felipe,
nuestro señor, Rey de Castilla y de Portogal y de las Indias
Occidentales y Orientales, descubiertas y por descubrir, hal-
ladas y por hallar, mediante la sobredicha potestad, juri-
dición y monarchía Apostólica y Pontifical, transfussa,
concedida y otorgada, encomendada y encargada, a los Reyes
de Castilla y Portogal y a sus sucessores desde el tiempo del
sumo Pontífice Alexandro Sexto, por divina y singular in-
spiración, como por la piedad Christiana enseña ser infali-
blemente assí, pues Dios a su Vicario, que representa su
persona y vezes en cosas graves, jamás falta, y la experiencia,
verdadera maestra y prueba de la verdad, en tan largos
tiempos a mostrado, lo qual testifica con infalible certid-
umbre el consentimiento, permiso y confirmación del so-
bredicho Imperio y dominio de las Indias Orientales y
Occidentales en los Reyes de Castilla y Portogal y sus subces-
sores, transfusso y colocado por manos de la Iglesia militante
de todos los demás sumos Pontífices, subcessores del dicho
santíssimo Pontífice, de gloriosa memoria, Alexandro Sexto,

Heaven and in the kingdoms of the earth, and in whose
hands he put the weight and measure, judicature, reward
and penalty, of the universal globe, making him not only
King and Judge, but also universal shepherd of the sheep,
faithful and unfaithful, of those who today believe in and
follow his voice and are within his fold and Christian people,
and of those who have not heard his voice and Evangelical
word, not to the day of today know him, whom he says it
suits him to bring to his divine acquaintance, because they
are his and he is their legitimate and universal shepherd,
for which, having to ascend unto his eternal Father in cor-
poral presence, he had to leave and he left as his Vicar and
substitute the prince of the Apostles, Saint Peter and other
successors, legitimately chosen, to whom he gave and left
the kingdom, power and empire and the keys of Heaven,
according to and as the same Christ God received them
from his eternal Father, in him, as its head and universal
lord, and in the others, as in his successors, servants, min-
isters, and vicars, and so he left them not only the eccle-
siastical jurisdiction and spiritual monarchy, but also he left
them habitually temporal jurisdiction and monarchy, and
the one arm and the other and the two-edged sword, so
that through themselves or through the means of their
children, the emperors and kings, when and as might seem
suitable to them, for urgent cause, they might reduce the
aforesaid jurisdiction and temporal monarchy to fact and
put it into execution as soon as the occasion and necessity
should be offered they execute it, using the entire temporal
power of the secular arm and power as well by itself as by
fleets and armies on land and sea, in his own and in different
and barbarous nations, with the pennons, banners, and
Imperial standard of the Cross, subjecting the barbarous
nations, leveling the way for the evangelical preachers, as-
suring their lives, avenging the injuries which they once
received, might receive, restraining and checking the im-
petus and bestial and barbarous wildness of the aforemen-
tioned; and in the name of the powerful Christ God who
ordered his Evangel preached to all the world, and by his
authority and right extending the boundaries of the Chris-
tian Republic and amplifying its Empire also by the hand
of the aforesaid its sons, emperors, and kings, among whom
the King don Felipe, our lord, King of Castile and of
Portugal and of the Oriental and Occidental Indies, dis-
covered and to be discovered, found and to be found, under
the aforesaid power, jurisdiction and Apostolic and Pontif-
ical Monarchy transferred, conceded, and handed over, en-
trusted and charged upon the Kings of Castile and Portugal
and to their successors since the time of the supreme Pontiff
Alexander the Sixth, by divine and singular inspiration, as
Christian piety teaches that he infallibly is, since God to

hasta el día presente, en cuio sólido fundamento estribo para tomar la sobredicha possessión destos Reynos y Provincias en el sobredicho nombre, a lo qual se allegan, como vassas y pilares deste edificio, otras muchas, graves, vrgentes y notorias causas y razones que a ello me mueven y obligan y dan segura entrada, y con aiuda de Dios y de su vendita Madre y el estandarte de su santa Cruz, por medio de los Evangélicos Predicadores, hijos de mi Seráphico Padre san Francisco, darán mucho más seguro, próspero, felice subcesso, y la primera y no de menos consideración para el caso presente es la inocente muerte de los Predicadores del santo Evangelio, verdaderos hijos de san Francisco, Frai Iuan de Santa María, Frai Francisco López y Frai Agustín Ruiz,[32] primeros descubridores desta tierra después de aquel gran Padre Frai Marcos de Niza, que todos dieron sus vidas y sangre,[33] en primicias del santo Evangelio, en ella, cuia muerte fue inocente y no merecida, pues siendo vna vez recebidos destos Indios y admitidos en sus Pueblos y casas, y quedándose los dichos Religiosos solos entre ellos para predicarles la palabra de Dios y mejor entender su lengua, confiados de la seguridad del buen rostro y trato que les hazían, y abiendo acudido en todas ocasiones a hazer bien a estos naturales, assí en todo el tiempo que los pocos Españoles que con ellos estuvieron, que fueron sólos ocho, duraron en la tierra, como el que después estuvieron solos, contra ley natural, dieron mal por bien y la muerte a otros hombres como ellos, inocentes y que no les hazían daño y que les daban como por entonces mejor podían y procuraban darles la vida mediante la palabra de la Ley de gracia más aventajadamente, causa y razón bastante, quando otra no vbiera, para justificar mi pretensión, demás de la qual la enmienda, corrección y castigo de los pecados contra naturaleza y la inhumanidad que entre estas bestiales naciones se halla, que a mi Rey y Príncipe, como a tan poderoso señor, conviene corregir y reprimir, y a mí en su Real nombre, dan mano al acto presente, y sin éstas, la piadosa razón y Christianíssima opinión del Bautismo y salvación de las almas de tantos niños como entre estos infieles padres al presente viven y nacen que a su verdadero Padre Dios y más principal Padre ni obedezen ni reconozen, ni pueden, moralmente hablando, reconozer sino es mediante este medio, como la larga experiencia en todas estas tierras ha mostrado, y quando pudieran reconozerle, entrando por la puerta del Bautismo, no pueden conservar la Fe ni perseverar en su bocación entre gente idólatra e infiel, contra cuia voluntad

his Vicar, who represents his person and supplies his place in such grave things, never fails, and true experience, master, and proof of the truth, has shown for long periods, which testifies with infallible certitude to the consent, permission, and confirmation of the above-mentioned empire and dominion of the Oriental Indies and Occidental in the Kingdoms of Castile and Portugal and their successors, transferred and placed by the hands of the Church militant of all the other Supreme Pontiffs, successors to the aforesaid most holy Pontiff of glorious memory, Alexander the Sixth, up to the present day, upon which solid foundation I strive to take the aforesaid possession of these kingdoms and provinces in the aforesaid name, for which are alleged, as bases and pillars of this edifice, many other grave, urgent, and notorious causes and reasons, which move me to it, and oblige me and give secure entry; and with the aid of God and of his blessed Mother and of the standard of his holy Cross, by means of the evangelical preachers, sons of my seraphic Father Saint Francis, giving much safer, more prosperous, happy success, and the first and of no less consideration for the present case is the innocent death of the preachers of the holy Evangel, true sons of Saint Francis, Fray Juan de Santa María, Fray Francisco López and Fray Agustín Ruiz,[10] first discoverers of this land after that great Father Fray Marcos de Niza, who all gave their lives and blood, as first fruits of the holy Evangel,[11] in it, whose death was innocent and undeserved, for, being once received by these Indians and admitted into their Pueblos and houses and the aforesaid monks remaining alone among them to preach to them the word of God and to better understand their language, trusting the safety of the good appearance and treatment that was shown them, and having come on all occasions to do good to these natives, so in all the time that the few Spaniards who were with them, who were only eight, remained in the land, as they were afterward alone, against the law of nature they gave evil for good and death to the other men as they, innocent and doing them no harm and who gave them what best they could and tried to give them life through the word of the law of grace more advantageously, cause and reason, were there no other, to justify my pretension, beside which the improvement, correction, and punishment of the unnatural sins and the inhumanity which among these bestial nations is found, which it seems proper to my King and Prince, as so powerful a lord, to correct and repress, and to me in his Royal name

32. Se equivoca Villagrá: Fray Agustín Rodríguez. Véase Hammond & Rey, *Oñate*, 333.

33. Se le olvidan los frailes mártires llegados mucho antes con la expedición de Coronado: Fray Juan de Padilla, Fray Luis de Escalona y Fray Juan de la Cruz. Véase Bolton, *Coronado*, 336.

10. Villagrá errs. Fray Agustín Rodríguez. See Hammond and Rey, *Oñate*, 333.

11. Villagrá forgets the martyrs resulting from the Coronado expedition: Fray Juan de Padilla, Fray Luis de Escalona, and Fray Juan de la Cruz. See Bolton, *Coronado*, 336.

se ha de hazer esta obra porque la voluntad de Dios es que
todos se salben y a todos llegue el son y efectos de su palabra
y Passión, y Dios debe ser obedecido y no los hombres,
aunque sean jueces o padres, o si tengan Reynos o Ciudades,
pues sola vn alma es más preciosa que todo el mundo ni
sus mandos, riquezas y propiedades; y sin éstas, ai otras
evidentes causas en que me fundo para este efecto, assí del
gran bien temporal, que el espiritual no tiene precio, que
estas bárbaras naciones con nuestro comercio y trato ad-
quieren y ganan en su trato pulítico y gobierno de sus
Ciudades, viviendo como gentes de razón, en pulicia y en-
tendimiento, acrecentando sus oficios y artes mecánicas y
algunos las liberales, aumentando sus Repúblicas de nuevos
ganados, crías y semillas, legumbres y bastimentos, ropas
y frutos, y ordenando discretamente el trato económico de
sus familias, casas y personas, vistiéndose los desnudos y
los ia bestidos mejorándose; y dexando otras causas, final-
mente, en ser gobernados en paz y justicia, con seguridad
en sus casas y en sus caminos, y defendidos y amparados de
sus enemigos por mano y a expensas de tan poderoso Rey,
cuia subgeción es verdadero provecho y libertad, y tener en
él proprio Padre, que a su costa y mediante sus gages y
mercedes de tan remotas tierras les embían Predicadores y
ministros, Iusticia y amparo, con instruciones, verdadera-
mente de Padre, de paz, concordia, suabidad y amor, la
qual guardaré yo a perder de vida y mando y siempre man-
daré se guarde, sopena della. Y por tanto, fundado en el
sólido fundamento sobredicho, quiero tomar la sobredicha
possesión, y assí lo haziendo en presencia del Reverendíssimo
Padre Fray Alonso Martínez de la orden del señor san Fran-
cisco, Comissario Apostólico, *cum plenitudine potestatis,* desta
jornada de la nueva México y sus Provincias, y de los Rev-
erendíssimos Padres Predicadores del santo Evangelio, sus
compañeros Fray Francisco de san Miguel, Fray Francisco
de Zamora, Fray Iuan de Rosas, Fray Alonso de Lugo, Fray
Andrés Corchado, Fray Iuan Claros y Fray Christóbal de
Salazar, y de mis amados Padres y hermanos Fray Iuan de
San Buenaventura y Fray Pedro de Vergara, frailes legos,
Religiosos, que van a esta jornada y conversion, y de mi
Maese de campo General, don Iuan de Zaldívar Oñate, y
de los oficiales mayores y de la maior parte de los Capitanes
y oficiales del campo y gente de paz y guerra dél, digo que
en voz y en nombre del Christaníssimo Rey don Felipe,
nuestro señor, vnico defensor y amparo de la santa madre
Iglesia y su verdadero hijo, y para la corona de Castilla y
Reyes que de su gloriosa estirpe Reynaren en ella, e por la
dicha e para la dicha mi gobernación, tomo y aprehendo,
vna, dos y tres vezes, vna dos y tres vezes, vna, dos y tres
vezes, y todas las que de derecho puedo e debo, la tenencia
y possesión Real y actual, cibil y criminal, en este dicho

give hand to the present act, and without them the pious
course and most Christian opinion of Baptism and salvation
of souls of as many children as among these faithless parents
at present live and are born, who to their true Father God
and chief Father neither obey or recognize, nor can, morally
speaking, recognize except through this means, as long
experience in these lands has shown, and when they can
recognize him, entering through the door of baptism, they
cannot preserve the faith nor persevere in their vocation
among a people idolatrous and unfaithful, against whose
will this work must be done because the will of God is that
all be saved and to all shall come the sound and effects of
his word and Passion, and God should be obeyed and not
men, although they be judges or parents or if they have
kingdoms or cities, for but one soul is more precious than
all the world nor its commands, riches, and properties; and
without these there are other evident causes on which I base
myself for this effect, such as the great temporal good, as
the spiritual has no price, that these barbarous nations with
our commerce and treatment may acquire and gain in their
political affairs and government of their cities, living like
reasonable folk in modesty and understanding, increasing
their professions and arts, mechanic and some the liberal,
augmenting their republics with new cattle, livestock, and
seeds, vegetables and provisions, clothing and fruits, and
ordering discreetly the economic affairs of their families,
houses, and persons, the naked being clothed and the now-
clothed bettering themselves; and leaving other causes, fi-
nally, in being governed in peace and justice, with safety
in their homes and on their highways, and defended and
sheltered from their enemies by hand and at the expense of
so powerful a king, subjection to whom is true advantage
and liberty, and to have in him an own father who at his
cost and by means of his pay and mercy to such remote
lands sends them preachers and ministers, justice and pro-
tection, with instructions truly of a father, of peace, con-
cord, suavity, and love, which I shall preserve at cost of my
life and I order and shall always order that it be kept under
pain of same. And therefore, based on the aforesaid solid
foundation, I wish to take the aforesaid possession, and
doing so, in the presence of the most reverend Father Fray
Alonso Martínez, of the Order of the lord Saint Francis, the
Commissary Apostolic, *cum plenitudine potestatis,* of this jour-
ney into New Mexico and its provinces, and of the most
reverend Fathers, preachers of the holy Evangel, his com-
panions, Fray Francisco de San Miguel, Fray Francisco de
Zamora, Fray Juan de Rosas, Fray Alonso de Lugo, Fray
Andrés Corchado, Fray Juan Claros and Fray Cristóbal de
Salazar, and of my beloved Fathers and brothers, Fray Juan
de Buenaventura and Fray Pedro de Vergara, lay friars,

Río del Norte, sin excetar cosa alguna y sin ninguna limitación, con las vegas, cañadas y sus pastos y abrevaderos. Y esta dicha possessión tomo y aprehendo en voz y en nombre de las demás Tierras, Pueblos, Ciudades, Villas, Castillos y casas fuertes y llanas que aora están fundadas en los dichos Reynos y Provincias de la nueva México y las a ellas circunvezinas y comarcanas, y adelante por tiempo se fundaren en ellos, con sus montes, Ríos y Riberas, aguas, pastos, vegas, cañadas, abrevaderos y todos sus Indios naturales que en ellas se incluieren y comprehendieren, y con la jurisdición cibil y criminal, alta y baja, horca y cuchillo, mero mixto imperio, desde la hoja del Monte hasta la piedra del Río y arenas dél y desde la piedra y arenas del Río hasta la hoja del Monte.

Y yo, el dicho Iuan Pérez de Donís, Escribano de su Magestad y Secretario susodicho, certifico y doi fee que el señor Gobernador, Capitán General y Adelantado de los dichos Reynos, en señal de verdadera y pacífica possessión, y continuando los actos della, puso y clavó con sus proprias manos en un arbol fijo que para el efecto se aderezó, la Santa Cruz de nuestro Señor Iesu Christo, y bolviéndose a ella, las rodillas en el suelo, dixo: "CRVZ Santa, que sois divina puerta del Cielo, Altar del vnico y essencial sacrificio del cuerpo y sangre del Hijo de Dios, camino de los Santos y possessión de su gloria, Abrid la puerta del Cielo a estos infieles, fundad la Iglesia y Altares en que se ofresca el cuerpo y sangre del Hijo de Dios; Abridnos camino de seguridad y paz para la conversión dellos y conversión nuestra, y dad a nuestro Rey, y a mí en su Real nombre, pacífica possessión destos Reinos y Provincias, para su Santa Gloria. Amén."

Y luego, incontinente, fixó y prendió, assimismo, con sus propias manos, en el estandarte Real, las Armas del Christianíssimo Rey don Felipe, nuestro señor, de la vna parte las Imperiales, y de la otra las Reales; y al tiempo y quando se puso e hizo lo susodicho, se tocó el clarín y disparó el arcabuzería con grandíssima demonstración de alegría, a lo que notoriamente pareció. Y su Señoría del dicho señor Gobernador, Capitán General y Adelantado, para perpetua memoria mandó que se autorice y selle, con el sello maior de su oficio, y signado y firmado de mi nombre y signo, se guarde con los papeles de la jornada y Gobernación y se saquen deste original los traslados que quisieren, assentándose en el libro de la gobernación, y lo firmó de su nombre, siendo testigos los sobredichos Reverendíssimos, Padre Comissario, Frai Alonso Martínez, Comissario Apostólico, Frai Francisco de San Miguel, Frai Francisco de Zamora, Frai Iuan de Rosas, Frai Alonso de Lugo, Frai Andrés Corchado, Frai Iuan Claros, Frai Christóbal de Salazar, Frai Iuan de San Buenaventura, Frai Pedro de Vergara y don Iuan de Zaldívar Oñate, mi Maese de campo General y los

monks, who go on this journey and conversion, and of my general Army Master, don Juan de Zaldívar Oñate, and of the chief officers and of the greater part of the Captains and officers of the camp and of the people of peace and war of it, I say that in the voice and in the name of the most Christian King Don Felipe, our lord, only defender and protector of the Holy Mother Church and its true son, and for the crown of Castile and of the kings who of his glorious stock may reign in it, and for the aforesaid my government I take and seize one, two, and three times, one, two, and three times, one, two, and three times, and all those which I can and ought, the Royal tenancy and possession, actual, civil, and criminal, at this aforesaid River of the North, without excepting anything and without any limitation, with the meadows, glens, and their pastures and watering places. And I take this aforesaid possession, and I seize upon it, in the voice and name of the other lands, towns, cities, villas, castles, and strong houses and dwellings, which are now founded in the said kingdoms and provinces of New Mexico, and those neighboring to them, and shall in future time be founded in them, with their mountains, rivers and banks, waters, pastures, meadows, glens, watering places, and all its Indian natives, who in it may be included and comprehended, and with the civil and criminal jurisdiction, high and low, gallows and knife, mere mixed power, from the leaf on the mountain to the rock in the river and sands of it, and from the rock and sands of the river to the leaf on the mountain.

And I, the said Juan Pérez de Donís, notary of his Majesty and above mentioned secretary, certify and give faith that the said Lord Governor, Captain General and Adelantado of the aforesaid kingdoms, in sign of the true and peaceful possession and continuing the acts of it, he set and nailed, with his own hands, on a fixed tree prepared for the purpose, the holy Cross of our Lord Jesus Christ, and returning to it, his knees on the ground, he said: "Holy Cross, who art the divine gate of Heaven, altar of the only and essential sacrifice of the body and blood of the Son of God, road of the saints and possession of their glory, open the gate of Heaven to these infidels, found the church and altars upon which are offered the body and blood of the Son of God, open for us a road of safety and peace for their conversion and our conversion, and give our King, and me in his Royal name, peaceful possession of these kingdoms and provinces, for His holy glory. Amen." And then, immediately, he fixed and set himself, with his own hands, the Royal standard, the Arms of the most Christian King don Felipe, our lord; on the one side the Imperial, and on the other the Royal; and at the time and when he placed it, and did the aforementioned, the trumpet sounded and the musketry fired

demás oficiales mayores, Capitanes y soldados del exército sobredichos, el dicho día de la Ascensión del Señor, treinta y vltimo de Abril deste año de mil y quinientos y noventa y ocho años.

Tomada esta possesión, otro día comenzó a marchar el campo para passar el Río del Norte en la forma que diremos.

with most great demonstration of joy, accordingly as notoriously appeared. And his Lordship, the said Governor, Captain General and Adelantado, for perpetual memory, ordained that there be authorized and sealed with the great seal of his office and signed and marked with my name and signet, be kept with his papers of the journey and government, and be taken from this original such transcripts as might be desired, setting it down in the Book of the Government; and he signed it with his name, being witnesses the above-mentioned, most revered Father Commissary Fray Alonso Martínez, the Apostolic Commissary, Fray Francisco de San Miguel, Fray Francisco de Zamora, Fray Juan de Rosas, Fray Alonso de Lugo, Fray Andrés Corchado, Fray Juan Claros, Fray Cristóbal de Salazar, Fray Juan de Buenaventura, Fray Pedro de Vergara and don Juan de Zaldívar Oñate, my Army Master general, and the other major officers, captains, and soldiers of the army aforesaid, the aforesaid day of the Ascension of the Lord, thirtieth and last of April of the year of one thousand five hundred and ninety-eight.

This possession taken, the next day the camp began to march, to pass over the River of the North, in the form we shall state.

CANTO XV

COMO SALIO EL CAMPO PARA PASSAR EL RÍO DEL
Norte y como se despachó el Capitán Aguilar a espiar la tierra,
y como estuvo para degollar por aber quebrado el orden que le
dieron, por cuya causa el Gobernador se adelantó para los
pueblos, y de las cosas que fueron sucediendo hasta que el
Gobernador quiso hazer assiento y poblar la tierra.

L A cumbre más subida y más gallarda
Que al buen soldado illustra y le lebanta

Dexo, la con que el alma se enrriqueze[1]

Es la noble nobleza de la honrra
Que por sólo valor, por excelencia,
Por prudencia, por ser y por esfuerzo
De virtud propria, vemos que se alcanza.
Y porque ay grandes honrras que deshonrran
Y vituperios ay también que honrran,
Sólo se advierte, nota y se pratica
Que aquélla que es perfecta y verdadera
Que no consiste en más que en merecerla.
Y si la grande alteza deste gusto
Faltase a los guerreros que professan
El bélico exercicio, casi apenas
Halláramos vn hombre que quisiera
Llevar alegremente los trabajos
Que el rigor de la guerra trae consigo,
Si el triunfo desta impressa no le hiziera
Ligera aquesta carga tan pesada,
Para arresgar por ella cien mil vidas
Y otras tantas con ellas si tuviera.
Y assí, llamados todos los soldados
Desta su vida, gloria lebantada,
Por sólo merecerla y alcanzarla,
Bueltos al gran trabajo, lebantaron
A todo vuestro campo y le pusieron
De essotra vanda de las aguas turbias
Que del Norte decienden, en vn puesto
Seguro y abundante, de buen pasto,
Cuia grandeza juntos la asentaron,
Desnudos y descalzos, quebrantados,
A fuerza de sudor y de los brazos,
Hechos pedazos todos, ya rendidos.
Y porque ya muy cerca de poblado
Sentía el General que el campo estaba,
Por prevenirse en todo, mandó luego

1. Con la que el alma se enriquece.

CANTO XV

How the camp went forth to pass the River of the North and
how Captain Aguilar was sent to spy out the land, and how he
was to be executed for having disobeyed the orders given him,
wherefore the Governor went ahead to the pueblos, and of the
things that happened afterward until the Governor chose to
make a dwelling place and populate the land.

T HE highest and most glorious peak
That brings to fame and raises up the good
soldier
I leave, that one with which the soul's
enriched
'Tis the noble nobleness of honor,
5   Which, through valor alone, through excellence,
Through prudence, through the effort
Of self-virtue we see to be obtained.
And as there are great honors that dishonor one
And, too, vituperations that do give honor,
10 It is but seen and noted and practiced
That that which is perfect and is true
Consists of no more than meriting it.
And if the great height of this pleasure
Should be lacking to warriors who profess
15 The warlike exercise, yet scarcely
Will we discover one man who will wish
Cheerfully to endure the woes
That the rigor of war involves
Unless the triumph of that enterprise should make
20 That load, so heavy, a light one,
To risk for it a hundred thousand lives
And other equal number had they them.
And all the soldiers being thus called
By this their life, glory most high,
25 Only to deserve and attain to it,
Turning to the great work, took up
All of your camp and set it on
This other side of the turbid waters
Which do descend from out the north, and in a place
30 Safe and abundant in good pastures,
Whose greatness they together 'stablished,
All naked and unshod, broken,
By dint of their sweat and their arms, now
Entirely tired out and exhausted.
35 And since the General did feel
The camp was now near to some peopled place,
To be forewarned in all, he then ordered

Que Pablo de Aguilar, con seys soldados
En caballos ligeros, se aprestase
Y con todo secreto y buen recato
La tierra le espiase, y que si viesse
Alguna población que luego al punto,
Qual la libiana jara que se arroja
A la subida cumbre, que en llegando
Al puesto donde el arco le permite
Luego la vemos todos que rebuelve,
Que assí luego bolviesse sin que en esto
Otra cosa ninguna dispensase.
Y para más forzarle y obligarle,
Mandole que con pena de la vida
Deste mandato expreso no excediesse.
Saliendo el Aguilar con este orden,
El campo fue marchando las riberas
Deste copado² Río caudaloso
Cuios incultos bárbaros grosseros,
En la passada edad y en la presente,
Siempre fueron de bronco entendimiento,
De simple vida, bruta, no enseñada
A cultivar la tierra ni romperla,
Y en adquirir hazienda y en guardarla
También de todo punto descuidados.
Sólo sabemos viven de la caza,
De pesca y de raízes que conozen,
Tras cuia vida todos muy contentos,
De las grandes Ciudades olvidados,
Bullicio de palacio y altas Cortes,
Passan sin más zozobra sus cuidados.³
Estos, con gusto, bien nos ayudaron
A passar por sus tierras sin rezelo,
Y estando ya, señor, para dexarlos,
Tomando otra derrota deste Río,
Llegó Aguilar y dixo aber entrado
En el primero pueblo de la tierra
Sin respecto ninguno de aquel orden
Que nuestro General mandó tuviesse.
Por cuia justa causa estuvo a pique
De⁴ darle allí garrote, sino⁵ fuera
Por la fuerza de ruegos que cargaron
Por él y por la gente que llevaba,
Excepto Iuan Piñero, porque quiso
Guardar en todo el orden que les dieron.
Y como no ay temor, si con prudencia
Prevenimos el golpe que amenaza,

That Pablo de Aguilar, with six soldiers,
On swift horses, should hasten forth
40 And with all secrecy and caution
Should spy upon the land, and should they see
Any town, then at once they should,
Like the light arrow which is sent
Into the upper air, which, arriving
45 At that point which the bow permits,
At once we all see it return,
Return thus instantly, and that in this
No other course would be granted.
And the more to enforce and oblige this
50 He ordered him that under pain of death
He should not exceed this express command.
Aguilar then departing with these orders,
The camp did march along the banks
55 Of this well-forested and rich river,
Whose unlearned, rude barbarians
In ages past, and in the present, too,
Were always of crude comprehension,
Of simple lives, brutish, untaught
To cultivate the earth or break it up,
60 And in acquiring farms and keeping them
Completely unaccustomed, too.
We know that they lived only by the chase,
By fishing and by roots they know,
In which life, all very content,
65 Unknowing of the great cities,
The noise of the palace and the high courts,
They pass over their cares without anxiety.¹
These, with good will, well aided us
To pass over their land without fearfulness,
70 And as we were, lord, on the point of leaving them,
Taking another course than the stream did,
Came Aguilar and said he had entered
Into the first town of the land
Without respect for that order
75 That our General had told him to obey,
For which just cause he was upon the point
Of having him garroted, were it not
For the mass of pleas that were made
For him and for the people that he took,
80 Except for Juan Piñero, since he tried
To keep in everything the orders they were given.
And since there is no heartfelt fear, if prudently
We do foresee the blow that threatens us,

2. Ha de entenderse que lleno de altos (copados) árboles.
3. Eco del *Beatus Ille*, tan tópico en la literature de la época.
4. A pique de = próximo a.
5. Sino = si no.

1. This is an echo of the *Beatus Ille* topos so widely used in Renaissance and post-Renaissance literature.

Que vn sossegado puerto no nos muestre,
Temiendo el General que luego alzasen
Todos los bastimentos con presteza
Los bárbaros y luego despoblasen,
Cincuenta buenos hombres, bien armados,
Con él mandó que fuessen, y dexando
Al Alférez Real por su teniente,
Llevando a nuestro Padre Comissario
Y al Padre fray Christóbal, fue marchando
Con tan ligero passo y presto curso
Que muy breve se puso por sus tierras.
Y estando a vista de los pueblos
Parece que la tierra, estremecida,
Sintiendo la gran fuerza de la Iglesia,
Sacudiendo los ídolos furiosa,
Con violencia horrible arrebatada
Y tempestad furiosa y terremoto,
Estremecida toda y alterada,
Assí, turbada fue con bravo asombro,
Cubriendo todo el cielo de entricadas[6]
Nubes tan densas, negras y espantosas
Que paboroso pasmo nos causaban
Viéndolas encender por cien mil partes
Con tremendos relámpagos y fuegos.
Y vertiendo gran lluvia, fue rompiendo,
Con truenos grimosíssimos,[7] los montes,
Los valles, cerros, riscos y collados,
Despidiendo de piedra tan gran fuerza
Que rendidos los Padres se pararon
Y al poderoso Dios, a grandes vozes,
Socorro le pidieron. Y acabada
Toda la letanía con sus preces,[8]
Sin otras oraciones que rezaron
Con suma reverencia allí contritos,
Condolido el Señor, mostró la fuerza
De aquel turbión grimoso, lebantado.
Qual poderoso mar soberbio, hinchado,
Que recogido el viento se sossiega
Y vna grande bonanza a todos muestra,
Assí dio buelta luego el alto Cielo,
Mostrándose tan claro y tan sereno
Qual suele estar el Sol quando sus rayos
Por medio de su curso nos descubre.
Con cuio noble tiempo fue llegando
El General al pueblo y luego, juntos,
Los bárbaros salieron a nosotros,

That a safe harbor does not show to us,
85   The General, fearing the barbarians
Might swiftly remove all provisions
And then all folk as well, did give order
That fifty good men, all well armed,
Should go with him; leaving behind
90   The Royal Ensign as his lieutenant.
And taking our Father Commissary
And Father Fray Cristóbal, he did march
With such a rapid pace, so swift a course,
That very soon he was within their lands.
95   And being well within sight of the towns,
It seemed the earth did tremble there,
Feeling the great force of the Church
Shaking the idols furiously,
With horrible, impetuous violence
100   And furious tempest and earthquake.
All trembling and altered,
It thus was troubled with fearsome shadow
Covering all the heaven with intricate
Clouds, and so dense, black, and fearful
105   They caused us an awesome amazement,
Seeing them burn in a hundred thousand spots
With lightnings tremendous and fires.
And, pouring down great rains, they seemed to burst
The mountains with most frightful thunderings,
110   The valleys, hills and cliffs and heights,
And hurling down such mass of rocks
That the devoted Fathers stopped
And of our powerful God, with mighty voice,
They did ask aid. And having said
115   All of the litany with all its prayers,
And other prayers which they prayed
With highest reverence, contrite, there,
The Lord, in pity, showed His power.
Of that frightful tempest that He had raised,
120   Like powerful sea, swelled up in pride,
Which, the wind going down, is calmed
And shows a great peace unto all,
So the high heavens turned about,
Showing themselves as calm and as serene
125   As the sun always is when his bright rays,
In the midst of his course, he does show us.
In which noble weather, the General
Arrived at the town and then, all together,
The barbarians came out to us

6. Entricadas = intrincadas, enredadas, confusas.
7. Grimosíssimos = grimosísimos, muy espantosos, amedrentadores.
8. Preces = ruegos, súplicas.

Y viendo al Comissario que llevaba
Arbolada vna Cruz en la derecha
Todos con gran respecto la vesaron.
Y a nuestro General obedecieron,
Alojándole dentro de su pueblo,
En cuias casas luego reparamos
En una grande suma que tenían
De soberbios demonios retratados,⁹
Feroces y terribles por extremo,
Que claro nos mostraban ser sus dioses
Porque al¹⁰ dios del agua junto al agua
Estaba bien pintado y figurado.
También al dios del monte junto al monte,
Y junto a pezes, siembras y batallas
A todos los demás que respetaban
Por dioses de las cosas que tenían.
Y tienen una cosa aquestas gentes,
Que en saliendo las mozas de donzellas
Son a todos comunes sin escusa
Con tal que se lo paguen, y sin paga
Es vna vil bageza tal delito,
Mas luego que se casan viven castas,
Contenta cada qual con su marido.
Cuia costumbre, con la grande fuerza
Que por naturaleza ya tenían,¹¹
Teniendo por certíssimo nosotros
Seguíamos tambíen aquel camino,
Iuntaron muchas mantas bien pintadas
Para alcanzar las damas Castellanas
Que mucho apetecieron y quisieron.
También notamos ser aquestas gentes
Manchadas del bestial pecado infame,
Y en esto fue tan suelta su soltura
Que sino¹² diera gritos vn muchacho
De nuestra compañía, le rindiera
Vn bárbaro de aquéllos que por fuerza
Le quiso sugetar, y sino¹³ fuera
Por la gran tierra que por medio puso,
Fuera caso impossible que quedara
Semejante delicto sin castigo.¹⁴
Con esto fuimos todos por los pueblos

130 And seeing the Commissary, who bore
A wooden cross in his right hand,
All kissed the same with great respect.
And they obeyed our General,
Lodging him within their town,
135 Within whose houses we then saw
A mighty store which they had there
Of haughty demons pictured,²
Ferocious and extremely terrible,
Which clearly showed to us they were their gods,
140 Because the god of water near the water
Was well painted and figured out.
The god of the mountains, too, near the mountains,
And next to fishes, seeds, battles,
Were all the rest that they revere
145 As gods of those things that they had.
And these folk have a certain thing,
That the maidens, when once they mature,
They are common to all without excuse,
Provided that they pay, but without pay
150 Such sin is a vile baseness,
But soon as they are married they live chaste,
Each one contented with her spouse.
Which custom, with the mighty strength
Which it already had in nature
155 Thinking most certainly that we
Should also follow that same road,
They gathered many well-painted mantles
To obtain the Castilian dames,
Whom they desired and much wished.
160 We also noted that these folk
Were stained by the infamous and bestial sin,
And in this they were so free and open,
That if a young boy from our troop
Had not yelled, he would have been overcome
165 By one of the barbarians who by force
Would take him; and had the Indian
Not quickly raced away from us
It would have been impossible
That he not suffer punishment for his sin.³
170 With this, we went through all the towns

9. Probablemente la primera descripción de las figuras llamadas kachinas. Véase Villagrá, *Historia*, edición de Junquera, 224.

10. Posible errata del original por "el," que haría mejor lectura.

11. Posible errata del original por "tenía," que daría mejor lectura: con la fuerza que semejante costumbre ya tenía en la naturaleza.

12. Sino = si no.

13. Sino = si no.

14. Sobre la tolerancia de la homosexualidad entre los antiguos Pueblos, y acerca de su poligamia, véase Villagrá, *Historia*, edición de Junquera, 229, 234.

2. Villagrá, *Historia*, Junquera edition, 224, correctly suggests that this is one of the earliest mentions of the kachinas.

3. The Curtis manuscript with which we work, found in the Coronado Room of the University of New Mexico Library, does not translate these lines. For the tolerance of homosexuality among the ancient Pueblo Indians, see Villagrá, *Historia*, Junquera edition, 229. See also p. 234 for Villagrá's reference to polygamy.

Con notable contento, aunque aguado[15]
Por no saber las lenguas destas gentes
Y darles a entender nuestros intentos.
Y por ser otro día aquella fiesta
Del gran San Iuan Baptista, luego quiso
El General que el campo se assentase
En vn gracioso pueblo despoblado
De gentes y vezinos y abundoso
De muchos bastimentos que dexaron.
Aquí, con gran recato prevenidos,
La mañana graciosa[16] celebraron
En los caballos de armas los soldados
En dos contrarios puestos divididos,
Cuias ligeras puntas[17] gobernaban,
En vna bien trabada escaramuza,
El buen Maese de campo y gran Sargento,
Las poderosas lanzas rebolviendo
Con vizarro donaire desembuelto.
Y luego que los vnos y los otros
Rompieron gruessas lanzas y probaron
Las fuerzas de sus pechos en torneos
Que con bella destreza tornearon,
Quedaron para siempre señalados
Por buenos hombres de armas y de impresas
El Maese de campo y el Sargento,
El Capitán Quesada, con Bañuelos,
El Capitán Marcelo de Espinosa,
Pedro Sánchez Monrroi y Antonio Conde,
El Alférez Romero, Alonso Sánchez,
Iuan de León, Damiero y los Robledos.
Acabadas las fiestas, luego entraron
Tres bárbaros graciosos, desembueltos,
Y estando el General con gran contento
Con todos los soldados platicando,
Assí los tres se fueron a su puesto
Y estando junto dél, algo risueño,
El vno dellos dixo en altas vozes:
"Iueves y Viernes, Sábado y Domingo."
Y qual si fuera aquella gran culebra
Que en la expulsión de los Tarquinos vieron
Ladrar dentro de Roma los Romanos,
Que atónitos quedaron del portento,[18]
Assí, desatinados nos colgamos
De la lengua de aquél, que más no quiso
Hablar otra palabra Castellana.

In notable content, though 'twas much marred
Through not knowing the language of these folk
And telling them our intentions.
And being, the following day, that feast

175   Of great Saint John the Baptist, the General
Did wish the expedition stop
In a town pleasant but abandoned
By all its folks and neighbors, but filled up
With many supplies they had left.

180   Here, taking precautions with great care,
They celebrated the fair morn,[4]
The soldiers on their war horses
Divided into two opposing groups
Whose nimble flanks were captained,

185   In a well-contested skirmish, by
The Army Master good and the Sergeant,
Whirling their powerful lances
With gay and carefree skill.
And when the others of the men

190   Had broken mighty lances and had proved
The courage of their hearts in tournament
Which they had ridden with great skill,
There did remain forever signalized
As mighty men of arms and enterprise

195   The Army Master, the Sergeant,
Captain Quesada, Bañuelos,
Captain Marcelo de Espinosa,
Pedro Sánchez Monrroi and Antonio Conde,
Ensign Romero and Alfonso Sánchez,

200   Juan de León, Damiero, the Robledos.
The celebration over, there came in
Three unafraid, pleasant barbarians,
And, the General being well content
And chatting there with all the soldiers,

205   The three went up to where he was
And, being near to him, smiling somewhat,
One of them said in a loud voice:
"Thursday, Friday, Saturday, and Sunday."
And, as it had been that great snake

210   Which, at the expulsion of the Tarquins, was
By Romans seen to bark at Rome,
So that they were at that portent amazed,[5]
So we, bewildered, hung upon
The tongue of him who would no more

215   Another word of Castilian speak.

15. Aguado = diluido, rebajado.
16. Con este adjetivo, en su acepción de "llena de gracias,"
identifica la virtud mítica de la mañana de San Juan.
17. Puntas = extremos, alas.
18. Se halla referido en Livio I.

4. Villagrá's *graciosa mañana*, referring to the morning after
Midsummer's Eve, clearly points (morning filled with grace) to the
traditional magical character of that date.
5. This is narrated in Livy, I.

Y visto el General su gran silencio,
A todos los prendió, por cuia causa
El mismo bárbaro, algo temeroso,
Dixo, "Thomás, Christóbal", señalando
Que los dos destos nombres dos jornadas
Estaban de nosotros bien cumplidas.
Y apurándole mucho conozimos
Que nunca jamás supo más palabras
Que aquestas que nos dixo Castellanas.
Con sola aquesta lumbre,[19] alegres todos,
Llevándolos con gusto y con recato,
Salió el Gobernador con toda priessa
En busca de los dos que baptizados
Por los dos Santos nombres parecían.
Y haciendo jornada en vn buen pueblo
Que Puarai[20] llamaban sus vezinos,
En él a todos bien nos recibieron
Y en unos corredores jalbegados[21]
Con vn blanco jalbegue[22] recién puesto,
Barridos y regados con limpieza,
Llevaron a los Padres, y allí juntos
Fueron muy bien servidos. Y otro dia,
Por aberse el jalbegue ya secado,
Dios, que a su santa Iglesia siempre muestra
Los Santos que por ella padecieron,
Hizo se trasluziesse la pintura.
Mudo Predicador aquí encubrieron
Con el blanco barniz porque no viessen
La fuerza del martirio que passaron
Aquellos Santos Padres Religiosos
Fray Agustín, Fray Juan y Fray Francisco,
Cuios illustres cuerpos retratados
Los bárbaros tenían tan al vivo
Que porque vuestra gente no los viese
Quisiéronlos borrar con aquel blanco,
Cuia pureza grande luego quiso
Mostrar con evidencia manifiesta
Que a puro azote, palo y piedra fueron
Los tres Santos varones consumidos.
Y como siempre prende el que assegura,[23]
Mandó el Gobernador, con gran recato,
Que allí desentendidos se mostrasen
Y que en manera alguna no pusiessen
La vista en la pintura, pues con esto,

220 The General, seeing his stubborn silence,
Had them all seized, and for this cause
The same barbarian, though somewhat afraid,
Said: "Tomás, Cristóbal," and pointed out
That they of those two names were yet two days
Of traveling from us, and long ones, too.
And, testing him sharply, we learned
That he had never known more words
Of Spanish than the ones he said to us.
225 With only that spark, we, overjoyed,
And bringing them with pleasure and with care,
The Governor in all haste set out
In search of those two who appeared
Baptized with those two holy names.
230 And making a stage in a good town
Which its neighbors do call Puarai,[6]
In it they did receive us well,
And in some whitewashed corridors,
With whitewash recently put on,
235 Well swept and watered, fully cleaned,
They put the Fathers, and together there
They were served well. And the next day,
The whitewash having now dried out,
God, who unto his holy Church doth ever show
240 The saints who for it have suffered,
Made a painting come shining through,
A mute preacher that had been covered
By the white glaze lest they might see
The martyrdom that was endured
245 By those holy, devout Fathers
Fray Augustin, Fray Juan, and Fray Francisco,
Whose famous bodies the barbarians
Had drawn so truly to the life
That, so your people might not see the same,
250 They wished to erase them with that white paint,
And His pure greatness then did wish
To show by evidence most manifest
How, strictly by the lash and club and stone,
Those three most holy men were slain.
255 Since he wins who makes others feel secure,
The Governor ordered with great care
That they should seem to be all ignorant
And that by no means should they send
A glance at the painting, since in this way,

---

19. Lumbre = indicio.
20. Acerca de Puarai, véase Bolton, *Spanish Exploration*, 146.
21. Jalbegados = blanqueados.
22. Jalbegue = arcilla blanca, cal.
23. Siempre consigue la captura el que ha hecho a la presa sentirse segura, descuidada.

6. For the early presence of Puarai in the history of the Spanish exploration of the region, see Bolton, *Spanish Exploration*, 146.

Assegurados todos,²⁴ passarían
Al pueblo de Thomás y de Christóbal.
Y assí, con el secreto que importaba,
Cuia custodia y guarda es vna cosa
Con gran razón de todos estimada,
Quando el bárbaro pueblo ya entregado
Estaba con reposo al dulze sueño,
Qual vn valiente tigre que agachado,
Con el oído atento y vista aguda,
Los gruessos pies y manos va sacando,
El poderoso lomo recogiendo
Para alentar mejor el presto salto
Sobre el ligero pardo descuidado,
Assí, quando rindieron la modorra,
Salió de aqueste pueblo recatado
Nuestro Gobernador y fue marchando
La noche toda en peso²⁵ y puso cerco
Al pueblo de los dos que se llamaban
Christobal y Thomás, en cuias casas
Aquéllos que prendimos nos pusieron.²⁶
Y luego dentro dellas se arrojaron
El provehedor Zubra²⁷ y Iuan de Olague,
El Alférez Zapata y León de Isasti,
Munuera, Iuan Medel, Alonso Nuñez
Y Pedro de Ribera, Gentilhombre
De vuestro General y de su mesa,
Francisco Vázquez y Christóbal López,
Manuel, Francisco, Vido y Montesinos,
Segundo Paladín²⁸ en bien serviros,
Que éstos dieron con ellos en la cama
Y della los sacaron y truxeron
A nuestro General, con quien hablaron
En Español y en lengua Mexicana,
Diziendo que ellos eran ya Christianos
Y que fueron de aquéllos que Castaño
Trujo de nueva España y que quisieron
Quedarse en aquel pueblo, donde estaban
A vsanza de la tierra ya casados.
Nunca jamás se halló tan gran tesoro
Ni bien tan lleno, rico y abundoso
Quanto el Gobernador sintió tenía
Con los dos baptizados que delante
Con él hablaban lengua que entendía

260 Thinking themselves safe,⁷ they'd go to
The pueblo of Tomás and Cristóbal.
Thus, with the secret which imported much,
Whose custody and keeping is a thing
By all esteemed with good reason,
265 The barbarian folk being now given up
To sweet slumber and in repose,
Like valiant tiger, crouching down
With ear attentive and keen sight,
That strikes out its deadly feet and paws,
270 Tensing its powerful muscles
To better speed its lightning spring
Upon the careless, swift leopard,
So, when deep sleep had conquered them,
There left that pueblo, cautiously,
275 Our Governor, and marched along
Throughout the entire night, laying
Siege to the pueblo⁸ of those two whose names
Were Cristóbal and Tomás, to whose homes
Those whom we captured then led us.
280 And into them there hurled themselves
The purveyor Zubía and Juan de Olague,
The Ensign Zapata and León de Isasti,
Munuera, Juan Medel, Alonso Núñez
And Pedro de Ribera, gentleman
285 Of your General and of his own table,
Francisco Vázquez and Cristóbal López,
Manuel, Francisco, Vido, Montesinos,
A second Paladin in serving you.⁹
These found their men in bed
290 And took them out and did bring them
To our General, with whom they spoke
In Spanish and in the Mexican tongue,
Saying they were now Christians
And they were of those whom Castaño
295 Brought from New Spain, and they had wished
To stay in that place, where they were,
According to the custom of the country, wed.
Never was found so great treasure,
Nor so full, rich, and abundant,
300 As the Governor knew that he had there
In those two baptized ones before him who
Spoke with him in a tongue he understood,

24. Se entiende que los indios, pensando que su ocultación había
tenido efecto.
25. En peso = enteramente.
26. Se trata del pueblo hoy llamado Santo Domingo.
27. Errata del original por Zubía.
28. Aludiendo a que el apellido, Montesinos, coincide con uno de
los paladines de la épica carolingia recordado en numerosos romances
de la época.

7. The reference is to the Indians feeling secure, not realizing that
the Spaniards had detected the paintings.
8. Today the Pueblo of Santo Domingo.
9. The analogy is to Montesinos, one of the paladins in Carolingian
literature.

Y que también sabían y alcanzaban
Aquélla que los bárbaros vsaban,
Mediante cuios medios luego pudo
Manifestar su intento y sus conceptos
Por toda aquella tierra, donde vimos
Muy buenas poblaciones assentadas
Por sus quartos[29] y plazas bien quadradas,
Sin género de calles, cuias casas
Tres, cinco, seys y siete altos suben,
Con mucho ventanaje y corredores
A la vista graciosa desde afuera,
Cuios vezinos tienen tantas hembras
Quantas les es possible que sustenten.
Son lindos labradores por extremo.
Ellos hilan y tejen y ellas guisan,
Edifican y cuidan de la casa,
Y visten de algodón vistosas mantas
De diversos colores matizados.
Son todos gente llana y apazible,
De buenos rostros, bien proporcionados,
Rebueltos,[30] prestos, sueltos[31] alentados;
No mancos, no tullidos, no contrechos,
Mas de salud entera reforzada,
De miembros muy bien hechos y trabados.
Y tienen vna cosa aquestas gentes
Digna de noble estima y excelencia,
Y es que nunca han tenido ni han vsado
Ninguna borrachera ni brebaje
Con que puedan privarse de sentido,
Argumento evidente que los tiene
La Magestad del Cielo ya dispuestos
Para el rebaño santo que, escogido,
Está para salvarse señalado.[32]
Son lindos nadadores por extremo
Los hombres y mugeres, y son dados
Al arte de pintura y noble pesca.
No tienen ley ni Rey ni conozemos
Que castiguen los vicios ni pecados.
Es toda behetría,[33] no enseñada
A professar justicia ni tenerla,
Y son supersticiosos hechizeros,
Idólatras perdidos. Inclinados

And who knew, too, and fully grasped
That tongue which the barbarians used,
305   By means of whom he then well could
Show his intentions and his thoughts
Throughout that land in which we saw
Most excellent cities set out,
Well sectioned and with squared plazas,
310   But with no sort of streets, and their houses
Rose up in stories, three, five, six, and seven,
With many windows, corridors,
Most pleasing to the sight from far,
Whose freemen had as many wives
315   As they could possibly support.
They are extremely skillful laborers.
They spin and weave, the women cook
And build and take care of the house,
And wear seemly cotton mantles
320   Of divers colors, many-hued.
They are all simple, peaceful folk,
Of good faces and all well-formed,
Restless, quick, bold, and spirited;
No cripples, no helpless, no maimed,
325   But of complete and robust health,
Of limbs right well-made and well-joined.
And these folk have a certain thing
Worthy of noble esteem and excellence
And 'tis that they have never had nor used
330   Any sort of drunkenness or of beverage
With which they might deprive themselves of sense,
Evident argument that they are kept
By Heaven's majesty and now disposed
For that holy flock of the chosen ones
335   Which is marked out for salvation.[10]
They are extremely graceful in swimming,
Both men and women, and are given
To the art of painting, noble fishing, too.
They have no law nor king, nor do we know
340   That they do punish vices or grave sins,
And every town is all untaught
In claiming justice or maintaining it,
And they are superstitious enchanters,
Damned idolaters. Much inclined

---

29. Quartos = cuartos, cada una de las partes en que se divide una extensión.

30. Rebueltos = revueltos, término que, aplicado a las caballerías, significa "dócil y presto al mando."

31. Sueltos = veloces

32. Esta sobriedad contrasta con la propensión a la bebida y borrachera con que, ya en Ercilla (*La araucana* I, 9) se identifica al indígena. Puede verse, asimismo, en *Arauco domado* II y *Argentina* XVI.

33. Behetría = estado político sin sujeción a señor.

10. This sobriety that Villagrá stresses contrasts with the drinking propensity of the Indians described, for example, in *La araucana* I, 9; *Arauco domado* II; and *Argentina* XVI.

A cultivar la tierra y a labrarla,
Cogen frisol,³⁴ maíz y calabaza,
Melón y endrina³⁵ rica de Castilla,
Y vbas en cantidad por los desiertos.
Y después que con ellos nos tratamos
Cogen el rubio trigo y hortaliza,
Como es lechuga, col, haba, garbanzo,
Cominos, zanaorias, nabos, ajos,
Zebolla, cardo, rábano y pepino.
Tienen graciosa cría de gallinas
De la tierra³⁶ y Castilla en abundancia,
Sin el carnero, baca y el cabrito.
Tienen caudales Ríos, abundosos,
De gran suma de pezes regalados,
Como es bagre, mojarra y armadillo,³⁷
Corbina, camarrón, róbalo, aguja,

Tortuga, anguila, truchas y sardinas,
Sin otra buena suma que notamos,
En tanta cantidad que a sólo anzuelo
Vn solo Castellano en un solo día
A venido con seys y más arrobas
De pezes regalados. Y no cuento
Otras cosas grandiosas que la tierra
Produze, abraza y tiene de nobleza,
Con cuias buenas partes muy gustosos
Hizimos el assiento que tenemos
Según que en otro canto lo veremos.

345 To cultivate the earth and work the same,
They harvest beans, corn, and squashes,
Melons and rich sloes of Castile,
And grapes in quantity through the desert.
And after we have dealt with them
350 They harvest the red wheat and garden stuff,
Such as lettuce and cabbage, beans and peas,
Cumins, carrots, turnips, garlic,
Onions, artichokes, radish, cucumbers.
They have pleasing herds of turkeys
355 In abundance, and fowl of Castile, too,
Beside sheep and cattle and goats.
They have full-flowing rivers, full
Of a great store of dainty fish,
Delicious, such as the mojarre and armadillo,¹¹
360 The conger eel, the prawn, the haddock and the
    needlefish,
The turtle, eel, trout, and pilchard,
Beside a good sum more that we noted,
In such a quantity that, just by hook alone,
A single Spaniard in a single day
365 Has come with six and more quarters
Of gratifying fish. Nor do I tell
Of other splendid things which that country
Produces, does contain and has, and noble ones.
Right pleased with good things in it
370 We made the dwelling place we have,
As in another canto we shall see.

34. Frisol = frijol, judia.
35. Endrina = ciruela.
36. Gallinas de la tierra = pavos, guajalotes.
37. No hemos hallado pez que se conozca con este nombre de "armadillo," que es mamífero americano no acuático.

11. Curtis omits the *bagre* and Villagrá appears to list the armadillo among the fish.

CANTO DIEZ Y SEYS

COMO HIZO ASSIENTO EL GOBERNADOR CON
TODO el Campo en vn pueblo de Bárbaros a quien pusieron por
nombre San Iuan de Caballeros y del buen hospedaje de los
Indios, y motín de los soldados, y fuga que hizieron quatro
dellos, y castigo que en los dos se hizo, saliendo el autor hasta
tierra de paz tras dellos, y de la primera Yglesia que se hizo.

NO tiene el mundo gusto tan gustoso
Que compararse pueda al que recibe
La gente de una flota contrastada
Quando, de bravos vientos combatida,
Seguro y dulze puerto va tomando
En sossegado albergue conozido.
No de otra suerte todo vuestro campo,
Al cabo de fortunas y sucessos,
Tiempo y desventuras tan pesadas,
Alegre y con gran gusto fue arribando
Hazia vn gracioso pueblo bien trazado
A quien san Iuan por nombre le pusieron,
Y de los Caballeros, por memoria
De aquéllos que primero lebantaron
Por estas nuevas tierras y Regiones
El sangriento estandarte donde Christo,
Por la salud de todos, fue arbolado.
Aquí, los Indios muy gustosos
Con nosotros sus casas dividieron.
Y luego que alojados y de assiento,
Haziendo vezindad, nos assentamos,
Estando el General comiendo vn día,
Lebantaron los bárbaros vn llanto
Tan alto y espantoso que pensamos
Aber llegado el vltimo remate
De la tremenda cuenta y postrer punto
Del fin vniversal de todo el mundo.
Por cuia causa todos alterados,
Confussos, preguntamos a las lenguas[1]
La causa de aquel llanto y nos dixeron
Que lloraba la gente por el agua,
Que mucho tiempo ya passado abía
O[2] las nubes jamás abían regado
La tierra, que de seca por mil partes
Estaba tan hendida y tan sedienta
Que no le era possible que criase
Ninguna de las siembras que tuviesse.

---

1. Lenguas = intérpretes.
2. Villagrá, con licencia poética, parece utilizar el "o" adverbial por
"en que" en vez de "en donde."

CANTO XVI

How the Governor made a dwelling place in a town of
barbarians to which was given the name of San Juan de los
Caballeros, and of the good hospitality of the Indians, and the
mutiny of the soldiers, and the flight of four of them, and the
punishment made upon two of them, the author going to the
land of peace in search of them, and of the first church that
was built.

THE world has no such pleasing joy
As may compare to that received
By the folk of a battered fleet
When, beaten by uproarious winds,
It takes a safe and pleasant port
In peaceful and well-known shelter.
Not otherwise all this your camp
At the end of adventures and events
And times of sorrow, misadventures, too,
10 Happy and in great pleasure did arrive
At a fine pueblo, well laid out,
To which they gave the title of San Juan
And "de los caballeros" to recall
The ones who first did elevate
15 In these new lands and regions
The bloody standard on which Christ
For general salvation was raised up.
Here all the Indians with pleasure
Did share their houses with our folk.
20 And when, all lodged and settled down,
We were endeavoring to be good neighbors,
The General being at his meal one day,
The barbarians set up a wail
So loud and fearful that we thought
25 The last moment had now arrived
To the tremendous judgment, final point
of universal end for all the world.
Wherefore, all being much perturbed,
Confused, we asked the translators
30 The cause of that wailing, and they replied
That 'twas for water all the people wept,
For much time now had passed away
In which the clouds had never watered
The earth, which, in a thousand places dry,
35 Was so cracked and so burnt with thirst
That 'twas impossible to raise
As much as one of the crops they had sown.

Por cuia causa luego el Comissario
Y el Padre Fray Christóbal, confiados
En aquel sumo bien por quien vivimos,
Mandaron que en voz alta les dixessen
Que no llorasen más ni se cansasen
Porque ellos rogarían a su Padre
Que estaba hallá en el Cielo se doliesse
De toda aquella tierra, y que esperaban
Que, aunque inobedientes hijos eran,
Que a todos muchas aguas les daría
Y que éstas que vendrían de manera
Que todos los sembrados se cogiessen.
Y assí como los niños tiernos callan
Quando ciertos los hazen de las cosas
Porque se afligen, lloran y fatigan,
Assí, callados todos, sossegaron
Esperando les diessen cierta el agua
Por quien lloraban tanto y se afligían.
Y apenas otro día fue llegando
La hora deste llanto quando el Cielo,
Cubriéndose de nubes, fue vertiendo
Por toda aquella tierra tantas aguas
Que espantados los bárbaros quedaron
De la merced que allí el Señor nos hizo.
Tras deste buen sucesso luego vino
Vn Indio bautizado que Iusepe[3]
Dixo que se llamaba y que venía
Huiendo de la gente que abía entrado,
Contra vando y sin orden, con Bonilla.
Y dio por nuevas que vn soldado, Vmaña,
Le dexaba ya muerto a puñaladas
Por vandos y passiones que tuvieron,
Y que éste por Gobernador quedaba,
También por General, de aquella gente,
Que Riberas de vn Río le dexaba
Tan ancho y caudaloso que tenía
Vna cumplida legua, y que distaba
De nuestro nuevo assiento y estalaje
Seyscientas largas millas bien tendidas.
Y díxonos, con esto, que, cebado[4]
De la noticia grande que tenía
De muchas poblaciones abundosas
De gran suma de oro, se yba entrando
La tierra más adentro y que pensaba
Passar con ciertas balsas aquel Río

For this reason the Commissary, then,
And Father Fray Cristóbal, trusting in
40 The highest Good through which we live,
Did order that it should be cried aloud
That they should weep no more nor be downcast,
Because they would ask their Father,
Who there in Heaven was, to have pity
45 On all that land, and that they hoped,
Though these were disobedient children,
He yet would give much water to them all
And they would come in such good time
That all the planting might be saved.
50 And just as tender babes are quieted
When once assured of the things
For which they weep and grieve and tire themselves,
So they, all silent, were at peace,
Hoping that surely water would be given
55 For which they wept and grieved so much.
Now hardly another day gone by
To the hour of that weeping when the heavens,
Being covered o'er with clouds, poured down
So much water on all that land
60 That the barbarians were amazed
At the mercy the Lord had shown us there.
After that good event there shortly came
A baptized Indian who told us
That he was called Jusepe[1] and had come
65 In flight from those folk entering
Against orders, without permit, with Bonilla,
And gave us news that a soldier, one Umaña,
Had left him dead from a knife thrust
Caused by factions and passions that they had,
70 And that they had this man for Governor
And also for the General of those folk,
Whom he had left on the banks of a stream
So wide and full that it measured
A complete league, and that it was distant
75 From our abiding place and halt
Six hundred long and weary miles.
And with this, he told us that, hungering
From the great news that they had heard
Of many and wealthy peoples
80 With mighty sums of gold, they did keep on
Further into the land, and that he thought
To pass that river upon certain rafts,

---

3. Este indio mexicano, acompañante de Bonilla y Humaña, se
entrevistó con Oñate despúes de la expedición que hizo Vicente
Zaldívar a los llanos de las vacas de Cíbola. Véase Hammond & Rey,
Oñate, 417.

4. Cebado = prendado.

1. This Mexican Indian, who had accompanied Bonilla's illegal
expedition to New Mexico, was found and interviewed later, after
Vicente de Zaldívar's exploration of the buffalo plains. See Hammond
and Rey, *Oñate*, 417.

Por entender que estaba bien poblado
Respecto de los humos que, visibles
De aquesta vanda, todos descubrían.
También nos dio noticia abían passado
Por vn pueblo tan grande que estuvieron
Vn día y medio en sólo atravesarle,
Y que de miedo que de Vmaña tuvo,
Respecto de los muchos que ahorcaba,
Quiso con presta fuga allí dexarlos.
En este medio tiempo, vnos soldados,
Amotinando el campo, fueron presos,
Y entre ellos Aguilar, por cuia causa,
Queriendo el General hazer castigo,
Fueron tantos aquéllos que cargaron
Con lágrimas, lamentos y con ruegos,
Que general perdón allí alcanzaron.
Por cuia causa, todos consolados,
Por sólo aqueste hecho se ordenaron
Vnas solemnes fiestas que turaron
Vna semana entera, donde vbo
Iuego de cañas, toros y sortija⁵
Y vna alegre comedia bien compuesta,
Regozijos de moros y Christianos,⁶
Con mucha artillería, cuio estruendo
Causó notable espanto y maravilla
A muchos bravos bárbaros que abían
Venido por espías a espiarnos.
Y a ver las fuerzas y armas que alcanzaban
Allí los Españoles, cuio brío
De ninguna nación fue más notado,
Como después veremos adelante,
Que de la fuerza de Acoma, que tuvo
Entre nosotros vna grande espía
Que muy larga razón llevó de todo.
Pues luego que estas fiestas se acabaron,
Como el perdón a vezes es gran parte
Para que nuevas culpas se cometan,
Parece que vnos pobres, olvidados
De la infamia y bageza que emprendían
En bolver las espaldas a la Iglesia,
A vuestro General y al estandarte
Y a sus hermanos, deudos y parientes,
Hurtando vna gran parte de caballos,
Hizieron fuga, siendo los primeros
Que a tal infamia abrieron el camino.
Mas Dios nos libre quando quiebra y rompe

Believing the land was peopled right well
Because of the smoke which, quite visible,
85 All had discovered from the bank.
He also told us they had passed
Through a town so great that they were
A full day and a half only in crossing it,
And that, because of fear that he had for Umaña
90 Due to many he had hanged,
He'd wished, by swift flight, to desert them there.
In the meantime some of the soldiery,
Mutinying within our camp, were seized,
Among them Aguilar, and for this cause
95 The General wishing to give punishment,
There were so many who did beg
With tears, lamentings, and with prayers
That they received a general pardon.
All being for this reason consoled,
100 For no more than this fact there was set
A solemn feast that did endure
For a whole week, in which there were
Tilts with cane spears, bullfights, tilts at the ring,
A jolly drama, well-composed,
105 Playing at Moors and Christians,²
With much artillery, whose roar
Did cause notable fear and marveling
To many bold barbarians who had
Come there as spies to spy on us,
110 To see the strength and arms possessed
By the Spaniards, whose manliness
Was by no nation noted more,
As we shall see here further on,
Than by the folk of Acoma, who had
115 There in our midst a mighty spy
Who took a long report of all he saw.
Well, when these feasts were completed,
As pardon is at times a potent cause
For new crimes to be committed,
120 It seems that some poor wretches, forgetful
Of the baseness and infamy they did
In turning their backs on the Church,
Your General, and the standard,
And on their brothers, kin, and relatives,
125 Stealing a great part of the horses there,
Took flight, being the first that opened that road.
Now God help us when there does burst and break
The sacred anchor of obedience

---

5. Sortija = competición hípica que consistía en enganchar un anillo con la lanza.

6. Para el sobrevivir de la fiesta de moros y cristianos en Nuevo México, véase Villagrá, *Historia,* edición de Junquera, 58.

2. For the survival in New Mexico of the Moors and Christians's reenactment, obviously a festival emanating from Spain's long reconquest, see Villagrá, *Historia,* Junquera edition, 58.

El háncora sagrada de obediencia
La nave y con fortuna se abalanza
Por lebantados riscos y assí, suelta,
Perdido ya el gobierno y arrastrando
Los poderosos cables donde assida
Estuvo y sin zozobra de anegarse,
Que quando assí perdida vemos pierde
El miedo a todo trance.[7] Dios nos libre
Que a tanta desventura nadie llegue.
Abiendo, pues, perdido la vergüenza
Y hecho fuga aquestos desdichados,
Mandó el Gobernador que luego al punto
Tras dellos yo saliesse y me aprestase,
Y porque aquesta causa bien se hiziesse,
Mandó que Iuan Medel, Ribera y Márquez,
Como leales siempre en bien serviros,
A castigar tan gran delicto infame
Saliessen assimismo y ayudesen,
Y que doquiera que el alcance fuesse
Que allí luego las vidas les quitase.
Con cuio mandamiento luego fuimos
Catorze días siempre por la posta,[8]
Gran suma de trabajos padeziendo,
Y dándoles alcance, qual Torquato,
Que al muy querido hijo mandó luego,
Por transgressor del vando quebrantado,
Que la cabeza de los tristes hombros
Allí le destroncasen[9] y quitasen,[10]
Assí a los dos mandamos degollasen
Y libres otros dos se libertaron[11]
Dexándonos allí la caballada.
Y como todo aquesto sucediesse
Cerca de Santa Bárbara, salimos,[12]
Forzados de gran hambre, a socorrernos,
Desde cuios assientos escrebimos
A vuestro Vissorrey lo que pasaba,
Assí en esta causa como en todas
Las que en tan largo tiempo nos passaron.
Y como el Real Alférez Peñalosa
Llegó con todo el campo sin disgusto
Al pueblo de san Iuan,[13] los Religiosos

The ship, swaying in the tempest
130 Amid high cliffs, and so loosed,
All control lost and dragging at
The powerful cables where it was
Made fast and without fear of being sunk,
Which, thus being lost, we see it lose
135 All fear for all perils. So may God free
Us and all men from such a pass.
Those miserable men thus having lost
All shame and taken them to flight,
The Governor ordered that at once
140 I go after them and make haste,
And so that thing should be done well
He ordered Juan Medel, Ribera, and Márquez,
As always loyal in well serving you,
To punish so great, infamous, a crime
145 Should also go as help for me,
And that wherever we should capture them
We should in that place take their lives.
With which command we then went on
For fourteen days, always posthaste,
150 Suffering many trials, too,
And, taking them, like Torquatus,
Who ordered that his own beloved son
As a transgressor of the broken law
Have his head from his sad shoulders
155 Detached and stricken off at once,[3]
So we ordered those two beheaded there,
And two more freely escaped us,
Leaving the horse herd to us there.
And as all this had taken place
160 Near Santa Bárbara, we went,
Forced by great hunger, to seek aid,
From which location we did write
Unto your Viceroy what had passed,
As well in this thing as in all
165 That had in so long time occurred to us.
And as the Royal Ensign, Peñalosa,
Arrived with all the camp without mishap
At the town of San Juan,[4] the holy men
Then made a church,[5] and it was blessed

---

7. A todo trance = resueltamente.
8. Por la posta = corriendo.
9. Destroncasen = cortasen.
10. Manlio Imperioso Torcuato, tribuno militar romano, hizo ajusticiar a su hijo por desobedecer sus órdenes.
11. Se libertaron = se escaparon.
12. Se entiende que con destino a la población señalada.
13. Peñalosa, se recordará, había quedado mandando el grueso del campo mientras que Oñate salió a los pueblos.

3. Manlius Imperiosus Torquatus, Roman general, had his son executed for disobeying orders.
4. Ensign Peñalosa, it should be remembered, had remained in charge of the main body of the expedition when Oñate went out into the pueblos.
5. This was the first church built in New Mexico, dedicated on the 8 September 1599.

Hizieron luego Iglesia¹⁴ y la bendijo
El Padre Comissario y baptizaron
Mucha suma de niños con gran fiesta.
En esto, el General mandó saliesse
El Sargento mayor y que arrancase
Cincuenta buenos hombres y que fuesse
A descubrir la fuerza de ganados
Que los llanos de Zíbola criaban.
Pues como aquesto luego se hiziesse,
Salió marchando y en vn fresco Río,
De ziruelas cubierto y de pescado,
Alegres descansaron, y se fueron
Por otros muchos Ríos abundosos
De muchas aguas, pezes y arboledas,
Donde con sólo anzuelo sucedía
Sacar quarenta arrobas de pescado
En menos de tres horas los soldados.
Pues yendo assí marchando, acaso vn día
Abiendo hecho alto por las faldas
De vna pequeña loma junto a vn Río,
Por vn repecho vieron que assomaba
Vna figura humana con orejas
De casi media vara y vn hozico
Horrible por extremo y vna cola
Que casi por el suelo le arrastraba,
Bestido con vn justo¹⁵ muy manchado,
De roja sangre todo bien teñido,
Con vn arco y carcax, amenazando
A toda vuestra gente con meneos,
Saltos y con amagos nunca vistos.¹⁶
Y mandando el Sargento que estuviessen
Apercebidos¹⁷ todos y aguardasen
A ver en qué paraba tal ensayo,
Notaron que era vn Indio que venía
A no más que espantarlos por que tuvo
Por cosa cierta que los Españoles
Dexaran el bagaje y se acogieran,
Y que él fuera señor de todo aquello
Que allí llevaban todos, descuidados
De la bárbara burla de aquel bruto.

170 By the Father Commissary, and they did baptize
Much sum of children with great holiday.
The General then ordered that
The Sergeant Major should set out, and take
Fifty good men, and he should go
175 To discover the herds of horned beasts
That the plains of Cibola held.
Now, as that should be done at once,
He marched away and at a fresh river,
Lined with plum trees and full of fish,
180 They rested pleasantly, and then went on
By many other rivers, abundant
With many waters, fish, and woods,
Where with but hooks alone the soldiers
Drew out forty quarters of fish
185 In less than three hours of fishing.
Now, marching thus, by chance one day,
A halt being made upon the skirts
Of a small upland hard by the river,
Upon a slope they saw there did appear
190 A human figure having ears
Almost half a yard long and with a snout
Extremely horrible, and with a tail
That almost dragged upon the ground,⁶
Dressed in a tight garment, much stained,
195 And all well-stained with red blood,
With bow and quiver, threatening
All of your folk with gestures,
With leaps and such capers as ne'er were seen.
And, the Sergeant ordering that they all
200 Should be prepared and wait to see
Where such performance might well stop,
They saw it was an Indian who came
For no more than to scare them, for he thought
It certain that the Spaniards
205 Would leave the baggage and take flight,
And that he would be lord of everything
All of them there had, undisturbed
By the barbarian humor of that brute.
Wherefore, huddled together, they did act

---

14. Esta primera iglesia contruida en Nuevo México fue consagrada el 8 de septiembre de 1599.

15. Justo = jubón, prenda que cubre hasta la cintura.

16. Parece que Villagrá, hombre instruido, se burla un tanto de los seres monstruosos que formaron parte de la leyenda de los nuevos pueblos hallados en el Nuevo Mundo. Para un ejemplo de semejantes leyendas (de hombres monipodos o de orejas como aquí describe el poeta) en la propia expedición de Oñate, véase la *Relación* de Escobar, C. Colahan y A. Rodriguez, *Missionalia Hispánica* 46 (1986): 388–90. Para una probable primera descripción del payaso sagrado de los Pueblos, véase Villagra, *Historia,* edición de Junquera, 51.

17. Apercebidos = apercibidos, preparados, avisados.

6. This humorous description of the exaggerated body parts of the approaching Indian suggests that Villagrá may have intended to satirize the many reports of outlandishly monstrous peoples then circulating. For an example of such legends, and their transmission, taking place in the very same Oñate expedition, see the *Relación* of Father Escobar, C. Colahan and A. Rodríguez, *Missionalia Hispánica* 46 (1986): 388–90. It should be noted that this description might well be the first recording by a European of the sacred clown figure of Pueblo religious dances (see Villagrá *Historia,* Junquera edition, 51).

Por cuia causa juntos se mostraron
Alebrestados,[18] tímidos, cobardes,
Fingiendo se escondían temerosos
Entre la misma ropa que llevaban.
Y assí, notando el Indio que temían,
Entre ellos se metió haciendo cocos,
Al cabo de los quales le cogieron
Y la máscara luego le quitaron.
Y assí, corrido, triste, avergonzado,
Llorando les pidió que le bolviessen
Aquel rebozo, el qual, con grande risa,
Chacota y passatiempo le bolvieron.
Y no quiso el Sargento que se fuesse
Hasta que, muy risueño, alegre y ledo,
Con todos se mostrase; y esto hecho,
El bárbaro se fue por su camino
No menos disgustoso que contento.
Tras desto luego fueron a otro Río
Donde vieron a vn bárbaro gallardo,
Mucho más blanco y zarco[19] que un flamenco,
Con vna buena esquadra de flecheros
Que con pausado espacio[20] se venía
Hazia los Españoles. Y en llegando,
Con grande gravedad y gran mesura
A todos los miró muy sossegado,
Y viendo allí el Sargento su descuido,
Su pausa y su silencio y poco caso
Que de todos hazía, y que apenas
Quiso alzar los ojos para nadie,
Mandó que se llegasen y a la oreja
Vn buen mosquete allí le disparasen
Con fin de que temiesse y se assombrase.
Pues haziéndose assí, qual sino[21] fuera
La fuerza del mosquete disparado,
Alzó la blanca mano y con el dedo
Escarbando el oydo con espacio
Al punto le quitó y quedó tan sesgo[22]
Como si de vn fino mármol fuera.
Viendo, pues, el Sargento tal prodigio,
Mandó que con respecto le tratasen
Y assiéndole del brazo cortesmente
Vn gran cuchillo quiso presentarle.
Y tomándole el bárbaro, mirole
Y bolviendo la mano poca cosa

210 Extremely fearful, all timid, cowardly,
Pretending they hid themselves in fear
Among the very clothing that they wore.
The Indian, seeing that they were thus afraid,
Did come among them, grimacing,
215 And, at the end of this, they seized him
And then they took his mask away
So that, downcast, sad, and ashamed,
Weeping, he begged them to return
That muffler, which, with great laughter,
220 With noisy mirth and joking, they gave back.
And the Sergeant wished not that he should go
Until he showed himself to all
As very happy, smiling, and cheerful. This done,
The barbarian went off upon his way
225 No less unhappy than content.
After this they soon reached another stream
Where they did see a gallant barbarian,
Much whiter and more blue-eyed than a Fleming
With a good squadron of archers,
230 Who with a slow and measured pace came on
Toward the Spaniards, and, arriving,
With a great gravity and serious countenance
He looked at all of them most peaceably.
The Sergeant, seeing there his carefreeness,
235 His repose, his silence, the little heed
He paid to all, and that he hardly wished
To raise his eyes to look at anyone,
Did order one to approach and by his ear
Discharge a musket-shot of a sudden,
240 That he might fear and be astonished.
Well, doing this, as though the force
Of the musket had never been discharged,
He raised his white hand and, with a finger
Scratching his ear deliberately,
245 He shortly drew it back and was as calm
As if he were of fine marble.
The Sergeant then, seeing such prodigy,
Ordered they treat him with respect
And taking him courteously by the arm
250 He wished to give him a large knife.
And, taking it, the barbarian did look at it
And, turning his hand a little bit,
He gave it to his men, upon which they

18. Alebrestados = acobardados.
19. Zarco = de ojos azules. Probable descripción de un albino.
20. Pausado espacio = despacio.
21. Sino = si no.
22. Sesgo = quieto.

A los suyos le dio y luego ellos
De su misma pretina²³ le colgaron.
Con esto, le pidieron que vna guía
Fuesse servido darles y que fuesse
Tal que a todos juntos los llevase
A los llanos que todos pretendían.
Apenas lo dixeron quando luego
Mandó que cierto bárbaro saliesse
De aquéllos que con él abían venido
Y que qual buen piloto los llevase
Hasta los mismos llanos que dezían.
Iamás se vio sentencia rigurosa
Ni pérdida de vida más temida
Que el bárbaro temió tan gran mandato,
Y qual si yunque fuera, no le vieron,
Aunque muy demudado y alterado,
Estremecido todo y sin aliento,
Que réplica tuviesse ni hablase.
Con esto, los dexó y qual se vino,
Con reposados passos, fue bolviendo.
Y luego con la guía fue marchando
El Sargento mayor, y siempre quiso
Que postas a la guía se pusiessen
Porque fuga no hiziesse y los dexase.
Pues velando Cortés²⁴ el triste quarto²⁵
Que dizen de modorra, fue rompiendo
La fuerza de prisión el Indio cauto
Y assí, como cometa que ligero
Traspone su carrera, assí traspuso
Y el Español tras dél, y con presteza
El curso apresuraron de manera
Que corrieron dos leguas bien tiradas,
Al cabo de las quales, ya rendido,
El Cortés se quedó desatinado,
Lleno de corrimiento y de vergüenza.
Pues como no supiesse ni entendiesse
El Sargento Mayor ni otro alguno
El camino y derrota que llevaban,
El vno tras del otro, disgustosos,
Esperando estuvieron hasta el alba.
Y estando con grandíssima tristeza,
Porque era medio día ya passado,
A cosa de las tres llegó sudando
Con doze bravos bárbaros dispuestos,
Y con gentil donaire y desenfado

Did hang it at his own girdle.
255 At this, they asked him if he would
Be pleased to furnish them a guide who would
Be such as could conduct them all
To those plains which they all were searching for.
Hardly had they said it when he at once
260 Ordered a certain barbarian to stand forth
From those who had come there with him
And that he should, as a good pilot, take
Them to the very plains they said.
Never was there a sentence harsh
265 Or loss of life more evidently feared
Than that barbarian feared such great command,
And, as he had an anvil been, we saw,
Although mute and changed in his countenance,
All trembling and panting hard,
270 That he had no reply, nor spoke.
With this he left them, and, as he had come,
With peaceful gait, he did return.
And then the Sergeant Major, with the guide,
Went marching and always wished
275 That guards be set over the guide
That he might not take flight and leave them there.
Well, Cortés⁷ watching in that sad quarter
They call the sleepy one,⁸ the clever Indian
Did break from us and his imprisonment,
280 And like a comet, which most rapidly
Moves on its course, so he did move,
The Spaniard after him, and right swiftly
They sped along their course, in such a way
That they ran two good leagues,
285 At end of which, now overcome,
Cortés had lost his bearings,
Full of discouragement and shame.
Well, since the Sergeant Major nor no other man
Did know or comprehend the route
290 And road that they had followed,
One after the other, in great disgust
They were waiting until dawn.
And being in most great sadness,
Because midday had now passed by,
295 About three he arrived, sweating,
With twelve brave barbarians well disposed,
And with great wit and ease of port
He said to all those hardy men:

23. Pretina = correa.
24. Para datos biográficos de Marco Cortés, véase Villagrá, *Historia*, edición de Junquera, 246.
25. Quarto = división del día, el de "modorra," tratándose de "velas," se puede suponer el de la alta noche.

7. For a biographical background of Marco Cortés see Villagrá, *Historia*, Junquera edition, 246.
8. The sleepy watch, probably that at midnight.

A todos denodado²⁶ fue diziendo:
"Si como fueran doze fueran ciento,   300
A todos los truxera y fuera paga
Conforme al Evangelio sacrosanto.²⁷
El vno se me fue y aquestos traigo,
Y no viniera acá sino supiera
Que bien puede suplir por vno solo   305
Qualquiera de los doze que aquí vienen."
Con esto, alegres todos y contentos,
Arrancaron de allí, cuia memoria
Será bien que se cante en nueva historia.

26. La reproducción mexicana trae "denodados."
27. Se refiere a que Dios, según el Evangelio, dara ciento por uno.

"If a hundred 'stead of twelve they'd been,
He would have brought them, and 'twas pay
According to the most holy Gospel.⁹
One got away from me and I bring these,
Nor would I have come here had I not known
That I could well furnish for that one man
Any of the twelve that you see here."
All happy and content, with this
They went from there, the memory of which
'Twere well should be sung in new episode.

9. The reference is to the biblical indication that God will pay a hundred to one.

*COMO SALIO EL SARGENTO CON LAS NUEVAS
GUIAS que trujo Marcos Cortés y como llegó a los llanos
de Zíbola, y de las muchas vacas que vio en ellos, y de la
obediencia que dieron los Indios al Gobernador, y salida que
hizo para los pueblos, en cuya vista[1] determinó que en llegando
el Sargento mayor al Real quedase gobernando y que el Maese
de campo saliesse para yr con él al Mar del Sur, para lo qual
despachó mensagero proprio para que saliesse tras dél con treynta
hombres.*

*How the Sergeant left with the new guides that Marcos Cortés
brought and how he came to the plains of Zíbola, and of the
many cows he saw in them, and of the obedience the Indians
rendered to the Governor, and the trip that he made to the
pueblos, for which he determined that, on the arrival of the
Sergeant Major at the capital, he should remain as Governor
and that the Army Master should go to the South Sea, for
which he sent a special messenger for him to come after him with
thirty men.*

¿VE quiebra puede ser en sí tan grande

   Que fácil no se enmiende y ponga en
      punto
   Si es hombre de valor y de vergüenza
   Aquél por quien sucede vn caso triste?
Abiendo, pues, el buen Cortés perdido
El bárbaro en la vela y en la fuga,
Ocupado de empacho y de vergüenza,
Se fue por vna senda muy hollada
De gente natural de aquella tierra,
y, acaso, derrotados[2] del camino
Vio sólos doze bárbaros desnudos
Con ímpetu furioso venir ciegos
Tras de vn valiente cierbo que venía,
También de temor ciego, por el puesto
Por donde cuidadoso yba marchando.
Y luego que le vido, desembuelto,
Dio buelta al arcabuz y alargó en trecho,[3]
Cogiéndole en el aire lebantado
Con la fuerza del salto poderoso,
Dio con él muerto en tierra. Y con el humo
De la encendida llave descubierto,
Los bárbaros le vieron y quedaron

No menos muertos que el que en tierra estaba,
Pensando que era Dios, pues con vn rayo
De sus valientes manos despedido
El animal ligero que seguían
Ynopinadamente fue privado
De la vida y aliento que llevaba.
Viéndolos, pues, suspensos y parados,
Atónitos del caso nunca visto,

HAT accident can be within itself so
    great
   As not to be easily fixed and set to rights

   If he by whom the accident occurs
   But be a man of courage, self-respect?
5   The good Cortés, then, having lost
The barbarian in watch and flight,
All overcome with shame, embarrassment,
Went on a path well trodden by
The people native to that land,
10 And, luckily, out of the road
He saw twelve naked barbarians alone
Coming blindly in furious charge
After a valiant deer that came,
Blind, too, with fear, straight toward the place
15 Where he was going carefully.
And when he saw it, aiming carefully,
He fired his harquebus and, at that range,
Hitting him, flying through the air
With the force of his powerful leap,
20 He struck him dead upon the ground.
And being discovered in the smoke
Of his fired musket, the barbarians saw him, and they
    were
No less dead than the beast there on the ground
Thinking he was God, since with the lightning
25 Sent from his valiant hand
The swift beast they were following
Was unexpectedly deprived
Of the life and breath that it had.
Seeing them, then, halted and in suspense,
30 Astonished by a thing ne'er seen before,

---

1. Vista = intento o propósito.
2. Derrotados = fuera.
3. Salvo errata del original, hemos optado por la lectura que da a
"alargó" el valor de efectuar el disparo, "en trecho" viniendo a señalar
que a una buena distancia.

A todos los llamó que se llegasen,
Y ellos, bien temerosos y encogidos,
Arrastrando los arcos por el suelo,
Mudos, suspensos, tristes, cabizbajos,
Por no ser sin pensar allí abrasados,
Pasmados y temblando, se acercaron
Al puesto y estalaje donde estaba
El valiente Español con bravo imperio.
En esto, quatro bárbaras vinieron
Por este mismo puesto atravesando
Con vna buena requa, bien cargada,
De perros, que en aquestas partes vsan
Traerlos a la carga y trabajarlos
Como si fueran mulas de requaje,
Y aunque pequeños, llevan tres arrobas
Y quatro y andan todos lastimados,
Qual suelen nuestras bestias, con la carga
Que se les va assentando con descuido.
A éstas dio Cortés el gran cierbo,
Y después que a los bárbaros hablaron,
Todas de miedo y de temor cubiertas,
Allí le lebantaron, encogidas,
Y ellos con gran respecto se vinieron
Con el fuerte extremeño que les dixo
Que con él se viniessen. Y assí, juntos,
A todos los llevaron a los llanos,
Donde vieron vn toro desmandado,
Con cuia vista luego los caballos,
Bufando y resurtiendo por mil partes,
A fuerza de la espuela y duro freno
Hizieron los ginetes se llegasen.
Y allí todos en cosso⁴ le truxeron
Con grande regocijo y con espanto
De la bárbara gente que notaba
Aquel imperio y magestad tan grande
Con que los Españoles apremiaban
El ímpetu y fiereza de animales
Tan fuertes y animosos como aquéllos
Que cada qual regía y gobernaba.
Y por sólo causarles mayor grima,
Mandó el Sargento todos sossegasen
Y, poniéndose enfrente desta bestia,
Vn ligero valazo, con el fuego
Del arcabuz ligero, fue impeliendo
Por medio de los sesos, que tenía,⁵
Con tan viva presteza que en vn punto,
Los quatro pies abiertos, puso en tierra

He ordered all to come to him,
And they, right fearful and awed,
Dragging their bows upon the ground,
Mute, in suspense and sad, with lowered heads,
35 Not to be there burned on the spot,
In terror and with trembling they approached
Toward the place and station where there stood
The valiant Spaniard in imperious pose.
Just then came four barbarian women,
40 Traveling on this selfsame trail
With a large and well-loaded drove
Of dogs, for in these parts they use
To employ them for burdens and work them
As though they were packmules,
45 And, although small, they carry three-quarters
Or four and they are all pack-galled,
As our beasts are with loads
That are put carelessly on them.
To these Cortés did give the goodly deer
50 And, after speaking with the barbarians,
All smitten with alarm and terrified,
They took it up in great amaze.
The men with great respect did then follow
The strong Extremaduran,¹ who told them
55 That they should come with him. So, together,
They took them all unto the plains
Where they saw an unruly bull,
At sight of which the horses then,
Snorting and bucking to and fro,
60 By use of spur or hard-held rein
Were made by the men to approach.
And there all charged and taunted it
With great rejoicing, though frightening
The barbarians who there witnessed
65 That power and majesty so great
By which the Spaniards controlled
The charge and wildness of animals
So strong and fiery as these
That each of them so did rule and govern.
70 And, simply to amaze them more,
The Sergeant Major ordered all to stand
And, taking post opposite to this huge beast,
He fired from his light harquebus
A swift ball with its fire
75 In the middle of the creature's brain,
With such swiftness that instantly
It spread its four feet, on the ground

4. En cosso = en coso, acosado, lidiado.
5. Se refiere al arcabuz y no a los sesos de la bestia.

1. Cortés, born in Extremadura, the area of Spain bordering on Portugal, renowned in the New World because the greatest conquerors, Cortez and Pizarro, came from that region.

El vientre, rebolcando y dando vuelta,
Quedó sin vida, hierto, estremecido,
Sobre el tendido lomo sustentado.[6]
Con esto, todos juntos se metieron
Los llanos más adentro y encontraron
Tanta suma y grandeza de ganados
Que fue cosa espantosa imaginarlos.
Son del cuerpo que toros Castellanos,
Lanudos por extremo, corcobados,
De regalada carne y negros cuernos,
Lindíssima manteca y rico cebo,
Y como los chibatos, tienen barbas,
Y son a vna mano[7] tan ligeros
Que corren mucho más que los venados,
Y andan en atajos[8] tanta suma
Que veynte y treynta mil cabezas juntas
Se hallan ordinarias muchas vezes.
Y gozan de vnos llanos tan tendidos
Que por seyscientas y ochocientas leguas
Vn sossegado mar parece todo,
Sin género de cerro ni vallado
Donde en manera alguna pueda el hombre
Topar la vista acaso o detenerla
En tanto quanto ocupa vna naranja,[9]
Si assí puede dezirse tal excesso.
Y es aquesto, señor, en tanto extremo
Que si por triste suerte se perdiesse
Alguno en estos llanos, no sería
Más que si se perdiesse y se hallase
Enmedio de la mar sin esperanza
De verse jamás libre de aquel trago.[10]
Queriendo, pues, en estos grandes llanos
El Sargento mayor coger algunas
De aquestas vacas sueltas y traerlas
Al pueblo de san Iuan porque las viessen,
Mandó que vna manga[11] se hiziesse
De fuerte palizada prolongada,
La qual hizieron luego con presteza
El Capitán Ruyz y Iuan de Salas,
Iuan López, Andrés Pérez y Iuan Griego,
Tras destos Pedro Sánchez Damiero,
Iuan Guerra, Simón Pérez y Escalante,
Alonso Sánchez Boca Negra y Reyes
Y Iorge de la Vega y Iuan de Olague
Y el buen Christóbal López, Mallea.

80

85

90

95

100

105

110

115

120

Set its belly, and, rolling over,
Remained dead, stiff and quivering,
Lying outstretched upon its back.
After this all did travel on
Further into the plains and found
Such sum and mighty herds of beasts
That 'twas a frightful thing to imagine them.
In size they are like Spanish bulls,
Wooly in the extreme and all humpbacked,
Of plenteous flesh and of black horns,
Most splendid lard and rich in fat,
And, like to he-goats, they have beards,
And they are so swift turning
That they do run much more than deer,
And so many do go in bands
That twenty, thirty thousand head at once
Are often and commonly found.
And they enjoy such widespread plains
That for six and eight hundred leagues
All seems to be a peaceful sea
With no sort of valley or hill
Where a man can in any way
Limit his vision or rest it
Upon as much height as an orange occupies,
If such excess may so be said.
And it is true, lord, to such an extent
That if by evil chance a man were lost
Upon these plains 'twould be the same
As though he were lost and did find himself
In the midst of the sea, beyond all hope
Of ever seeing himself freed from the strait.
The Sergeant Major then, wishing
On those great plains to capture some
Of those wild cows and to bring them
To the town of San Juan that others might see them,
Ordered a trap to be made there
Of strong palisades, spreading far,
Which straightway was constructed by the men:
Captain Ruiz and Juan de Salas,
Juan López, Andrés Pérez and Juan Griego,
With them Pedro Sánchez Damiero,
Juan Guerra, Simón Pérez, Escalante,
Alonso Sánchez Boca Negra and Reyes,
And Jorge de la Vega, Juan de Olague,
And the good Cristóbal López, Mallea.

6. La reproducción mexicana trae "sustentando."
7. A vna mano = con movimiento circular.
8. Atajos = grupos de ganado.
9. Que ni el bulto de una naranja impide el horizonte.
10. Trago = dificultad o peligro.
11. Manga = estrecho entre palos que conducen a un corral.

Y Luego que la manga se compuso
Salieron para dar el aventada¹²
Todos los sobredichos y con ellos
El provehedor y aquellos Capitanes
Aguilar y Marcelo de Espinosa,
Domingo de Lizama con Ayarde,
Christóbal Sánchez y Francisco Sánchez,
Iuan de León, Zapata y Cabanillas,
Pedro Sánchez Monrroi y Villabiciosa
Y Francisco de Olague y los Robledos,
Iuan de Pedraza con Manuel Francisco,
Carabajal, Carrera y los Hinojos,
Iuan de Vitoria, Ortiz y los Varelas,
Francisco Sánchez, el Caudillo, y Sosa.
Todos en buenas yeguas voladoras
Aventando salieron el ganado,
Y assí como la manga descubrieron,
Qual poderoso viento arrebatado
Que remata en vn grande remolino,
Assí fue reparando¹³ y rebolviendo,
La fuerza del ganado lebantando
Vn terremoto espeso, tan cerrado
Que si junto a vnas peñas no se halla
La soldadesca toda guarecida
No quedara ninguno que hecho piezas
Entre sus mismos pies no se quedara.
Por cuia causa luego dieron orden
Que el ganado en paradas¹⁴ se matase,
Y todo assí dispuesto, hizieron carne
Para bolverse luego, y despidieron
Con notables carizias a los doze
Que el buen Marcos Cortés abía traído,
Dándoles muchas cuentas y abalorios,
Con que todos se fueron espantados
De ver la fuerza y armas de Españoles.
Los quales vieron siempre en estos llanos
Gran suma de vaqueros¹⁵ que apie matan
Aquestas mismas vacas que dezimos
Y dellas se sustentan y mantienen,
Toda gente robusta y de trabajo,
Desenfadada, suelta y alentada,
Y tienen lindas tiendas por extremo
Y lindos y luzidos pabellones
Del cuero de las vacas, cuio adobo
Es tan tratable y dozil que mojado
Aqueste mismo cuero que dezimos

And when they had set up the trap
They then went out to make the drive,
125 All the above and with them, too,
The purveyor and those captains,
Aguilar and Marcelo de Espinosa,
Domingo de Lizama with Ayarde,
Cristóbal Sánchez and Francisco Sánchez,
130 Juan de León, Zapata and Cabanillas,
Pedro Sánchez Monrroi, Villabiciosa,
Francisco de Olague and the Robledos,
Juan de Pedraza with Manuel Francisco,
Carabajal, Carrera, the Hinojos,
135 Juan de Vitoria, Ortiz, the Varelas,
Francisco Sánchez, el Caudillo² and Sosa.
All mounted on swift and good mares,
They sailed forth to drive the herds
And, as soon as these saw the trap,
140 Precipitate as a powerful wind
Which ends up in a great whirlwind,
They did stop and whirled to the rear,
The force of the beasts, raising up
An earthquake so heavy and so blinding
145 That, had the soldiers not found themselves
Protected by some nearby rocks,
There would not have been one of them
Not cut to pieces neath their hoofs.
Wherefore an order then was given
150 That these cattle should be killed as they stood,
And, all being thus arranged, they made meat
For their return and said farewell
With great affection to the twelve
Whom the good Marcos Cortés had brought them,
155 Giving them many trinkets and beads,
And they were all greatly amazed
To see the strength and arms of the Spaniards.
We always saw upon these plains
Great sums of cowboys,³ who did kill, on foot,
160 Those same cows we have spoken of,
And from them maintained and sustained themselves,
All robust folk and hard workers,
Unembarrassed and free and spirited,
And they have tents, extremely gay,
165 And gay and splendid pavilions
Made of the hides of cows, which are treated
To such a smooth and soft consistency that, wet,
That very leather we are speaking of,

12. Aventada = ahuyentada del ganado.
13. Reparando = parando.
14. Paradas = donde los ganados se paran.
15. Se refiere a apaches, que eran los cazadores de bisontes.

2. Curtis doesn't translate the epithet here, which means "leader."
3. The reference is to buffalo hunting Apache.

Buelve después de seco más suabe
Que si fuera de lienzo o fina olanda.[16]
En este medio tiempo y coiuntura,
Estando hallá en san Iuan que no dormían,
Iuntos el General y el Comissario,
De parte de la Iglesia sacrosanta
Y de vuestra grandeza generosa,
Vnánimes los dos, determinaron
Que allí los Capitanes principales
De todas las Provincias se juntasen,
Por cuia causa luego despacharon
El libro de memoria,[17] que era el sello
Con que era el General obedezido
De toda aquella tierra, porque en viendo
Los bárbaros el libro se rendían
A todo lo que aquél que le llevaba
De parte el General les proponía.
Pues como sin tardanza obedeciessen,
Sin exceder en cosa de aquel tiempo
Que a todos les fue puesto y señalado,
Iuntos en vna plaza les propuso
El noble General con buena gracia,
Presente el Secretario y todo el campo
Y el Padre Comissario y Religiosos,
Que la causa de aberlos él llamado
Era sólo el amor que les tenía
Y que éste le oprimía y le forzaba
A que les enseñase vna gran cosa
Que mucho le pesaba que tan ciegos
En ella tantos tiempos estuviessen,
Pues sin que la supiessen y alcanzasen
No era possible que ninguno dellos
Después que muerto fuesse que dexase
De arder para siempre en los infiernos.
Y que para librarlos deste fuego
Y que gozasen de vn descanso alegre
Era fuerza supiessen y alcanzasen
Que estaba vn gran señor allá en el Cielo
De tan grande poder y tanto imperio
Que con sólo querer aquello hazía,
Queriendo que se hiziesse y que se obrase,
Y que con este mismo señorío
Deshazía y quitaba todo aquello
Que tenía ya hecho y lebantado.
Cuia verdad muy claro les mostraba

170

175

180

185

190

195

200

205

210

Becomes, when dry, even more soft
Than if it were of linen or fine Holland cloth.
In the meantime and conjuncture,
There being those there in San Juan who did not sleep,
The General and the Commissary, together,
Upon the part of the most holy Church
And of your generous greatness,
Unanimous the two, did determine
That there the principal Captains
Of all the provinces should come,
Wherefore they then did send about
The Book of Memory,[4] which was the seal
By which the General was obeyed
In all that land, for, on seeing
The Book, the barbarians obeyed
All that the one who carried it
Proposed to them on the General's part.
Now, as they did obey without delay,
Without in any way missing the time
That was to all given and pointed out,
The noble General, with goodly grace,
The Secretary present there, with all the camp,
The Father Commissary and the monks,
Together in one place, announced to them
That the cause of their being called
Was but the love which he had for them,
And that this weighed on him and forced him there
That he should teach them a great thing
Which grieved him much to think that they
Should have been blind to for so long a time,
Since unless they knew this, and grasped it, too,
It was not possible that one of them
After he should have died, could 'scape
Burning forever there in hell.
And that to free them from this fire
So that they might enjoy a happy rest
'Twas necessary that they know and learn
There was a great Lord there in Heaven,
Of such great power and such empire
That only wishing a thing done 'twas done
Because He wished it done and made,
And that with this same power of His
He unmade and destroyed all those things
That now were made and erected.
The truth of this He showed to them clearly,

16. Olanda = holanda, lienzo muy fino.

17. Libro de memoria = diario, crónica. Siendo la escritura y el libro elementos tan exóticos entre los indios, no es de extrañar que, como afirma Villagrá, pasara a ser símbolo para aquéllos de la autoridad de Oñate.

4. This *libro de memoria* was the diary or chronicle of the expedition. Its coming to symbolize the authority of the governor must be understood in terms of the impact that writing and books must have had upon the native population.

Aqueste gran señor, que les dezía
A ellos mismos, si notar quisiessen,
Pues sin obra de manos vían todos
Crecer las miesses, árboles y plantas,
Marchitarse después y deshazerse,
Llover y granizar el alto Cielo
Y mostrarse después claro y sereno,
Venir el Sol y luego las Estrellas,
Tener salud el hombre y en vn punto
Perderla sin que manos le tocasen.
Cuias obras grandiosas y admirables
Era razón supiessen y entendiessden
Eran hechas y obradas todas ellas
Con sóla voluntad y no otra cosa,
Y que de aquesta suerte, traza y modo
Este mismo señor, sin más ayuda,
Abía hecho el Cielo, Sol y Luna,
Estrellas y los campos y las aguas,
Los pezes y las aves y los montes
Y vna gran suma de Angeles que estaban
Sirviéndole en el Cielo, y a los hombres
Que abitaban en la tierra, y que importaba
Saber que en todas partes assistía
Aqueste gran señor y se mostraba
Más dentro de las cosas que criaba
Que ellas estaban dentro de sí mismas,
Sabiendo y penetrando el pensamiento
Y voluntad que cada qual tenía
En obrar bien o mal y qué camino
Era aquél que llevaba y qúe cuenta
Hazía de la ley que no podía
Negar[18] que la ignoraba y no supiesse,
Pues todos dicernían y sabían
Quál era malo o bueno, cuias obras,
En bien o mal, ninguno se escusaba
De dar estrecha cuenta en la otra vida.
Porque aunque libres Dios a todos hizo
Para escoger aquello que quisiessen,
A todos les forzó a que alcanzasen,
Y juntamente claro conociessen,
Ser llegado a razón[19] seguir lo bueno
Y culpa y ceguedad seguir lo malo.
Y por si en la elección destas dos cosas
Alguno discrepase, les hazía
Ciertos de gloria y pena, según fuesse,
Malo o bueno, el camino que llevasen,
Y que por sólo aquesto acá en la tierra

This great Lord, who spoke there to them,
If they themselves would but note it,
For, without work of hands, they all did see
The grain and trees and plants did grow
And afterward did wither and decay,
The high heaven did rain and hail
And, afterward, clear and serene,
The sun did show himself and then the stars,
Man have his health and, all at once,
To lose it without hands having touched him.
These mighty works, admirable,
It was but right that they should know and understand
Were, all of them, performed and done
Through will alone and by no other thing,
And that in this way, shape and means
This selfsame Lord, without more aid,
Had made the Heavens, sun and moon,
The stars, the fields, and the waters,
The fish, the birds, and the mountains,
And a great sum of angels who were
Serving Him there in Heaven, also men
Who dwell on earth, and there was need
To know that that great Lord
Was present everywhere and showed Himself
More in the things that He had made
Than these had being of their own,
Knowing and penetrating to the thought
And will that each one had
In doing well or ill, and on what road
It was he went and what account
He took of that law he could not
Deny that he knew of and did not know,
For all discern and knew right well
What things were good or bad, whose works,
For good or evil, were excused to none
From giving strict account in the next life.
For though God had made all men free
To choose whatever they might wish,
He had forced all to grasp the fact,
And all to clearly recognize,
That it was right to follow good
And sin and blindness to do ill.
And if in choice of these two things
They should disagree in some things,
Certain of glory or of pain, as it might be,
Evil or good, the road they followed,
For this thing only on the earth

18. Negar = decir negando.
19. Llegado a razón = conforme a la razón.

Tenía este señor grandes ministros
Para que castigasen y premiasen
A todos los que mal o bien hiziessen.
Y que pues ellos eran libertados
Y no estaban sugetos a ninguno
Que justicia ni ley les enseñase,
Que si en estas dos cosas pretendían
Ser todos industriados y enseñados
Que era fuerza que todos libremente
Diessen la libertad y la obediencia
A vuestra Real corona y que entendiesen
Que a los que bien viviessen les daría,
En vuestro nombre, premios muy honrrosos
Y que estarían siempre defendidos
Y de sus enemigos amparados,
Y assimismo también aprovechados
En muchas cosas de importancia grande
Para el cuerpo y el alma que tenían.
Y que assimismo que era bien supiessen
Que a los que hiziessen mal que sin escusa
Abían de ser todos castigados
Según que los delictos cometiessen,²⁰
Y que los que vna vez se sugetasen
Y diessen la obediencia a vuestras leyes
Que en ninguna manera no podían,
Con pena de la vida, hacerse afuera.
Todas aquestas cosas les propuso
Allí el Gobernador, bien declaradas,
Y a todas ellas luego respondieron
Los bárbaros a vna que gustaban
De dar la libertad y sugetarse
A vuestra Real persona, y que querrían
Dar luego la obediencia de buen grado
Porque a todos muy bien les parecía
Lo que el Gobernador les proponía.
Y luego se hizieron y escribieron
Públicos instrumentos y escrituras
A cerca desta causa ya tratada.
Con esto, alegre, el noble Comissario
Allí también a todos les propuso
Que dexasen su vil idolatría
Y adorasen a Christo, Dios y hombre,
Cruzificado, muerto y sepultado
Por la salud de todo el vniverso.
A lo qual juntos todos replicaron
Que quisiessen primero doctrinarlos
En aquello que assí les proponían
De aquel hombre mortal, passible²¹ y muerto;

This Lord had mighty ministers,
That they might punish or reward
The ones who had done good or ill.
And since they were completely free
And were not subject unto anyone   265
That might teach them either justice or law,
That if they tried in these two things
To be industrious and learn
That it was necessary that all should freely
Resign their liberty and obedience   270
Unto your Royal Crown, and understand
That to those who lived well he would offer,
In your name, most honorable rewards
And that they would always be defended
And sheltered from their enemies   275
And also given great advantages
In many things of high importance
For the bodies and souls they had.
And it was also well they know
That those who should do ill, without excuse   280
Should all be punished according to
What crime they might commit,
And that the ones who once had submitted
And given obedience to your laws
Could never in any manner   285
Release themselves upon the pain of death.
All these things, then, were put to them
There by the Governor, well declared,
And to them all they then did make reply
Those barbarians, as one, that they were pleased   290
To give their liberty and be subject
Unto your Royal person, and they wished
To give obedience with good pleasure
Because it had seemed very good to all
That which the Governor set forth to them.   295
And then were made and written down
Public documents and writings
Concerning the case just dealt with.
Happy at this, the noble Commissary
There also did propose to all   300
That they should leave their vile idolatry
And adore Christ, the God and man,
Crucified, dead, buried,
For the salvation of all the universe.
To which they, all together, did reply   305
That they wished first that he would instruct them
In that which he thus had set forth to them
About this mortal man, suffering and dead,

20. Según los delitos que cometiesen.
21. Passible = pasible, capaz de padecer.

Y que si bien a todos estuviesse	And that if it were well for all
Dexar su ley por recebir aquélla	To leave their law to receive this
Que allí les enseñaban y mostraban,	That he did teach and show them there,
Que todos con gran gusto lo harían,	That they would so do with much pleasure,
Y que si viessen no les combenía,	And that should they see it was not fitting,
Que no mandasen que ellos recibiessen	To order not they should receive
Cosa que no entendiessen y alcanzasen.	A thing they did not understand and grasp.
Con cuia puerta²² luego el Comissario	Through this open door the Commissary
Sembró sus Religiosos, como Christo	Did sow his monks the same as Christ
Sembró el Apostolado, por Provincias,	Once sowed the Apostles, in provinces,
Y assí a san Miguel luego le dieron	And so to San Miguel was given
La Provincia de Pecos y a Zamora	The province of Pecos and to Zamora
La Provincia de Queres y al gran Lugo	The province of Queres, to great Lugo
La Provincia de Emes y a Corchado	The province of Emés, and to Corchado
La Provincia de Zía y al buen Claros	The province of Zía, to good Claros
La Provincia de Tiguas, y con esto	The province of Tiguas, and with this
Dieron a Fray Christóbal la Provincia	They gave to Fray Cristóbal the province
De aquellos nobles Teguas donde el campo	Of those noble Teguas with whom the camp
Quiso hazer assiento. Y allí, juntos,	Chose to make halt. And there, together,
Los soldados a vna hizieron fiestas	The soldiers, as one man, made holiday
Por bien tan inefable y tan grandioso,	For such ineffable and mighty good.
Con cuio buen principio, sin tardanza,	With this good beginning, delaying not,
Salió el Gobernador por las Provincias	The Governor left for the provinces
Que estaban lejos y apartadas destas.	That were far off and separate from
Que assí, señor, os dieron la obediencia,	Those who had rendered you, O lord, obedience.
Y viendo quan bien todos se rendían	And seeing how well all did give themselves
A vuestra Real justicia y leyes della,	To your Royal justice and to your laws,
Al Maese de campo escibió luego	He then did write to the Army Master
Que, no bien el Sargento se apease	That as soon as the Sergeant should appear,
De buelta de las vacas, le dixese	Returning from the cows, should tell him
Que en su lugar quedare gobernando	That he should stay and govern in his place,
Y que él, sin detenerse, le siguiesse	And he, without delay, should follow him
Con treinta buenos hombres bien armados,	With thirty good men, all well armed,
Porque determinaba yrse²³ breve	As he had determined to go shortly
A ver el mar del Sur, y que entretanto	To see the Ocean of the South, and that, until
Que los dos se juntasen que él quería	The two should join, he had a wish
Hazer visita entera de los pueblos	To make complete inspection of the towns
Que por amigos todos se mostraban.	That had all showed themselves friendly.
Y como es cosa cierta que entre buenos	And as it is a certain thing that 'mid the good
No faltan siempre malos que deshazen	There never lack some bad ones to destroy
Aquello que los buenos apetecen,	Whatever the good men desire,
Salió el Gobernador para la fuerza²⁴	The Governor then came unto the stronghold
De Acoma famosa, cuia gente,²⁵	Of famous Acoma,⁵ whose folk,
Alborotada toda, van tomando	All agitated, were running to arms

The line numbers in the right column are: 310, 315, 320, 325, 330, 335, 340, 345, 350.

22. Puerta = oportunidad.
23. Posible errata del original omitiendo "en" que haría mejor lectura y medida del verso.
24. Fuerza = fuerte.
25. Para un resumen etnológico del pueblo Querés, y de sus anteriores contactos con los españoles, véase Villagrá, *Historia,* edición de Junquera, 19–20.

5. For an ethnological summary of the Queresan people of Acoma, and of earlier contacts with Spanish explorers, see Villagrá, *Historia,* Junquera edition, 19–20.

Las poderosas armas, incitados
Del bárbaro más bajo que tenía
Aquesta brava fuerza, cuio encanto
Será bien que se cante en nuevo canto.

And had been powerfully stirred up
By the most base barbarian there was
355 In that brave fortress, whose fascination
'Twere well were sung in new canto.

Canto Diez y Ocho

COMO FVE EL GOVERNADOR PARA LA FUERZA DE
Acoma y alboroto que causó Zutacapán, y traición que tuvo
fabricada.

libre libertad, como te ofendes

Si duro iugo viene amenazando,
Con qué solicitud la altiva frente
Y cerviz brava vemos que sacudes

Al punto que le sientes y conozes!
No sube en Tibar[1] ni en Arabia tanto
El oro sus quilates lebantados,
Quanto los tuyos vemos que lebantas,
Y no es mucho, pues toda su grandeza
No es valor suficiente ni bastante
Que pueda emparejar al alto precio
De lo mucho que vales y te estimas.
Apenas se movió y salió marchando
Para el Peñol[2] soberbio todo el campo,
Quando Zutacapán salió de passo,[3]
Y digo assí, señor, 'salió de passo',
Por no aber sido bárbaro de cuenta,
Mas antes comunmente reputado,
El y todos sus deudos y passados,
Por gente más vil, baja y más grossera
Que toda essotra chuzma conozida.
Y assí, en las juntas graves que tuvieron,
Por ser todos humildes y encogidos,
Iamás ninguno dellos fue llamado.
Pues siendo aquéste de ambición cautivo,
Invidioso, soberbio y aleboso,
Amigo de mandar y ser tenido,[4]
Pareciole ser ya llegada la hora
De que libertad fuesse medianera
Para poder subirse y lebantarse.
Y para dar principio a su flaqueza
Determinó de hablar a todo el pueblo,
Y subiéndose a lo alto de vna casa
En altas vozes empezó a dezirles:
"Escuchadme varones y mugeres,
Vezinos desta fuerza desdichada,

---

1. El oro de Tibar, como el de Arabia, se consideraba especialmente fino y valioso.
2. Peñol = peñón.
3. Salió de passo = actuó impertinentemente.
4. tenido = considerado, respetado.

Canto XVIII

How the Governor went to the fortress of Acoma and the tumult
that Zutacapán caused, and the treason that he had prepared.

thou, free liberty, how thou dost take offense

If a hard yoke approaches threatening,
With what solicitude do we see thee
Shaking thy haughty front and stubborn neck

5   As soon as you do feel and know the same!
Nor in Tivar nor in Arabia[1] does the gold
Raise up so high its pristine quality
As we do see you raise up yours,
And 'tis not much, for all its mightiness
10 Is not enough, sufficient of value,
That it may equal the high price
Of all that thou art worth and esteemed at.
Hardly had all the camp moved off
And started for the haughty rock
15 When Zutacapán did quickly spring forth,
And I say thus, lord, "did quickly spring forth,"
As he had not been of aught account,
But rather commonly looked on,
He and all his family and ancestors,
20 As folk more base, low and more gross
Than all the other rabble that was known.
And in the grave councils that had been held,
All being humble and timid,
Not one of them had ever been called on.
25 But this man, being captive of his ambition,
Envious, proud, and treacherous,
Eager for power and to be considered great,
It seemed to him that now the hour had come
To be able to mount and raise himself.
30 And, to give a beginning to his frailty,
He determined to speak to all the town,
And going up to the top of a house,
He there began to speak aloud to them:
"Listen to me, ye men and ye women,
35 Dwellers in this unhappy place
That to a miserable harsh slavery

---

1. The gold of Arabia and of Tibar was, since antiquity, considered especially fine.

Que a dura servidumbre miserable
Hos siento ya sugetos y abatidos,
¿Por quál razón abéys assí querido
Dormir a sueño suelto sin cuidado?
¿Será bien que perdamos todos juntos
La dulze libertad que nos dexaron
Nuestros difuntos padres ya passados?
¿No sentís los clarines y las cajas
De la soberbia gente Castellana
Que a toda priessa viene ya marchando?
¿Quál es aquél que piensa de vosotros
Quedar con libertad si aquéstos llegan,
Estando como estamos descuidados?
Tomad, tomad, las armas y esperemos
La intención, mala o buena, con que vienen,
Que en nuestra mano está después dejarlas
Si conviene, assí, que las dexemos."
Apenas lo vbo dicho quando luego
Furiosos todos fueron embistiendo,
Los vnos con gran priessa descolgando
Del alto techo la fornida maza,[5]
Otros el gruesso leño bien labrado,
Qual la rodela y hasta, bien tostada,[6]
El arco y el carcax de agudas puntas,
Con otras muchas armas que a su modo
Han conserbado siempre y han guardado,
Y con ellas salieron a la plaza
Turbados de alboroto y de rebuelta.
Y el bárbaro, qual vn astuto lobo,
Por la nariz y boca resollando,
Latiendo los hijares con braveza,
Vn ñudoso bastón en la derecha,
Rebentando por[7] verse ya rebuelto
En cosas de ambición y de gobierno,
De lo alto de la casa donde estaba
Al bárbaro esquadrón bajó diziendo
Con grandes alaridos: "¡Guerra, guerra,
A sangre, fuego y arma, sin remedio
Ni dilación alguna se lebante
Contra estos alebosos que pretenden
Pisar los bravos términos vedados
No sólo a todo el mundo y su grandeza,
Mas a los mismos dioses prohibidos;
Que muerte y vida traigo aquí rendidas
Al valor deste brazo poderoso,
Para que por mi sólo gusto vivan
O mueran, tristemente miserables,

I feel you are now doomed and subjected,
Wherefore is it you thus have wished
To sleep a deep slumber, without a care?
40 Will it be well we all, together, lose
The sweet freedom that was left us
By our dead fathers, now gone on?
Do you not hear the trumpets and the drums
Of those haughty Castilian folk
45 Who now come marching in all haste?
What one of you is there who thinks
To keep his liberty if they arrive,
Being, as we are, all unprepared?
Take, take your arms and let us wait
50 The intention, good or bad, with which they come,
For it is in our hands to lay them down
If it shall seem best that we lay them down."
Hardly had he said this when, instantly,
All, furious, did rush away,
55 Some, in great haste, then taking down
From neath the roof the stout war club,
Others the mighty beam, well-worked,
Some the shield and even, well-charred,[2]
The bow, the quiver with its whetted points,
60 With many other arms that, in their way,
They have always preserved and have kept well,
And with them they came to the public square
Disturbed with uproar and revolt.
And the barbarian, like a clever wolf,
65 Snorting aloud through nose and mouth,
Beating his flanks in his ferocity,
A knotted stick in his right hand,
Bursting to see his fortunes now reversed
In things of ambition and government,
70 From the top of the house where he did stand
He came down to the barbarous troop, saying,
With mighty screeching: "War, war, war,
By blood, fire, and arms, without recourse
Nor with any delay, be raised
75 Against those traitors who intend
To tread rudely the goal that is forbid
Not only to the world and its greatness
But to the very gods themselves forbid!
But I bring here both life and death, subdued
80 Unto the valor of this powerful arm,
Wherefore by my sole will shall live
Or die sadly and miserably
Those daring ones who now direct

---

5. Maza = arma de palo con cabo grueso.
6. Las flechas se quemaban para endurecer y afilarlas.
7. Rebentando por = deseoso de.

2. This probably refers to the fact that the arrows were charred to harden them.

Aquestos atrebidos que enderezan
Sus mal seguros passos a nosotros!"
Muchos dellos allí se le arrimaron,
Que aquesto tiene el mundo, que no faltan
Amigos de renzillas y alborotos
Y quien atize, sople y cresca el fuego.
Y porque también todo lo digamos,
Entre los malos muchas vezes vemos
Algunos que de suyo son muy buenos.
Tuvo Zutacapán vn noble hijo,
El primero que en todo su linaje
Mostró tener valor y buen concierto,
Llamado Zutancalpo, mozo afable
Que veinte años cumplidos no tenía,
Gracioso, gentilhombre y bien hablado,
Amigo de su Patria y muy compuesto
Y en cosas de importancia reportado.
Aquéste fue el primero que se opuso
A resistir al Padre en sus intentos,
Hablando desta suerte a todo el pueblo:
"Nobleza de Acomeses valerosos,
Aunque es verdad, y todos conozemos,
Que la fortuna siempre faborece
A los que son ossados y atrevidos,
Con esto,[8] también todos alcanzamos
Que no es cosa segura ni discreta
Ser, sin maduro acuerdo, el hombre ossado,
Porque donde el peligro no se teme
Allí muestra su fuerza mayor golpe,
Y éste es tanto más grave y más pesado
Quanto con más confianza fue emprendido.
Bien os consta que entraron los Castillas,
Según grandes guerreros, en la tierra
Bien prevenidos todos, con cuidado,
La noche toda en peso, con sus velas,
Sabemos duermen juntos bien armados,
Y en pueblos que han entrado conozemos
Que en paz gustosa a todos los dexaron.
Pues si ellos alcanzasen que nosotros
Las sossegadas armas lebantamos,
Viniendo como vienen prevenidos,
Quién duda ser la guerra cierta en casa,
Y si aquésta no bien nos sucediesse
Y éstos son, como dicen, inmortales,
¿Quál disculpa será la que disculpe
El ser todos nosotros los primeros
En encender la tierra que de suio
Esta toda gustosa y sossegada?
Tened las armas, no queráis con ellas

Their insecure feet unto us."
85 Many of them there joined with him,
Since the world is so built there never lack
Friends of ill-feeling and uproar,
Someone to poke, blow, and increase the fire.
And also, that we may tell all,
90 We often see among the evil men
Some who are good by their nature.
Zutacapán did have a noble son,
The first in all his lineage
To show that he had valor and good sense,
95 Called Zutancalpo, an agreeable lad,
Who yet was in his twentieth year,
Gracious, a gentleman and well-spoken,
A friend of his country and right thoughtful
And, in things of importance, forbearing.
100 He was the first one who opposed himself
To resist his father in his intent,
Speaking to all the people in this wise:
"Ye noble, valorous men of Acoma,
Although 'tis true, and we all know it is,
105 That fortune always favors those
Who are daring and truly bold,
With this we also know it to be true
That it is not a safe nor a discreet thing
For men to dare without mature judgment,
110 Because where peril is not feared
There its strength shows its greatest blows,
And this is the more grave and more weighty
Proportionate to the trust with which 'twas undertook.
'Tis evident enough to you that the Spaniards
115 Entered into the land like great warriors,
All well on guard, very careful,
All the entire night with their guards out,
And in the towns that they have entered we know
That they have left all men in pleasant peace.
120 But if they come to know that we
Are taking up our arms, that were at peace,
Coming, as they will come, forewarned,
Who doubts war will be certain in our home?
And if that go not well with us,
125 And they be, as they say, immortal ones,
What pardon will there be that can pardon
The fact of our being first of all
To set on fire the land which of itself
Was all joyous and full of peace?
130 Put by your arms, nor think with them
To cause a fire which afterward could not
By all of us be extinguished."

8. Con esto = a pesar de esto.

Causar incendio que después no pueda
Ser de todos nosotros apagado."
Y cessando con esto el brabo joben,
Estaba en esta fuerza vn noble viejo[9]
Que ciento y veinte años alcanzaba,
En sus tiempos varón de muy buen seso,
Aviso y discreción bien concertada
Y principal también de seys que abía
En toda aquella fuerza señalados.
Este por nombre Chumpo se llamaba
Y porque algún gran daño no causasen
Con el bullicio de armas lebantadas,
De aquesta suerte a todos les propuso:
"Hijos caros, valientes y escogidos,
De donde el honor de Acoma deciende,
Y flor de aquella gente esclarecida
De donde vuestro esfuerzo y ser depende,
Que con yra seáis embravecidos
Contra todos aquéllos que pretenden
Por algún mal camino perturbaros
Es cosa en sí tan justa quanto injusta
Querer vosotros mismos encenderos
Y assí encendidos aguardar el viento
Y que con él los vnos y los otros
Quedemos después todos abrasados.
Yo soy de parecer que luego, auna,[10]
Las armas se sossieguen y descansen,
Que, como os tiene dicho Zutancalpo,
Si en otros pueblos guerras no han tenido
Aquestos Españoles que esperamos,
Hijos, ¿qué causa puede aber bastante
Para que aquí nosotros los temamos?"
Y con esto que el viejo les propuso,
Demás de las razones del mancebo,
Todos las armas luego suspendieron
Y libres de temor se sossegaron.
Sólo Zutacapán, embravecido,
Fue tal su furia, fuego y frenesía[11]
Que muy vivas centellas de su cuerpo,
Y por los ojos llamas, despedía.
Y qual furioso toro que, bramando,
La escarba[12] de la tierra vemos saca

And, the brave youth ceasing with this,
There was in that place a noble old man
135 Who had reached one hundred and twenty years,
In his time a man of very good talent,
Intelligence and discretion well-matched,[3]
And chief, moreover, of six men there were
In that place set apart from all.
140 This man was called by name Chumpo,
And, so no great injury might be caused
With the uproar of arms taken,
He spoke to all in this fashion:
"My dear children, valiant and chosen ones
145 From whom the honor of Acoma comes
And flower of that valiant folk
On which your efforts and your strength depends,
That you should be stirred up with wrath
Against all those who do intend
150 With evil ways to disturb you
It is a thing as just as 'tis unjust
To wish to set yourselves afire
And, thus blazing, wait for a wind,
And, with it, every one of us
155 Would, afterward, be all burnt up.
I am of the opinion that, unanimous,
You should lay down and set aside your arms,
For, as Zutancalpo has said to you,
If these Spaniards whom we await
160 Have in the other pueblos had no war,
My children, what cause can there be
That we here should have fear of them?"
And with this that old man said to them,
Beside the reasons given by the youth,
165 All then did lay aside their arms
And, free from fear, were quite at peace.
Only Zutacapán, enraged,
Such was his fury, fire and frenzy
That from his body and his eyes
170 Bright, living sparks of fire were cast
And from his eyes he threw out flames.
And, like a furious bull which, bellowing,
We see tear up the surface of the earth
And throw it over his broad sides,

9. La figura del noble anciano, prudente por la edad, procedente del Nestor de Homero, tiene presencia señalada en la épica americana, empezando por el Colocó de Ercilla (*La araucana* I, 2). Sin descartar la importancia de precedentes literarios, ello probablemente refleja, asimismo, la prominencia del anciano entre los pueblos descubiertos por los españoles.

10. Posible errata del original por "aína."

11. Frenesía = frenesí.

12. La escarba = lo escarbado.

3. The figure of the noble ancient, symbolizing prudence and wisdom, is probably rooted, for Western literature, in Homer's Nestor, and is very prominent in the New World epic, beginning with Ercilla's Colocó (*La araucana* I, 2). To some extent, but without disregarding purely literary precedents and models, this prominence reflects anthropological and social aspects of the peoples the Spaniards encountered.

Y sobre el espacioso lomo arroja,
Y firme en los robustos pies ligeros
El ayre en vano azota, hiere y rompe
Con vno y otro cuerno corajoso,
Assí salió este bárbaro sañudo,
Al hijo maldiciendo y blasfemando
Y a Chumpo, si pudiera, con los dientes
Allí, hecho pedazos, le dexara.
Mas qual vivo raposo, hastuto y diestro,
Disimulose todo lo que pudo,
Fingiendo darle gusto lo tratado,
Y al descuido, las redes bien tendidas,
Fue con todas sus fuerzas procurando
De agasajar amigos bulliciosos.
Y supo darse en esto tanta maña
Que no quedó mozuelo belicoso
Que su opinión y vando no siguiesse.
Viéndose, pues, de fuerzas reforzado,
Creciole la soberbia de manera
Que trató con algunos de secreto
Que al General, sin réplica ninguna,
Dentro de aquella fuerza le matasen,
Dando entre todos traza que, en entrando,
A cierta estufa[13] luego le llevasen
Y dentro doze bárbaros secretos
Allí la vida juntos le quitasen.
Hecho aqueste concierto y trato doble,
Llegó el Gobernador con todo el campo
Y admirado de ver la brava fuerza,
Grandeza y fortaleza que mostraban
Los poderosos muros lebantados,
Torreones, castillos espantosos,
Baluartes y braveza nunca vista,
Pasmado se quedó por vn buen rato
Mirando desde afuera las subidas
Y bajadas grimosas, no pensadas.
Y estando allí mirando y remirando,
Assí como el artífice que el sitio
Del edificio nota y toma al punto
Y advierte bien los vientos, Sol y quadros,[14]
Medidos con los anchos y los largos,
Y en proporción debida traza y forma
La planta con destreza bien sacada,
Llegó Zutacapán con todo el pueblo
A ver al General y a todo el campo.
Y si admirados todos estuvieron,

175 And, firm on his robust, swift feet,
In vain lash at the air, wound and tear it
With both his formidable horns,
Thus this barbarian, enraged,
Cursing, blaspheming, at his son,
180 And Chumpo would, could he have, with his teeth,
Left bloody, torn to pieces there.
But, like the clever and astute dog-fox,
Dissimulated all he could,
Pretending the discourse had pleased him well,
185 And, his nets well-prepared for careless men,
With all his strength he went on attempting
To win to him quarrelsome friends,
And in this knew how to display such skill
That there was not a warlike youth
190 Who did not follow his warlike opinion and command.
Seeing himself thus reinforced
His pride increased to such extent
That he did plan in secret with some more
That they should kill the General
195 Inside the fortress, unopposed,
The plan being that, as he entered,
They should take him to a certain Kiva
And, twelve barbarians being hid within,
They there should take away his life.
200 This agreement for double-dealing made,
The Governor arrived with all the camp
And, wondering to see the great stronghold,
Its hugeness and the strength demonstrated
By powerful walls, erected high,
205 Great towers, castles, inspiring fear,
Bulwarks, such strength as ne'er was seen,
Amazed, he stood for a good while
Looking from far upon the heights
And depths, cliffs most incredible.
210 And, being there staring, staring again,
Like to an architect who notes
The building site, and marks details
And sees well to the winds, sun, and squares
Measured in all their length and width,
215 And, in proportion due, traces and forms
His plan with skill right well applied,
Zutacapán with all the people came
To see the General and all the camp.
And if they all were much amazed,
220 Much more amazed, and frightened, too,

13. Estufa = kiva, lugar subterráneo usado para ritos religiosos de los indios Pueblo.

14. Quadros = cuadros, la cuarta parte del círculo en la posición de los astros.

Mucho más admirados y espantados
Se quedaron los bárbaros de verlos
A todos tan cubiertos y vestidos
De poderoso azero y duro hierro
Y en ligeros caballos animosos
De fina piel curtida encubertados,[15]
Cuyos bravos relinchos les causaron
Vn terrible pabor y sobresalto,
Medrosos de que aquellos animales
Alguna cosa grande les dixessen.
Y porque el General assí lo quiso,
No más que por causarles más espanto,
Con gallarda destreza los probaron
En ligeros manijos desembueltos,
Y pasmados los bárbaros de verlos
Los ojos no movieron ni hablaron.
Y luego que don Iuan en pie se puso,
Todos con gran presteza se pusieron
En formado esquadrón, sin que ninguno
Allí los gobernase ni mandase,
Por la mucha destreza que tenían
En ocupar sus puestos con cuidado.
Y notando los bárbaros el orden
Con que empezó a subir la grande cumbre
Y guarda que quedaba en los caballos,
Aviso y prevención que en todo abía,
Y que a la retaguardia los pusieron
Por llevarles el alto ya ganado,
Avergonzados todos se mostraban
De ver en los Castillas tanto aviso.
Y, con esto, les dio también cuidado
Que luego que llegaron a la cumbre,
Disparando y cargando, vna gran salva
A todos los del pueblo les hizieron.
Demás desto advirtieron y notaron
El orden con que fueron por las plazas
Y como, hechos todos una piña,
En vna dellas fueron reparando.
Y conoziendo el bárbaro que aquello
Era por don Iuan solo gobernado,
Y que si su persona les faltase
Abían de ser todos sus rendidos,
Arrojose al intento comenzado.
Y por poder mejor salir del hecho
Llegose al General y por el brazo
Con gusto le prendió y rogó que fuesse
A ver vna gran cosa que tenía
Metida en vna estufa bien guardada.
Y luego el General con buen semblante,

Were the barbarians on seeing them
All covered and completely clothed
In mighty steel and hard iron
And on horses swift and high-spirited
225 And covered with well-tanned leather,
Whose spirited neighing did cause them
Terrible fear and sudden dread,
Being fearful that those animals
Were saying some great thing to them.
230 And, as the General so wished,
No more than to cause them more fear,
With gallant skill they displayed them
In swift and free maneuvering.
The barbarians, astonished at the sight,
235 Nor ever moved their eyes or spoke.
And when Don Juan rose in saddle,
All instantly arranged themselves
In a formed squadron, with no one
Giving an order nor command,
240 Through the great skill that they possessed
In properly taking their place.
And the barbarians, seeing the order
With which he 'gan to climb the lofty peak
And the guard with which the horses remained,
245 The care and foresight that there was in all,
And that they had placed them to rear
To keep the heights already gained,
They all did show themselves ashamed
To see such caution in the Castilians.
250 And they were also much alarmed
Because, arriving at the top,
They fired and discharged a great salute
To all the people in the pueblo.
Beside this they observed and well noted
255 The order in which they passed plazas
And, as they had all made up a pinecone,
In one of them they all came together.
And the barbarian, knowing that all this
Was governed by Don Juan alone,
260 And that, if his person were but lacking,
They all would be entirely helpless,
Sprang to the plan he had begun,
And, better to accomplish it,
Came to the General and by the arm took him
265 To go and see a mighty thing he had,
Kept in a well-guarded kiva.
The General then, with a good countenance,
That he might not show any signs of weakness there,
Went off with him but did not lose from sight

15. Encubertados = cubiertos.

Por no dar de flaqueza algún indicio,
Con él fue junto, sin perder de vista
Al formado esquadrón que allí dexaba.
Y assí como llegaron a la estufa,

Alegre le rogó que dentro entrase,
Y visto el soterrano[16] y boca estrecha,
Qual suele aquél que por camino incierto
Echa de ver, ynopinadamente,
Que de muy alta cumbre se despeña
Y con prestas repressas[17] se retira,
Assí se retiró y, con contento,
Al bárbaro le dixo que quería
Bajar el esquadrón de aquella fuerza
Y, puesto abajo todo y alojado,
Daría luego buelta a ver la estufa.
Y por assegurarse más le dixo
Que con él se bajase porque juntos,
Mano a mano, a la cumbre se bolviessen.
Y con aquesto el bárbaro, contento,
Con ellos se bajó para lo llano,
Donde don Iuan le despidió diziendo
Que por venir cansado y ser ya tarde
Ya no podría subir, que tiempo abría
Para poder bolver a darle gusto.
Y visto el lance en vano, entristecido,
El bárbaro quedó con gran cuidado.
Y esta traición jamás, señor, se supo
Hasta que vbo gran tiempo ya passado.
Y assí, contentos de que mal saliesse
Zutacapán del hecho mal pensado,
Luego Purguapo, Chumpo y Zutancalpo,
Con todos sus amigos, le truxeron
Los más regalos que les fue possible
Y gran cantidad de agua que bebiesse
Toda la caballada que venía.
Y estando todo aquesto prevenido,
Luego el General quiso proponerles
Si pretendían daros la obediencia.
Y assí, como los otros, sin rezelo
La dieron con gran gusto y gran contento,
Siendo Zutacapán y sus consortes
Los primeros que en darla concedieron.
Con esto, se partió de aquella fuerza,
Passando a Mohoze,[18] Zíbola y Zuni,

270 The formed squadron that he did leave behind.
And as they came to the kiva
He cheerfully asked him to enter in;
And having seen the underground chamber, its narrow
    mouth,
Like he who on an unknown road
275 Sees suddenly and unexpectedly
That it plunges over a lofty precipice
And with a sudden spring draws back,
So he retired, but in a quiet way,
And said to the barbarian he wished
280 To lead his squadron from that fortress
And that, once it was down and in the camp,
Then he would return to see the kiva.
And, to assure him more, he said to him
That he should come down with him so they two
285 Might, hand in hand, re-scale the heights.
And with this, the barbarian, content,
Went down with them unto the plain,
Where Don Juan bade farewell to him, saying
That being tired from his trip and it being
290 Now late, he now could not go up, but there would be
A time when he again could pleasure him.
And seeing his trick in vain, greatly cast down,
The barbarian was very sad.
This treachery, O lord, was never known
295 Until much time had passed away.
Pleased that Zutacapán's malicious plan
Had thus had such a bad outcome,
Purguapo, Chumpo and Zutancalpo,
With their friends, then brought the General
300 All the gifts that were possible for them
And a great quantity of water to give drink
To all the horses which had come.
And, all this being provided for,
The General then wished to ask of them
305 If they would give you their obedience,
And, like the rest, without hesitation,
They gave it with great pleasure and content,
Zutacapán and his fellows being
The first who did agree to render it.
310 With this, he went from that stronghold,
Passing Mohose,[4] Zibola, Zuni,
Amid whose noble lands we discovered
A great troop of Indians who came with

---

16. Soterrano = subterráneo.
17. Repressas = represas, pasos retrocedentes.
18. Mohoze, también conocido como Mohoqui, Mohuqui y Moqui se refiere a los indios Hopi. Véase Hammond & Rey, *Oñate,* 36. Los pueblos de Zíbola y Zuni, mencionados a continuación, se cree que eran el mismo. Véase Villagrá, *Historia,* edición de Junquera, 265.

4. Mohoze, also called Mohoqui, Mohuqui and Moqui, refers to the Hopi Indians, the westernmost Pueblos. See Hammond and Rey, *Oñate,* 36. The following pueblos, Cíbola and Zuni are generally considered to have been one and the same. See Villagrá, *Historia,* Junquera edition, 265.

Por cuias nobles tierras descubrimos
Vna gran tropa de Indios que venía
Con cantidad[19] harina que esparcían
Sobre la gente toda muy apriessa.[20]
Y entrando assí en los pueblos, las mugeres
Dieron en arrojarnos tanta della
Que dimos en tomarles los costales,
De donde resultó tener con ellas
Vnas carnestolendas[21] bien reñidas,
De grande passatiempo y muy trabadas.[22]
Y luego que, cansados, vbo pazes
Entre ellas y nosotros por concierto,
Con sumo regozijo nos truxeron
A todos que comer en abundancia.
Y estando assí, comiendo, nos dixeron
Que aquella cerimonia[23] se hazía
Por darnos a entender con más certeza
Que assí como no puede ser que el hombre
Pueda passar viviendo alegremente
Aquesta vida triste sin sustento,
Que assí no era possible que passasen
Sin sernos siempre amigos verdaderos.
Y viendo que vna Cruz allí arbolamos,
Como nosotros todos la adoraron,
Y para más mostrar su buen intento
Al General y a todos combidaron
Para vna illustre caza que hazían.
Y dándoles en esto todo gusto
Tomamos los caballos y partimos,
Y llegados al puesto, estaban juntos
Más de ochocientos bárbaros amigos,
Y assí como nos vieron arrancaron.
Haziendo dos grandiosas medias lunas
Y cerrando los cuernos, se mostraron
En círculo redondo tan tendidos
Que espacio de vna legua rodeaban
De sóla travesía, y en el medio,

A quantity of meal which they sprinkled

315 With great rapidity on all our folk.
And entering in their towns thus, the womenfolk
Did throw upon us so much of the same
That we[5] began taking their sacks
And, thereby, had with those women

320 Carnival battles,[6] bravely fought,
Of great amusement, strongly contested.
And when tired out, there being peace
Between them and ourselves by agreement,
They brought, with the height of rejoicing,

325 All sorts of things to eat in abundance.
And as we thus were eating, they told us
That this ceremony[7] was done
To make us understand more certainly
That just as it cannot be that a man

330 Should keep on living happily
In this sad life without some nourishment,
It was not possible that they exist
Unless always true friends of ours.
And seeing that we there did bear a Cross,

335 They all adored it like ourselves,
And, better to show good intentions,
They did invite the General and all
Unto a famous hunt they were making.
And, granting their pleasure in this,

340 We took our horses and set out.
Arriving at the place, there were gathered
More than eight hundred of barbarian friends,
And, soon as they saw us, they all spread out.
Making two mighty half-moon lines

345 And closing in the wings, they then did form
A complete circle, so stretched out
As to surround the full space of a league
In sole circumference, in whose midst,
With all our squadron, we halted.

350 And when they began the beating,

19. Posible errata del original omitiendo "de."

20. Aunque Villagrá utilice aquí la primera persona del plural, y
alguna vez hasta el singular, el hecho es que, como se advertirá, él no
anduvo personalmente con Oñate en su escapada hacia los pueblos del
oeste.

21. Carnestolendas = carnaval, y, por extensión, las acciones, libres
y licensiosas, que con él se asociaban. Ha de tenerse en cuenta, al
respecto, que Villagrá narra aquí basado en lo que sus compañeros le
dijeran, quizás jactanciosamnte.

22. Trabadas = agarradas, de contacto físico.

23. Para el significado religioso del rito de la lluvia de harina entre
los indios Pueblo, véase Villagrá, *Historia*, edición de Junquera, 50–
51. Para el lanzamiento de harina como costumbre carnavalesca de la
España del siglo XVII, véase A. Redondo, "De molinos, molineros y
molineras," en *Literatura y folklore: problemas de intertextualidad*
(Salamanca: Editora de la Universidad de Salamanca, 1983), 111.

5. Although Villagrá uses the first person plural here, he was not a
member of Oñate's expedition to the Pacific.

6. This allusion to carnival time in the Spaniards's encounter with
the Indian women perhaps suggests a certain licentiousness, proper to
carnival activities, in that contact. It must be remembered, of course,
that Villagrá narrates here based on hearsay, on the no doubt bragging
stories told him later by his companions.

7. For the religious and ritual significance of the *lluvia de harina* or
throwing of corn meal among the Pueblo Indians, see Villagrá, *Historia
de Nuevo México*, Junquera edition, 50–51. For the Spanish carnival
custom of throwing flour, see A. Redondo, "De molinos, molineros y
molineras," in *Literatura y folklore: problemas de intertextualidad*
(Salamanca: Editora Universidad de Salamanca, 1983), p. 111.

Con toda nuestra esquadra, nos tuvimos.
Y luego que empezaron el ogeo,[24]
Cerrando todo el círculo, vinieron
A meter donde juntos nos quedamos
Tantas liebres, conejos y raposos
Que entre los mismos pies de los caballos
Pensaban guarecerse y socorrerse.
Bien quisieran algunos por su gusto
Andar allí a las bueltas con la caza
Y dar a los raposos ciertos golpes,
Mas fue mandato expresso que ninguno
Dexase de estar bien apercebido,
Los pies en los estribos con cuidado,
Por no saber de cierto si sus pechos
Fuessen tan buenos, nobles y cenzillos
Como ordinariamente se mostraron.
En esta alegre caza vimos muertas
Largas[25] ochenta liebres muy hermosas,
Treinta y quatro conejos, y no cuento
Los raposos que allí también juntaron.
Y no sé yo que tenga todo el mundo
Liebres de más buen gusto y más sabrosas,
Mas crecidas, más bellas ni más tiernas
Que esta tierra produze y sus contornos.
Con esto, se bolvieron para el pueblo
Y luego al Capitán Farfán mandaron
Que fuesse a descubrir ciertas salinas
De que grande noticia se tenía,
Y poniendo por obra aquel mandato
Con presta diligencia y buen cuidado,
En brebe dio la buelta y dixo dellas
Que eran tan caudalosas y tan grandes
Que por espacio de una legua larga
Mostraba toda aquélla sal de gruesso
Vna muy larga pica bien tendida.
Y con tan buena mano como tuvo,
Mandole que segunda vez saliesse
En busca de vnas minas muy famosas
Porque dellas también se abía tenido
Bastante relación de muchas gentes.
Y porque todo bien se encaminase,
Con él salió Quesada bien armado,
Don Iuan Escarramal y Antonio Conde,
Marcos García, en mil trabajos fuerte,
Y en[26] ellos Damiero, bien sufrido,
Y Hernán Martín, con otros compañeros
Que juntos con presteza se partieron.

24. Ogeo = ojeo, espantar la caza con voces y ruido.
25. Largas = más de.
26. En = con.

Closing the circle in, they drove
Toward the point where we all together stood
So many hare, rabbit, and fox
That mid the very feet of the horses
355 They thought to hide and save themselves.
Some for their pleasure did much wish
There to dismount and follow up the hunt
And to strike down the foxes there,
But 'twas express command that no one should
360 Cease to be well upon his guard,
His feet kept carefully in the stirrups,
Not knowing certainly whether their hearts
Were as good, noble, and simple
As they seemed ordinarily.
365 In this joyous hunt we saw killed
Some eighty large, beautiful hares,
Rabbits some thirty-four, nor do I count
The foxes that were also gathered there.
And I do not know that the whole world has
370 Hares of a better taste, more savory,
Larger, more beautiful, or more tender
Than this land and its neighborhood produce.
With this, they returned to the town
And then did order Captain Farfán
375 To go discover certain saline lakes
Of which they had heard great reports.
And putting into practice that command
With rapid diligence and goodly care,
He shortly did return and talk of them,
380 That they were so well-filled, so very large,
That for the space of a long league
All was covered with salt and to the depth
Of a very long pike in full length.
With such good luck as he had had
385 He was ordered to leave a second time
In search of certain very famous mines,
Because of them, too, we had had
A many tales from many folk.
And that all might go well with him
390 There went with them Quesada, the well-armed,
Don Juan Escarramal and Antonio Conde,
Marcos García, in a thousand trials strong,
And Damiero, well-tried by the same,
Hernán Martín, too, with other companions
395 Who quickly set out all together.
And after they had wandered many leagues,
Suffering very great trials,

Y después que anduvieron muchas leguas,
Padeciendo grandíssimos trabajos,
La buelta dio Quesada, muy contento,
Diziendo grandes vienes de la tierra
Y que era de metales abundosa,
De lindos pastos, montes, fuentes, Ríos,
Cañadas, vegas, sitios y llanadas,
Por cuios puestos cantidad toparon
De gallinas monteses de la tierra,
Iguanas y perdizes de Castilla,
Conchas de perlas, porque cerca estaban
De la perlada costa que en silencio
Quiere el inmenso Dios que esté guardada,
El sabe para qué y por qué se calla,
Y mucha gente, toda bien dispuesta,
Hermosa por extremo, y no era mucho
Porque no abía ninguno que dexase
De ponerse en mitad de la cabeza
Vna Cruz bella, hecha de dos cañas
Y a los mismos cabellos bien prendida.[27]
Y estándonos diziendo todo aquesto,
Llegó Farfán y, sin faltar en nada,
Aquellas mismas cosas fue contando.
Y quisieron los dos adelantarse,
Dexando muy atrás los compañeros,
Por sólo dar aquellas buenas nuevas.
Y como el gran contento siempre causa
Gran largueza en aquél que le recibe,
Por más bien celebrar las buenas nuevas,
Nombró el Gobernador por Capitanes
Al Alférez Romero y Iuan Piñero.
Y porque, ¡ya he llegado!,[28] temo y siento
Que aquí se me apareja vn gran quebranto,
Quiero esforzar la boz en este canto.

Quesada did return, very content,
Saying much good about the land

400 And that it was abundant in metals,
With beauteous pastures, mountains, springs, rivers
And glens, meadows, small camps, and plains
Where they had come upon a quantity
Of the wild chickens of the land,

405 Lizards and Spanish partridges,
And pearl-shells, for they had been near
That land of pearls which mighty God
Has wished to be kept in silence,
He knows for why and he tells not,

410 And many people, all of them friendly,
Extremely beautiful. Nor was this strange
Since there was none of them who did not have
Placed on the middle of his head
A beauteous cross made of two canes

415 And well-attached unto the hair.[8]
And as he told us all these things
Farfán arrived, and, without missing one,
Told us these very selfsame things.
And these two had chosen to come ahead,

420 Leaving their fellows very far behind,
Only to give us this good news.
And as great satisfaction always brings
Great largesse from the receiver,
To better celebrate this splendid news,

425 The General made captains of
Ensign Romero and of Juan Piñero, too.
And as I now have come, I think and fear,
To where a great affliction came to me,
I wish to raise my voice for this[9] canto.

430

27. Para la relación de estos indios cruzados, véase Colahan y Rodriguez, "La Relación del padre Escobar," *Missonalia Hispánica* 43 (1986): 373-93.

28. Se refiere el autor, en aparte a sí mismo, al recuerdo de su trabajosa aventura personal.

8. For a detailed description of these *cruzados*, Indians wearing crosses on their heads, see the *Relación* of Father Escobar, Colahan and Rodriguez, *Missonalia Hispánica* 43 (1986): 373–93.

9. Villagrá is here referring to the coming canto.

CANTO DIEZ Y NVEVE

COMO BOLVIO EL AVTOR DEL CASTIGO DE
AQUELLOS que degollaron y como los Indios de Acoma le
cogieron en vna trampa, y trabajos que padeció por escapar la
vida, y socorro que tuvo hasta llegar al Real del Gobernador.

N O se ha visto jamás que la fortuna
Aya vn punto la rueda assegurado,
Y assí los de su mal segura cumbre,
Por más bien que se tengan, no es possible
Dexar de verse todos rebolcados,

Puestos de lodo, tristes y afligidos,
Cuya gran desbentura siempre nace
De ser en sí invidiosa, fementida,
Improba, melancólica, inconstante,
Dudosa, cautelosa, movediza,
Frenética, furiosa, débil, flaca,
Y fuerte, si de vicios se socorre.[1]
Y, al fin, si a muchos toca su braveza
Todo es sufrible, todo es comportable,
Mas si viene a ser solo quien la sufre
Dios nos libre que aquí ninguno llegue.
Bolviendo, pues, señor, de aquel castigo
De los pobres soldados que dexamos
Abiertas las gargantas, ya difuntos,
Abiéndonos bien todo sucedido,
Como en fortuna frágil nunca ay gusto
A quien alegre rato le suceda,
Abiéndose passado tanto tiempo
Que el General y todos los del campo
No tenían de nosotros nueva alguna,
Pareciome ser bien adelantarme
A dar cuenta al Gobernador del hecho
Que assí tuvo por bien de encomendarme.
Pues siendo deste acuerdo todos juntos,
Luego tomé el camino trabajoso
Y llegando a Puarai, pueblo de amigos,
Allí vine a saber por cosa cierta,
De vn niño Castellano que llamaban
Francisco de las Nieves, como abía
Salido el General de aquel assiento
Antes que yo llegase solo vn día.

---

1. La veleidad de la Fortuna, simbolizada en la rueda girante de los clásicos, era tópico de la literatura de la época. *El laberinto de la fortuna* de Juan de Mena era, todavía en el siglo XVI, libro muy leído, y de la imagen de la rueda trata concretamente Antonio de Torquemada, *Jardín de flores curiosas* IV.

CANTO XIX

How the author returned from the punishment of those who were
executed and how the Indians of Acoma caught him in a trap,
and the toils he underwent to escape with his life, and the
assistance he had until he came to the camp of the Governor.

N EVER has it been seen that Dame Fortune
Has fixed her wheel at any single point,[1]
And thus, those on its insecure summit,
However tight they hold, 'tis beyond hope
5   That they should fail to see themselves
thrown down,
Set in the mud, sad and afflicted much,
Which great misfortune always doth arise
From being in herself envious and faithless,
Wicked and melancholy, inconstant,
10 Doubtful, suspicious, unstable,
Frenetic, furious, feeble, weak,
And strong if she seeks aid from vice.
And, finally, if one's courage is much,
All is bearable, all endurable,
15 But if the one who suffers is alone,
Then God free anyone from landing there.
Returning, lord, back from the punishment
Of those poor soldiers whom we left
With their throats open and now dead,
20 All things having gone well with us,
As fickle fortune never takes pleasure
In him to whom successful times have come,
So long a time having passed by
That the General and all those of the camp
25 Had not had any news of us,
It seemed to me good I should go ahead
To give the Governor a report upon the work
That he had thought it well to assign to me.
All being in accord with this,
30 I then set out upon the toilsome way,
And coming to Puarai, a town of friends,
I there did learn it was a certain fact,
From a Castilian lad they called
Francisco de las Nieves, how the General
35 Had taken his departure from that place
Only a single day before I came.

---

1. The fickleness of Fortune, symbolized in the classics by the turning wheel, was a commonly used image since the Renaissance. Juan de Mena's well-known *Laberinto de la fortuna* was very widely read into the seventeenth century, and Villagrá may well have been familiar with Antonio de Torquemada's writing on that symbol, *Jardín de flores curiosas* IV.

Y assí como lo supe, sin tardanza,
Tras dél me fuy marchando, cuidadoso
De darle breve alcance si pudiesse.
Y apenas, alto Rey, me fuy llegando
A la gran fuerza de Acoma nombrada
Quando vi que los bárbaros estaban,
Según sentí, no nada descuidados,
Que esto tienen los pechos cautelosos,
Que siempre dexan rastros y señales
Con que avisan, despiertan y previenen
A los que dellos viven recatados.
Y assí, con el recato que llevaba,
Eché de ver me estaban aguardando
Como diestros lebreles, agachados
A la vereda, todos desseosos
De verse ya rebueltos y ocupados
Con la gustosa pressa bien assidos.
Y por temor que tienen estas gentes,
Con seys tendidas brazas² no se llegan
Al hombre de acaballo, temerosos
Del animal gallardo porque piensan
Que allí los ha de hazer cien mil pedazos.
Y aquél que yo llevaba tengo, oy día,
Que más bello animal nunca parieron
Castizas yeguas, diestras, bien probadas
En alentado curso desembuelto,
Por cuia causa todos rezelosos,
Con muestras y señales rebozadas,
El bien venido juntos me mostraron.
Y más Zutacapán, a quien propuse
Necesidad vrgente que tenía
De sólo bastimento que aprestaba³
La mísera flaqueza desabrida.
Con cuia mano luego, rebozado,
Mirando, me pidió desocupase
La silla del caballo y me daría
En todo mucho gusto, y esto dixo
Algo risueño y nada sossegado.
Y porque dél estuve rezeloso,
Por escapar la vida si pudiesse
Allí le di a entender que mucha priessa
Era la que llevaba y no podía
Parar solo vn momento en aquel puesto.
Y viendo que no pudo, demudado,
El brazo sacudiendo con enojo,
Me dixo que me fuesse y no aguardase.

And, soon as I knew this, without delay,
I set out marching, cautious, after him,
To catch up with him quickly if I might.
40 And hardly, mighty King, had I arrived
At the fortress of Acoma, renowned,
When I saw the barbarians were,
Or so I felt, in no way unprepared,
For so suspiciously inclined hearts are,
45 That they do always leave traces and signs
With which they warn and wake and set on guard
Such men as live on watch for them.
So, with the prudence I maintained,
I saw that they were waiting my coming,
50 Like swift greyhounds who do crouch down
Upon the trail, all desirous
To see themselves excited, occupied,
With the savory prize seized fast.
Now, through the fear which these folk have,
55 They will not come to six arm's lengths
Of a man on horseback, being afraid
Of the brave animal, whom they think
Will tear them to a hundred thousand shreds.
And that one I had then I feel today
60 That animal more beautiful was never born
Of splendid, speedy, mares, well-proved
Upon the swift and flying course,
Wherefore they, all most fearful,
With motions and signs deceptive
65 They, all together, welcomed me,
Especially Zutacapán, to whom I told
The great, urgent necessity I had
For food alone that might assuage
My sharp and exhausted weakness.
70 He then, deceptive, with his hand
Gesturing, asked me to dismount
From out the saddle of my horse and he
Would give me all with much pleasure, and he
Said this smiling a little, and nonchalant.
75 And since I was distrustful of him,
To escape with my life if I but might,
I made him understand that I then was
In a great hurry and could not
Stop even for one moment in that place.
80 And, seeing he could not change me,
Shaking his arm in annoyance,
He told me I should go and should not wait.

2. Brazas = medida de extensión de unas dos varas, metro y medio.
3. Aprestaba = necesitaba.

Y vista su desgracia,[4] despedime,
Fingiendo el rostro alegre quanto pude.
Y estando ya yo dellos tanto trecho
Quanto vna gran carrera bien tirada,
A grandes bozes todos me llamaron,
'Castilla' muy apriessa pronunciando,
Y aunque les entendí que me llamaban,
Reparé mi caballo y con el brazo
Hize señal de allí si me pedían
Que mi camino fuesse prosiguiendo
O que a su puesto luego me acercase.
Y llamándome juntos con las manos,
Sacando fuerzas de flaqueza, al punto,
Fiado en el caballo que llevaba,
Bolví luego las riendas, demudado,
Y, vna veloz carrera atropellando,[5]
El animal gallardo, desembuelto,
Salió con presto curso poderoso,
Y allí, los crudos trapos[6] sacudiendo,
Batiendo con braveza el duro suelo,
Haciéndose[7] pedazos con las manos,
Brioso y alentado, fue parando,[8]
Haziendo vna gran plaza bien tendida
Por la canalla bárbara medrosa.
En cuio puesto, lejos, desde afuera,
Allí Zutacapán me preguntaba
Si atrás otros Castillas me seguían
Y que fuesse contando por los dedos
Qué número venía y quántos días
Tendría de demora su tardanza.
Yo, con algún temor, fingí venían
Ciento y tres hombres bien aderezados[9]
Y que sólos dos días tardarían
En llegar a sus muros lebantados.
Pues como bien me vbiessen entendido,
Mandáronme que fuesse mi camino,
Y viendo ya que el Sol de todo punto
Sus claros y hermosos rayos yba
Descubriendo al Antípoda remoto,
Apresureme todo quanto pude
Hasta que ya la triste noche obscura
Apagada la luz al mundo tuvo.
Y por hazer mi causa más segura

And, seeing his anger, I said farewell,
Pretending in my face what joy I could.
85   And being now as far away from them
As the length of a long racecourse,
All called to me in loud voices,
"Castilla," very rapidly pronounced,
And, though I knew that they were calling me,
90   I stopped my horse and with my arm
I signaled them from there if they asked me
Just to continue on my way,
Or that I should draw near to them.
And, all beckoning to me with their hands,
95   Drawing strength from my weakness then,
Trusting in the horse that I rode,
I then did loose the reins upon his neck
And, taking up a rapid run,
The brave and gallant animal
100   Set off in powerful and rapid course
And stretching out his powerful limbs,
Striking the hard ground with fury,
Breaking it into pieces with his hoofs,
Spirited, panting, he came to a stop,
105   Opening a well-extended space
Among the cowardly barbarian crowd.
In this place, from good distance off,
Zutacapán did question me
If other Spaniards were following me,
110   And said I should count upon my fingers
What number was coming, how many days
Delay there would be in their arrival.
I, with some fear, pretended that there came
A hundred and three men, well-equipped,
115   And that they would delay only two days
In coming to their lofty walls.
Now, as they well had comprehended me,
They ordered me to go away,
And, seeing now the sun was with all speed
120   Going with his bright, beauteous rays
To discover remote Antipodes,
I hurried all that I well could
Until the sad and darkening night
Had shut off the light from the world.
125   And then, to make myself more safe,

4. Desgracia = desagrado, aspereza.
5. Atropellando = yendo a tropel, rápido.
6. Posible errata del original por "brazos." Lo sugiere el adjetivo "crudos" y el contexto inmediato.
7. Posible errata del original por "haciéndole," que haría más sentido y mejor lectura.
8. Parando = empinándose.
9. Aderezados = preparados.

Vna gran milla quise derrotarme
A vn lado del camino que llevaba,
En cuio puesto, triste, solitario,
El caballo animoso assegurando
Con gruessa y fuerte amarra, sólo quise
Quitarle el pecho, freno y la testera,
Dexándole pazer a su albedrío.
Y viéndome del sueño ya vencido
Después de media noche ya passada,
Tendido en aquel suelo, fuy arrimando
Los quebrantados miembros fatigados
Al azerado hielmo desabrido.[10]
Y como el alma siempre está despierta
Al tiempo que el terrestre cuerpo duerme,
Della misma despierto y recordado,
Lebantándome fuy, despavorido,
Y viendo todo el tiempo en sí rebuelto
Aderezé de presto mi caballo
Y apenas los estribos fuy cobrando
Quando del alto Cielo grandes copos
De blanca nieve todo me cubrían.
Y assí me fuy saliendo a la vereda
Y rastro que el Gobernador dexaba,
Y llegando a vna grande palizada[11]
En forma de barrera bien tendida,
Vi que por medio della mi camino
Por vn portillo estrecho yba saliendo.
Y assí, sin más acuerdo, con descuido,
Por él quise salir sin más cuidado.
Y assí como al relámpago sucede
Vn repentino rayo arrebatado,
Assí fue, gran señor, mi triste suerte,
Que apenas fui passando quando, a pique,[12]
La tierra que pisaba y que corría
Abriendo vna gran boca poderosa
Sentí que me sorbía y me tragaba.
Y viendo que el caballo, entre sus labios
Sorbido a dentro todo, le tenía
Sin género de vida, atravesado,
De todo punto muerto y sin sentido,[13]
Qual flaco marinero que perdida
Siente la pobre nave zozobrada,
Que apriessa y sin vagar[14] se desempacha

I went a long mile from my course
To one side of the road I took,
In which sad, solitary place,
Securing the spirited horse

130   With strong and heavy fastenings, I chose
To take off breastpiece, bridle, and crownpiece,
Letting him pasture at his will.
And seeing myself all overcome with sleep,
Midnight now having long gone by,

135   I then laid down upon the ground,
My broken and fatigued limbs
Coming near to my vexing helm of steel.[2]
Now as the soul doth always keep awake
During what time the earthly body sleeps,

140   Awakened and recalled by that same,
Rising, I was all terrified,
And seeing the weather about to storm,
I quickly did prepare my horse,
And hardly had I put foot in stirrup

145   Before from the high heaven monstrous flakes
Of white snow covered me all o'er.
And so I went, departing for the trail
And track the Governor had left.

150   Coming unto a mighty palisade
In the form of barrier, extending far,
I saw that through the middle of the same
My way went by a narrow pass.
And so, without more thought, all carelessly,
I wished to go through it without precaution.

155   And just as on the lightning bolt follows
A thunder crash, precipitate and swift,
So was, great lord, my sorry fate,
For hardly was I passing when, at once,
The land I trod and over which I went

160   Opening a mighty, powerful mouth,
I felt myself drawn down and swallowed.
And seeing that my horse between its lips
Had been entirely drawn in and held,
And pierced, without a sign of life,[3]

165   Entirely dead and motionless, then I,
Like some exhausted mariner who knows
That his poor ship is sunk and lost
And quickly and without delay grows bold

10. La postura que indica parece ser la fetal.
11. Palizada = sitio cercado de estacas.
12. A pique = hundiéndose.
13. Es una trampa excavada con afiladas estacas en su fondo. La aventura recuerda algo la mencionada por Saavedra Guzmán, *El peregrino indiano* X.
14. Vagar = lentitud, pausa.

2. Villagrá indicates that he achieved a fetal sleeping position.
3. Although not otherwise indicated, the pit-trap had stakes on its floor. This adventure, although very probably historical, echoes another found in *El peregrino indiano* X.

Y al poderoso y bravo mar se arroja,	And gives himself to the strong and rough sea,
Tragada ya la muerte sin remedio,	Tasting of death beyond all remedy,
Assí, la corta vida ya rendida	Considering my short life now done
Y la esperanza rota, fue¹⁵ saliendo	And all hope lost, did still creep out
Del horrible sepulcro temeroso	Of that horrible, sudden sepulchre
Que Zutacapán hecho me tenía	That Zutacapán had prepared for me
Para cogerme vivo si pudiesse.	To take me living if he could.
Y fue la magestad de Dios serbida	And it did serve the majesty of God
Que por suceder esto entre dos luzes	That, this occurring at evening
Y que gran nieve el Cielo derramaba,	And since heaven poured down much snow,
Retirados los bárbaros estaban,	The barbarians had all retired,
Donde alcanzar ninguno dellos pudo	So that not one of them did know
Aquello que en la trampa peligrosa	What, in their perilous pitfall,
A solas y sin ellos padezía.	I suffered all alone and without them.
Y temiendo que presto allí viniessen	And fearing that they might soon come
Y sin remedio juntos me matasen,	And, without remedy, together kill me there,
Qual suelen con tormenta y gran borrasca	As they tend to do in storms and tempests,
Los pobres contrastados y oprimidos	The poor sailors, storm-tossed and overwhelmed,
Alijar¹⁶ con presteza la más ropa,	Who quickly leave most of their clothes,
Assí determiné de despojarme,	I thought my armor to remove,
Y escondido al socarre¹⁷ de vna peña	And, hidden out of view behind a rock,
Allí dexé la cota y escarcela,	I there did leave my cuirass and cuisses,
El lebantado yelmo y el adarga,	My lofty helmet, and my shield,
El arcabuz con frasco¹⁸ y su frasquillo,¹⁹	My harquebus and flask and priming flask,⁴
Y sólo con la espada y con la daga	And only with my sword and my dagger
Quise tomar de presto mi camino.	I chose swiftly to go my way.
Y por no ser sacado por el rastro	And, not to be caught by my tracks,
Los zapatos bolví sin detenerme,	I turned my boots around without delay,
Poniendo los talones a las puntas,	Putting my toes into the heels,
Con cuia diligencia deslumbrados	With which stratagem the barbarians
Los bárbaros quedaron todo el tiempo	Remained deceived for all the time
Que me fue necessario, muy al justo,	That was duly needed by me
Para poder librarme de sus manos.	To be able to free me from their hands.
Quatro días naturales fuy marchando,	Four entire days I kept walking,
Terrible sed y hambre padeciendo,	Suffering horrible hunger and thirst,
Rendido de flaqueza, y²⁰ que perdida	Worn out with weakness, having lost
Tenía la esperanza que alentaba	The hope I had that kept me up
El mísero vivir de aquesta vida.	In miserable living of this life.
Que quando aquí se llega, desdichado	For when one comes to this point, unhappy
De aquél que assí se ve tan afligido,	The sad person who sees himself so tried,
Porque no tiene el mundo insulto ni torpeza,	Since the world has no insult nor baseness,
Delicto, crimen, vicio ni pecado,	Nor wickedness, crime, vice, nor deadly sin,
Si Dios no le socorre, que no emprenda	Unless God aids him, he will not think of
Y ponga por la obra si en hazerlo	And carry out if but in doing it

Line numbers: 170, 175, 180, 185, 190, 195, 200, 205, 210

15. Patente errata del original por "fui."
16. Alijar = aligerar, aliviar la carga.
17. Posible errata del original por "socaire" = abrigo o defensa.
18. Frasco = cajuela en que el arcabucero llevaba la pólvora.
19. Frasquillo = cajuela más pequeña en que éste llevaba la pólvora muy menuda que servía para cebar las armas de fuego.
20. Posible errata del original por "ya."

4. The reference is to the flask in which the gunpowder was carried.

Consiste el escaparse y verse libre.
¡O vida humana, débil, quebradiza!
No creo que con más maganta[21] hambre
Al hijo dio la muerte aquella triste
Que al vientre le bolvió en la gran ruina
De aquella Ciudad santa que perdida
Quedó, por sus pecados assolada,[22]
Qual sucedió por mí en este hecho.
Llevaba, pues, un perro que a mi lado
Anduvo mucho tiempo y que velaba
Quando de noche acaso me dormía;
Y porque ya la hambre me afligía
De suerte que la vida me acababa,
Determiné matarle y dos heridas
Le di mortales con que luego el pobre
De mí se fue apartando vn largo trecho.
Llamele con enojo y olvidado
Del vergonzoso hecho, inadvertido,
Gimiendo mansamente y agachado,
A mí bolvió el amigo mal herido,
Lamiéndose la sangre que vertía.
Y assí, con desconsuelo y lastimado,
Por agradarme en algo si pudiesse,
Lamió también mis manos, que teñidas
Me puso, de su sangre bien bañadas.
Mirele, pues, señor, y avergonzado
De aberle assí tratado y ofendido,
Con tan crasa ignorancia que no vía
Que fuego para assarlo me faltaba,
Bajé los ojos tristes y bolviendo,
Del hecho arrepentido, a acariciarlo,
Muerto quedó a mis pies. Con cuio susto,
Dexándolo tendido y desangrando,
Passé aquel trago amargo y fui siguiendo
El golpe de fortuna que acababa[23]
La miserable vida que vivía,
Hasta que por gran suerte fuy llegando
Al pie de vnos peñascos lebantados,
En cuio assiento y puesto vi que estaba
Vn apazible estanque de agua fría,
Sobre cuios cristales, casi ciego,
Apenas fuy venciendo la gran furia
De la insaziable sed que me acababa,
Quando temblando, todo estremecido,
El húmido licor lancé forzado.

215	He may escape, see himself free.
	Oh human life, so feeble and frail!
	I do not think that with more hunger
	That sad woman dealt death unto her son
	Who ate him in the monstrous ruin
	Of that holy City, which, lost
220	Through its great sins, was quite destroyed,[5]
	Than came to me in this experience.
	I had a dog, then, the which at my side
	Had been for a long time and which did watch
	What times it might be that I slept at night;
225	And since hunger now threatened me
	So as to take away my life, I then
	Determined to kill him and gave two wounds,
	Both mortal, at which the poor wretch
	Fled from me away some distance.
230	I called him angrily, and, forgetful
	Of the shameful and inconsiderate deed,
	Whining in friendly sort and crouching down,
	My badly wounded friend came back to me,
	Licking the blood that he poured out.
235	And, though in pain and wounded sore,
	To please me in something if he but could,
	He also licked my hands, till they
	Were stained and well-bathed with his blood.
	I looked at him then, lord, and much ashamed
240	That I had treated him and wronged him thus,
	With such crass ignorance as not to see
	That I did lack a fire to cook his flesh,
	I lowered my sad eyes and, beginning,
	Repenting of my deed, to caress him,
245	He lay dead at my feet. And with this shock,
	Leaving him stretched out in his blood,
	I gave a bitter gulp and went to find
	That stroke of fortune which might end
	The miserable life I led,
250	Until, by great good luck, I reached
	The foot of certain lofty cliffs,
	In which place I did see there was
	A pleasant pool of cold water,
	Over whose crystal depths I, almost blind,
255	Scarcely could conquer the great fury
	Of that insatiable thirst that all but ended me
	When, trembling all over, quivering,
	I forcibly threw up the damp fluid.

21. Maganta = triste.
22. Se trata de Roma cuando fue tomada por los godos, y la descripción de Villagrá esta muy ajustada a la que trae Pero Mexía, *Silva de varia lección* I, 30. Hay una descripción muy similar, tratando de Numancia, al final mismo de *El satiricón* de Petronio.
23. Posible errata del original por "acabara."

5. Probably a reference to the Visigothic sacking of Rome since Villagrá's description is close to that found in Pero Mexía, *Silva de varia lección* I, 30.

Y estando allí algún tanto suspendido,
No libre de temor y trassudado,
A caso eché de ver que cerca estaba
Vn poco de maíz que por ventura
Alguno con descuido abía dexado.
Y a mi Padre san Diego²⁴ gracias dando,
A quien con veras siempre fuy pidiendo
Que allí me socoriesse y amparase,
Hincado de rodillas fuy cogiendo
Dos puños bien escasos, mal cumplidos.
Pues viéndome de hecho ya perdido,
Los pies hinchados, torpes, destroncados,
Y que esperanza humana no podía
En tanta desbentura socorrerme,
Con el sustento corto que sembrado
Estaba por el suelo bien tendido,
Al Real de san Iuan quise bolverme,
Más de cincuenta leguas muy bien hechas
De aquel assiento y puesto donde estaba.
Y abiendo entrado ya el silencio triste
De la obscura noche, que cargaba,
Dios que en sus grandes santos resplandeze
Y socorro por ellos nos embía,
Empezando a marchar para bolverme,
A mí llegaron tres amigos nobles,²⁵
Valientes, esforzados y animosos,
Y de todos por tales conozidos,
Que acaso y sin pensar allí llegaron
En busca de caballos que, perdidos,
Andaban codiziosos de hallarlos.
Francisco de Ledesma fue el primero
Y luego, detrás dél, Miguel Montero,
Iuan Rodríguez, el bueno, también vino,
Y como el toldo oscuro ya tendido²⁶
A todos en tinieblas nos tenía,
Allí me preguntaron que quién era.
Y luego que mi nombre yo les dixe,
Alegres todos juntos dispararon
Los prestos arcabuzes de contento.
En este mismo instante y coiuntura,
Siguiéndome, los bárbaros llegaron
Sedientos de acabarme ya la vida,
Y sintiendo la fuerza de los tiros,
Entendiendo que el campo junto estaba
En aquel mismo puesto, temerosos,

And, waiting there a little bit,
Not free from fear and sweating much,
By chance I noticed that nearby there was   260
A little corn which, by some chance,
Someone had carelessly left there.
And giving thanks to San Diego, my Father,⁶
Of whom I always had implored
That he would aid and shelter me,   265
And kneeling there I gathered up
Two scant handsful, scarcely, hardly filled.
Seeing myself in fact now lost,
My feet swollen, heavy, torn to pieces,
And that no human expectation could   270
Aid me in such a misfortune,
With that scant sustenance there sown
And well spread out upon the ground
I wished to return to San Juan, the capital,
More than some fifty lengthy leagues   275
From that place and location where I was.
And now there having come the sad silence
Of the dark night, so oppressive,
God, who in his great saints shines forth
And by them doth send aid to us,   280
Beginning on the march for the return,
Three noble friends made come to me,
Valiant and strong and spirited,
And all well-known to be such ones,
Who, by mere chance and unthinking, came there   285
In search of horses which, being lost,
They wandered with purpose of finding them.⁷
Francisco de Ledesma was the first
And then, after him, Miguel Montero;
Juan Rodríguez, the Good, did also come.   290
And as the robe of darkness, now stretched out,
Did keep us all in deep obscurity,
They there did ask me who I was.
And then, when I told them my name,
Joyful, they all together fired off   295
Their ready harquebuses with content.
At this same instant and this conjuncture
The barbarians who followed me arrived,
Thirsting to take away my life,
And, hearing the noise of the shots,   300
Believing that the camp was near,
Stricken with fear there where they stood,

24. Santiago.
25. Para la narración, en otras crónicas, de este incidente, véanse Bolton, *Spanish Exploration,* 236 y Villagrá, *Historia,* edición de Junquera, 276.
26. La oscuridad de la noche ya extendida.

6. Saint James, Santiago, patron saint of warriors.
7. For accounts of Villagrá's rescue in other chronicles, see Bolton, *Spanish Explorers,* 236, and Villagrá, *Historia,* Junquera edition, 276.

Antes que la tiniebla el Sol rasgase
Los presurosos passos rebolvieron,
Dexándome allí libre y sin peligro.
Alábente los Angeles, Dios mío,
Que vn caballo ensillado y enfrenado,
Sin qué ni para qué, acaso, trujo
Iuan Rodríguez, el grato,²⁷ por pagarme,
Por secreto juizio no entendido,
Aquel grande socorro que le hize
En otra, tal qual ésta, desbentura,
Quando atrabesado en vn caballo,
Rendido ya de hambre, le trayan,²⁸
Esperando su muerte y que acabase.
Secretos son ocultos que nos muestran
Ser todo por su sacrosanta mano
Socorrido, amparado y remediado.
Truxeron, demás desto, los amigos,
En muy grande abundancia, todo aquello
Para matar la hambre necessario,
Y sacando del pedernal fogoso
Vivas centellas, luego los pegaron
A la yesca y con paja que encendieron,
Desgajando los tres con mucha priessa
De los antiguos árboles las ramas,
Vn grande fuego juntos lebantaron,
A cuia lumbre luego fue rendida
La miserable hambre que llevaba.
Y contándoles todos mis trabajos,
Otro día siguiente luego fuimos
A donde el General con todo el campo
Estaba de nosotros apartado
Dos muy grandes jornadas, y en llegando,
Dándole larga cuenta del sucesso,
En todo, allí, se dio por bien serbido.
Y, pues, de mis trabajos he querido
Daros, como a señor, estrecha cuenta,
Suplícoos me escuchéis también aquéllos
Que sufren y padezen mis amigos
Y pobres camaradas quebrantados
Por todas estas tierras remontados.

27. Grato = agradecido.
28. Trayan = traían.

Before the sun put the shadows to flight
They did turn back their hasty steps,
305   Leaving me free there and out of peril.
May the Angels praise Thee, my God,
That a saddled and bridled horse
The which had been brought there by chance
By Juan Rodríguez, the grateful, to pay me for,
310   By secret judgment not well understood,
That great aid I had given him
In that other misfortune, like this one,
When, slung across the saddle of a horse,
They brought him in, by hunger overcome,
315   Expecting his death and that he would end.
Hidden secrets that show to us
All being by His most holy hand
Aided, sheltered, and remedied.
And, beside this, my friends had brought
320   In very great abundance all the things
Necessary to slay hunger,
And drawing from the fiery flint
Living sparks, they did strike them then
Into the tinder, and with straw that they did light,
325   The three tearing in mighty haste
The branches from some ancient trees,
Together did build up a roaring fire,
By whose flames there was then dispersed
The raging hunger that I had.
330   And telling them all my trials,
Upon the following day we went
Toward where the General, with all the camp,
Was, at a distance from ourselves
Of two long day's marches; and, arriving,
335   Giving him long account of what had chanced,
In all considered himself well served.
Since of my trials I have wished
To give to you, as lord, a brief account,
I beg that you will listen, too, to those
340   Which my friends suffer and endure,
My poor comrades, all broken down
By all these far and remote lands.

CANTO VEYNTE

DE LOS EXCESIBOS TRABAJOS QUE PADEZEN LOS
soldados de nuevos descubrimientos y de la mala correspondencia
que sus servicios tienen.

TODO el valor, alteza y excelencia
Que puede acaudalar el buen guerrero
De los gloriosos triunfos que se alcanzan

En la sangrienta guerra belicosa
Es quedar para siempre bien premiado
Por el gallardo brazo de la espada
Y por el bravo pecho valeroso
Que en padezer trabajos a tenido
Entre cien mil peligros no esperados.
Y assí, alto y heroico Rey, sabemos
Que no ay trabajo duro en la milicia
Ni tiempo en padecerle mal gastado
Si la correspondencia deste fruto
Viene a ser tal qual es razón se tenga
Con aquellos gallardos corazones
Que muy bien en las guerras os sirbieron.
Aunque para mi tengo, Rey sublime,
Que es mucho mejor suerte la de aquéllos
Que por más bien serbiros acabaron
Entre enemigas armas destrozados,
Hechos menudos quartos y pedazos,
Que no aguardar la triste suerte y paga
Que algunos destos Héroes han tenido
De sus muchos quebrantos padezidos.
Y por mostrar mejor si son soldados
Aquestos valerosos por quien digo,
Que como los estimo y reverencio
Por mucho más que hombres, más que hombres[1]
Fuera bien se encargara y que escribiera
Sus claros y altos hechos hazañosos,
Mas como inculto, bronco y mal limado,
Dellos informaré lo que supiere,
Que assí satisfaré con sólo darles
Todo aquello que valgo, alcanzo y puedo.
No trato por agora que dexaron,
Por serbiros, señor, como es justicia,
A su querida y dulze patria amada,
Padres, hermanos, deudos y parientes,
Ni que ya sus ligítimas[2] y haziendas
Están de hecho todas consumidas,

---

1. Patente errata del original por "hombre."
2. Ligítimas = legítimas, herencia obligada de derecho.

CANTO XX

Of the excessive trials suffered by the soldiers in new discoveries,
and of the poor rewards of their services.

ALL the value, the pride, the excellence
That a good warrior can store up
From all the glorious triumphs that are
    won
In bloody and bellicose war
5   Is to remain for always well repaid
For gallantry of his sword arm
And for the brave and valorous heart
Which he has shown in suffering hardships
Through a hundred thousand dangers unforeseen.
10 And so, most lofty and heroic King, we know
That there is no hard work in military life,
Nor time ill-spent enduring it,
If the requital for its fruits
Is such as should be merited
15 By those courageous, gallant hearts
Who served you very well in all the wars.
Although I, sublime King, do consider
That a much better fate is that of those
Who, better to serve you, have died,
20 Destroyed amid the hostile arms,
Cut into fragments and pieces,
Not to await the sorry fate and pay
That some of those heroes have had
For the great ills they have endured.
25 Better to show if they are true soldiers,
Those valorous ones for whom I speak,
Since I esteem and reverence them
As more than men, more than a mere man
'Twere well should set about it and write here
30 Their famous, high, and daring deeds;
But as one uncultured, rude, unpolished,
I shall relate of them what I do know,
And thus be satisfied in giving them
All I am worth, attain and can.
35 I do not now exalt the fact they left,
To serve you, lord, as is justice,
Their sweet, dear and beloved Fatherland,
Their parents, brothers, family, and kin,
Nor that their property and goods
40 Are now in fact entirely consumed,

Trocando por trabajos el descanso
Que pudieron tener sin sugetarse
Los días y las noches que se ocupan
En pesados oficios trabajosos,
Miserias y disgustos nunca vistos,
Donde veréis, señor, que se sustentan
No más que por su pico³ y fiel trabajo,
Mediante el qual adquieren todo aquello
Para passar su vida necessario,
Aventajando siempre sus personas
A la de aquel Tebano⁴ memorable
Que por no más de sólo aberle visto
Quedaron muchos cortos y afrentados
Quando en el monte Olimpo, en sus vertientes,
Vieron que quanto sobre sí traya
Eran grandiosas obras de sus manos,
Porque él abía cortado los zapatos
Y puéstolos en punto bien cosidos,
Y assí, como si fuera sastre, el sayo
Fue por sus proprias manos acabado.
Y él también la camisa abía tegido
Y de su valor mismo, punto y corte,
Salió toda cumplida y acabada.
Y los insignes libros que traía,
Qual illustre filósofo prudente,
El los abía compuesto y trabajado,
Y con esto otras muchas cosas nobles,
Dignas, por cierto, todas de estimarse.
Assí también, señor, estos varones
No traen consigo cosa que no sea
Hechura y obra de sus bellas manos.
El sayo, calzón, media y el calzado,
El jubón,⁵ cuello, capa y la camisa,
Con todas las demás cosas que alcanzan⁶
La femenil flaqueza por su aguja,
De todo dan tan diestra y buena cuenta
Como si en coser siempre, y no otra cosa,
Vbieran sus personas ocupado.
Y no ay de qué espantarnos, pues sabemos
Que fue el primer oficio que se supo
En esta vida triste, miserable.
Y con esto, ellos mismos por sus manos
Guisan bien de comer, laban y amasan,

Exchanging for hard toil the rest
They might have had without submitting to
The days and nights they occupied themselves
In heavy and laborious duties,
45 In miseries, misfortunes, such as ne'er were seen,
Where you may see, lord, they maintained themselves
By no more than their industry, hard work,
Through which they did acquire all that
Was necessary to sustain their lives,
50 Always improving their persons
After the fashion of that Theban memorable
At no more than the sight of whom
Many were affronted and displeased
When, on Mount Olympus and its fringe,
55 They saw that all he wore on his body
Was the proud work of his own hands,
For he himself had cut his shoes
And shaped them well, and sewed them, too,
And, as he had a tailor been, his cloak
60 Was made by his own hands.
And he also had wove his shirt,
And from his own efficiency the style and cut
Had all proceeded and been done.
And the famous books which he had brought there,
65 As a philosopher prudent and famed,
He had composed and worked them out,
And, with these, many other noble things,
Surely all worthy of esteem.¹
So, too, O lord, these men of yours
70 Had nothing with them which was not
The work and product of their hands.
Their cloaks, their hose, trunks, and their shoes,
Their jupons, collars, capes, and shirts,
With all the other things achieved
75 By feminine weakness with the needle,
All giving such skillful and good account,
As if in sewing always, and no other thing,
Their persons had been occupied.
Nor should we be alarmed, since it is known
80 That 'twas the first employment that was known
In this sad, miserable life.
With this, they with their own two hands
Dress victuals well to eat and wash and knead,

---

3. Pico = instrumento de trabajo.
4. La referencia es a Hipias de Elis, filósofo sofista a quien Socrates describe, casi en las mismas palabras de Villagrá, en el diálogo, "Hipias menor," atribuido a Platón, *The Collected Dialogues of Plato,* eds por E. Hamilton y H. Cairns (New York: The Bollingen Foundation, 1961), 206.
5. Jubón = prenda que viste desde los hombros a la cintura.
6. Posible errata del original por "alcanza" = consigue.

1. The reference is to Hippias of Elis, a sophist described by Socrates, in language very similar to that employed by Villagrá, in the dialogue "Lesser Hippias," attributed to Plato in *The Collected Dialogues of Plato,* ed. E. Hamilton and H. Cairns (New York: The Bollingen Foundation, 1961), 206.

Y, en fin, toda la vida siempre buscan
Desde la sal hasta la leña y agua
Si gusto han de tener en la comida.
Ellos rompen la tierra y la cultivan
Como diestros, famosos, labradores,
Y como hospitaleros siempre curan
Las más enfermedades con que vienen
Sus pobres camaradas quebrantados
De los muchos trabajos que han sufrido.
Y cosa alguna aquesto les impide
Para que todo el año no los hallen,
A qualquier hora de la noche y día,
Tan cubiertos de hierro y fino azero
Como si fueran hechos y amasados
De poderoso bronce bien fornido,
Trabajo que por mucho menos tiempo,
Quando diamantes todos se mostraran,
Los vbiera deshecho y acabado,
Quanto más a la mísera flaqueza
Del que de carne y güesso está compuesto.
Viven y passan casi todo el tiempo
Como si fueran brutos por el campo,
Sugetos al rigor del Sol ardiente,
Al agua, al viento, desnudez y frío,
Hambre, sed, molimientos y cansancio,
Cuio lecho no es más que el duro suelo,
Adonde muchas vezes amanecen
En blanca nieve todos enterrados.
Passan crueles y grandes aguazeros
Sin poderse albergar en parte alguna,
Y sécanse en las carnes los vestidos.
Sucédeles que llevan en costales
El agua para sólo su sustento,
Algunas vezes hecha toda nieve,
Carámbano, las más, empedernido.⁷
Sufren todos eladas de manera
Que ya por nuestras culpas hemos visto
Rendir el alma y vida todo junto
Al gran rigor del encogido tiempo.⁸
No ay aguas tan caudales por los Ríos
Que no los passen, naden y atrabiessen,
Ni páramos ni fieras ni vallados
Que a puros palmos todo no lo midan.⁹
No ay bárbara nación que no descubran
Ni gran dificultad que no acometan,
Y no cuidan jamás estos varones
De maestros y oficiales para cosas

And, finally, always seek their whole living
85 From salt on to wood and water
If they are to have pleasure in eating.
They break the earth, cultivate it
Like famed and skilled laborers,
And as hospitalers they always cure
90 Most of the sicknesses that come
To their poor, worn-out companions.
Nor does anything prevent them
From being found at any time of year,
At any hour of night or day,
95 As covered in iron and tempered steel
As though they were all made, molded,
Of powerful and robust bronze,
A trial which in a short time,
Though all had been of adamant,
100 Would have destroyed and ended them,
And all the more the miserable feebleness
Of what is made of flesh and bone.
They live and pass almost all their time
Out in the field as though they were brute beasts,
105 Subjected to the rigor of the burning sun,
Of water, wind, of nakedness and cold,
Of hunger, thirst, weariness, and fatigue,
Their bed being no more than rugged ground,
Where many times they do awaken
110 All buried in white snow.
They pass through many heavy rains,
Being unable to shelter anywhere,
And their clothes dry upon their flesh.
It often happens that they must take in bags
115 The only water for their sustenance,
Sometimes all frozen into snow,
More often turned to stony icicles.
All are frozen and to such extent
That, for our sins, we have already seen
120 Some give up life and soul at once
To the great rigor of this freezing weather.
There are no waters so high in the streams
That they do not pass, swim, and cross o'er,
Nor high plains, animals, valleys,
125 They do not measure inch by inch.
There is no barbarous nation they discover not,
Nor great difficulty they do not meet,
Nor do these men ever need go
To craftsmen or artificers for things
130 That may be necessary for their military work.

7. Empedernido = endurecido.
8. Encogido tiempo = tiempo de frío.
9. Se dice "medir a palmos" cuando se explora algo detalladamente.

Al militar oficio necessarias.
Ellos cortan las armas y las hazen
Para qualquier caballo bien seguras.
Saben aderezar sus arcabuzes
Y echarles lindas cajas[10] por extremo.
Remallan bien sus cotas y escarcelas
Y pintan[11] sus zeladas de manera
Que quedan para siempre provechosas.
Y como diestros cirujanos curan
Heridas peligrosas, penetrantes,
Y son también boníssimos barberos.[12]
Y quando es menester también componen
De la gineta y brida las dos sillas.[13]
El aluzitar[14] jamás les haze falta,
Porque ellos hierran todos sus caballos,
También los sangran, cargan y los curan,
Domándolos de potros con destreza,
Y por ser buenos hombres de a caballo,
En ellos hazen grandes maravillas.
Y en las sangrientas lides y contiendas
Quál o quál[15] ha dexado de mostrarse
Ser hombre de valor y grande esfuerzo;
Y aquesto muchas vezes sustentados
De raízes incultas, desabridas,
De hierbas y semillas nunca vsadas,
Caballos, perros y otros animales
Inmundos y asquerosos a los hombres.
Y por nevados riscos y quebradas,
Qual suelen los arados que, arrastrados,
Rompiendo van la tierra, deshaziendo
Las azeradas rejas que, enterradas,
Haziendo van sus sulcos prolongados,
Assí los Españoles valerosos,
A colas de caballos arrastrados
Por no morir, de hecho, entre las nieves,
Muchos assí las vidas escaparon,
Temerarias hazañas emprendiendo
Y hechos hazañosos acabando,
Qual cantaré, señor, si Dios me dexa
Ver la segunda parte a luz echada.[16]

10. Cajas = piezas de madera en que se aseguran el cañón y la llave.

11. Pintan = figuradamente, construyen; aunque es posible que, también figuradamente, se refiera Villagrá a que las untaran para impedir que enmoheciesen.

12. Recuérdese que los barberos eran los sangradores y dentistas de aquel tiempo.

13. Los dos tipos de silla de montar, gineta y brida.

14. No hemos hallado la voz, pero el contexto sugiere "herrador," que entonces hacía también las veces de veterinario.

15. Quál o quál = cuál o cuál, qué pocos.

16. Esta segunda parte anunciada nunca se llevó a cabo.

They cut harnesses and do make them up,
And safe enough for any horse.
They know how to repair their harquebuses
And make them stocks extremely beautiful.
135 They mend well their corselets and coats of mail,
And paint[2] their sallets in such sort
That they are ever afterward useful.
And, like to skillful surgeons, they do cure
Most dangerous and penetrating wounds,
140 And are also most excellent barbers.[3]
And, when 'tis necessary, too,
They mend their two types of saddles.
They never have need of a veterinarian
As they all shoe their mounts themselves,
145 And also bleed, physic, and cure them,
Breaking them in as colts with mighty skill
And, being excellent horsemen,
When mounted they perform many marvels.
And in the bloody battles and contests
150 Hardly a single one has failed to show
That he is a courageous man and of great zeal;
And this though many times they are sustained
By wild and bitter roots or else
By herbs and seeds unaccustomed,
155 By horses, dogs, and other animals
Filthy and repugnant to man.
And over snowy crags, ravines,
Like to plows, which, when dragged along,
Parting the earth, erode away
160 The steel ploughshares that, being buried,
Go turning up long, straight furrows,
These valorous Spaniards of yours,
Pulled on by the tails of horses
That they might not die there among the snows,
165 Many thus escaped with their lives,
Undertaking most risky feats
And doing many risky deeds,
Which I shall sing, lord, if God permits me
To see the Second Part put into print,[4]
170 Where you shall see, great king, great prodigies

2. The verb Villagrá employs, *pintan*, could both mean that they made their own sallets or that they oiled them against rust.

3. It must be remembered that, at the time, surgeons performed the functions of bleeders and dentists and were often barbers as well.

4. Villagrá's second part, if written, was never published.

Donde veréis, gran Rey, prodigios grandes
De tierras y naciones nunca vistas,
Trabajos y aventuras no contadas,
Impressas inauditas y desdichas
Que a fuerza de fortuna y malos hados   175
También nos persiguieron y acosaron.
Que desto mostraron inmensas pruebas,
Demás de los varones que hemos dicho,
Los Capitanes Vaca y Iuan Martínez,
Rascón y Iuan Rangel y Iuan de Ortega,   180
Gimón[17] García, Ortiz y Iuan Benítez,
El Capitán Donís y Iuan Fernández,
Guevara, Luzio y Alvaro García,
Giménez, Iuan Ruyz, Sosa, Morales,
También Pedro Rodríguez y otros bravos,   185
Valientes y esforzados caballeros
Que bien en paz y guerra trabajaron.
Sin los heroicos y altos Comissarios,
El Padre fray Francisco de Velasco,
Francisco de Escobar, con Escalona,   190
Fray Alonso Peinado, cuias fuerzas
En cultivar la viña bien mostraron
Ser hijos del Seráfico Francisco,
Pues más de siete mil abemos visto
Que tienen bautizados por sus manos.[18]   195
Mas qué importa, Rey inmenso y justo,
Si ya los veo a todos destroncados,
Estropeados, cansados y tullidos,
Bueltos todos en pobres hospitales
De males y dolencias incurables,   200
Sin género de amparo ni remedio,
En cuio gran conflicto miserable
Si buelven para sus antiguas casas
Sucede, a bien librar,[19] por todos ellos,
Lo mismo que de Vlixes valeroso,   205
Que después de servicios tan honrrados
Escapó de la guerra de manera
Que no fue de ninguno de su casa
Mas que de sólo el perro conozido,
Según bolvió de viejo y destrozado.[20]   210
¡O flor de jubentud, o verdes años,
Qué presto la belleza se marchita!
Notad qual buelven estos esforzados
Que ya no los conozen en sus casas,
Rotos, pobres, cansados y afligidos,   215

Of lands and nations never seen,
Toils and adventures never told,
Unheard-of enterprises, misfortunes
That through bad weather and ill fate
Also pursued and accosted us.
Of which enormous proofs are shown,
Beside the men that we have spoken of,
In those captains Vaca and Juan Martínez,
Rascón and Juan Rangel and Juan de Ortega,
Simón García, Ortiz, and Juan Benítez,
Captain Donís and Juan Fernández,
Guevara, Luzio, and Alvaro García,
Giménez, Juan Ruiz, Sosa, Morales,
Also Pedro Rodríguez and other brave men,
Valiant and energetic cavaliers,
Who did their work right well in peace or war.
Nor do I omit the hero Commissaries,
Father Fray Francisco de Velasco,
Francisco de Escobar and Escalona,
Fray Alonso Peinado, whose zeal
In cultivating the vineyard shows well
That they were sons of seraphic Francis,
For more than seven thousand did we see
Who were baptized by their hands.
But what is this worth, immense and just King,
If now I see them all destroyed,
Crippled, worn out, sorely wounded,
All now become poor hospitals
With ills and sicknesses incurable,[5]
With no sort of protection or refuge.
In which miserable and great conflict,
If they return unto their former homes,
It occurs, at best, to all of them
The same as with Ulysses valorous,
Who, after services so honorable,
Returned from war in such a sort
That there was no one in his house
Except his dog alone that might know him,
Since he was so old and worn out.[6]
O flower of youth, o verdant years,
How soon your beauty withers up!
Note how these gallant men return
So they are unknown in their homes,
Broken and poor, worn out and afflicted,
Old, sick, and sad, in misery.

17. Errata del original por "Simón."
18. Está claro que Villagrá se mantuvo al tanto de los
acontecimientos de Nuevo México después de acabada su presencia allí.
19. A bien librar = en el mejor de los casos.
20. Se refiere al final de *La odisea* de Homero.

5. It is clear that Villagrá, probably through his connections with
the Oñate family, was knowledgeable about the fate of many of the
members of the expedition in the years after it ended. It is true, of
course, that, with the poem, Villagrá was making a case for his own
compensation.
6. The reference is to the end of the *Odyssey.*

Viejos, enfermos, tristes, miserables.
Y si por vltimo y postrer remedio
Quieren, señor, valerse y socorrerse
De vna migaja de los muchos panes
Que con tan liberal y franca mano
Mandáis que se les dé sin escaseza,
No son más ellos que los otros pobres,
Hijos perdidos, nietos y viznietos
De aquellos esforzados que os sirbieron
Y aqueste nuevo mundo conquistaron,
Que a todos falta la segunda tabla²¹
Que despúes del naufragio se pretende.
Llamo segunda tabla, Rey insigne,
A los Gobernadores y Virreyes,
Que ay algunos, algunos, señor, digo,
Que para sólo aber de proponerles
Su mísera demanda y causa justa
Primero es fuerza sufran y padezcan
Vna eternidad de años arrimados
Por aquellas paredes de palacio,
Muertos de hambre, cansados y afligidos,
Adorando a los pajes y porteros,
Sirvientes y oficiales de su casa
Por ver si por aquí tendrán entrada
Para su larga pretensión perdida.
Y si caso²² por gran ventura alcanzan
A ver el lugar del *santa santorum,*
Si es que aquel puesto assí puede llamarse,
A donde está la magestad intacta,
Que, qual si fuera aquella soberana
Que no puede ser vista de ninguno
Que tenga alguna mancha o cosa fea,²³
Porque a de ser más limpio, puro y bello
Que el ampo de la nieve no tocada,
Assí, no puede ser que nadie alcance
A ver grandeza y celestial²⁴ tan alta
Si no es gente muy limpia y olorosa,
Almidonada, rica y bien luzida,
No con algunas manchas de pobreza,
Necessidad, trabajo y desbentura,
Que éstos, como incapazes²⁵ de su vista,
Inmundos, pobres, viles y leprosos,
No es possible merescan bien tan grande.
Sabe el inmenso Dios, Rey poderoso,

And if, for a last remedy,
They wish, lord, to help and aid themselves
By a crumb from the many loaves
Which, with a free and liberal hand,
You order they be given without stint,
They are held no more than the other poor,
The ruined sons, grandsons, and great-grandsons
Of those strong men who have served you
And conquered this new-found world,
For all do lack that second board⁷
Which after shipwreck may be sought.
I call, O famous King, the second board
The Governors and the Viceroys,
For there are some, some, lord, I say,
That just in order to present to them
One's cry of misery and most just cause,
'Tis first needed one suffer and endure
Eternity of years leaning
Against the walls of the palace,
Dying of hunger, tired and worn out,
Adoring pages and porters,
Servants and household officers,
To see if through them they may gain entry
For their large claims, now lost.
And if by great good fortune they attain
To see the place of that sancta sanctorum,
If that place may well be called so,
Where complete majesty resides,
Which, as though it were that, godlike,
Which cannot be seen by any unfortunate
Who may have any stain or ugly thing
Since it must be more clean and pure and beautiful
Than a snowflake of untouched snow,
So 'tis impossible that anyone attain
To see such high, celestial, mightiness
Except it be some very clean, sweet-smelling folk,
Well-starched and rich and very brilliant
And not with any stain of poverty,
Necessity or toil and misfortune,
For these, as most unworthy of his sight,
Filthy, poor, vile, and leprous,
'Tis not possible they deserve so great a good.
The high God knows, O powerful King,
That I have wished with heart and soul

Line numbers: 220, 225, 230, 235, 240, 245, 250, 255

---

21. Esta segunda tabla es la que requiere el náufrago para salvarse; la primera habiendo sido el barco desaparecido.
22. Caso = acaso.
23. Se refiere a Dios.
24. Celestial = perfección. Es posible, asimismo, que la "y" sea errata.
25. Incapazes = incapaces, sin mérito, indignos.

7. The second board or plank was that which saved one after shipwreck. It is understood that the first was the ship itself.

Que con corazón y alma he desseado
Veros, señor, Virrey de nueva España,
Por no más de que viéssedeys el cómo
Se haze un puro²⁶ hombre dios del suelo.
Aquél que está en el Cielo lo remedie
Y aliente los balidos y gemidos
De tantos miserables como claman.
Porque aunque es cierto, y todos lo sabemos,
Que han gobernado muchos como buenos
Y que oy el Reyno todo se gobierna
De manera que ya ninguno ignora
Que a vozes por las casas de palacio
Buscan los negociantes²⁷ porque tengan
Sus causas con justicia buen despacho,
Cosa que jamás nunca abemos visto,
Dexando aqueste bien tan grande en vando,
Algunos otros vemos que han passado,
Sin hazer cuenta de los muchos perros,²⁸
Que, en púlpitos haziéndose pedazos
A muy grandes ladridos y amenazas,
No hizieron más impressión en ellos
Que si fueran de bronze o duro azero.
Siete años continuos me detuve
En vuestra illustre y lebantada corte
Y no vi pobre capa ni mendigo
Que con facilidad no se llegase
A vuestro caro Padre y señor nuestro
A contalle sus cuitas y fatigas
Con esperanza cierta y verdadera
De bellas²⁹ remediadas y amparadas.
Dios, por quien es, os tenga de su mano
Y conserve el illustre y alto nombre
Que por acá se suena y se publica
De que soys muy gran Padre de soldados,
Que yo, como el menor de todos ellos
Y que a señor y Padre me querello,
He querido contaros los trabajos
Que por acá se sufren y padezen.³⁰
Que como bien sabéys, Rey poderoso,
No ay hombre que después de aber sufrido
Fatigas y miserias tan pesadas

260 To see you as the Viceroy of New Spain,
For no more than that you might observe how
A mere man may be made a god on earth.⁸
May He who is in Heaven better it
And aid the moaning and the groans
265 Of all those miserable who cry.
For though 'tis certain, and though we all know,
That many have ruled as good men
And that the whole kingdom is governed now
In such a way that no one fails to know
270 That there before the palace with loud yells
They seek the claimants that they may
Secure swiftness and justice for their pleas,
A thing we ne'er before have seen,
Leaving aside that good so great,
275 We see others who have gone on,
Not unlike so many dogs in church,⁹
That those from the pulpits preaching fiercely,
With barkings terrific and threats,
Did make no more impression upon them
280 Than if they were of bronze or tempered steel.
Seven years continuous was I
In your illustrious and lofty court
And saw no poor gentleman or beggar
That did not come, and with great ease,
285 To your beloved father and our lord
To tell him of his troubles and fatigues
With certain and most genuine hope
Of handsome remedy and sheltering.
May God, for who He is, keep you in hand
290 And keep the famous, elevated name
That here is sounded and set forth
That you are to your soldiers a father,
For I, as the least of them all,
And who complain to my father and lord,
295 Have wished to tell you of the sufferings
That hereabouts¹⁰ are felt and are endured.
That as you well know, powerful King,
There is no man who, after suffering
Fatigues and miseries so deep,
300 Does not wish some pay, recompense,

---

26. Puro = mero.
27. Negociantes = los que acuden con asuntos.
28. La imagen del perro en la iglesia, como algo fuera de lugar y que, lógicamente, nada aprende, se la aplica Villagrá a algunos virreyes y políticos que, como tales, nada aprenden del mensaje de caridad de la religión.
29. Bellas = verlas.
30. Aunque Villagrá escribe como si lo hiciera desde el Nuevo Mundo, no hay otros indicios de que estuviera, al escribir su obra, efectivamente allá.

8. Although softened immediately after, as it might refer to the then viceroy of New Spain, this Villagrá attack on the institution itself is very strong.
9. The image of the dog in church, of heedlessness, is a common one in the Spanish world.
10. Although Villagrá seems to suggest that he is in Mexico as he writes this part of his poem, there is no proof that he was not already in Spain.

No quiera alguna paga y recompensa
De sus muchos serbicios y trabajos,
Por cuio memorable sufrimiento,
Las manos puestas,[31] pido y os suplico
Que aya memoria destos desdichados
Cuio valor heroico, lebantado,
Merece, clementíssimo Monarca,
Perpetua gloria y triunfo esclarecido
Que lebante la alteza y excelencia
De sus gallardos pechos esforzados.
Y por no cansar más, señor, ya he dicho,[32]
Y assí será razón que yo me buelva
Al hilo de la historia que llevaba.[33]
Llegó el Sargento alegre y muy contento
De los grandes ganados descubiertos
En los llanos de Zíbola[34] famosos,
Y, suspendiendo vn tanto los trabajos,
Quedando en el Real por buen gobierno,
Sin detenerse luego fue saliendo
El buen Maese de campo con desseo
De dar en breve alcance, si pudiesse,
A vuestro General, que ya cansado
Estaba de esperarle muchos días.
Pues yendo assí marchando su derrota
Llegó a la fuerza de Acoma famosa,
Donde Zutacapán tratado abía
Con algunos del pueblo belicosos
Que por señor y Rey de aquella fuerza
Tratasen de secreto le nombrasen
Entre los más amigos que pudiessen,
Ofreciendo por esto les daría
Honrras y libertades preminentes.
Para cuio principio concertaron
Que la mano Zutacapán tomase
En defender la patria y libertarla
De manos de Españoles, y con esto
Sería fácil cosa que le diessen
La pretensión segura y sin rezelo,
Que nadie se mostrase su contrario,
Pues lebantarle todos por cabeza
Era la libertad de todo el pueblo.

For his much serving and his toil.
For these memorable, great sufferings,
With my hands joined, I beg and plead that you
May hold in memory these hapless ones
305 Whose lofty, heroic valor
Deserves, most clement of Monarchs,
Perpetual glory and noble triumph
To show the loftiness and excellence
Of their gallant and noble hearts.[11]
310 And not to tire you more, lord, I have done,
And so 'tis right I should return
To the thread of the story that I told.
The Sergeant came, joyous and well content,
From those great herds he had discovered
315 Upon the famous plains of Zíbola,[12]
And, leaving off his toiling for a while,
Remaining at the capital to govern well,
Immediately there left, without delay,
The good Army Master, desiring
320 To quickly reach, if so he might,
Your General, who was tired
Of waiting for him many days.
Well, marching thus upon his route
He reached the famous fort of Acoma,
325 Where Zutacapán had essayed
With some of the warlike people
That as the lord and king of that fortress
He be in secret named by them
Among as many friends as they could gain,
330 Offering for this to give them
Honors and liberties preeminent.
To begin this they had agreed
Zutacapán should take the chief hand
In defending the fatherland and freeing it
335 From the hands of the Spaniards, and with this
'Twould be an easy thing they grant to him
His wish, secure and without suspicion,
That no one show himself an opponent,
Since for all to make him the head
340 Was liberty for all the folk.
With this, then, they gathered round them

31. Las manos puestas = con humildad.
32. He dicho = he terminado.
33. Estos más de trescientos versos, dedicados a defender los méritos de los conquistadores originales y sus familias criollas frente a los poderosos llegados después de la península, refleja, en la épica de la época (*El peregrino indiano* XV y Francisco de Terrazas, *Nuevo mundo y conquista* XV) un conflicto que, con los años, pasaría, de semilla, a árbol de independencia.
34. Se le daba este nombre, por extensión, a toda la zona identificada con las siete ciudades de Zíbola reportadas por Cabeza de Vaca.

11. These more than three hundred verses dedicated to defending the grievances of the old settlers in the face of the always recently arrived viceroys and their hangers-on is found in much of the New World epic. See, for example, *El peregrino indiano* XV, and Francisco de Terraza's *Nuevo Mundo y conquista* XV.
12. The name of Zíbola (Cíbola) was given, by extension, to all the area of the "seven cities of Zíbola" reported by Cabeza de Vaca.

Con esto, luego a una se juntaron
Todos los más amigos que pudieron,
Donde el bárbaro a todos les propuso
Que en ninguna manera permitiessen
Que gente advenediza y forastera
Los pies pusiesse dentro de aquel fuerte,
Y más para pedirles bastimentos,
Pues nunca jamás ánima viviente
Tal les abía pedido ni sacado,
Y que aunque los Castillas pereciessen
Y muertos de hambre todos acabasen,
Era razón que todos por las armas
Aquel partido juntos defendiessen.
Otompo y Meco luego concedieron,
Que fueron los del trato y del secreto,
Con lo que aquel traidor allí dezía,
A Mulco³⁵ y otros pocos sediciosos,
Amigos de rebueltas y alborotos,
Que aquéstos nunca faltan, porque es tanta
La braveza del hombre miserable
Que si falta quien sople y lo rebuelva
El mismo se rebuelve y alborota,
Abrasa, enciende, quema y se destruie.
Y esta desdicha siempre la notamos
Después de aquella culpa lamentable
Que a todos nos deshizo y descompuso,³⁶
Y assí el mayor contrario que tenemos
Es a nosotros mismos, porque somos
Los que solos podemos derribarnos,
Sin que las fuerzas del infierno juntas
Basten, si no queremos, a rendirnos,
Porque las mismas fuerzas que alcanzamos
Para emprender el mal que cometemos
Aquesas mismas siempre nos assientan³⁷
Para emprender el bien si le queremos.
Y assí nadie es tan torpe que no sabe
El premio que por sólo el bien alcanza
Y el mal que por la culpa se merece.
Y assí, por esta causa temerosos,
Todos aquestos bárbaros a vna,
Por ser menos culpados, acordaron
Que, pues allí faltaba la más gente,
Que todos los del pueblo se juntasen,
Cosecha propria de ánimos doblados³⁸
Cubrir siempre con capa de inocentes

All of their friends, the most they could,
Where the barbarian proposed to them
That they should in no way permit
That foreigners and strange people   345
Should set a foot inside that fort,
Especially to ask provisions,
For never had a living soul
Asked or obtained such thing from them,
And though the Castilians perished   350
And dead from hunger should all end,
'Twas but reason that by their arms
All should defend that policy.
Otompo and Meco then did agree,
Who were those of the plan and the secret,   355
With all that traitor had said there,
Amulco and a few seditious more,
Friends of revolt and of uproar,
For such are never lacking, so great is
The brazenness of miserable man   360
That if there's none to blow and stir things up,
He will revolt and agitate himself,
Provoke, glow, burn, and be destroyed.
And this misfortune we do note always
After that lamentable fault   365
That destroyed and overturned us all,¹³
And so the greatest enemy we have
Is we ourselves, because we are
The only ones can overturn ourselves,
And all the joint forces of hell   370
Were not enough, did we not wish to yield,
Because the same forces we use
To undertake the evil we commit,
Those very same, are always at our call
To undertake the good, if we wish it.   375
So there is none so wicked not to know
The prize that is for good alone
And the evil that is deserved by wrong.
And so, for this reason fearing,
All those barbarians at one,   380
To be less blamable, agreed
That, since most of the people were not there,
They should assemble all of the pueblo,
A proper process for deceitful minds
To cover with the cape of innocence   385
The huge gravity of their sins.

35. Errata del original por "Amulco."
36. Se refiere al pecado original.
37. Nos assientan = nos asientan, sirven de base. Posible errata del original por "asisten."
38. Acción propia de ánimos engañosos.

13. The reference is to man's original fall from grace.

La mucha gravedad de sus delictos.
Y assí, bien disfrazados y cubiertos,
A todo el pueblo junto congregaron,
Donde luego veréis lo que trataron.

And so, well-disguised and covered,
They called together the whole town,
Where you shall soon see what they said.

390

CANTO VEYNTE Y VNO

*COMO ZVTACAPAN HIZO IVNTA DE LOS INDIOS
ACOMESES y discordia que entre ellos vbo, y de la trayción
que fabricaron.*

O gloria humana, en cuia instable cumbre
La presunción hinchada y vil soberbia
Quiere siempre subirse y assentarse!
¿Dime, soberbia infame, cómo ygualas
El poderoso cetro y Real corona
Con vn tan bajo bárbaro perdido,
De bárbara y vil bárbaro engendrado?
¿Di, qué tiene que ver el alto trono
Con bárbara canalla y behetría?
¡O ciega vanidad, o vana pompa,
De altos, medianos, vajos y abatidos
Sin distinción, razón ni cuenta alguna
Ygualmente buscada y pretendida!
Dígalo aqueste bárbaro furioso,
De tan humilde sangre produzido,
Si como Luzbel quiere lebantarse
Y el gobierno de todo atribuirse.
Y assí, sin disistirse de su intento,
Ordenó que a consejo se juntasen,
Y juntos todos dentro de una plaza,
Como la cruel soberbia, desmedida,
Continuamente siempre se adelanta,
Sin dilatarlo, luego en pie se puso,
En sí todo encendido y abrasado,
Y tendiendo la vista por el pueblo,
Desbergonzado, libre y desembuelto,
Assí tomó la mano[1] y fue diziendo:
"Varones esforzados y valientes,
Los postreros trabajos y peligros
Dan franca entrada y campo bien abierto
Para que cada qual aquello diga
Que más le duele, aprieta y le lastima.
Decid, ¿quál más infamia y vil afrenta
Puede venir por toda aquesta fuerza
Que permitir tan dura servidumbre
Como es dar de comer a forasteros,
Siendo, como ellos, todos libertados?[2]
Yo juro por los dioses todos juntos
Y por quien vidas todos alcanzamos
Que no ha de quedar hombre en esta tierra
Que tal bageza aya imaginado."

1. Tomó la mano = comenzó a discurrir.
2. Libertados = libres.

CANTO XXI

*How Zutacapán called an assembly of the Acoma Indians
and the discord there was among them, and of the treason
they made.*

OH human glory, to whose peak
Swollen pretension and vile pride
Doth always wish to mount and to attain!
Tell me, infamous pride, how do you square
5 The powerful scepter and the Royal crown
With such a base, ruined barbarian,
Begotten of other vile barbarians?
Say what the lofty throne may have to do
With barbarous riffraff and confusion?
10 Oh blind conceit, oh empty pomp,
By high and middle, low and crestfallen,
Without distinction, reason, reckoning,
Sought equally and so solicited!
Let that furious barbarian say,
15 Brought forth from such a humble strain,
Who, like to Lucifer, did wish to rise
And to obtain all government.
So, not leaving off his intention,
He ordered all should be in council joined,
20 And, all being joined in a plaza,
As such cruel, unmeasured haughtiness
Continually, always erupts,
Not hesitating, he did then stand up,
Burning and glowing in himself,
25 And, gazing out over the folk,
All unashamed, bold, and brazen,
Thus he began and thus he spoke:
"Ye valiant and gallant men,
The last of our trials and our dangers
30 Give a free entry, leave an open field,
For each man to declare the thing
That pains, presses, and hurts him most.
Say what more infamous and vile affront
Can come upon all of this fort
35 Than to permit so harsh a servitude
As giving food to strangers is,
We all being as free as they?
I swear by all the gods at once,
From whom we all receive our lives,
40 There cannot be a man on earth
Who would imagine such baseness."

Y viendo que las armas embrazaban,[3]
Sin dexarle acabar, salió diziendo
Su hijo Zutancalpo, demudado,
A su Padre mirando con enojo:
"El más seguro bien que el hombre alcanza
Es que quiera rendirse a todo aquello
Que a la razón va bien encaminado.
No soy de parecer que a los Castillas
Enemistad ninguna se les muestre,
Porque es temeridad hazer agravio
A quien nunca jamás nos a ofendido.
Tenerlos por amigos, con recato,
Es más sano consejo y sin peligro.
Lo demás es patente desatino,
Y para no ser todos imputados
Digo que la obediencia les guardemos,
Pues ya la abemos todos professado.
Y pues la ocasión freno nos permite,
Reprímase la cólera indiscreta,
Que la paz es el punto más discreto
Que puede remediar el mal que aguarda
Aquél que está en peligro de sufrirle."
Y, con esto, cesó el noble joben,
Y luego comenzó vn rumor confusso
De toda aquella gente congregada.
Y aprobando por bueno lo que dixo,
Nunca passó palabra por crugía[4]
Más respetada, libre y más essenta,[5]
Ni más obedecida ni acabada,[6]
Que aquel acuerdo expresso, porque luego,
Iuntas,[7] obedecieron y dejaron
Las poderosas armas lebantadas.
En esto, el viejo Chumpo, rezeloso
De que la paz y tregua se rompiesse,
Cargado de vejez y de trabajos,
Con palabras discretas y seberas
La fatigada voz alzó, diziendo:
"Mirad, mis hijos, que el consejo es sano
Y es quien alcanza siempre la victoria
En peligrosas guerras conozidas.
Y pues que Zutancalpo, en verdes años,
Os a ya dicho aquello que os combiene,
Pues vemos que el morir no es más que vn soplo
Y en bien morir consiste nuestra gloria,

Seeing that they were taking arms,
Not letting him finish, there then spoke out
His son Zutancalpo, enraged
And gazing at his father angrily:
"The surest good that man can grasp
Is to be willing to give in to all
That may seem well on reason's road.
It is not my opinion we should show
Any enmity to these Castilians,
For it is rashness to insult
One who has never injured you.
To keep them carefully as friends
Is more sane counsel and less dangerous.
The other course is patent foolishness
And, not to be accused of this,
I counsel that we keep obedience
Since we have all professed the same.
And, since occasion gives us rein,
That we repress indiscreet wrath,
For peace is the most discreet course
That can ward off the evil expected
From him who is in danger of its fall."
With this the noble youth did cease,
And a confused murmur commenced
From all those people gathered there.
And, approving his words as good,
Never did word run through gauntlet
More respected, more free, or more exempt,
Nor more obeyed nor carried out
Than that accord expressed, for then
They all obeyed and did lay down
The powerful arms they took up.
At this, old Chumpo, fearful lest
The peace and truce should be broken,
Burdened with age and with trials,
With words discreet and severe, too,
Raised up his tired voice, saying:
"Behold, my children, the advice is good,
And 'tis what always gains the victory
In perilous wars we have known.
And since Zutancalpo, in his young years,
Has told already what is best for you,
Since we see dying is no more than an instant,
And our glory consists in dying well,

45

50

55

60

65

70

75

80

85

---

3. Embrazaban = abrazaban.
4. Por crugía = entre personal mal dispuesto. El castigo en galeras consistía en pasear la crugía entre golpes.
5. Siguiendo la imagen de castigo en galeras, indica que pasó exenta, "essenta," de ataque.
6. Posible errata del original por "acatada."
7. Iuntas parece modificar "armas."

Para morir buen tiempo se procure,
Sazón y coiuntura bien mirada,
Y escúsese tan grande inconveniente
Como es tratar con furia y movimiento
Cosas tan graves, grandes y pesadas
Como éstas que tenemos entre manos."
Aquí bolaron luego las palabras
Y torpes fanfarronas amenazas
De aquellos indiscretos conjurados,
Llamando al viejo Chumpo de atreguado,[8]
Caduco, infame, loco y hechizero.
Oyendo aquesto, todo embravecido
Zutacapán arremetió furioso,
Poniendo al pobre viejo en tal aprieto
Que si Cotumbo presto no repara
La fuerza de la maza que bajaba,
La espalda toda entera le derriba.
Vístose,[9] pues, cargado con palabras,
Que le dixo también, de grande afrenta,
Qual si sobre él valientes y altos montes
Se vbieran juntos puesto y assentado,
Assí se echó de ver su sentimiento.
Mas qual si fuera, él mismo, centro y vassa
Para llevar vn peso tan pesado,
Disimulose todo quanto pudo,
Sufriendo el corage concebido
Y dando a la templanza larga rienda.
Assi compuesto, habló con todo el pueblo:
"Nunca jamás me vi tan inclinado
A satisfazer mi honrra ya difunta
Qual oy lo estoy con tanta desbergüenza
Como conmigo veys que se ha tenido,
Y si aquel jubenil ardor tuviera
Que en mi passada edad tener solía,
Que es en que aqueste vil traidor estriba,[10]
Ya de su vana presunción tuviera
La enmienda y el castigo merecido.
Mas ¿qué puedo hazer en mi descargo
Si ya de tanta edad estoy cargado
Y la vejez a más andar me aflige?
Aquesta afrenta no es a mi persona,
A vosotros se ha hecho por ser hijos
De aquéllos cuios padres yo he criado."
Y saltando enmedio de la plaza,
Qual serpentín[11] famoso que cargado
Está de fina pólvora, suspenso

A proper time to die let us achieve,
A season and occasion well chosen,
And forego such great inconvenience
As talking furiously and movingly
90 Of things so great, grave, and weighty
As these we now have neath our hands."
Here, now, there flew about the words
And wicked and swaggering threats
Of those foolish conspirators,
95 Calling old Chumpo one deranged,
Senile, infamous, crazy, a wizard.
Hearing this, and being all enraged,
Zutacapán, furious, attacked,
Putting the old man in such peril
100 That, had Cotumbo not quickly detained
The force of the mace that he swung,
He would have crushed his whole back in.
Seeing himself, then, charged with words
Of great insult that he said, too,
105 As if upon him mountains high and valiant
Then had all fallen and been cast,
He did allow his feelings to be seen.
But as though he were center and the base
To bear up such a heavy weight,
110 He did dissimulate all that he could,
Bearing the anger poured on him
And giving a free reign to temperance.
Being thus composed, he spoke to all the folk:
"Never have I seen myself so inclined
115 To satisfy my honor, now gone by,
As I am this day at such impudence
As you have seen was shown to me,
And if I had the juvenile ardor
That in my past age I did have,
120 Which is what this vile traitor counts upon,
His vain presumption would already have received
Its correction and deserved punishment.
But what can I do to avenge myself
If I am so burdened with age
125 And old age in its course afflicts me?
This insult is not made to my person,
But made to you, being children
Of those whose fathers I brought up."
Leaping, then, to the middle of the square,
130 Like a famous musket which is
Full charged with fine powder, waiting,

8. Atreguado = el loco con períodos de lucidez.
9. Vístose = viéndose.
10. Que es en lo que este vil traidor se apoya.
11. Serpentín = pieza con que se mueve la llave en armas de fuego.

Su taco¹² y gruessa vala, y sossegado
Está mientras el fuego no le mueve,
Y luego que le llega, con ruido
Assí se desembuelve, sale y rompe
Qual rayo de las nubes escupido,
Assí, sin detenerse ni tardarse,
Zutancalpo por él tomó la mano
Y, el reforzado leño rebolviendo,
Para el Padre se fue desatinado.
La gran maza el Padre aferró¹³ luego
Y al encuentro Parguapo fue saliendo.
Pilco allí también se desembuelve,
Otompo y luego Meco, con Guanambo,
A Mulco¹⁴ y otros muchos Acomeses,
Y cada qual su vando sustentando,
Derribando los mantos de los hombros,
Probar quisieron todos sus personas,
Mas fueles impedido el allegarse
Por los muchos que juntos estuvieron.
Con esto, la canalla se deshizo
Y cada qual se fue para su casa.
¡O vanidad, vil tósigo¹⁵ sabroso
Sugeto a cruel invidia y muerte azerba,
Qué mar de sangre vemos derramada
Por sólo pretenderte el vano altibo!
Qué presta¹⁶ la Real sangre, la hidalga,
La villana, la bárbara y serrana,
Si, como de aquel Padre decendientes,¹⁷
Toda es vna materia y vna fuente,
De vn color y vna misma semejanza,
Que en cada qual la cruel soberbia altiva
Sabemos que se anida y se atesora
Qual hambrienta polilla peligrosa
O sedienta carcoma que, royendo
De sus venas y entrañas a su gusto,
Derrama, rompe y vierte la que quiere.
Y assí, este vil idólatra sangriento,
Llevado de frenética soberbia,
Luego determinó que se rompiessen
Las pazes y las treguas concertadas
Y a los Castillas todos acabasen
Sin que ánima viviente en pie quedase.
Y por enderezar mejor su intento
Determinaron todos que en entrando
La gente Castellana en sus assientos

Its wadding and great ball, and is at peace
So long as fire does not move it,
And, when it comes, with a great noise,
135   It springs to life, bursts forth and cracks
Like lightning spat out by the clouds,
E'en so, not waiting and without delay,
Zutancalpo took up his cause for him
And, whirling in air his mighty club,
140   Went wildly toward his own father.
The father quickly seized his mighty mace,
And to meet him Purguapo went out.
Pilco there, too, did go forward,
Otompo, then Melco and Guanambo, too,
145   Mulco and many other Acomans,
Each one supporting his party.
Throwing their blankets off from their shoulders,
They all did wish to prove their persons there,
But their approach was hindered
150   By the many there gathered.
With this the rabble did break up,
And each one went to his own house.
O vanity, tasty vile poison,
Subject to cruel envy, bitter death,
155   What seas of blood we see are shed
By the vain, haughty, aspiring to you!
How fixed on it is royal blood, noble,
Plebeian, barbarian, or highland,
Being descended from that one father
160   Is all of one material and one source,
Of one color and of one same likeness,¹
For in each one the cruel, haughty pride,
We know, is nourished and is treasured up
And like the hungry, dangerous moth
165   Or thirsty cancer that, eating
At its pleasure at one's veins and entrails
Destroys, breaks down, and ruins what it will.
And thus, this vile, bloody idolater,
Borne on by a frenzy of pride,
170   Then did determine they should break
The peace and truce which they had made,
And destroy all Castilians
So that no living soul might still remain.
Better to accomplish their intent
175   All determined that, on entrance
Of Spanish folk into their towns,

---

12. Taco = vaqueta con que se aprieta la carga del arcabuz.
13. Aferró = agarró.
14. Errata del original por "Amulco."
15. Tósigo = veneno.
16. Presta = dispuesta.
17. Se refiere a la común descendencia de Adán.

1. The reference here is to Adam as father of all mankind. But Villagrá expounds forcefully upon that common origin of all men, so that it almost comes across as a defiant democratic critique of the rigid social hierarchy of his day.

Que cada qual hiciesse por su parte
Que todos por las casas se sembrasen,
Y estando bien sembrados y esparcidos,
Iuntos acometiessen de manera
Que pelo de ninguno se escapase.
Estando todo aquesto assí tratado,
Zutancalpo, con todos sus amigos,
Y Chumpo, con los suyos, se salieron
Fuera de todo el pueblo por no verse
En trato tan infame y vergonzoso.
Desto Zutacapán tomó contento,
Porque assí todo el pueblo le dexaban
Casi sin fuerza alguna que pudiesse
Contradezirle aquello que ordenase.
En este punto crudo[18] fue llegando
Aquel Maese de campo que vendido[19]
Aquestos alebosos le tenían,
Y por hazer su causa más en breve,
Iuntos a recibirle le salieron.
El pobre caballero, descuidado
De aquel rebozo estraño[20] y encubierta,[21]
A todos abrazó con gran contento,
Y luego que los vbo acariciado
Pidioles que le diessen por rescates[22]
Algunos bastimentos que tuviessen.
A esto todos alegres le dixeron
Que assentase el Real y que otro día
Todo muy bien cumplido lo ternían.
Con esto se bolvió y el día siguiente,
En fin, por orden del precioso hado,
Para el pueblo bolvió, que no debiera
Aquél que, careciendo de sospecha,
Acercándose fue para el engaño.
Que todo aquesto tiene el trato doble,
Llamar sobre seguro al inocente.
Dios nos libre del mal que nos aguarda
Y con muestras de bien nos assegura,[23]
Porque puestos en prueba tan difícil
No ay discreción, aviso ni destreza,
Armas, virtud, verdad ni resistencia
Que puedan contrastar su gran violencia.
Propuso, pues, el sin ventura joben,
Assi como a la fuerza fue llegando,

180

185

190

195

200

205

210

215

Each one should take upon himself
To scatter all 'mongst the houses,
And, being well-scattered and spread,
They would attack together, in such wise
That not a hair of them should 'scape.
All being thus agreed upon,
Zutancalpo with all his friends
And Chumpo with his did then depart
From the pueblo, that they might not be seen
In such an infamous and shameful scheme.
From this Zutacapán drew much content,
For thus they left to him the whole pueblo
Almost without a force that could
Oppose the thing he had ordered.
At this critical point arrived
That Army Master who had been betrayed
Already by those traitors there,
And, to accomplish their cause in a shorter order,
They all went out to receive him.
The poor gentleman, off his guard
For that strange snare and deception,
Embraced them all with great content,
And, after he had caressed them,
He asked them to give him in barter
Such provisions as they might have.
At this, they all rejoicing, said
That he should pitch his camp and the next day
They would have everything prepared.
At this he went on back, and the next day,
Finally, by the order of rude fate,
He went to the pueblo, as he should not,
That man who, lacking suspicion,
Went approaching the deception.
For double-dealing always does
Make feel secure poor innocents.
God free us from the evil waiting us
And with signs of good secure us,
For put into so difficult a test
There is no discretion, warning, or skill,
Arms, virtue, truth, or resistance
That can oppose its mighty violence.
The unfortunate youth set forth,
As soon as he came to the fort,

18. Crudo = cruel.
19. Vendido = traicionado.
20. Extraño = inhumano.
21. Encubierta = ocultación, fraude.
22. Rescates = dineros o su equivalente. En México, "rescate" se dice a la prueba de valor de una muestra mineral, de cuya acepción podría venir a significar aquí "prueba de amistad."
23. Posible errata del original por "asegure."

Vna gustosa plática amorosa
Para que allí los bárbaros le diessen
El bastimento que le abían mandado.
Ellos con gran descuido respondieron
Que fuessen por las casas a pedirlo,
Que todos con gran gusto le darían.
Luego el Maese de campo, sin sospecha,
Porque fuese más breve aquesta causa,
O, por mejor dezir, su corta vida,
Quedándose con sólos seys soldados,
Mandó que todos fuessen por las casas
Y el bastimento todo le juntasen,
Cuia traición, si abemos de dezirla,
Quiero alentar,[24] señor, para escrebirla.

24. Alentar = tomar alientos.

220 A pleasing and friendly discourse
That the barbarians might give
The provisions that he had asked.
They, with great easiness, replied
That they should go to their houses to seek
225 What all would give to him with great pleasure.
The Army Master, then, without suspicion,
That this thing might be sooner done,
Better to say, his own short life,
Remaining with but six soldiers,
230 Ordered that all should go to the houses
And gather up all the provisions.
If we are to tell of this treachery,
I wish, lord, to rest to write it.

CANTO VEYNTE Y DOS

DONDE SE DECLARA LA ROTA[1] *DEL MAESE DE
CAMPO y muerte de sus compañeros, causada por la trayción
de los indios Acomeses.*

O mundo instable, de miserias lleno,
Verdugo atroz de aquél que te conoze,

Disimulado engaño no entendido,
Prodigiosa tragedia portentosa,
Maldito cáncer, solapada peste,
Mortal veneno, landre[2] que te encubres!
¿Dime, traidor aleve, fementido,
Quántas traiciones tienes fabricadas,
Quántos varones tienes consumidos,
De quánto mal enrredo estás cargado?
¡O mundo vano, o vana y miserable
Honrra, con tantos daños adquirida,
O vanas esperanzas de mortales,
O vanos pensamientos engañosos,
Sugetos siempre a míseros temores
Y a mil sucessos tristes y accidentes!
¡O muy terrible caso lamentable
Que no se le conceda más de vida
A la noble lealtad, alta, gallarda,
De vn esforzado corazón valiente,
De quanto vn vil traidor, cobarde y bajo,
Quiera, con encubierta y trato doble,
Dar con su esfuerzo en tierra y derribarle
A pesar de los brazos belicosos,
Cuias illustres prendas desbanecen,
Qual presuroso viento que traspone,
Luego que traición quiere atravesarse
Y con secreto tósigo cubrirse,
Para mayor ponzoña, del estrago
Con que después se muestra y embrabece!
Dexemos los autores que escribieron
Gran suma de sucessos desdichados
Por manos de traidores fenecidos,
Y tomemos aqueste miserable
Caso por accidente sucedido.
No bien, señor, los vieron derramados
Y a todos por el pueblo divididos,
Propria y común dolencia de Españoles
Meterse en los peligros sin recato,
Sospecha ni passión de mal sucesso,

1. Rota = derrota.
2. Landre = tumor.

CANTO XXII

*Where is told the destruction of the Army Master and the
death of his companions, caused by the treachery of the
Acoma Indians.*

O world unstable, full of misery,
Atrocious headsman to him who knows
  you,
Unknowable dissembling deceit,
A prodigious, portentous tragedy,
5   A cursed cancer, a concealed pest,
Mortal poison, a tumor hidden deep!
Tell me, false, treacherous traitor,
How many treasons you have made,
How many men you have consumed,
10 With how great evil falsehoods you are charged?
O thou vain world! O vain and miserable
Honor, acquired with so much harm!
O ye vain hopes of mortal men!
O ye vain and deceptive thoughts,
15 Subject always unto a thousand fears
And to a thousand sad events and accidents!
Oh most terrible, lamentable case,
That there should be given no more of life
To the high, noble loyalty
20 Of a most brave and valiant heart
Than that vile traitor, coward, and villain
Should wish, by stealth and trickery,
To strike his courage down and prostrate it,
In spite of those most warlike arms
25 Whose famous strengths vanish away
Like the swift wind that doth blow past
When treason wishes to come forth
And with secret poison conceals,
For greater evil, the destruction,
30 With which it afterward shows forth and boasts!
Now let us leave the authors who write of
A great sum of unfortunate events
By hands of traitors now long dead,
And let us take that miserable case
35 Which happened by the merest accident.
Hardly, lord, did they see them all dispersed
And all divided throughout the pueblo,
A common and proper failing of Spaniards
To go into dangers without caution,
40 Suspicion, or feeling of ill success,

Cuio grande descuido con cuidado
Los bárbaros notaron y con esto
Advirtieron que sólos seys soldados
Con el Maese de campo abían quedado,
Y temiendo que presto se juntasen,
Poniendo en aventura[3] su partido,
La furia popular fue descubriendo
La fuerza del motín que estaba armado.
Y mormurando todos la tardanza,
Sedientos de acabar las flacas fuerzas
Que allí los Españoles alcanzaban
Por sólo aber querido derramarse,
Alborotados todos lebantaron
Vn portentoso estruendo de alaridos
Tan altos, tan valientes y grimosos
Que a todos causó espanto imaginarlos.
Viendo el Maese de campo la braveza
De la bárbara gente rebelada,
Con reportado rostro, grave, ayrado,
Para los suyos se bolvió diziendo:
"Caballeros, cuia grandeza encierra
Todo valor, esfuerzo y buen consejo,
Bien claro veys la grande desbergüenza
De toda aquesta chusma desmandada,
Pues a nosotros vemos que rebuelven
Las omicidas armas lebantadas.
Notad que toda viene al descubierto,[4]
La fee quebrada, rota la obediencia,
Las treguas y los pactos quebrantados,
Violado el vassallage que nos dieron,
Por cuio manifiesto desengaño[5]
Siento la cruda guerra ya encendida
Y vn diabólico fuego lebantado.
¿Qué consejo os parece que tomemos
Que más a nuestra causa satisfaga,
Guardando el punto,[6] que es razón se guarde,
Al bélico exercicio y al gobierno
Del grave General que nos encarga
Que siempre imaginemos y pensemos
En quán sin sangre tiene assegurada
Cosa de tanta afrenta y grave peso
Como es toda la tierra que pisamos?
Y si por qual que desdichada suerte
Nosotros derramasemos alguna,
Sería desdorar la gran grandeza
De la más sossegada paz que alcanza,

Whose great carelessness carefully
Was noted by the barbarians, and then
They noted that but six soldiers
Had stayed with the Army Master,
45 And, fearing that the others would return,
Putting their plot into great risk,
The popular fury did then reveal
The strength of the mutiny that was raised.
And, all murmuring, then, at the delay,
50 Thirsty to do away with the weak force
Which the Spaniards had gathered there
Through only having wished to so disperse,
All, in a tumult, did raise up
A portentous outbreak of cries
55 So loud, so valiant and horrid,
That it caused fear to all to think of it.
The Army Master, seeing the boldness
Of the rebelled barbarians,
With temperate countenance and serious air
60 Turned to his men and said to them:
"Ye gentlemen, whose greatness doth comprise
All courage, effort, and counsel,
You see clearly the mighty shamelessness
Of all this disobedient crowd
65 And also that for us they shake
The homicidal arms they raise.
Note that all of them come openly,
With broken faith, broken obedience,
Treaties and pacts being broken, too,
70 The homage they gave us violated,
Through which manifest and eye-opening truth
I feel that brutal war is now aflame
And diabolic fires alight.
What counsel seems it best to you we take
75 That will best satisfy our cause,
Keeping in mind, as we should do,
The warlike practice and the rule
Of the grave General, who orders us
Always to keep in mind and think
80 Of how he has secured without bloodshed
A thing of such hardship and such great weight
As is most all the land we tread?
And if, by some unhappy fate,
We should shed any blood at all
85 'Twould be to tarnish the greatness
Of the most happy peace he won.

3. Aventura = riesgo.
4. Al descubierto = abiertamente.
5. Desengaño = verdad.
6. Guardando el punto = teniendo cuidando de respetar.

Por cuia justa causa soy de acuerdo,
Pues tan buena ocasión el tiempo ofrece,
Que luego nos salgamos retirando,
Recogiendo al descuido nuestra gente,
Pues para todo ay tiempo y coiuntura."
Y como jamás vemos que a faltado
Para las cosas bien encaminadas
Vn fiscal que repruebe y contradiga,
Parece que la sobra de arrogancia
De vn torpe Capitán que cerca estaba
Dixo, porque más bien se descubriesse
Su vana presunción y vano esfuerzo:
"No es bien, Maese de campo, que sigamos,
Por honrra de Españoles, tal afrenta.
Y si no, sólo a mí se dé licencia
Y versea⁷ como solo me antepongo
A toda esta canalla y la sugeto
Para que, sin que nadie se retire,
Decienda quando más le diere gusto,
Sano y salbo, a lo llano desta cumbre."
Pasmado el de Zaldívar, sin aliento,
De la sobrada⁸ réplica encendido,⁹
Suspenso, difirió la justa enmienda¹⁰
Para mayor bagar¹¹ del que le daba
La furia de la tropa que embestía,
Por aberle aquel necio entretenido
Con sus necias palabras mal digestas.
Pues como si¹² le vbiesse ya passado
La precissa ocasión de retirarse,
Cuya pérdida triste, lastimosa,
Por maravilla vemos que la cobran¹³
Aquéllos que la pierden sin rezelo
Del grave inconveniente que se sigue
Después de ser perdida y acabada,
Assí, por no perderla,¹⁴ desembuelto,
Salió Zutacapán, feroz, diziendo:
"¡Mueran, mueran a sangre y fuego, mueran
Todos estos ladrones que han tenido
Tan grande atrebimiento y desbergüenza
Que, sin ningún temor ni buen respecto,
Han querido pisar los altos muros
De aquesta illustre fuerza poderosa!"
Luego, tras dél, salieron replicando

For this just cause, my judgment is,
Since time offers such good occasion,
That we could easily retreat,
90 Collecting our folk casually,
Since there is time and opportunity."
As we have never seen lacking
In anything set well on course
A meddler who reproves and contradicts,
95 It seems the surplusage of arrogance
Of a stupid captain who stood nearby
Said, better to reveal to all
His vain presumption and vain forwardness,
"It is not well, Army Master, for us
100 And for our Spanish honor to accept
This insult, and, if I may be allowed,
You shall see I alone shall place myself
Before this rabble and shall subdue it
So that, no one retreating from this spot,
105 You may descend when it most pleases you,
Both safe and whole, to the plain near this height."
Zaldívar, breathless, astonished,
Inflamed at this most audacious reply,
Deferred the reward it deserved, waiting
110 A greater leisure than was given by
The fury of the mob who did attack
While he was listening to that fool
With his foolish and ill-digested words.
Now, as for him there had passed by
115 The precious occasion for retreat,
Whose sad and painful loss we see
But by a miracle retrieved
By those who lose it without thought
Of the great ruin that might come.
120 Once it was lost and gone,
Not to lose his chance, now, wildly,
Zutacapán came forth, ferocious and shouting:
"Death! Death by blood and fire! Death
To all these robbers who have had
125 Such great daring and shamelessness
As, without any fear or decency,
To wish to tread the lofty walls
Of this famous and powerful fort!"
Then after him came, shouting too,

7. Posible errata del original por "verse a."
8. Sobrada = innecesaria.
9. Encendido = sonrojado.
10. Enmienda = castigo.
11. Para mayor bagar = para mayor vagar, para tener más tiempo.
12. Posible errata del original por "se."
13. Muy rara vez vemos que la recuperen.
14. La ocasión, se entiende.

Ezmicaio, Amulco y también Pilco,
A quien siguieron Tempal y Cotumbo,
Diziendo: "¡Mueran estos fementidos,
Infames, viles, perros alebosos,
Perturbadores del común sossiego!"
Esforzó aquesta voz la brava turba
De la infernal canalla belicosa,
Las poderosas armas embrazando.
Viendo el Maese de campo sin remedio
El rigor de las armas lebantadas,
Buelto a los suyos, dixo, a grandes vozes:
"No me dispare nadie, y sólo apunten,
Que con sólo apuntar será possible
Detener la gran fuerza que descarga
De la bárbara furia que arremete."
La qual se abalanzó con tanto aliento
Qual suele vna deshecha[15] y gran borrasca
Quando a la pobre navezilla embiste,
Cuias más encumbradas y altas gavias[16]
Al profundo del hondo mar derriba
Y luego al mismo Cielo las lebanta.
Assí, rabiosos todos, embistieron,
Las poderosas mazas descargando.
Viendo el Maese de campo sin remedio
Cosa de tanto peso y grave afrenta,
Y que por bien no pudo reduzirlos,
Qual ponzoñosa víbora pisada
Del ancho pie del rústico villano
Que, viéndose perdida y quebrantada,
En sí toda se enciende y embravece,
Tendida y recogida, amenazando
Con la trisulca[17] lengua y corbo diente,
Assí el Zaldívar, todo embravecido,
A los suyos mandó con grande priessa
Que las fogosas llaves apretasen,
Y escupiendo los prestos arcabuzes
Las escondidas valas, derribaron
De la enemiga gente grande parte.
Mas poco les valió tan buen efecto,
Porque todos al punto se mesclaron
Sin que pudiessen darlos otra carga.
Y assí, la soldadesca en tanto aprieto,
Qual suelen, con fortuna, los forzados[18]
Bogar sobre los cabos,[19] rebentando
Por no desamarrarse y desassirse,

130 Ezmicaio, Amulco and Pilco,
Whom Tempal and Cotumbo followed,
Shouting, "Death to the false and unfaithful,
Infamous, vile, and treacherous dogs,
Disturbers of our common peace!"
135 That cry raised up a bold uproar
Of the infernal, warlike mob,
Grasping their powerful weapons.
The Army Master, seeing beyond all help
The power of the upraised arms,
140 Turned to his men and cried aloud,
"Let no one fire now, but only aim,
For by aiming alone 'tis possible
To hold back the great force discharged
By the barbarian fury that attacks."
145 But it attacked with such élan,
As does a mighty tempest and great wind
When it attacks a poor, small ship,
Whose loftiest and highest sails
It levels with the deepest sea
150 And then raises to the highest heaven.
Thus, all, in a fury, attacked,
Striking with powerful maces.
The Army Master, seeing the affair
Of such gravity, grave outrage, now beyond all help,
155 And that by gentle means he could not reduce them,
Like poisonous viper trod upon
By the broad foot of rustic plebe,
Which, seeing itself lost and injured,
Takes fire and is all enraged,
160 And coils and uncoils, threatening
With three-forked tongue and poison tooth,
So Zaldívar, now all enraged,
Ordered his men that with all haste
They fire their vehement muskets,
165 And, the quick harquebuses then vomiting
The hidden balls, did strike to earth
A great part of the enemy.
But such a good effect availed little
Since all were instantly o'erwhelmed
170 Without being able to reload again.
And so the soldiery in such a plight,
As galley slaves in a tempest
Row set upon the oars, straining
Not to be unchained and swept away,

15. Deshecha = violenta.
16. Gavias = cestos en lo alto del mástil.
17. Trisulca = trisurca, dividida en tres partes.
18. Forzados = galeotes.
19. Bogar sobre los cabos = remar puesto sobre los remos.

Y a fuerza de los puños y los brazos,	175
Con roncos azezidos[20] y gemidos	
Contra el rigor del mar soberbio arfando,[21]	
Embisten con las hondas y las rompen	
Con sobra de corage, lebantando	
Al Cielo espumas de agua, assí, oprimidos,	180
Los fuertes Españoles arrancaron	
Las valientes espadas rigurosas	
De las gallardas cintas en que estaban.	
Y assí, resueltos, todos desembueltos,	
Por medio la canalla se lanzaban,	185
Desquartizando a diestro y a siniestro	
Inormes cuerpos, bravos y espantosos,	
Con horribles heridas bien rasgadas,	
Sangrientas cuchilladas desmedidas,	
Profundas puntas, temerarios golpes,	190
Con que los vnos y otros bien mostraban	
De sus heroicos brazos raras pruebas.	
En esto, el bravo Tempal, que corrido	
Estaba ya, sin seso, avergonzado	
De ver en Españoles tal esfuerzo,	195
Al suelo se abajó por vn gran canto	
Y atrás el pie derecho fue haziendo,	
La espalda derribada,[22] y fue lanzando	
El canto de manera que hundida	
Dexó la triste boca de Pereira.	200
Y no bien vio los dientes derramados	
Quando sobre él bolvió y, regañando,[23]	
Pedazos la cabeza con vn leño	
Le hizo al miserable, y viendo todos	
Los cascos que, mesclados con los sesos,	205
Sangrientos se esparcieron por el suelo,	
Tan gran corage a vna concibieron	
Que assí como la pólvora, de hecho,	
Lebanta vn gran castillo y lo destroza,	
Siembra y lo derrama por mil partes,	210
Assí la chusma bárbara, furiosa,	
La Castellana fuerza fue embistiendo,	
Por cierta la victoria allí cantando.	
Quán bueno es el callar y qué importante	
Quando la dura guerra se platica,	215
Porque aunque con gran fuerza pretendamos	
Se ygualen las palabras con las obras,	
No son los nobles hechos tan tenidos	
Quanto aquéllos que, sin parlar, se acaban.	
Todo esto digo por aquel furioso	220

175	By force of mighty arms and hands,
	With hoarse and harsh curses and groans
	Against the rigor of the proud and heaving sea,
	Strive with the waves and break through them
	With more than enough courage, throwing up
180	To heaven spray from water, thus attacked,
	Those strong Spaniards did then draw out
	Their valiant, death-dealing swords
	From the gay belts in which they were.
	And so, freely, without a fear,
185	They threw themselves into the midst
	Of the mob, slashing to the right and left
	Enormous, brave bodies in frightful wise,
	With horrid wounds that bit right deep,
	Bloody and measureless slashes,
190	Deep thrusts of points, terrific blows,
	With which they all displayed right well
	Rare proof of their heroic arms.
	At this, the brave Tempal, bothered
	By then and shamed beyond his senses to
195	Behold such courage in Spaniards,
	There bending to the ground for a rock,
	Threw to the rear his strong right leg,
	Lowered his shoulders and did cast
	The rock in such a way that it left crushed
200	Pereira's most sorrowful mouth,
	And hardly did he see his broken teeth
	Before he sprang upon him and shattered
	The head to pieces with a club
	Of that miserable man, and, all seeing
205	The skull fragments which, mingled with the brains,[1]
	Were scattered, bloody, on the ground,
	At once they all took such courage
	That, like the powerful gunpowder
	Which hoists a great castle and destroys it
210	And scatters it to a thousand pieces,
	The Spanish force was thus set on
	By all the furious barbarian crowd,
	Singing assured victory there.
	How good is silence and how important
215	When horrid war is exercised,
	Because although we try with mighty force
	To equal our words with our deeds,
	Our noble deeds are not considered such
	As those which are done without any talk.
220	I say all this for that furious

20. Azezidos = acezidos, jadeos.
21. Arfando = cabeceando, como los buques.
22. Derribada = caída, arqueada hacia atrás.
23. Regañando = mostrando los dientes, como los perros.

1. This type of rather gory description of battle wounds, common to the New World epic, may possibly be traced to its usage in the then very popular romances of chivalry.

Capitán, indiscreto, mal mirado,
Que por ganar gran fama blasonaba,
Que está de todo punto ya rendido,
Alebrastado, mudo, temeroso,
Suspenso, manso, pálido, cobarde
Y sin género de armas en las manos,
La vil, bana, cabeza descubierta
Y escudando su tímida persona
Con el Maese de campo valeroso
Que en la sangrienta guerra desdichada
Vn invencible Godo[24] se mostraba.
Mas poco le turó el escudarse,
Que al fin le dieron muerte vergonzosa,
Pues sin que lastimasen su persona
De las manos las armas le quitaron,
Y qual si fuera oveja miserable
Assí también la vida le rindieron.
¡O soldados que al bélico exercicio
Soys con grande razón aficionados,
Advertid que es grandíssima grandeza
No ser nada muy pródigos de lengua,
Y serlo por la espada es cosa noble
Si con razón se ajusta y se compone!
Notad aquesta historia porque os juro
Que si Dios nuestra causa no repara[25]
Como bondad inmensa, poderosa,
Que fuera este hombre causa suficiente
Para que, sin que cosa en pie quedara
En aquel nuevo mundo y nueva Iglesia,
Todo se destruyera y se assolara,
Y esto sin que viva ánima pudiera
Salir a dar la nueva desdichada.
Y para no venir con tanta afrenta,
Dos cosas con grandíssimo cuidado
A siempre de notar el buen guerrero:
La vna es que considere bien si manda
Y la otra si es de aquéllos que obedecen.
Y mire quál de aquestos dos oficios
Le es fuerza que exercite y que professe,
Y no permita quiebra ni se atreba
A perder ni salir tan sólo vn passo
Del término que a cada qual se debe,
Teniendo siempre por opuesto y blanco[26]
Al mismo poderoso Dios eterno,
A cuia alteza inmensa y soberana
No está bien se gobierne por nosotros
Y menos no es bien que gobernemos

225

230

235

240

245

250

255

260

265

Captain, the indiscreet, the impudent,
Who boasted to gain reputation,
Who now is quite surrendered,
Cowering and dumb and timorous,
Crouching and quiet, pale and cowardly,
No sort of weapon in his hands,
The vile, vain head uncovered
And shielding his cowardly person
Behind the valorous Army Master,
Who in bloody and unlucky war
Did show himself an invincible Goth.[2]
But little good did shielding do this man,
Because in the end they gave him shameful death,
For, without harming his person,
They took his arms away from him
And, as he were a miserable sheep,
So, too, they took his life away.
O soldiers who of warlike exercise
Are fond, and with much reason, too,
Note that it is of greatness the greatest
To be of speech in nothing prodigal,
While it is noble to be so with sword,
If it be done within reason!
And note this story, for I swear to you
That, should God not restore our cause,
As an immense and powerful good,
This man alone would be sufficient cause
That, without anything left standing up
In this new world and this new Church,
All should be desolated and destroyed,
And this so that no living soul should be
Able to carry the unhappy news.
And not to come into such dishonor
The good warrior must always note
Two things with the minutest care:
The one is to think well if he commands;
The other, if he is of those who do obey.
And note which of these two duties
'Tis most proper that he exercise and profess,
And not permit the slightest change or dare
To lose or go astray a single step
From the end that is due to each,
Having always before him as model
That same all-powerful, eternal God
Whose immense loftiness and sovereignty
It is not well should be governed by us
And it is less good we should rule

---

24. Godo = noble.
25. Repara = arregla.
26. Opuesto y blanco = modelo.

2. The Spaniards, feeling themselves successors to the Visigoths, employed that designation in the most laudatory fashion.

A magestad tan alta y lebantada.
Y porque sé muy cierto que me entienden
Los que mandan y aquéllos que obedecen,
Cada qual exercite con imperio
La fuerza del oficio que tuviere,
Y mande la cabeza poderosa
Y obedezcan los bajos pies, humildes,
Si quieren ver en todo buen gobierno.
Pero dexemos esto, gran Monarca,
Que sale Pilco echando espumarajos
Por la rabiosa boca desmedida,
Y vn gran bastón en torno rebolviendo,
Biene ciego, de cólera encendido,
Con sobra de corage amenazando
La lebantada frente de Bibero,
Cuia fuerza fue en alto reparando,
Cubriendo la cabeza con dos manos,
Iunta la guarnición²⁷ con el adarga,
La rodilla derecha en tierra firme,
Todo el costado yzquierdo descubierto,
Sobre cuio desocupado espacio
Descargó el brazo del ferrado²⁸ leño
Con tan violenta fuerza y gran pujanza
Que le quebró la hiel dentro del cuerpo,
Haziéndole pedazos las costillas.
Y a penas dio consigo el pobre en tierra
Quando de lo más alto de vna casa,
De encima del pretil, vna gran piedra
Fue de vna flaca vieja rempujada.
Esta se vino aplomo²⁹ de manera
Que le hizo pedazos la cabeza.
Viendo al triste Español allí tendido
Y, qual el compañero que hemos dicho,
Los escondidos sesos derramados,
Tan fuertes vozes todos lebantaron,
Y con vn tan horrible y bravo estruendo,
Que los más altos y encumbrados Cielos
Por vna y otra parte parecían
Que tristemente todos se rasgaban,
Dexándose venir de todo punto,
Rotos y destrozados, para el suelo.
Y como todo andaba de rebuelta,
Popolco arremetió para Costilla,
Mulato de nación³⁰ y tan muchacho
Que armas nunca jamás abía ceñido,
Y abriéndole de vn hijar al otro

Such high and lofty majesty.
And as I well know they may understand,
270 Those who command and those who do obey,
Let each one exercise with power
The terms of the office he has,
And let the head rule powerfully
And let the humble feet obey
275 If they do wish to see good government in all.
But let us leave this, great Monarch,
For Pilco comes frothing out foam
From his mouth, raging measureless
And whirling in circles a mighty club.
280 He comes blind and inflamed with wrath,
With overflowing courage threatening
The lofty head of Bibero,
Who, seeing his strength over him,
Covering his head with both hands,
285 Joined the hilt of his sword to his shield,³
His right knee firmly set to ground
And all his left side uncovered.
Upon this unprotected space
He brought his iron-pointed lance
290 With such a violent force and heavy thrust
It broke the bile in his body,
Smashing his ribs into pieces.
And hardly had the poor man fallen to the earth
When from the topmost of a house,
295 From on its parapet, a mighty rock
Was by a weak old woman thrust.
This fell straight down in such a way
As smashed his head into pieces.
Seeing the Spaniard thus sadly stretched out
300 And, like his companion we mentioned,
His hidden brains now scattered wide,
All set up such a mighty shout
And with such terrible and horrid noise
That the highest and stateliest heavens
305 Did seem upon all sides to be
Most sorrowfully pierced through
And letting themselves entirely
Be broken and shattered down to the ground.
And as all was in a melee,
310 Popolco did attack one Costilla,
A mulatto by race and so young yet
He never had borne any arms,
And, slashing him from side to side,

27. Guarnición = defensa de las espadas para guardar la mano.
28. Ferrado = armado de hierro.
29. Aploma = a plomo, vertical.
30. Nación = nacimiento.

3. The plastic image clearly projects the man's defensive posture.

Todas las tripas le vertió en el suelo.
El mísero muchacho lastimado,
Que junto al cuerpo de Bivero estaba,
La daga le arrancó de la pretina
Y, qual suele imprimirse y estamparse
La figura del sello en blanda cera,
Assí imprimió la llaga aquel mulato
En su mismo omicida de manera
Que, en las rebueltas tripas tropezando
El vno con el otro muy rabiosos,
A los brazos vinieron ya difuntos,
Y estando bien assidos y abrazados
Por las terribles bocas sangrentadas
Las inmortales almas vomitaron.
En esto, Chontal, bárbaro arriscado[31]
Que acaso fue passando por do estaba
El Alférez Zapata, en yra ardiendo,
Con mil salbajes bravos peleando,
Alzó el serrado[32] leño y en el yelmo
Tan gran golpe le dio que estuvo en punto
De dar consigo en tierra casi muerto.
Y luego que algún tanto fue cobrado,
De verse assí tratado y ofendido,
No la braveza y furia desatada
Del corajoso toro ya vencido,
Vertiendo gruessas babas por vengarse,
Assí se vio jamás, qual vimos todos,
Al Español furioso rebolviendo
El hierro de la espada, avergonzado,
Sobre el valiente bárbaro atrevido,
Y embebiéndola[33] toda, casi ciego,
Seys vezes la bañó y tinta y roja
Sacó de los costados poderosos,
Vertiendo vn mar de sangre denegrida
Do el alma zozobró y, assí, rabiosa,
Salió de la vertiente sangrentada.
No bien el fuerte bárbaro, difunto,
En tierra dio consigo, quando todos,
Alzando vn alarido, arremetieron,
"¡Muera, muera!", diziendo, y assí, juntos,
Qual el soberbio mar quando combate
La lebantada roca y ella, fuerte,
Las poderosas aguas contrastando,
Inhiesta queda siempre, estable y firme,[34]
Assí su grande esfuerzo fue mostrando

315
His bowels poured out upon the ground.
The miserable, wounded boy,
Who fell by Bibero's body,
Did seize his dagger from his belt
And, as a figure of a seal in wax
Is often impressed and stamped,
320
That mulatto then stamped his wound
On his own murderer, so that,
Now tripping over their own entrails,
One to the other, both raging,
Fell each in the others arms, dying,
325
And, having seized each other fast,
They gave up their immortal souls
Through their terrible, bloody mouths.
At this, Chontal, a bold barbarian
Who passed by chance the spot where stood
330
Ensign Zapata, blazing in his wrath,
Fighting a thousand savages,
Raised up his serrated club and on his helm
Gave such a blow as barely failed
To fell him to the ground half-dead;
335
And when he had recovered a little,
Seeing himself thus treated and injured,
The anger and unleashed fury
Of the courageous, battered bull,
Dripping thick spit, seeking revenge,
340
Was never such as then was seen
In this Spaniard, who, furious, turned
The steel of his sword, ashamed,
Upon the valiant, daring barbarian,
And piercing with it, blind with rage,
345
Six times he dipped and red, scarlet,
He drew it from his mighty sides,
Shedding a sea of blackish blood,
Whence his soul sank and so, raging
Departed from the bloody fount.
350
Hardly was this strong savage dead
And fallen to the ground when all,
Raising a mighty shout, attacked,
Shouting, "Death, death!," and all at once,
Like the proud sea when it combats
355
The lofty rock, and it, in strength,
Giving resistance to the powerful waves,
Always remains steep, firm, stable,[4]
So in this conflict the gallant Spaniard

31. Arriscado = atrevido, valiente.
32. Serrado = dentado.
33. Embebiéndola = embutiéndola.
34. Esta imagen, favorita de Villagrá, se halla en Virgilio, *Eneida* VII, 771–74).

4. This image of a storming sea battering a firm rock, a favorite of Villagrá and of all the New World epics, is found in Virgil, the *Aeneid* VII, 771–74.

El Español gallardo en tal conflicto.
Zutacapán, furioso, viendo aquesto,
Con toda su quadrilla fue embistiendo
A tres solos fortíssimos guerreros,
Y por ser la ventaja tan sobrada
A su pesar los fueron retirando
Para vn grimoso y gran despeñadero
Adonde les fue fuerza que probasen
Los oprimidos Héroes, afligidos,
El vltimo rigor y postrer trance
Que pudo la fortuna embravecida
Dar a sus tristes cuerpos esforzados.
El primero de todos fue Camacho,
Detrás dél, luego, se arrojó segura,[35]
Y a la postre aquel pobre de Ramírez,
Que todos de la mal segura cumbre
Se fueron despeñando y lanzando,
Culpando en vano y sin ningún remedio
A su triste ventura y mala suerte.
Triste, pues antes de llegar al suelo
Muertos llegaron, dando cien mil botes
Por los más crudos riscos lebantados.
Pues como el valor de armas se encendiesse
Y el rigor de los dientes se apretase,
Escalante, con Sebastián Rodríguez,
Mostrando la fineza de quilates
De sus bravos, gallardos, corazones,
La más cruenta refriega sustentaron
Hasta que faltos de vigor y aliento,
Apedreados, los dos nobles guerreros
Iuntos al otro mundo se partieron.
El bueno de Araujo, peleando
Con vn valiente bárbaro que quiso
Fortuna que estuviessen retirados,
Dos poderosos lobos se mostraron
El vno contra el otro, y se embistieron
Tan esforzadamente que ponían
Horror en sólo verlos tan heridos
Y de ambas partes tan ensangrentados.
Y después que vendieron bien sus vidas
Sin ninguna ventaja o diferencia,
Rendidos, los dos bravos fenecieron.
En esto, con gran furia descargaban
Sobre el Maese de campo fieros golpes,
Cuio triste progreso a nuevo canto
Será bien difirir porque me faltan
Fuerzas para escrebir mi gran desdicha,
Pues de dos camaradas y señores

Displayed his mighty energy.
360 Zutacapán, furious, seeing this,
Was making an attack with all his men
On only three most sturdy warriors,
And with such overwhelming advantage
They forced them to retreat despite themselves
365 Upon a horrible, steep precipice
Where it was necessary that
The hard-pressed, spent heroes should prove
The last rigor, the ultimate crisis
That a contrary fortune could
370 Give to their sad and worn bodies.
The first of all was Camacho,
After him, then, Segura threw himself,
And last of all that ill-starred Ramírez,
So that all from the insecure summit
375 Did leap down and did hurl themselves,
Blaming in vain and beyond any help
Their sad fortune and evil fate,
Sad, since before they struck the ground
They were dead from a hundred thousand blows
380 Upon the harsh and lofty rocks.
Now, as valor in arms is fired
And teeth are pressed together tight,
Escalante and Sebastián Rodríguez,
Showing the most exquisite quality
385 Of their brave, gallant hearts,
Did still maintain the bloody fight
Until, all out of strength and breath,
Struck down by stones, that pair of noble warriors
Together went into another world.
390 The brave Araujo, battling
With a brave barbarian, who tried
Their fortunes in a separate fight,
Showed themselves as two powerful wolves
Each against other, and they fought
395 So furiously that they did strike
Horror only to see them wounded so
And both of them so stained with blood.
And after they had well bartered their lives,
With no advantage and no difference,
400 The two brave men, exhausted, fell down dead.
Meantime they were delivering with great fury
Fierce blows upon the brave Army Master,
Whose sad progress unto a new canto
It were well I defer, since I do lack
405 Strength here to write my great unhappiness,
Since of two comrades and superiors

35. Errata del original por "Segura."

Que por buena y gran suerte me cupieron
En toda aquesta guerra trabajosa,
Me es fuerza llore al vno y con quebranto
Viva de oy más en vn azerbo llanto.

That by great good fortune I had
In all of that laborious war
'Tis necessary that I mourn this one
410 And live now sorrowing in bitter tears.

Canto Veynte y Tres

*DONDE SE DIZE LA MVERTE DEL MAESE DE
CAMPO y lo que después sucedió hasta llevar la nueva al
Gobernador.*

R ENUEVESE el dolor y el ronco azento
Con fúnebre dolor salga llorando
La fiera y brava muerte lamentable
De aquel varón heroico que, rompiendo
Por mil furiosas bárbaras esquadras
Por la terrible espada poderosa
Vn mar de fresca sangre va bertiendo.
Tres largas horas con valor sostuvo
Todo el inorme peso portentoso
De la cruenta batalla el nuevo Marte
Con tan sobrado ánimo y esfuerzo
Como si de vn fino bronce fuera.
Pues, viendo aquel membrudo y fiero Qualpo
La fineza del Español gallardo,
Con sobrado corage fue a dos manos
Del arco las dos puntas encorbando
Para que con mayor violencia y fuerza
La poderosa flecha se arrancase
De la tirante cuerda belicosa.
Y assí la despedió con tal braveza
Que rompiéndole toda la escarcela
Atrabesada se quedó temblando
Por el derecho muslo bien assida.
Aquí el Zaldívar rebolvió furioso,
Qual rabioso león atrabesado
Del riguroso dardo que le clava
El hastuto montero que le sigue,
Tras cuio brazo[1] vemos que se enciende
Y se arma, sacude y embrabece
Rabioso, lebantando y herizando
El áspero crestón del alto cerro,[2]
El bedijoso cuello rebolviendo
Y con roncos bramidos y gemidos,
Fuertes vñas y dientes corajosos,
Para todos arranca y se abalanza.
No de otra suerte y traza la braveza
Del bravo Español crece y se lebanta,
Haziendo vn bien tendido y ancho campo
Por do quiera que embiste y arremete.
Aquí derriba, tulle y estropea;

---

1. Es difícil determinar si se refiere al atacante brazo del cazador o a
la pata delantera del cuadrúpedo.
2. Cerro = espinazo.

Canto XXIII

*Wherein is told the death of the Army Master and what
happened afterward until the news came to the Governor.*

L ET sorrow be renewed. Let hoarse accents
Of weeping come with funeral sorrow
For the lamentable, cruel, brave death
Of that most brave man who, bursting
Through a thousand furious barbarian troops,
With his terrible, powerful sword
Did spill forth a whole sea of fresh blood.
Three long hours, brave, he sustained
All the enormous and portentous weight

10 Of that most bloody battle, a new Mars,
With such surpassing courage and effort
As he were all of one pure bronze.
Now, strong and fiery Qualpo, seeing
The zeal of the gallant Spaniard,

15 With soaring courage and both hands
Drew back the ends of his bow,
That with more violence and force
The powerful arrow might be sped
From that warlike and tight-drawn cord.

20 And so he sent it with such force
That, breaking quite through the cuisses,
It pierced and, quivering, remained
Fastened deep into his right thigh.
At this, Zaldívar, furious, turned

25 Like a ravening lion pierced through
By a mordant dart driven into him
By the astute hunter who pursues,
Behind whose arm[1] we see he is inflamed,
Furious, erecting, and displaying high

30 The rough crest on his lofty back,
Turning his shaggy neck from side to side,
And with harsh howling and with roars,
Mighty claws, and ravening teeth,
Against all he races and strikes.

35 Now, in no other way and sort the bravery
Of that bold Spaniard grows and is increased,
Cutting a well-extended and wide field
Wherever he attacks and charges in.
Here he postrates, gives wounds and maims;

40 There, fleeing him, all seek refuge

---

1. It is difficult to tell whether the reference here is to the striking
arm of the pursuing huntsman or to the shoulder of the beast itself.

Allí, huyendo dél, se acogen todos
Qual vanda de palomas que, esparcidas
Huyendo del vilano,[3] van tendiendo
Las alas por el ayre y van buscando
Los avigados[4] nidos, puerto libre
Donde seguras puedan ampararse
Y libres de sus garras socorrerse,
Assí los Acomeses, temerosos,
Apriessa se retiran y recogen.
Mas como lo violento no es perpetuo,
La gran braveza fue desfalleciendo.
Qual en vn fiero toro desfalleze
Quando, en estrecho coso agarrochado,[5]
Se ve por todas partes afligido,
Arroyado de sangre denegrida,
Ya falto de vigor, fuerza y aliento,
No menos el raudal bravo, famoso,[6]
De aquel brioso ánimo valiente
Vino a menguar sus esforzadas fuerzas,
Que ya, como atrás queda referido,
Sobre él furiosos golpes descargaban.
Pilco embistió con todos sus guerreros;
Zutacapán también fue descargando,
Ayudado de Amulco y Ezmicaio;
Cotumbo y Tempal fueron rebolviendo.
Y assí, todos se fueron ya mezclando
Con la popular tropa que embestía
Sobre el bravo caudillo destroncado,
Cobrando en su flaqueza nuevos bríos,
Tanto más alentados y esforzados
Quanto menos esfuerzo y resistencia
Sintieron en el pobre caballero,
Condición propria y natural cosecha
De torpes brutos, ánimos bestiales,
Ensayar su foror[7] en vn rendido
Y que en él sean sus golpes señalados,
Fingiéndose valientes y animosos,
Como si por allí no se dexara
Mucho más descubierta la bageza
De sus infames ánimos cobardes.
Pues siendo tan apriessa lastimado,
Luego que por tres vezes, ya perdido,
Del suelo se cobró con nuevo esfuerzo
El animoso y fuerte combatiente,
Haziendo en todas tres, por tres leones,

Like a flock of doves, which, scattered wide
Fleeing the sparhawk, do spread out
Their wings unto the air and fly, seeking
Their raftered nests, a safe harbor
45 Where they may refuge in safety
And find a place safe from his claws,
Just so the fearful Acomans
Quickly retreated and withdrew.
But, as violence is not perpetual,
50 His great fury kept weakening.
As in a wild bull it weakens
When, pricked in a narrow bullring,
He sees himself attacked from all sides,
All covered with his blackening blood,
55 Now failing in vigor and strength and breath,
No less the brave and famous bloodletting
Of that courageous, valiant soul
Came to diminish his straining strength,
For, as has previously been stated,
60 There rained upon him furious blows.
Pilco attacked with all his warriors;
Zutacapán, too, was attacking there,
Aided by Amulco and Emizcaio;
Cotumbo and Tempal came on as well.
65 And then they were all in a melee
With the troops of the people who did charge
Upon the brave, wounded leader,
Recovering new courage from his plight,
The more encouraged and spurred on
70 As they saw in the wretched cavalier
Less of endeavor and of resistance,
The proper condition and natural result
Of wicked brutes and bestial minds
To vent their fury upon one worn out
75 And deal most renowned blows to him,
Pretending themselves valiant, courageous,
As if they did not, in that work,
Make much more evident the true baseness
Of their own infamous and cowardly souls.
80 For, so repeatedly being wounded,
After he had three times, all lost,
The courageous and strong fighter,
Risen from the ground with new strength,
Making in each of them, like three lions,
85 Three wide, depopulated rings,

---

3. Vilano = milano.
4. Avigados = entre/sobre vigas.
5. Agarrochado = herido de garrocha, vara con gancho en la punta.
6. De sangre, se entiende.
7. Errata del original por "furor."

Tres bien desocupadas y anchas plazas,
Al fin, con gran cuidado, fue bajando
De aquel Zutacapán la fiera maza
Con tan valiente fuerza que, assentada
Sobre las altas sienes del Zaldívar,
Allí rendido le dexó, entregado
Al reposo mortal y largo sueño
Que a todos nos es fuerza le durmamos.
¡O vida miserable de mortales,
Sugeta a mil millones de miserias,
Peligros, desbenturas y desastres,
Naufragios y otros tristes accidentes
De míseros subcessos que notamos
Aquéllos que, aunque libres los sentidos,⁸
Dios sabe si otra cosa nos aguarda
De más dolor, miseria y más quebranto
Que aquéllos que muy graves nos parecen!
Pues viendo aquel guerrero allí tendido,
Como rabiosos perros lebantaron
Vn grande estruendo, bárbaro, confusso,
De aullidos y alaridos temerosos,
Y rempujándose, desatinados,
Los vnos a los otros, se estorbaban
Por sólo ensangrentar las fieras armas
Que cada qual mandaba y gobernaba
De la inocente sangre del Christiano.
Y tantos golpes fueron descargando,
Qual suelen los herreros quando en torno,⁹
Gimiendo, junto al yunque van bajando
Los poderosos machos¹⁰ y a porfía¹¹
Assientan con esfuerzo mayor golpe,
Y tantos sobre él dieron y cargaron
Quantos sobre aquel noble Anaxarco¹²
Quando por vista de ojos vio molerse¹³
En vn gran mortero bien fornido
Adonde en lastimosa y tierna pasta
La carne con los güessos le dexaron.
Viendo al Maese de campo ya rendido,
El valiente Zapata y Iuan de Olague,
El gran León y fuerte Cabanillas
Y aquel Pedro Robledo, el animoso,
Abiendo como buenos señalado
Sus imbenzibles brazos no domados

Finally, with good aim, there did descend
The furious mace of that Zutacapán
With such fierce strength that, striking on
The lofty temples of that Zaldívar,
90 It left him there prostrate and given o'er
To mortal rest and that long sleep
That needs be all of us must sleep.
Oh miserable life of mortal men,
Subject to thousand million miseries,
95 Perils and misadventures, disasters,
Shipwrecks and other sorry accidents
In miserable events that we note down,
We who, although at present free of pain,
God knows if other things await
100 Of more sorrow and misery and woe
Than those that so grave seem to us.
Well, seeing that warrior lying stark there,
Like raging dogs they did set up
A great uproar, a barbarous confusion
105 Of howls and horror-striking shrieks,
And, pushing forward crazily,
They struggled with each other there
Only to stain the haughty arms
That each one wielded and possessed
110 In innocent blood of that Christian.
And they rained down as many blows
As do the smiths when, gathered round
The anvil, grunting, they bring down
Their mighty hammers and, in rivalry,
115 Each tries to strike the hardest blow.
As many struck and mangled him
As ever did noble Anaxarces²
When, in the sight of all, he was ground up
In a great mortar, huge and stout,
120 Where in a sad and bloody paste
They left his body and his bones.
Seeing the Army Master was now dead,
The valiant Zapata, Juan de Olague,
The great León and strong Cabanillas,
125 And that Pedro Robledo, the courageous,
Having, like good men, made famous
Their invincible arms never subdued
And beaten back the crowd that charged,

8. Los que, aunque en el presente libres de dolor.
9. En torno = por turno.
10. Machos = mazos grandes usados en las herrerías.
11. A porfía, = porfiando entre sí.
12. Anaxarco, filósofo griego de la escuela de Demócrito y acompañante de Alejandro Magno, es leyenda que fue molido por el tirano. Nicocreón: Diógenes Laercio, *Vidas* IX.
13. Se vio moler.

2. Anaxarces, a Greek philosopher and member of the school of Democritus and companion to Alexander the Great, who in legend was said to have been pulverized by the tyrant Nicocreon. Diogenes Laertius, *Lives* IX.

Resistiendo a la turba que cargaba,
Se fueron a gran priessa retirando
Hasta llegar a vn salto lebantado,
De más de cien estados[14] descubiertos,[15]
De donde todos cinco se lanzaron,
Por milagro las vidas escapando,
Ecepto el miserable de Robledo,
Que, derramados los bullentes sesos,
Por las peñas bajó sin ambos ojos.
Y como Sosa y Tabora, con priessa,
Y con ellos Antonio Sariñana,
Se fueron a buen tiempo retirando,
Libres y sin zozobra decendieron
Al llano de la cumbre lebantada,
Donde el Alférez Casas quedó en guarda
De la importante y fuerte caballada,
El qual fue recogiendo a grande priessa
Aquellos quatro amigos despeñados,
Que casi muertos los halló, molidos,
Sin género de pulso ni sentido,
Con los quales salió sin detenerse
Al puesto y vando amigo que dejaron,
Donde los recibieron con gran llanto.
Y después que curaron los heridos
Acordaron que Tabora saliesse
A dar al General la triste nueva,
Y luego despacharon por la posta
Por todas las Provincias comarcanas
Porque a los Religiosos, descuidados,
Alguna tropa no les embistiesse
Y a todos sin las vidas los dexasen.
Y para obiar tan grande incombiniente
A todos escribieron y avisaron
Que a más andar se fuessen recogiendo
Al Real de san Iuan con toda priessa,
Donde ya con ligero y presto buelo
La vil parlera fama abía llegado
Con la infelix nueva desdichada.[16]
Allí luego el Sargento, descuidado,
De nueva tan atroz quedó suspenso,
Los brazos en el pecho bien cruzados
Y, teniendo el aliento por buen rato,
Con profundos gemidos fue vertiendo
Vna gran lluvia, con que fue apagando
Las brasas en que su alma se abrasaba,
De vna tan grande pérdida encendida.

Did then retreat, and with much haste,
130 Until they came to a high leap
Of more than a hundred fathoms,
Over which all five threw themselves,
By miracle escaping with their lives,
Except the miserable Robledo,
135 Who, with his flustered brains knocked out
Among the rocks, came down losing both eyes.
And as Sosa and Tabora, in haste,
And with them Antonio Sariñana,
Had made retreat all in good time,
140 They had descended freely, without risk,
From off the lofty peak unto the plain,
Where Ensign Casas had remained on guard
Of the important, numerous horse herd.
He gathered in mighty haste
145 Those four friends who had made the leap,
And found them broken, almost dead,
With no sort of pulse and senseless.
With them he left without delay
For that post and shelter of friends he'd left,
150 Where they were received with weeping.
And when the wounded had been cured,
It was agreed that Tabora should go
To give the General the sorry news,
And then quickly dispatched posthaste
155 To all the neighboring provinces
So that the monks, unwarned, might not
Be overwhelmed by some troop
And all left lifeless at their posts.
To obviate such an unbecoming thing,
160 They wrote them all and gave warning
To gather themselves at full speed
Unto the capital, San Juan, at once,
Where now on swift and ready wing
Ill-speaking rumor[3] had arrived
165 With the unhappy, sorrowful news.
There, then, the Sergeant, all unsuspecting,
At such terrible news was astounded,
His arms crossed tight across his breast
And, holding his breathing for a goodly time,
170 He poured out, amid deepest groans,
A mighty rain of tears that extinguished
The coals that burned within his soul,
Lighted by such a heavy loss.
And after his exhausted eyes

14. Estados = medidas, la estatura de un hombre.
15. Descubiertos = de caída.
16. Este adelantarse de la "fama" a las noticias es eco de los clásicos. Puede verse, por ejemplo, en Lucano, *La Farsalia* IV.

3. Villagrá uses *fama* here. Fame, depicted as rushing to anticipate news, is an echo from the classics. Its use, in a text most probably known to Villagrá, can be seen, for example, in Lucan, *Pharsalia* IV.

Y después que sus ojos, fatigados,
Vbieron un gran golfo ya vertido,
Todo lo más que pudo fue sufriendo[17]
Por no desconsolar a las mugeres,
Que en vivos gritos todas se encendían
Y, assí como leonas que bramando
Sus muertos cachorrillos rezucitan,[18]
No menos, dando vozes, pretendían
Dar vida a sus difuntos malogrados.
Y cada qual sintiendo su desdicha,
Gritos a sus maridos están dando
Y otras al dulze hijo y caro hermano,
Otras al bien hechor y deudo amado,
Con tanto sentimiento que ya el pueblo
Con lastimoso llanto se hundía
De las pobres señoras que mesaban[19]
Las hebras de oro fino que tenían
Y con sus blancas manos azotaban
Las rosadas mexillas de sus rostros
Con vno y otro golpe que se daban,
Haziendo tanta confussión y estruendo
Como quando con furia y con braveza
El poderoso mar resurte y vate
En las cóncabas rocas y peñascos
Que contra su gran fuerza se anteponen.
Vista tan gran desdicha y desbentura,
Reprimiendo el Sargento como pudo
Del sexo femenil el tierno llanto,
Sacando algunas fuerzas de flaqueza,
Bien lastimado, triste y afligido,
Mandó por los difuntos se hiziessen
Vnas tristes obsequias funerales.
En este medio tiempo y coiuntura,
Llegó el Capitán Tabora diziendo
No aber podido dar con el camino
Y rastro que el Gobernador llevaba.
Visto el recado con que abía venido,
Sin más acuerdo se mandó que Casas
Y que Francisco Sánchez, el caudillo,
Francisco Vázquez y Manuel Francisco,
Soldados de valor y de vergüenza,
Saliessen con grandíssima presteza
Y la nueva al Gobernador llevasen.
Y apenas se les dixo quando luego
En sus caballos bien encubertados
Marchando juntos, con valor, salieron,

175 Had now shed forth a sea of tears,
He then bore all as best he might
So as not to discourage the women,
Who all burst forth into screaming
And, like to lionesses who, roaring,
180 Restore to life their little cubs who die,[4]
They tried no less by loud screaming
To give life to their men, ultimately dead.
And each one feeling her own misfortune,
Some crying out for their husbands
185 And others for a sweet son or loved brother,
Others for benefactor and for loved kinfolk,
With such sorrow that all the town
Was sunk in sorrowful weeping
Of the poor women, who did tear
190 The hair of finest gold they wore
And with their white hands they did beat
Their rosy cheeks and their faces
With many blows they gave themselves,
Making as much confusion and uproar
195 As when with fury and ferocity
The powerful sea beats and rebounds
Upon the hollow rocks and cliffs
That do oppose its mighty force.
Seeing such great unhappiness and woe,
200 The Sergeant, checking as he could
The tender weeping of the female sex,
Taking some strength from his weakness,
Though sad enough, mournful and much downcast,
Ordered that for the dead be held
205 The sad funeral obsequies.
In the meantime and conjuncture
Captain Tabora arrived, telling him
That he had failed to find the road
And track by which the Governor had gone.
210 Seeing the message with which he had come,
Without more talk he ordered that Casas
And Francisco Sánchez, the Commander,
Francisco Vázquez and Manuel Francisco,
Soldiers of valor and of self-respect,
215 Should go in very greatest haste
And to the Governor should take the news.
And hardly had he spoken when at once,
Upon their well-caparisoned horses,
They left, marching together with courage,
220 And, breaking through a thousand hindrances

17. Sufriendo = resistiendo.
18. La misma imagen, de inequívoca procedencia clásica, se halla en *El peregrino indiano* XIX.
19. Mesaban = arrancaban.

4. This image, unequivocally from classical sources, is also found in *El peregrino indiano* XIX.

Y rompiendo por mil dificultades
Que los bárbaros siempre les pusieron
Sin poder ofender a sus personas,
Aunque algunos caballos les mataron,
Al fin, con buena y presta diligencia,
Llegaron estos quatro valerosos
Al mismo assiento, puesto y estalage
Donde en mi gran trabajo riguroso
Fuy por mi buena suerte socorrido.
Pues viniendo el Gobernador al puesto,
De aquella triste nueva descuidado,
Marchando con grandíssimo contento
Con acuerdo de hazer allí jornada
Y de hospedarse en Acoma otro día,
Abiendo prevenido grandes fiestas
Para quando el Real se descubriesse
Y otras para después que dentro entrase,
Estando, como digo, prevenido
Y todo con acuerdo platicado,
Llegaron los amigos sin consuelo,
Muy tristes, cabizbajos y llorosos.
Y antes que puedan dar la triste nueva
Quiero tomar reposo si pudiere,
Si es que por mi desgracia y corta suerte
He de bolver de nuevo a lamentarme
Para más afligirme y lastimarme.

Which the barbarians ever made for them
Without being able to injure them in person,
Although they killed a few horses,
At last, with good and speedy diligence,
225 These four right valiant ones arrived
Upon the very spot and location
Where, in my great and rigorous toil,
I was aided by my good fate.
The Governor then coming unto that place,
230 All unsuspecting that sad news,
Marching in the greatest content,
Thinking to halt for the night there
And shelter the next night at Acoma,
Having arranged a great celebration
235 For when the capital could be made out
And others for after he entered it,
Having, as I say, planned all this,
And all talked over in accord,
The friends arrived, all unhappy,
240 Most sad, heads lowered, all tearful.
And before they can give out the sad news
I wish to take repose, if I but may,
Since for my own misfortune and bad luck
I must once more make my lament
245 The more to grieve and hurt myself.

CANTO VEYNTE Y QVATRO

COMO SE DIO LA NUEVA AL GOUERNADOR Y DE
lo que fue sucediendo hasta llegar a San Iuan
de los Caballeros.

O más que loca, incierta, débil y dudosa

Esperanza variable de los hombres
Y sus vanos y altivos pensamientos,
Pues que en mitad de la carrera vana,
Quando con más braveza la atropellan,[1]
De súbito se vnde y zozobran
Primero[2] que en seguro y dulze puerto
Puedan de su barquillo, tenue, flaco,
Dando fondo, aferrar la pobre amarra![3]
Porque como begigas muy hinchadas
Que con agua y jabón los nínos tiernos
Por libiano canuto al aire esparzen,
Que quando más vistosas y agradables
En vn instante vemos desbanecen
Tan sin rastro de aquello que mostraron
Qual si nunca jamás obiessen sido,
No menos, Rey sublime y poderoso,
Todas las más humanas esperanzas,
Al fin como mortales, desbanecen
Y entonces se consumen y se acaban[4]
Quando dellas estamos más assidos,
Más prendados, más firmes y más ciertos,
Y menos sospechosos de perderlas.
Cuia verdad nos muestra y manifiesta
Aqueste claro exemplo que tenemos,
Pues abiéndonos puesto la fortuna
En la más alta cumbre de su rueda,
Teniendo ya pacífica la tierra
Sin ver gota de sangre derramada,
Como nunca jamás se vio parada,
Abiéndose mostrado faborable,
En enemiga buelta fue bolviendo,
Dándonos, quando menos entendimos,
De su mudable fee patente indicio.
Y assí, llegaron juntos los amigos
Y dando al General la triste nueva,
Siendo Casas de vista buen testigo
Para mayor dolor y sentimiento

---

1. Atropellan = derriban, alcanzan.
2. Primero = antes.
3. La imagen de la barquilla en mar tormentoso, representación de la vida, llegó a ser, como de Horacio, tópico en el Siglo de Oro.
4. Eco de las famosas coplas de Jorge Manrique.

CANTO XXIV

How the news was given to the Governor and what happened
afterward until arriving at San Juan de los Caballeros.

OH more than mad, uncertain, weak,
    doubtful,
And variable hope of men
And their most vain and haughty thoughts,
For in the midst of the vain race,
5   When they press on with the utmost fury,
They suddenly sink down and disappear
Before they can anchor the poor cable
Of their fragile, weak, little bark,[1]
Finding secure berth in a safe and pleasant port!
10   For like the much-swollen bubbles
Which, with water and soap, tender children
Spread to the air with a light cane,
Which, when most beautiful and most charming,
We see vanish in an instant,
15   So without trace of what they were
As if they never had been there,
No less, sublime and powerful King,
Do all the most of human hopes
Vanish at last, being merely mortal,
20   And then are consumed and are done[2]
When we are most attached to them,
Most pledged, most firm, and most certain,
And least suspicious of losing them.
The truth of which is shown and manifest to us
25   By that famous example that we have,
For fortune, having now set us
Upon the very summit of her wheel,
Having the land now pacified
Without a drop of blood being shed,
30   As she was never seen to stop,
Having shown herself favoring,
Turned to an enemy, she whirled about,
Giving us, when least expected,
A patent indication of her fickle faith.
35   So, together, the friends arrived
And, giving the sad news to the General,
The sight of Casas being good witness,
For greater anguish and sorrow,

---

1. The image of the bark in a tempestuous sea as a representation of life, from Horace, became commonplace in Renaissance and Siglo de Oro literature.
2. This verse, *se consumen y se acaban,* echoes another from the famous *Coplas* of Jorge Manrique, which Villagrá undoubtedly knew.

Del desastrado caso que contaba,
Cuio progresso apenas fue acabando
Quando se derribó⁵ de su caballo,
Que encubertado todo le traía,
Y por sus ojos lágrimas vertiendo
Y el rostro para el Cielo lebantando,
Hincadas las rodillas por el suelo,
Puestas las manos, todo demudado,
Assí esforzó la boz, desalentada,
Hablando a Dios el triste caballero:
"Gran señor, si la pobre navezilla
Que aquel grande piloto de tu Iglesia
Quiso y tuvo por bien de encomendarme
La tienes ya, por mí, aborrecida,
Si por mis graves culpas no merece
Le des tu mano santa, generosa,
Por esta vez suplico la perdones
Y no permitas paguen inocentes
La mucha gravedad de mis delictos.
Y si combiene todos zozobremos,
A tu voluntad santa, poderosa,
Estoi aquí sugeto y muy rendido.
Mas pues llegado abemos a estas tierras,
Suplícote, señor, que nos aguardes,
Suspendiendo el rigor de tu justicia
Y el grande y grave azote que descarga,
Y serenando nuestras pobres almas,
Gozemos del valor de tu clemencia."
Con éstas y otras cosas lamentables,
Alzándose del suelo, sollozando,
Tomó el caballo bien enternecido,
Y assí como llegamos al parage,
Solo a su tienda quiso recogerse,
Hincado de rodillas y en las manos
Vna Cruz pobre, hecha de dos trozos,
Ambos con su corteza, mal labrados,
Que a falta de otros me mandó buscase
Y que a su tienda luego los truxesse,
Donde passó la triste y larga noche
Gimiendo amargamente y suplicando
A Dios, nuestro señor, le diesse esfuerzo
Para poder llevar tan gran trabajo.
Y luego que la luz entró rompiendo
De la obscura tiniebla el negro manto,
Mandó que me llamasen y dixessen
Iuntos los compañeros le llevase.
Y estando a una todos recogidos
Y sin consuelo lágrimas vertiendo,
Salió del pabellón todo cubierto

In the disastrous things he told,
40 Whose telling he had hardly done
When he threw himself from his horse,
Which was right well caparisoned,
And pouring tears from his eyes
And raising up his face to Heaven,
45 His knees bending unto the ground,
His hands together, pale of countenance,
He thus forced out a feeble voice,
The sad knight, speaking to his God:
"Great Lord, if the poor, little ship
50 Which the great Pilot of Thy Church
Wished and thought well to trust to me
Thou dost detest now for my sake,
If for my heavy sins I deserve not
That Thou give it not Thy holy, generous hand,
55 I beg Thee that this time Thou pardon it
And permit not that innocents should pay
For the great weight of my transgressions.
And if it pleaseth Thee we all be in danger,
Before Thy holy, powerful will,
60 I here am subject and surrendered.
But since we have arrived among these lands,
I beg Thee, Lord, Thou suffer us,
Suspending the rigor of Thy justice
And the great, heavy lash that falls,
65 And, making our poor souls serene,
We may enjoy the power of Thy clemency."
With these and other lamentable things,
Rising from off the ground, sobbing,
He took his horse, most piteous,
70 And as soon as we reached the stopping place
He went into his tent alone,
Kneeling upon the ground and in his hands
A poor cross made out of two sticks,
Both badly worked in the cutting,
75 Which, lacking others, he commanded me to seek
And then bring to him in his tent,
Where he did pass the long, sad night
Groaning bitterly and praying
To God our Lord to give him strength
80 That he might bear so great a task.
And when the light appeared, breaking
The black mantle of dark shadows,
He ordered them to summon me and say
That I should call to him our companions.
85 And, all being gathered together
And shedding tears, disconsolate,
He left his tent, completely sunk

---

5. Se derribó = se bajó. Oñate, se entiende.

De fúnebre dolor, manso, lloroso,
Los ojos hechos carne y viva sangre,
Hinchados, tristes, tiernos, mal enjutos,
Descolorido todo y trasnochado.
Y afligido, apretándose las manos,
Estando allí parado por buen rato,
Assí como del áspero tomillo,
Azedo⁶ y desabrido, vemos saca
Miel para el panal la cauta abeja
Y della se socorre y faborece
Quando los tiempos cargan más sin jugo,⁷
Assí el Gobernador, a sus soldados,
Desconsolados, tristes y afligidos,
Queriendo por tres vezes esforzarse
A dezir su razón, quedó suspenso,
Con todas las palabras atoradas
A la pobre garganta y tierno pecho.
Y luego que el tormento fue aflojando
Algún tanto la cuerda que apretaba,
Dexándole alentar con más sossiego,
Assí habló a los flacos corazones:
"Señores compañeros, sabe el Cielo
Que me lastima el alma verlos todos
Desconsolados, güérfanos y tristes
Viendo la gran columna que nos falta
En el Maese de campo ya difunto
Y en los demás amigos valerosos
Cuias vidas, sin par y sin medida,
Sirbiendo a las dos grandes magestades
Sabemos fenecieron y acabaron.
La pobre carne ha hecho ya su oficio
Y assí será razón también que el alma
Prosiga con el suyo, pues es justo
Que en todo siempre vaya por delante.
No siento aquí varón que no se precie
De soldado de Christo verdadero,
Pues como tal, su sangre, Cruz y muerte
Viene a comunicar con grande esfuerzo
Por todas estas bárbaras naciones.
Sé dezir que no tiene todo el campo,
Soldadesca y exército de Christo,
Vn tan solo soldado en su estandarte
Que, según tuvo cada qual las fuerzas,
No fuesse fuertemente molestado
Y rigurosamente combatido.
Dexo todos aquéllos que oyeron
Y que por vista de ojos se hallaron
A vn millón de desastres prodigiosos

In funereal sorrow, weeping quietly,
His eyes much bleared and much bloodshot,
90   Swollen, sad, tender, hardly dried,
Discolored, showing signs of sleepless nights.
Clasping his hands, absorbed in grief,
Standing still there for a good while,
Just as from out the rough wild thyme,
95   Though it be tart and ill-tasting,
We see the prudent bee draw honey for its comb
And help and aid itself therewith
When the time of nectar is gone,
So was the Governor to his soldiers,
100 Disconsolate, sad, grieving as they were,
Trying three times in an effort
To say his say, he still said naught,
With all his words entirely choked
In his sad throat and grieving breast.
105 And when the torment somewhat loosed
The stricture with which it had pressed,
Letting him breathe more easily,
He thus spoke to their feeble hearts:
"My gentlemen companions, Heaven knows
110 It pains my very soul to see you all
Disconsolate, orphaned, and sad
At seeing the great pillar we do lack
In him, the Army Master, who is dead,
And in the rest of our brave friends
115 Whose lives, unequaled and without measure,
We know ended and were finished
Serving the two great Majesties.
The poor flesh has now done its work,
And thus 'tis right that the soul also
120 Should keep on with its own, for it is just
That it in all things should go first.
I know there's no man here that is not prized
As a soldier of the true Christ,
And so His blood and cross and death
125 Do come with such effort to be made known
Through all these barbarous nations.
I know that I can say not all the camp,
The soldiery, and the army of Christ,
Has not a single soldier beneath its standard
130 Who has not, in proportion to his strength,
Been troubled to the very utmost
And been opposed with a mighty rigor.
I leave aside all those who heard
And those who saw themselves with their own eyes
135 A million prodigious disasters

---

6. Azedo = acedo, ácido.

7. Jugo = nectar.

Con que quedaron todos lastimados
Y assí como nosotros afligidos,
Dezidme, los demás, ¿por dónde fueron
Y quál fue la derrota que llevaron?
Los vnos vivos fueron enterrados
Y también aserrados otros vivos.
A otros desollaron el pellejo.
Descoiuntados otros acabaron,
Y a bocados de cruel tenaza viva
Vna gran suma dellos fenecieron.
Otros crucificados y azotados,
Desquartizados otros valerosos,
Tanto más esforzados y estimados
Quanto mayor martirio padezieron.
Si es que tenéys espíritu de Christo,
Señores compañeros, lluevan muertes,
Carguen trabajos, vengan aflicciones,
Porque el que de nosotros más sufriere
Más triunfo, más alteza, más trofeo
Es verdad infalible que le aguarda.
Y pues esto es assí, varones nobles,
Deseche cada qual la vil tristeza
Y a Dios lebante el alma, y no desmaye
En quien sin duda alguna espero y fío
Que si con veras todos le seguimos
Que con veras y por su misma mano
Abemos de ser todos consolados."
Y luego que el Gobernador, prudente,
Acabó con su plática parece
Que, qual marchito campo que se alegra
Y brota, crece, sube y se lebanta
Con fuerza de las aguas que derraman
Las poderosas nubes a su tiempo,
Que assí todos se fueron consolando,
Sacudiendo de sí el disconsuelo
Y dolor melancólico, pesado,
Con que sus almas tristes lastimaban
Viendo a su General con tanto pecho,
Esforzado, animado y alentado.
El qual luego empezó a ponerlo todo
En buen concierto y orden por si acaso
A nosotros los bárbaros saliessen.
Y assí, determinó Tomás entrase,
Como de aquella tierra buen piloto
Y lengua de los Indios naturales,
A dar aviso a todos los amigos
Que allí, golosos del metal sabroso,
A descubrir las grandes minas fueron,

By which they all were most gravely injured
And were afflicted like ourselves,
The rest, tell me where they went
And what the route was that they took?[3]
140 Of them, some were interred alive,
And some, alive, were sawed in two.
Others had their skin flayed from them;
Others died torn to pieces,
And from the bites of the cruel pincers
145 A great number of them perished.
Others were crucified, beaten to death;
Other brave ones cut in quarters,
The greater thought of and esteemed
As they had suffered greater martyrdom.
150 If you possess the true spirit of Christ,
My gentlemen companions, let death rain,
Toils multiply, afflictions come,
For he of us who suffers most,
Most triumph, most highness, greatest trophy,
155 Awaits him. This is truth infallible.
And since it is thus, noble men,
Let each cast off his vile sadness
And lift his soul to God, nor yet despair.
In Him, beyond all doubt, I trust and hope,
160 For if we all do follow Him truly,
Then truly, and by His own hand,
We all shall yet be comforted."
And when the prudent Governor
Had finished his speech, it appeared
165 That, like a withered field which takes pleasure,
Bursts out, increases, grows and rises up
With the strength of the waters shed
By powerful clouds in their season,
All there were likewise comforted,
170 Shaking their sorrow from themselves
And heavy, melancholy grief
With which they wounded their sad souls,
Seeing their General with such courage
Supplied, driven on, and supported.
175 He then began to arrange all
In good concert and in order, lest by chance
The barbarians should attack us.
He also ordered that Tomás should go,
Being a good guide for that land
180 And translator to the native Indians,
To give warning to all our friends,
Who, eager for the most pleasing metal,
Had gone to discover the mighty mines,

3. These verses imitate the *Ubi sunt* topos, also greatly reworked in Renaissance and post-Renaissance Spanish literature.

Para que derrotados[8] se bolviessen
A san Iuan con grandíssimo recato.
De cuia esquadra quiso adelantarse
El Capitán Farfán en compañía
Del Capitán Quesada, porque juntos
Salieron con la nueva de las vetas,
Según que atrás lo abemos ya contado.
Hecha esta prevención, que fue importante,
Alzose todo el campo y fue marchando,
Llevando en la banguardia gran cuidado,
Y cuerpo de batalla y retaguardia.
Y porque todo fuesse más seguro,
Ligeros corredores despachaba
Que tierra descubriessen y abisasen
De qualquiera subcesso que importase.
Y como siempre vemos que aborrecen
La belleza del sol los mal hechores,
No libres de traición y de encubierta,
De noche a punto todos nos velamos
Con cuidadosas postas desembueltos
Y grandes centinelas bien partidas,[9]
Con que al quarto del alba juntos todos
Continuamente siempre nos hallamos
Vigilantes y bien apercebidos.
Y con este orden fuimos a alojarnos,
Fatigados de sed, a vna cañada,
Por cuias peñas fuimos recogiendo
Cierta parte de nieve, retirada,
Donde el rigor del Sol no pudo entrarle.
Aquésta con el fuego regalamos[10]
Puesta en los hielmos, cascos y zeladas,
Y al fin hizimos razonable aguage
Con que nuestra gran sed satisfizimos.
Y aquél que no desamparó los suyos,
Qual verdadera senda,[11] fue guíando
Nuestros cansados passos de manera
Que llegó a salvamento todo el campo
Muy cerca de san Iuan, adonde estaba
El Sargento bien triste y cuidadoso
Porque nunca jamás abía tenido
De todo nuestro campo nueva alguna.
Viendo el Gobernador quan cerca estaba,
Mandó salir al niño don Christóbal
Para que de su parte visitase
Al Sargento mayor por su persona.

That they, by other route, return
185   To San Juan with the very greatest haste.
From which group had already come
Captain Farfán, and with him, too,
Captain Quesada, since they together
Had come with the news of the lode,
190   As we have related before.
The warning given, which was important,
The whole camp rose and took the march,
Maintaining care in the vanguard,
The main body, and the rear guard,
195   And that all might be yet safer
He sent out light-armed skirmishers
Who should spy out the land and send in news
Of any event that was important.
And as we always see evildoers
200   Abhor the beauty of the sun,
Not free from treason and deceit,
At night we sent out guards at once
And set out posts most carefully,
And strong vedettes set well apart,
205   So that 'til dawning, together,
We invariably found ourselves
Continually vigilant and on the watch.
And in this order we did lodge one night,
Much worn with thirst, in a canyon,
210   Along whose rocky sides we collected
A little bit of snow, preserved
Where the sun's heat could not reach it.
This we entrusted to the fire,
Placed in our helmets, casques, sallets,
215   And finally we had a small supply
Of water, satisfying our great thirst.
And He who never abandons his own,
As a true path,[4] did guide
Our tired feet in such a way
220   That all the camp arrived safely
Right near San Juan, where there then was
The Sergeant, very sad and in deep care
Because he never yet had had
A bit of news of all our camp.
225   The Governor, seeing how near he was,
Ordered the child, Don Cristóbal, to go
And in his behalf to visit
The Sergeant Major as his representative.

8. Derrotados = fuera del camino usual; es decir, no pasando por Acoma.
9. Partidas = repartidas.
10. Regalamos = derritimos.
11. Villagrá, poéticamente, dado el contexto, usa "senda," sinónimo de Dios en la terminología religiosa.

4. John 14:1–12.

Y porque su edad tierna no le daba
Lugar a lo que el Padre pretendía,
Para que aquesta falta se supliesse[12]
Y que por él vbiesse quien hablase
Encomendose toda aquesta causa
Al Capitán Quesada y juntamente
Que fuesse yo con él al mismo efecto.
Mandonos que con veras se pidiesse
A todos los amigos que escusasen
De salir al camino a recebirle,
Porque sería ocasión de lastimarle
Más de lo que él venía, aunque esforzando
A todos los del campo fatigado.[13]
También nos encargó que con cuidado
Viessemos de su parte a las biudas
Y a todos los demás que perdidosos
Obiessen, por desastre o mala suerte,
De la desdicha de Acoma salido,
Y a todos ofreciessemos, con veras,
De su misma alma y vida todo el resto,
Porque con alma y vida procuraba
Hazer en su consuelo tanto efecto
Quanto era bien hiziesse por[14] salbarse.
Llegamos, pues, a casa del Sargento,
Cuia vista me puso en gran tristeza
Porque de tres que juntos estuvimos
Dentro de aquel albergue, descuidados,
Ya güérfanos los dos quedado abemos,
Aguardando encogidos nuestra suerte.
Dios sabe quál será y también el quándo.
Visitamos también a las biudas
Y fue tal el dolor que en todas vimos
Que, assí como al Sargento no hablamos,
Menos a ellas palabras les diximos.[15]
En esta sazón, luego, tras nosotros
Llegó el Gobernador con todo el campo,
Y estando en su presencia todos juntos
No se escapó garganta que añudada,
Enzolbada[16] y suspensa no se viesse,
Ni ojos que allí no se quebrasen,
Rebentando de lágrimas copiosas,
Viendo el Gobernador que abía llegado.
Y sin que hombre razón allí dixesse,
Sólo vbo abrazos tiernos y apretados,

230

235

240

245

250

255

260

265

270

And since his tender age would not permit
All that his father desired,
And that this lack might be supplied
And he might have someone to speak,
He entrusted all this affair
To Captain Quesada, and with him
Ordered I go, to that same end.
He ordered that we should sincerely beg
All of our friends that they would not
Come out upon the road to receive him
As it would occasion him more sorrow
Than he already bore, although it bother
All those within the tired camp.
He also ordered us that we should carefully
Visit, on his behalf, widows
And all the rest who had emerged
With loss, through disaster or evil fate,
Arising from the misfortune at Acoma,
And we should truly offer them
All of his very soul and life,
For with his life and soul he tried
To work such things, that they might be consoled,
As he might do for his own salvation.
We came, then, to the house of the Sergeant,
The sight of which caused me great grief,
For of we three who lived together there,
Within that shelter, without care,
Two of us now remained orphans,
Awaiting, timidly, our fate.
God knows what it will be and, also, when.
We visited the widows, too,
And such the sorrow that we saw in them
That, as we had not talked to the Sergeant,
Still less said we a word to them.
In the meantime, following us,
The Governor arrived with all the camp,
And, being all gathered in his presence,
There was no throat escaped being seen
To tighten, contracted and all useless,
Nor eyes that did not there burst out
And shed most copious tears
Seeing the Governor who had arrived.
And, without any man there speaking word,
There were only tender, close embraces,

12. La reproducción mexicana trae "supiesse."
13. Aunque el no salir a recibir y remediarlos esforzara a sus hombres fatigados.
14. La reproducción mexicana trae "par."
15. A ellas aún menos palabras les dijimos.
16. Enzolbada = ensolvida, contraída.

Crianza de buena gorra[17] y no otra cosa.

Y assí, juntos, al Templo le llevamos,

Donde también los santos Religiosos,

Sin dezirle palabra, le abrazaron

Y, rindiendo al inmenso Dios las gracias

Por su buena venida, le cantaron

Te Deum laudamus, todos muy contritos.

Y acabado el oficio todos fuimos

Con él hasta su casa bien llorosos,

Y dexándole allí, fue repartida

La cuidadosa vela por sus quartos,

Y cada qual se fue, qual nunca vaya

Alárabe ni moro,[18] a su posada,

Desconsolado, triste y afligido,

En su confusso pecho rebolviendo

Cien mil quimeras tristes, lastimosas,

Y las zozobras grandes y trabajos

Ordinarios que siempre nos cargaban.

El pesado desastre sucedido,

La soledad del campo sin su abrigo,[19]

La tierra rebelada y alterada,

El pequeño socorro y gran peligro,

Nuestro flaco partido y corta fuerza,

La enemiga pujanza si quisiesse

Proseguir en la rota comenzada,

Todas aquestas y otras muchas cosas

Las lastimadas almas rebolvían

Dentro de sus albergues, alteradas.

Y el General prudente, que asistía

Velando y no durmiendo en esta causa,

Y en cuio ossado y animoso pecho

Los cuidados de todos se encerraban,

Aguardando a la luz de la mañana

Estaba el esforzado caballero.

Y para ver el orden que ha trazado,

Pues viene ya rayando el claro día,

Será razón que yo también me aguarde

Y en advertirlo todo no me tarde.

275 The service of good manners and no other thing.

And so we took him near to the temple,

Where also the holy religious,

Saying no word, did embrace him,

And, giving thanks unto Almighty God

For his safe arrival, they sang

Te Deum laudamus, all most contrite.

280 And, services over, we all did go

With him up to his house, all weeping much,

And, leaving him there, we distributed

The watchful guard about these, his quarters,

And each one went, as never may

285 An Arab or a Moor,[5] to his lodgings,

Disconsolate, sad, and grieving,

Revolving in his confused mind

A hundred thousand sad and gloomy chimeras

And the many anxieties and toils

290 That always, ordinarily, did weigh on us.

The great disaster that occurred,

The solitude of the camp, his protection gone,

The land rebelled and greatly changed,

The little aid, the great danger,

295 Our weak party, our little strength,

The enemy's power should he wish

To follow up the route he had begun,

All these and many other things

The saddened souls reflected on,

300 Disturbed, within their homes.

The prudent General, too, who much pondered

Awake, not sleeping, upon this affair,

And in whose daring and courageous breast

The cares of all were fast locked up,

305 This energetic cavalier

Was waiting for the morning light.

And so to see the order he had planned,

As clear day now comes shining forth,

'Twere right that I should also wait

310 And not delay in noting all.

17. Crianza de buena gorra = saludos.

18. Parece maldición contra enemigo: que los citados nunca tengan posada, refugio.

19. Abrigo = defensa. Se refiere al muerto maese de campo.

5. This appears to be a form of malediction: wishing the enemy bereft of home and haven.

Canto Veynte y Cinco

COMO SE HIZO CABEZA DE PROCESSO[1] CONTRA
LOS Indios de Acoma y de los pareceres que dieron los
Religiosos, y de la instrucción que se le dio al Sargento mayor
para que saliesse al castigo de los dichos Indios.

NO bien la fresca Aurora entró rindiendo

El encogido quarto[2] quando estaba
El fuerte General, sin desarmarse,
Hablando con las velas y ordenando,
Por aberse ya muerto el Secretario,
Iuan Pérez de Donís, vn gran sugeto
Y que sirvió muy bien en esta entrada,
Hiziesse Iuan Gutiérrez Bocanegra,
Alcaide y Capitán, por ser muy diestro,
Contra la gente de Acoma y su fuerza
Cabeza de processo. Y ésta hecha,
Estando ya la causa sustanciada,
Antes de dar sentencia quiso diesse
El Padre Comissario y Religiosos
Su voto cada qual sobre estas dudas,
Cuios escritos graves me parece
Que sin mudar estilo aquí se pongan.

Caso que puso el Gobernador para que sobre él diessen
su parecer los Padres Religiosos

DON Iuan de Oñate, Gobernador y Capitán general
y Adelantado de las Provincias de la nueva México:
Pregunta ¿qué se requiere para la justificación de
la guerra y, supuesto que es la guerra justa, qué podrá hazer
la persona que la hiziere acerca de los vencidos y sus bienes?

Respuesta del Comissario y Religiosos

LA pregunta propuesta contiene dos puntos: el pri-
mero es, ¿qué se requiere para que la guerra sea
justa? Al qual se responde que se requiere, lo pri-
mero, autoridad de Príncipe que no reconozca superior,
como lo es el Pontífice Romano, el Emperador y los Reyes
de Castilla, que gozan de previlegio de Imperio en no re-
conocer superior en lo temporal, y otros; assí ellos, por su

---

1. Cabeza de processo = cabeza de proceso, oficio que provee el juez para investigar un delito.
2. Se refiere a la segunda y última mitad de la noche, pero su uso de "fresca Aurora" y "encogido" para designar a ese último cuarto del día sugiere una referencia mitológica, a Aurora y Titono. Este se fue reduciendo (encogiendo) en la avanzada decrepitud.

Canto XXV

How a process was drawn up against the Indians of Acoma and
of the opinion the monks gave, and of the instructions given the
Sergeant Major that he might go forth to the punishment of the
aforesaid Indians.

SCARCE had the fresh dawn entered, defeating

The spent quarter[1], when the strong General
Was, without having taken off his arms,
Conversing with the sentries, ordering
5 That, since the secretary now was dead,
Juan Pérez de Donís, your true subject,
One who had served well on this expedition,
Juan Gutiérrez Bocanegra should,
Being a judge and captain and well skilled,
10 Draw up against the folk and fort of Acoma
Beginning of a suit. And, this being done,
The cause being substantiated well,
Before giving sentence he wished
The Father Commissary and the monks
15 Should each give vote upon his doubts,
Whose serious writings, it seems to me,
Should be placed here unchanged in style.

The case which the Governor put, that the holy
Fathers might give their opinions upon it.

DON Juan de Oñate, Governor and Captain General
and Adelantado of the provinces of New Mexico,
asks what is required for the justification of war,
and, supposing that the war is just, what the person who
makes it may do concerning the conquered and their goods?

Reply of the Commissary and monks.

THE question proposed contains two points. The first
is, what is required for war to be justified? To
which is replied that there is required, first, the
authority of a prince who does not recognize a superior,
such as is the Roman Pontiff, the Emperor, and the rulers
of Castile, who enjoy the privilege of empire in not rec-
ognizing a superior in temporal affairs, and others; they in

---

1. The reference is to the last quarter of the night. The poetic reference (fresh dawn/spent night) appears to be to the Aurora/Tithonus myth.

persona, o quien su poder obiere para este efecto, porque persona particular no puede mover guerra, pues se requiere combocar gente para ella, que es acto de sólo el Príncipe, y él puede pedir su justicia ante su superior.

Lo segundo, se requiere que aya justa causa para la sobredicha guerra, la qual es en vna de quatro maneras: o por defender a inocentes que injustamente padecen, a cuia defensa están los Príncipes obligados siempre que pudieren; o por repetición[3] de bienes que injustamente les han tomado; o por castigar a delinquentes y culpados contra sus leyes, si son sus súbditos, o contra las de naturaleza, aunque no lo sean; y vltima y principalmente por adquirir y conservar la paz, porque éste es el fin principal a que se ordena la guerra.

Lo tercero, se requiere para la omnímoda justificación de la guerra justa y recta intención en los que pelean, y será justa peleando por qualquiera de las quatro causas que acabamos de dezir y no por ambición de mandar ni por venganza mortal ni por codicia de los bienes agenos.

El segundo punto de la pregunta es, ¿qué podrá hazer la persona que hiziere la dicha justa guerra de los vencidos y sus bienes? Al qual se responde que los dichos vencidos y sus bienes quedan a merced del vencedor en la forma y manera que requiere la causa justa que mobió la guerra, porque si fue defensión de inocentes puede proceder hasta dexarlos libres y ponerlos en salvo y puede satisfazerles y satisfazerse de los daños que han padecido y de los que han contraído en este hecho, a semejanza de Moisén en la defensión del Hebreo maltratado del Egipcio.

Y si la causa de la guerra fue repetición de bienes, puede satisfazerse tanto por tanto en la misma especie o en su valor en toda justicia; y si quiere vsar de autoridad de ministro de la divina justicia y juez de la humana, puede, como tal ministro y juez, estender más la mano en los bienes de su contrario, penando y castigando su delicto, sin obligación de restitución, a semejanza del Iuez que ahorca a vno porque hurtó algunos maravedís o Reales.

Si la causa de la guerra es castigo de delinquentes y culpados, ellos y sus bienes quedan a su voluntad y merced conforme a las justas leyes de su Reyno y República si son sus súbditos, y si no lo fuessen, los puede reducir a vivir conforme a la ley divina y natural por todos los modos y medios que en justicia y razón le fuere visto convenir, atropellando todos los inconvenientes que a esto se le pudiessen ofrecer de qualquier modo que fuessen, siendo tales que le pudiessen estorbar el justo efecto que pretende.

Y finalmente, si la causa de la guerra es la paz universal o de su Reyno y República, puede muy más justamente hazer la sobredicha guerra y destruir todos los incombi-

person, or whoever may possess their power for this effect, for a private individual cannot make war, for the collection of people for it is required, which is the act of the prince alone, and he can plead to justice before his superior.

The second requires that there shall be just cause for the aforesaid war, which is in one of four manners: either to defend the innocent who suffer unjustly, to whose defense princes are obligated whenever they are able, or for the recovery of property which has been unjustly taken from them, or to punish delinquents and guilty persons under his laws if they are his subjects or under those of nature if they are not, and, finally and principally, to secure and preserve peace, for that is the principal end for which war is ordained.

Thirdly, there is required, for the entire justification of war, a just and right intention in those who fight; and it will be just fighting for any of the four causes which we have just stated and not through ambition to rule nor for mortal vengeance, nor for the desire for the property of others.

The second point of the question is: what can the person who may make the aforesaid war do in regard to those conquered and their possessions? To which it is replied that the aforesaid conquered and their goods remain at the mercy of the conqueror, according to the form and manner required by the just cause which moved the war, for if it was defense of the innocent, he can proceed until he leaves them free and places them in safety, and may satisfy them and satisfy himself for the damages they have suffered and for those they have incurred in this deed, like Moses in the defense of the Hebrew ill-treated by the Egyptian.

And if the cause of the war was the recovery of property, he may satisfy himself measure for measure in the same kind or in its value in all justice, and if he wishes to use the authority of a minister of divine justice and judge of human, he may, as such minister and judge, extend his hand further, penalizing and chastising his crime, without obligation of restitution, like the judge who hangs a man because he stole some maravedís or reales.

If the cause of the war is the punishment of delinquents and those guilty, they and their goods remain at his will and mercy, according to the just laws of his kingdom and republic, if they are his subjects; and if they should not be, he may reduce them to live according to the law divine and natural by all the methods and means which in justice and reason may seem proper to him, overcoming all hindrances which may be offered to this, of whatever sort they may be, these being such that they may disturb the just result which he intends.

---

3. Repetición = reclamación.

nientes que estorbaren la sobredicha paz hasta conseguirla con efecto, y conseguida, no debe de guerrear más, porque el acto de la guerra no es acto de elección y voluntad, sino de justa ocasión y necessidad, y assí debe requerir[4] con la paz, antes que la empieze, si guerrea por sólo ella, y si también guerrea por otras causas de las ya dichas, puede repetir y tomar la debida satisfación a ellas, absteniéndose de no dañar a los inocentes, porque éstos siempre son salvos en todo derecho, pues no han cometido culpa, y absteniéndose todo lo que fuere possible de muertes de hombres, lo vno porque es odiosíssima a Dios, tanto que de mano del justo David, por aber sido omicida, no quiso recebir Templo ni morada. Lo segundo, por la manifiesta condenación de cuerpo y alma que, en los contrarios que injustamente pelean, con la muerte se causa, de los quales pudiera aber muchos convertidos o justificados, andando el tiempo, si allí no morían. Puesto caso que es assí verdad, que, cessando la necessidad o manifiesto peligro a muertes,[5] o por ser impossible de otra manera la victoria o por justa sentencia de Iuez competente en tal caso, no es la culpa de los matadores que, como ministros de la divina justicia, executan, sino de los muertos que, como culpados, lo merecieron. Y este es mi parecer, salvo otro mejor.

Fray Alonso Martínez, Comissario Apostólico.

Esto mismo sintieron y firmaron todos los demás Padres.

CON cuios pareceres, bien fundados
En muchos textos, leyes y lugares
De la Escriptura santa, luego quiso,
Viendo el Gobernador que concurrían
Todas aquestas cosas en el caso
Y dudas que assí quiso proponerles,
Cerrar aquesta causa y sentenciarla,
Mandando pregonar, a sangre y fuego,
Contra la fuerza de Acoma, la guerra.
Y por querer hazerla y ordenarla
Por su propria persona, y fenecerla,
Vbo sobre este acuerdo grandes cosas
Muy largas de contar; mas por yr breve,
Al fin, a fuerza grande de la Iglesia
Y de todo el Real, fue suspendida
La voluntad precisa que tenía
De salir en persona, y puso luego
Sobre los fuertes hombros del Sargento

And, finally, if the cause is universal peace, either of his kingdom or republic, he may much more justly wage the aforesaid war and destroy all impediments that may disturb the aforesaid peace, until effectually securing it, and, having secured it, he should not make war further, because the act of war is not an act of choice and will but of just occasion and necessity, and so he should seek peace before he begins it if he makes war only for it; and also, if he makes war for other causes than those already stated, he may demand and take the satisfaction due them, abstaining from injuring the innocent, because they are always secure in all right, since they have committed no fault; and avoiding, as far as possible, the death of men, first, because it is most hateful to God, so much so, that from the hand of the just David, on account of his having been a homicide, He did not wish to receive a temple nor a dwelling place; the second, through the manifest condemnation of body and soul which in the opponents who unjustly combat by death is caused, of whom there might be many converted or justified in the course of time if they had not died there. Notwithstanding that it is thus true that, discounting the necessity or manifest peril of death, or victory being impossible in any other way, or by a just sentence of a competent judge, in such case, it is not the fault of the slayers, who as ministers of divine justice execute, but of the dead who, as culprits, deserved it. And this is my opinion, lacking a better one.

Fray Alonso Martínez, Apostolic Commissary.

This was agreed to and signed by all the other Fathers.

With whose opinions, well-founded
On many texts, laws and places
20   In holy Scripture, then the Governor,
Seeing how all these things agreed
Upon the case and doubts that he had wished
To be proposed to them, he wished
To close that case and give sentence,
25   Ordering war, with fire and blood,
Proclaimed against the fort of Acoma.
And since he wished to do and order it
In his own person, and to finish it,
There was in this matter debate
30   Too long to tell, but, to be brief,
At last, by the Church's great strength,
As well as that of all the camp,
The dutiful will that he had to go
In person was suspended, and he put
35   Upon the mighty shoulders of the Sergeant

4. Requerir = intimar.
5. Descontando los casos en que haya peligro de muerte.

El peso y gravedad de aqueste hecho.
Para cuyo buen fin mandó saliesse
Por su lugar teniente y castigase
A toda aquesta gente por las muertes
Que dieron y causaron tan sin causa
A vuestros Españoles ya difuntos,
De donde total quiebra se seguía
De la vniversal paz que ya la tierra
En sí toda tenía y alcanzaba,
Demás del gran peligro manifiesto
De tantos niños, todos inocentes,
Tiernas donzellas con sus pobres madres,
Sin los Predicadores y ministros
De la doctrina santa y Fe de Christo
Y libertad que todos alcanzaban
Con el fabor y amparo que tenían
En su misma persona, a cuio cargo
Sería qualquier daño que viniesse
Si aquestos alebosos se quedasen
Sin la debida enmienda que pedía
Delicto tan inorme y tan pesado.
Por cuia justa causa luego quiso
Que a toda diligencia se aprestase,
Y, pues su autoridad toda le daba,
Tomase en sí la comissión y diesse
Recibo al Secretario del entrego.
Mandándole, con esto, que estorbase
A todos los soldados, lo primero,
Las ofensas de Dios, y que hiziesse,
Llevando vía recta su derrota,
Fuessen los naturales bien tratados
Por doquiera que fuesse y que passase;
Y luego que la fuerza descubriesse,
Notase, con acuerdo, sus assientos,
Entradas y salidas, y en la parte
Que más bien le estuviesse que plantase
La fuerza de los tiros y mosquetes,
Y, en sus lugares puestos y ordenados
Todos los Capitanes y soldados
Por sus esquadras diestras prevenidos,
Sin que en manera alguna permitiesse
Ruido de arcabuzes ni otra cosa,
Con mucha suavidad allí llamase
De paz aquella gente, pues abía
Rendido la obediencia, y entregasen
Todos los movedores que causaron
El passado motín, y que dexasen
La fuerza del Peñol y en vn buen llano,
Seguro de que mal hazer pudiessen,
Assentasen su pueblo, donde fuessen

The weight and the gravity of that deed.
For which good end he ordered him to go
As his lieutenant and to castigate
All of those people for the deaths
40 That they had dealt and caused, so without cause,
Unto your Spaniards now dead,
Whence there had followed total breach
Of that peace universal which the land
Had possessed and attained throughout,
45 Beside the great danger, most manifest,
Unto so many innocent children
And tender damsels with their poor mothers,
Beside the preachers and the ministers
Of holy doctrine and the faith of Christ
50 And liberty which all possessed
With the shelter and favor which they had
In his own person, to whose charge
Would fall what damage might occur
If those traitors should continue
55 Without the due payment required
For such enormous and serious crime.
For this just cause he then did wish
That he should hasten with all diligence
And gave to him all his authority
60 To take upon himself the commission and give
Receipt unto the secretary for his charge,
Ordering him, moreover, to forbid
To all the soldiers, above everything,
Any offense to God, and telling him
65 That, taking the most direct route,
The natives should be treated well
Wherever they should go or pass;
And when he should approach the fort
He should note carefully its form,
70 Its entrances and exits, and what place
It might be best for him to plant
His ordnance and his force of musketeers,
And, set in place and well-ordered,
The captains and all the soldiers
75 Made ready in their skilled squadrons,
And that, without any way permitting
A noise of harquebuses or other things,
He was to summon, with much gentleness,
Those people unto peace, because they had
80 Given obedience, and was to order them
To give up all the leaders who had caused
The recent mutiny, and to come down
From the fort on the rock and on the plain,
Safe from the possibility of doing ill,
85 To set their town, to which should come

A sólo predicarles los ministros
Del Evangelio santo la doctrina,
Pues por sólo este fin abían venido
De tierras tan remotas y apartadas,
Y que los cuerpos, armas y los vienes
De los pobres difuntos entregasen.
Y si en aquesto todo se viniesse,[6]
Que, quemada la fuerza y abrasada,
A los culpados presos los truxesse.
Y si rebeldes todos se mostrasen
Y viesse se arresgaba y se ponía
En condición y punto de perderse,
Que mucho se abstuviesse y que mirase
Cosa tan importante y tan pesada
Con muy maduro acuerdo y buen consejo.
Y si faborecidos y amparados
Fuessen de nuestro Dios y la victoria
Allí por vuestra España se cantase,
Que a todos juntos presos los truxesse,
Sin que chico ni grande se escapase,
Y que a los de edad entera que hiziesse,
En todos, sin que nadie se escapase,
Vn exemplar castigo, de manera
Que todos los demás con tal enmienda
Quedasen para siempre escarmentados.[7]
Y si después de presos combiniesse
Hazer algún perdón, que se buscasen
Todos los medios, trazas y caminos
De suerte que los Indios entendiessen
Que aquel perdón que sólo se alcanzaba
Por no más que pedirlo al Religioso
Que acerca deste caso intercediesse,
Porque notasen todos y advirtiessen
Que eran personas graves y de estima
Y a quien muy gran respecto se debía.
Y porque bien en todo se acertase,
Del consejo de guerra mandó fuessen,
Y al Sargento mayor acompañasen,
El Contador y Provehedor Zubía
Y Pablo de Aguilar, Farfán y Márquez,
Y yo también con ellos quiso fuesse
Porque con tales guías me adestrase

The ministers only to preach to them
The doctrine of the holy Evangel,
Since they had come here for this end alone
From lands so far and so remote.
90 They were, moreover, to give up
The bodies, arms, and goods of those poor dead.
And if in all this they should come about,
That, razing and burning the fort,
He should bring the guilty back prisoners.
95 If all should show themselves rebellious,
And it be seen that he risked much and placed himself
In a position where he might be lost,
That he should forbear much and should observe
So important and weighty a matter
100 With careful judgment, good counsel.
And if we should be favored and aided
By our God, and if victory
Should be sung there for your Spain,
He should bring all together, prisoners,
105 Without one, great or small, escaping him,
And that upon those of mature age he should make,
On all, without one escaping,
An exemplary punishment, so that
All of the rest, at such indemnity,
110 Might take a warning for all time.[2]
If, after they were taken, he should choose
To grant some pardons, they should seek
All the ways, means, and all the roads
So that the Indians might understand
115 That pardon could be gained only
Through no more than asking it of the monk
Who should intercede in the case.
Thus they would all note and observe
That these were persons of high esteem
120 To whom most great respect was due.
That he might succeed well in all,
He ordered out from the council of war
To go in company with the Sergeant Major
The paymaster and the purveyor Zubía
125 And Pablo de Aguilar, Farfán, Márquez,
And wished me, too, to go with them
As with such guides I might gain skill

---

6. Viniesse = viniese, conviniese.

7. Del castigo feroz que impuso Zaldívar, por el cual él y Oñate fueron posteriormente juzgados, no se hace mención. Se explica, y la historia de la humanidad a ningún pueblo dominante excusa de ello, que los que, siendo pocos, pretenden controlar a muchos tengan el escarmiento como medida necesaria. Aparte el sinnúmero de ejemplos de la historia, antigua y moderna, puede verse, por ejemplo, el castigo impuesto a los indios en Ercilla, *La araucana* II, 22, 26. Para detalles sobre el castigo efectivamente impuesto a los acomeses, véase Villagrá, *Historia,* edición de Junquera, 407.

2. Nothing is mentioned in the poem of the harsh punishment eventually meted out by Zaldívar, and for which he and Oñate would later be tried in Mexico City. The degree of harshness involved may perhaps be best gauged by a comparison within the context of the times, as, for example, with the punishment given captive Indians in *La araucana* II, 22, 26. For details about same, see Villagrá, *Historia,* Junquera edition, 407.

En vuestro Real serbicio y no estuviesse
Tan torpe como siempre me mostraba
En cosas de momento y de importancia.
También mandó que Iuan Velarde hiziesse,
Por ser sagaz, prudente y avisado
En todas nuestras juntas, el oficio
De Secretario fiel, pues por la pluma
No menos era noble y bien mirado
Que por la illustre espada que ceñía.
Después de todo aquesto se nombraron
Setenta valerosos combatientes,
Cuias grandiosas fuerzas se aumentaron
Mediante la destreza y el trabajo
De Iuan Cortés, Alférez tan valiente
Quanto muy diestro y prático en las armas,
Que a fuerza de sus brazos puso en punto
Para poder romper,⁸ sin que hiziessen
Al combatiente falta,⁹ en la refriega
En que después nos vimos y hallamos.
Cuia persona de contino hizo
Muy grande falta a todo vuestro campo
Por la poca salud que siempre tuvo,
Mas aquí quiso el Cielo la tuviesse
Tan entera y cumplida que sin ella
Tengo por impossible que este hecho
En ninguna manera se acabara.
Y porque largo trecho dibertido
Estoy ya de los bárbaros, sospecho
Que juntos en su fuerza van tratando
De nuevo nuevas cosas, yo de nuevo,
Para mejor notarlas y escrebirlas,
En nuevo canto quiero proseguirlas.

8. Romper = rasgar, cortar, abrir.
9. Falta = fallo.

In your Royal service and might not be
So stupid as I always showed myself
130 In things of moment and of importance.
He also ordered Juan Velarde should,
As being wise, prudent, and sagacious,
Perform in all our councils the work
Of faithful secretary, for with pen
135 He was no less noble and admired
Than with the famous sword that he girt on.
After all these, were appointed
Some seventy valorous fighters,
Whose splendid forces were increased
140 By the skill and the energy
Of Juan Cortés, an ensign as valiant
As he was skilled and wise in weaponry,
Which by his toil he very well prepared
To function properly, cutting and piercing,
145 Without their ever failing the combatant in that fight
In which we later saw and found ourselves.
His person had habitually been
A very great lack unto all your camp
Because of the poor health he always had,
150 But here heaven granted he should be
So thoroughly, completely well that without him
I think it quite impossible this deed
Could have been done in any way.
Since I have been diverted a long time
155 From the barbarians, I do suspect
That they, together, in their fortress, plan
New things anew, and I, anew,
To better note and write them down,
Wish to pursue them in a new canto.

Canto Veynte y Seys

COMO LLEGO LA NUEVA DEL MAESE DE CAMPO A
oydos de Gicombo, vno de los Capitanes Acomeses que ausente
abía estado, y de las diligencias que hizo, juntando a los Indios
a consejo, y discordia que tuvieron.

L A cosa que más duele y más lastima

El alma y la consume es que le imputen,
Quando más quieta y sossegada,
Culpa que nunca hizo ni propuso.
Y este dolor y caso desastrado
En sí es tanto más grave quanto tiene
De peso y gravedad aquel excesso
Con que quieren mancharla y desdorarla.
Luego que sucedió el caso triste
Que en Acoma los bárbaros hizieron,
No bien sólas dos horas se pasaron
Quando Gicombo,[1] vn bárbaro valiente,
Afable, gentilhombre y avisado
Que treinta leguas de la fuerza estaba,
Por arte del demonio, que no duerme,
Supo lo que passaba, y sin tardanza,
Temiendo le imputasen tal delicto
Por ser varón de cuenta y estimado
Por Capitán en esta misma fuerza,
Donde estaba casado con Luzcoija,
Vna famosa bárbara gallarda
Que por su gran belleza y trato noble
Era reverenciada y acatada
De todo aqueste fuerte y sus contornos,
Por cuias justas causas y otras muchas
Que en su noble persona concurrían,
Afrentado del hecho y caso infame,
Mandó a Buzcoico luego se partiesse
A los Apaches,[2] que eran estrangeros,
De su nación remotos y apartados,
Y a Bempol, gran su amigo, le llamase,
Nacido y natural de aquella tierra,
Valiente por extremo y gran soldado,
Y de su parte sólo le dixesse
Que dentro de seys soles convenía

Canto XXVI

How the news about the Army Master came to the ears of
Gicombo, one of the Acoman captains, who had been absent,
and of the activity he showed gathering the Indians in council,
and of the discord they had.

T HE thing which gives most pain and most
injures
The soul, and consumes it, is imputation,
When 'tis most quiet and peaceful,
Of fault it never did, nor yet proposed.
5 And this pain and disastrous case
Is in itself more grave in proportion
To the weight and import of the excess
With which they wish to stain and tarnish it.
When that sad offense had occurred
10 That was done by the Acoman barbarians,
Not even two hours had passed by
When Gicombo, a valiant barbarian,
A gentleman, affable, sagacious,
Who then was thirty leagues from the fortress,[1]
15 Through the arts of the devil, who sleeps not,
Learned what had happened, and without delay,
Fearing such crime would be ascribed to him
As being a man of influence, esteemed
As captain in that same fortress,
20 Where he was married to Luzcoija,
A famous, beauteous barbarian,
Who for her great beauty and noble air
Was reverenced and respected
In all that fortress and its neighborhood,
25 For this just cause and many more
That were all joined in his noble person,
Affronted at the deed and infamous affair,
He ordered Buzcoico to depart at once
For the Apaches, who were foreigners,
30 Remote and set apart from his nation,
And call to him Bempol, his greatest friend,[2]
A native born in that land there,
Extremely valiant and a great soldier,
And he should say as his message
35 That within six suns 'twas convenient

---

1. Hay en Gicombo algo del Caupolicán de Ercilla. Véase Villagrá, *Historia*, edición de Junquera, 39.

2. Esta comunicación entre los indios pueblo y los apaches parece invención poética de Villagrá, quizás en imitación de las comunicaciones y alianzas entre diferentes caciques que, en imitación de la épica clásica, recoge, empezando con Ercilla, la épica americana. Sí consta, históricamente, que había algunos indios zuni en Acoma.

1. Gicombo is perhaps somewhat patterned on Ercilla's great indigenous hero, Caupolicán. See Villagrá, *Historia de Nuevo México*, Junquera edition, 39.

2. This friendship between the Pueblo Indians and the Apache appears to be a Villagrá poetic invention, perhaps imitating the alliances between caciques that the New World epic, itself in imitation of the classics, often presented.

En Acoma se viessen, sin que vbiesse
En esto quiebra alguna ni tardanza
Porque tenía cosas muy pesadas
Que tratarle y dezirle de importancia.
Y apenas las seys bueltas fue cerrando
La poderosa lámpara del Cielo
Quando los dos guerreros animosos
En Acoma se vieron, donde a una
Fueron bien regalados y servidos
De la noble Luzcoija; y allí juntos,
Después de aber tratado y conferido
Por toda aquella noche el caso feo,
Determinaron que en abriendo el día
Los Capitanes todos se juntasen,
Que eran sólos seys bárbaros valientes,
Popempol, Chumpo, Calpo y gran Buzcoico,
Ezmicaio y Gicombo, aqueste bravo
Por cuio ruego todos se juntaron.
Y assí como parece que derrama
El sembrador el grano y que lo arroja
Perdido por el suelo, assí, al descuido
Hablando con la junta, fue diziendo:
"Varones poderosos, bien os consta
Que aquél que ofende es fuerza siempre traiga
La barba sobre el hombro,³ recatado
De todo mal sucesso y caso triste.
Bien veys que quien a honze Castellanos⁴
Hizo sin causa alguna se partiessen
De aquesta vida triste, miserable,
Que puede ser que a su pesar le fuercen,
Quando más descuidado y más seguro,
Que tras de todos ellos vaya y siga
La mísera derrota que llevaron.
Y pues para que buelvan no ay remedio
Aquéllos que de aquesta vida parten,
Yo soy de parecer que con recato,
Si en lo hecho queréis asseguraros,
Que nuestros hijos todos y mugeres
Salgan de aqueste fuerte y nos quedemos
No más que los varones entretanto
Que los Castillas dan indicio o muestran
El corage que tienen y las fuerzas
Que ponen en vengar a sus amigos.
Por cuia causa quise que viniesse
Bempol y con nosotros se juntase

40

45

50

55

60

65

70

75

80

They should both meet at Acoma, nor should there be
Any failure or delay in this,
Because he had serious things
To tell him and discuss with him, of importance.
And hardly was the powerful lamp of heaven
Closing the sixth of his revolutions
When the two spirited warriors
Did meet in Acoma, where, together,
They were well served and well supplied
By noble Luzcoija, and, together there,
After having considered and conferred
Through all the night upon the ugly case,
They determined that at the break of day
All the captains should be called in,
Who were but six valiant barbarians,
Popempol, Chumpo, Calpo, Buzcoico,
Ezmicaio, and Gicombo, that brave man
By whose command all were gathered.
And seeming like the sower who scatters
The grain and spreads it well about,
Lost in the soil, so, seeming quite carefree,
Addressing the assembly, he thus spoke:
"Ye powerful men, right well you know
'Tis necessary an offender always wear
His chin upon his shoulder,³ suspicious
Of all misfortune and all sad outcome.
You see well that he who has made
Eleven Spaniards⁴ leave without a cause
This sad and miserable life
May well expect them, 'spite of him, to force,
When he is most careless and most secure,
Him to depart and follow after them
Upon the sorry route which they pursued.
And since there is no remedy to recall them,
Those who depart from out this life,
It seems to me that with all due prudence,
If you would make yourselves safe in fact,
All our children and our wives, too,
Should leave this citadel, and we remain,
No more than we men, in the meantime, till
The Spaniards indicate or show
The courage which they have and the forces
They will set to avenge their friends.
It was for this cause that I wished
Bempol should come and join himself with us

---

3. La expresión popular es gráfica, mirando hacia atrás, receloso de enemigos.

4. Fueron trece los "españoles" muertos en Acoma. Véase Hammond & Rey, *Oñate*, 460. Parece que los indios, como quizás los propios españoles, no contaban como tales a los dos criados suyos que murieron, uno mulato, como el texto narra, y otro indio mexicano.

3. The popular Spanish expression graphically suggests one constantly looking back in apprehension.

4. Thirteen Spaniards were killed on that occasion: see Hammond & Rey, *Oñate*, 460. It appears that neither the Indians nor the Spaniards included as such two servants that were killed, one a mulatto and the other a Mexican Indian.

Y que su parecer y voto diesse
Como quien en las armas siempre tuvo
Lugar más preminente, y más en cosas
Que son de tanto peso y tanta estima
Quales son éstas donde tantas honrras
Vemos que penden, sin las muchas vidas
Que es fuerza que peligren y se pierdan
Si muy breve remedio no se aplica
A mal tan peligroso quanto el tiempo
Dirá si con presteza no se ataja
Su mísera dolencia conozida."
Y assí como frenético que buelve
Su saña contra el médico y furioso
Pretende deshacerlo y acabarlo,
Sin ver que se desbela, busca y traza
Orden para curarle y darle sano,
Assi, rabioso, fiero y sin sentido,
Oyendo estas palabras desde afuera,
Zutacapán se fue luego acercando
Con vna falsa risa y al desgaire[5]
Y dixo desta suerte, con descuido:[6]
"Cierto que estoy corrido y que me pesa
Que para cosa tan cobarde y baja
Ayan tan bravos y altos Capitanes
Juntádose a consejo, pues de siete
Que están en esta illustre y noble junta
Qualquiera de los cinco generosos
Que estoy por señalarlos con el dedo
Es muy bastante amparo y suficiente
Para poder en este puesto y fuerza
Desbaratar a todo el vniverso
Y destruirlo sin que quede cosa
Que no se le sugete y avasalle.
Y si Gicombo tanto miedo tiene,
Arrímese a la sombra desta maza,
Que aquí tendrá su vida bien segura
Y escusará también que forasteros
Vengan a defendernos y a dar voto
Donde las fuerzas y el consejo sobra,
Y más entre soldados tan valientes
Quanto cobardes todos los temores
Con que vienen agora alebrastados."
Los dos guerreros, con el bravo golpe
De vna sola piedra lastimados,
Desocuparon luego los assientos
Y como prestos sacres embistieron,

85

90

95

100

105

110

115

120

125

And give his opinion and vote
As one who always had, in arms,
Place most prominent, and more in things
That are of so great weight and import
As these are, upon which we see
The honor of so many hang, not to speak of
The many lives that will be risked and lost
Of stern necessity unless quick remedy be used
To ill so dangerous as time will tell
Right speedily unless it be cut short,
Its miserable sickness known."
Now, like the madman who does turn
His rage against his doctor and, enraged,
Tries to destroy and make an end of him,
Not seeing that he watches, seeks, attempts,
A method to cure him and give him health,
Thus, raging, wild and without sense,
Hearing these words from the outside,
Zutacapán was approaching
With a feigned and disdainful laugh
And spoke in this wise, with disdain:
"Surely I am ashamed and it galls me
That for so cowardly and base a thing
Such brave and lofty captains should
Have joined in council, for of seven
Who are in this noble, famous body,
Any of the five honorable men
Whom I shall soon point out with my finger
Is shelter enough and sufficient
To be, within this post and fort, able
To break to pieces all the universe
And quite destroy it, leaving naught
Not subject and vassal to him.
And if Gicombo has so great a fear,
Let him shelter beneath the shadow of this mace,
For here his life will be preserved all safe
And also will prevent a foreigner
From coming to defend us and to vote
Where forces and advice more than suffice,
Especially among soldiers as brave
As all those fears are cowardly
With which they now come skulking in."
The two warriors, alike wounded
By the rude stroke of but one stone,
Immediately left their seats
And, like swift sakers, they attacked,

5. Al desgaire = de mal talante.
6. Con descuido = con menosprecio.

Las palmas bien abiertas,⁷ y si presto
Popempol, Chumpo y Calpo no bajaran
La cólera rebuelta ya encendida,
Allí Zutacapán de todo punto
Quedara para siempre deshonrrado.
Y buelto contra él le dixo Bempol:
"¿De quándo acá te atreves, dime, infame,
Hablar donde jamás nunca tuviste
Manos para librar por fuerza de las armas
Lo que quieres librar por sola lengua?"
Cotumbo dixo, en esto, desembuelto:
"No ay para qué ninguno se aventaje,
Que sólo aqueste brazo en esta fuerza
Basta para rendir a todo el mundo.
Y pensar otra cosa es cobardía,
Infamia y vil afrenta con que mancha
El valor y la grandeza que alcanzamos,
Qual si fueramos dioses, en lo alto
Destos valientes muros poderosos."
Tras déste, luego Tempal, demudado,
Assí como escorpión rabioso y fiero,
De venenosa hierba apacentado,
Vibrando las tres lenguas⁸ desgarradas
Y el espinazo todo lebantado,
Dixo ser gran bageza gobernasen
Armas todos aquéllos que tuviessen
Temor sobre seguro⁹ tan notorio.
Qual brotan pedernales las centellas
Con golpes del azero, y chispas vivas,
Otros también, sin éstos, aprobaron
Este partido juntos y dixeron
Ser pobres de valor y de vergüenza
Aquéllos que temiessen ni pensasen,
Puestos en aquel puesto, les viniesse
El¹⁰ mal que a las Estrellas, cuia cumbre
No permite que cosa jamás llegue
Que pueda escurecerlas ni mancharlas.
Oyendo aquesto el noble Zutancalpo,
Assí qual diestro músico que abaja
La lebantada prima¹¹ y la afloja,
La poderosa maza fue lanzando

Their palms open widely,⁵ and if
Popempol, Chumpo, and Calpo had not
Swiftly smoothed o'er their roused and kindled wrath,
There would Zutacapán entirely   130
Have lost forever his honor.
And, turning to him, Bempol said:
"Tell me, infamous wretch, since when you dare
To speak where you have never had
The hands to do by force of arms   135
What you wish now to do by tongue alone?"
At this, Cotumbo said, enraged:
"There is reason for no one to excel,
For, in this fort, this arm alone
Suffices to conquer the entire world.   140
And to think otherwise is cowardice,
Infamy, and vile affront that stains
The valor and the grandeur which we have,
As though we were the gods, on top
Of these valiant and mighty walls."   145
Then, after this, Tempal, insidious,
Like cruel, poisonous scorpion
Grazing amid the poisoned grass,
Whirring its three impudent tongues⁶
And with its sting elevated,   150
Said it would be great baseness should
Their arms be governed by all those who had
Fears for a place so notoriously safe.
As bits of flint do strike out sparks
With blows from steel, and glowing flakes,   155
Others beyond these few approved,
Joining their party, and they said
That those were poor in valor and in shame
Who ever feared or even thought
That, placed in that position, there could come to them 160
Any more evil than to the stars, whose great height
Does not permit that anything should come
Which might obscure them or stain them.
Hearing this, the noble Zutancalpo,
Like skillful musician who doth lower   165
The high first string and loosen it,⁷
Did throw his powerful war club

---

7. La imagen corresponde al ave de presa, con garras abiertas; aunque es también la propia, en el hombre mediterráneo, para abofetear.

8. El escorpión, alacrán, pica con la cola, luego Villagrá parece mezclar aquí la imagen de la serpiente, citada a menudo junto con el escorpión: *super serpentes et scorpiones.*

9. Seguro = seguridad.

10. Posible errata del original por "más," que es el sentido que parece tener aquí.

11. El aflojar la "prima," en instrumentos de cuerda la más aguda, supone bajar la tensión ambiente.

5. The image corresponds well to the bird of prey, with its talons spread, and with the Mediterranean offensive norm of slapping instead of punching.

6. Villagrá mixes the image of the serpent (three-pronged tongue) with that of the scorpion, not unusual since both are so often cited together: *super serpentes et scorpiones.*

7. The image indicates an intention to relieve tensions.

Enmedio de la junta y fue diziendo:
"Si ser pudiera por valiente brazo
Aquesta pobre patria defendida,
Por éste sé que fuera libertada.
Mas dezidme, varones no vencidos,
¿Quántos en alta cumbre entronizados
Con mísera ruina abemos visto
Caer de sus assientos lebantados?
¿Quántos valientes, bravos y animosos
Vemos de flacas fuerzas consumidos?
¿Quántas altas estrellas, desclavadas
De los grandiosos cielos poderosos,
En breve espacio vemos apagadas?
¿De qué sirve, señores, que mi padre
Con sóla sombra de su maza haga
Seguras nuestras vidas y con esto
Quieran otros también, con sólo vn brazo,
Derribar todo vn mundo y sugetarle,
Si puestos en las veras, todos juntos,
Quales milanos tristes,¹² sin respecto,
Han de ser despreciados y arrastrados
Qual veys aquesa maza por el suelo,
Muda, cobarde, flaca y sin gobierno
De mano belicosa que la mande?"
Sin dexarle acabar, al mismo instante,
Echando vivo fuego por los ojos,
Salió diziendo Bempol, corajoso:
"No piense aquí ninguno que su esfuerzo
En sí tanto se estiende y se lebanta
Quanto el más bajo polvo despreciado,
Porque haré que donde yo la planta,¹³
A su pesar, sus viles ojos ponga."
Gicombo se arriscó,¹⁴ con otros muchos,
Y este partido todos, por las armas,
Quisieron defender; y porque el fuego
No se encendiesse más y se abrasasen,
Después de aber passado con enojo
Muchas grandes demandas y repuestas,
Desafiados tres a tres quedaron
Gicombo y Zutancalpo y el gran Bempol
Contra Zutacapán, Cotumbo y Tempal,
Cuio bravo combate suspendieron
Hasta alcanzar de España la victoria.
Por cuia causa Amulco, vn hechizero,
Que era por tal de todos estimado,

In the midst of the council, and he said:
"If this poor fatherland could be
170   Defended by a single valiant arm
I know that it would be set free by this.
But tell me, you unconquered men,
How many, throned upon a lofty peak,
Ourselves have seen in miserable wreck
175   Fall from their elevated seats?
How many, valiant, strong, and courageous,
We see consumed by weak forces?
How many lofty stars, unfixed,
From out the huge and mighty heavens
180   We see extinguished in a little time?
What boots it, gentlemen, that my father
With but the shadow of his mace doth make
Our lives secure, and that, beside,
Others, too, wish with but a single arm
185   To overthrow and conquer a whole world,
If, coming to the truth, they, together,
Like sorry kites,⁸ without respect,
Must be despised and so demeaned,
As you see that club on the ground,
190   Mute, cowardly, and without management
Of the bellicose hand that governs it?"
Not letting him finish, at that instant,
Discharging living fire from his eyes,
Bempol stood forth, saying defiantly:
195   "Let no one think that his own strength
Extends or in itself is raised as far
As is the lowest, most despised, dust,
For I shall make him place his worthless eyes,
Spite of himself, where I do place my foot."
200   Gicombo then was ired, with many more,
And this party all did desire
To plead through arms, and, that the fire
Might not be kindled more and so burst out,
After they had exchanged with much anger
205   Many great demands and replies,
There did remain three against three opposed,
Gicombo, Zutancalpo, and the great Bempol
Against Zutacapán, Cotumbo, and Tempal,
Whose fierce combat was suspended
210   Until they gained a victory from Spain.
Because of this a wizard, Amulco,
Who was as such esteemed by all,

12. Tristes = miserables. El milano se consideraba cobarde. Es posible, asimismo, que la imagen se refiera a la flor seca del cardo, también "milano," que vuela por los aires sin gobierno.

13. Se refiere a la del pie.

14. Se arriscó = se enojó.

8. Among birds of prey, the kite is considered cowardly by Spaniards.

Assí como se exsala,[15] afloja y templa
El encendido horno destapando
La cóncava bravera,[16] assí templando
La bárbara canalla descompuesta,
Dixo: "Muy bien sabéis, nobles varones,
Que el futuro sucesso que esperamos
Por hado adverso o próspero que es fuerza
Que yo le sepa, entienda y le conozca
Muy grandes tiempos antes que suceda.
Y bien sabéis también que a mí los dioses
En aplacar las armas dieron mano
Y en alterarlas siendo conveniente.
Si esto es assí, ¿por qué queréis en vano
Litigar estas cosas si está en casa
Quien con patente y claro desengaño
Puede manifestaros todo aquello
Que puede disgustaros o agradaros?
Por cuia justa causa quiero luego,
Por quitaros de dudas y sospechas,
Consultar a los dioses porque a todos
Pueda desengañaros sin tardanza
Del bien o mal que ya determinado
Es fuerza que le tengan. Y no dudo
Daros alegres nuevas faborables."
Todos los Capitanes aprobaron,
Con el resto del pueblo, aquel intento,
Y abiendo entrado en cerco,[17] confiado,
Aqueste bruto presago[18] adivino,
Estando todos juntos aguardando
El prodigioso oráculo suspensos,
Como si en el horrible infierno bravo
Vbiera estado, assí salió encendido,
Diziéndoles a todos con enfado:
"¿Qué miedos son aquéstos, qué pantasmas,
Qué sombras, qué visiones abéys visto,
Dezidme, valerosos Acomeses?
Y tu, Gicombo y Bempol, esforzados,
Cuios grandiosos y altos corazones
Nunca jamás temieron como agora,
Veo que estáys los dos desalentados.
¿Abemos puesto todos, por ventura,
En olvido perpetuo al bravo Qualco
Quando fue por espía y le embíamos
Al pueblo de san Iuan que dizen ellos
Ser de los Caballeros? ¿No nos dixo
Que en ciertos regozijos que tuvieron

Just as the fiery furnace doth evaporate,
Relax, and temper by uncovering
215 Its hollow stack, so, tempering
The overwrought barbarian mob,
Said: "Well you know, you noble men,
That what future events we all await
By evil fate or prosperous, perforce
220 I know it, understand it and grasp it
A very long time before it occurs.
And well you know the gods to me
Assign a part in pacifying powers
And changing them, if it be meet.
225 This being so, why do you wish in vain
To struggle on these points if there be here
One who with patent and clear truthfulness
Can manifest to you all that
Can give to you displeasure or yet joy?
230 For which just cause I wish at once,
To free you from doubts and suspicions,
To counsel with the gods, because this can
Set you all right without delay
Concerning good or evil which, needs must,
235 They have already planned. Nor do I doubt
To give you happy, favorable, news."
The captains all gave approval,
With the rest of the people, unto that intent,
And having entered his magic circle,[9] confident,
240 That ignorant and guessing soothsayer,
All standing by and awaiting
Prodigious oracle in great suspense,
As if he might have been within
Hell, savage, horrible, he came out in a rage,
245 Saying most angrily to all:
"What fears are these? What phantasms,[10]
What shadows, what visions have you seen?
Tell me, you valiant men of Acoma,
And you, Gicombo and Bempol, brave men
250 Whose glorious and lofty hearts
Have never feared as now, when I
Observe that both of you are discouraged?
Then have we all, by chance, resigned
Brave Qualco to perpetual forgetfulness
255 When he went as a spy and we sent him
To that town of San Juan, which they do say
Is 'de los Caballeros'? Saw he not
That in certain rejoicings which they had

15. Exsala = exhala, despide gases.
16. Bravera = ventana o respiradero del horno.
17. Cerco = círculo ceremonial para los conjuros.
18. Presago = agorero.

9. The reference is to the circle that the seer draws about himself in witchcraft.
10. Curtis pluralizes normally. The plural of *phantasma* is *phantasmata*.

Estos mismos Castillas que dezimos
Que muy soberbios tiros se tiraron
Los vnos a los otros y no vido
Caer ninguno dellos, donde todos
Bien claro conozimos y entendimos
No ser sus armas más que sólo asombro,
Estrépitu, ruido, grima espantosa
Y al fin todo alboroto, pues sus rayos,
Si assí queréis llamarlos, no hirieron
A ninguno de todos los que andaban
Enmedio de sus truenos paborosos?"[19]
"Por sólo esta razón," dixo Gicombo,
"Que no se lastimaron ni tocaron
Con armas tan grimosas y espantosas
Abemos de entender que como dioses,
Que nada les ofende, combatieron,
Y assí es muy justo todos les temamos."
Aquí Zutacapán replicó luego:
"Yo quiero que con rayos muy ardientes,
Quales soberbios dioses, nos arrojen
Todos estos Castillas que tú temes,
Pero será razón también me cuentes
Por cada cien mil truenos ¿quántos rayos
Has visto que han llegado a nuestros muros?
Y si has visto alguno, ¿qué destrozo
Hizo aquél que más? Pues vna arroba
Jamás nos han mermado todos juntos
De sus valientes riscos lebantados.
Pues si el poder del Cielo no se estiende
A más de lo que oyes, ¿por qué tratas
De vnos infames, todos más mortales
Que aquéllos que sin almas vemos dexan
Los miserables cuerpos ya difuntos?"
"Ya sé que son mortales," dixo luego
El valiente Gicombo, reportado,
"Pues por sola tu causa, como tales,
Honze en aquesta fuerza fenecieron.
Y sabes tú también que no ay peñasco
Ni fuerza tan soberbia en esta vida
Que no pueda assolarse y abrasarse
Si debajo de engaño y trato alebe
Queremos combatirla y derribarla."
"Muy bien estoy con esso," dixo Amulco,
"Mas quando viene el bien es cosa justa
Que todos su grandeza conozcamos.
No es tan cierto el Sol en darnos lumbre
Quanto tenemos cierta la victoria.

260

265

270

275

280

285

290

295

300

305

These same Castilians whom we speak about
Did fire many angry shots
The ones against the others? Saw he not
That none of them fell down? From this
We knew and understood clearly
Their weapons were no more than fright alone,
A clamorous noise, fearful horror,
And, finally, all sound, for their lightnings,
If thus you wish to call them, wounded not
A single one of those who walked about
Amid their frightful thunderings."
"For this reason alone," said Gicombo,
"That they were not wounded nor touched
By weapons so fearful and terrible,
We ought to understand that, like gods,
They fight and nothing injures them,
And so 'tis very just we should fear them."
Here Zutacapán made reply at once:
"I wish that these Castilians whom you fear
Might, like gods in a passion,
Hurl their most ardent lightnings upon us,
But it would be proper for you to tell
Of each one hundred thousand bolts how many you
Have seen that have struck on our walls?
And if you have seen one that did
More damage ever than to tear away
A few pounds, counting it at most,
From our valiant and lofty cliffs?
Now if the power of Heaven does not extend
Further than you have heard, why speak
Of infamous wretches, all more mortal
Than those we have seen left without their souls,
Their miserable bodies being dead?"
"I know that they are mortal," then declared
The valiant, temperate Gicombo, "For,
Because of you alone, being such,
Eleven in this stronghold died.
And you know also that there is no rock
Nor strength so haughty in this life
That it cannot be leveled and destroyed
If with deceit and treacherous dealing
We wish to fight and destroy it."
"I know this very well," said Amulco,
"But when good comes it is but just
That all acknowledge its greatness.
The sun is not so sure to give us light
As it is sure we shall have victory.

19. Se refiere a los juegos de armas y escaramuzas que practicaban
los españoles.

Cálense²⁰ luego puentes y piquemos²¹
Todos los passadizos,²² sin que cosa
Quede para Castillas reserbada,
Que desta vez abemos de assentarnos
En el más alto cuerno de la Luna.
Y a ti, fuerte Gicombo, yo te mando,
No obstante que Luzcoija es muy hermosa,
Doze donzellas bellas Castellanas,
Y seys al bravo Bempol porque buelva
Con tal despojo honrrado a sus amigos,
Deudos, patria y parientes más cercanos."
Aquí los dos a una replicaron
Por no dar de flaqueza más sospecha:
"Armas nos han de dar y no mugeres
Si abemos de aber premio en las batallas.
Mas porque no se entienda que queremos,
Por miedo de la muerte, aquí escusarnos
De ver a los Castillas, prometemos
Por nos, y por los muchos que quisieran
Salirse deste puesto y no aguardarlos,
De quedarnos aquí con más firmeza
Que están los altos montes quando aguardan
A quien los rompa, tale y los abrase."

Y porque ya la gente Castellana
Apriessa se dispone, quiero luego
Disponerme, señor, porque me es fuerza
Venir con todos ellos a esta fuerza.

20. Cálense = ciérrense.
21. Piquemos = demolamos.
22. Passadizos = pasadizos, pasos estrechos entre lugares.

Break down the bridges, then, and block
All passageways so that nothing
May be left for the Spaniards,
For from henceforward we must settle on
310 The moon's most elevated horn.
To you, strong Gicombo, I give,
Though Luzcoija is most beautiful,
Twelve beautiful Castilian maids,
And six to brave Bempol, that he may go
315 Back honored with such booty to his friends,
His kinsmen, fatherland, and his near relatives."
At this point, both at once replied,
Not to give more suspicion of weakness,
"Arms shall you give to us and not women
320 If we are to have prize of battle.
And lest it be thought that we wish,
From fear of death, to be exempted here
From seeing the Castilians, we promise
On our part, and for those who wished
325 To leave this place and not to wait for them,
To remain here more firmly than
The lofty mountains do when they await
Those who would break and penetrate and destroy
     them."
And since the Spanish folk do now
330 Prepare themselves in haste, I wish at once
To prepare me, lord, for I must
Come with them all unto this fortalice.

Canto Veynte y Siete

*COMO SALIO EL EXERCITO PARA EL PEÑOL DE
ACOMA y de las cosas que fueron sucediendo, y rebato[1]
que dieron en el pueblo de San Iuan.*

QVANDO con buena y presta diligencia
La braveza del cáncer no se ataja,
No es possible que el mísero paciente
Escape con la vida, porque es cierto
Que la aya de rendir a tal dolencia.
Y si la atrozidad de los delictos
Justicia con rigor no los reprime,
También es impossible que gozemos
De la gustosa paz en que bivimos.
Desto dechado grande nos han dado
Aquellos bravos bárbaros de Arauco,[2]
Pues por no más de aberles dilatado
El debido castigo a tales culpas
Sincuenta largos años son passados
Que en efusión de sangre Castellana
Sus omicidas armas no se han visto
Enjutas ni cansadas de verterla.
Temiendo, pues, aquesto, dando alarma,
El bravo General mandó tocasen
Los gallardos clarines lebantados,
De los valientes soplos impelidos
De los trompetas diestros, que, en coloquios
Respondiendo a los pífanos y cajas,
La fuerza de las armas encendían
Y a los valientes pechos provocaban
Al rigor de los brazos y los golpes
Que en la cruenta batalla se executan.
Turbáronse, con esto, las provincias,[3]
De las quales salieron con presteza
A dar aviso todas las espías,
Pidiendo a los amigos socorriessen
Y contra España juntos conjurasen,
A fuego y sangre, guerra y la rompiessen.
Con cuia fuerza luego fue creciendo
En toda la libiana y moza gente
Vn ánimo y corage desmedido
De bárbara braveza desgarrada.[4]
Los nuestros, viendo aquesto, se cubrieron

1. Rebato = tocar a rebato, convocar al pueblo ante un peligro.
2. Los "bárbaros de Arauco," indios chilenos cuyas guerras con los conquistadores españoles había poetizado Ercilla en *La araucana*.
3. Con el término "provincias," se refiere Villagrá a los distintos pueblos indios.
4. Desgarrada = licenciosa, rebelde.

Canto XXVII

*How the army left for the Rock of Acoma and of the things
that happened, and of the alarm they had in the pueblo
of San Juan.*

WHEN with a good and rapid diligence
The spreading of a cancer is not stopped,
'Tis not possible that the sad patient
Escape with his life, for 'tis certain
That he must give it up to such disease.
And if justice does not strictly
Repress the wickedness of crime,
It is impossible that we enjoy
The pleasant peace in which we live.
Of this those rude barbarians of Arauco[1]
Have given us a notable standard,
Since, for no more than delaying
The punishment due to such crimes,
Fifty long years have now gone by
When in effusion of Castilian blood
Their homicidal arms have not been seen
Or dry or tired of shedding it.
Fearing this, then, the valiant General
Ordered alarm be given and sounded
By spirited trumpets raised up
And blown by valiant lips
Of skillful trumpeters, who, in a colloquy
Replying to the fifes and drums,
Do rouse the very force of arms
And do provoke the valiant hearts
To the power of arms and blows
Which are delivered in a bloody strife.
At this the provinces[2] were all perturbed,
From which there came out, in all haste,
To give their warning, all the spies,
Asking their friends to give them aid
And all to plot together against Spain,
Fought in fire and blood, war, and so crush her.
With this idea, then, they increased
In all the fickle and young folk
Immeasurable spirit and courage
Of impudent barbarian bravado.
Seeing this, our men did clothe themselves

1. The reference is to the Araucanian Indians of Chile, whose wars with the Spanish conquerors, the basis of Ercilla's *La araucana*, lasted into the nineteenth century.
2. Villagrá refers to the other pueblo communities.

De fino azero limpio y anta⁵ doble,
Y dentro de las mallas sacudieron
Los poderosos tercios y colgaron
De los valientes hombros las adargas.
Las lanzas empuñaron de dos hierros,⁶
Las medias lunas⁷ otros aprestaron
Y de los caballos bravos, animosos,
Las bridas y ginetas⁸ compusieron,
Los bastos,⁹ los estribos, los aziones,¹⁰
Los fustes,¹¹ las corazas, los pretales,¹²
Los frenos,¹³ con las riendas y azicates,
Los pechos, las hijadas, las testeras,¹⁴
Y de los gruessos, crudos, correones
Recorren y refuerzan las hebillas.
Ciernen el polvorín¹⁵ y al Sol le ponen,
Y otros al serpentín la cuerda ajustan,
Aprestan las mochilas y las balas,
Y, en fin, no dexan cosa que les pueda
Hazer alguna falta o quiebra puestos
En la difícil prueba y estacada.¹⁶
Y porque sin buen orden el soldado
No es más que bruto cuerpo sin el alma,
El noble General les fue diziendo
Que sin passión tomasen el delicto
De la bárbara gente y que ninguno
Fuesse con sólo blanco de vengarse,
Pues era cosa cierta que llamaba
Venganza a la venganza y muerte a muerte,
Por cuia causa a todos encargaba
Que sólo se estendiessen y alargasen
A la enseñanza y corrección debida,
De suerte que el delicto y no otra cosa
Quedase castigado y la justicia
De todos amparada y socorrida.
Mediante cuios medios esperaba,
En Dios, nuestro Señor, muy buen sucesso,
Por cuias vivas llagas sangrentadas
Assimismo pedía con el alma

With steel, fine, clean, and thick leather
40 And in their mail they did enwrap
Their powerful limbs, and they did hang
The targes from their valiant shoulders.
They seized the lances, double-ironed;
Others made ready the half-moons
45 And for the brave and spirited horses
Prepared the bridles and the cinches, too,
Packsaddles, stirrups, stirrup straps,
Lance shafts, cuirasses, breast leathers,
Bits with their reins and Moorish spurs,
50 Breastplates, flank pieces, crown pieces,
And inspected and reinforced buckles
Upon the thick and rudely made great straps.
They sift the fine powder and set it in the sun,
And others fit the matches to gunlocks,
55 Prepare the pouches and the balls,
And, finally, leave nothing which they might
Have need or want of being in
The midst of the crucial test and challenge.
And since without good order the soldier
60 Is no more than brute body without soul,
The noble General directed them
That without passion they should take the crime
Of the barbarians, and none of them
Should go with sole purpose of vengeance,
65 For 'tis a certain thing, they call,
Vengeance to vengeance, death to death,
Wherefore he did instruct them all
That they should strain and bend themselves only
To teaching and correction that was due,
70 So that the crime, and nothing else beside,
Should be punished, and justice should
Be aided and protected by them all.
By which procedure he did hope
In God, our Lord, for good success.
75 By Whose living, blood flowing wounds
He also begged them from his very soul

5. Anta = ante, cuero de este mamífero o piel curtida de cualquier animal.
6. Lanzas con doble punta.
7. Medias lunas = fortificaciones que se construyen delante de los baluartes.
8. Ginetas = jinetas, cinchas.
9. Bastos = albardas.
10. Aziones = aciones, correas del estribo.
11. Fustes = armazones de la silla de montar.
12. Pretales = fajas de cuero puestas al caballo en el pecho.
13. Frenos = el bocado de hierro.
14. Se refiere a la armadura del caballo en las partes señaladas.
15. Polvorín = pólvora.
16. Estacada = desafío.

Que todos confessasen, pues la Iglesia,	That all go to confession, for the Church
En peligros tan graves y pesados,	In such grave and weighty dangers
Assí lo disponía y lo mandaba,	Arranged it so and ordered it,
Y que no permitiessen que ninguno	80 And they should not permit that any man
Partiesse desta vida y que dexase	Should leave this life and leave behind
Afrenta y sambenito[17] tan infame,	An affront and disgrace[3] as infamous
Quanto penoso y triste, para el pobre	As 'twould be painful, sad, for the poor wretch
Que contra sí tan gran maldad hiziesse.[18]	Who should against himself do such a wrong.
Apenas lo vbo dicho quando todos	85 Hardly had he said this when all,
Labaron como buenos sus conciencias,	As good men, cleared their consciences,
Comulgando después devotamente,	And, after, took communion devoutly,
Ecepto vn desdichado que no quiso,	Except one wretched man who yet would not,
Por más que sus amigos le apretaron,	However much his friends would urge him on,
Y assí le dexo aquí, que, pues se olvida,[19]	90 And so I leave him here: if he forgets,
Dios, que murió por él, terná[20] el cuidado.	That God, who died for him, will care.
Salimos, pues, marchando, y otro día	Thus we marched off and on another day
Mandó el Sargento luego me partiesse	The Sergeant ordered that I go
Con doze compañeros y aprestase	With twelve companions and collect,
En el pueblo de Zía bastimentos	95 Within the pueblo of Zia, supplies
No más que para sólas dos semanas,	Sufficient for two weeks alone,
Sin que en esto otra cosa dispensase,[21]	And not, in this, to grant another thing,
Porque mediante hambre pretendía,[22]	For by the means of hunger he would try,
Si no pudiessemos hazer subiessen	If we could not get your Spaniards
A lo más alto del peñol soberbio	100 To climb unto the very top
A vuestros Españoles, sin que vbiesse,	Of that proud rock, there not being
Para escapar la vida trabajosa,	Some means or hope of something else
Remedio ni esperanza de otra cosa.	To escape such a weary life.[4]
Hízelo, pues, ansí y en tiempo breve	I did his bidding and in a short time
Por vna boca estrecha fue asomando	105 I was observing, through a narrow gulch,
El campo Castellano, no dos millas	The whole Castilian force, now not two miles
Del soberbio Peñol jamás vencido.	Away from the proud, never conquered rock.
Nunca pilotos vieron viento en popa,	Never did pilots see a favoring wind
Después de larga calma desabrida,	After a long and weary calm
Más alegre, contento ni gustoso	110 With more of pleasure, joy, content
Que el que estos bravos bárbaros tuvieron	Than those rude barbarians displayed
De vernos ya tan cerca de sus manos.	On seeing us now so near to their hands.
Y luego que nos vieron lebantaron	And when they saw us they set up
Vna algazara y grita tan grimosa	A huge hurrah and cry so horrible
Que allí todo el infierno parecía	115 That it seemed that all hell was there
Estaba con su fuerza rebramando.	And bellowing with all its force repeatedly.

17. Sambenito = saco, señal del penitente en la antigua iglesia. Covarrubias hace notar que aunque señal ignominiosa para el vulgo, que es el sentido que aquí lleva, no lo debiera ser por tratarse de señal de arrepentimiento.

18. Indica que ninguno se deje morir sin confesión.

19. Se olvida = se descuida.

20. Terna = tendrá.

21. Dispensase = distribuyese.

22. Lo que pretendía no era rendir a los acomeses por hambre, para lo cual hubiese sido ilógico limitar sus propios bastimentos. Lo que pretende es que el espectro del hambre, si no conquistaban a Acoma en dos semanas, fuera incitación para los españoles.

3. Villagrá's term, *sambenito*, properly translated by Curtis as "disgrace," was the sackcloth worn by the penitent as a sign of repentance. Covarrubias correctly notes that, although an emblem of disgrace for the populace, such a manifestation of repentance should not have had that stigma attached to it.

4. It would be illogical for Zaldívar to have ordered a limited store of food collected if, as a last resort, he planned to starve out the Acomans. This passage makes sense only if it is understood that the hunger mentioned was to serve as a spur to the Spaniards themselves to risk their lives in storming Acoma.

Y assí, marchando en orden, nos llegamos
Al poderoso fuerte, el qual constaba
De dos grandes peñoles lebantados,
Más de trecientos passos devididos
Los terribles assientos no domados,
Y estaba vn passamán[23] del vno al otro,
De riscos tan soberbios que ygualaban
Con las disformes cumbres nunca vistas,
Desde cuios assientos fue contando
Zutacapán la gente que venía
En orden dando buelta a sus murallas.
Y viendo ser tan pocos, dixo luego
Con grande regozijo: "No es possible
Que dexen de ser locos todos éstos,
Pues con tan cortas fuerzas han venido
A meterse en peligro tan notorio."
Aquí dixo Gicombo, rezeloso:
"Bien sé que para cuerdos son muy pocos
Y muchos para locos. Y esto es cierto,
Que jamás vido el mundo tantos locos
Iuntos, qual tú los hazes, en vn puesto.
Y pues las frentes todos enderezan
A nuestras casas con tan poca gente,
Grande misterio tiene su venida."
Tras desto, dixo luego Zutancalpo:
"Bien os consta, señores, que éstos vienen
De muy remotas tierras y que es fuerza
Que en distancia tan larga ayan tenido
Grandiosas ocasiones de disgustos,
Encuentros y batallas peligrosas,
Con cuios duros trances, pues que vienen
Assí para nosotros, yo no dudo
Sino que dexan hechas grandes pruebas
De sus soberbios brazos poderosos."
Y atajando la plática furiosa,
Dixo Zutacapán que le dexasen
Con sólos sus amigos, que él quería,
Sin su fabor y ayuda, dar principio
A gozar de aquel tiempo y coiuntura
Que su buena fortuna le ofrecía.
Y assí, salió bramando con su gente,
Qual jugando la maza y gruesso leño,
Qual la soberbia galga[24] despedida
Del lebantado risco peñasco,[25]
Qual tiraba la piedra, qual la flecha,
Qual de pintados mantos se adornaba

120

125

130

135

140

145

150

155

160

Thus, marching in order, we did arrive
Before the mighty fort, which consisted
Of two great, lofty rocks upraised,
The terrible, unconquered sites
Divided by more than three hundred feet,
And from one to the other was a neck
Of rocks so lofty they equaled
The outsized peaks, such as were never seen.
From these summits Zutacapán
Was counting the people who came,
In order marching round those walls,
And seeing them so few, he then announced,
With great rejoicing; "'Tis not possible
That all these can be other than insane
Since with such scanty forces they have come
To put themselves in such well-known peril."
Here Gicombo said, cautiously:
"I well know that for sane men they are few,
And many for insane. That is certain,
But never saw the world so many mad
Together, as you think them, in one place.
And since they direct their steps
Toward our houses with so few folk,
Their coming has much mystery in it."
Then, after this, spoke out Zutancalpo:
"'Tis evident to you, my lords, they come
From very distant lands, and that perforce
In such long distance they have had
Many occasions of annoyances,
Encounters, and of battles perilous,
With which hard dangers, since they come
Thus against us, I do not doubt
That they have left behind great proofs
Of their powerful and proud arms."
Cutting short this furious conversation,
Zutacapán said they should leave
Him with only his friends, for he did wish
Without their aid and favor to begin
To enjoy that time and conjunction
Which his good fortune offered him.
And so he went, raging, with his people,
Some playing with their maces and thick clubs,
Some with great boulders fallen down
From off the lofty, rocky cliffs,
Some hurled down stones and some arrows.
Some were adorned with painted bands,

23. Passamán = pasamano, pasadizo.
24. Galga = peñasco despedido de lo alto.
25. Errata del original por "peñascoso," que hace más sentido y completa la medida.

Y de diversas pieles y pellicos[26]
Otros también allí se entretejían,
Entre cuias libreas se mostraba
Vna grandiosa suma nunca vista
De bárbaras bizarras, muy hermosas,
Las partes bergonzosas enseñando
A vuestros Castellanos, confiadas
De la victoria cierta que esperaban.
También, entre varones y mugeres,
Andaban muchos bárbaros desnudos,
Los torpes miembros todos descubiertos,
Tiznados y embijados[27] de vnas rayas
Tan espantables, negras y grimosas
Qual si demonios bravos del infierno
Fueran, con sus melenas, desgreñados,
Y colas arrastrando y vnos cuernos
Desmesurados, gruessos y crecidos;
Con cuios trajes todos, sin vergüenza,
Saltaban como corzos por los riscos
Diciéndonos palabras bien infames.[28]
Y a todas estas cosas el Sargento,
Qual aquel gran David que las palabras
Sufrió de Semei,[29] assí, sufriendo
La bárbara canalla, mandó luego
Llamar al secretario Iuan Belarde
Y a Tomás, el interprete ladino[30]
En la bárbara lengua y Castellana,
Para que les dixessen se bajasen
A dar razón y cuenta de las muertes
Que dieron y causaron tan sin culpa
A nuestros compañeros. Y al momento
Que fue por todos ellos entendido,
Con boz terrible y ronca dixo luego
Zutacapán, soberbio y arrogante:
"¿Qué tempestad, qué viento, qué pujanza,
Os ha traído, pobres, a las manos
Y matadero triste, desgraciado,
Que es fuerza que sufráis? ¿No abéis vergüenza
De aberos allegado a nuestros muros,
Sino que pretendéis pedirnos cuenta
De las muertes de aquéllos cuias vidas
Tuvimos, qual tenemos de presente
Las vuestras miserables, desdichadas?"

With various hides and pelisses.
Others, too, there were mingled there,
165 Among whose different dress were seen
Such great sum as were never known
Of spirited barbarian women, very beautiful,
Who displayed their shameful parts
To your Castilians, confident
170 Of certain victory which they foresaw.
Also, among men and women,
There wandered many naked barbarians,
Their unchaste members all displayed,
Sooty and painted with broad streaks,
175 As fearful, black, and horrible
As if they were brave demons out of hell,
With long, loose hair all disheveled
And wearing tails and also horns
Immeasurable, long and huge;
180 And in this dress, all without shame,
They leaped like deer among the rocks,
Shouting to us in words right infamous.[5]
The Sergeant, amid all these things,
Like great David, who did endure
185 The words of Shimei,[6] so endured
The barbarous rabble, and then ordered
Juan Belarde, the secretary, to be called,
And Tomás, the knowing interpreter
In the barbarian language and in the Castilian,
190 That they might tell them to come down
To give reasons and causes for the deaths
Which they had given and caused so without provocation
To our companions. And, as soon
As all were understood by them,
195 Zutacapán, proud, arrogant, did say
Immediately, in a terrible harsh voice:
"What tempest, what wind, what impulse
Has brought you wretches to the hands
And to the sad and miserable slaughtering
200 You needs must suffer here? Have you no shame
At having gathered here beneath our walls,
But you must try to seek account from us
For deaths of those whose lives we took
As we shall presently take, too,
205 Your own unhappy, miserable ones?"

26. Pellicos = zamarras de pastor, pieles que se le parecen.
27. Embijados = pintados.
28. Para las costumbres de los indios Pueblo respecto a la pintura de sus cuerpos, al vestir y a la danza, algunas de las cuales han sobrevivido hasta nuestros días, véase Villagrá, *Historia,* edición de Junquera, 38–39.
29. Semei fue el pariente de Saul que insultó a David: *Reyes* 16:6.
30. Ladino = apto en varias lenguas.

5. For an indication of the pueblo ritual, as regards dress, painting, and dance, much still preserved today, see Villagrá, *Historia de Nuevo México,* Junquera edition, 38–39.
6. Shemei, Saul's relative, insulted David: see *Kings* 16:6.

En esto todos juntos lebantaron
Las armas y las bozes en confusso,
Diziendo: "¿A qué aguardamos? ¡Mueran, mueran,
Mueran aquestos perros atrebidos
Y no quede ninguno que no sea
Hecho menudos quartos y pedazos
Por nuestras mismas manos y cuchillos!"
Viendo, pues, el Sargento su dureza
Y pertinacia brava que mostraban
Y que la luz del día derribada
Estaba al Occidente, mandó luego
Assentar su Real en vn buen puesto,
Donde, las postas todas repartidas,
Me es fuerza que le dexe por contaros
Lo que esta misma noche fue passando
El fuerte General allá en su assiento,
Donde dieron alarma con gran fuerza
Los bárbaros del pueblo, temerosos
De aquéllos sus vezinos comarcanos,
Diziendo que venían con pujanza
A destruirlos todos y assolarlos,
Si ya no fue ruydo y trato alebe
Que entre todos trataron y acordaron.
Mas como quiera que esto sucediesse,
El pueblo no constaba ni tenía
Más que una sola plaza bien quadrada,
Con quatro entradas sólas, cuios puestos,
Después de aberlos bien fortalecido
Con tiros de campaña[31] y con mosquetes,
Mandó que el vno dellos le guardase
El Capitán Moreno de la Rua
Y Francisco Robledo y Iuan de Salas
Y aquel Esteban, noble hijo caro
Del gran Carabajal, a quien seguía
Iuan Pérez de Bustillo y el Alférez
Iuan Cortés con Antonio Sariñiana;
Y essotra esquina quiso defendiesse
El Capitán y Alcaide Bocanegra
Y su Hijo, Gutiérrez, y Medina,
Don Iuan Escarramal, Ortiz y Heredia,
Francisco Hernández, Sosa y don Luis Gasco;
Y el otro puesto tuvo, con buen orden,
El Capitán Marcelo de Espinosa,
Con Gerónimo Márquez y Iuan Díaz,
Pedro Hernández y Francisco Márquez,
Hermanos todos quatro, y con ellos
Bartolomé González y Serrano,
Baltasar de Monzón y los Barelas
Y Iuan de Caso y Pedro de los Reyes;

At this they all together raised
Their arms and voices in confusion,
Saying: "What do we await? Death, death,
Death to those ever daring dogs!
210 Let there be none who shall not be
Made fragments, quarters, and pieces
By our own hands and by our knives!"
The Sergeant then, seeing their stubbornness
And the stern pertinacity they showed,
215 And that the light of day was lowering
Into the west, at once ordered
His camp to be pitched in a goodly place,
Where, sentries being placed about,
Needs be I leave this to relate to you
220 What was occurring that same night
To the brave General, there within his town.
The barbarians of the pueblo, timorous
Of those their neighbors bordering,
Gave an alarm with great uproar,
225 Saying they came with a large force
To overthrow them all and destroy them,
If it was not a rumor, treacherous dealing,
Made up, agreed on 'mong themselves.
But, however this might have been,
230 The town did not consist of nor possess
More than one plaza, well squared off,
With only four entries, which posts,
Having well-garrisoned the same
With fieldpieces and muskets, too,
235 He ordered one of them should be guarded
By captain Moreno de la Rua,
Francisco Robledo, and Juan de Salas,
And that Esteban, noble, well-loved son
Of great Carabajal, who were followed
240 By Juan Pérez de Bustillo and the ensign
Juan Cortés, with Antonio Sariñiana.
He chose to defend this other corner
Bocanegra, the captain and the judge,
And his son, Gutiérrez, and Medina,
245 Don Juan Escarramal, Ortiz, and Heredia,
Francisco Hernández, Sosa, and Don Luis Gasco.
The next post in order he gave
To captain Marcelo de Espinosa,
With Gerónimo Márquez and Juan Díaz,
250 Pedro Hernández and Francisco Márquez,
These four all brothers, and with them
Bartolomé González and Serrano,
Baltasar de Monzón and the Barelas,
Juan de Caso and Pedro de los Reyes.

31. Tiros de campaña = piezas de artillería.

Y el último mandó que se encargase
Al Capitán Ruyz y al buen Cadimo,
A Gonzalo Hernández y al Alférez
Iuan de León y Hernán Martín, el mozo;
Y el cuerpo de guardia,[32] el Real Alférez,
El General y gente de su casa,
Antonio Conte, Vido, Alonso Nuñez,
Christóbal de Herrera y Iuan de Herrera,
Brondate, Zezer y Castillo, todos
Muy bien apercebidos. Y assí juntos,
Alborotados todos con la grita
Y confusso tropel de aquella gente,
Alarma dando todos con gran priessa,
Requirieron los puestos y notaron
Que estaban ya los altos de las casas
Tomados y ocupados. Y assí, luego
El General a bozes mandó fuessen
Algunos Capitanes y mirasen
Qué gente fuesse aquélla y que distino
En aquel puesto puesto los abía.
Mas luego doña Eufemia, valerosa,
Hizo seguro el campo, con las damas
Que en el Real abía,[33] y fue diziendo
Que si mandaba el General bajasen,
Que ellas defenderían todo el pueblo,
Mas que si no, que solas las dexasen
Si assegurar querían todo aquello
Que todas ocupaban y tenían.
Con esto, el General, con mucho gusto,
Dándose el parabién de aber gozado
En embras vn valor de tanta estima,
Mandó que doña Eufemia se encargase
De toda aquella cumbre, y assí todas,
Qual a la gran Martesia[34] obedecían
Las bravas amazonas, assí, juntas,
Largando por el ayre prestas valas,
Con gallardo donaire passeaban
Los techos y terrados lebantados,
Al fin, como mugeres, prendas caras,
De aquellos valerosos corazones:
El Alférez Real y Alonso Sánchez,
Zubía y don Luys Gasco y Diego Nuñez,
Pedro Sánchez Monrroi, Sosa, Pereira,
Quesada, Iuan Morán y Simón Pérez,

255

260

265

270

275

280

285

290

295

The last he ordered to be given
To captain Ruyz and the good Cadimo,
Gonzalo Hernández and the ensign
Juan de León and Hernán Martín, the boy.
As the body guard,[7] the Royal Ensign,
The General, and the people of his house,
Antonio Conte, Vido, Alonso Núñez,
Cristóbal de Herrera, Juan de Herrera,
Brondate, Zezar, and Castillo, all
Right well provided. And, together thus,
All, much excited by the cries
And confused troopings of that folk,
The alarm given, in great haste
Took up their posts and then noticed
That all the tops of the houses
Were garrisoned and occupied. And then
The General shouted an order that
Some captains go out and observe
What folk those were and what intention
They had, at that moment, upon that post.
And then valorous Doña Eufemia
Put the camp at ease, with ladies
That were then in the camp,[8] saying
That, if the General ordered them all down,
They would defend all of the town,
But, if not, he should then leave them alone,
If they wished to keep safe all that
Which they now occupied and held.
At this, the General, with much pleasure,
Congratulating himself that he had
In women a courage of such esteem,
Ordered that Doña Eufemia command
All of that summit, and thus all,
As the brave Amazons obeyed
Great Martesia,[9] thus, as one,
Discharging flying balls into the air,
With gallant spirit they did promenade
The roofs and lofty terraces,
As the wives, after all, the dear pledges
Of those valorous hearts I name:
The Royal Ensign and Alonso Sánchez,
Zubía and Don Luis Gasco, Diego Núñez,
Pedro Sánchez Monrroi, Sosa, Pereira,
Quesada, Juan Morán, and Simón Pérez,

32. El cuerpo de guardia es un conjunto de soldados designados para defender un punto. En este caso parece tratarse del cuerpo de reserva, capaz de acudir a cualquier punto.

33. Doña Eufemia, con las damas que en el campamento había, devolvió, al identificarse, la tranquilidad al mismo.

34. Esta reina de amazonas la menciona Pero Mexía, *Silva de varia lección* I, 10.

7. Villagrá's expression, *cuerpo de guardia,* is used for any body of soldiers set to defend a given point. Here it appears to refer to the reserve.

8. Doña Eufemia and the women identified themselves.

9. This Amazon queen is mentioned by Pero Mexia, *Silva de varia lección* I, 10.

Asensio de Archuleta y Bocanegra,
Carabajal, Romero, Alonso Lucas
Y San Martín, Cordero y el Caudillo
Francisco Sánchez y Francisco Hernández,
Monzón y Alonso Gómez Montesinos
Y Francisco García, con Bustillo
Y la de aquel membrudo y fuerte Griego
Que, como gran genízaro[35] valiente,
Allí muy bien mostró su bravo esfuerzo.
Y visto los contrarios el recato,
Aviso y prevención que en todo abía,
Bolvieron las espaldas sin mostrarse.
Y porque nos bolvamos al Sargento,
Que cerca de la fuerza está alojado,
Será bien que paremos entretanto
Que la obscura tiniebla pierde el manto.

35. Genízaro = extranjero, del mediterráneo oriental particularmente, pero con alusión también a miembro del cuerpo de choque turco reclutado entre jóvenes cautivos cristianos. Villagrá no utiliza el término en su posterior acepción nuevo mexicana, de indios cristianizados fijados en las afueras de las poblaciones españolas.

300 Asencio de Archuleta, Bocanegra,
Carabajal, Romero, Alonso Lucas,
And San Martín, Cordero, and the chief,
Francisco Sánchez, and Francisco Hernández,
Monzón, Alonso Gómez Montesinos,
305 And Francisco García, with Bustillo,
And the wife of that robust, strong Griego,
Who, like a valiant, strong janissary,[10]
Showed there right well his brave spirit.
The adversaries, seeing the caution,
The warning, preparation, in all things,
310 Did turn their backs and not reveal themselves.
And that we may return to the Sergeant,
Who now is lodged near to the fort,
It will be well we stop, in the meantime,
'Till the dark shadow loses its mantle.

10. Although used generally as "foreigner," especially from the eastern Mediterranean, the reference is to a member of the Turkish corps of greatly feared shock troops, usually recruited from captive Christian youths. Villagrá clearly does not employ the term in its later use in New Mexico, as converted and assimilated Indians who, for defensive purposes, were made to settle on the periphery of Spanish settlements.

DE LAS COSAS QUE PASSARON Y SUCEDIERON
ANTES de subir al Peñol y dificultades que pusieron.

Of the things which occurred and happened before climbing
the rock, and the difficulties they made.

N O las muestras, hazañas, no prohezas
De corazones grandes y hechos bravos,
Quilatan los soldados si ganosos
De verse y estimarse por valientes
Arriesgan sus personas y las ponen
En punto de perderse y deslustrarse,
Mas el valor, alteza y excelencia
De aquél que con esfuerzo y con prudencia
Emprende, reportado, vn hecho honrrado.
Y' assí, cuando el esfuerzo va y se pone
Enmedio del peligro con recato
Y aquestos requisitos que hemos dicho,
Y dél sabe salir sin empacharse,
No hay para qué tratar si sus prohezas
Y altos, heroicos, hechos hazañosos
Fueron muy bien o mal acometidos.
Mas quando está perplejo y muy dudoso
Del fin de sus impressas, aquí cargan
Las dudas y vergüenza de vn discreto
Y honrado Capitán, fuerte, valiente,
Cuios cuidados graves afligieron
A todos los del campo fatigado,
Considerando bien la gran braveza
Del poderoso fuerte y enemigos
Tan proterbos y altibos que abrazaba
Y las grandes entradas y salidas
Que para ganar honrra descubrían,
Y el aguage, que estaba de aquel puesto
Muy largas cinco millas bien tendidas,
Y que agua de pie[1] la fortaleza
Tenía allá en la cumbre bien sobrada,
Y el poco bastimento, pues tassado
Para no más que sólas dos semanas
Me mandó que truxesse y no passase
Vn punto más de aquello que ordenaba,
Y con esto notaron que tenían
Mas de para seys años los cercados
Bastantes bastimentos recogidos.
Tenían todas éstas y otras cosas
A todos los de acuerdo cuidadosos,

NOT the display, the deeds, nor the prowess
Of mighty hearts, nor yet brave deeds,
Do assay soldiers, if desirous
Of being thought and judged as valiant
   men
5 They risk their persons and do place themselves
In danger of ruin or tarnishing,
But the courage, the loftiness, and excellence
Of him who, with energy and prudence,
Doth moderately undertake an honored deed.
10 And when his effort goes and does progress
Into the midst of danger cautiously
And with the other requisites we name,
And knows how to come out without a stain,
There is no reason to ask if his deeds
15 And his high, heroic, courageous works,
Were undertaken very well or ill.
But when he is perplexed, very doubtful,
About the end of his emprise, then come
The doubts and modesty of a discreet
20 And honored captain, strong and valiant,
Whose heavy cares caused sorrow to
All of the whole exhausted camp,
Considering well the mighty strength
Of the powerful fort and enemies
25 As forward and haughty as he did face,
And the difficult entrances and exits
That, for gaining honor, they could see,
And the water which was beyond that place
Five very long and well-extended miles,
30 And that the fortress had water,[1]
More than enough, there at the top,
And of the scant provisions, for an estimate
For no more than for two weeks alone
He ordered me to bring, nor to exceed
35 A single point beyond his ordering,
And at the same time he knew that they had
In their enclosures for more than six years
Enough provisions collected.
All these and other things did keep
40 All of the council in great care;

1. Agua de pie = agua de fuente. Pero el agua de Acoma era, al parecer, de aljibe. Véase Villagrá, *Historia,* edición de Junquera, 18, 348.

1. Villagrá uses *agua de pie,* which would suggest some manner of spring at the top of the rocky summit. Even so, the Acoman water was apparently provided by cisterns. See Villagrá, *Historia,* Junquera edition, 18, 348.

Y viendo demás desto que acordaba
El Sargento mayor hazer, de hecho,
Subir a escala vista[2] a lo más alto
Del poderoso risco peñascoso,
Temiendo se perdiesse todo el resto,
Algunos me pidieron que tratase
Con el dicho Sargento que advirtiesse
Aquello que intentaba y no arresgase
Cosa tan importante y que pedía
Acuerdo muy maduro y muy pesado,
Porque en saliendo mal de aquel intento
Era fuerza perderse y assolarse.
Y dándole razón de todo aquesto
Y de otras muchas cosas que passamos,
Tomando mal aquello que propuse,
Sin más considerar, me dixo ayrado:
"Yo trazaré esta causa de manera
Que más no me repliquen estas dueñas,"
Llamándonos assí a los de acuerdo
Porque él determinaba con cuidado
Assegurar primero nuestras vidas,
Con cuio buen seguro, sin rezelo,
También asseguraba que ninguno
Haría más de aquello que él quisiere.
Y aunque es verdad que dixo todo aquesto
Por algún mal,[3] seguro no ignoraba
Que venían con él illustres hombres,
Valientes y discretos y animosos.
Y assí fue prosiguiendo y dixo luego:
"Aquí no ay qué tratar, sino apliquemos
Los vltimos[4] remedios, pues lo pide
La dolencia,[5] que es vltima y, de todos,
Por tal, desahuziada. Y pues a ossados
Es fuerza que fortuna faborezca,
Tentemos luego el vado pocos hombres
Para que a menos costa y menos sangre
Escapen con las vidas y se buelvan
Los señores de acuerdo a su presidio."[6]
Luego que aquesto dixo, confiado,
Qual suele el leñador que al alto pino
Con vno y otro golpe reforzado
De la segur[7] aguda lo estremece
Hasta que a puros golpes ya vencido,

And seeing, beside this, that 'twas the intent
Held by the Sergeant Major to attempt, in fact,
To climb by escalade unto the top
Of that immense and rocky cliff,
45 Fearing lest all the rest be lost,
Some asked of me that I should try
To make the aforesaid Sergeant see
What he attempted and not risk
So important a thing, needing
50 Opinion more mature and weightier,
For, coming badly out of that attempt,
They would, of need, be ruined and destroyed.
And, telling him of all these things
And many more we had discussed,
55 Taking badly what I proposed,
Without considering more, he said, angry:
"I shall attempt this thing in such a way
That these duennas shall not answer me."
Thus calling us of the council,
60 For he determined carefully
To protect our lives first of all,
With which good safety, without fear,
He also made sure that no one
Should do more than he should desire.
65 And though 'tis true he said all this
For some cowardly ones,[2] he never did ignore
That with him there came famous men,
Valiant, discreet, and courageous,
And so he continued, and finally said:
70 "Here there is naught to talk of. We must try
The extreme cure, for it is demanded
By the disease,[3] terminal and by all,
As such, deemed as hopeless. And since fortune
Must needs give favor unto daring men,
75 Let us, then, try this recourse with few men
So that with the least cost and the least blood
The thoughtful council may thereby escape
With their lives and return to their barracks."[4]
When he had said this, confident,
80 As the woodsman who has attacked
The lofty pine with blow raining on blow
From his sharp axe, and set it trembling
Until, now conquered by his blows,

2. A escala vista = asaltar de día y a vista del enemigo.

3. Este "mal" lo mismo puede referirse a enfermedad del cuerpo que del espíritu, y que el poeta lo modifique con el impreciso "algún" sugiere que no pretende saberlo.

4. Vltimos = últimos, extremados.

5. La dolencia a la que se refiere es la deshonra.

6. Presidio = guarnición, fortaleza. Zaldívar sigue burlándose de los soldados reflexivos ("de acuerdo").

7. Segur = hacha.

2. Villagrá's text, *por algún mal*, may perhaps more likely suggest a reference to a malady he purposely does not identify, and which one may conjecture to have been either "deep grief" or "blind vengeance."

3. The deathly disease referred to is dishonor.

4. Zaldívar continues to ridicule his conservative counselors.

Temblando por la cima y por los lados,
En tierra da con él y hecho rajas
Allí lo ve a sus pies, assí el Zaldívar,
Para traerlos todos a su gusto,
Al punto señaló doze guerreros
Para que como tales se aprestasen
Y a escala vista todos emprendiessen
La más difícil cumbre lebantada.
En esto, aquellos bárbaros, contentos
De ver los Castellanos tan vezinos,
Vn grande vaile todos ordenaron
Y vna opulenta cena regalada
Donde Zutacapán salió el primero,
De mantas regaladas[8] adornado.
No menos que él salieron muy vizarros
Cotumbo y Tempal, llenos de alegría;
También aquel Amulco y grande Pilco
Y otros muchos con éstos que mostraban
Vn no pensado gusto, rebozando
De placer y contento jamás visto
De ver los Españoles alojados
Tan cerca de sus muros lebantados.
Estando, pues, cenando todos juntos
Para empezar el vaile señalado,
Como quiera que siempre la fortuna
Aborrece los gustos y contentos
Que celebran lo que ella quiere darnos,
Temiendo Zutancalpo rebolviesse,
En enemiga buelta, la inconstante
Y mal segura rueda prodigiosa,
De parecer de Bempol y Gicombo,
Entró con sus amigos, demudado,
Y tendiendo la vista por aquéllos
Que con tan gran descuido allí cenaban,
Qual otro Scipión, que al Campamigo[9]
No quiso permitirle tal excesso
Quando a Numancia vino,[10] assí este joben,
Pareciéndole mal aquellas fiestas,
A todos desta suerte les propuso:
"Barones descuidados, bien os consta
Que para bien hablar en cosas justas
Es a qualquiera edad muy permitido
Que diga lo que siente y le lastima,

Trembling in its top and its sides,
He strikes it to the earth and, all shattered,
Sees it there at his feet, thus Zaldívar,
To bring them all to his pleasure,
Immediately told twelve warriors
That, as such, they should go in haste
And by an escalade were to attempt
The most difficult, lofty peak.
At this, those barbarians, content
To see the Spaniards so nearby
Did all prepare a mighty dance
And bounteous, plentiful banquet,
Where Zutacapán came out first
Adorned with the most splendid mantles.
No less than he, there came, most gay,
Cotumbo and Tempal, both full of joy,
Also that Amulco and great Pilco,
And many others with them, who displayed
A joy beyond thought, fair bursting
With pleasure and contentment unbelievable
At seeing the Spaniards lodged there,
So near unto their lofty walls.
All, then, together sitting at the feast,
About to make beginning of the famous dance,
Since it always occurs that Dame Fortune
Abhors the pleasure and contentment
Which celebrate what she is yet to give,
Zutancalpo, fearing a rapid change
Into a hostile phase by that unsafe,
Inconstant, and prodigious wheel,
His act favored by Bempol and by Gicombo,
He entered with his friends, greatly enraged,
And, sweeping with his glance over those folk
Who there were dining in such heedlessness,
Like a new Scipio, who did not wish
To permit Campamigo[5] such excess
When he came to Numantia,[6] so this youth,
This revel seeming ill to him,
Did speak to all in this fashion:
"You heedless men, right well you know
That for good speaking on just things
It is permitted unto any age
To say what hurts and injures it,

85

90

95

100

105

110

115

120

125

---

8. Regaladas = suaves, delicadas.

9. Parece errata del original, puesto que el verso queda corto. En todo caso, se refiere al campamento propio, amigo.

10. Se refiere a la dura disciplina castrense del conquistador de Numancia, Publio Emiliano. Ello consta en los historiadores romanos que de Numancia trataron (Livio, Florio, etc.) y también en Ambrosio Morales, *Crónica general de España* VIII, 8.

5. The original text's *Campamigo* is probably a printing error for *campo amigo,* which renders a better measure to the verse and better sense ("his own camp") to the line.

6. Scipio's harsh discipline upon taking command at Numancia is recorded by Roman historians (Livy, Florian, etc.) and also by the widely read historical text at that time, Ambrosio Morales's, *Crónica general de España* VIII, 8.

Y assimismo sabéys que alcanza y tiene
La fuerza de razón en sí más alma
Quanto por menos años se propone
Aquello que es justicia y es derecho.
Y si a lo que yo agora propusiere
No diere autoridad la fresca sangre,
Tomad, señores, todas mis palabras
Como de hijo que a su mismo padre
Repugna y contradize en lo que haze,
Cuia desemboltura no se toma
Si no es herrando el padre y arrastrando
La fuerza de razón por los cabellos.
Ya sé que es impossible reduziros
A la gustosa paz que pretendemos,
Y siendo aquesto assí, ¿dezidme agora
Por quál razón vivís tan descuidados
Teniendo al enemigo tan a pique?[11]
¿Quién vio jamás banquetes y libreas,
Bailes y regozijos por aquéllos
Que lastimosa guerra les aguarda?
Mirad, soldados nobles, esforzados,
Que están ya los Castillas dentro en casa,
Y aunque tengáis muy cierta la victoria
Es justo no ignoréis de todo punto
Que della nace siempre nueva guerra.
Apercibid las armas, reforzemos
Todas las partes flacas con presteza.
Haced luego reparos[12] y empezemos
A apercibir ingenios y trincheas,[13]
Pongamos luego postas, no durmamos.
Demos luego principio, cuidadosos,
A dar en qué entender[14] al enemigo.
Mirad que de centellas muy pequeñas
Se suelen lebantar muy grandes llamas."
Aquí Zutacapán, algo risueño,
Colmado de contento, dixo luego:
"Dirás a tus amigos, Zutancalpo,
A Gicombo, te digo, y al gran Bempol,
Que riñan[15] sus pendencias con palabras
De gran comedimiento y cortesía,
Bajas las dos cabezas y los ojos
En tierra bien clavados y los brazos
Sueltos por los costados, sin que cosa
Ocupen con las manos, que con esto
No esperen que jamás les venga cosa

And you know, likewise, that the force of reasoning
Does gain and have within itself more strength
Proportionate to the youth of him who shows
130 That which is just and is the right.
And if to what I now set forth to you
My youthful blood give no authority,
Take, gentlemen, all these my words
As from a son who contradicts, repudiates,
135 His own father in whatever he does,
An effrontery only tolerable
When the father is in error and drags
The force of reason by its very hair.
Since 'tis impossible to reduce you
140 Unto the pleasant peace that we desire,
In such a situation, tell me, now,
For what reason you live so heedlessly
Having the enemy so near?
Who ever saw banquets and gaudy dress,
145 Dancings and rejoicings in those
Whom doleful war was awaiting?
Look, soldiers, noble, gallant men,
The Spaniards are within our very home,
And though you are so sure of victory,
150 'Tis right, above all, that you know
New war is always born from this.
Take up your arms. Let us strengthen
All the weak places and do so in haste.
Make you repairs. Let us begin
155 To make our hazards ready and trenches.
Let us put sentries out, not sleep.
Let us begin at once, most carefully,
To encounter the enemy.
Remember that from tiny coals
160 The greatest flames do oft spring forth."
Zutacapán, then, with a smile,
Filled with contentment, said quickly:
"Say to your friends, Zutancalpo,
To Gicombo, I mean, and great Bempol,
165 To fight their quarrels out with words
Of great civility and courtesy,
Their two heads lowered and their eyes
Fixed well upon the ground, their arms
Hanging loose at their sides, nor must
170 They occupy their hands, for so,
They hope, nothing may ever come

11. A pique = cerca.
12. Reparos = reparaciones.
13. Trincheas = trincheras.
14. Dar en qué entender = hostigar.
15. Riñan = disputen.

Que pueda dar disgusto a sus personas."
Oyendo, pues, aquesto el noble joben,
Venciendo aquel disgusto con prudencia,
Dejándolos a todos, dio la buelta,
Y ellos empezaron luego el baile
Y entraron tan briosos y gallardos
Qual suelen los caballos que, tascando[16]
Los espumosos frenos, van hiriendo,
Con las herradas manos lebantadas,
Los duros empedrados, y assí, bravos,
Hollándose[17] ligeros, mil pedazos,
Ganosos de arrancar, se van haziendo.
Assí los bravos bárbaros, soberbios,
Haziendo mil lindezas y saltando,
Hiriendo aquel peñasco a puros golpes
De las valientes plantas que assentaban,
Y con fuerza de gritos y alaridos
Vn infernal clamor allí subían
Tan horrendo y grimoso que las almas
De todos los dañados[18] parecían
Que allí su triste suerte lamentaban.
Este baile turó hasta que el Alba
La mísera tiniebla fue venciendo,
Y dando buelta al muro por lo alto
Dixo Zutacapán en altas bozes,
Viendo que abía bien abierto el día,
Que a qué aguardaban tanto los Castillas,
Que ya estaban cansados de aguardarlos.
Y lebantando todos grandes gritos,
Diziéndonos palabras afrentosas,
A la batalla todos incitaban.
En esto, vnos caballos se acercaron
A vnos charquillos de agua llovediza,
Y estando allí bebiendo, nos flecharon
Algunos dellos y otros nos mataron.
Mas no les salió el hecho tan barato,
Que, al descuido,[19] Cordero con Zapata,
Por orden del Sargento, les salieron[20]
Y al Capitán Totolco, su caudillo,
Del gran Gicombo suegro regalado
Y de Luzcoija padre muy querido,
Muerto le trujo a tierra el buen Zapata,
Siendo el primero que mostró el esfuerzo
Del Castellano vando belicoso.
En esto, los demás se retiraron

175 Leaving them all, departed thence,
And they at once began the dance,
Becoming as lively and spirited
As horses do when, grinding at
180 The foamy bits, they keep pawing
With their upraised and iron-shod hoofs
Upon the hard pavements and, so aroused,
Stomping themselves, they make a thousand bits,
Themselves, desirous to be off.
185 Thus these brave, haughty barbarians
Performed a thousand pretty tricks, leaping,
Wounding that rock by the sheer blows
Of their own flying feet, which they set down,
And with a violence of cries and yells
190 They set up such an infernal roar,
So horrid and so fearful, that the souls
Of all the damned did seem to be
Lamenting there their sorry fate.
This dance lasted until the dawn
Was conquering the miserable darkness,
195 And, running to the topmost of the wall,
Zutacapán inquired in a loud voice,
Seeing that it was quite daylight,
Why they so long awaited, the Spaniards,
Since they were now tired of awaiting them.
200 And, all setting up monstrous cries,
Saying to us insulting words,
They all urged us into battle.
Just then some horses did approach
Some little pools of rainwater
205 And, drinking there, with their arrows
They wounded some and killed others.
But they did not come off so cheap,
For suddenly Cordero, Zapata,
By order of the Sergeant, sallied forth
210 And their leader, the captain Totolco,
Famous father-in-law of Gicombo
And much loved father of Luzcoija,
The good Zapata struck dead to the earth,
Being the first who did display the strength
215 Of all the bellicose Castilian band.
At this, the others then retired,

To give displeasure unto their persons."
The noble youth, then, hearing this,
Repressing his displeasure prudently,

16. Tascando = mordiendo, pues se dice de los caballos cuando comen.
17. Hollándose = pisándose.
18. Dañados = condenados.
19. Al descuido = inadvertidamenrte.
20. Salieron = confrontaron.

A muy gran priessa todos de aquel puesto.
Viendo, pues, el Zaldívar tal sucesso
A consejo mandó que se juntasen,
Y estando juntos todos con cuidado,
Assí les fue diziendo, reportado:
"Quando todos partimos del presidio,
Discretos caballeros, no ignoramos
Que supieron los bárbaros salimos
A sóla la venganza y el castigo
De aquéstos que este fuerte abraza y tiene,
Cuias balientes fuerzas todos juntos
Supimos y alcanzamos no ser menos
Que agora se nos muestran y descubren.
Si puestos en el puesto donde estamos
Alzasemos la mano y sin enmienda
Dexassemos la causa comenzada,
¿Quál será aquel seguro que assegure
Nuestras honrras y vidas si tal mancha
Viessemos²¹ en Españoles los vezinos
De todas estas tierras comarcanas?"
Y por salir mejor de aqueste hecho
Púsoles por delante vuestro ceptro,²²
Con omenage eterno obedecido,
Y la Española sangre, no cansada
De ser siempre leal, y los disgustos
De tan prolijos tiempos padecidos.
Trújoles assimismo a la memoria
Aquel inmenso premio y altas cruzes²³
Con que, señor, honrráis los nobles pechos
De aquellos valerosos que en las lides,
Entre temor dudosos y esperanza,
Triunfaron como buenos de los hechos
Que assí como valientes alcanzaron.
Por cuias justas causas les dezía
Que pues por flacos medios pocas vezes
Grandes cosas se alcanzan y consiguen,
Que a escala vista doze permitiessen
Que aquestos muros juntos escalasen,
Que señalados todos los tenia.
Para cuio buen fin dixo assimismo:
"Señores compañeros, advirtamos
Que razonar vn grande cortesano
Con vn vil, bronco, bárbaro, grossero,
Y tratar con él cosas que no caben
Más que en vn limpio, claro y cultivado,

220

225

230

235

240

245

250

255

260

All in great haste, from that station.
Zaldívar, then, seeing such a success,
Ordered the council to gather
And, all worried, assembling,
Thus he did boldly speak to them:
"When we all left the garrison
We were not ignorant, ingenious gentlemen,
That these barbarians knew that we had gone
For vengeance only and for punishment
Of those this fort embraces and contains,
Whose valiant forces all summed-up
We knew and comprehended were no less
Than now they discover and show themselves.
If, having come, then, to our present state,
We should withdraw our hands without amends
And leave the cause we have commenced,
What would be the assurance to assure
Our honor and our lives if such a stain
Should be seen in Spaniards by the inhabitants
Of all these lands here neighboring?"
The better to come out of this affair
He called to their attention your scepter,
Obeyed with eternal homage,
And the Spanish blood, never tired
Of being ever loyal, misfortunes
Suffered throughout such tedious times.
Likewise he brought before their memory
That immense prize, the high crosses⁷
With which, lord, you do honor noble breasts
Of those brave men who, in battles,
Doubtful between their fear and hope,
Did triumph, like good men, by deeds
Which they, like valiant men, had done.
For these just reasons he asked them
That, since by timid means very few times
Great things have been accomplished and performed,
They would permit twelve, by an escalade,
To climb those walls in a body,
Those he had pointed out to all.
For which good end he also said:
"My gentlemen companions, let us note
That for a great courtier to talk
With a vile, wild, and gross barbarian
And with him treat of things that have no place
Except in a bright, clear, and well-instructed,

---

21. Errata del original por "viessen," que da mejor sentido y mejor medida.

22. Hizo alusión a la magestad real.

23. Se refiere a las cruzes de las órdenes militares con que podían quedar premiados los héroes.

7. The reference is to any of the crosses that were insignia of the military orders, granted by the king for meritorious service.

Sagaz, discreto y alto entendimiento,
Es querer que los pezes se apacienten
Por los subtiles ayres delicados
Y que los cierbos sueltos por el agua
Con presuroso curso la atropellen.
Y assí, por esta causa, soy de acuerdo,
Imitando si puedo en este hecho
Al madrigado²⁴ simple de tragedia,
Cuio fingir taimado,²⁵ desembuelto,
Es como si otra cosa no encubriesse,²⁶
Que assí, cubierto todo y rebozado,
Será bien que yo hable²⁷ aquestos Indios,
Diziéndoles que quiero por la cumbre
Más alta del Peñol subir arriba
Con todos los soldados de a caballo,
Con cuio trato doble, deslumbrados
Viendo que juntos todos emprendimos
La difícil subida peligrosa,
Será possible todos desamparen
Sus puestos y al socorro partan luego,
Y assí los doze salgan, señalados,
Para escalar los muros lebantados
Sin que persona alguna los impida."
Pues aprobando todos este acuerdo,
Salió el sagaz Sargento y junto al muro,
Cuia vertiente casi cien estados
De grimosa caída descubría,
Mandó que les dixessen y avisasen
Que, pues que no le daban cuenta alguna
De las muertes injustas que causaron
A nuestros compañeros, que él quería,
Por sólo que supiessen y alcanzasen
Las fuerzas y valor de los Castillas,
Subir por aquel puesto y darles muerte,
Passándolos a todos a cuchillo.
Y porque no dixessen ni alegasen
Que no les avisaba, abía querido
Señalarles el puesto y prevenirlos.
Y assí, bolvió las riendas y al descuido
A todos los dexó con gran cuidado.
Y porque aqueste hecho más se entienda
Ya tengo, señor, dicho y declarado
Que estaban dos peñoles lebantados
Más de trecientos passos divididos
Los terribles assientos no domados

265

270

275

280

285

290

295

300

305

Wise, discreet, and lofty understanding,
This is to wish that fish should feed
Amid the air, subtle and delicate,
And that the wild deer in water
Should press their way in rapid course.
And so, for this reason, I hope
To imitate in this thing, if I can,
The practical fool of the comedy,
Whose astute cleverness is to pretend
As though he were not hiding something else,
For thus, covering and masking all,
'Twere well I should speak to these Indians,
Telling them that I wish to climb
Up to the very topmost of the rock
With all the soldiers of the cavalry.
Put off their guard by this double-dealing,
Seeing we all together undertake
The difficult and perilous ascent,
It may be possible that they will leave
Their posts unguarded and go to help them,
And so the chosen twelve may sally forth
To scale those huge and lofty walls
Without a single person hindering them."
All then approving of this plan,
The wise Sergeant went out and next to the wall,
Whose slope did show nearly a hundred fathoms
Of standing rock, a fearful fall,
He ordered they be told and warned
That, since they gave him no account
Of the unjust deaths they had caused
To our companions, he now would,
Solely that they might know and grasp
The strength and valor of the Castilians,
Climb up unto that place and deal out death,
Passing them all beneath the knife.
And lest they might say or allege
He had not warned them, he had wished
To indicate the place and prepare them.
And so he reined about, quite nonchalant,
And left them all in deepest care.
That this deed may be better understood
I have already told, lord, and declared
That there were two rocks raised aloft,
By more than three hundred feet divided
Their fearful tops yet unconquered,

24. Madrigado = malicioso, del toro padre que se deja envejecer y
que llega a cobrar gran malicia.
25. Taimado = astuto.
26. Hace parecer que nada encubre.
27. Posible errata del original omitiendo la "a."

Y estaba vn passamán del vno al otro
De rocas tan soberbias que ygualaban
Con las más altas cumbres que tenían.
Entendido, pues, esto, con secreto
Dexó doze Españoles escondidos
Al socaire de vn risco muy pegado
Al primer peñol, y luego al punto
Mandó quitar las tiendas, de manera
Que todos claro viessen y notasen
Que, sin que Castellano allí quedase,
Al prometido hecho todos juntos
Determinados yban a matarlos.
Y assí partieron todos de arrancada,
Rasgando los costados poderosos
De los bravos caballos animosos,
Y viendo allí los bárbaros que juntos
Los Españoles yban denodados
A subir por el puesto señalado,
Como bárbaros todos, luego al punto,
Teniendo por verdad aquel engaño,
Dexando sus assientos arrancaron
A defender el passo más seguro
Que toda aquella fuerza allí alcanzaba.
En esto, aquellos doze que escondidos
Al socaire del risco abían quedado
Salieron con esfuerzo, acometiendo
La fuerza del Peñol jamás vendido,[28]
Según veréis, gran Rey, si soys servido.

28. Probable errata del original por "vencido."

And there, between the two, was a passage
Of rocks so lofty they equaled
The very highest tops of them.
310   This understood, then, secretly
He left twelve Spaniards in hiding
Upon the lee of a crag very near
To the first rock, and then at once
He ordered the tents struck for the purpose
315   That all might see clearly and note
That, no Castilian staying there,
All, joined for this the promised deed,
Were coming determined to slaughter them.
Now all set forth in a great charge,
320   Spurring hard on the powerful sides
Of the brave, spirited horses,
And the barbarians, seeing that
The Spaniards boldly came on there
To climb up at the indicated spot,
325   All, like barbarians, instantly
Taking that deceit for truth,
Leaving their own posts, hastened forth
To hold the most secure passage
That all that fortress possessed there.
330   At this, those twelve who had remained
Hidden upon the lee side of the cliff
Came out, attacking with fury
That rocky fortress never lost,
As you shall see, great King, if you but please.

CANTO VEYNTE Y NVEVE

COMO LOS DOZE COMPAÑEROS ESCALARON EL
PRIMER Peñol y batalla que tuvieron con los Indios, y junta
que tuvieron para lebantar por General a Gicombo, y acetación
que hizo del cargo, y condiciones que sacó para exercerlo.

COSA es patente, clara y manifiesta,
Poderoso señor, si bien notamos,
Que muchas vezes vemos se aventaja
A toda discreción, saber y aviso
Vn necio razonar, si con prudencia
Sabe disimularse y proponerse.
Cuio disfraz discreto vimos tuvo
Aquí el sagaz Sargento, hastuto y cauto,
Porque viendo los bárbaros que juntos
Los Castellanos todos arrancaban
Y al poderoso muro acometían
Y que ánima viviente no quedaba
Por todo nuestro assiento, cuias tiendas,
Para más encubrirnos, derribamos,
Temiendo ser verdad aquel portento,
De tropel todos juntos arrancaron
A defender el passo más guardado
Que pudo dessearse en todo el mundo.
Viendo, pues, que dejaban despoblado
El primer Peñol aquellos bravos,
Salieron de tropel y a escala vista,
Quales al rico palio¹ arremetían
Ligeros corredores, assí juntos
Los doze Castellanos arrancaron,
Cuios nombres es justo que se escriban
Pues no piden sus obras que se callen:
El Sargento mayor y León de Isasti,
Marcos Cortés, Munuera, Antonio Hernández,
También el Secretario Iuan Belarde,
Christóbal Sánchez y Christóbal López,
Hernán Martín, Cordero y aquel Pablo
Que dizen de Aguilar y yo con ellos,
Que assí fue necessario porque el colmo
No fuesse tan cumplido y que mermase.²
Pues, como³ aquestos fuertes embistiessen
El más valiente muro y lo escalasen
Estaba⁴ el gran Gicombo y Bempol juntos

---

1. Palio = paño de seda que se daba al vencedor en algunas carreras.
2. Indica, humildemente, que su presencia mermaba, reducía, la altura, "colmo," del conjunto de los hombres que subieron.
3. Como = según, mientras.
4. El verbo en singular es licencia poética.

CANTO XXIX

How the twelve companions scaled the first rock and the battle
they had with the Indians, and the council held to raise
Gicombo as General, and his acceptance of the charge,
and the conditions he expected to exercise it.

IT is a thing clear, patent, manifest,
O powerful lord, if we but notice it,
That many times we see advantage won
Over discretion, wisdom, and learning
5   By a foolish reasoning, if prudently
It knows how to dissimulate, convince.
We see that this disguise was taken on
By the sagacious Sergeant here, astute, cunning,
For the barbarians, seeing that together
10   The Castilians had moved forward,
All rushing to the mighty wall,
And that no living soul remained
At our encampment, where the tents
Had all been struck, the better to conceal our plan,
15   All fearing that our threat was true,
They hastened, all in a great troop,
To guard the pass, the best guarded
That could, in all the world, be wished.
Seeing, then, that they left vacant
20   The whole first rock, those gallant men
Did sally out at once and to scaling,
Like the swift runners who do strive
For a rich prize, so together
Those twelve Castilians did set themselves,
25   And 'tis but just their names be writ
Since their deeds call for no silence:
The Sergeant Major and León de Isasti,
Marcos Cortés, Munuera, Antonio Hernández,
Also the secretary, Juan Velarde,
30   Cristóbal Sánchez and Cristóbal López,
Hernán Martín, Cordero, and that Pablo
They call de Aguilar, and I with them,
So that their true greatness be somewhat less
Complete and e'en perhaps somewhat lessened.¹
35   Now when these stalwart men attacked
The strongest wall and climbed up it,
The great Gicombo and Bempol were together,

---

1. Villagrá again, in narrating his own presence, strikes the exaggeratedly humble pose expected.

Y el viejo Chumpo y noble Zutancalpo
Con todos los amigos que las pazes
Pidieron con instancia y procuraron,
Por cuia causa a todos despreciaron
Aquestos pobres bárbaros perdidos.
Y assí, sin hazer dellos cuenta alguna,
Como bruto animal, sin más sospecha,
Dexando aquel peñol desocupado,
Salió Zutacapán con todo el pueblo
A defender la entrada a los Castillas
Que estaba a solas aves reserbada.⁵
Notando, pues, Gicombo que ocupaban
El primer peñol los Castellanos
Y que era fuerza allí los acabasen,
Por pensar que eran todos sus contrarios⁶
Mandó que Bempol luego arremetiesse
Con cuatrocientos bárbaros. Y al punto
Que todos embistieron y a las⁷ doze
La cumbre del peñol abían ganado
Y luego al passamán acometieron
Y en vn angosto estrecho todos juntos
Las armas sangrentaron de manera
Que, si qual ellos yo me señalara,
El número de doze dentro en Francia
De todo punto es cierto se perdiera
Y en este angosto estrecho se hallara.⁸
Viendo, pues, el Sargento tal braveza
En brazos tan valientes y esforzados,
"Caballeros de Christo," les dezía,
"Oy es de san Vicente el santo día,⁹
Con cuio santo nombre soy honrrado,
Y en este heroico, illustre y grande santo
Espero, valerosos Españoles,
Que abemos de salir de aqueste hecho
Triunfando como bravos desta gente
Idólatra, perdida, vil, infame."
Oyendo, pues, aquesto, todos juntos,
Apretando los dientes, soportaban
De flecha y piedra espesa tan gran lluvia
Que pedazos a todos los hazían,
Hasta que el gran caudillo dio con Polco,
Vn bárbaro valiente, en tierra muerto,

And old Chumpo, noble Zutancalpo
With all their friends who did desire
40 And work for peace insistently,
For which the rest did all despise
Those poor, ruined barbarians.
And so, taking no thought of them,
Like a brute beast, without suspicion,
45 Zutacapán, with all the town,
Went to defend an entrance from the Castilians
That was reserved unto the birds alone,
Leaving that rock unoccupied.
Gicombo, noting the Spaniards
50 Were occupying the first rock
And that 'twas necessary they be slain,
Thinking that these were all his opponents,²
Ordered that Bempol should attack at once
With four hundred barbarians. And, just when
55 They all attacked, all of the twelve
Had gained the summit of the rock,
And they did meet upon the neck
And, in a narrow place, they all
Did flesh their weapons in such wise
60 That, had I distinguished myself
Like them, 'tis certain the number
Of twelve would have been lost to France
And found in this narrow passage.³
The Sergeant then, seeing such zeal
65 In arms so valiant and so courageous,
Said unto them: "Ye cavaliers of Christ,
This is the holy day of Saint Vincent,⁴
With whose most holy name I am honored,
And by this great, heroic, famous saint
70 I hope, ye valorous Spaniards,
That we are to come out of this affair
Triumphing like brave men over these folk,
Idolaters, lost, vile, and infamous."
We, all together, hearing this,
75 Gritting our teeth, did submit to
A furious rain of arrows and of rocks
That was cutting us to pieces
Until our great chief struck Polco,
A valiant barbarian, dead to earth,

5. Otra vez repite que el paso que defendían los indios era de sí inexpugnable.
6. Villagrá justifica que el bravo Gicombo mandase tantos hombres sugiriendo, un tanto inverosímilmente, que pensaba que todos los españoles habian subido.
7. Probable errata del original por "ya los," que da sentido al texto.
8. Dice que si él hubiera estado a la altura de sus once compañeros la fama de los doce pares se hubiera perdido para Francia, pasando a los doce que escalaron.
9. El 22 de enero.

2. This seems to wish to justify Gicombo's sending so many men, four hundred, as he was thinking that he was confronting the entire Spanish force and not just twelve men. The poet, in good epic tradition, maintains the perception of the enemy hero.
3. Villagrá humbly indicates that had he been as brave as his eleven companions France would have lost its famous Twelve Peers and they would have been found in that place.
4. The feast of Saint Vincent is January 22.

Con cuia buena suerte el Secretario,
Marcos Cortés, Cordero y León Isasti,
Con cada quatro balas despedidas
De los prestos cañones, derribaron
Diez bárbaros gallardos, y tras destos
Otros catorze juntos despacharon
El buen Christóbal Sánchez con Munuera
Y Pablo de Aguilar y Antonio Hernández
Y aquel Hernán Martín al qual seguía
El gran Christóbal López, a quien vimos
De vna grande pedrada tan ayrado
Que apenas en el suelo fue tendido
Quando se puso en pie y, assí, encendido,
Hizo tan gran destrozo que no abía
Quien ya esperar ossase su osadía.
En esto, Antonio Hernández, Lusitano,
Ganoso de estimarse por valiente,
En sus soberbias fuerzas confiado,
Tanto quiso meterse y arriscarse[10]
Que a palos y a pedradas, assí[11] muerto,
Abiendo destrozado grandes cuerpos,
Fue por sólo el Sargento socorrido.
Pues como Bempol viesse la braveza
De aquel pequeño número de espadas,
Arrastrando los cuerpos ya difuntos
Y a cuestas los heridos retirando,
Socorro fue pidiendo. Y luego en esto,
Assí como de Irlanda vn bravo perro,[12]
Con vna grande esquadra de guerreros
Gicombo fue embistiendo y Zutancalpo.
Y viendo allí el Sargento que traía
Vn bárbaro gallardo aquel bestido
Del caro hermano muerto, ensangrentado,
Assí como Iacob quedó suspenso
De ver la bestimenta tinta en sangre
De su Ioseph querido y regalado,[13]
Assí le vimos todos suspendido.
Y luego que algún tanto fue cobrado,
Poniendo en aquel bárbaro los ojos
Para él arremetió con tal braveza
Qual suele vn bravo sacre arrebatado,
Que de muy alta cumbre se abalanza
Sobre la blanca garza y de encuentro
La priva de sentido y luego a pique,

80 At which good luck the secretary,
    Marcos Cortés, Cordero, and León de Isasti,
    With every four bullets discharged
    From their swift barrels, did strike down
    Ten brave barbarians, after whom
85 Fourteen more were at once dispatched
    By good Cristóbal Sánchez with Munuera,
    Pablo de Aguilar, and Antonio Hernández,
    And that Hernán Martín, and after this
    The great Cristóbal López, whom we saw
90 So angered by a great blow from a rock
    That had just scarcely stretched him on the ground
    When he arose, and thus, furious,
    Made such great slaughter there was none
    Who dared there to challenge his daring.
95 At this, Antonio Hernández, he of Lusitania,[5]
    Desirous of esteem as a brave man,
    Trusting in his own proud strength,
    So chose to place himself and risk himself,
    That, almost dead from blows of clubs and stones,
100 He was rescued by the Sergeant alone,
    Although he slew great multitudes.
    Now, as Bempol beheld the bravery
    Of the small number of swordsmen,
    Disposing of the bodies of those dead
105 And sending off his wounded to one side,
    He sent for help, and, upon this,
    Like a brave dog of Ireland,[6]
    With a great troop of warriors,
    Gicombo hastened up and Zutancalpo, too.
110 The Sergeant, seeing a bold savage there
    Was wearing a bloody garment
    Belonging to his dear and dead brother,
    Was, like to Jacob, overcome
    On seeing the dress, red with blood,
115 Of his beloved, dear Joseph,[7]
    We all observed, disconcerted.
    And when he had somewhat recovered,
    Fixing his eyes on that barbarian,
    He forced a way to him with such fierceness
120 As a brave and swift hawk doth show
    Which hurtles from the top of some high peak
    Upon the white heron and, meeting it,
    Strikes it senseless, then, sinking down,

10. Arriscarse = arriesgarse.
11. Posible errata del original por "casi."
12. La braveza del perro irlandés se nota ya en *La araucana* I, 3, donde se indica que se usaban para cazar al jabalí.
13. Los hermanos de José, después de venderlo, hicieron creer al padre que lo había matado un animal, *Génesis* 30.

5. Lusitania was and is Portugal.
6. The ferocity of Irish hounds was a commonplace of the times. See *La Araucana* I, 3, where it is indicated they were used to hunt boar.
7. *Genesis* 30.

Hecha un ovillo,[14] toda a tierra viene,
Assí, de aquesta suerte, sin acuerdo,
Para él se abalanzó desatinado
Y tulliendo[15] y matando fue rompiendo
La bárbara canalla reformada[16]
Hasta que por mortaja aquella ropa
Quedó del miserable, que en vn punto
Dexó sin vida y alma allí difunto.
En esto, el gran Gicombo, desembuelto,
Furioso a todas partes rebolvía,
La bárbara canalla allí alentando
Con vno y otro grito, y fue embistiendo
Con todos sus soldados de manera
Que la pequeña esquadra Castellana
De todo punto rota allí quedara
Si el Sargento mayor con gran presteza
Pedazos de vn valazo no le haze,
Por lo alto del molledo,[17] el diestro brazo,
Con cuia buena suerte venturosa
Nunca se vio jamás que assí bramase,
Bertiendo espumarajos por la lengua,
La braveza y fiereza desatada
Del corajoso toro jarretado,[18]
Que a todas partes vemos arremete
La destroncada corba sacudiendo,
Los muy agudos cuernos lebantando,
Qual vimos a Gicombo embravecido,
Por vna y otra parte rebentando
De cólera deshecha, y assí, bravo,
Esforzando a los suyos, les hazía
Que de los prestos brazos despidiessen
De flecha, palo y piedra tal vertiente
Qual vemos vn gran polvo quando, espeso,
Los poderosos vientos nos derraman.
Y en el inter, aquellos valerosos
Que de falso embistieron al gran muro
Apenas arrancaron quando luego
De los caballos presto se apearon
Aquel Francisco Sánchez, el Caudillo,
Tras dél Diego Robledo y Simón Pérez,
Guillén y Catalán, Mallea y Vega,
También Martín Ramírez y Montero,
Ayarde con Iuan Griego. Y assí, juntos
Sacudiendo las crestas lebantadas

A ball of feathers, it doth strike the earth.[8]
125 Now, in this very way, regarding naught
He wildly hurled himself toward him
And, wounding and killing, he burst
Through the ceding barbarian mob
Until the garment was the winding-sheet
130 Of that poor wretch whom he at once
Left dead there, without life or soul.
Now great Gicombo, furious,
Went recklessly about, in every place
Encouraging the savage rabble there
135 With shout on shout, and then attacked
With all his troops in such manner
That the small Castilian squadron
Would there have been all overwhelmed
Had not the Sergeant Major suddenly,
140 With shot of musket, broken in pieces
His mighty arm high in the upper part.
At this good fortune, come by chance,
There ne'er was seen such bellowing
Nor spurting foam from out the mouth
145 From the fury and boundless savageness
Of raging bull that has been houghed
And whom we see attack in all directions
Dragging his severed hocks behind
And raising up his pointed horns,
150 As we did see Gicombo, furious,
Now here, now there, and bursting forth
With violent wrath and, thus, furious,
Encouraging his men, he ordered them
To send upon us from their ready arms
155 Such storm of arrows, clubs, and stones
As we see of great dust when thick
The powerful winds drive it at us.
Now in the meantime those brave men
Who falsely made attack on the great wall
160 Had hardly drawn rein when at once
They quickly dismounted their horses.
There was Francisco Sánchez, the leader,
And, too, Diego Robledo and Simón Pérez,
Guillén and Catalán, Mallea and Vega,
165 Also Martín Ramírez, Montero,
Ayarde, and Juan Griego. So, they all,
Maneuvering shut the lifted crests

14. Hecha vn ovillo = hecha una masa informe (de plumas), que sigue muy de cerca la imagen que emplea Virgilio, *Eneida* XI, 954–59.
15. Tulliendo = hiriendo.
16. Reformada = retirada.
17. Molledo = parte carnosa del brazo.
18. Jarretado = cortadas las piernas por la corva.

8. The image is very close to that employed by Virgil in the *Aeneid* XI, 954–59.

De las bravas zeladas, se apegaron,
Qual trepadora yedra, al fuerte muro
Y, fingiendo escalarle, soportaban
De piedra desgalgada[19] tal tormenta
Que, assí como se rompe el alto Cielo
Con vno y otro trueno pavoroso
Y con fuerza de rayos nos assombra,
Assí, todos temiendo, prohejaban
Contra la gran tormenta, jamás vista,
De cantos y peñascos que embiaban,
Atónitos los bárbaros, confussos
De ver en Castellanos tal prodigio,
Creyendo ser verdad que vía el ciego
Y que bolava el que alas no tenía.
Y para más engaño, desembueltos,
El poderoso muro acometían
Los Capitanes Márquez y Quesada,
El Contador Romero y Iuan Piñero,
También el provehedor y gran Zapata,
Farfán y Cabanillas, cuios brazos,
Apriessa, espesas balas despedían
Contra Zutacapán, Cotumbo y Tempal,
Amulco y gran Parguapo y bravo Pilco,
Derribando del alto muchos dellos,
Que a pique se venían sin el alma
Que en la cumbre dexaban con la fuerza
De los gallardos brazos, ayudados
De Iuan Medel, Ribera y de Naranjo,
Francisco de Ledesma y de Carrera,
Iuan de Pedraza, Olague y de Zumaia,
Francisco Vázquez y Manuel Francisco,
Marcos García y Pedro de los Reyes
Y, a bueltas,[20] Pedro Sánchez Damiero,
Simón de Paz, Iuan López y Andrés Pérez,
Pero Sánchez, Monrroi, también Villalba
Y Francisco Martín y aquel Alonso
Que del Río llamamos, cuias aguas
A muchos, anegando, zozobraban.[21]
Y el Alférez Bañuelos, rodeando
El poderoso muro, yba blandiendo
Vna terrible lanza de dos hierros.
Tras dél el fuerte brazo lebantaba,
En vn caballo bayo remendado,[22]
De blancas manchas todo bien manchado,
Aquel gallardo Inojos. Mal sufrido,

170

175

180

185

190

195

200

205

210

Of their good sallets, placed themselves
Like climbing ivy upon the strong wall
And, with a pretense of scaling, they endured
Such storm of rocks thrown down on them
As when high heaven doth break forth
In fearful roaring of thunder
And stuns us with its swift lightning,
All, though afraid, did thus forge on
Against the great, incredible tempest
Of stones and rocks which they sent down.
And the barbarians were astonished and confused
To see such prodigies in the Spaniards,
Believing it was true that the blind saw
And those flew who had no wings.
For greater lure in the deceit
The powerful wall was bombarded
By captains Márquez and Quesada,
Romero, the paymaster, Juan Piñero,
The purveyor, and great Zapata, too,
Farfán, Cabanillas, whose strong arms
Swiftly set balls to flying thick
Against Zutacapán, Cotumbo, and Tempal,
Amulco, great Parguapo, brave Pilco,
Striking from off the heights many of them,
Who, falling, came without their souls,
Which they had left above through the great strength
Of those heroic arms, aided
By Juan Medel, Ribera, de Naranjo,
Francisco de Ledesma, and de Carrera,
Pedro de Pedraza, and Olague, de Zumaia,
Francisco Vázquez, and Manuel Francisco,
Marcos García, Pedro de los Reyes,
And also Pedro Sánchez Damiero,
Simón de Paz, Juan López, Andrés Pérez,
Pedro Sánchez, Monrroi, and Villalba,
Francisco Martín, and that Alonso
Whom we did call del Río, whose waters
Did overwhelm a many and sink them,[9]
And the ensign Bañuelos, going round
The mighty wall, was brandishing
A fearful lance, double-pointed.
Behind him there raised his strong arm,
There mounted on a light bay horse,
Well spotted o'er with white patches,
The gallant Inojos. And long-suffering

19. Desgalgada = precipitada desde lo alto.
20. A bueltas = a vueltas de, además.
21. Jugando sobre el nombre, Alonso del Río, indica que sus aguas, léase acciones, inundaban a muchos y los hundían.
22. Remendado = manchado.

9. Villagrá plays on the man's name: Río/river.

Carabajal y Casas, reportado,
También Alonso Gómez Montesinos,
La fuerza de las armas fue sufriendo
Hasta que ya la noche fue tendiendo
Su lóbrega tiniebla, con que todos,
Suspendiendo la cólera encendida,
Las armas reposaron fatigadas.
Y encargando el Sargento, cuidadoso,
La fuerza de aquel alto ya ganado
A Pablo de Aguilar y a León de Isasti,
A quien Villaviciosa y otros buenos
También acompañaron como bravos,
El Sargento mayor bajó y en peso
Rondó toda la noche. Y porque estaban
Dos muy profundas zanjas que partían
El alto passamán que abían ganado,
Para poder passarlas mandó presto
Que vn buen madero luego se subiesse.
Y haziéndose assí, sin que quedase
Más que aquel pertinaz²³ que abemos dicho,
Todos se confessaron y, en rompiendo
La luz de la mañana, comulgaron.
Y viendo aquellos bárbaros las muertes
Y estrago desgraciado, y que vencidos
Yban de hecho ya y destrozados,
A consejo llamaron, y assí, juntos,
Notaron que Gicombo y Zutancalpo
Y el valeroso Bempol no venían,
Por cuia causa juntos acordaron
Que Mencal fuesse luego y los llamase
Por ser de todos tres muy grande amigo.
Y saliendo al efecto vio que estaba
La pobre de Luzcoija lamentando
El destroncado brazo de su amigo,
A quien con alma y vida le rogaba
Que más a la batalla no bolviesse,
Pues güérfana sin él allí quedaba.
En esto, llegó Mencal y de parte
De toda aquella junta les propuso
Que a todos los llamaban y que fuessen,
Pues sin ellos el fuerte, mal parado,
Era fuerza perderse y acabarse.
Y al fin supo tan bien encarecerlo
Que fue Bempol con él y Zutancalpo,
Sin que possible fuesse que Gicombo
Con ellos se hallase. Y por si acaso
Bolviessen a llamarlo no le viessen,
A Bempol le avisó se retiraba
A cierta parte oculta de aquel risco,

²³. Pertinaz = terco, obstinado.

Carabajal and moderate Casas,
Also, Alonso Gómez Montesinos there
215 Was suffering the weight of heavy arms,
Until the night began spreading
Its mournful shades, upon which all,
Setting a pause to their enkindled wrath,
Did lay aside their weapons, much fatigued.
220 And the Sergeant did carefully entrust
The force upon that height which he had won
To Pablo de Aguilar and León de Isasti,
Whom Villaviciosa and other good men
Also accompanied, being brave.
225 The Sergeant Major went down and in thought
Did walk about all night, because there were
Two very deep ditches which did divide
The high passage which we had gained.
That we might pass them, he then gave orders
230 To bring a goodly beam at once.
And, this being done, without one refusing
Except the pertinacious one we have mentioned,
All did confess, and, at break
Of morning light, took communion.
235 Those savages, seeing the death
And the fearful destruction, and how they
Were now conquered in fact and all destroyed,
Called all to council and, all being met,
They saw Gicombo and Zutancalpo
240 And brave Bempol had not come there.
For this reason they all did there agree
Mencal should go at once and call them in,
As he was a great friend of all the three.
And, going for this purpose, he observed
245 Poor Luzcoija making much lament
Over the shattered arm of her husband,
Whom by her life and soul she did implore
He would no more go into the battle
Since she would be an orphan without him.
250 Just then Mencal arrived and on the part
Of all the council he announced to them
That all were called and they should go,
For without them the much endangered fort
Would necessarily be lost and overcome.
255 And, finally, he knew so well how to treat them
That Bempol and Zutancalpo did go,
Though 'twas impossible that Gicombo
Should go with them. And if by chance
They should return to call him and should not
260 See him, he told Bempol he would retire
Unto a certain hidden spot upon that rock

Donde los aguardaba si bolviessen.
Y partiendo los dos para la junta,
Viendo que allí Gicombo no venía,
Con grande instancia juntos les pidieron
Que luego le truxessen, pues que vían
Que sin él era fuerza que aquel fuerte
Quedase para siempre deshonrrado.
Y diziendo con esto otras razones
Con que les obligaron, luego fueron
Al retirado puesto donde estaba
Y tanto le dixeron que les dixo:
"Por vosotros yré, y nunca fuera
Si assí los dioses juntos lo mandaran."
Y diziendo a Luzcoija se quedase
Y en aquel puesto sola se estuviesse,
En lastimosas lágrimas deshecha,
Allí le respondió, toda turbada:
"Si el Sol mil vezes sale y se me esconde
Y las altas estrellas otras tantas
Vinieran y ausentaren sus antorchas,
No faltaré, señor, aunque yo muera,
Del solitario puesto en que me dejas."
Y dejándola allí llegó a la junta,
Y assí como le vieron, con cuidado,
Luego Zutacapán en pie se puso
Y dixo: "Bien será, varones nobles,
Que antes que cosa alguna se proponga
Que sea de Gicombo remediado
El poderoso brazo mal herido."
Oyendo, pues, aquesto, dixo luego:
"Yo tuviera mi brazo remediado
Si, como de enemigo,²⁴ yo tomara
El primero consejo que me diste,
Diziendo que a la sombra de tu maza
Tendría yo mi vida bien segura.
Mas dexemos aquesto por agora,
Que pide más respuesta lo que callo.²⁵
Sepamos qué mandáis agora juntos
Al que quiso tan mal aconsejaros
Quando dixe ser bien que a los Castillas
En ninguna manera se aguardasen."
Por cuia causa luego replicaron:
"Por sóla esa razón queremos todos
Sugetar nuestras vidas y rendirlas
A no más que tu gusto, y desde luego

Where he would wait for their return.
The two coming to the council,
When it was seen Gicombo had not come
They all asked of them with great insistence
That they should bring him there, for they must see
That without him that fort would, of necessity,
Forever be dishonored.
With this they gave other reasons
With which they obliged them to go
To that retired spot at which he was
And they told him so much that he then said:
"For you I go, and I would never go
If all the gods together should command."
And telling Luzcoija to remain
And stay in that place all alone,
She, all dissolved in sorry tears,
And much perturbed, replied to him:
"Now, if the sun should rise a thousand times and sink,
And all the stars as many times
Should bring and take away their lights,
I shall not fail you, lord, although I die
Upon my solitary post where you leave me."
Leaving her there, he came to the council
And, when they saw him, carefully
Zutacapán got to his feet
And said: "It will be well, ye noble men,
That ere anything be proposed
The powerful arm, now sore wounded,
Of Gicombo be tended to."
Hearing these words, he then replied:
"My arm would be entirely healed
If I had taken, as an enemy,¹⁰
The first advice which you gave me,
Saying that in the shadow of your mace
My life would be entirely safe.
But let us leave this for the nonce,
For what I speak not of requires reply.¹¹
Let us now know what you, in council, wish
Of him who would have counseled you so ill
When I said 'twould be well we should not wait
For these Castilians in any way."
Now, upon this, they all replied:
"For this sole reason we all wish
To give our lives and to surrender them
To no more than your pleasure, and at once

265
270
275
280
285
290
295
300
305

---

24. Se refiere, aunque irónicamente, al dicho que sugiere que el listo atiende el consejo del enemigo.

25. Parece decir, refiriéndose a la irónica indicación que acaba de hacer, que esa jactancia de Zutacapán merecería, en otras circunstancias, una respuesta.

10. The ironical reference is to the adage that a wise man heeds his enemy.

11. Gicombo ironically indicates that what he does not say would be cause for a duel.

Por General de todos te nombramos
Y todos como a tal te obedecemos."
Y después que passaron grandes cosas
Y el oficio por fuerza fue acetado
Del gallardo Gicombo, fue debajo
De condición y pacto, firme, expresso,
Que si el dicho Gicombo memorable
Y el noble Zutancalpo y bravo Bempol
En las presentes lides y batallas
Sus vidas acabasen, y con ellos
También Zutacapán, Cotumbo y Tempal,
Que en vn sepulcro juntos, con sus armas,
Fuessen sin más acuerdo sepultados,
Porque en essotra vida los enojos
Y desafíos graves que tenían
En las entrañas fijos y arraigados
Fuessen de todos juntos fenecidos;²⁶
Y que si con victoria allí saliessen,
Que entrasen en batalla y, acabada,
Que fuesse aquella fuerza gobernada
Por sólo el General, sin que ninguno
Ningún otro dominio pretendiesse;
Y que si caso juntos la perdiessen,
Que hasta morir ninguno se entregase
Y después de vencidos se matasen
Los vnos a los otros, sin que cosa
Dentro del fuerte viva les quedase.
Con cuias condiciones fue exerciendo
El valiente Gicombo el nuevo oficio,
Y pues nuevo gobierno ya tenemos,
De nuevo nueva pluma aquí cortemos.

We here do name you General of all,
All of us will obey you as such."
And after many great things had occurred
And the office was accepted perforce
By gallant Gicombo, it was
Under condition and compact, express and firm,
That if the said illustrious Gicombo
And noble Zutancalpo, brave Bempol,
Should in the present struggle and battles
Give up their lives, and beside them
Zutacapán, Cotumbo, and Tempal, also,
Together in one sepulcher, with all their arms,
Should be buried without discussion
So that in the next life the passions and
The mortal challenges they had
Most firmly fixed within themselves
Might be finished by all of them;¹²
And that if they should win a victory
They should engage in battle and, that done,
The whole fortress should be governed
By only one General and no one
Should pretend to any dominion;
And that if they perchance should lose,
No one should give up until death,
But, after being conquered, they should kill
Each other, and thus nothing should
Remain alive for us within the fort.
With these conditions, valiant Gicombo
Began to exercise his new office,
And since we now have a new government,
Again let us cut a new pen.

310

315

320

325

330

335

26. Recuérdese que habían quedado desafiados los mencionados, y Gicombo pretende llevar a cabo ese desafío en la otra vida.

12. Gicombo does not forget, even for after death, the duel those six had entered into.

CANTO TREINTA

COMO AVIENDO ORDENADO EL NUEVO GENERAL
A SUS soldados se fue a despedir de Luzcoija, y batalla que
tuvo con los Españoles, y cosas que en ella sucedieron.

How the new General, having given orders to his soldiers,
went to take leave of Luzcoija, and the battle he had
with the Spaniards, and the things that happened.

VANDO contra razón se enciende el
    hombre
Y fuerza a su apetito a que se incline
A emprender vna cosa que es sin traza,
Con qué facilidad advierte y nota
Lo que es en pro y en contra de aquel hecho
Que assí quiere emprender contra justicia.
Temiendo, pues, Gicombo, y tracendiendo,
Como prudente, diestro y recatado,
Que allí Zutacapán y todo el pueblo,
Iuntos, al mejor tiempo le faltasen,
Hizo comprometiesen y jurasen,
Según sus leyes, ritos y costumbres,
Assí como Aníbal juró en las haras
Y altares de sus dioses, que enemigo
Mortal sería siempre de Romanos,[1]
Que assí, inviolablemente, guardarían,
Con grandes penas, vínculos y fuerzas,
Las condiciones puestas y assentadas.
Hecha la cerimonia y celebrado
El vil supersticioso juramento,
Fue por su propria mano allí escogiendo
Quinientos bravos bárbaros guerreros,
Y en vna gran caberna todos juntos,
Que por naturaleza estaba hecha
Cerca de las dos zanjas que hemos dicho,
Mandó que se metiessen con intento
Que, luego que los vuestros la passasen,
Saliessen de emboscada y allí juntos
A todos sin las vidas los dejasen.
Y luego que ubo puesto y encargado
Al bravo Bempol, Chumpo y Zutancalpo,
A Calpo y a Buzcoico y a Ezmicaio,
A cada qual su esquadra bien formada,
Para mejor meternos en sus manos
Con discreto recato dio a entendernos[2]
Que estaba todo el pueblo despoblado.
Y al tiempo que traspuso el Sol luziente
Y los opacos cuerpos, apagados,
Tenían ya sus sombras, y en silencio
Quedaron los vivientes sossegados,

HEN man enkindles himself against right

And forces his desires to bend themselves
To undertake a thing that has no plan,
With what ease he doth mark and note
5   What is in favor, what against that thing
That he wills to undertake against justice.
Gicombo, then, fearing and foreseeing,
Being prudent, skillful, and cautious,
That Zutacapán and all the people
10 Together would fail him at any time,
Did make them bind themselves and take an oath
According to their laws, rites, and customs,
As Hannibal once swore upon the fanes
And altars of his gods that he would be
15 Ever a mortal foe to the Romans,[1]
So that they would keep inviolate,
Subject to penalties, controls, and force,
The conditions made and agreed.
The ceremony done and done also
20 The vile and superstitious oath taking,
He, with his own hand, did select
Five hundred brave barbarian warriors
And ordered them to go in a body
Unto a great cavern, by nature made,
25 Near to the two ditches we have mentioned,
Purposing, when your men should pass that place,
That they should sally forth from their ambush and
Deprive them, then and there, of all their lives.
And when he'd posted them and entrusted
30 To brave Bempol, Chumpo, Zutancalpo,
To Calpo, Buzcoico, and Ezmicaio,
To each of these a squadron well-chosen,
The better to trap us into their hands
He carefully gave us to understand
35 That all the town was deserted.
And when the shining sun had gone to rest
And the dark bodies had been plunged
Into deep shadows, and in silence deep
All living things remained at rest,
40 From the sea came forth the night,

---

1. Juramento que le impuso su padre. Se halla en Livio XXI.
2. Nos dio a entender.

1. Oath required of him by his father. See Livy XXI.

Salió del mar la noche presurosa,
Embolviendo la tierra en negro velo.
Y antes que las Estrellas traspusiessen
El poderoso curso que llevaban,
A despedirse fue de su Luzcoija,
Que esperándole estaba en aquel puesto
Donde quiso dejarla mal herida
De la fuerza de amor que la abrasaba.³

Y assí como le vido, lastimada,
Qual simple tortolilla que, perdida
La dulze compañía, no se assienta
En los floridos ramos ni reposa
Si no es en troncos secos deshojados,
Buelta, qual madre tierna que contino
Al hijo regalado trae colgado
Del cristalino cuello y, encendida,
Con él se desentraña y se derrite
En amoroso fuego y se deshaze,
Vencida de su amor, assí, la pobre,
Derramando de lágrimas dos fuentes,
Allí soltó la boz desalentada:
"Si el grato y limpio amor que te he tenido,
Amándote mil vezes más que al alma,
Merece que me des algún alibio,
Suplícote, señor, que no permitas
Que venga en flor tan tierna a marchitarse
La que entender me has dado que fue siempre
Para ti más gustosa, grata y bella
Que la vida que vives y que alcanzas.
Por cuia cara prenda te suplico
Que si vienes, señor, para bolverte,
Que el alma aquí me arranques, que no es justo
Que viva yo sin ti tan sola vn hora."
Y assí, la boz, suspensa, colocando,⁴
Aguardando respuesta, fue diziendo
El afligido bárbaro: "Señora,
Iuro por la belleza de essos ojos,
Que son descanso y lumbre de los míos,
Y por aquesos labios con que cubres
Las orientales perlas regaladas,
Y por aquestas blandas manos bellas
Que en tan dulze prisión me tienen puesto,
Que ya no me es possible que me escuse
De entrar en la batalla contra España.
Por cuia causa es fuerza que te alientes
Y que también me esfuerzes porque buelva
Aquesta triste alma a sólo verte,

Enveloping the earth in a dark veil.
And before all the stars had run
The mighty course which they do take,
He went to take leave of Luzcoija,²

45   Who was awaiting him in that same place
Where he had chosen to leave her, wounded
Deeply by that love which did burn in her.
And when she saw him, overcome,
Like a mild turtledove which, lost

50   From its sweet company, roosts not
Nor takes repose on flowering branches,
But on the dry and leafless trees,
And like a tender mother who carries
Her tender child about with her, hanging

55   About her lovely neck, and, filled with love,
Yearns over him and grows tender
In loving fire, and wastes away,
So this poor woman, conquered by her love,
Making two fountains of her tears,

60   Did there raise her discouraged voice:
"If the dear pure love I have had for you,
A thousand times more loving you than my own soul,
Deserveth that you give me some comfort,
I beg of you, my lord, not to permit

65   A flower so tender to wither
Which you have made me think was e'er
To you more pleasing, sweet, and beautiful
Than the life which you live and do enjoy.
By which dear gift I beg of you

70   That if you come, lord, but to go,
You take my life, for I cannot
Live without you a single hour."
And she became expectantly quiet,
Awaiting a reply, and then spoke out

75   The sad barbarian: "Madam, I swear
Now by the beauty of those eyes
Which are the peace and light of mine,
And by those lips with which you hide
Those lovely oriental pearls,

80   And by those soft, delicate hands
Which hold me in such sweet prison,
That now I cannot make excuse
From going to battle against Spain.
Wherefore you must rouse your courage

85   And strengthen mine, so this sad soul
May return but to look on you,
For though 'tis true it fears your loss

---

3. La despedida del héroe y su amante hace en mucho eco de *La araucana* XIII.

4. Colocando = acomodando.

2. The hero's leave-taking from his beloved is probably based on that of the Araucanian hero. See *La araucana* XIII.

Que, aunque es verdad que teme de perderte,
Firme esperanza tiene de gozarte.
Y aunque mil vezes muera te prometo
De bolver luego a verte y consolarte,
Y porque assí, querido amor, lo entiendas
El alma y corazón te dexo en prendas."
Y assí se despidió porque venía
La luz de la mañana ya rayando,
Y entrando en la caberna con los suyos
Entró luego la luz y fue bordando
De ricos arreboles todo el Cielo.
En cuyo tiempo, suerte y coiuntura,
Diziendo Missa el Padre fray Alonso
La fiesta de su nombre celebraba,[5]
Y abiéndonos a todos comulgado,
Del Altar se bolvió y assí nos dixo:
"Caballeros de Christo valerosos
Y de nuestra ley santa defensores,
No tengo que encargaros a la Iglesia,
Pues como nobles hijos abéys siempre
Preciados de serbirla y respetarla.
Por Iesu Christo pido y os suplico,
Y por su sangre santa, que se enfrenen,
En verter la que alcanza el enemigo,[6]
Los agudos cuchillos lo possible,
Que aquése es el valor de Castellanos,
Vencer sin sangre y muerte al que acometen.
Y pues a Dios lleváis en vuestras almas,
A todos os vendiga y os alcance
Su mano poderosa, y yo en su nombre
A todos os vendigo." Y alcanzada
La vendición del Padre Religioso,
Al alto passamán subimos luego,
Donde todos notamos desde afuera
Que el pueblo despoblado todo estaba
Y que ánima viviente no se vía.
Por cuia causa luego las dos zanjas
Del fuerte passamán passaron treze
Sin orden ni permiso del Sargento,
Y no bien todos juntos ocuparon
Los términos vedados,[7] quando luego
De la horrible caberna fue embistiendo
El valiente Gicombo, rebramando.
Y qual el vallenato[8] que, herido
Del áspero harpón y hierro bravo,
Vn humo espeso de agua en alto esparce

It has firm hope to enjoy you.
And though I die a thousand times I swear

90 I shall return to see and console you,
And that, dear love, you may understand this
I leave you as ransom my heart and soul."
And so he took his leave, for now
The morning light was appearing,

95 And, entering the cavern with his men,
The light came fast and embroidered
All of the sky with bright red clouds.
At this great time and conjuncture
The Father Fray Alonso, saying mass,

100 Did celebrate the day of his name saint,[3]
And having given communion to us all,
Turned from the altar and addressed us thus:
"Ye valiant cavaliers of Christ
And of our most holy laws defenders,

105 I have not to exhort you to the Church
For as her noble sons you have always
Taken great pains to serve and respect her.
By Jesus Christ I ask and beg of you,
And by His holy blood, that you restrain

110 Your keen swords, in so far as possible,
From shedding the blood of the enemy,
For thus the valor of the Spaniards is,
To conquer without blood and death whom they attack.
And since you carry God within your souls,

115 May He bless all of you and may His powerful hand
Protect you, and I, in His name,
Do bless you all." And having thus
Received the blessing from this holy Father there,
We then climbed to the lofty passageway,

120 Whence we all saw from afar off
That all the pueblo was deserted quite
And that no living soul was seen.
For this reason thirteen immediately
Did pass both ditches from the passageway

125 Without the Sergeant's order or his permission,
And hardly had they, all together, occupied
The further side when all at once
There charged from the horrible cave
The valiant Gicombo, roaring loud.

130 And, like the young whale which, wounded
By keen harpoon and deadly steel,
Projects on high thick clouds of spume
And lashes the sea with his tail and cleaves

---

5. La cronología no puede resultar muy exacta en razón del santoral, ya que el 23 de enero es San Ildefonso y el 26 de enero, San Alfonso.
6. En derramar la del enemigo.
7. Términos vedados = terrenos prohibidos, desautorizados.
8. Vallenato = ballenato, ballena joven.

3. The feast of Saint Ildephonse is January 23 and that of Saint Alphonse January 26.

Y azota con la cola el mar y hiende
Por vna y otra parte, sobre aguando⁹
El espacioso lomo y, desabrido,¹⁰
Bufando y sin sosiego, va haziendo
Mil remolinos de agua, assí, sañudo,
Las poderosas armas lebantadas,
Con todos embistió y fue rompiendo.
Y viendo al enemigo tan a pique,
Los nuestros todos juntos dispararon
Los prestos arcabuzes, y aunque a muchos
Por tierra derribaron, fueles fuerza,
Por no poderles dar segunda carga,
Venir a las espadas y, rebueltos
Los vnos con los otros, no pudimos
Darles ningún socorro, porque abían
Llevado aquel madero que subieron
A la segunda zanja y no notaron
Dejaban sin passage a la primera.
Y assí, todos rebueltos en confusso,
Soterrando¹¹ las dagas y los filos
De las vivas espadas, grande gifa¹²
De miserables cuerpos destrozados
Y vn matadero horrendo ya tenían.
Y assí, soberbios, bravos, encendidos,
Allí los dos hermanos valerosos,
Christóbal Sánchez y Francisco Sánchez,
Y el Capitán Quesada y Iuan Piñero,
Francisco Vázquez y Manuel Francisco,
Cordero, Iuan Rodríguez y Pedraza,
Assí como los dedos de la mano,
Que siendo desiguales se emparejan
Los vnos con los otros y se ajustan
Quando, cerrado el puño, despedazan
Alguna cosa fuerte y la destrozan,
Assí, conformes todos, se aunaron
Los vnos con los otros y embistieron.
Y abriendo grandes fuentes, derramaron
Por los bárbaros pechos y costados,
Ojos, cabezas, piernas y gargantas,
De fresca sangre arroyos caudalosos,
Por cuias bravas bocas espantosas
Las almas temerosas presta fuga
Yban haziendo todas por no verse
En manos tan soberbias. Y tras desto,
Carrasco, Isasti, Casas, Montesinos,
Hasta los codos rojas las espadas,

The water here and there, rising
His spacious back, and, in anger
Snorting and restless, doth stir up
A thousand whirlpools in the deep, so he,
Enraged, his mighty weapons lifted high,
Attacked with them and struck at all.
Seeing the enemy so near at hand
Our men did, in a volley, fire
Their ready harquebuses and, though many
Were stricken down, they yet were forced,
Unable to load a second time,
To come to swords, and in the hot melee,
Mixed with each other, we could not
Give any aid to them because they had
Taken that beam by which they crossed
Unto the second ditch and did not note
They left the first without means of crossing.
All thus involved in such confusion,
Plunging their daggers and the sharp edges
Of their swift swords into a great slaughter
Of miserable, shattered bodies,
They made a fearful butchery.
And so, proud, brave, and fiery
There the two valorous brothers,
Cristóbal Sánchez and Francisco Sánchez,
Captain Quesada and Juan Piñero,
Francisco Vázquez and Manuel Francisco,
Cordero, Juan Rodríguez, Pedraza,
Like to the fingers of the human hand,
Which, being unequal, yet combine
Each with the others and do form,
When closed, a fist that doth destroy
Some strong substance and crushes it,
All joined together in one band,
Each with the others, and charged in.
And, opening great wounds, they shed
From the barbarian breasts and sides,
Eyes, heads, and legs, and from their throats,
Swift-flowing streams of their fresh blood,
And through these great and fearful mouths
Their fearful souls did take swift flight,
All going thence so not to fall
Into such powerful hands. And then
Carrasco, Isasti, Casas, Montesinos,
Their swords red up to their elbows,
Were plying well their brawny arms

135
140
145
150
155
160
165
170
175

9. Sobre aguando = sobreaguando, en la superficie.
10. Desabrido = disgustado.
11. Soterrando = enterrando, en los cuerpos enemigos.
12. Gifa = jifa, desperdicio de la matanza.

Los poderosos brazos exercían,
Hasta que Zutancalpo y gran Buzcoico
Entraron de refresco y retiraron
A vuestros Españoles con tal fuerza
Que, arrinconados todos a vn repecho
Que estaba vn tanto hondo y reparado[13]
De la fuerza de piedra que sobre ellos,
Sin lastimar a nadie, descargaban
Con priessa tan sobrada que enterrados
Allí quedaron todos sin remedio.
Viendo, pues, zozobrada y anegada
Aquella navecilla, el bravo joben
A grandes vozes dixo que vn madero
Al punto se subiesse y se guindase.[14]
Oyendo, pues, aquesto, retireme,
Porque entendí, señor, que a mí dezía,
Cosa de nueve passos, y qual Curcio,[15]
Casi desesperado, fue[16] embistiendo
Aquella primer zanja, y el Sargento,
Pensando que pedazos me haría,
Asiome del adarga y, si no suelta,
Sin duda fuera aquél el postrer tiento
Que diera a la fortuna yo en mi vida.
Mas por largarme presto fui alentando
La fuerza de aquel salto de manera
Que al fin salvé la zanja, y el madero,
No libre de temor y de rezelo,
Fuy como mejor pude allí arrastrando
Y, puesto en el passage, los dos puestos
Passaron con presteza allí los vuestros.[17]
Y apenas el clarín alto tocaron,
Quando de aquel repecho donde estaban
Nuestros caros amigos soterrados
Iuntos salieron todos, qual es fuerza
Que al son de la trompeta se lebanten
El día de la cuenta postrimera
De sus sepulcros todos los difuntos.
Y viendo, assí, la plaza, que perdida
Estaba, por nosotros ya ganada,
Rebentando de empacho y corrimiento,
Como encendidas brasas que, enterradas,
De las cenizas salen abrasando,
Assí, furiosos, vivos, desembueltos,
Mas fieros que bravíssimos leones,
Arremetieron todos, ayudados

180   When Zutancalpo and great Buzcoico,
      With reinforcements, came and did drive back
      Your Spaniards, and with so great a force
      That, all cornered upon a slope
      Which was a trifle deep and protected,
185   By rain of rocks which they discharged
      Upon them, though they wounded none,
      Yet so swift and so overwhelming
      They were burying them beyond all help.
      The brave youth then, seeing that little ship
190   So overwhelmed and now about to sink,
      Shouted with a great voice that someone should
      Immediately go and bring a beam.
      Hearing this, then, I did fall back,
      For, lord, I thought he spoke to me,
195   Some nine paces and, like to Curtius,[4]
      I was running, near desperate,
      Toward the first ditch and the Sergeant,
      Thinking that I would be dashed to pieces,
      Did grasp me by the shield, and, had he not
200   Loosed me no doubt that had been
      The last test I had made of fortune in my life.
      But, as he loosed me quickly, I gathered
      Momentum for that leap to such effect
      That finally I jumped the ditch and then,
205   Not free from fear and trembling, I took
      The log as best I might and dragged,
      And, passage made between the ditches,[5]
      Your men did quickly pass over.
      And hardly had the trumpet blared aloud
210   When, from the slope on which they were,
      Our friends so dear who were buried
      Did all come forth, as needs must be
      Upon the trumpet's sound shall rise,
      On that day of the ultimate judgment,
215   All of the dead from out their sepulchers.
      And seeing that all the lost ground
      Was now regained by our men,
      Bursting with shame and with sense of disgrace,
      Like fiery coals that were buried
220   And came from the ashes ablaze,
      Fiercer than courageous lions
      They all did charge, being aided by
      Captain Romero and Juan Velarde,
      Carabajal, Bañuelos, and Archuleta,

13. Reparado = protegido.
14. Se guindase = se subiese con cuerda.
15. Joven romano que se arrojó en la zanja del foro como sacrificio humano. Lo narra Livio VII.
16. Errata del original por "fui."
17. Hay que recordar que había dos zanjas, razón por la cual los primeros que cruzaron quitaron el madero de la primera.

4. A Roman youth who sacrificed himself by leaping into the trench of the Forum. See Livy VII.
5. It must be recalled that there were two ditches and only one plank.

Del Capitán Romero y Iuan Velarde,
Carabajal, Bañuelos y Archuleta,
De Lorenzo Salado y de Zubía
Y de otros muchos nobles Españoles
Que a diestro y a siniestro despachaban
Idólatras apriessa de esta vida.
Por cuia causa el fuerte Zutancalpo
Con el bravo Gicombo y con Buzcoico,
Qual suele el mar rebuelto y alterado
Hervir por todas partes, lebantando
Valientes cumbres de agua y cimas bravas,
Bañando el alto Cielo, y que, soberbio,
En sí se hincha, crece, gime y brama
Y en poderosas rocas quiebra y rompe
Su furia desatada y no sossiega
En tanto que los vientos no reprimen
La fuerza de sus soplos y se muestran
En sossegada calma reportados,
Assí estos bravos bárbaros feroces,
Que, los suyos alentando, les dezían
Que de los prestos arcos despidiessen
De flecha tanta suma como suele
Llover y granizar el alto Cielo
Espesas gotas de agua y de granizo.
Con cuia brava fuerza, mal heridos
Dexaron a Quesada y al Alférez
Carabajal y buen Antonio Hernández,
A Francisco García y a Lizama.
En este medio tiempo, fue poniendo
Asencio de Archuleta firme al pecho
La coz¹⁸ del arcabuz y fue tomando
La brújula y el punto de manera
Que, sin saber por dónde o cómo fuesse,
Atravesó con quatro bravas balas
Al mayor camarada y más amigo
Que jamás tuvo el pobre en esta vida.
¡O divino pastor, y cómo arrojas
Tu muy santo cayado y le enderezas
Para la oveja triste, desmandada,
Que lejos del rebaño, a su albedrío
Muy largo trecho vemos se remonta!
Cuio castigo justo bien nos muestra
El infelix Salado, pues que viendo
Ocho mortales bocas respirando
Por sus espaldas, pechos y costados,
Encogiendo los hombros y los ojos
Al lebantado Cielo desplegando,
Assí esforzó la boz a Dios el pobre:
"Señor, dos años ha que no confiesso
Por más que mis amigos me han rogado.

225   by Lorenzo Salado, and de Zubía
And many other noble Castilians
Who to the right and left dispatched
Idolaters most swiftly from this life.
Because of this the strong Zutancalpo,
230   With brave Gicombo and Buzcoico,
Just as the sea in tumult and tempest
Doth boil all over, raising up
Huge crests of water, high summits
Wetting the high heaven, and haughtily
235   Swells and increases, moans and roars,
And breaks and foams its wild fury
On mighty rocks, and does not rest
So long as the winds temper not
The force of their blasts nor do show themselves
240   All temperate in peaceful calm,
So were these brave, ferocious barbarians,
Who, urging on their men, did order them
To speed from their swift ready bows
A flight of arrows full as numerous
245   As the thick drops of water and hailstones
That the high heaven rains or hails.
By whose sharp force sorely wounded
They left Quesada and the ensign, too,
Carabajal and good Antonio Hernández,
250   Francisco García, and Lizama.
At this, Asencio de Archuleta
Did set firmly against his breast
The stock of his harquebus and did align
The rear sight with the front sight in such wise
255   That, not knowing how 'twas or where he shot,
He shot through, with four heavy balls,
The greatest comrade and the dearest friend
Whom the poor man had ever in his life.
O divine Shepherd, how You stretch
260   Your most holy crook out and direct it
To that sad, disobedient sheep
Which we have seen of its free will
Departing very far from out the fold!
Their just punishment is well shown
265   By unhappy Salado, for, seeing
Eight deadly mouths there open wide
In back and breast and in his sides,
Shrugging his shoulders and raising
His eyes unto the lofty Heavens,
270   The poor wretch thus did raise his voice to God:
"Lord, it is two years since I have confessed
No matter how my friends have begged me to.
I know, my Lord, I have offended Thee
And I beg only that Thou wait for me

18. Coz = culata.

Conozco, mi Señor, que te he ofendido
Y sólo te suplico que me aguardes
A que limpie las manchas que manchada
Tienen el alma, triste, redimida
Por la preciosa sangre que vertiste."
Sabida la desgracia, luego vino
El Sargento mayor a mucha priessa
Y porque confessase luego quiso
Que seys buenos soldados le bajasen.
Y entendido por él aquel socorro,
Allí le suplicó con muchas veras
Que pues a solas siempre abía ofendido
A Dios, nuestro Señor, que le dexassen
Que a solas su remedio procurase.
Y viendo cuan de veras le pedía,
Dándole gusto en esto, con descuido[19]
Mandó que con él fuessen los nombrados.
Pues yéndole siguiendo dio en vn risco
De soberbia caída, donde vido
Vn demonio grimoso que le dixo:
"Soldado valeroso, si pretendes
Salir triunfando desta triste vida,
Arrójate de aquí, que yo en las palmas
Sustentaré tu cuerpo, sin que pueda
Recebir detrimento en parte alguna."[20]
Oyendo aquesto el triste baptizado,
Turbado de temor y de rezelo,
Assí le respondió, cobrando esfuerzo:
"¡Vete de aquí, maldito, no me tientes,
Que soy de Dios soldado y si he seguido
Tus banos estandartes, ya no es tiempo
De tanta desbentura!" Y rebolviendo
Las fatigadas plantas, fue tomando
El camino derecho y fue bajando
Al pabellón del Padre, donde luego
Que confessó sus culpas y fue absuelto,
Allí quedó sin alma y sin sentido.
¡Vendígante los Angeles, Dios mío,
Que assí las llagas curas y nos muestras
Que quando más afliges y deshazes
Al miserable cuerpo que nos diste,
Que entonces vive el alma y se lebanta
Para la suma alteza y excelencia
Que a todos nos espera y nos aguarda!
Y porque a más andar se va encendiendo
La fuerza de batalla y yo me siento
Sin fuerzas ni valor para seguirla,
Quiero parar aquí para escrebirla.

275 'Till I wash off the stains with which I have
Contaminated my sad soul, redeemed
By that most precious blood You shed."
Hearing of this misfortune, then did come
The Sergeant Major in a mighty haste,
280 And that he might confess he then ordered
That six good soldiers should take him down.
And he, understanding that aid,
Did beg of him with much sincerity
That since he had alone given offense
285 To God, our Lord, it be allowed to him
To seek his remedy alone.
Seeing how sincerely he begged
He pleased him in this, but, appearing nonchalant,
He ordered that those men should go with him.
290 Now, as they followed, he came to a cliff
Of a great height, whereon he saw
A fearful demon who did say to him:
"O valorous soldier, if you now desire
To leave this sad life in triumph,
295 Throw yourself off here, for I, in these hands,
Will hold your body so that it cannot
Receive an injury in any place."[6]
The sad christian one, hearing this,
Though filled with fear and suspicion,
300 Summoning courage, answered thus:
"Begone from here, accursed! Tempt me not,
For I am God's soldier, and if I have followed
Your vain standards, this is no time
For such calamity." And, turning back
305 His tired feet, he then followed
The proper road and clambered down
Unto the Father's tent, where, just as soon
As he confessed his faults and was absolved,
He there lay senseless, for his soul had gone.
310 The Angels praise you, O my God,
That You thus cure our wounds and show to us
That however You afflict and destroy
The miserable body You gave us,
The soul yet lives and is raised up
315 Unto the highest height and excellence
That doth await and expect us.
And since the storm of battle as it goes
Grows hotter, and since I do feel myself
Without the strength or courage to continue it,
320 I wish to stop here that I may write it.

19. Con descuido = sin atender.
20. Dado el contexto de altura montañosa, Villagrá recuerda la tentación de Satanás a Cristo.

6. Given the lofty setting, Villagrá appropriately uses a satanic temptation close to that undergone by Jesus.

Canto Treinta y Vno

COMO SE FVE PROSIGVIENDO LA BATALLA HASTA
alcanzar la victoria y como se pegó fuego a todo el pueblo, y de
otras cosas que fueron sucediendo.

SIEMPRE la prevención y diligencia,
Hastuta vigilancia y el cuidado
De no perder jamás vn sólo punto,
Estando en la batalla el buen guerrero
Es lo que más encumbra y más lebanta
El claro resplandor y la grandeza
De los heroicos hechos hazañosos
Que assí vemos emprende y acomete.
Con cuias buenas partes el Sargento,
Pedro Sánchez Monrroi, Marcos García,
Martín Ramírez y Christóbal López,
Iuan Lucas, Iuan de Olague y Cabanillas,
Iuan Catalán, Zapata y Andrés Pérez,
Francisco de Ledesma y el buen Márquez,
No tienden, apañando,¹ con más ayre
La corba hoz los diestros segadores
Quando apriessa añudan sobre el brazo
Vna y otra manada² y assí, juntos,
Lebantan por mil partes sus gavillas,
Como estos bravos y altos combatientes,
Que, en vn grande ribazo tropezando
De cuerpos ya difuntos, no cessaban
De derramar apriessa grande suma
De fresca y roja sangre, con que estaba
Por vna y otra parte todo el muro
Bañado y sangrentado, sin que cosa
Quedase que teñida no estuviesse.
Mas no por esto amainan³ y se rinden
Los bárbaros furiosos; mas, qual vemos
Crecer y lebantar las bravas llamas
De poderosos vientos combatidas,
Que mientras más las soplan y combaten
Más es su brava fuerza y gran pujanza,
Assí, feroces, todos rebramando,
A boca de cañón arremetían
Sin miedo ni rezelo de la fuerza
De las soberbias balas que, a barrisco,⁴
A todos los llevaban y acababan.
Y viendo el de Zaldívar tal fiereza,

---

1. Apañando = recogiendo, la mies, se entiende.
2. Manada = puñado.
3. Amainan = aflojan.
4. A barrisco = sin distinción.

Canto XXXI

How the battle was carried forward until gaining victory
and how fire was set to all the pueblo, and of other things
that happened.

ALWAYS astute prevision, diligence,
A careful watchfulness and care
Never to lose a single point,
This, for a warrior in fight,
5   Is what most elevates and raises up
The clear resplendency and the greatness
Of deeds heroic and adventurous
That we see him embark upon.
With such qualities, the Sergeant,
10   Pedro Sánchez Monrroi, Marcos García,
Martín Ramírez, Cristóbal López,
Juan Lucas, Juan de Olague, Cabanillas,
Juan Catalán, Zapata, Andrés Pérez,
Francisco de Ledesma, and the good Márquez,
15   No skillful reapers do more swiftly wield
Their curving sickles, flashing rapidly,
When they do quickly knot within their arms
One handful after other and do so
Set up their sheaves in a thousand places,
20   As these brave, haughty combatants
Who, stumbling upon a lofty mound
Of bodies now dead, never ceased
To shed apace a mighty sum
Of fresh red blood, by which the wall
25   Was everywhere, upon all sides,
Bathed and ensanguined, and nothing
Remained that was not sprent with it.
Yet not for this the furious barbarians
Would yield or surrender, but as we see
30   Fierce flames increase and tower high
Combated by the powerful winds,
And the more that they blow and fight
The greater is their force and their power,
So they, ferocious, all roaring,
35   Did charge the very musket's mouth
Without fear or caution before the storm
Of deadly balls which struck them down
Unto that dust and killed them all.
He of Zaldívar, seeing such ferocity,

Como valiente tigre que acosado
Se ve de los monteros y rabioso
Contra los hierros buelve y perros bravos
Que assí le van siguiendo y hostigando,
Y a fuerza de los dientes y los brazos
A todos los retira, esparce y hiere,
Assí, vuestro Español furioso, ayrado,
La poderosa diestra allí rebuelve.
Y anduvo la batalla en sí tan fuerte
Y de ambas partes tanto ensangrentada
Que sólo Dios inmenso allí les era
Bastante a reprimir su fuerza brava,
Por cuia gran braveza, luego quiso
El hastuto Sargento se guindasen
Dos piezas de campaña. Y en el inter,
Hablando con los suyos, les dezía:
"Fundamento de casas solariegas,⁵
Columnas de la Iglesia no vencida,
Espejo de esforzados, cuios pechos
Merecen con razón estar honrrados
Con rojas cruzes, blancas y con verdes,⁶
Oy suben vuestras obras a la cumbre
Y más alto omenage que Españoles
Nunca jamás assí las lebantaron.
No las dexéis caer, tened el peso⁷
Que assí sustenta y pesa la grandeza
Del hecho más honrroso y más gallardo
Que jamás nunca vieron brazos nobles."
En esto, las dos piezas se subieron,
Y assentadas al puesto y a la parte
Por donde a caso fueron embistiendo
Trecientos bravos bárbaros furiosos,
Terribles gritos todos lebantando,
Y assí como de hecho arremetieron,
De presto las dos piezas regoldaron,
Cada, dozientos clavos y, con esto,
Qual suelen las hurracas que, espantadas,
Suspenden los chirridos y grasnidos
Con la fuerza de pólvora que arroja
De munición gran copia, con que vemos
Escapar a las vnas y a las otras
Quedar perniquebradas y otras muertas
Y otras barriendo el suelo con las alas,
El negro pico abierto y con las tripas
Arrastrando, rasgadas las entrañas,
No de otra suerte, juntos todos vimos,

40 Was like the valiant tiger which beholds
Itself pressed closely by huntsmen and, mad,
Turns on the spears and the fierce dogs
That follow it so close and, scourging them
By dint of teeth and claws, it drives
45 Them back and scatters and wounds them,
And so your Spaniard, furious in wrath,
Did lay about him with his good right arm.
And round him, then, the battle raged so fierce
And was so bloody upon both the sides
50 That only immense God was there enough
For them to hold against the savage force.
Because of their great fury the astute
Sergeant did order that there be brought up
Two fieldpieces, and, in the interim,
55 Addressing his men, he thus spoke to them:
"Ye founders of manorial houses,¹
Ye columns of the Church invincible,
Ye mirrors for brave men, whose breasts
Deserve with reason to be honored
60 With crosses red and white and green,²
Today your deeds attain the highest point
And to the highest homage that Spaniards
Have ever yet raised them on high.
Let them not fall, sustain the scale
65 That thus sustains and weighs the true greatness
Of the most honorable, gallant deed
That noble arms were ever seen to do."
Just then the two pieces came up
And were set at the place and spot
70 Where an attack, by chance, was being made
By three hundred brave, furious barbarians,
All delivering terrible shouts.
And as they made their charge, at last,
The two pieces did suddenly belch forth
75 Two hundred spikes from each, at which,
Just as we see the magpies, terrorized,
Suspend their chirping and their cackling
At the charge of powder which scatters
Great store of small shot, and we see
80 A few escaping and others
Remain with shattered limbs, and others dead,
And others beating their wings on the ground,
Their black beaks gaping and their bowels
Pouring from out their torn bellies,
85 We then beheld, not otherwise than this,

5. Por las cédulas de concesión a la expedición de Oñate, todos los pobladores adquirían hidalgúia.
6. Se refiere a las encomiendas de las ordenes militares de Calatrava, Alcántara y Santiago.
7. Peso = balanza.

1. As conceded by Oñate's royal authorization, all the colonizers in his expedition acquired the rank of *hidalgo,* roughly equivalent to the English squire.
2. The reference is to the insignia of the military orders of Calatrava, Alcántara, and Santiago.

De súbito, gran suma de difuntos,
Tullidos, mancos, cojos, destroncados.
Abiertos por los pechos, mal heridos,
Rasgadas las cabezas y los brazos,
Abiertos por mil partes y las carnes
Vertiendo viva sangre, agonizando,
Las inmortales almas despedían,
Dexando allí los cuerpos palpitando.
Con cuias muertes Qualco, corajoso,
Qual suele el espadarte[8] que en la fuerza
Del espeso cardume[9] embiste y rasga
Las mallas de las redes y las rompe
Y a los opressos pezes assegura
Y libre libertad les da, y gallardo,
Blandiendo el ancho lomo y fuerte espada,
Las cristalinas aguas va hendiendo,
Desempachado, alegre, suelto y ledo,[10]
Assí, el fuerte bárbaro inbencible,
En sus valientes fuerzas sustentado,
Y con razón, pues dos valientes toros
En los llanos de Zíbola rendidos
A sus valientes brazos vieron tuvo,
Abiendo derramado allí a los nuestros
Y hecho vna ancha plaza, como vn toro,
Para Diego Robledo fue embistiendo
Con vna corta maza, y en llegando
Para el valiente Roble,[11] fue largando
La hoja el Español y fue bajando
La maza poderosa, y todo aquello
Que la espada excedía fue colando
Por el bárbaro pecho y ancha espalda
La rigurosa punta, de manera
Que, de vna y otra vanda atravesado,
El poderoso Qualco, mal herido,
Allí largó la maza y con el puño,
Abiéndole otra vez atrabesado,
Le dio tan grande golpe en el costado
Que dio con él, hipando[12] y boqui abierto,
Casi por muerto en tierra. Y con presteza,
Antes que recobrase algún aliento,
Assiole por la pierna y, como vemos
Al rústico villano quando assienta
El mazizo guijarro en lo más ancho
De la rebuelta honda y sobre el brazo
Dándole en torno vueltas, le despide,

90

95

100

105

110

115

120

125

130

A sudden great heap of the dead,
Mangled, without hands, legs, shattered,
Deep wounds opened into their breasts,
Their heads laid open and their arms,
Pierced a thousand times, their flesh
Pouring out blood in mortal agony,
Took leave of their immortal souls,
Leaving the bodies quivering there.
Upon this slaughter brave Qualco,
As does the swordfish, which in midst
Of shoals of fish doth charge and strike
The meshes of the net and so break them
And renders safe the fish captured in them
And gallantly and freely gives them liberty,
Writhing his mighty sides and his strong sword,
And goes away, cleaving the crystal deep,
Contented, happy, free and gay,
So he, the strong, invincible, barbarian,
Depending on his valiant strength,
And justly, for two stalwart bulls
Upon the plains of Zibola had been
Subdued by his own valiant arm,
Having dispersed our men somewhat
And made a wide space, like a bull
Did charge on Diego Robledo
With a short mace. And as he came
Upon the valiant Roble,[3] the Spaniard
Thrust with his sword; the mace came down
And all by which the sword was longer
Did glide onward and so did pass
Its deadly point through the barbarian,
Through breast and back, in such a sort
That powerful Qualco, pierced through
From one side to the other, wounded sore,
Then dropped his mace, and with his fist,
Though run through once again before he struck,
Did deal him such a blow upon the side
As struck him down openmouthed
Upon the earth, near dead. And rapidly,
Before he could recover any breath,
He seized him by the leg and, as we see
The rustic man when he places
A massive stone in the broad part
Of whirling sling and, with his arm
Whirling it round, lets it go

8. Espadarte = pez espada.
9. Cardume = banco de peces.
10. Ledo = alegre, contento.
11. Robledo.
12. Hipando = resollando.

3. Villagrá plays on the Spaniard's name: Roble/oak.

Zumbando, por el Cóncabo del ayre,
No de otra suerte Qualco, rebolviendo
Con vna y otra buelta al bravo Roble
Por encima del brazo y la cabeza,
No bien le despedió dos largas hrazas[13]
Quando sin alma el bárbaro difunto
Caió tendido en tierra. Y tras desto,
Viéndose el Español allí arrastrado,
De generosa[14] afrenta ya vencido,
Cobrándose, furioso fue embistiendo,
Qual regañado[15] gato que a los bofes[16]
Con la maganta hambre se abalanza
Y allí los dientes clava y se afierna[17]
Con las agudas vñas, lebantando
La cola regordida[18] y pelo hierto,
Y en el difunto cuerpo tropezando
Suspenso se quedó allí temblando,
Notando la gran fuerza que alcanzaba
Y la poca que muerto allí tenía.
En esto, el gran Zapata y buen Cordero,
Cortés, Francisco Sánchez y Pedraza,
Ribera, Iuan Medel y Alonso Sánchez,
Iuan López y Naranjo y noble Ayarde,
Simón de Paz, Guillén, Villaviciosa,
Carabajal, Montero, con Villalba,
Dieron en pegar fuego por las casas
Por ponerles temor, mas no por esto
Algún tanto amainaban, o temían,[19]
La fuerza de las armas que cargaban.
Viendo, pues, el Sargento la braveza,
Dureza y pertinacia con que a vna
Los bárbaros furiosos combatían,
Por no ver ya tan gran carnizería,
Qual suele el podador hastuto y cauto
Que juzga bien la cepa, tiende y pone
La vista cuidadosa en cada rama
Y, luego que ha visto, corta y tala
Los mal compuestos brazos y rebiejos,
Con todo lo superfluo, mal trazado,
Y dexa con destreza y buen acuerdo

Humming into the empty air,
Not otherwise, strong Qualco whirling round
Brave Roble in a series of circles
At full arm's length above his head
135 Had hardly hurled him two men's lengths
When the barbarian, dead, soulless,
Fell down upon the earth. And after this
The Spaniard, seeing himself stretched out,
By such noble action thus defeated,
140 Recovering himself, charged furiously,
Like snarling cat which on offal
Doth prey from ravening hunger
And in it sets its teeth and grapples it
With its sharp claws, and raises high
145 Its swelling tail and bristling back,
And, stumbling upon the dead corpse,
He stood there trembling, hesitant,
Noting the great strength it possessed
And how narrowly he 'scaped death.
150 Then great Zapata and good Cordero,
Cortés, Francisco Sánchez, Pedraza,
Ribera, Juan Medel, Alonso Sánchez, too,
Juan López, Naranjo, and noble Ayarde,
Simón de Paz, Guillén, Villaviciosa,
155 Carabajal, Montero, and Villalba,
Did set on fire some of the houses there
To frighten them, but not for this
Did they abate a whit or slack
The power of the arms they swung.
160 The Sergeant, then, seeing the bravery,
Endurance and persistence with which all
Of the barbarians yet fought furiously,
That he might see no more of butchery,
Just as the clever, cautious pruner does
165 Who judges well the vine and looks and runs
His careful glance over each spreading bough,
And when he has surveyed, doth act and prune
The ill-shaped branches and the withered ones,
With all superfluous and useless ones,
170 And leaves with skill and good judgment

13. Errata del original por "brazas."
14. Generosa = noble, refiriéndose a la calidad de Qualco y de su acción.
15. Regañado = sañudo.
16. Bofes = pulmones. Los pulmones y otras entrañas de animales sacrificados servían de comida a los gatos.
17. Errata del original por "afierra," "aferra."
18. Regordida = abultada.
19. Por evitar la rima, amainaban/ cargaban, queda un hipérbaton: no por esto temían o amainaban la fuerza de las armas que cargaban.

Las varas con las vcas²⁰ y pulgares²¹	The stems with runners and new shoots
Que dicen esquilmenas,²² provechosas,	Which are considered fruitful ones,
Assí, mirando el campo, el gran guerrero	That great soldier, surveying all the field,
La soldadesca toda entresacando	Withdrawing all the soldiery
De sus debidos puestos señalados,	From their appointed stations,
Mandó que de su parte les dixessen	He ordered that from him the foe be told
Mirasen el estrago y el destrozo	They should observe the slaughter, the destruction
De tantos miserables como estaban	Of all the miserable wretches that there were
Tendidos por el suelo y se doliessen	Stretched out upon the ground and they should grieve
De aquella sangre y cuerpos, que él les daba	At such corpses and blood, and he gave them
Palabra y fee de noble caballero	The word and faith of noble gentleman
De guardarles justicia y con clemencia	To do them justice and with clemency
Mirar todas sus causas qual si fuera	To hear their case as if he were
Su verdadero padre. Y luego al punto,	Their own true father. And immediately
Arrojando de flechas grande suma,	Loosing a great flight of arrows,
Como rabiosos perros respondieron	Like to mad dogs, they made reply
No les tratasen desto y que apretasen	They would not speak of this, but they would take
Las armas y los dientes con los puños	Their arms and teeth and fists, as well,
Porque ellos y sus hijos y mugeres	Because they, their wives and children
Era fuerza acabasen y rindiessen	Perforce would die and would give up
Sus vidas y sus almas y sus honrras	Their lives and souls and their honor
En las lides presentes. Y con esto,	In this struggle. And, upon this,
Combatiendo furiosos, embestían,	They, fighting furiously, did charge
A morir o vencer, con tanta fuerza	To die or conquer with such force
Que pasmo y grima a todos nos causaba.	That they caused fear and terror to us all.
Por cuia causa luego, acobardado,	Now at this time, turned cowardly
Pensando por aquí tener salida,	And thinking to find safety here,
Zutacapán se vino y pidió pazes	Zutacapán did come and beg for peace
Al gallardo Sargento, y él, contento,	Before the gallant Sergeant; he, content,
Sin conocer quién fuesse aquel aleve,	Not knowing who that traitor was,
Luego le dixo diesse y entregase	Told him that he should give and hand over
Sólos los principales que causaron	Only the chief ones who had caused
El passado motín, y que, con esto,	The recent mutiny and that with this
Haría todo aquello que pudiese.	He would do all that he well could.
Nunca se vio jamás que assí temblase,	The tender cinquefoil⁴ was never seen
De vn sólo toque manso y blanda mano,	To tremble so at single gentle touch
La tierna argentería²³ qual temblaba	Of a soft hand as he then shook,
Aqueste bruto bárbaro, del dicho.²⁴	That brutal savage, at the word.
Y assí, suspenso, triste y rezeloso,	And so, hesitant, sad, suspicious,
No bien por el ocaso derribaba,	Hardly had there driven to his settling,
Con poderoso curso arrebatado,	In mighty and precipitous course,
El Sol su bello carro y trasponía	The sun his beauteous chariot and hid
La lumbre con que a todos alumbraba,	The light with which he lighted us,
Quando el triste poblacho todo estaba	When in the sorry town all was
En dos partes diviso y apartado,	Divided and set off in two parties,

Line numbers in right margin: 175, 180, 185, 190, 195, 200, 205, 210, 215

---

20. Probable errata del original por "uvas."

21. Pulgares = parte del sarmiento con yemas.

22. Esquilmenas = esquilmeñas, fructíferas.

23. Con "tierna argentería" es posible que Villagrá se refiera al azogue (argento vivo).

24. Del dicho = de lo dicho.

4. Curtis translates *argentería* as this delicate plant, but the plant, in Spanish, is called *argentina*. The reference may well be to quicksilver.

Los vnos y los otros temerosos
De la fuerza de España y su braveza.
Y luego que la luz salió encendida,
Despés de aber los bárbaros tratado
Sobre estas pazes todos grandes cosas,
Viendo Zutacapán ser el primero
Que el passado motín abía causado
Con todos sus amigos y sequaces,
Quales hojosos bosques, sacudidos
Del poderoso boreas y alterados,
Que assí, en montón confusso, se rebuelven
Por vna y otra parte y se sacuden
Las pajas,²⁵ lebantando y alterando
Sus lebantadas cimas, y en contorno²⁶
Todos por todas partes se remecen,
Assí estos pobres bárbaros, perdidos,
Bolvieron a las armas, de manera
Que tres días en peso los soldados
No comieron, durmieron ni bebieron,
Ni se sentaron ni las fuertes armas
Dexaron de los puños, derramando
Tanta suma de sangre que anegados
Estaban ya y cansados de verterla.
En esto, ya yba el fuego lebantando
Vn vapor inflamado, poco a poco
Todas las tristes casas calentando.
Y luego, en breve rato, fue cobrando
Vigor bastante, y por el seco pino
De las teosas²⁷ casas y aposentos
Restallando los techos por mil partes,
Vn muy espeso, denso y tardo²⁸ humo,
Como gruessos vellones, las ventanas
Por vna y otra parte respiraban
Y como fogosíssimos bolcanes
Bolando hazia el Cielo despedían
Gran suma de centellas y de chispas.²⁹
Y assí, los brutos bárbaros, furiosos,
Viéndose ya vencidos, se mataban
Los vnos a los otros, de manera
Que el hijo al padre y padre al caro hijo
La vida le quitaba, y, demás desto,
Al fuego, juntos, otros ayudaban
Porque con más vigor se lebantase
Y el pueblo consumiesse y abrasase.
Sólo Zutacapán y sus amigos,

220

225

230

235

240

245

250

255

260

Both one and the other being timorous
About the Spaniards' strength and their courage.
And when the light did grow once more
The barbarians, having discussed
All the grave matters of this peace,
Seeing Zutacapán had been the chief
Who had brought on the recent mutiny,
With all his friends and all his followers,
Like leafed forests that are rustled
By powerful Boreas, shaken,
So in a confused mass they move
Hither and thither, shaking off
Their dust, raising and altering
Their lofty tops, and all about
Are all moved to and fro and everywhere,
These poor barbarians, ruined,
Took refuge in their arms to such effect
That for three whole days the soldiers
Nor ate nor slept nor drank a drop,
Nor sat down nor laid aside
Their strong weapons from out their hands,
Shedding such store of blood they now
Were flooded, tired out with shedding it.
And now the fire kept sending up
A ruddy vapor, bit by bit,
Attacking all the sad houses,
And then in a short time it mustered up
Sufficient vigor and in the dry pine
Of the resinous houses and dwellings
It crackled in the roofs and in a thousand spots,
A very thick and dense and sluggish smoke,
Like great fleeces, was puffing out thickly
From windows here, there, and everywhere,
And like the most ardent of volcanoes
They poured out, whirling toward the sky
Great store of embers and of sparks.⁵
And thus, those wild and mad barbarians,
Seeing themselves now conquered, 'gan to kill
Each other, and did so in such fashion
That sons from fathers, fathers from their loved children,
Took life away, and further, more than this,
Others in groups did give aid to the fire
So that it might leap up with more vigor,
Consume the pueblo and destroy it all.
Only Zutacapán and they his friends,

25. Pajas = polvo.
26. En contorno = alrededor.
27. Teosas = inflamables.
28. Tardo = lento.
29. El incendio de Acoma guarda semejanzas con la descripción que
Virgilio, *Eneida* II, da de la caída de Troya.

5. This described burning of Acoma is, not surprisingly, somewhat
similar to the burning of Troy as narrated in Virgil. See the *Aeneid* II.

Huiendo de cobardes por no verse	Fleeing as cowards lest they see themselves
En manos de Gicombo, se escondieron	Within Gicombo's hands, did hide themselves
En las cuevas y senos que tenía	Within the caves and hollows which there were
La fuerza del peñol, cuia grandeza	Upon the fortress rock, whose great extent
Segundo labirinto³⁰ se mostraba	Did show itself a second Labyrinth[6]
Según eran sus cuevas y escondrijos,	Because of many caves and hiding holes,
Sus salidas y entradas y aposentos.	Their entrances and exits and chambers.
Y viendo el General y bravo Bempol	The General and brave Bempol, seeing
Que todos se mataban y cumplían	That all did kill themselves and seal
La fuerza de aquel pacto que jurado	Truly the pact which all had sworn
Estaba de matarse si vencidos	To suicide if they as conquered should
Saliessen de los brazos Castellanos,	Come from the struggle with the Castilians,
Juntos determinaron de matarse.	Determined jointly they would kill themselves.
Y assí, por esta causa, temerosos	And so, fearful, because of this,
De mal tan incurable, por no verse	Of such incurable evil, not to see all
En brazos de la muerte, les hablaron	In death's own arms, some of their friends,
Ciertos amigos, tristes, encogidos,	Sad, much dismayed, did speak to them,
Pidiéndoles con veras se rindiessen	Begging sincerely they would surrender
Y que las vidas, juntos, rescatasen.	And so, together, they might save their lives.
Por cuia causa luego replicaron	At this appeal they instantly replied,
Los pertinaces bárbaros, furiosos:	Those furious, obstinate barbarians:
"Dezidnos, Acomeses desdichados,	"Tell us, ye Acomans unfortunate,
¿Qué estado es el que Acoma oy tiene	What state is this of Acoma today
Para emprender vn caso tan infame	To undertake so infamous a thing
Qual éste que pedís? Decid agora,	As this you ask us? Tell us now
¿Qué refugio pensáis que os dexa el hado	What refuge you do think that fate doth leave
Luego que aquestas pazes celebradas	As soon as peace might be secured
Estén con los Castillas con firmeza?	All firmly with these Castilians?
¿No hecháis de ver que abemos ya llegado	Do you not see that we have now arrived
Al vltimo dolor y postrer punto,	At that last sorrow and that final point
Donde sin libertad es fuerza todos	Where we all must, without our liberty,
Vivamos, como infames, triste vida?	Live out our sorry life as infamous wretches?
Acoma vn tiempo fue, y en alta cumbre	Acoma was once, and upon the peak
Vimos su heroico nombre lebantado,	We saw her name, heroic, lifted high,
Y agora aquellos dioses que la mano	And now the very gods who gave
Le dieron por honrrarla y lebantarla	Their hands to her, to raise and honor her,
Vemos que la subieron porque fuesse	We see only did so that her ruin
Su mísera ruina más sentida	Might be more miserably felt
De aquellos miserables que esperamos	By those poor wretches who did hope
En tan débil flaqueza³¹ tal firmeza,	For such firmness in such feeble weakness.
Por cuia causa juntos acordamos,	For this reason, we, all of us, agreed,
Si estáis, como nostros entendemos,	If you are, as we two do feel you are,
Firmes en la promesa que juramos,	Firm in the promise which we swore
Que a la felice muerte las gargantas	That we would give our throats to happy death
Las demos y entreguemos, pues no queda,	and submit them since there remaineth not
Para nuestra salud, mayor remedio	Another greater remedy for this our health
Que perder la esperanza que nos queda	Than to give up the hope that yet remains

Line numbers in margin: 265, 270, 275, 280, 285, 290, 295, 300, 305

---

30. Se refiere al laberinto, por antonomasia, de Creta.
31. Lo de "débil flaqueza" puede referirse a la de sus dioses o a la de la subida posición que habían alcanzado.

6. The reference is to the Labyrinth of Crete.

De poder alcanzarle y conseguirle."³²
Y luego que con esto otras razones
El bravo General les fue diziendo,
Maximino, Macrino ni Maxencio,
Procrustes, Dioclеciano ni Tiberio,
Nerón³³ ni todo el resto de crueles
Con ninguno mostraron su braveza
Más brava, más atroz ni más terrible
Que éstos consigo mismos se mostraron,
No sólo los varones, mas las hembras.
Las vnas, como Dido,³⁴ abandonaron
Sus cuerpos y en las llamas perecieron.
Y assí, como espartanos, sus hijuelos
También a dura muerte se entregaron.
Otras los arrojaban y lanzaban
En las ardientes llamas, y otras, tristes,
Con ellos abrazadas³⁵ desde el muro
Las vimos con esfuerzo despeñarse.
Otras, qual Porcia,³⁶ apriessa satisfechas
De brasas encendidas acababan.
Otras el tierno pecho, qual Lucrecia,³⁷
Con dura punta roto, despedían
Las almas miserables, y otras muchas
Con otros muchos géneros de muertes
Sus vidas acababan y rendían.
En este medio tiempo, las hermanas
Del bravo Zutancalpo, desvalidas,
Fuera de sí, salieron a buscarle
Por acabar con él la triste vida,
Cuio dolor acerbo y triste llanto³⁸
Quiero cantar, señor, en nuevo canto.

For us to gain it and to secure it."⁷
And when, with this, the haughty General   310
Had also told them other arguments,
Maximian, Macrinus, Maxentius,
Procrustes, Diocletian, nor Tiberius,
Nero, nor all the rest of cruel men,⁸
Displayed upon no one ferocity   315
More harsh, atrocious, nor more terrible
Than these displayed upon their very selves,
Not only men, but the women as well.
Some, like to Dido,⁹ took leave of
Their bodies and did perish in the flames,
And, like the Spartans, they also   320
Gave up their tender babes unto harsh death.
Others did hurl and cast their babes
Into the burning flames, and others, sad,
With them held tight, from off the wall
Hurled themselves dashing down, as we could see.   325
Others, like Portia,¹⁰ quickly satisfied
With living coals, did end their lives.
Others, like Lucrece,¹¹ with a keen dagger
Piercing their tender breasts, did thus speed forth
Their miserable souls, and many more   330
By very many other sorts of death
Did end and render up their lives.
In the meantime, the fair sisters
Of Zutancalpo brave, in great distress
Beside themselves, went out to seek   335
Their brother, to end their sad lives with his.¹²
Their bitter grief, their sad weeping,
I wish, lord, in a canto new to sing.

32. Se refiere al "remedio" antes mencionado.

33. Maximino, emperador romano, se entretuvo con las torturas de sus enemigos; Macrino, emperador romano a quien se le sublevó el ejército por los castigos severos que imponía; Maxencio, emperador romano de proverbial crueldad; Procrustes, legendario bandolero atico que, puestas sus víctimas en una cama, les cortaba lo que de sus cuerpos sobrara; Diocleciano, Tiberio y Nerón, emperadores romanos asociados con las crueldades sufridas por los mártires cristianos. Véase Pero Mexía, *Silva de varia lección* I, 34, capítulo sobre la crueldad, en que aparecen éstos.

34. Indica que se mataron antes ("abandonaron sus cuerpos") de que las llamas las consumieran, ya que Dido, reina legendaria de Cartago, se mata primero (la *Eneida* IV, 915).

35. La reproducción mexicana trae "abrasadas."

36. La historia de Porcia, esposa de Bruto, que se suicidó tragando brasas encendidas, se halla en Plutarco, *Vidas,* en la biografía de su marido, Marco Bruto.

37. Lucrecia, tras ser ultrajada por Tarquino, se suicidó como indica el texto. Se halla el relato en Livio I.

38. El tema de las hermanas buscando el cuerpo del heroico hermano muerto en batalla, relacionado con el de Antígone, se halla también en Tasso. Véase Villagrá, *Historia*, edición de Junquera, 61.

7. The "it" here appears to have "remedy" as its precedent.

8. Maximian: Roman emperor who enjoyed torturing his enemies; Macrinus: Roman emperor against whom the army rebelled because of the severe punishments he imposed; Maxentius: Roman emperor of proverbial cruelty; Procrustes: legendary Attic assaulter who tied his victims to a bed and cut off parts of their body that did not fit it; Diocletian, Tiberius, and Nero: Roman emperors associated with the cruelty endured by the Christian martyrs. For references, in this respect, to the above, see Pero Mexia, *Silva de varia lección* I, 34.

9. Indicating they killed themselves before burning. For that sequence in Dido, legendary queen of Carthage, see the *Aeneid* IV, 915.

10. The story of Portia, Brutus's wife, who committed suicide by swallowing live coals, is found in Plutarch's *Lives,* in the biography of Marcus Brutus.

11. Lucrece, raped by Tarquin, committed suicide in the indicated manner. See *Livy* I.

12. The sisters seeking out the heroic brother after battle, perhaps going back to the Antigone theme, is also found, as indicated by Junquera (Villagrá, *Historia,* 61) in Tasso's *Jerusalem Delivered.*

COMO ZVTANCALPO FVE HALLADO POR SVS
QVATRO *hermanas y del fin y muerte de Gicombo y
de Luzcoija.*

*How Zutancalpo was found by his four sisters and of
the end and death of Gicombo and Luzcoija.*

VE peña lebantada o fuerte roca
Puede ser del soberbio mar ayrado
Más brava y atrozmente combatida
Que nuestra vida triste miserable,
Si lo miramos bien los más mortales,   5
A quien la cruel soberbia desmedida
Y ambición vil, frenética, furiosa,
Iamás pudo hartar: al alto ceptro,
A la Real corona y bravo trono,
Al pobrecillo assiento[1] y bajo estado?   10
¡O triste condición de humana vida,
Sugeta y puesta a bestias tan sedientas,
En cuia abara fuente, vil, infame,
De su canina sed jamás contenta,
Pretende cada qual sacar hartura!   15
¿Qué prestaron[2] al noble Zutancalpo
Aber con tanta fuerza contradicho
Los furiosos intentos paternales
Que tantas vidas tienen acabadas
Y tantos buenos hombres consumidos   20
Y tantas nobles casas abrasadas?
¡O cruel Zutacapán, por qué quisiste
Yr contra la corriente que llevaba
El sossegado pueblo ya perdido
Y aquel gallardo joben que engendraste!   25
¿Qué prestaron los retos y braveza
Con que turbaste tantos inocentes,
Qué el bravo y fiero orgullo que pusiste
Para que Castellanos lebantasen,
Contra tu corto esfuerzo, armadas?   30
¿Qué prestó[3] aber la tregua quebrantado,
Palabra y fee de paz aber rompido?
¿De qué vil furia fuiste arrebatado
Para que con altivo pensamiento
Moviesses tan sin causa injusta guerra?   35
¡O soberbia, que porque siempre sobras
Assí fue bien que el nombre te pusiessen!
Y assí, como sobrada, te lebantas
Y tanto más te subes y te encumbras

HAT lofty rock or towering cliff
Can by the wrathful, haughty sea
Be battered harder, more atrociously,
Than our own sad and miserable life,
If we but note it, most mortals,   5
Whom cruel pride, exaggerated,
And vile ambition, raving, furious,
Could never satisfy: the great scepter,
The royal crown, and its brave throne,
The poorest commoner of lowliest estate?   10
Oh sad condition of our human life,
Subjected, prostrate, to such thirsty beasts,
From whose most greedy fountain, vile and infamous,
Never contented of their thirst inordinate,
Each one pretends to take satisfaction!   15
What did it serve noble Zutancalpo
To have opposed with such great strength
The furious designs of his father
Which had ended so many human lives
And had consumed so many goodly men,   20
And burned down so many noble homes?
Cruel Zutacapán, why did you choose
To go against the current that did bear
The peaceful people who are now ruined
And that brave youth whom you begot!   25
What profited the threats and bravado
With which you did perturb so many innocents,
And what the harsh, wild pride you showed
In wishing the Castilians might come
In arms against your little strength?   30
What profited to have broken the truce,
Your word, and oath that you had given for the peace?
By what vile fury were you dragged along
That you with such lofty ideas
Did move an unjust war so carelessly?   35
O pride, for since you have more than enough
'Twere well that you were named so![1]
And thus, as excess, you do rise,
Soaring always to ever greater heights

---

1. Villagrá hace poético juego, para contrastar con "trono," entre
silla ("asiento") y hogar/residencia ("asiento").
2. Prestaron = aprovecharon.
3. La reproducción mexicana trae "presto."

1. Villagrá plays on the phonetic similarity between *soberbia,* pride,
and *sobra,* excess.

Quanto es más bajo aquél que te pretende.
No siente la ambición bruta, furiosa,
Deste atreguado bárbaro perdido
La pérdida y desgracia miserable
Que por sóla su causa le ha venido
Al desdichado pueblo desgraciado
Cuias plazas y muros lebantados
Sólos arroyos, charcos y lagunas
De fresca sangre vemos rebozando,
Con gran suma de cuerpos ya difuntos,
Por cuias fieras llagas temerarias
Terribles quajarones regoldaban,
Témpanos[4] y sangraza[5] nunca vista,
A bueltas del[6] sustento mal digesto
Que por allí también le despedían
Por do las pobres almas escapaban.
Por cuio atroz estrago no hecha menos[7]
Al noble Zutancalpo, a quien salieron
No más que por buscarle de su casa
Quatro hermanas donzellas que tenía,
Pressas de mortalíssimas congojas
Y desfogando por su ausencia, en vano,
De lo íntimo del alma ya cansada,
Entrañables suspiros y gemidos,
Rebolviendo los cuerpos desangrados
Por ver si entre ellos a su caro hermano
Acaso ver pudiessen, porque abía
Passado vna gran pieza[8] sin que fuesse
De algún amigo visto o descubierto.
Mocauli, la mayor de todas ellas,
Rebolvió por seys vezes un difunto,
Y como es cierto que la sangre llama,
Otra quiso tomarle y rebolverle,
Y viendo ser aquel tesoro grande
Y por quien siempre todas fueron ricas,
Sin que pudiessen descubrir quál[9] fuesse
La fuerza del espada rigurosa
Que por tan fieras bocas desmedidas
Le hizo despedir el alma brava,
Con presurosos gritos esforzados,
A palma abierta y puño bien cerrado
Comenzó a lastimar su rostro bello.
Y qual vemos que acuden al ladrido

40 The baser the subject who thus aspires.
It regrets not, that brute, the ambition
Of that insane and lost barbarian,
The pitiable loss and misfortune
Which, caused by it alone, has come
45 Upon the unhappy, ill-fated town
Whose public squares and lofty walls we see
Mere rivulets and puddles, aye, and lakes
All overflowing with fresh human blood,
And a great store of bodies of the dead,
50 From whose deep, terror striking wounds
Terrible clots of blood emerged,
Congealed and liquid blood unheard of, too,
And bits of undigested food, as well,
From whence also had way been made
55 Through which their poor souls had escaped.
And in this dreadful slaughter, yet unmissed,
Was noble Zutancalpo, for whom came,
That they might seek for him, from out their house
Four maiden sisters whom he had,
60 Given up to most deadly anxiety
And uttering in vain at his absence,
From the innermost of their weary souls,
The most heartrending sighs and moans,
Turning over the bloodless bodies there
65 To see if among them they might perceive
Their dearly loved brother, because there had
Now passed a long time when he had not been
Seen nor observed by any of his friends.
Mocauli, the oldest of them all,
70 Did six times examine one corpse
And, as 'tis certain that blood calls to blood,
Once more she chose to take it and turn it,
And seeing that it was that great treasure
By which they always reckoned themselves rich,
75 Though she could not discover whose had been
The strength of that most deadly sword
Which by such deep, measureless mouths
Had made him give up his brave soul,
With prompt and with most piercing cries,
80 With open palm and with tightly-clenched fist
She did begin to wound her beauteous face.
And as we see haste unto the barking

4. Témpanos = sangre cuajada.
5. Sangraza = sangre acuosa.
6. a Bueltas de = a vueltas de, además de.
7. Salvo errata del original, "Hecha menos" (echa de menos) se refiere a que, dado el estrago, Zutacapán, el antecedente más próximo, no echa de menos a su hijo.
8. Pieza = rato.
9. Quál = cuál, de quién.

De la presta y solícita podenca	Of some quick eager-nosed hound
Las demás, codiciosas de la caza,	The rest, all of them, eager for the chase,
Con lebantados saltos alentados	85 Speeding on with astounding leaps
Y vna y otra corrida presurosa,	And many a rapid burst of swift running,
Assí las tres hermanas, desbalidas,	So the three other sisters, overcome,
Partieron con presteza y sin sentido,	Set out in haste and, half out of their wits,
Con desapoderado[10] curso, al puesto	With speed incalculable, to the spot
De aquélla que pedazos se hazía	90 Where she was tearing her fair flesh
Sobre el querido hermano desangrado.	Above her dear brother, now all bloodless.
Y juntas todas quatro, a manos llenas	And there the four together did tear out
Las más crecidas hebras arrancaban	In handfuls the long, beauteous hair
De las pobres cabezas inocentes,	From their poor, sad, innocent heads,
Las rosadas megillas golpeando	95 Striking upon their rosy cheeks
Con vna y otra mano lebantada.	With one hand and the other, lifted high.
Y después que le vbieron bien llorado,	And after they had wept for him right well
Sobre vn gran tablón luego le pusieron	They then laid him upon a heavy plank
Y encima de sus hombros le llevaron	And carried him upon their shoulders
Con fúnebre dolor, triste, afligido,	100 With funeral grief, all sad and downcast,
Para su antigua casa ya abrasada.	Unto his former home, now burnt to earth.
Y luego que la madre desdichada	And when the unfortunate mother
Tuvo delante de sus tristes ojos	Beheld before her own sad eyes
El horrendo espectáculo que vido,	The horrible spectacle which she saw,
Sin piedad desgarrándose la cara	105 Tearing her face without the least mercy,
Y la madeja suelta de cabellos,	As well as her loose, flying locks of hair,
Assí empezó la pobre a lamentarse:	The poor creature began thus to lament:
"Dioses, si en flor tan tierna abéis querido	"Ye gods, if in his tender flower ye wished
Quitar[11] aquesta pobre desdichada	To take away from this unhappy wretch
Vn hijo malogrado que le distes,	110 The son, untimely dead, whom you gave her,
¿Decid si[12] aqueste punto he ya llegado	Tell me, if I have now reached such a point
Y a tan perdido estado he ya venido,	And come now into such a ruined state,
Quál otro mal podéis tener guardado?	What other evil you may yet reserve?
Este vltimo quebranto y postrer duelo	It remained only that this last trial,
Solamente restaba que viniesse	115 This final sorrow, should have come to me
A mi pobre vegez, triste, afligida."	In my old age, poor, sad, and afflicted."
Y vertiendo de lágrimas gran lluvia,	And shedding a great rain of tears,
Con el bravo dolor y amor fogoso	Through bitter sorrow and through fiery love
Del trágico furor enternizada,[13]	Being deeply moved by her tragic distress,
Cien mil gemidos tristes redoblaba	120 She gave a hundred thousand grieving sighs
Que del ansiado pecho le salían.	From out the depths of her anguish-wrung breast.
Y como la desesperada furia	And as the madness of desperation
Es el más cruel y capital verdugo	Is the most cruel executioner
De aquél que semejante mal padece,	Of him who suffers from such an evil,
Assí, desesperada y con despecho,	125 So, desperate and utterly heedless,
Sobre vn gran fuego se lanzó de espaldas.	She cast herself backward into the flames.
Y tras della las quatro hermanas tristes	And after her the four grieving sisters
También allí quisieron abrasarse	Did also choose to be consumed there,

10. Desapoderado = precipitado.
11. Posible errata del original omitiendo "a."
12. Posible errata del original omitiendo "a."
13. Enternizada = enternecida.

Sobre el querido hermano ya difunto,
Que assí, juntas con él se abalanzaron
Iunto a la misma madre que se ardía.
Y qual suelen grosíssimas culebras
O ponzoñosas víboras ayradas
Las vnas con las otras retorcerse
Con aprretados ñudos y enrroscarse,
Assí las miserables se enlazaban
Por aquellas cenizas y rescoldo,
Que, amollentado y fofo, a borbollones
Hirviendo por mil partes resoplaba,
Y restribando[14] sobre vivas brasas
Con hombros, pies y manos juntamente,
Instaban por salir. Mas era en vano,
Porque assí como vemos yrse a fondo
A aquéllos que en profundo mar se anegan,
Que con piernas y brazos, sin provecho,
Cortan el triste hilo de sus vidas
Y, en tiempo desdichado, corto y breve
Las inmortales almas oprimidas
De las mortales cárceles escapan,
Assí estas malogradas fenecieron.
Dando, en aquella vltima partida,
Los postreros abrazos bien ceñidos
Y despidiendo assí la dulze patria,
Dieron el *longum vale*[15] a las cenizas
En que todas quisieron resolverse.
Passado aqueste mísero sucesso,
Otro le sucedió también estraño,
Que esso tiene la mal segura rueda,
Ser incierta en que el bien nos venga estable
Y cierta en que el mal siempre nos persiga;
Y assí podéis notar, Rey poderoso,
Que, como en este mundo antojadizo
Vnos con ansias buscan y apetecen
Aquello que los otros aborrecen,
Por escapar la vida fue saliendo
Vn conozido bárbaro valiente
Con tan desatinado y presto curso
Que, assí como se escribe que corrieron
Efisido y Orión[16] con gran presteza,

130 Together with their dead, beloved brother.
Thus they, with him, did hurl themselves
In, next their mother, who burned there.
And like to the most monstrous snakes
Or poisonous, deadly vipers,
135 Who with each other intertwine
In clinging knots and twist about,
So these poor wretches were entwined
Among those ashes and embers
Which, crumbling and soft, seething
140 Fiercely, did burst out in a thousand spots,
And they, struggling up on the glowing coals,
With shoulders, hands, and feet, jointly
Attempted to get out. But all in vain,
For as we see sink neath the waves
145 Those who are overcome upon the deep,
Who, uselessly, with arms and legs
But shorten the sad thread of life,
And in a time unfortunate, short, brief,
Their souls, immortal yet oppressed,
150 Escape from their mortal prisons,
So these did make untimely end.
Yet giving in that last farewell
Their last embraces mid the coals,
And thus, leaving their fatherland beloved,
155 They gave a long farewell to its ashes
Mid which they all had willed to die.
This pitiful event over,
Another, also strange, followed,
For 'tis the character of that uncertain wheel
To be unsure when good seems sure to us
160 And certain when evil pursues;
And thus you may note, O powerful King,
How in this topsy-turvy world
Some anxiously seek and desire
The very thing which other men abhor.
165 A barbarian, known as a valiant man,
Was hastening to leave this life
With such precipitate and rapid course
That, as 'tis written Efisidus ran
And Orion,[2] with such astounding speed

14. Restribando = apoyándose.
15. Villagrá, con utilizar *longum vale* (larga despedida) sugiere una prolongada agonía.
16. La carrera de Orión, gigante mitológico y después constelación, sería en su persecución de las Pléyades, que terminaron acompañándole en los cielos. No hemos hallado referencia de Efisidio, pero quizás sea equivocación de Villagrá, ya que la habilidad que describe (de correr tan velozmente por encima de los sembrados) se asocia, en Virgilio, *Eneida* VII, 1060–64, con Camila, dedicada a Diana, asociada con Efeso y que, por ello, pudiera llamarse "Efesida."

2. Orion, the mythological giant turned constellation, raced after the Pleiades, who later joined him in the heavens. We have found no reference to Efisidus and suppose that it is a printing error, possibly for a word close to *Efesida,* Ephesidan, since the ability described, racing speedily over the heads of grain is associated with Camila (*Aeneid* VII, 1060–64) who was dedicated to Diana, in turn associated with Ephesus.

El vno por encima de las aguas
Y el otro por las puntas de los trigos
Sin que ninguna arista se doblase
Y sin que el agua en parte se sintiesse,
Assí, con esa misma ligereza,
Corriendo por encima de las llamas
Vimos al bravo Pilco, presusoro,
Qual fiera salamandria que en el fuego
Sin pesadumbre passa y se sustenta.[17]
Y por sólo estorbarle la corrida,
Antes que se saliesse y ausentase
Gran suma de balazos le tiraron,
Y abiéndose escapado de las brasas
Y del rigor y fuerza de pelotas
Vino a parar a manos de vn soldado,
León por nombre y por su grande esfuerzo.
Estos dos combatieron larga pieza
Con gran fuerza de golpes denodados,
Y descargando el bárbaro la maza
Con furia arrebatada, fue saliendo
El gallardo Español con tal destreza
Que la hizo pedazos el membrudo,
Traiendo el golpe en vano y sin provecho
Sobre vna grande piedra que aferrada
Estaba con el muro poderoso,
Con cuio buen sucesso y con que vido
Que por el suelo casi le arrastraba
Al salvage la greña que tenía,
Por ella le prendió con fuertes garras,
Y qual suele evadirse y deslizarse
La suelta anguila de la fuerte mano,
Assí de entre sus fuertes brazos vimos
Salir al bravo bárbaro guerrero,
Lanzándole de sí como si fuera
Muy libiana pelota despedida
Con lebantada pala gobernada
De vn poderoso brazo bien fornido.
Pasmado el Español de aquel sucesso,
Vencido de vergüenza y corrimiento
De verse de tal pressa desasido,
Assí como libiana y triste sombra
Que sigue al cuerpo opaco y no se empacha
En la carrera, buelo y presto curso,
Que va sin detenerse, assí, siguiendo
Al miserable bárbaro perdido,
Tanta priessa le dio con el espada
Quanta el membrudo alárabe, ligero,
Con vno y otro salto le dexaba

170 The one upon the top of the water,
The other on the heads of the standing grain,
The one so that no head was ever bent,
The other without the water parting,
So, with this very same lightness,
175 We saw the brave Pilco nimbly
Running on top of the flames there,
Like fiery salamander which through fire
Does pass without a hurt and is all whole.[3]
Solely to hinder his running,
180 Before he should go on and so escape,
They fired at him a goodly stock of balls,
And, having escaped from the flames
And from the force and power of the bullets,
He fell into the hands of a soldier,
185 León in name and also in his strength.
These two did struggle a long time
With great exchange of heavy blows,
And the barbarian hurling his mace
With violent fury, the bold Spaniard
190 Did escape it with so much skill
That his opponent shattered it,
The blow falling in vain upon
A mighty rock that was fixed in
The structure of the mighty wall,
195 With which good fortune he also did see
That there was hanging almost to the ground
In front the long hair which the savage had,
And seized it and held on with strong fingers.
And as the slender eel escapes
200 And glides away from the strong hand,
So we did see the bold barbarian warrior
Escape from the grip of his brawny arms,
Hurling him from himself as though he were
A mere light playing ball driven
205 By the upraised, well-strung racket
Wielded by powerful and skillful arms.
The Spaniard, astounded at that event,
All overcome with shame and with embarrassment
At seeing his hold broken so quickly,
210 Like to an insubstantial, swift shadow
Which follows an opaque body nor is
Delayed in its career, its turns and its swift course,
But follows without stopping, so did he
The miserable, lost barbarian,
215 And howe'er he pressed him with his sword
The strong and light Arab, equally quick,
By leaping here and there, did leave to him

17. Se pensaba desde Plinio, recogido por los más bestiarios medievales, que la salamandra podía vivir en el fuego.

3. A common indication of medieval bestiaries, based on Pliny.

Los golpes en el ayre desmentidos.
Hasta que, por grandíssima ventura,
Se le vino a meter por vn estrecho
Por donde el muro, con aguda punta,
Más de setenta estados derramaba
De terrible vertiente bien cumplidos,
Desde cuia alta cumbre poderosa,
Estando todo el campo bien atento,
Se arrojó aquel indómito guerrero
Con tan vizarro aliento que suspensos,
Los leales corazones palpitando,
A todos nos dexó desatinados,
Porque con braza y media bien tendida
No se sintió soldado que quisiesse
Asomar ni poner el rostro firme
Por donde quiso el bárbaro escaparse.
Y apenas, con el grande sobresalto,
Le vimos ocupar el duro suelo,
Quando de golpe todos arrancamos
A ver el alto y portentoso salto
Que, sin pensar, el Indio memorable
Allí le acometió con bravo esfuerzo.
Y qual la gruessa lanza despedida
Del poderoso brazo, que clavada
Quedó temblando entera y bien assida
En aquel gran caballo que Troianos
Tan por su mal en Troia les metieron,[18]
No de otra suerte Pilco, valeroso
Quanto[19] pudo blandir la larga lanza,
Sobre los firmes pies, algo perdido,[20]
Quedó temblando en tierra bien clavado.
Y rebolviendo en sí qual suelto pardo,
Sacudiendo algún tanto la melena
Con ímpetu furioso, fue corriendo
A campo abierto por el ancho llano,
Donde Diego Robledo, con cuidado,
Vatiendo con priessa los hijares
De vn ligero caballo desembuelto,
Al puesto le salió con vn benablo
De temerario hierro, bien tendido,
Y vibrando sobre él la fiera diestra
Tres vezes le mojó, con que quedaron
Por los gruessos costados poderosos
Seys anchas puertas rojas bien rasgadas,
Por donde el cuerpo y alma desdichada
El natural diborcio celebraron
Con no pequeña lástima de aquéllos

His blows striking upon the empty air.
Until, by the greatest of good fortune

220 He happened to chance on a narrow place
Where the wall, at a sharp angle,
Went down more than full seventy fathoms
Of fearful cliff, all perpendicular,
And from this high, dreadful summit,

225 The whole army there watching him,
That warrior indomitable threw himself
With such bizarre daring that, in suspense,
Our loyal hearts palpitating,
He left us all in confusion,

230 Because within a fathom and a half
There was no soldier who did dare
To peep nor glance with a firm face
Where that barbarian chose escape.
Hardly, after our great astonishment,

235 Had we seen him land on firm ground
When, all together, we did turn about
To see the lofty and portentous leap
Which, unthinking, the memorable Indian
Had there attempted with a brave effort.

240 And like the heavy lance which, thrown
By powerful arm, did remain fixed
And trembling, stuck fast and deep rooted
In the huge horse which the Trojans
To their great harm had taken into Troy,[4]

245 Not otherwise the valorous Pilco,
Brave when brandishing the long lance,
Set firm upon his feet, though somewhat hurt,
Stood trembling, imbedded in the ground.
And turning about then, like freed leopard,

250 His long locks streaming out behind,
With furious speed set out running
Toward open ground across the spreading plain,
Where Diego Robledo, watchful,
Beating in haste upon the flanks

255 Of a swift and ready charger,
At once attacked him with a javelin
Of tempered iron, long and strong.
And, brandishing his right hand over him,
He struck him three times so there were

260 In his heavy and powerful flanks
Six wide red doorways, stricken deep,
Through which his body and unlucky soul
Did then perform a divorce of nature,
To no small sorrow of those men

18. Se narra el hecho en Virgilio, *Eneida* II, 70–75.
19. Probable errata del original por "quando."
20. Perdido = fuera de sí, perturbado.

4. The incident is narrated by Virgil, the *Aeneid* II, 70–75.

Que al horrendo espectáculo asistían,
Doliéndose de verle destroncado
El miserable tiempo que de vida
Llevaba ya ganado y adquirido
Y por justa justicia prolongado.
Passada esta tragedia prodigiosa,
Paréceme, señor, que nos bolvamos
Al sin ventura puesto donde queda
El pobre General y bravo Bempol
Que, como apunto y queda referido,
Qual aquellos illustres Bruto y Casio,²¹
Que quisieron privarse de la vida
Por sólo que se vieron ya vencidos,
Assí, por no vivir jamás sugetos,
El vno fue saliendo a despeñarse
Y el otro a sólo dar injusta muerte
A su amada Luzcoija, por no verla
En manos de Españoles que pudiessen
Gozar de su belleza malograda.
Pues, saliendo del grande labirintho,
Desesperados, bravos y furiosos,
Desta suerte los dos fueron diziendo:
"¡O como nos quebrantan duros ados
Y tempestad violenta nos perturba
Y a viva sangre y fuego nos molesta,
Oprime, rinde, vence y nos contrasta!
Y vosotros, infames Acomeses,
Seréis horriblemente castigados,
Con pena tal qual es muy bien que venga
Por semejantes ánimos cobardes.
Y a ti, Zutacapán, cebil,²² que has sido
Instrumento de tanta desbentura,
Sábete que te aguardan y te esperan
Desta maldad y vergonzosa afrenta
Cruelíssimos azotes y castigos,
Y, en los más sustos²³ dioses confiados,
Que les darás de tus enormes culpas
Enmienda muy tardía y sin provecho."
Diziendo esto, los dos se dividieron.
Gicombo enderzó para su casa,
Que en humo y viva llama estaba embuelta,
Y rompiendo las enemigas brasas,
Rescoldo, y por las llamas lebantadas,
Llegó al mismo aposento donde estaba

265 Who saw that horrid spectacle,
Grieving to see destroyed for him
The miserable period of life
Which he had gained and well acquired
And had prolonged by true justice.
270 This tragedy prodigious being done,
I think, lord, that we should return
To the unhappy spot where yet remain
The poor General and the brave Bempol,
Who, as I say and said before,
275 Were like illustrious Brutus and Cassius,
Who wished to take away their lives
Because they saw themselves conquered.⁵
Thus, never to live as subjects,
The one departed to leap off the cliff,
280 The other to give undeserved death
To his dear Luzcoija, lest he might see her
In hands of Spaniards who could
Enjoy her beauty, now wasted.
Now, coming from the mighty labyrinth,
285 Desperate, reckless, furious,
They then spoke to each other in this wise:
"Oh how the harsh fates do now destroy us
And violent tempest doth batter us
And troubles us with living fire and blood,
290 Oppresses, subdues, conquers, ruins us!
And you, infamous men of Acoma,
Shall be most horribly punished,⁶
With such penalty as 'tis well should come
Upon such coward spirits as yours are.
295 And you, vile Zutacapán, who have been
The instrument of such calamity,
Know that for you there are waiting, prepared,
Most cruel beatings, cruel punishments,
For this evil and this shameful disgrace,
300 And are entrusted to most fearsome⁷ gods,
Who for your monstrous crimes will give to you
A very late and profitless reward."
Having said this, the two did separate.
Gicombo made his way to his own house,
305 Which was enveloped in smoke and live flames,
And, forcing passage through the hostile coals
And embers, and through leaping flames,
He came into the very room where was

---

21. Bruto y Casio se suicidaron, el primero echándose sobre su
arma, el segundo mandando que otro le atravesara, después de la
batalla de Filipo contra Julio César. Plutarco, entre otros muchos
historiadores y poetas romanos, narra los hechos.
22. Cebil = civil, vil, despreciable.
23. Probable errata del original por "justos."

5. Both Brutus and Cassius committed suicide after being defeated
by Caesar. The first running himself through, the second having an
aide do it for him. The details can be seen in Plutarch under the
appropriate biographies.
6. This is the closest that Villagrá comes to referring to the
punishment eventually meted out to the surviving adult males.
7. Villagrá has *sustos*, which may well by an errata for *justos*, just.

Su más querida esposa lamentando,
Con gran suma de dueñas y donzellas,
Que boqui abiertas todas desfogaban
Aliento calidíssimo del pecho
Y en las paredes tristes besos daban.
Y entrando dentro no le fue possible,
Por los confusos gritos y lamentos
Y el humo espeso que tendido estaba,
Dar con ella, y assí, por esta causa,
Tomó la puerta porque todas juntas
Allí se consumasen y abrasasen.
Y acercándose el fuego embravecido
Al mísero palacio, sin consuelo
Llegó en busca del bárbaro el Sargento
Con vna buena esquadra de guerreros,
Y como el bruto alárabe le vido
Para él alzó los ojos encendidos
Y en muy rabiosa cólera deshechos.
Qual corajoso jabalí cercado
De animosos lebreles y sabuesos,
Tascando la espumosa boca apriessa,
Con el colmillo corvo amenazando,
Assí el General bravo se mostraba,
Obiando la salida a los que estaban
Dentro del aposento peligroso.
Y assomando Luzcoija el rostro bello,
Como aquéllos que toman el atajo
Por abreviar el curso del camino,
Assí la pobre bárbara, afligida,
Sugetó la espaciosa y ancha frente
Al rigor de la maza poderosa
Que los dos más hermosos ojos bellos
Le hizo rebentar del duro casco.
Nunca se vio en solícito montero
Contento semejante cuando tiene
La codiciosa caza ya rendida
Como el que el bárbaro tomó teniendo
A su querida prenda ya sugeta
Y de todos sentidos ya privada.
Viendo, pues, el Sargento la braveza
Del General valiente riguroso,
Con fuerza de promesas y razones
Instó por hazer dél vn fiel amigo,
Dándole la palabra de soldado
Y fee de caballero bien nacido
De reduzir sus causas de manera
Que él solo gobernase aquella fuerza
Por vuestra Magestad, sin que otro alguno,
Más que don Iuan, en ella le mandase.
Y qual si fuera más que viva brasa

His most beloved wife, she lamenting
310 With a great store of matrons and maidens
Who, openmouthed, were all gasping
Most heated breath out of their lungs
And implanting sad kisses on the wall.
As he entered, it was impossible
315 Amid the confused cries and lamentings
And the thick smoke that hovered over all,
For him to find her, and because of this
He held the doorway so that all of them
Might there consume and be burnt up.
320 As the fire, gaining strength, approached
The miserable palace, unconsoled,
The Sergeant came in search of the barbarian
With a good squadron of our warriors,
And when the brute Arabian saw him
325 He fixed his eyes on him, inflamed with rage
And violent with insane anger.
Like a ferocious boar hemmed in
By speedy greyhounds and foxhounds,
Grinding foam freely from his mouth
330 And threatening with his curving tusks,
Thus did the General display his rage,
Obstructing the exit for those who were
Within that perilous dwelling.
And Luzcoija's beauteous face showing,
335 Like those who go by a shortcut
To shorten the course of the road,
So the poor, afflicted savage
Offered her broad, spacious forehead
To the force of the powerful mace
340 That caused her two most beauteous eyes
To spring from out her solid skull.
Never was seen in the eager hunter
Greater content when he possessed
His longed-for game, already caught,
345 Than this barbarian had having
Now quite destroyed his dearest pledge
And deprived her of all feeling.
The Sergeant, then, seeing the hardihood
Of that valiant, stern General,
350 Attempted to make a true friend of him
By dint of promises and reasoning,
Giving to him his word as a soldier
And faith as cavalier of noble birth
To settle his affairs in such fashion
355 That he alone should govern that fortress
For your Majesty, and no other one
Except Don Juan should give commands in it.
As he himself had been a living coal,

Que al tiempo de morirse y apagarse
Enciende más su luz y la descubre,
Assí el furioso ydólatra sangriento,
Risueño y al desgaire, le responde:
"Ya no me puedes dar mayor disgusto
Que vida, estando aquesta ya difunta.[24]
Mas si queréis hazerme vn buen partido,
Dejadme combatir con seys o siete,
Los mejores soldados de tu campo,
Y mátame tú luego, que no es justo
Negar este partido tan pequeño
A mí, que ves ya tan de partida.
Y más haré por ti, pues ves que es fuerza
Que todas éstas mueran abrasadas,
Que salgan todas libres deste incendio,
Sin que vna sola quede por mi cuenta."
Y viendo aquesta causa mal parada
Por estas y otras cosas que passaron,
Mandó que Simón Pérez le tirase,
Dándose mucha priessa, vn buen valazo,
Y, sin que fuesse visto ni entendido,
Dio con el pobre General en tierra,
En fea amarillez el rostro embuelto.
Y luego que acabó y quedó difunto,
Atónitas las bárbaras que tuvo,
Abochornadas, casi sin sentido,
Vertiendo arroyos de sudor hirviendo,
Abiertos todos los cerrados poros
Y las fogosas bocas y narizes,
Satisfaciéndose de sólo el ayre,
A grande priessa todas escaparon.
Y porque el bravo Bempol me da priessa,
Será bien, gran señor, desocuparme
Por ver aquel diabólico destino
Que llevó quando quiso desasirse
Deste difunto pobre y dividirse.[25]

24. Se refiere a Luzcoija.
25. Se refiere al cuerpo.

360 Which at its time of dying, going out,
Doth kindle its light higher and show it,
The furious, bloody idolater,
Smiling disdainfully, thus replied to him:
"You now can give me no greater sorrow
365 Than life, this woman being now dead.
But if you wish to do me a favor,
Then allow me to fight with six or seven
Of the best soldiers found within your camp,
And then kill me yourself, for 'tis unjust
370 To refuse such a trifling favor
To me whom you see now so bound for death.
I shall do more for you, as you must see
That all these women must be burnt,
Let them all be freed from this fire
And not one of them stay on my account."
375 Seeing that his cause was hopeless,
By this and other things which had happened,
He ordered Simón Pérez to shoot him
Right quickly and with certain aim,
And, without being seen nor understood,
380 He struck the unhappy General to the earth,
His face all tainted in ugly yellow.
When he had ended and was quite lifeless,
Those savage women, amazed, whom he kept
In killing heat, almost unconscious,
385 Pouring out streams of sweat, boiling,
All their closed pores now open wide
And their hot mouths and their nostrils
Being satisfied by air alone,
Did then escape in greatest haste.
390 And since brave Bempol hastens me,
It would be well, lord, I break off
To see that diabolic fate
Which he had when he chose to part
From this dead man and go his way.

Canto Treinta y Tres

DEL MISERABLE FIN QVE TUVO BEMPOL Y DE
OTROS que con él sus días acabaron, y del sentimiento que
hizo el Sargento mayor, buscando los güessos de su hermano.

IOS nos libre del áspero castigo

Con que su gran grandeza nos lastima,

Lebantando su mano poderosa
Para que como réprobos sintamos
Mal del gran bien y bien del mal que es grande,
Porque apenas abremos allegado
A fuerte tan perdida y desdichada
Quando de todo punto zabullidos
En el abismo y centro nos hallemos
De todo lo que es vltima miseria,
Dolor, tristeza y vltimo quebranto.[1]
Dexemos las historias que están llenas
De mil sucessos tristes ya passados
Y dígalo este ydólatra perdido,
Suelto, desamparado y ya dexado
De tan santa, divina y alta mano,
¿Quál es el paradero en que le vemos?
¡O gran bondad inmensa, no permitas,
Por tus llagas rasgadas, tal castigo,
Por los que tu ley santa professamos!
Que si los que andan fuera del rebaño
Merecen, mi señor, los desampares,
Otros castigos tiene tu justicia
Que pueden molestarnos y afligirnos
Y no el que aqueste mísero padece,
Cuia desdicha, si queréis notarla,
Bolved, Rey poderoso, allí los ojos.[2]
Mirad al pobre Bempol desdichado
Que está sobre aquel risco temeroso,
Desde cuia alta cumbre lebantada
Assí comienza el triste a despedirse:
"Oy me da ya reposo mi desdicha,
Si es que desdicha puede dar sossiego
Al que a sus pies se rinde zozobrado,
Y mi temprana muerte me apareja
Seguro y dulze puerto con alibio,
Si es que el morir también puede alibiarme

---

1. Contrasta la altura de Acoma con el abismo, espiritual,
aleccionador, de lo que va a referir.
2. Villagrá emplea aquí la actualización espacial (allí), técnica
asociada, como llamada de atención al público, con los juglares y,
después, con cantores de romances.

Canto XXXIII

Of the miserable end of Bempol and of others who ended their
days with him, and of the sorrow of the Sergeant Major
seeking the bones of his brother.

AY God free us from the harsh
    punishment
With which His great omnipotence doth
    punish us,
His powerful hand being uplifted
That we may feel, as sinful men,
5 Evil in great good and good in great evil,
For hardly will we have approached
A fort so ruinous, unfortunate,
When we are plunged entirely
Into the abyss and center of it all,
10 Of all that is total misery,
Grief, sadness, ultimate destruction.
Let's leave the histories, so full
Of thousand sad events, now done,
And let us look at this ruined heathen,
15 Loosed, unshielded, now abandoned
By so holy, divine, and lofty hand.
What is the situation in which we find him?
O great and immense Good, do permit not
Such punishment, for grace of Your deep wounds,
20 For us who do profess Your holy laws!
But if those who do wander from the fold
Deserve, O Lord, abandonment,
Thy justice has yet other punishments
That can trouble and afflict us
25 And not the one which that poor wretch suffers,
Whose misfortune, if you would observe it,
Turn your eyes there,[1] O powerful King,
And see poor Bempol, miserable,
Who stands upon that dread declivity
30 From off whose high and towering top
He early made his farewell thus:
"Today my misfortune gives me repose,
If misfortune can give tranquility
To one who at its feet surrenders, crushed,
35 And my too-early death prepares
A safe and pleasant harbor of relief,
If death indeed can relieve me

---

1. Villagrá again employs the spatal actualization featured by the
epic's oral narrative tradition.

De tan inorme carga como llevo.
Y sólo con perpetua sepultura
Saliendo, como espero, desta afrenta,
Pueden faltarme obsequias funerales
Si, como estoy determinado, siembro
Las míseras cenizas, ya perdidas,
Deste triste mortal corpóreo velo,[3]
Vertiéndolas sin lástima, pues puedo
Desta tan alta cumbre despeñarme.
Y, cerrando el postrer día de mi vida,
No faltará quien a mi dulze patria,
Con esta sin ventura nueva, rompa
El ayre[4] en vano porque presto llegue
A las orejas tristes, miserables,
De aquélla que, por corta y mala suerte,
Le cupo aqueste pobre por esposo.
Y cada qual, sintiendo con tristeza
O sobra de alegría y de contento,
De mi vltimo fin triste, miserable,
Dirá lo que quisiere y le agradare;
Y luego que esto se aya ventilado,
Después que el Sol por doze Lunas corra,
Ya no abrá quien de mí jamás se acuerde.
Que esto es muy cierto quando el tiempo corre,
Que se enjugan las lágrimas caudales[5]
Y cansan los suspiros más ansiosos
Y acaban los dolores que se sufren
Por aquéllos que fueron más amigos,
Más padres, más hermanos, más parientes,
Más queridos, más hijos y más deudos,
Más amparo, consuelo y más firmeza
De buenos y caríssimos maridos.
¡O Acoma, a qué Dios has ofendido
O por qué causa assí los altos dioses
Quieren contra nosotros enojarse!
¿Súfrese que tal yra y tal corage
Muestren dioses, y más contra vna fuerza
Que es inmortal, qual ellos inmortales,
Y en las cosas de guerra y preheminencia
Tan insigne, tan fuerte y poderosa
Que si sus fuerzas no nos contrastaran
Fuera cosa muy fácil el hazerse
De todo el mundo vniversal señora?[6]

From such enormous burden as I bear.
And by perpetual burial alone

40   Escaping, as I hope, from this disgrace,
I may lack funeral obsequies
If, as I am resolved, I sow
The miserable ashes, all unseen,
Of this sad, mortal, and corporeal veil,[2]

45   Without regret destroying them, for I
Can cast myself from this high peak.
And, closing thus the last day of my life,
I shall not lack someone in my dear land
To rend, at this new misfortune,

50   The air in vain[3] so soon 'twill come
Unto the grieving and unhappy ears
Of her who through perverse and evil fate
Must needs have this wretch as her spouse.
And each one hearing, with sadness

55   Or more of joy and of content,
Of my sad, miserable, final end,
Say what he will and what he please;
And after this has been well-aired,
After the sun goes through twelve moons,

60   No one will ever think of me.
For this is very true: as time goes by
The flowing tears are all dried up
And the most bitter sighs do tire,
So end sorrows which are endured

65   For those who were our greatest friends,
Our parents, brothers, relatives
Most loved, our children, dear kinsmen,
Protectors, counselors, and the strongest ties
Of dearest and most loved spouses.

70   O Acoma, what god have you defied,
What reason is there that the lofty gods
Should wish to be angered at us!
Can it be gods would show such rage
And fury, more so toward a fortress

75   As immortal even as the gods
And in the things of war and dominance
So famous and so strong and powerful
That if their forces had not opposed us
It would have been easy to make itself

80   The universal mistress of the world?[4]

3. Se refiere al cuerpo, cobertura ("velo") efímera del alma.
4. Difícil determinar si con "rompa el ayre" quiere decir Villagrá, poéticamente, "herir el aire," es decir, lamentarse; o si con esa expresión quiere dar sentido de velocidad, "atravesando el aire."
5. Caudales = abundantes.
6. La hipérbole respecto a las posibilidades del enemigo parece eco de la propuesta conquista de España por los araucanos en Ercilla, *La araucana* I, 8.

2. The body is viewed as a temporary veil covering the soul.
3. It is difficult to determine whether the image of "rending the air" is to be interpreted as "shouting through it" or "racing through it."
4. This hyperbole regarding the potential of Acoma echoes the Araucanian threat of conquering Spain. See Ercilla, *La araucana* VIII.

Mas como dizen que en los graves males
Ay consuelo si muchos le padecen,
Si aquésta es regla cierta, que consuelan,
¿Cómo no vivo agora consolado?"
Y estando assí hablando y replicando,
Para él enderezaron, desbalidas,
Cosa de diez donzellas con sus madres,
Y atónitas, corriendo en competencia,
Para el triste se fueron acercando.
Como suelen las simples mariposas
Quando a la lumbre vemos que se acercan
Y alegres se abalanzan y se apegan
Y allí fenecen todas abrasadas,
Assí, desalentadas, se apegaron
Las míseras al mísero afligido,
A quien con alma y corazón clamaban,
Con gran suma de lágrimas amargas,
Sollozos y terníssimos suspiros,
Que quisiesse de tanto afán librarlas,
Llevándolas, perdidas, a la parte
Que fuesse de su gusto, y que juraban
De no desampararle por trabajos,
Angustias y miserias que viniessen
Y por más que fortuna descargase
Con poderosos golpes esforzados
Su riguroso brazo y las truxesse
Debajo de su rueda rebolcadas;
Y si no, que les diesse compañía
Con quien todas pudiessen escaparse.
Y para más moverle a sus clamores
Delante le pusieron vna hija
Que de su patria trujo quando vino,
Por gusto de Gicombo, a aquella fuerza.
La qual acaso quiso entremeterse,
Con el bravo temor y sobresalto,
Con las demás donzellas que clamaban,
Y poniendo la vista en todas ellas,
Clavola y la detuvo en sóla aquélla
Que era la misma lumbre de sus ojos
Y de tan tierna edad que no tenía
Diez miserables años bien cumplidos.[7]
Y qual si fuera firme y alta roca
En el ancho mar puesta y assentada,
Que con su ynorme peso y grave assiento
Al tempestuoso mar y a todos vientos
Con gran fuerza resiste y se antepone,

But as they say that in great sufferings
There is relief if many suffer them,
If this is true, that they console,
Why live I now beyond consolation?"
85 As he was speaking, answering himself,
Some ten maidens with their mothers,
Being unprotected, came toward him
And running swift, in competition,
They did approach the wretched man.
90 As do the simple butterflies
When we see them approach the fire
And fly in happily and of their choice
And there they all die in the flames,
Thus these poor things attached themselves,
95 All breathless, to that miserable man,
And him they begged with heart and soul
And with great store of bitter tears,
With sobs and with most tender sighs,
That he would please to free them from distress,
100 Taking them, lost, unto what place
Might be his pleasure, and they swore
They would not leave him through trials
Or anguish or though misery might come,
However fortune might discharge
105 Its powerful heavy blows on them
With rigorous arm or might hurl them
All crushed beneath its whirling wheel;
And, if not, to offer them an escort
With whom they might all escape.
110 And better to move him to their appeals,
They set before him his daughter,
Whom he had brought from his country
When he came to this fort for Gicombo's pleasure.
Now she, by chance, had been involved,
115 Amid the dreadful fear and sudden dread,
Among the other damsels pleading there.
He, casting his glance over them,
Did halt and fix it upon her alone
Who was the very apple of his eye,
120 Of age so tender that she had not yet
Completed quite ten miserable years.
And like a firm and lofty rock
Set firm and fixed in the wide sea,
Which, with enormous weight and strength,
125 Resists most forcefully and overcomes
The strong sea and all the winds,

7. Este uso de la vida de la hija para afectar la decisión del padre
hace eco del tema de Guzmán el Bueno en la historia de la
Reconquista. La reacción heroica se la atribuye Villagrá, aquí, al
enemigo.

Assí, contraviniendo a su plegaria,
Furioso, desta suerte les responde:
"Mezquinas de vosotras, miserables,
Si es fuerza que salgáis de aquesta vida,
¿Quál compañía podéis tomar que os sea
Más que ésta que tenéis aventajada,
Y dónde queréis que no os espere
Mayor quebranto que éste que os aflige?"
Con cuio susto[8] absorto y elebado,
Quedó pasmado y fuera de sentido,
Hiriendo con la vista aguda y brava
Los lebantados Cielos, corajoso,
Con vna y otra punta[9] que embiaba.
Y assiendo a la muchacha por el brazo,
Con la pobre se despeñó, diziendo:
"Si queréis libre libertad, seguidme."
Y qual si fueran simples ovejuelas
Que viendo se abalanza y se despeña
El que es manso cencerro y que las guía,
Que todas tras dél vemos arrojarse
Sin género de miedo ni rezelo,
Assí, todas se fueron despeñando,
Dando fin a sus días miserables,
Y llorando su grande desbentura
Para el segundo albergue caminaron,
Que ocupan, según dize el gran lombardo,[10]
Allá en los calabozos del infierno
Los que sin merecer alguna culpa
De su voluntad fueron omicidas
De sus infames almas desdichadas.
Y como el mismo Héroe se lamenta,
Quánto mejor les fuera ya en la vida,
De que los pobres tristes se privaron,
Sufrir sin libertad duros trabajos.
Mas como él mismo dize y nos enseña,
Por orden de los hados se les veda,
Y es viva Fe cathólica inviolable
Que en miserable llanto permanezcan.
Passado lo que abemos referido,
Luego la veloz fama fue corriendo,
Llevando aquella amarga y triste nueva
A la afligida madre de Gicombo,
Cuio vital calor sus flamos[11] güessos

He there refused to grant their prayer,
Replying furiously to them thus:[5]
"Ye miserable, petty minded things,
If ye must needs depart from out this life   130
What company can ye take that will be
Of more advantage than this that ye have,
And where expect ye not to find
Far greater sorrows than afflict ye here?"
With which great effort, absorbed and uplifted,   135
He stood benumbed and quite beside himself,
Striking, with glances keen and sharp,
The lofty heavens, much enraged,
With the many arrows that he lofted.[6]
And then, seizing his daughter by the arm,   140
He hurled himself down with her, crying out:
"If you wish proper freedom, follow me!"
They, as if they were simple sheep
Who seeing that their gentle bellwether,
Which guides them, ventures on and falls headlong,   145
We see all hurl themselves after
Without a sig.. of fear or suspicion,
Did all hurl themselves down likewise
And so ended their miserable days.
Weeping their crushing misfortune   150
They went unto that second dwelling place,
Peopled, as the great Lombard[7] has declared,
There in the Inferno's dungeons,
By those who, deserving no blame,
Were murderers through their own wills   155
Of their own damned, unhappy souls.
And, as the same hero laments,
How much better it were if in this life,
Which these poor wretches cast away,
They had borne without ransom heavy tasks.   160
But as he also says, and teaches us,
It is forbid by order of the fates,
And is inviolable universal[8] faith
That they remain in miserable weeping.
What we have told having been done,   165
Immediately swift rumor went forth,
Taking that bitter and sad news
To the grieving mother of Gicombo,
Whose vital heat from flaming limbs

---

8. Susto = crisis nerviosa.

9. Punta = flecha; vale por "mirada."

10. Villagrá, refiriéndose a Dante, *Infierno* XIII usa "lombardo" en sentido genérico de italiano.

11. Difícil determinar si el antecedente es Gicombo o su madre. Posible errata del original por "flameos" (encendidos), en un caso, o "flacos" en el otro.

5. The bringing forth of the child to influence the father's decision, availing naught, recalls the prominent Guzmán el Bueno topos from Spanish reconquest history. It is interesting that Villagrá should ascribe it here to the great Indian warrior.

6. The metaphor (looks/arrows) underscores the rage indicated.

7. The reference is to Dante (*Inferno* XIII), although Lombard, generic for Italian, is used.

8. Curtis translates Villagrá's *catolica* etymologically rather than with reference to a specific religion.

Por todas partes fue desamparando.
Y afligida del gran dolor causado
De las atrozes muertes desdichadas
De su muy dulze hijo y cara nuera
Y del pobre marido que tenía,
Sin sentido salió la miserable
Dando terriblísimos aullidos,
Mesando fuertemente sus cabellos,
Rompiendo por las armas Castellanas
Sin ningún pabor, miedo ni rezelo,
Y rasgando los ayres con querrellas,
Sentida de dolor, assí dezía:
"Desdichada de mí, triste, afligida,
Miserable, sin hijo y sin marido,
Ya güérfana y también desamparada
De aquestas dulzes prendas[12] que tenía.
Dezid, Castillas, pues que estáis tan cerca
Que si[13] hablar siquiera con su madre
No dio lugar al hijo malogrado,[14]
¿Dónde está la belleza de Luzcoija
Que a mi triste vejez entretenía?
¿Este es el galardón que yo esperaba
Quando más esperé mi buena suerte,
Pensando, dulzes hijos, de gozaros?
¡O Castillas, si por ventura os mueve
Aquesta miserable desdichada,
Pido que me quitéis aquí la vida!
Mas en lo que yo puedo y tengo mano,
¿De qué me sirve seros importuna?"
Y qual gran marinero o diestro buzo,[15]
Que de la lebantada y alta entena,[16]
Bueltas las duras plantas hazia arriba,
Al profundo del ancho mar se inclina,
Assí la triste bárbara, furiosa,
Desde aquel lebantado y alto muro
Inclinó, con gran rabia y con despecho,
La muy blanca cabeza desgreñada,
Dexándose yr a pique y sin remedio
A los bravos profundos infernales,
Vnico alberque, centro y paradero
De todos los que aquí se despeñaron.
En esto, salió el noble viejo Chumpo,
Como quien la paz siempre pretendía,
A ponerse en las manos del Sargento.

170 Was everywhere disappearing.
And downcast at the heavy sorrow caused
By the terrible and unhappy deaths
Of her sweet son and dear daughter-in-law,
And of her poor old husband, moreover,
175 The miserable woman sallied forth,
Half senseless, giving terrible outcries
And tearing her hair fearfully,
Bursting through the Castilian ranks
Without a tremor or a fear
180 And rending the air with her screams,
Broken with sorrow she sadly cried out:
"Ah, woe is me, unhappy, afflicted,
Childless and husbandless and miserable,
Now orphaned and unprotected as well
185 By those dear pledges which I had![9]
Tell me, Castilians, since you are so near
There was no time for my unhappy son
To even speak with his mother,[10]
Where is the beauty of Luzcoija
190 Which so gladdened my sad old age?
This is the recompense I waited for
When I did most expect a happy lot,
Thinking, sweet children, to have joy in you?
O ye Castilians, if by chance you are
195 Moved by this miserable, unhappy wretch,
I beg you here to take away my life!
But in that which I can well do myself
What gain I in imploring you?"
Then, like great mariner or skilled diver
200 Who from the lofty lateen yard,
Turning upward his hardened soles,
Dives to the depths of the wide sea,
This sad and maddened barbarian
From the most high and lofty wall
205 Did bend in madness of distress
Her aged, white disheveled head
And let herself go down, beyond all hope,
Into the fearful depths of hell,
The only halting place and home
210 Of all those who cast themselves down.
Now came the noble old Chumpo,
Who had always striven for peace,
To place himself in the good Sergeant's hands.

12. Eco del verso garcilasiano tan repetido en la época.
13. Probable errata del original por "ni."
14. Esta madre que lamenta no haberse despedido del hijo recuerda a Virgilio, *Eneida* IX, 640–45.
15. Buzo = el que trabaja debajo del agua.
16. Entena = mástil.

9. This expression is an echo of Garcilaso's famous verse, the most cited in Spanish literature.
10. This mother, lamenting not having received her dead son's farewell, recalls a similar passage from Virgil, the *Aeneid* IX, 640–45.

Gibado[17] de vejez, las piernas corbas,
Secos los brazos y la piel pegada
A sóla la ossamenta que tenía,
Ayudado de vn pobre caiadillo
Sobre que el flaco cuerpo sustentaba
Y puesto en su presencia, temeroso,
Temblando con la fuerza de los años,
Assí esforzó la débil voz cansada:
"Hijo gracioso,[18] el Cielo me es testigo,
Y esta sangre que ves aquí vertida,
Que nunca, por mí, fuera derramada
Si Zutacapán sólo se arrimara
A mi voto, qual yo, señor, me arrimo
A aquesta vara tierna, quebradiza,
Que treinta vezes han los campos dado
De nuevo flores y continuo
A siempre mi flaqueza sustentado . . ."
Y luego que esto dixo, enternecido
Y en lastimosas lágrimas deshecho,
Prosiguió con su plática, diziendo:
"Para sólo venir a lastimarme,
Con desdicha tan grande como veo,
Por estas tristes almas miserables.
Aflígenme sus cuerpos destrozados
Y de sus mismos perros ya comidos.
Duélenme sus abuelos y sus padres
Y más sus visabuelos, que nacieron
Quando, triste, nací, para quedarme
A sólo ser testigo de la sangre,
Muertes y gran destrozo que han sufrido
Todos éstos que están aquí tendidos,
Reliquias de los tristes que han passado,
Que aunque es possible sepan el estrago
Allá donde sus almas se recojan,
No es tan grande el dolor y sentimiento
Quanto recibe el pobre miserable
Que por sus proprios ojos ve las llagas
Que aquí vemos abiertas y rasgadas
Por querer vn traidor solo llevarlos
A sus vanos intentos, porque quiso
Ser él solo señor de aquesta fuerza.
Y por querer por fuerza lebantarse,
Assí te está por fuerza ya rendido,
Y yo también lo estoi, señor, y advierte
Que assí, como él, rendido y afrentado
En público palenque,[19] y ofendido."

215
220
225
230
235
240
245
250
255

Bent down with age, his legs crooked,
His arms dried up, his skin shriveled
Upon the bony frame of him,
Helped on by a poor shepherd's crook,
Which held up his weak, aged frame,
And in his presence, all fearful
And trembling with his weight of years,
He thus spoke, in a feeble, weary, voice:
"Most gracious son, Heaven is my witness,
And this blood which you see shed here,
That, for me, it would never have been spilled
Had Zutacapán only given support
Unto my vote as I, lord, have sought support
Of this most fragile tender rod
That, while the fields thirty times have bred
New flowers anew, has so continually,
Always, supported my weakness . . ."
Now when he said this, being much saddened,
Dissolved in sorrowful weeping
He continued his speech, saying:
"Only to come to be thus grieved
With such great evils as I see
Among these sad and miserable souls.
I grieve for their bodies destroyed
And eaten now by their own dogs.
I grieve for their parents and grandparents,
Their great-grandparents, too, for they were born
When I, wretched, was born but to remain
To be the only witness of the blood,
The deaths, the great destruction, they suffered,
All these who are lying dead here,
The relics of those sad ones who are gone,
For though 'tis possible they know the woe
There where their sad souls do gather,
Their sorrow and grief is yet not so great
As that of this poor, miserable wretch
Who sees with his own eyes the wounds
That we see here, open and deeply gashed,
Merely because a traitor wished to carry them
To his vain purposes, because he wished
To be the only lord of this fortress.
And, wishing to exalt himself through force,
He now, through force, surrenders unto you,
And I also, my lord, and, you may note,
That, like him, surrendered and dishonored
In a public arena and humbled."

17. Gibado = corcovado.
18. Gracioso = atractivo, airoso. Es posible que Villagra le dé el
sentido a esta palabra, dadas las circunstancias, de "repartidor de
gracias o mercedes."
19. Palenque = conjunto de tablas levantado para hechos públicos.

Cuia cabeza estuvo ya sugeta
Y a merced de la espada rigurosa
Que allí pudo acabarle y deshazerle
Y vida quiso darle. Es cosa cierta,
Y en lides de importancia bien probada,
Que muerto allí quedó, pues muerta dexa
La honrra, el ser, valor y todo quanto
Lebanta al buen soldado y le abilita
Y en cosas de la guerra le acridita.
Y teniendo, qual suelen los mendigos,
Los flacos brazos secos algo abiertos,
Arrodillarse quiso a su presencia.
Y convertido de áspero en clemente,
Su ánimo benigno allí apercibe
Y con palabras dulzes, regaladas,
Salidas sin sospecha ni rebozo
De vn blando corazón y entrañas tiernas,
Echándole los brazos, el Sargento
En peso le tomó y con gran respecto
Abrazado le tuvo por buen rato.
Y después que con mucho amor le dixo
Razones y palabras de consuelo,
Con que el mísero viejo lastimado
Reprimió la vertiente de sus ojos,
Pidiole el noble joben que le diesse
Aquel illustre cuerpo que mataron
Del caro hermano y caros compañeros.
Y abiendo con grandíssimo cuidado
Puesto en esto grande diligencia,
Venimos a saber cómo, en la parte
Que vino a rendir cada qual su vida,
En el mismo lugar, a pura fuerza
De palos y pedradas que cargaron,
En blanda y tierna masa combirtieron
Su miserable carne con los güessos,
Y en confusso montón los recogieron.
Y en vna gran hoguera, lebantada
Con pujanza de leños que arrimaron,
Los rayos del Sol fueron embolviendo
En vna obscura sombra temerosa,
Y en este funeral y triste incendio,
Alegres de aquel hecho que acabaron,
Dando altíssimos gritos y alaridos,
Assí, sin distinción, honor ni cuenta
Los pobres Castellanos arrojaron
Enmedio de las llamas portentosas.
Y por honrra del Dios de las batallas
Con ellos presentaron y ofrecieron
Muy ricas mantas, plumas y pellicos,
Con gran chacota, risa y algazara
De la plebeia gente que ofrecía

260 His head is now bowed lowly down
And at the mercy of the horrid sword
That there may end his days and destroy him,
And chose to give him life. It is certain,
And by important battles very well proved,
265 He was as dead, for he leaves dead
His honor, being, and all that
Lifts up the good soldier, makes him skillful,
And in affairs of war gives him credit.
Then he, extending, as the beggars do,
270 His feeble arms, withered, somewhat apart,
He wished to kneel in his presence.
Changed from asperity into clemency
His benign will he there prepares,
And with words sweet and comforting,
275 Pronounced without suspicion or deceit
From a soft heart and tender sensibilities,
The Sergeant, giving him his hands,
Bore up his weight and, with greatest respect,
Held him embraced for a good space of time.
280 And afterward he lovingly gave him
Reasons and words for consolation,
At which the miserable, sad old man
Did stanch the torrent from his eyes.
The noble youth asked to be given
285 That famous body they had killed
Of his dear brother and dear companions.
And having, with the greatest care, then given
Attention to this point with highest diligence,
We came to know how in the place
290 Where each one had given up his life
In that same place, by the mere force
Of logs and rocks which they had thrown on him,
They had converted to a viscid mass
His miserable flesh and bones
295 And then collected them in one heaped mass.
And by a great bonfire which they had built
With a huge pile of logs which they threw on,
They did obscure the clear rays of the sun
Within a very dark and fearsome cloud.
300 In this funereal and sorry blaze,
Happy at that deed, just finished,
Giving their loudest cries and shouts,
Without distinction, honor, nor account,
They hurled the poor Castilian dead
305 Into the midst of those portentous flames.
To honor the god of battles,
With them they presented as offerings
Rich blankets, feathers, and jackets,
With noisy mirth, laughter, and loud hurrahs
310 Of the plebeian folk, who also gave

También al invencible Dios furioso	To the invincible and furious god
Grande suma de flechas y macanas,	Great store of arrows and of swords,
Arcos, bastones, mazas y carcages,	Bows, war clubs, maces, and quivers,
Contentos de que el fuego consumiesse	Contented since the fire consumed
Los miserables cuerpos baptizados.	The miserable baptized corpses.
Sabido ya el fin triste, miserable,	Now that we knew the sad and grievous end
De nuestros infelices compañeros,	Of our unhappy companions,
Pedímosles que al puesto nos llevasen	We asked them straight to take us to the place
Donde al Maese de campo dieron muerte,	Where they had dealt the Army Master death,
Sobre el qual, sin tardanza, nos pusieron,	And they did take us there without delay,
Y en él tan gran manchón de sangre vimos	And there we saw as large a stain of blood
Que dos tendidas brazas ocupaba.[20]	As two extended arms might well compass.[11]
Vista por el Sargento desdichado	The unfortunate Sergeant having seen
La sangre del hermano ya difunto,	The blood of his dear brother, now deceased,
Aunque ya fría, elada y denegrida,	Though it was now congealed and all turned black,
Sin ningún fuego comenzó a hervirle	Without fire he did yet begin to feel
En lo más hondo de su tierno pecho,	A seething deep in his sensitive heart,
Y luego al mismo punto se le puso	And at the same time there did come
Vn grosíssimo ñudo atravesado,	A choking lump that quite filled up
A la pobre garganta bien assido,	His grieving throat and held it fast,
Y los enjutos ojos combertidos	And his austere eyes then were changed
En dos mares sin fondo derramaban	Into two boundless seas and shed
Mil arroyos de lágrimas caudales,	A thousand rivulets of copious tears,
Con que a doloroso y tierno llanto	With which to dolorous and sad weeping
A todos nos movía y lebantaba.	He moved us and did bring us all.
Y no bastando nadie a detenerle,	As no one had the strength to restrain him,
Por enmedio de todos fue rompiendo	He then burst through the midst of all
Y tendiéndose encima de la mancha,	And throwing himself on the stain,
Gimiendo amargamente, rebentaba[21]	Groaning most bitterly, he did give way
Sobre la triste sangre ya vertida.	To grief for the sad blood spilled there.
Y después que por vna larga pieza	And after he for a long period
Bañó aquel fuerte passo[22] de amargura,	Bathed that hard place of bitterness,
Y luego que el dolor azerbo y duro	And when his keen and sharp sorrow
Con gran dificultad abrió la puerta	Had with great difficulty made a way
A la pobre garganta fatigada,	To his much grieved and overburdened throat,
Assí empezó, afligido, a lastimarse:	He thus began to wail his affliction:
"No era aquéste el fin que yo esperaba	"This was no end that I was hoping for
Quando a tantos trabajos y miserias	When for such labors and for such miseries
Quisimos ofrecernos y entregarnos.	We wished to offer ourselves and enlist,
Porque en aquellos tiempos bien pensaba,	For in those times I truly thought,
Qual soldado nobel, pobre, bisoño,	Like a new soldier, a recruit,
Que los dos adquiriéramos gran fama,	That we two should acquire great fame
Prometiéndonos suertes muy honrrosas,	And promised us right honorable lots
Colmadas de victoria y triunfo cierto.	Filled up with victory and sure triumph.
Mas, ¡ay de mí!, que por demás han sido	But woe is me that all to this have come

Line numbers: 315, 320, 325, 330, 335, 340, 345, 350, 355

20. En esto del "manchón de sangre" Villagrá parece seguir muy de cerca a Virgilio, *Eneida* III, 57–60.

21. Rebentaba = reventaba, descargaba su sentimiento.

22. Passo = paso, lugar de encuentro; figuradamente, "passo de amargura," aludiendo a las estaciones de la pasión de Cristo.

11. The description of the blood here parallels that of Virgil, the *Aeneid* III, 57–60.

Mis vanas esperanzas fabricadas,
Pues bullirse la más pequeña hoja
Del más remontado árbol desta vida
Es quererlo quien todo lo gobierna.
Y pensar otra cosa es desatino,
Cuia verdad bien claro me has mostrado,
Señor y hermano mío, anhelando
A muy gloriosos fines onorosos,
Rotos y destroncados por el suelo,
Con medios y principios desdichados.
Y por mejor dezir, fueron dichosos,
Pues que con muerte felix y agradable
Seguro puerto diste a tus cuidados,
Siendo primer primicia que se ofrece
En esta nueva Iglesia Mexicana,[23]
Y no yo, cuia pobre, triste, vida
Al duro hado, fiero y peligroso,
La traigo por momentos sometida.
¡Quién a tu lado fuerte se hallara
Quando la corta vida feneciste,
Aunque el gran furor bárbaro acabara
Aquésta miserable que me queda
Y escusara siquiera lastimarme
Con ver este lugar todo teñido
En la inocente sangre que dejaste
Para mayor quebranto y más tormento
Destos cansados ojos que llegaron
A ver tan gran desdicha y tal estrago!
¡O Acoma, no quiera Dios te impute
Aquella falsa fee y hospicio[24] alebe
Que a mi amado y caro hermano diste
Con tan terrible engaño y trato doble,
Porque esta miserable y dura suerte
Yo solo la causé con graves culpas
Que contra el alto Dios he cometido!
Mas qué digo yo, triste, miserable,
Si es que abías de gustar amarga muerte,
¿Qué más corona y palma lebantada
Que aber venido, hermano, a merecerla
Donde no se les sigue más ventaja
A los que con alegre y bravo triunfo
Cantan la gran victoria que alcanzaron
Que a los vencidos, si sus cuerpos quedan
Enmedio de las armas destrozados?
Y assí es fuerza digan todos fuiste
Muy bienaventurado en tal jornada,

My empty hopes, which I had raised so high,
For when the smallest leaf doth fall
From off the highest tree in this our life
It is the will of Him who governs all.
And to think otherwise is but folly,   360
The truth of which I have been clearly shown
By you, my lord and brother, desirous
Of very glorious and honored ends
Broken and shattered on the ground
By means and beginnings unfortunate.   365
Yet I might better call them fortunate
Since with a happy and agreeable death
You found a secure haven for your cares,
Being the initial first fruit offered
To this new Church of Mexico;[12]   370
Not, unhappily, I, whose poor, sad life
Is borne each moment subject to the call
Of harsh fate, dangerous and fierce.
O, to have been at your strong side
When you ended your too-short life,   375
E'en if the barbarian fury finish
This miserable life which I yet have
And so at least spare me the pain
Of seeing this place all stained thus
With that innocent blood which you have left   380
As greater sorrow and greater torment
For these eyes, tired to have seen
Such great unhappiness and such slaughter!
O Acoma, may God yet not impute to thee
That broken faith and treacherous welcome   385
Which thou didst give my dear, beloved brother
With such fearful deceit and such double-dealing,
For his most miserable and harsh fate
I alone did cause with the heavy faults
Which I against high God have committed!   390
But what do I say, sad, miserable,
If you needs have tasted bitter death,
What higher crown or what more lofty palm
Than to have come, brother, to attain it
Where no more profit has followed   395
To those who with rejoicing and triumph
Sing the great victory they have achieved
Than to the conquered, if their bodies lie
Broken in the midst of their arms?[13]
And so all needs must say you were   400
Most fortunate in such journey

23. El hermano trata al maese de campo de primer mártir, aunque
ya habían muerto algunos frailes en anteriores intentos de cristianizar a
Nuevo México.
24. Hospicio = hospitalidad.

12. Zaldívar suggests his brother as the first martyr in those lands,
although a number of friars had suffered death at the hands of the
Indians over the previous sixty years.
13. The poet can give no higher praise to the defeated Acomans.

Donde no puede ser que la grandeza
De todo el vniverso que gozamos
Pueda darte sepulcro más pomposo
Ni más gallardo y alto enterramiento   405
Que el que en aqueste muro memorable
Quiso la fuerza de Acoma ofrecerte,
A quien yo estimo, tengo y reverencio
Por preciosíssima Ara y Monumento
Donde por tu ley santa, poderosa,   410
Por Dios y por tu Rey, alto, invencible,
A su gran Magestad sacrificaste
El resto de la sangre que tuviste."
Y bolviéndose allí para nosotros,
Algo esforzado, prosiguió, diziendo: 415
"Aquí fue Troia,²⁵ nobles caballeros.
Aquí, por su alto esfuerzo y zelo ardiente
Y por su gran valor, insigne y raro,
Quedará para siempre eternizado
Y por el consiguiente²⁶ conocido,   420
Para que²⁷ el claro nombre que han mostrado
Todos sus mayores y passados."
Y con esto arboló vna Cruz en alto,
Y contritos, llorando, de rodillas
Todos juntos allí nos derribamos   425
Y a la gran Magestad de Dios pedimos
Que de sus pobres almas se doliesse
Y que a su santa gloria les llevase.
Y pues al fin, señor, de la jornada
Y canto postrimero he ya llegado,   430
Quiero parar vn tanto porque pueda
Cantar aquesto poco que me queda.

Where, sure, it cannot be that the entire grandeur
Of all the universe which we enjoy
Can give you more pompous sepulcher
Nor more gallant and lofty burial   405
Than that which in its memorable walls
The fort of Acoma has given you,
Which I esteem, keep, and shall reverence
As altar most precious and monument
Where, for the powerful and holy law,   410
For God and for your great, unconquered King,
To His great Majesty you made the sacrifice
Of all the blood that yet was in your veins."
Now, turning from there to us all,
With some effort he continued to speak: 415
"Here was Troy,¹⁴ noble cavaliers.
Here, for his high effort and ardent zeal,
And for his great valor, famous and rare,
He shall remain forever eternized
And known throughout all later times   420
Continuing the great reputation gained¹⁵
By all his great ancestors and forbears."
He then set up a cross on high
And, contrite, weeping, on our knees,
We all, together, sank down there   425
And asked of God's great Majesty
To take pity on those poor souls
And take them into His sainted glory.
And since, lord, I have now arrived
At end of the journey and last canto,   430
I wish to halt a little that I may
Sing what little remains to me.

25. La expresión ha pasado a ser común para señalar alguna gloria
ya pasada.

26. Por el consiguiente = en virtud de lo antecedente.

27. Salvo errata del original, "para que el"/ "parangón del," la
lectura exige un verbo y hemos de pensar que Villagrá, muy barroco,
lo dio elípticamente, referido al verbo principal que antecede: para que
"quede" (continue, permanezca) el claro nombre, etc.

14. The expression was commonly used to indicate a past glory,
afterward defeated and destroyed.

15. Villagra's text is unclear. Possibly an errata in the original
substituting *para que* for *parangón*, paragon of.

CANTO TREINTA Y QVATRO

COMO SE FVE ABRASANDO LA FUERZA DE ACOMA
y como se halló Zutacapán muerto de vna gran herida, y de los
demás sucessos que fueron sucediendo hasta llevar la nueva de la
victoria al Gobernador, y muertes de Tempal y Cotumbo.

CANSADO del viage trabajoso,
El estandarte santo no vencido
Dexemos ya de Christo allí arbolado.

Reprímanse las lágrimas, pues dexan
Las almas lastimadas y afligidas,
Y vos, Filipo sacro, que escuchando
Mi tosca musa abéys estado atento,
Suplícoos no os canséis, que ya he llegado
Y al prometido puesto soy venido.
Fiado, gran señor, en la excelencia
De vuestra gran grandeza y que, qual padre
Del bélico exercicio trabajoso,
Vn apacible puerto abéys de abrirme,
Con cuio inmenso aliento reforzado
Las velas doi al viento, rebolviendo
Al temeroso incendio, cuias llamas,
Vibrando poderosas y escupiendo
Vivas centellas, chispas y pavesas,[1]
Las lebantadas casas abrasaban.
Notad, señor, aquí, los altos techos,
Paredes, aposentos y sobrados[2]
Que abiertos por mil partes se desgajan
Y súbito a pedazos se derrumban,
Y cómo en vivo fuego y tierra entierran
Sus míseros vezinos, sin que cosa
Quede que no se abrase y se consuma.
Mirad, señor, también, los muchos cuerpos
Que de las altas cumbres del gran muro,
Assí, desesperados, se abalanzan
Y rotos por las peñas, quebrantados,
Hechos menudas piezas y pedazos,
Assí, en el duro suelo se detienen;
Los bárbaros y bárbaras que ardiendo
Están, con sus hijuelos lamentando
Su mísera desgracia y triste suerte.
Con cuias muertes el Sargento,
Movido de piedad y de alto zelo,
Qual suele con tormenta y gran borrasca
Vn gran piloto diestro rebolverse,

1. Pavesas = restos ligeros de la combustión.
2. Sobrados = las partes más altas de la casa.

CANTO XXXIV

How the fortress of Acoma continued to burn and how
Zutacapán was found dead from a great wound, and of other
events which happened until the news of the victory was carried
to the Governor, and of the deaths of Tempal and Cotumbo.

BEING fatigued by this our toilsome voyage,
Let us now leave the holy, unconquered
Standard of Christ, which we had set up
    there.
Hold back your tears for they do leave
5   Your souls grieving and afflicted,
And you, most holy Philip, who have been
Listening to my rude muse thus attentively,
I beg you to tire not, for I have come
And arrived now upon the promised spot.
10 Trusting, great lord, unto the excellence
Of your great greatness, that, as the father
Of all the toilsome exercise of war,
You will open a pleasant door for me,
With which immense encouragement strengthened
15 I spread sail to the wind and thus return
Unto the fearful fire, whose flames,
Trembling with power and spitting forth
Live coals and embers and ashes,
Did rapidly consume the tall houses.
20 Behold, lord, there, the lofty roofs,
The walls, the rooms, the high garrets
Which, open at a thousand points, do break
And suddenly crumble into pieces
And bury, both in living fire and earth,
25 Their miserable neighbors, that nothing
Remains that is not burnt up and consumed.
Behold the many corpses, also, lord,
Who from the lofty summit of the wall
Have hurled themselves down in desperation
30 And, smashed and broken there among the rocks,
Lie there in pieces and in small fragments.
Likewise upon the hard ground there do lie
Barbarian men and women who, burning,
Lament, together with their little babes,
35 Their miserable misfortune and sad fate.
The Sergeant, at this spectacle of death
Being moved with pity and with lofty zeal,
As in the storm and the great hurricane
A great and skillful pilot goes about,

Saltando a todas partes, y esforzarse,
Mandando al marinaje y passajeros
Con vno y otro grito, y assí, juntos,
Con hervorosa priessa se socorren
Y al flaco navichuelo combatido
De la fuerza del mar y viento ayrado,
Entre mil sierras de agua, faborecen,
Assí, esforzando a Chumpo y otros pocos
Bárbaros que las pazes pretendían,
A vozes les promete y assegura,
En fee de caballero, que las vidas
A todos les promete si se abstienen
Del riguroso estrago y crudas muertes
Que assí los miserables se causaban.
No bien el pobre viejo las palabras
De aquel ardiente joben fue advirtiendo
Quando, clamando a vozes, con los pocos
Bárbaros que con él allí assistían,
A todos persuade y encarece,
Haziéndose pedazos con señales
Y muestras, muy de padre, que se abstengan
Y que a tan tristes muertes no se entreguen,
Porque a todos las vidas les promete
Y noble trato a todos assegura,
Sin género de duda ni sospecha,
Encubierta, rebozo o trato aleve.
Y assí como después del rayo vemos
A todos suspenderse mal seguros,
Difuntos ya en color y palpitando
Los vivos corazones dentro el pecho,
Y assí, encogidos, todos rezelosos,
Por vna parte el vno y qual por otra,
Con passos espaciosos,³ van saliendo
A ver si están seguros y el destrozo
Causado de la fuerza ya passada,
Assí salieron muchos, poco a poco,
Alertos, pavorosos, encogidos,
Con passos atentados⁴ y advirtiendo
De no pisar los cuerpos desangrados
De tanto caro amigo y fiel amparo
De aquellos pobres muros que teñidos
Estaban, de su sangre ya bañados.
Assí, temblando, tristes, afligidos,
Por vna y otra parte rodeados
De pálido color y muerte acerba,
Se fueron acercando. Y viendo estaba
El vando Castellano acariciando
A todos sus vezinos y que daban

40 Leaping everywhere with energy,
Ordering mariners and passengers
With many shouts, so that they all
Come to his aid with an impetuous haste
And help the weak and tiny ship, attacked
45 By the sea's mighty force and by the wind
Driven among a thousand watery mountains,
So he, strengthening Chumpo and a few
More savages who did desire peace,
Doth shout out promises and assure them
50 The lives of all if they will but abstain
From the horrid destruction and harsh death
Which these wretches were causing for themselves.
Hardly had the poor old man well noted
The words of that ardent young man when he,
55 Shouting aloud together with the few
Barbarians who were there to help him,
Tries to persuade and recommend to all,
Making the strongest efforts with his signs
And most paternal gestures that they stop
60 And not give themselves to such sorry deaths,
Because their lives are promised them all,
And he assures them of noble treatment
Without a shade of doubt or suspicion,
Deceit, trickery, or double-dealing.
65 As after lightning stroke we all have seen
Everyone in suspense, insecure,
In color like the dead, their fearful hearts
Beating like hammers at the breast,
So they, all timid, all in suspicion,
70 Some from one side, from the other some,
Come creeping out with laggard steps
To see if they are safe, the destruction
Caused by the now ended struggle.
So, many came, few at a time,
75 Alert, fearful, and right timid,
With furtive steps, yet taking care
Lest they should step upon the bloodless corpse
Of some dear friend or faithful protector
Of those poor walls which now were stained
80 And bathed all over with their blood.
Thus, trembling and sad and afflicted,
Surrounded as they were on every side
By the pale hue of death and death itself,
They made approach. And the Castilian band
85 Beheld them all caressing with much joy
All their neighbors and saw them give
Sure and great signs of their content

3. Espaciosos = lentos.
4. Atentados = moderados.

Seguro y muestras grandes de contento
De verlos reduzidos y apartados
De aquel cruento estrago que emprendían.
Qual vemos que se abaten y se humillan
Los lebantados trigos, azotados
Con vno y otro soplo reforzado
Del poderoso viento que, sulcando
En remolcadas[5] hondas sus espigas,
Al suelo las amaina, abate y baja,
Assí, vencidos, llanos, desarmados,
Más de seycientos dieron en rendirse
Y dentro de vna plaza, con sus hijos
Y todas sus mugeres, se postraron
Y como presos, juntos, se pusieron
En manos del Sargento y sossegaron,
Movidos del buen Chumpo, que seguro
A todos prometió y dio la vida,
Sin cuia ayuda dudo, y soy muy cierto,
Que aquella gran Numancia trabajosa,
Quando más desdichada y más perdida,
Quedara más desierta y despoblada
Que aquesta pobre fuerza ya rendida.[6]
Estando ya, pues, todo sossegado
Y puestas ya las treguas sin rezelo
De algún bullicio de armas o alboroto,
Los pactos assentados y de assiento
Los vnos y los otros sossegados,
De súbito las bárbaras, rabiosas,
Qual vemos deshazerse y derrumbarse,
Dexándose venir con bravo asombro,
Vna terrible torre poderosa,
Recién inhiesta, puesta y lebantada,
Y con terrible espanto rebolvernos
La sossegada sangre y alterarnos,
Assí, señor inmenso y poderoso,
Alzando vn alarido, arremetieron,
Y apeñuscadas[7] todas, qual se aprietan
Sobre la chueca,[8] juntos, los villanos,
Con los caiados corbos procurando
De darle con esfuerzo mayor bote,
Assí las vimos, todas hechas piña,
A palos y pedradas deshaziendo

At seeing them saved and removed
From that cruel slaughter they undertook.
90 As we see downcast and humbled
The high-uplifted heads of wheat when lashed
By gust on gust, ever stronger,
Of mighty winds which go plowing
Its spiky heads into great rippling waves
95 And bend them to the ground and beat them down,
So, conquered, humbled, and disarmed,
More than six hundred surrendered
And in one plaza, with all their children
And all their women, they did put themselves
100 Into the Sergeant's hands and were at peace,
Moved by the good Chumpo, who had given
A promise of safety and life to all,
Without whose aid I doubt, nay, I'm sure,
That great, laborious Numantia,
105 E'en when most unfortunate and lost,
Would have been no more desert and empty
Than this poor fort now surrendered.[1]
All being now quite pacified
And truce now made without suspicion
110 Of any armed turmoil or uprising,
Agreements signed and to be signed
And all on both sides well appeased,
Suddenly the barbarian women, mad,
As we see suddenly falling and breaking up,
115 Coming on us to our astonishment,
A terrible and mighty tower
But recently erected, placed, and set,
And with a terrible fear all our blood
Flows back upon our hearts and we grow pale,
120 So, lord, immense and powerful,
Raising a fearful cry, they all set off,
And all crowding, as the peasants
Do crowd together round a hockey ball
And all do try with curving sticks
125 To give it greater impulse with their strength,
So we did see them, gathered in a knot,
With sticks and blows of stones smashing
A miserable body. So at once
We all set out for their squadron

---

5. Remolcadas = que se empujan o tiran las unas de las otras.
6. Se compara Acoma a la ciudad celtíbera que tomaron los romanos, tras varios asedios, en 133 antes de la era cristiana. Los numantinos, negándose a ser prisioneros, se suicidaron colectivamente. A través de la historia de España se ha usado como emblema del carácter indómito de los hispanos, y Villagrá, en honor de los acomeses, no utiliza el ejemplo fortuitamente.
7. Apeñuscadas = apiñadas.
8. Chueca = bolita pequeña con que juegan los campesinos.

1. Acoma is favorably compared in its stoic valor to the Celtiberian city that the Romans besieged three times before Scipio Africanus finally took it in 133 B.C. The Numantians decided upon collective suicide before surrender, and the feat was always a symbol of heroism in Spanish history and legend.

A vn miserable cuerpo. Y assí, juntos,
Para la esquadra todos arrancamos
Por ver si era Español y dar venganza
A hecho tan atroz y desmedido.
Y luego que nos vieron, sin aliento,
Alborotadas todas, nos dixeron:
"Varones esforzados, generosos,
Si abernos entregado en vuestras manos
Merece que nos deis algún contento,
Dejadnos acabar lo comenzado.
Aquí Zutacapán está tendido,
Y gracias al Castilla que tal alma
Hizo que se arrancase por tal llaga.
Este causó las muertes que les dimos
A vuestros compañeros desdichados.
Este metió cizaña y alboroto
Por todos estos pobres que tendidos
Están por este suelo derramados."
Y poniendo la vista en sus difuntos
Y luego en el traidor, rabiosas todas,
Assí como en tajón[9] la carne pican
Los diestros cozineros y deshazen,
Assí, con yra, todos[10] rebolvieron
Y en muy menudas piezas le dexaron,
Con cuio hecho, alegres, satisfechas,
En su primero puesto sossegaron.
Y nosotros, señor, jamás podimos
Saber quál fuesse el brazo que de vn tajo
Cinco costillas cerce[11] le cortase.
Y assí como con ansia cobdiciosos,
Después de la batalla ya vencida,
Vn gran varón famoso, que escondido,
De muy grande rescate, procuramos,
Y assí, sin alma, seso y sin sentido
Salimos a buscarle y reparamos
En todos los vencidos y ponemos
La vista bien atenta por hallarle,[12]
Assí, los bárbaros, atentos y las bocas
Abiertas y los ojos que pestaña
Iamás movió ninguno, vimos todos
Que con asombro y pasmo nos miraban.
Y no vien asomaba algún soldado,
Que fuera del quartel acaso estaba,
Quando de golpe todos, qual se allegan
Las moscas a la miel, assí llegaban

130 To see was it a Spaniard and avenge
So treacherous and excessive a deed.
And when they saw us then, all out of breath
And all excited, did cry out to us:
"Ye valiant and generous men,
135 If to have given ourselves into your hands
Deserves that you give us some satisfaction,
Then let us finish what we have commenced.
Here Zutacapán lies stretched out
And thanks to the Castilian who has made
140 Such soul be snatched from such a wound.
He caused the deaths which we have dealt
To your unfortunate companions.
He sowed discord and disturbance
Among all those poor creatures who
145 Are lying lifeless on this ground."
And gazing now upon their dead
And then upon the traitor, all, raging,
As on the chopping block skilled cooks
Do mince up meat and sunder it,
150 So, in their rage they all gathered around
And left him battered into small pieces;
Happy and satisfied at this their deed,
Returned unto their former peaceful state.
And we, lord, never could find out
155 Whose was the arm that with one mighty cut
Had shorn through five of his ribs at one time.
As we most anxiously and greedily
Do seek, after a battle has been won,
Some great and famous man from whom we hope
160 To get great ransom, finding him hidden,
And thus soulless, madly, out of our wits,
We go to seek for him and examine
All of the conquered and eagerly fix
Our gaze attentively to find that man,[2]
165 So these barbarians, attentive, with their mouths
Open and eyes that never moved
An eyelid, were then seen by us
To look at us in fear, astonishment.
And hardly would some soldier appear
170 Who had by chance been absent from the group
When all of them, as flies to honey crowd,
Would instantly run and crowd around him
And look into his face attentively.
Seeing the great care which they took

9. Tajón = tronco de madera sobre el que cortan los carniceros.
10. Probable errata del original por "todas."
11. Probable errata del original por "cercén," a cercén, enteramente.
12. Describe la búsqueda de soldados victoriosos por un rehén rico que pudiera rescatarse.

2. The wartime practice, condoned as described, was an incentive to underpayed soldiers almost into modern times, and was not a peculiarly New World phenomenon.

Y el rostro sólo, atentos, le miraban.
Y viendo el gran cuidado que ponían
En no dexar a nadie reservado[13]
Que bien no le notasen y advirtiessen,
Fue fuerza preguntarles qué distino,
Qué blanco o por qué causa, assí, sedientos,
A todos nos miraban. Y suspensos,
La mano dando a Chumpo, que por ellos
A todos respondiesse, dixo el viejo:
"Buscan éstos, mis hijos, a vn Castilla
Que estando en la batalla anduvo siempre
En vn blanco caballo suelto, y tiene
La barba larga, cana y bien poblada
Y calva la cabeza. Es alto y ciñe
Vna terrible espada, ancha y fuerte,
Con que a todos por tierra nos ha puesto,
Valiente por extremo. Y, por extremo,[14]
Vna bella donzella también buscan,
Más hermosa que el Sol y más que el Cielo.[15]
Preguntan dónde está y qué se han hecho."
El caudillo Español, oyendo aquesto,
Movido, por ventura, del que pudo
Mostrar la duda clara y socorrernos
En casos semejantes y ampararnos,[16]
Qual vn blandón[17] o antorcha cuia lumbre
La vista haze clara y quita el velo
De la ciega tiniebla, assí, alumbrando,
Al grato viejo Chumpo fue diziendo:
"Responde a éstos, tus hijos, noble padre,
Que en esso no se cansen ni fatiguen
Ni más los dos que buscan los procuren,
Que son bueltos al Cielo, donde tienen
De assiento su morada, y que no salen
Si no es a defendernos y ayudarnos
Quando assí nos agravian y se atreven,
Qual ellos se atrevieron, a matarnos
Con muertes tan atrozes y crueles
Los pocos Españoles que subieron
A lo alto desta fuerza descuidados.
Que miren lo que hazen y no buelvan

175 Not to leave anyone aside
     Whom they should not well note and scrutinize,
     'Twas necessary to ask for what mark,
     What sign or what cause they did gaze
     Thus anxiously and thirstily on us.
180 Giving authority to Chumpo, that for all
     He might reply, the old man said to us:
     "These sons of mine seek a Castilian
     Who, being in the battle, always rode
     Upon a great white horse and has
185 A great long beard, both white and thick,
     And a bald head, is tall and wears
     A terrible and broad and mighty sword
     With which he has stricken us all to earth,
     A man extremely valiant. And also
190 My people seek, as well, a beauteous maid,
     More beautiful than the sun or the heavens.[3]
     They ask where these may be, where they have gone."
     The Spanish leader then, hearing these things,
     Being moved, perhaps, by He who could
195 Make that doubt clear, also help us
     And protect us in similar affairs,
     like to a taper or a torch whose light
     Makes our sight clear and cleaves the veil
     Of blind darkness, so he, shining,
200 Said to the grateful old Chumpo:
     "Reply to these your children, noble sire,
     That they should not tire or fatigue themselves
     Nor should they try to seek these more,
     For they have now returned to Heaven,
205 Where they do keep their dwelling, nor leave it
     Except to come to our aid and defense
     When we are injured or one dares,
     As those men dared, to slaughter ours
     With such atrocious and such cruel deaths,
210 Those few poor Spaniards who did climb
     To the height of this fortress heedlessly.
     Let them watch what they do, and not repeat
     A second time of that their work begun."
     The Trojan had not ended, had not drawn

13. Reservado = encubierto.
14. Por extremo = por último. En este segundo uso en el mismo verso, podría interpretarse adverbialmente referido a "bella" del verso siguiente.
15. La referencia es a la Virgen, socorro, aunque nunca bélico, de los castellanos. La aparición de la Virgen y Santiago, con antecedentes, especialmente la del último, en la literatura de la Reconquista, se halla prominentemente, asimismo, en la epica americana: *La araucana* I, 9; *Mexicana* XII. En *El peregrino indiano* XIII, aparecen la Virgen y Santiago juntos.
16. Se refiere a Dios.
17. Blandón = receptáculo de antorchas.

3. The appearance of Santiago and/or the Virgin (the latter never armed, of course) in aid of the Castilian cause, had many antecedents in the history and literature of the Reconquest. It was incorporated, as well, especially in the case of Santiago, into the American epic: *La araucana* IX; *Mexicana* XII. In *El peregrino indiano* XIII, as here, Santiago and the Virgin appear together.

Segunda vez al hecho comenzado."
No suspendió el Troiano ni redujo
La rienda del silencio con más fuerza
Quando a la illustre Reyna los sucessos
De Troia y su desgracia recontaba[18]
Qual hizo aquí el Zaldívar, que pasmados
Y mudos los dexó, que más palabra
Hablaron ni chistaron. Y assí sólo
Dixo: "Señor inmenso, que alcanzamos
Aquesta gran victoria el mismo día
Del vasso de elección,[19] a quien la tierra
Tenía por patrón,[20] y assí entendimos
Que vino con la Virgen a ampararnos."
Iuizios son ocultos que no caben
En mí, Señor, que siempre soy y he sido
Vn gusanillo triste, despreciado.
Y assí, Señor, me buelvo a mi caudillo,
Que está con toda priessa despachando
Al provehedor Zubía porque lleve
Desta victoria insigne alegre nueva
A nuestro General, a quien abía
Vna bárbara vieja, por sus cercos,
Héchole cierto della el mismo día
Que fue por vuestro campo celebrada.
Y estando, assí, aguardando el desengaño,
Marchando el provehedor, acaso Tempal
Y el pobre de Cotumbo, destrozados,
Corriendo gran fortuna a árbol seco,[21]
Abiendo de la fuerza ya escapado,
Yban atravesando,[22] y viendo el golpe
Que allí el rigor del hado descargaba
Tras tanta desbentura, rebozados
Con máscara de paz, los dos fingieron,
Como hastutos cosarios, que ellos eran
De allá la tierra adentro y que robados
Venían de vnas gentes que huiendo
Salían del Peñol. Y assí, encogidos,
Pidieron con gran lástima les diessen
Con que la triste hambre que llevaban
Socorrida quedase y no acabasen.
Con esto, el Español mandó prenderlos
Por no errar el lance, que perdido,

215 The rein of silence with more vivid force,
When to the famous queen he did relate
The tale of Troy and of its misfortunes,[4]
As Zaldívar had here, for he left them
Astonished and silent, so they spoke not
220 Another word nor muttered, whereat he
Did say: "Immense Lord, since we won
This great victory on the very day
Of the Sacred Vessel,[5] the saint that this land
Had as a Patron,[6] we do comprehend,
225 Did then come with the Virgin to guard us."
There are things hidden that are not
Clear to me, lord, for I have always been
And am a sad and despised trifling worm.
And so, lord, I return to my leader,
230 Who is dispatching, in the hottest haste,
The purveyor Zubía to carry
The famous, joyous news of victory
Unto our General, who had been
Informed of it upon the very day
235 That it had been won by these forces
By an old Indian woman within her ring.[7]
And as he was waiting for certain news,
The purveyor being upon the way,
By chance Tempal and poor Cotumbo, destitute,
240 Riding a terrible storm without sails,[8]
Having now escaped out of the fortalice,
Did happen to cross his path and, seeing
The blow that the rigor of harsh fate had struck
After so much misfortune, covering themselves,
245 The two did feign, behind a mask of peace,
Like astute pirates, that they were natives
From far within the land and that they had
Been robbed by some who came fleeing
From the great rock. And thus, most timidly,
250 They asked with much grieving that they be given
Something by which their fierce hunger might be
Alleviated so they might not die.
At this the Spaniard had them seized
Not to err in the juncture, for, once lost,
255 It might detract from a great soldier,
And so they were taken and, arriving

---

18. La *Eneida* II.
19. Se refiere a la Virgen. El día 24 de enero se celebra Nuestra Señora de la Paz.
20. Santiago, patrón de España y, por ende, de aquella tierra también. El pasaje habría que leerse: "y así entendimos que a quien la tierra tenía por patrón vino con la Virgen a ampararnos."
21. Esta imagen marinera parece significar: sufriendo gran tormenta sin velas o con mala arboladura.
22. Atravesando = pasando, cruzando.

4. See Virgil, the *Aeneid* II.
5. January 22 is the feast day of Our Lady of Peace.
6. Santiago, as patron saint of Spain, was, by extension, that of the Spanish New World.
7. The old woman, by this reference to the enchanting circle, is identified as a witch/seer.
8. This maritime image, *a palo seco*, appears to mean "mast without sails."

Suele por él perder vn gran soldado,²³
Y presos los llevó y en vna estufa,
Después de aber llegado y dado el pliego,
Mandó que los pusiessen y encerrasen.
Y abiendo con gran gusto recibido
El General la nueva, fue informado
De ciertos nobles bárbaros amigos
Que aquellos prisioneros que forzados
Estaban en la estufa y oprimidos
Eran de los más bravos y valientes
Que²⁴ Acoma mostraron y pusieron
La cólera en su punto y lebantaron
El sossegado fuerte ya perdido.
Con esto, los dos bárbaros sañudos,
Viéndose descubiertos, deshizieron
La escala de la estufa y, hechos fuertes,
A palos y pedradas no dexaron
Que nadie les entrase por tres días
Que assí se defendieron y guardaron.
Y viendo que era fuerza se rindiessen
Por hambre y sed rabiosa que cargaba,
Las armas sossegaron y dixeron:
"Castillas, si del todo no contentos
Estáis de abernos ya bebido toda
La generosa sangre que, gustosa,
tiene²⁵ vuestra braveza no cansada,
Y sóla aquesta poca que nos queda
Mostráis que os satisfaze, dadnos luego
Sendos cuchillos botos,²⁶ que nosotros
Aquí vuestras gargantas hartaremos
Privándonos de vida, porque es justo
Que no se diga nunca, por mancharnos,
Que dos guerreros tales se pusieron
En manos tan infames y tan viles
Quales son essas vuestras despreciadas."
Con esto, el General, y con que todos
Los bárbaros amigos le dixeron
Si allí los perdonaba que ponía
En condición la tierra de alterarse,
Abiendo hecho en vano todo aquello
Que pudo ser por verlos reduzidos
Al gremio de la Iglesia y agregados,
Mandó que los cuchillos les negasen,
Por más assegurar, y que les diessen
Dos gruessas sogas largas, bien cumplidas.
Y echándoselas dentro, las miraron,

And having then delivered the message,
He had them placed and locked in a kiva.
And, having now with much pleasure received
260 The news, the General was then informed
By certain noble, friendly barbarians
That those prisoners whom he had shut up
Inside the kiva and retained in custody
Were of the bravest and most valiant
265 That Acoma could show and they had raised
The outbreak to its highest point and roused
The peaceful fortress that was now destroyed.
At this, the two barbarians, enraged,
Seeing themselves discovered, did destroy
270 The ladder of the kiva and, grown strong,
With clubs and blows of rocks they prevented
The entrance of anyone for three days,
So well they did defend and keep themselves.
And seeing that they must needs surrender
275 Through the hunger and the raging thirst they felt,
They then laid down their arms and said:
"Castilians, if you are not content
As yet, though you have drunk up all
The generous blood that, succulent,
280 Your tireless bravery has already had,
And only this bit that is left to us
Will satisfy you, then give us
Two blunt knives, one for each, that we
May here appease your throats for you,
285 Taking our lives ourselves, for it is right
That no one may say, to stain us,
That two such warriors placed themselves
In hands so infamous and vile
As are your hands, which we despise."
290 At this the General was told
By all of his barbarian friends
That if he gave them pardon he would put
All of the land in a mind to revolt.
As he had done in vain all that
295 Could have been done to see them surrendered
And added to the bosom of the Church,
He ordered that they be refused the knives
For greater safety, and that they be given
Two long, strong halters, well and truly made.
300 And throwing these inside, they looked at them
With eyes bloodshot and pressing tight
Their lips and their strong teeth,

23. Un gran soldado pierde en su fama si deja pasar un buen lance.
24. Posible errata del original omitiendo "en."
25. Tiene bebida.
26. Botos = desafilados.

Los ojos hechos sangre y apretando
Los labios y los dientes, corajosos,
Hinchados los hijares y narizes,
Absortos, mudos, sordos, se quedaron.
Y estando assí, suspensos breve rato,
Sacudiendo el temor y despreciando
A todo vuestro campo y fuerte espada,
Nunca se vio jamás que assí pusiesse
Al corredizo lazo la garganta
Aquél que desta vida ya cansado
Partirse quiso della alegre y presto,
Qual vimos a estos bárbaros, que al punto,
La mal compuesta greña sacudiendo,
Las dos sogas tomaron y al pescuezo
Ceñidas por sus manos y añudadas,
Salieron de la estufa y esparciendo
La vista por el campo, que admirado
Estaba de su esfuerzo y condolido,
Iuntos la detuvieron y pararon
En vnos altos álamos crecidos
Que cerca, por su mal, acaso estaban.
Y no bien los notaron, quando luego
Dellos, sin más acuerdo, nos dixeron
Querían suspenderse y ahorcarse.
Y dándoles la mano abierta en todo,
Los gruessos, ciegos, ñudos apretados
Allí los requirieron,²⁷ y arrastrando
Las sogas por detrás partieron juntos
Del campo Castellano, ya rendidos
Y del bárbaro pueblo acompañados.
No los fuertes hermanos que, en Cartago,
Corriendo presurosos, alargaron,
A costa de sí mismos, los linderos,²⁸
Assí a la triste muerte se entregaron,
Dexándose enterrar en vida, vivos,
Qual estos bravos bárbaros que, estando
Al pie de aquellos troncos, lebantaron
La vista por la cumbre y en vn punto,
Como diestros grumetes que, ligeros,
Por las entenas, gavias y altos topes²⁹
Discurren con presteza, assí, alentados,
Trepando por los árboles arriba,
Tentándoles los ramos, se mostraron
Verdugos de sí mismos. Y amarrados,
Mirándonos a todos, nos dixeron:
"Soldados, advertid que aquí colgados

305

310

315

320

325

330

335

340

345

Their sides swollen, their nostrils wide,
Absorbed, deaf, dumb, they did remain.
And being thus in quiet for a time,
Throwing off fear and despising
All of your army and your mighty sword,
Never was seen thus to give up
His neck unto the running noose
A man who, being tired of this life,
Desired to leave this life swiftly and soon,
As we saw these barbarians who, at once,
Loosing their badly tangled hair,
Took the two nooses and, setting
The same upon their necks and knotting them,
They came out of the kiva, and casting
Their glance over the camp, which wondered much
At their courage and sympathized with them,
They halted it and centered it upon
Some lofty poplar trees that were well grown
And were, by some evil chance, near.
And hardly had they noted them when they
Informed us instantly they wished
To hang themselves and die upon those trees.
And, giving them an open hand in all,
The great and choking knots, hard drawn,
There they examined, and, dragging
Their halters behind them, they went
From the Castilian camp, worn out,
Accompanied by the barbarian folk.
Not the strong brothers of Carthage⁹
Who, running rapidly, increased
The boundaries to their own dole, did thus
Give themselves up unto dark death,
Allowing themselves to be buried though alive,
As these barbarians, who, arriving
At the foot of those tree trunks, lifted up
Their gaze unto the top and, instantly,
Like skillful cabin boys who run lightly
Upon the masts and yards and high tops,
Climbed the poplars to a great height,
And then, testing the branches, appeared as
Their own hangmen; and having tied the ropes,
Looking upon us all, they said to us:
"Soldiers, take note that hanging here
From these strong tree trunks we leave you
Our miserable bodies as spoils
Of the illustrious victory you won

---

27. Requirieron = examinaron.
28. No hemos dado con quiénes serían los hermanos cartagineses a los que alude Villagrá.
29. Topes = extremos superiores de los palos de arboladura.

9. We have not been able to identify these two Carthaginian brothers.

Destos rollizos troncos os dexamos
Los miserables cuerpos por despojos
De la victoria illustre que alcanzastes
De aquellos desdichados que podridos
Están sobre su sangre rebolcados,
Sepúlcro que tomaron porque quiso
Assí fortuna infame perseguirnos
Con mano poderosa y acabarnos.
Gustosos quedaréis que ya cerramos
Las puertas al vivir y nos partimos
Y libres nuestras tierras os dexamos.
Dormid a sueño suelto, pues ninguno
Bolvió jamás con nueva del camino
Incierto y trabajoso que llevamos.
Mas de vna cosa ciertos os hazemos,
Que si bolver podemos a vengarnos
Que no parieron madres Castellanas,
Ni bárbaras tampoco, en todo el mundo
Más desdichados hijos que a vosotros."
Y assí, rabiosos, bravos, desembueltos,
Saltando en vago, juntos se arrojaron,
Y en blanco ya los ojos, trastornados,
Sueltas las coiunturas y remisos
Los poderosos nierbios y costados,
Vertiendo espumarajos, descubrieron
Las escondidas lenguas regordidas
Y entre sus mismos dientes apretadas.
Y assí, qual suelen dos bajeles sueltos
Rendir la ancha borda,[30] afrenillando[31]
La gruessa palamenta[32] y en vn punto,
Las espumosas proas apagadas,
En jolito[33] se quedan, assí, juntos,
Sesgos y sin moverse se rindieron
Y el aliento de vida allí apagaron.
Con cuio fuerte passo desabrido,
Dexándolos colgados, ya me es fuerza
Poner silencio al canto desabrido.
Y por si vuestra Magestad insigne
El fin de aquesta historia ver quisiere,
De rodillas suplico que me aguarde
Y también me perdone si tardare,
Porque es difícil cosa que la pluma,
Abiendo de serviros con la lanza,
Pueda desempacharse sin tardanza.[34]

FIN

30. Borda = vela mayor de las galeras.
31. Afrenillando = amarrando con frenillos.
32. Palamenta = conjunto de remos.
33. Jolito = calma.
34. Se refiere a la prometida segunda parte.

Over those wretched ones who are
350   Rotting amid their weltering blood,
The sepulcher they chose since infamous
Fortune chose so to pursue us
With powerful hand and end our days.
You will remain joyful for we now close
355   The doors of life and take our leave,
And freely leave to you our lands.
Sleep sure and safe because no one
Ever returned with news about the road,
Uncertain and laborious, we now take,
360   But yet of one thing we do assure you:
That if we can return for our vengeance,
Castilian mothers shall not bear,
Barbarian either, throughout all the world,
Sons more unfortunate than all of you."
365   Thus raving, angry, all heedless,
Together they both leapt out into space,
And now their eyes, turned back, displayed the whites,
Their joints were all loosened and slack,
As were their mighty thews and sides.
370   Spurting out foam they discovered
Their hidden tongues, now all swollen
And tightly clenched between their teeth.
And, as may two separate and free vessels,
Lower their broad main sails and bridle up
375   The mighty banks of oars and all at once
The foaming prows do come to rest
And all is calm, so, together,
Calm, without motion, they remain
And there give up the breath of life.
380   And at this harsh and severe pass,
Leaving them hanging, I must now
Bring silence to this harsh canto.
And if your famous Majesty
Should wish to see the end of this story
385   I beg upon my knees that you will wait[10]
And pardon me, also, if I delay,
For 'tis a thing difficult for the pen
To lose all shyness instantly,
Having to serve you with the lance.
390

10. Villagrá again refers to a second part that was, if written, never published.

APPENDIX A

Keyed to the English translation, the italicized phrases or words below belong to Fayette S. Curtis's unfinished 1923 translation and show how the editors of the current volume differed with this earlier version.

Canto I

I.a
Which sets forth the *argument* of the history and

I.c
Of the *antiquity* of the Indians,

I.3
Of him whose patience *never broke,*

I.4
Though *burdened with a mass* of cares,

I.6
Which still doth cloud prowess and deeds,

I.8
Through India of the West *went forth,*

I.10
Go further yet, in courage strong,

I.12
As much in shock of arms experienced,

I.15
Be Phoenix of New Mexico,

I.18
By the most ardent faith, in whose hot coals

I.19
Under your sainted Father and our lord

I.21
Suspend a moment *for us men*

I.26
Thou here shalt see the load of *work,*

I.32
I having you, *a* Monarch, listener,

I.37
The deeds of which I write being no less worthy

I.39
To undertake those which *shall be* no less

I.50
Some thirty-three degrees, which *counted*

I.51
Are, we know, *from* sainted Jerusalem,

I.58
The furious sun, *in Cancer his beginning,*

I.59
For in his zenith he doth pass the ordinary

I.63
And shows to us *his district* in *his* longitude,

I.70
Approach the most and nearest *in its* coast

I.71
On the *southwest;* and *in that part*

I.74
Toward where the southwest wind *blows* the *sea;*

I.76
Some fifteen hundred full long leagues;

I.78
Beneath the parallel, *when as* we take

I.79
The thirty-six degree to North,

I.94
That painting, the most ancient,

I.102
And there *enforces* and corroborates *antiquity*

I.114
Just as midst us the coming here *from* Spain

I.121
The hollow cavern, *harassed*

I.122
By vigorous and hasty Boreas,

I.127
Discovering *their excellence to* the world,

I.128
And *to* its kings illustrious and *to* its lords,

I.131
Like gentle *shepherds in* the fold,

I.132
Bringing obedient and subject

I.151
Involved in pretty, graceful, games

I.161
And gentlemen and well *made*, all,

I.163
Such sum of finery and *of uniform*

I.165
Are customed to be *seen* on festal days

I.166
And pointed out by curious courtiers.

I.167
And *even this* the mighty squadrons

I.168
Showed *among their oddities so rare*

I.170
Of transformations wonderful from beasts:

I.177
The fox, the hare and *elk*, the rabbit shy,

I.182
A *truly* old invention, one that's used

I.193
Mischievous slings, *swift* in the air,

I.204
Kept marching *in the column long*

I.210
In blinding *whirling*, dust,

I.211
Of swift and sudden earthquake,

Canto II

II.3
It is a sign most evident, *unknown to man,*

II.10
This one accursed thus placed himself before

II.11
In form of an old woman *muffled up,*

II.31
Just as they picture *to* us and do show

II.36
So far as they have learned of them

II.37
In *diligent* and learned Astrology,

II.38
Thus of this fierce old woman *astrological*

II.43
Exceeded some eight hundred quintal weight,

II.45
And when the column to the stranger came

II.46
It *stopped* attentive and in *much* suspense,

II.49
"I am not *moved*, oh valiant Mexicans,

II.51
Which rises *from a* summit high,

II.52
You *may not be* less moved or *dissuaded*

II.53
From that rude haughtiness and gallantry

II.54
Of your illustrious, *fame* and noble blood,

II.65
For thus is spread, extends and is made known

II.72
As *quickly as the* arrow which flies fast

II.82
Has come *upon him, feeble weak,*

II.90
His separate destiny, and make his place,

II.95
To close within its mighty *span*

II.98
Near to the waters crystalline

II.101
A red-tailed eagle sits, *in beauteous deformity*

II.102
And *he is* eating greedily

II.107
Of the strong state *that's pointed out,*

II.109
That Mexico Tenuchtitlan be *built.*

II.113
And *since that* greed, a wicked vice

II.114
Is well accustomed because of misery

II.118
The borders and the boundaries of *your* lands

II.119
So that each one may know his own

II.120
And yet may not pretend

II.126
And, giving to his monstrous load a *twist,*

II.140
Like as the Romans and the Greeks

II.142
Whose great and wonderful *estate*

II.143
Th'imperial Eagle, double-headed, *represents,*

II.176
For some stood on their hind legs, *straight upright,*

II.197
Nor scoria, *burn,* nor any rock

II.204
And *that* same story which I here have told

II.208
They all were strangers, and *they all pointed out*

II.209
The *starting place* of those two brethern,

II.214
And they do say their *masses* do contain

II.219
Tabascans and the folk of Guinea.

II.224
Of that *unknown* Plus Ultra which they raise,

II.225
Folk more for distaff and for *throne-room* fit,

II.229
And *being gone* from these new lands,

II.230
The shrewd Mexicans do show to us

II.232
Which we all *saw* in New Galicia,

II.234
And they, the natives of the land,

II.237
Out of the new land that we *sought.*

II.238
And we sought for its cities and high walls,

II.239
In all the *places* that New Spain contains

II.240
Until *we found* the very towns

II.242
Just like the *ones who search in dreams,*

II.243
Until from no more than the wind *they draw*

II.244
The lofty house that has been hid,

II.245
Thus did the *sturdy* soldiery

II.246
By pressing on discover and draw out,

II.247
Of the broad boundaries I *name,*

II.249
Of this truth we *were searching for,*

II.263
Some pictures, aye, and edifices,

II.264
Derived from Ancient Mexican.

II.266
The much desired card *by secret mark,*

II.267
The rest being sure 'twas luck,

II.268
E'en so, by these same *paintings* and these signs

II.269
The whole camp sat us down

II.279
Of whom *the wandering indian* says

II.281
And very rightly doth *he* set us right

II.291
From having sung quite all of what

II.299
For here, for now, we leave the matter.

II.300
And *so that* your Castilian folk,

II.302
That we *delight*, to tread and to discover

II.304
May for themselves grasp a great part

Canto III

III.4
And in the *military* shelter where we live

III.7
Who followed *its* immortal flag.

III.10
That, as *a* scutcheon heroic and sublime,

III.16
Should *keep* it *for Him* and esteem it much

III.17
If *one* should wish to see most things

III.19
And thus no work *should* there be seen,

III.20
Truly by *the* heroic breasts 'twould be received,

III.21
That God Himself *would never* shine *upon*,

III.24
And *these*, like to resplendent suns,

III.33
For all these men most singular.

III.34
In the most fierce and raging *storms*

III.35
In all their miseries and trials sharp,

III.36
For them the Highest Power chose to work

III.38
And with His Diety as his sole base

III.39
He breathed the living spirit into men

III.41
And these brave men thus passing on

III.47
For through their sainted mouths they did breathe forth,

III.48
Live saffron, treacle, medicine

III.55
Did *conservate* and give and offer them

III.64
For, nothwithstanding that it is *a little thing*

III.70
Nor yet the little *thing* that's man

III.71
It is the base and *earliest fundamental*

III.75
That, as it must be passed and registered

III.77
In *whose past* the senses all preside,

III.78
Whatever to the greatest height and excellence

III.80
Thus comes it nothing *enters there*

III.84
For *that* is the last thing to die

III.97
And all *the* other men of strength

III.98
Who follow in *their* blessed steps,

III.106
Under the hot and famous province

III.109
And in *their* famous century of gold

III.122
A matter of *twelve* hundred leagues or more

III.150
Done with such effort and such daring

III.153
Of his *own heart*, never o'ercome,

III.162
Well, *pointing* the prow of his intent

III.165
Since loving and ruling never *give*

III.166
A competence to those who follow them,

III.167
The same *thing came* to him as to the famous Caesar

III.172
Telling him that to him alone the *journey,*

III.179
As it grows furious on the point it seeks

III.188
Because no mortal ever *dares*

III.191
Who *he shall* be that we *must* praise him

III.197
And, *having seen* the matter *ended* ill,

III.199
Through being Governor of the South Sea,

III.205
Of your *adventurous* grandfather,

III.216
Like powerful ship that *to the bottom goes*

III.218
We see *him* sink and without hope,

III.220
Speaking in loud and upraised voice,

III.221
With none made peace nor pardoned none

III.222
Taking the *journey* from before his gaze.

III.228
When they have never ceased to live

III.232
A *gift of* glass from out our hands

III.239
To see that man *extended on* the earth,

III.240
All *twined* to dust and ashes vile,

III.243
But who shall be so strong, *a* lord,

III.244
That his great strength *can* still resist

III.245
The furious force of *fate*

III.249
Much less, since we know it took the life

III.250
Of *living* Son of living God,

III.254
Beneath his *craft* and mighty spade.

III.268
And one of greatest gifts and valor

III.272
As to the soldier most *elegant,*

III.287
A *modest* soldier and as much long-suffering

III.293
Where *fortune* very great came to them

III.297
Meanwhile the *clever man* Mendoza

III.298
Foresaw need of great aid, being a man astute,

III.300
With sturdy soldiers, *so* excellent

III.301
More could not be desired

III.302
By those who *had gained and did employ*

III.318
And *since* they *had* reverence for him

III.326
Of good two hundred *leagues*, long ones,

III.328
The Captain Zaldívar, all broken down

III.329
By the harsh and laborious *way,*

III.330
He, *who* had just explored *it* and discovered *it*

III.334
And saying to the Viceroy that *that* land

III.343
Make it their custom, with great pleasure, *as mere passtime,*

III.351
The news came to the Viceroy's ear

III.352
And, like a prudent and cautious man,

III.354
Doth often come *on iron paths,*

III.358
A man who lives quite *at his ease,*

III.365
This he forbade because the expense

III.366
Would be quite lost and all consumed,

III.367
With *fifteen* thousand dollars of good gold

III.371
Second—it would be of advantage.

III.372
As *always it is of advantage*

III.373
To challenge a tired hunter,

III.375
In challenge then, he ordered on the spot

III.377
Should break his camp, and march.

III.380
The Royal expedition took its way

III.401
Just so the soldiery, *did feel*

III.402
The force of the endangered government,

III.405
To stop and curtail *the great* work.

III.416
The proof and on the ground,

III.431
The Doña Isabel who did incorporate

III.432
A virtue deep, *and high*

III.433
Of Sovereign love, with which she glows,

III.434
Having recourse to the *glowing* martyr

III.453
Cakes gilded, cakes of ore, more than enough,

III.459
Their meanness, worthy of dishonor,

Canto IV

IV.1
He who does not feel *all-sufficient gifts*

IV.2
In the degree of perfectness and *valor that he has*

IV.8
In sudden sound of trumpets of the war,

IV.10
For just as soon as the great pikes

IV.11
With rapid step do come into their quiet peace

IV.13
Throw in the air their swiftly flying balls,

IV.15
The gallant steeds and bannerets,

IV.16
Of those who bear the lance,

IV.17
Then 'tis the pompous haughtiness, the words,

IV.19
Those who do say themselves impermeable to fear,

IV.20
Then coming, as they do come, *at the truth,*

IV.28
Than to *assume* nobility in arms

IV.29
And be unable to attain that honor.

IV.30
And thus there can be no such vainglory

IV.31
Or *pride as well* can be compared

IV.33
Doth occupy *a single lofty* post,

IV.37
If, on occasion, before all the camp,

IV.39
From those about who point him out

IV.40
And know *the very names of those,*

IV.41
Whose grave delinquency *is quite ignored*

IV.42
This is more damaging and more outrageous

IV.44
Stripped, *by* the hangman's arm,

IV.48
This sad return of this famed enterprise,

IV.57
But a thing to feed their *knowing skill*

IV.58
In matters of importance and *that this might show*

IV.60
And *he who saw* them at full speed return

IV.65
Turned from *the* vain intent

IV.69
So the afflicted *monks,*

IV.74
His forces upon the brink of ruin,

IV.75
Others that all *his* work was vain,

IV.78
Denying, with great show of *right,*

IV.79
That they were made for lives of wandering,

IV.80
Since the divine and powerful hand,

IV.86
The fearful cold, the snow, *snowdrifts,*

IV.90
Watches and *sentry-go* most perilous,

IV.103
Created from the fertile grape,

IV.108
There in the future life *as he pretends,*

IV.118
That ancient, warlike, Roman *word*

IV.123
As Phaeton wished to *place* himself

IV.126
Taking such height *because* his soaring pride

IV.127
Was yet more wise than that

IV.132
To all war's fury and *profess* himself:

IV.135
And *fought* by powerful winds

IV.136
Yet, while they *fight* it most and most afflict,

IV.137
Doth show their rudeness firmer face

IV.140
He must set his face to *work,*

IV.142
And, *'stead of losing courage,* let him understand

IV.145
For the military laws, in truth,

IV.146
Expect and pardon nothing else,

IV.147
And thus do signify the shields

IV.154
To us the *wickedness* of those who *seem*

IV.155
To take a pleasure in such great disgrace.

IV.160
In *learning* how to season victuals sweet,

IV.164
Supply their lack with other virtues.

IV.165
And if to seem worth more, they *try to be*

IV.166
They go against the current and upstream,

IV.172
That he might higher raise his empire great,

IV.173
And he spent all his time

IV.179
Wrongly these undertook the work

IV.183
That they *paint us* that sentinel

IV.185
His gun well-held, with care.

IV.186
And always, never failing, they did give

IV.188
Of *massy* silver, stout enough,

IV.191
By falling *in a basin that* he had

IV.195
Who were afflicted by such misadventures,

IV.196
They shed those *famous* tears

IV.202
And time would *fail*, of need,

IV.210
Leaving his post, *as well he* might

IV.211
To take another of more profit yet

IV.213
By that same sovereign God *he loved*

IV.215
It would have been a great load on his conscience

IV.216
To have laid aside the holy *work*

IV.217
Which could *be done* for those

IV.247
One holy, lofty-minded, anchorite

IV.249
By *whom* it well may be supposed

IV.264
The scanty *gifts* of your weak arms,

IV.265
The which we see you indiscreetly *throw*

IV.266
Before the warlike, bloody, Mars,

IV.272
For those heroic ones who, *still remain,*

IV.273
And remedy your miserable lacks

IV.278
By one soul of the ones you left

IV.285
By that great God who wished to *ransom us,*

IV.287
To help and *ransom* it,

IV.291
You can deduce the esteem and the *valor* great

IV.294
When you did not erect in these new lands

IV.297
And *ended* all your works

IV.301
Prohibited, condemned forever

IV.302
To a perpetual exile *being banned*

IV.304
Say, where we shall place the work

IV.306
And 'tis a truly *graceful* thing, oh King sublime,

IV.307
That, *as* to cover more their baseness great,

IV.331
That this is all the good work of the Church

IV.343
The which have been the light of all this land,

IV.348
By the great first-fruits that were left

IV.359
Who give and scatter *from* full hands

IV.372
To find this same new work,

IV.377
Artus and Charles the great and other *brave*

IV.380
'Tis certain its antiquity ennobles

IV.391
And *were it* not allowed in Spain

IV.399
What may *come from* your Spain

IV.400
And if you *wish well to* these lands

IV.401
To favor them and give them aid

IV.402
In many a miserable misfortune

IV.403
That God permit to happen *them*

IV.404
From powerful and haughty *kings.*

IV.414
The Don Alonso, glory great and light and triumph

IV.416
And Gutierre Bernardo, who *stands*

IV.417
Forth named the oldest of the Quirós,

IV.419
At once with courage great subdued Bohorques,

IV.423
Those of the vile heretic camp *of Roman,*

IV.425
Most pestilential nests and *springs*

IV.429
Devotions for your sainted Father,

IV.432
Of one dissolute fiery, Joseph,

IV.441
And *since* our faith is plant so new,

IV.455
And since, *quite routed* from the road

IV.456
I've been scared off a goodly way,

IV.457
Returning *on* the route I started on,

IV.460
And haughty discoverers of *the* land,

IV.461
Defeated by such weary folk,

Canto V

V.62
Or so it seemed, *below* with sheets of gold.

V.77
Of the good *treatment* that he owed

V.85
They would have died then, without *help.*

V.98
'Tis certain in this year *as we relate,*

V.123
How great a martyrdom was given

V.133
Of that *red* metal, toothsome sweet,

V.139
Almost four thousand well-made robes

V.143
That that Friar Diego Márquez, persecuted

V.145
Made for the Church, our Queen,

V.146
In this new land we speak about,

V.148
Because of which within *your* court,

V.157
Attending to the news he gave,

V.158
That never *was* that noble land

V.162
Did order *that a colony* be sent.

V.169
Being there the *oldest* lieutenant

V.172
Whose *Master-of-the-Camp* was named

V.176
These the Viceroy did order should take

V.186
Brought down from their height of pride

V.197
According to the rank of the *offender,*

V.212
Upon the humble *food* of barnyard fowl,

V.226
From those brave, *generous,* barbarians

V.232
They made surrender to this prudent man,

V.244
To undo all and *throw* to earth

V.249
Within the inmost of the *unshapen* soul

V.254
Should *follow* any, *whom* we see

V.258
For valorous men do hold it true,

V.273
For things of *a laborious* importance.

Canto VI

VI.d–e
impede his good intentions, *those who took counsel to be*
favored . . .

VI.5
Since in the voyage there *is* nothing left

VI.19
That those means which it uses *symbolize*

VI.23
Within our hands, because *your* mighty Majesty

VI.28
It *being* to be discovered, note ye how

VI.34
That force, of Kings now dead

VI.35
And *of* those men we've spoken of,

VI.37
Are those who now take up the work again;

VI.39
Rulers of these dependent states,

VI.43
The noble Marquis of the Valley *took to wife,*

VI.53
He conquered by so notable a deed

VI.54
And *this* likewise was ruled with wisdom great,

VI.62
To the King's granddaughter, the *aforesaid* daughter

VI.63
Of the good Marquis, from whose *side* was born

VI.66
Which man, without an equal

VI.71
In whom you may see, *figured to the life,*

VI.77
Pretended to these distant lands.

VI.78
For *whose* just cause, without delay,

VI.91
So he did claim *that* enterprise

VI.99
Since he did know about *it,* knew that he

VI.100
Had just those *gifts* which would suffice

VI.101
For such grave matter, *and* such import,

VI.102
Just as he asked and begged of him.

VI.105
For *kindness* that he offered him

VI.106
With words alone (for lack of deeds),

VI.107
But reasons and most courteous favors,

VI.112
That 'twas impossible *for them to start*

VI.113
But the he surely showed to him

VI.116
For he had always a full memory

VI.117
Of *what* was owed to his forbearers

VI.119
Were also cause for choosing him,

VI.120
For all which reason he would give his aid

VI.121
And for the increasing longing that he had

VI.139
Into the month of August, and the year we *say*

VI.145
About the intention of the cause begun.

VI.155
Considering those who did desire

VI.158
To give *them* pleasure, gratify *them,*

VI.159
As much, on all occasions, as he *could*

VI.160
Had they *been with* his son Don Francisco,

VI.161
These things, *were* to him all of much import.

VI.163
The fact that *their* good works would merit it,

VI.164
To *them,* he said, he would adjudge

VI.172
Of all that he then *wished to write*

VI.178
Whom he did order that *they lend the aid,*

VI.179
Of those illustrious gifts they had,

VI.193
And then he sent *commands* to Don Fernando,

VI.196
All wealthy men and *with the same*

VI.199
These *draw* a contract for the *journey,*

VI.203
Columns of the Audiencia and *the* civil law,

VI.204
As well, *as very* great and deep observers.

VI.217
And finally most descendants of those Heroes

VI.224
A hundred millions were *drawn*

VI.225
From its *resources,* never tired

VI.228
Subdues the one it *saw* surrendered without pride,

VI.229
And Don Juan asked that but one point

VI.235
For it were possible *well to have thought*

VI.236
That such a noble action would be just

VI.248
And *as he made* in all most prompt dispatch,

VI.260
In skillful and in gainful *hawking,*

VI.276
So he wished that the *pleasing gift*

VI.277
Of his dear Fatherland and *duties loved*

VI.278
Should make so deep impression on the boy.

VI.280
Each one's alive, made happy, agitated,

VI.281
Triumphs, spends, pours out, exerts *himself,*

VI.284
And with no more haste do the *birds*

VI.285
Bestir, *them* at their labors in the sun,

VI.286
At the time when their *flocks* appear

VI.290
Life-giving, and ordained *for its effect,*

VI.293
Each other and *in utmost haste,*

VI.294
Impatient all, all *out of breath,*

VI.295
Pledging their properties, they *straight prepared*

VI.296
To *teach* the proper use and exercise

VI.298
And then they sent out joyous groups,

VI.300
To herald forth the liberties

VI.313
The fleet arrived and *as in it*

VI.319
And always wicked envy seeks

VI.328
Making a tale of our 'entrada'

VI.332
And knew so well how to hint to him a case

VI.333
That left him in suspense and in much doubt.

VI.334
Now, double-dealing gaining access to a noble heart

VI.335
By that proportion in which 'tis concealed,

VI.339
Asking that he *depart with feet of lead*

VI.341
He should *return to* Mexico,

VI.344
Unto your Royal Council, *asking* if they *knew*

VI.345
Of this Don Juan and whether they approved,

VI.346
And this affair and cause already *given,*

VI.347
Was all suspended and put off

VI.353
And *as for us 'twas* not enough to have

VI.354
Clean souls and consciences, if *so*

VI.355
We *could* not, with all diligence, keep down

VI.360
Suspicion falling on his wife,

VI.361
But would that she be free of *calumny,*

VI.370
The person, wisdom, *gifts* and parts,

VI.378
Kept Krying up and withering

VI.398
To dare to rival God, look thou what *injury,*

VI.399
And threw down all that we now see

VI.406
In that which they had entered on,

VI.409
Send off before the wind and quite surrender to

VI.412
And quite surrendered without *advice.*

VI.418
Saying the entry would *never* be made

VI.420
For all had been deceived in that respect?

VI.421
And others *publishing* aloud

VI.423
And never could make *head* again;

VI.430
Whose tongues, it seemed, *might furnish*

VI.431
Honey *to the* bees themselves,

VI.433
That Plato and wise Homer did,

VI.438
At which *place the* Don Luis de Velasco

VI.441
And the explanation been seen thus manifest,

VI.451
And *as* the mighty haste that he was in

VI.455
Only to offer himself *in* his sole service,

VI.456
Going without delay, as *still he would*

VI.457
But he considered that quite hopeless now

VI.458
Which he asked him with such vehemence.

VI.462
He *could* permit, without his blessing and approval,

VI.474
He now had changed his mind

VI.475
Toward what affairs Don Luis de Velasco

VI.476
Had left unfinished, since he could,

VI.488
Experience and time *could* teach

VI.494
May *bring to light* so great a work.

Canto VII

VII.16
The gallant, reckless, Californian,

VII.17
Del Cántabro the valiant whom they named

VII.27
And such as could no longer be withstood,

VII.38
And miseries and labors *now passed by,*

VII.40
And so remain forever *so* interred

VII.43
An army so resplendant and so large

VII.46
That *asks* a mighty pen to cover it,

VII.47
As good news of a thing

VII.48
Doth promise good success to *that which comes,*

VII.49
And more when 'tis agreed the purposes

VII.50
Are two most favored ones,

VII.57
For confirmation of his *news,*

VII.63
Men of good life and fame, *so that* with them,

VII.77
And *of* the tribunal of the Holy Office

VII.80
By those same Lutherans, *through whom* he came

VII.81
To be the one prime mover and the *whole*

VII.90
Had some things to reform,

VII.103
Received with most profound *disgust*

VII.115
And *the which* should be inviolably kept,

VII.121
And so, all *changed and altered,*

VII.124
And, ruined now, *thrown out-of-doors.*

VII.131
What the Count *said* to them,

VII.132
The poor gentleman being grieved,

VII.183
Through his illustrious gifts and parts,

VII.184
As his own person and his kinfolk merited.

VII.185
And as that showed in terms most clear

VII.186
The trend of his intentions toward us,

VII.194
That thus for diligence Don Juan would be

VII.195
Filled up as full and be as honorable

VII.196
As *for* the discharge of the duty

VII.197
He owed unto your Viceroy.

VII.202
This splendid *favor* they *met* well,

VII.203
With celebrating feasts and touraments

VII.204
Fifteen hundred able men

VII.205
Were collected for this expedition,

VII.209
Do disappear and *remain fixed in calm*

VII.210
Which always, durable, remains,

The King
pg. 65

. . . if *he* should come here to ask it of *you with* the said
Don Juan de Oñate, . . . a gentleman whom *you* say is *of*
the town of Bailén, had offered to make the said discovery,
I have *and you had* determined to suspend what had been
agreed upon with the said Don Juan de Oñate.

Order of the Viceroy
pg. 66

. . . President of the Royal Audience and Chancellory which
sit therein:

. . . with *nomination* as my lieutenant to prevent, obviate
and punish the disorders

. . . and of the Provinces and way to New Mexico,

. . . so that they shall not in any way use, nor can use
them, observing that by doing the contrary

. . . this my order, may appear before you, let the Captains
and officers of the aforesaid camp who are bent on the
aforesaid journey and as soon as this comes into your hands,
that it may come to the notice of the rest of the soldiers
and aforesaid people;

. . . the second of August of the year one thousand five
hundred and ninety-six.

. . . At this news the Governor *remained in suspense,* and-
because I am also, I wish to slacken until the next canto.

Canto VIII

VIII.16
The Viceroy *because he had obtained*

VIII.26
By so grave news, and *he be ruined quite,*

VIII.27
By stopping of the enterprise that cost

VIII.29
He then *wished* with all diligence

VIII.34
So, doing this, without *more difficulty,*

VIII.37
He soon *had* those two writings

VIII.53
According to *its* contents, and he would

VIII.58
And finished with great *quietness,*

VIII.64
As the *most crafty* bees do make their custom

VIII.69
"Gentlemen, whom we make companions.

VIII.70
Let us enter and not sleep upon entering,

VIII.71
For, spite of *fortune,* we are all

VIII.77
On trying for academic honors,

VIII.86
The two most valiant parties being ruled

VIII.89
And mid *the rest* the gallant General,

VIII.93
Rejoicing and their careless pleasuring,

VIII.102
As soon as he alighted, he *did give as* a reward

VIII.107
Pompey, *Cilla*, Marius and Lucullus,

VIII.110
Nor in them more *directly* acted

VIII.113
When thou with good *advice* dost so deceive

VIII.126
Of all the *points* that had been raised

VIII.132
Without excessive compliment they offer you

VIII.133
Each year a fifth of *their* estates,

VIII.136
Expert to serve you well,

VIII.149
And *never shows* within *its* forceful heart

VIII.151
For he it was who did provide

VIII.156
He *saw to it* that there should be kept

VIII.163
Gave to his words a great import

VIII.167
Where no provisions were, but hills and waters,

VIII.185
This disregard, he must understand

VIII.189
By all his disappointments *troubles and*

VIII.194
Diversity of *odorless* flowers,

VIII.197
Not otherwise the Count, *in course of duty,*

VIII.204
The powerful, compelling, *depths*

VIII.205
Against whose *hardness* we did see

VIII.206
That he *received* good letters always,

VIII.207
Asking him to be strong in truth

VIII.209
And hope much for what desperate seemed,

VIII.210
If he would *joy in* good outcome

VIII.215
The he should *trust* in God with firmness great

VIII.220
And, lord, I rightly *call* it twisted, for

VIII.221
As at first it carefully

VIII.222
Disturbed us in *our* zeal to serve you,

VIII.223
When afterward *it* wished to favor us

VIII.231
To see his children dear beset,

VIII.236
The poor monks, now in sorry *case,*

VIII.250
That he passed over gaily, though

VIII.255
The excess went to such extremes

VIII.258
"This property is mine", *however much*

VIII.259
Others said "ours", if *there* were two

VIII.263
So all *were* being *ruined,*

VIII.264
Losing all here and there.

VIII.276
Brought into shame the little *force*

VIII.281
"Tell *how you esteem* the noble worth

VIII.292
If you leave all to these *coifed dames,*

VIII.293
Who, seeing such baseness, such insult,

VIII.294
I know them all affronted sore,

VIII.297
When all *is* lost and we lack all,

VIII.298
Do we lack widely-stretching land,

VIII.330
Juan Guerra de Ressa, *knew* so well

VIII.331
How to arrange the leavings of their force,

VIII.352
And so a second time *he* was *losing*

VIII.358
Were so establishing themselves

Canto IX

IX.2
The memorable deeds we *undertook*

IX.4
The most gallant and lofty *deed*

IX.5
That always shines and glows *on* them

IX.7
Is the important *help and* assistance

IX.9
Remains dead and exhausted in itself.

IX.16
Of great injunction laid on him

IX.22
Should turn *its head,*

IX.25
To give his prelate some account

IX.26
Of certain serious and secret things,

IX.30
Following footsteps in displeasure.

IX.35
That certain soldiers, somewhat *elevated*, wished

IX.38
Was *by* the highest speed and diligence

IX.42
And in this time they did provide

IX.45
Should go as General to China, and, *at once*

IX.46
Astounding all of us, came news

IX.57
Behind which word, with no delay,

IX.76
But if not, that he *should* at once send word

IX.86
Should be *placed* and see fit to undergo

IX.92
Had *not* in full his contract's terms

IX.105
For as they had all ready then

IX.107
Like all the rest it passed *its flower,*

IX.109
The Commissary *of* the Court in time,

IX.145
Because they knew *from it* a mighty father

IX.163
Making two errands of one way,

IX.167
Did ask with great insistence he observe

IX.168
That, *beyond* this great inconvenience,

IX.171
That were so long time kept *in hope,*

IX.172
'Twere necessary, in the *gathering*

IX.177
And then all leave *for* there at once

IX.187
Had it not been such as we saw it come.

IX.225
Were carried off with *tight-packed* herds,

IX.227
The *bulls*, the horses, asses, *too,*

IX.240
Although all *were* enlisted there.

IX.244
And not divided from the camp by guards,

IX.245
And *at the break of dawn* he ordered us

IX.252
And if, *with no more hope,* some group

IX.272
And from the list *all those* were then discharged,

IX.273
And some not wishing to keep on,

IX.277
Were serving with *advantage* there

IX.278
And I know, too, great King, that some went back

IX.281
And at this time this your inspector chose

IX.292
And reasonable he should honor there,

IX.293
Your inspector and any other man,

IX.296
But such as those, for purposes so high,

IX.297
Did never come in infamy

IX.299
One for whom, in *the pleasant times of* peace,

IX.300
They sowed the *streets* with silver

IX.301
And that though in your Royal service he

IX.306
And one who surely knew well how to excuse

IX.313
Which, draining off the water, must *appear,*

IX.314
So he *appeared* and so *appeared* his cause.

IX.315
For more than all this we have said,

IX.319
In which there never *took a hand*

IX.323
The one *by* clear illustrious pen,

IX.324
The other by the *force* of his strong lance,

IX.343
Fulfilled his contract, and this *rudely,* too,

IX.344
Nor give a glimmer of what he had writ.

IX.346
And his wife Doña Ana be *allowed* to pledge

IX.356
And, should he wish it, they stood ready, too,

IX.357
To give up or alter anything

IX.359
And for the permission to be given him

IX.365
He *gave up all,* his eyes turned up

IX.386
After he had well seen the *powers,*

Canto X

X.10
Having, though with disgust, the muniments

X.12
In many places were assembling again,

X.15
Along with wagons and with coaches, went

X.31
Behind the *close-packed* cattle, following

X.36
Here, after the *wild* mares, there neighed

X.51
In graceful, sightly, pearl-mother,

X.52
And, too, *in* mighty store of fish.

X.56
He goes by winding roads and trails

X.57
To give *his* waters back unto the sea.

X.63
Because it all *was soundable,*

X.64
For which, together with the depth

X.65
They wished to find *an entry* safe.

X.89
If for the credit and the valor which

X.90
The insistent, mighty, labor we pursue demands

X.91
He has spirit enough, if he deserves

X.98
And, *breathing* on the other shore,

X.105
To all a safe ford was *before,*

X.114
And strain their powerful limbs,

X.121
To *wrap up* all that in the water might

X.124
And *in* the broad and spacious flanks

X.125
Of *mighty* oxen set the same,

X.127
In the olympian fields, *those carts,*

X.135
Upon the *submerged* poles did swing

X.146
Because of *their* strong hubs and spokes

X.156
And *as* a good example raises us

X.158
So that we easily may imitate

X.159
When 'tis *presented* with appropriate works,

X.160
Yet how weak we find *his* reasoning,

X.168
And needed little to bestir themselves,

X.184
All burden bearers, used to pain,

X.185
As being obedient to the yoke they bore,

X.186
Thrusting with their stout necks, *to pull and draw*

X.188
Now being all tired as they were,

X.198
And some the *beef* herd and the cows,

X.201
And all the numerous *droves* that came.

X.202
And with the weight of all their wool

X.266
To *follow out* his entry with relief.

X.277
His sorry end and impolite departure

X.284
But as there is and *grows* within the seed,

X.285
And through its mighty power makes the fruit,

X.288
Triumph and glory are raised up

X.294
Released the galling reins from us,

X.295
And left us all in much *suspense*

X.296
To see how without love he there *might* speak

X.303
And all made sudden start, and spurred

X.305
Light-footed, all together, *raced*

X.306
Until they caught up to their *goal.*

X.322
Let *go* the toilsome rigors of *the* weather

X.323
Though we can bear them now no more

X.324
Nor *may we* stand against their fury,

X.328
For God will *see that* He is a good Father,

X.332
For men of courage and of self-respect,

X.337
And *well risked* are the *injuries*

X.340
The more that if you *note it well,*

X.348
His sorrowful complaint, *of sufferings,*

X.349
As here to write them *to the full.*

Canto XI

XI.1
Whate'er the wounded soul may wish

XI.12
That this long *journey* had endured,

XI.15
Which he had always had, and *that anxiety*

XI.19
Which *to* a million disappointments and insults

XI.28
Because of *which* he had *set out*

XI.29
On this adventure with the mighty pledge

XI.40
The crown, the glory and the triumph *that he hoped,*

XI.41
Those who also deserved reward,

XI.42
Were seen so far behind, he did infer

XI.52
That had *been done upon* this expedition,

XI.54
If for thus *bearing on* the Church, extending it

XI.68
For so he chose to write and let him know.

XI.92
Well, *then* farewell to all *being* said

XI.93
The blessed Father *left* disconsolate,

XI.98
Marching with speed to reach us, *whom*

XI.99
He would forewarn with information

XI.100
By telling them the race of Tepehuan

XI.103
The which was given to the charge

XI.111
That without *map* still ploughs along

XI.116
He *stopped* to await the Fathers,

XI.145
That they might *do their part* in visiting

XI.168
With purpose to *find* out the turbid flood

XI.171
And which we call the R10 Bravo, too.

XI.172
Departing, then, the guides *found* out

XI.184
So, fixed upon *this difference,*

XI.186
To take a backward step nor thought

XI.195
That all *were* lost and stranded there,

XI.198
That *most came to* their hands,

XI.217
That, *as* they saw them, they would give them then

XI.232
And, *plunged into* the water, like to fish

XI.233
They there *remained*, half unconscious,

XI.235
This satisfied, the following day

XI.237
To go back with some friends of *theirs,*

XI.242
Publishing good news unto all,

XI.244
With pasture excellent and waters and good *hills,*

XI.250
Provisions now *in every point.*

XI.274
He hoping for his death to end it all.

XI.308
In it *was* buried and enclosed

XI.314
A discipline *sanguine* and great,

XI.323
Into New Mexico, *remote*

XI.324
A *work* so important, so salutary,

XI.329
And lest His goodness *might reject,*

XI.346
A sea of *purple* blood while imploring

XI.352
Until the dawn came, *and did show*

XI.353
The noble General *at the ministry*

XI.354
He needs must *do* in order to *see clear.*

XI.359
For that cause *had been* entrusted

XI.361
Their *great vagueness* doth *prove of use*

XI.362
To those who are more learned and discreet.

XI.364
What heavy load was laid on them,

XI.366
That it may not be thought I am,

Canto XII

XII.3
To be so famed, illustrious, that *of but that*

XII.4
Would *speak* that magnanimous one,

XII.8
By the repentant arm, *that doth return*

XII.10
Above the grave and memorable *signs*

XII.28
And, going on, *it may be said:*

XII.35
And *as* this doctrine teaches us

XII.60
That after the suspicious sun was hid

XII.64
But for such things *that* work is good.

XII.65
In *which* necessity doth rule,

XII.71
Just as each one his crustiness,

XII.77
Subject to error and to *oversights,*

XII.97
And did not *choose to think* of water,

XII.103
That heated some two hundred *farms.*

XII.113
Go forth to spy upon those *farms*

XII.125
The barbarous *farms* toward which we went.

XII.137
Him who *on* seeing it *was* most safe,

XII.152
Nor come and take us back with them,

XII.164
And so, all falling in and *joining it,*

XII.171
Who conquered the brave Emperor with *salute*

XII.186
And quick and swift in open field,

XII.192
Like Spaniards brave who *hurled* themselves

XII.195
And they should dismount from their steeds

XII.202
Nothing left to them *by intention*

XII.206
But not in this thing wasting time,

XII.237
Like *brawlers*, two barbarians bold;

XII.238
Bañuelos had *cut down* two more;

XII.247
And, seizing on his valiant limbs,

XII.248
Plying his teeth and *eke* his fists,

XII.254
And *in* their valiant *hearts* they both held firm.

XII.265
And, seeing the slight advantage he *might gain,*

XII.274
Well, going to their *work* a second time,

XII.275
The Spaniard, with a violent *wrench*

XII.276
Attacked the barbarian with such force

XII.284
With tenderness and loving *gifts,*

XII.292
That they should *think it good* to agree

XII.298
And that might seem to them good course,

XII.301
Loading them with glass beads and *rosaries,*

XII.311
And, like *men who submit to force,*

XII.315
So, meek *enforced*, we bore them off.

XII.318
Boiled meats, foxes, rabbits and roots,

XII.324
From those abandoned *ranches.*

XII.326
That I was sorry then, am sorry now,

XII.328
So that I do lack words and terms

XII.332
All like *round* shields and of a depth

XII.366
Praise to the Angels, oh my God,

XII.369
And given a soul and his beauty as well,

XII.370
'Tis possible, *oh* Lord, 'tis not enough

XII.376
And from this *miserable* misfortune,

XII.377
As, Lord, You suffer and permit

XII.379
Prefer it to Your image in such sort

XII.380
That there is *nothing felt* within this life

XII.381
That they *prefer not* in advantage?

XII.382
To eat, to drink, be clothed, be shod, content,

XII.383
That such is what we men most seek,

XII.384
Like brutes in all we prefer not to this?

XII.411
There we *made gifts unto* the prisoners,

XII.425
Who said that he was called Mompil *by all*

XII.451
He painted for us there a *spreading* pass

XII.453
And *more than that* he gave to us no path

XII.460
Making us understand *by* all

XII.461
That he was a most learned guide.

XII.465
And for the great part that I *did hold in,*

Canto XIII

XIII.6
Without it, all breaks and *disgusts,*

XIII.13
All is refined, sublimed, *assayed.*

XIII.25
She *set to rights* what she did bring,

XIII.30
A woven basket at her back

XIII.31
And hanging at her back also

XIII.44
Deceitful flower that quickly fades away,

XIII.47
And one to whom greatest respect is due.

XIII.51
For with no more than this love can break down

XIII.53
And there, too, love produces victories,

XIII.59
She came, like faithful, skillful, *dog*

XIII.64
The sad beast goes to him, *consoled*

XIII.65
For its vexatious, sad, absence,

XIII.75
Then she did ope the pouch and, *wiped the* dust

XIII.86
Her eyes *cast down,* she made us understand

XIII.98
If only we could *covenant for* life

XIII.125
The one most distinct from others:

XIII.132
To give *resources* and not plague the sad,

XIII.140
One miserable from fear and sustains him

XIII.141
So that *he* doth not furiously despair,

XIII.147
With grace and *then are still,*

XIII.150
Wished to assure him of her great content.

XIII.162
Whose *mighty* pledge remained behind with us,

XIII.164
Like a ferocious, *scheming,* horse,

XIII.182
Along the edge of that rough cliff

XIII.195
He left as pay for freeing *her*

XIII.197
Into whose hole he rashly went

XIII.198
And left it in a thousand pieces there

XIII.212
The fathers no more matter than the sons,

XIII.218
One with the other and *do burn*

XIII.225
That always mount to blood and fire.

XIII.226
I care no more for cultivated men

XIII.227
Than rude, wild, barbarous and gross,

XIII.229
And know that, *they are of* the Fiend himself,

XIII.230
And can be the worst beast, when they do wish,

XIII.240
The afflicted girl cannot *stay* in the camp,

XIII.249
What was the freest, safest, *step*

XIII.250
That in *his inmost* miserable *eye*

XIII.251
He did not grieve a hundred thousand times.

XIII.262
Was covering poor afflicted soul,

XIII.282
From the weak, tired, *herd of* steeds

XIII.283
The tired fourth watch to rouse up from sleep,

XIII.284
The weary first now overcome,

XIII.288
With mighty shouts *he* waked us up.

XIII.292
We *stopped at once,* our timorous hearts

XIII.330
And so there is no cause here for *dismay,*

XIII.331
And *we may* know, my gentle companions,

XIII.350
The very greatness of conduct did cause

XIII.354
Thinking more confidence *is given*

XIII.355
By shedding of *their* flowing tears

XIII.356
Than *by their* many words, *much speech,*

XIII.357
Although they might know much to say,

XIII.366
Increasing from a benefit,

XIII.377
And, giving it more *rosaries* and beads,

XIII.380
With which *dainty* performance,

XIII.381
As the deer the antlered stag

XIII.383
And eager to o'ertake *him* all at once

XIII.385
The trail of love and *his* dear track

Canto XIV

XIV.3
In such proportion *all* that is esteemed

XIV.12
At which high excellence 'tis very just

XIV.14
How they for others bear trials,

XIV.16
That bloody war *bears with itself*

XIV.17
If in the middle of *their* course *beyond all help*

XIV.27
Storing up great anxieties,

XIV.30
Without a memory of his recent *flight,*

XIV.33
So went the beautiful barbarian, *knowing.*

XIV.74
We did our work, while hoping, for

XIV.75
Some lighter, more endurable and easier borne.

XIV.108
Creeping, *foot after foot,* approached

XIV.137
From their own prostrate trunks nearby

XIV.140
The *most industrious* bees did go,

XIV.142
Travelling from one *bush* to the next

XIV.151
A furious current, roaring stream,

XIV.195
Did take him by the hand, and as a comfort

XIV.199
And as one of them truly told

XIV.200
How the camp came to the edge of ruin.

XIV.240
Such blessed gift and work it is,

XIV.242
Out of their season *did* pour water down,

XIV.244
Did move and change their locations

XIV.245
And the swift-flying sun *did* halt

XIV.248
At whose feet there *did* yield and crouch

XIV.250
Finally, as a *thing* upheld

XIV.286
And, travelling all together, *very gay,*

XIV.295
And as giving *always* breaks rocks,

Of how we took and seized upon possession of the new
  land.
pgs. 131–138

. . . and to *your* honor and glory and of *your* most sacred
  and blessed Mother,

. . . *through* the King, our lord, I say that, inasmuch as in
  virtue

. . . which his Majesty gives me, *from hence forward,* as such
  Governor,

. . . *without* other greater which he promises me

. . . in which, in opposition to *parties,*

. . . and other great number of necessary apparatus, carts,
  wagons, *compasses,* horses, oxen,

. . . kings *that his* glorious stock may reign in it,

. . . sons of my seraphic Father Saint Francis, will give
  much safer, more prosperous, happy, success,

. . . possession of *his* glory,

Canto XV

XV.6
Through prudence, *being, struggling,*

XV.7
Of *virtue's self* we see to be obtained.

XV.10
Let it be seen and noted and practised

XV.11
That *only what* is perfect and is true

XV.12
Although it be no more should deserve it.

XV.18
That the rigor of war *leads on*

XV.32
All naked and *unclothed, well drenched,*

XV.33
With pouring sweat and their arms, now

XV.65
Forgotten by the great cities,

XV.68
These, with good will, *gave aid to* us

XV.69
To pass over their land without *suspicion,*

XV.80
Except for Juan Piñero, since he *wished*

XV.82
And since there is no *cause for* fear, if prudently

XV.84
When a safe harbor *is* not *shown* to us,

XV.118
The Lord, in pity, showed *the force.*

XV.126
In the midst of his course, *discovers* us.

XV.147
That the maidens, *coming from girlhood,*

XV.153
Which custom, with the mighty *force*

XV.154
Which they consider natural,

XV.174
And being, *on another* day, that feast

XV.180
Here, *being prepared* with *greatest* care,

XV.184
Whose nimble *bands* were *governed,*

XV.188
With gay and *careless* skill.

XV.253
How, *simply* by the lash and club and stone,

XV.255
And as the man who grasps is always safe,

XV.260
All might go on in safety to

XV.276
Throughout the night with heavy heart, and set him down

XV.277
Beside the pueblo of those two whose names

XV.295
Brought from New Spain, and *that they* wished

XV.309
Well-planned in their rooms and their squares,

XV.356
Without sheep and cattle and goats.

XV.362
Beside a good sum more *than* we noted,

XV.363
In such a quantity that, *with a single hook,*

Canto XVI

XVI.25
The *final end* had now arrived

XVI.26
To the tremendous *tale and* final point

XVI.69
Through the factions and passions that they had,

XVI.90
Through the many he had hanged,

XVI.91
He'd wished, by swift flight, to desert them there.

XVI.105
Mirth of the Moors and Christians,

XVI.110
To see the *force* and arms possessed

XVI.129
The ship, *doth swing at fortune's hest*

XVI.141
And *since* that thing should *must* be done well

XVI.157
And two more freely *were set free,*

XVI.183
Where with *a single hook* the soldiers

XVI.200
Should *observe it* and wait to see

XVI.206
And that he would be lord of *all of it*

XVI.207
All of them there *were,* undisturbed

XVI.209
Wherefore, huddled together, they did *seem*

XVI.210
Being huddled down, all timid, cowardly,

XVI.214
Did come among them, *coquetting,*

XVI.234
The Sergeant, seeing there his *carelessness,*

XVI.271
With this *we* left them, and, as he had come,

XVI.299
"That were they twelve or a hundred,

XVI.308
'Twere well should be sung in new *history.*

Canto XVII

XVII.3
If he *to* whom the accident occurs

XVII.10
And, *perhaps lost* out of *their* road

XVII.16
And when he saw *him unsuspecting there,*

XVII.35
Not being thoughtless though amazed,

XVII.58
At sight of which the horses *straight,*

XVII.59
Snorting and bucking *made their riders,*

XVII.60
In spite of spur or hard-held rein

XVII.61
Go in a thousand different ways.

XVII.62
And there all *held him in a square*

XVII.66
By which the Spaniards *overcame*

XVII.69
So that each {of them so} one did rule and govern them.

XVII.77
It *put* its four feet, on the ground

XVII.78
Wallowed upon its belly and, rolling,

XVII.90
And they are so swift *of foot*

XVII.100
Relieve his eyes or detain it

XVII.101
Upon as much *space* as an orange occupies,

XVII.102
If such excess may *well* be said.

XVII.141
Which overthrows the high windmill,

XVII.142
They *reared up* and whirled to the rear,

XVII.144
An earthquake *packed together so tightly*

XVII.155
Giving them many *rosaries* and beads,

XVII.158
Who always saw upon these plains

XVII.222
Man *had* his health and, all at once,

XVII.223
He lost it without hands having touched him.

XVII.239
Than they did show within themselves,

XVII.266
Neither in justice nor in law, he would teach them,

XVII.272
That you would give to those who had lived well,

XVII.308
About this mortal man, *alive* and dead,

XVII.311
That he *should* teach and show them there,

XVII.312
Which they would *all* do with much pleasure,

XVII.313
And that *he should* see it was not fitting,

XVII.314
To order *that* they should receive

Canto XVIII

XVIII.7
Pile up its mounting coins to such a height

XVIII.8
As we do see you *pile* up yours,

XVIII.10
Has not enough, sufficient of value,

XVIII.25
But this man, being *wicked in* his ambition,

XVIII.36
For to a miserable harsh slavery

XVIII.58
Some the well-tanned buckler

XVIII.73
To blood, fire and arms, without recourse

XVIII.74
Nor *let* any delay, be raised

XVIII.80
Unto the valor of *the* powerful arm,

XVIII.111
There its *force* shows its greatest blows,

XVIII.147
Which on your efforts and your strength depends,

XVIII.148
You shall now be stirred up with wrath

XVIII.150
To agitate you by bad means,

XVIII.181
Left *those two* torn to pieces there.

XVIII.186
With all his *force* he went on attempting

XVIII.219.
And *truly* all were much amazed,

VIII.225
And covered with *well-curried hair,*

XVIII.236
And when Don Juan *had dismounted,*

XVIII.246
And that they had placed *a rearguard*

XVIII.255
The order in which *all were stationed*

XVIII.257
Were grouped about one man to protect him.

XVIII.318
That we *gathered it into* sacks

XVIII.319
And, *with them,* had with those women

XVIII.322
And when tired out, there *was a* peace

XVIII.323
Between them and ourselves by *previous plan,*

XVIII.332
It was not possible that they *keep on*

XVIII.339
And, *all taking* pleasure in this,

XVIII.348
In sole circumference, in *the* midst,

XVIII.366
Eight hundred large, beautiful, hares,

XVIII.389
And that all might go well with him *up on the rock*

XVIII.390
There went with *him* Quesada, the well-armed,

XVIII.402
And glens, meadows, small *farms* and plains

XVIII.429
I wish to *still* my voice for this canto.

Canto XIX

XIX.d
. . . until he came to the *capital* of the Governor.

XIX.8
From being in *itself* envious and faithless,

XIX.12
And strong if *it* seeks aid from vice.

XIX.45
That they do always *have* traces and signs

XIX.59
And that one I had then I *have* today

XIX.60
For animal more beautiful was never born

XIX.63
Wherefore they, all *suspicious,*

XIX.64
Prodigal of gestures and signs,

XIX.70
He then, *eagerly,* with his hand

XIX.74
Said this smiling a little, and *careless.*

XIX.75
And since I was greatly desirous,

XIX.91
I signalled them *to come and seek me there*

XIX.92
As I was going on my way,

XIX.93
Or that I *would* draw near to them.

XIX.105
Making a well-extended space

XIX.137
And laid aside my vexing helm of steel.

XIX.142
And, looking all the time all round about,

XIX.177
That, this occurring *'tween two days*

XIX.185
As they are used, with torture and uproar

XIX.186
Poor creatures, overwhelmed and captured,

XIX.187
And quickly leave most of *my* clothes,

XIX.188
I *then determined* to remove,

XIX.189
And, hidden *in the hollow of* a rock,

XIX.207
For when one comes to this point, *without hope*

XIX.208
Of that for which he sees himself so tried,

XIX.214
Oh human life, *and feeble frailty!*

XIX.215
I do not think that with *less* hunger

XIX.222
Had been for a long time and which *had watched*

XIX.228
Fled from me *to a long* distance.

XIX.236
He also licked my hands, *that* they

XIX.275
More than *five hundred* lengthy leagues

XIX.278
Of the dark night, *in which God grants*

XIX.279
That his great saints in splendor shine

XIX.282
Three noble friends *did* come to me,

XIX.291
And as the robe of darkness, *still* stretched out,

XIX.306
Praising the Angels and my God,

XIX.316
Hidden secrets *are shown* to us

XIX.342
By all these lands *they have raised up.*

Canto XX

XX.1
All the *valor*, the pride, the excellence

XX.6
By gallantry of his sword arm

XX.7
And *by* the brave and valorous heart

XX.9
Among a thousand dangers unforeseen.

XX.14
Is such as *it* should be *esteemed*

XX.15
With those courageous, gallant, hearts

XX.27
As I esteem and reverence them

XX.28
For much and much more than mere men

XX.29
'Twere well *I* set about it and write here

XX.47
By no more than their *courage and* hard work,

XX.74
With all the other things *they owned*

XX.75
Being from their needles, feminine foible,

XX.116
Sometimes, *when all is snow-covered*

XX.117
And many things to icicles are turned.

XX.124
Nor high plains, *wild places*, valleys,

XX.142
They mend their saddles *and bridles.*

XX.150
Neither this one nor that has failed to show

XX.158
Like plows dragged on, with which we use

XX.159
To break and overturn the earth

XX.160
The steel ploughshares being buried *deep*,

XX.161
And turning up long, straight, furrows,

XX.163
Were dragged at the tails of horses

XX.173
Unheard-of enterprises, *ill-fated*

XX.174
By evil fortune and ill-fate

XX.178
There were captains Vaca and Juan Martínez,

XX.187
Nor do I *question* the hero Commissaries,

XX.198
All now *retired into* poor hospitals

XX.230
Where only to have to propose to them

XX.244
Which, as though it were that, *sovereign*

XX.245
Who cannot be seen by any unfortunate

XX.248
Than *blanket* of *the* untouched snow,

XX.255
For these, as *incapable* of his sight,

XX.260
For you to see the Viceroy of New Spain,

XX.271
They seek the *traders* that they may

XX.276
Nor paid attention to the many dogs,

XX.277
Who, in pulpits tearing themselves to shreds

XX.283
And saw no poor beggar *or harborer*

XX.289
May God, of Whom you are, hold to your hand

XX.297
That *since* you well know, powerful King,

XX.336
'Twould be an easy thing *to give* to him

XX.337
Secure pretension, beyond jealousy,

XX.338
That no one *shows* himself an opponent,

XX.341
With this, then, they *joined to themselves*

XX.342
All of their friends, *more that* they could,

XX.353
That party should defend itself.

XX.357
To Mulco and a few seditious more,

XX.361
That if one lacks to prompt and to raise up,

XX.366
Has destroyed and overturned us all,

XX.370
Although the joint forces of hell

XX.384
A proper *harvest* for deceitful minds

Canto XXI

XXI.21
As *his* cruel, unmeasured, haughtiness

XXI.22
Continually, always, *advanced,*

XXI.23
Not to hinder it, he did then stand up,

XXI.34
Can come upon all of this *force*

XXI.68
Never did word run through *a crowd*

XXI.84
We see *since* dying is no more than an instant,

XXI.86
A proper time to die *will come to us,*

XXI.88
And *pardon* such great inconvenience

XXI.104
Of great insult he said *them*, too,

XXI.105
As if upon *the* mountains high and valiant

XXI.106
They had all fallen and been cast,

XXI.121
The fact is this vile traitor would receive

XXI.122
The bettering and deserved punishment.

XXI.123
Of this his vain presumption.

XXI.141
The father *instant* seized his mighty mace,

XXI.144
Otompo, then Melco and *Guanamibo,*

XXI.153
Oh vanity, *vile-savoring* poison,

XXI.156
Only to reach for you, the empty pride!

XXI.157
That royal blood does lend, noble,

XXI.158
Clownish, barbarian or highland,

XXI.168
And thus, this vile, bloody, *idolatry,*

XXI.205
They would return with it, and the next day,

XXI.211
Call to innocents upon security.

XXI.212
God *frees* us from the evil waiting us

XXI.214
For put into so difficult a *proof*

XXI.224
That they *would* go to their houses to seek

Canto XXII

XXII.3
To be a treacherous deceit not understood,

XXII.21
When a vile traitor, coward and villain

XXII.25
Whose famous *gifts* vanish away

XXII.27
When treason wishes to *dispute*

XXII.28
And be defended with secret poison,

XXII.29
For greater *poison*, *of* destruction,

XXII.36
Hardly, lord, did they see *themselves* dispersed

XXII.46
Putting their plot *to adventure,*

XXII.48
The *force* of the mutiny that was raised.

XXII.52
Through only having wished to *overthrow,*

XXII.67
Note that all *this is a discovery,*

XXII.68
Of broken faith, broken obedience,

XXII.71
Through which manifest *disillusionment*

XXII.80
Of what may be secured without bloodshed,

XXII.81
A thing of such *affront* and such great weight

XXII.82
As *great as* all the land we tread?

XXII.89
That we *should now have in* retreat,

XXII.90
Collecting our folk *as by chance,*

XXII.93
In anything set well on *foot*

XXII.117
Was by a miracle retrieved

XXII.118
By those who *lost* it without *fear*

XXII.123
"Death! Death *to* blood and fire! Death

XXII.142
Thinking by the aim alone 'twere possible

XXII.144
By the barbarian fury that *attacked."*

XXII.145
This hesitated for a breath

XXII.151
Then all in a fury, attacked,

XXII.152
Hurling their powerful maces.

XXII.157
By the broad foot of rustic *clown,*

XXII.172
Like those condemned by fortune who

XXII.173
Do row for land 'mid splashing waves

XXII.174
Not to be sunk and overwhelmed

XXII.180
To heaven spray from water, *they force through,*

XXII.193
At this, the brave Tempal, *who had*

XXII.194
Come up, was shamed beyond his senses to

XXII.196
And bending to the ground for a rock,

XXII.199
The rock in such a way that it *struck down*

XXII.200
Pereira, sorrowful upon his face,

XXII.203
His head to pieces with a club

XXII.204
For that miserable man, and, all seeing

XXII.211
The Spanish force *made an attack*

XXII.212
Upon the furious barbarian crowd,

XXII.215
When horrid war is *spoken of,*

XXII.258
And note *that* of these two duties

XXII.259
'Tis *necessary* that he exercise and profess *both,*

XXII.260
And not permit *that he break them* or dare

XXII.262
From the end that is due to *all,*

XXII.263
Having always before him as *target*

XXII.272
The *force* of the office he has,

XXII.283
Whose strength was raised, seeing this,

XXII.285
Joined 'neath the fortress of his shield,

XXII.289
An arm brought iron-pointed lance

XXII.308
Be broken and shattered *from the earth here.*

XXII.310
Popolco did attack one *Castilla,*

XXII.321
In his own murderer, so that,

XXII.322
He tripping over *his* own entrails,

XXII.332
Raised up his *iron-bound* club and on his helm

XXII.339
Shedding much blood in his vengeance,

XXII.342
The steel of his *abased* sword,

XXII.344
And *thrusting* with it, blind with rage,

XXII.345
Six times he *sank it,* red, scarlet,

XXII.348
Whence his soul *fled* and so, raging

XXII.372
After him, then, *the second* threw himself,

XXII.384
Showing the *fineness of their perfection,*

Canto XXIII

XXIII.4
Of that *heroic* man who, *burst*

XXIII.7
And shedding a whole sea of fresh blood.

XXIII.8
Sustained with courage the long hours

XXIII.28
With which arrow we see he is inflamed,

XXIII.30
The rough crest on his lofty *neck,*

XXIII.31
Turning his shaggy *head* from side to side,

XXIII.33
Prepares for all his mighty claws,

XXIII.34
And with his gleaming teeth attacks.

XXIII.44
Their *pleasant* nests, a safe harbor

XXIII.47
And so the fearful Acomans

XXIII.56
No less the brave and famous *abundance*

XXIII.58
Came to diminish *its* straining strength,

XXIII.59
And those who had held back before,

XXIII.60
Did rain upon him furious blows.

XXIII.80
For, *quickly* being wounded, *three times more,*

XXIII.81
And though he was completely ruined now,

XXIII.83
Did take new courage from the earth,

XXIII.84
Making *for* each of them, like three lions,

XXIII.85
Three wide, *unoccupied, spaces,*

XXIII.89
The lofty temples of *the* Zaldívar,

XXIII.98
And though we know that we are free of them,

XXIII.149
For that post and shelter of friends *he* left,

XXIII.154
And that they should send out post-haste

XXIII.169
And, holding his *courage* for goodly time,

XXIII.184
Is crying out for her husband

XXIII.186
Others for benefactor and for loved *parent,*

XXIII.193
And many blows they gave themselves,

XXIII.245
And once again grieve and complain.

Canto XXIV

XXIV.9
Finding *the bottom* in a safe and pleasant port!

XXIV.19
Vanish at last, *as mortals do themselves,*

XXIV.33
Making us at least understand

XXIV.40
Whose *progress* he had hardly done

XXIV.62
I beg Thee, Lord, Thou *wait for* us,

XXIV.67
In these and other lamentable things,

XXIV.95
Though it be *sour* and ill-tasting,

XXIV.121
That it in all things should go *on.*

XXIV.124
And *since* His blood and cross and death

XXIV.138
Let the rest tell me where they were

XXIV.180
And in the tongue of native Indians,

XXIV.184
That they, *retreating, might* return

XXIV.186
And in his company he wished to send

XXIV.194
The main *battle* and the rearguard,

XXIV.205
With which in that watch of dawn

XXIV.206
I always found myself assigned

XXIV.218
Was guiding on a real path

XXIV.239
As it would *be* occasion *for* sorrow

XXIV.240
More than his coming, though encouraging

XXIV.251
As it was good he do to succor them.

XXIV.255
Within that shelter, *carelessly,*

XXIV.284
And each one went, *more quiet than*

XXIV.300
Within their *altered* homes.

XXIV.301
The prudent General, too, who *considered*

XXIV.302
Watching, not sleeping, upon this affair,

XXIV.307
And so to see the order he had *traced,*

Canto XXV

XXV.1
Hardly had the fresh dawn entered, *filling*

XXV.2
The *narrow room*, when the strong General

XXV.10
Draw up against the folk and *force* of Acoma

Reply of the Commissary and monks.
pgs. 222–224

. . . *so* that they may disturb the just result which he in-
tends.

. . . and so *it* should *be required of* peace before he begins
it

. . . other causes *of* those already stated,

. . . *safe* in all right,

. . . the death of men, *the one*, because it is most hateful
to God,

. . . *whom they* unjustly combat *to* death is caused,

. . . the necessity *ceasing* or manifest peril *regarding* death,

XXV.18
With *these* opinions, well founded

XXV.27
And *though* he wished to do and order it

XXV.29
There was in this matter *great things*

XXV.32
And all that of the capital,

XXV.33
The *exact desire* that he had to go

XXV.52
In *their own persons*, to whose charge

XXV.63
To all the soldiers, *at the very first,*

XXV.69
He should note carefully *his camps,*

XXV.70
Their entrances and exits, and what place

XXV.73
And, set in place and *with orders*

XXV.76
And that he was by no means to permit

XXV.92
But if in all this *it* should come about,

XXV.99
That force burning and smouldering,

XXV.94
Should still keep the culprits its prisoners.

XXV.95
And all should show themselves rebellious,

XXV.116
Through no more than *a monk beseeching it*

XXV.117
Who should intercede in *this* case.

XXV.142
As he was skilled and *well-practiced in arms,*

XXV.143
Who with his strength of arm was well prepared

XXV.144
To be able to force his way in a melee

XXV.146
In which we *afterward* saw and found *him.*

Canto XXVI

XXVI.6
Is in itself more grave *as it contains*

XXVI.7
That excess of moment and gravity

XXVI.19
The captain in that same fortress,

XXVI.36
He should be seen at Acoma, nor should there be

XXVI.56
Lost in the soil, so, seeming quite *careless,*

XXVI.89
To ill so dangerous *that* time will tell

XXVI.101
And spoke in this wise, *carelessly:*

XXVI.115
Let him shelter beneath the shadow of this *man,*

XXVI.127
Their *hands clutching* widely, and if

XXVI.144
As though we were the gods, on *high*

XXVI.161
Any evil that could not reach the stars, whose height

XXVI.188
Must be despised and *rascally,*

XXVI.200
Gicombo then was *vain*, with many more,

XXVI.227
One who with patent *disillusionment*

XXVI.239
And having entered *a secure and enclosed place,*

XXVI.285
A *quarter*, counting it at most,

Canto XXVII

XXVII.33
To fire and blood, *and* war, and so crush her.

XXVII.39
With steel, fine, clean, and *reinforced*

XXVII.46
Prepared the bridles and the *saddles,* too,

XXVII.47
Pack-saddles, stirrups, *driving-whips,*

XXVII.57
Have need or *loss* of being in

XXVII.58
The proof most difficult and escalade.

XXVII.80
And they *would* not permit that any man

XXVII.90
And so I leave him here: *for* he forgets,

XXVII.91
That God, who died for him, *yet cares.*

XXVII.101
Of that proud rock, *unless there was*

XXVII.118
Before the mighty *force*, which consisted

XXVII.124
The *deformed* peaks, such as were never seen.

XXVII.133
Here Gicombo said, *jealously*:

XXVII.138
And since they *all turn* their *faces*

XXVII.151
Attacking furiously this conversation,

XXVII.153
Him and but six friends more, for he did wish

XXVII.160
From off the lofty, cliffs *and rocks,*

XXVII.164
Others, too, there were mingled *in*

XXVII.165
Among whose *uniforms* were seen

XXVII.170
Of certain victory which they *hoped for.*

XXVII.174
Sooty and painted with *lightnings*

XXVII.188
And Toms, the *cunning* interpreter

XXVII.208
Saying: "There awaited us, death, death,

XXVII.227
For this was not a rumor, treacherous dealing,

XXVII.259
The body-guard, *and* the Royal Ensign,

XXVII.268
Took up their posts and *saw to it*

XXVII.276
Made the camp safe with the ladies

XXVII.277
Who were in the city, and further said

XXVII.278
That, if the General ordered *more to go,*

XXVII.280
But, if not, he *would* then leave them alone,

XXVII.281
Since they wished to keep safe all that

XXVII.289
Great Martesia, *did likewise*

XXVII.293
Like women, after all, the dear pledges

XXVII.307
Showed there right well *her* brave spirit.

Canto XXVIII

XXVIII.4
To be observed, esteemed, as valiant men

XXVIII.26
And the great opportunities and means

XXVIII.27
That they presented for winning honor,

XXVIII.28
And the *great stream* which was beyond that place

XXVIII.49
So important a thing, *but ask*

XXVIII.61
To make our lives secure at first,

XXVIII.66
For some cowardly ones, he *was not ignorant*

XXVIII.71
The *last resource*, for it is demanded

XXVIII.72
By that pain which is final, and common

XXVIII.73
For such a hopeless case. And since fortune

XXVIII.75
Let us, then, try this *resource* with few men

XXVIII.77
We may escape, and let the gentlemen

XXVIII.78
Of my council, return to their command."

XXVIII.86
Sees it there at his feet, *the* Zaldıvar,

XXVIII.111
Zutancalpo, fearing *revolution*

XXVIII.115
He entered with his friends, *in deep silence,*

XXVIII.128
Does gain and have within itself more *force*

XXVIII.136
Whose forwardness should not be considered

XXVIII.137
Except as binding his father and dragging forth

XXVIII.155
To make our *engines* ready and trenches.

XXVIII.157
Let us begin at once, *to be careful*

XXVIII.158
To know what the foe is doing.

XXVIII.163
"*Speak* to your friends, Zutancalpo,

XXVIII.164
To Gicombo, I *say*, and great Bempol,

XXVIII.165
Who fight their quarrels out with words

XXVIII.169
Hanging loose at their sides, nor *do*

XXVIII.182
Stomping *nimbly*, they make a thousand bits,

XXVIII.183
Of them, desirous to be off.

XXVIII.230
If, put into the place where we are now,

XXVIII.251
That, since by *scanty* means *at no* few times

XXVIII.267
And so, for this *cause*, I intend

XXVIII.269
Whose *careless* cleverness is to pretend

XXVIII.270
And so he reined about, quite *carelessly,*

XXVIII.305
More than three hundred feet *and* divided

XXVIII.320
Spurring hard *in* the powerful sides

XXVIII.333
The force of the rock, never lost,

Canto XXIX

XXIX.5
By a *loquacious fool*, if prudently

XXIX.6
He knows how to dissimulate, *and talk.*

XXIX.9
For, seeing the barbarians together, whom

XXIX.10
The Castilians had *drawn away,*

XXIX.13
Toward our encampment, where the tents

XXIX.33
For it was necessary so as the number

XXIX.34
Was not filled up and it should be no less.

XXIX.82
Each one discharging four bullets

XXIX.91
That, almost stretched him out upon the ground,

XXIX.92
When he arose, *being* furious,

XXIX.94
Who dared *to hope to equal* his daring.

XXIX.116
We all observed, *him with suspense.*

XXIX.126
He wildly hurled himself *at* him

XXIX.128
Through the *re-formed* barbarian mob

XXIX.163
Behind Diego Robledo and Simón Pérez,

XXIX.167
First taking off the *lofty* crests

XXIX.168
From their good sallets, placed themselves

XXIX.175
All, though afraid, did *so* forge on

XXIX.178
That the barbarians were astonished and confused

XXIX.197
Francisco de Pedraza Olague, de Zumaia,

XXIX.215
Was suffering the *force* of *their weapons,*

XXIX.216
Until the night *was now* spreading

XXIX.253
For without them the *badly-prepared* fort

XXIX.290
Of Gicombo be *quite healed."*

Canto XXX

XXX.4
With what *skill* he doth mark and note

XXX.10
Together would fail him *in better times,*

XXX.17
Upon great penalties, *of chains* and force,

XXX.36
And *now* the shining sun had gone to rest

XXX.73
And so she stilled her voice, standing

XXX.85
And strengthen mine, *for* this sad soul

XXX.86
Has come here but to look on you,

XXX.92
I leave you as *a gift* my heart and soul."

XXX.104
And of our laws *the holy* defenders,

XXX.134
The water here and there, *sinking*

XXX.139
Attacked with them and *came crashing.*

XXX.175
All going thence not to *be seen*

XXX.176
As captives of such *haughty* hands. And then

XXX.184
Which was a trifle *steep* and protected,

XXX.203
The courage for that leap to such effect

XXX.207
And, passage made between *these points*

XXX.288
He pleased him in this, *with a studied carelessness*

XXX.289
But ordered that those men should go with him.

XXX.310
Blest be the Angels, oh my God,

Canto XXXI

XXXI.8
With such good things as these, we see

XXXI.9
A bold, charging, attack made by the Sergeant,

XXXI.15
The skillful reapers *no* more swiftly wield

XXXI.20
Than these brave, haughty, combatants

XXXI.61
Today your deeds attain *their* highest point

XXXI.62
And to the highest homage *for* Spaniards

XXXI.63
Have *never* yet raised them *so* high.

XXXI.64
Let them not fall, sustain the *weight*

XXXI.65
For thus *bears down* and weighs the true greatness

XXXI.127
The rustic *clown* when he places

XXXI.139
Now conquered and most openly disgraced,

XXXI.172
Which *seem useful and* fruitful ones,

XXXI.217
About the Spaniards' *force* and their courage.

XXXI.224
Like *forest leaves* that are rustled

XXXI.225
By powerful Boreas, *removed*

XXXI.226
And in a confused mass are whirled

XXXI.227
Hither and thither, *snatched about,*

XXXI.228
Blown high with chaff, alternating

XXXI.229
From high to low, and all about

XXXI.248
From windows *upon this hand and that,*

XXXI.255
That sons *for* fathers, fathers *for* their loved children,

XXXI.275
Of such incurable evil, not to see *them*

XXXI.297
We see *have withdrawn them* that her ruin

XXXI.302
If you are, as we two do feel *ourselves,*

Canto XXXII

XXXII.5
If we observe most of mortals

XXXII.6
Whom cruel and inmeasurable

XXXII.8
Could never satisfy: *with* great sceptre,

XXXII.9
With royal crown *or a* brave throne,

XXXII.10
After a poor beginning or a low estate?

XXXII.17
To have opposed with such great *force*

XXXII.38
And as you raise yourself so high,

XXXII.39
The more you rise and take upon yourself

XXXII.40
The baser is that thing you undertake.

XXXII.51
Terrible clots of blood *had oozed,*

XXXII.52
Their vital organs, too, and the black blood

XXXII.54
For thence also had way been made

XXXII.56
And in this dreadful slaughter, *moreover,*

XXXII.75
Though she could not discover *what* had been

XXXII.76
The *force* of that most deadly sword

XXXII.196
That *he had almost fallen* to the ground

XXXII.197
Then by the long hair which the savage had,

XXXII.198
He seized *him* and held on with strong fingers.

XXXII.246
Shook his long lance as best he could,

XXXII.248
Stood trembling, *though safe upon* the ground.

XXXII.295
And you, Zutacapn, who have been

XXXII.321
The miserable palace, *all unplanned,*

XXXII.368
Or else kill me yourself, for 'tis unjust

XXXII.370
To me whom you see now so *handicapped.*

XXXII.381
His face showing amid the yellow flames.

Canto XXXIII

XXXIII.6
For hardly *do we feel approach*

XXXIII.7
Of fate so ruinous, unfortunate,

XXXIII.9
Into the abyss and center of *the same,*

XXXIII.10
Of all that *makes us find* misery,

XXXIII.12
We leave the histories, so full

XXXIII.14
And let us *speak of* this ruined heathen,

XXXIII.15
Free, unsheltered, now abandoned

XXXIII.16
By *the* holy, divine and lofty hand.

XXXIII.17
Which is the halting-place in which we see?

XXXIII.18
Oh great and immense good, *you* permit not

XXXIII.19
Such punishment, *because* of Your deep wounds,

XXXIII.45
Without regret destroying them, *yet* I

XXXIII.50
The air in vain *for* soon 'twill come

XXXIII.54
And each one *feeling*, with sadness

XXXIII.55
Yet more of joy and of content,

XXXIII.56
At my sad, miserable, final end,

XXXIII.57
Say what *she* will and what *she* please;

XXXIII.59
After the sun goes through *two* moons,

XXXIII.63
And the most bitter sighs *are tired,*

XXXIII.64
And those sorrows which are endured

XXXIII.70
Oh Acoma, *who hast offended god,*

XXXIII.71
Why has thou caused it that the lofty gods

XXXIII.73
And caused the gods *should* show such rage

XXXIII.74
And fury, *and against such powers*

XXXIII.75
As *are* immortal even as the gods

XXXIII.78
For if their forces had not opposed us

XXXIII.79
It would have been easy to make *ourselves*

XXXIII.83
If this is true, *then may they be consoled,*

XXXIII.84
For I live now beyond consolation?"

XXXIII.85
As he was speaking, *as if in reply,*

XXXIII.133
And where expect ye *ye may hope*

XXXIII.134
For greater sorrows then afflict ye here?"

XXXIII.135
With this idea, absorbed and uplifted,

XXXIII.137
Searching with glances keen and sharp,

XXXIII.138
The lofty heavens, much *heartened,*

XXXIII.139
By one or other thought which they inspired.

XXXIII.169
Whose vital heat from *trembling* limbs

XXXIII.187
Was there no time for my unhappy son

XXXIII.188
To speak with his mother *at least,*

XXXIII.189
Where is the *beautiful* Luzcoija

XXXIII.190
Who did sustain my sad old age?

XXXIII.197
With all the strength I have and can apply

XXXIII.198
To serve me in imploring you?"

XXXIII.200
Who having made the hard journey,

XXXIII.201
Up to the lofty lateen-yard,

XXXIII.225
Had Zutacapn only given *assent*

XXXIII.226
Unto my *prayer for* I, lord, have *adhered*

XXXIII.227
To this most fragile tender rod

XXXIII.228
While the fields thirty times have *given*

XXXIII.229
New flowers anew, *and yet I continue*

XXXIII.230
Forever living though I may be weak . . ."

XXXIII.258
And like *one* surrendered and dishonored

XXXIII.259
In *the* public arena and *injured."*

XXXIII.260
Whose head is now bowed lowly down

XXXIII.264
And in the battle of well-proved importance,

XXXIII.272
Changed from *its hardness* into clemency

XXXIII.273
And there he sees that benign soul,

XXXIII.357
Well when the smallest leaf doth fall

XXXIII.362
By *Thee, Lord* and *my* brother, desirous

XXXIII.365
Their beginnings and midst misfortune.

XXXIII.368
Thou gavest safe entry into Thy cities,

XXXIII.369
Being the *foremost primacy* offered

XXXIII.370
In this new Church of Mexico;

XXXIII.371
And yet it was not I, whose poor, sad, life

XXXIII.374
Who was found there at your strong side

XXXIII.376
Nor would the barbarian fury finish

XXXIII.377
That miserable life which I yet have

XXXIII.392
If you *must needs taste* bitter death,

XXXIII.397
Sang the great victory they *had* achieved

XXXIII.398
Than to the conquered, *since* their bodies lie

XXXIII.399
In the midst of their broken arms?

XXXIII.417
Here, for *its* high effort and ardent zeal,

XXXIII.418
And for *its* great valor, famous and rare,

XXXIII.419
It shall remain forever eternized

XXXIII.421
Because of the great reputation gained

XXXIII.422
By all *its* great ancestors and forbears."

Canto XXXIV

XXXIV.47
So he, *ordering* Chumpo and a few

XXXIV.72
To see if they are safe, *if* destruction

XXXIV.73
Caused by *our army is now past,*

XXXIV.105
However more unfortunate and lost,

XXXIV.194
Being moved, *by chance so that he* could

XXXIV.195
Make that doubt clear, *and so* help us

XXXIV.202
That they *shall* not tire or fatigue themselves

XXXIV.203
Nor *shall* they try to seek these more,

XXXIV.212
Let them watch what they do, *lest these return*

XXXIV.213
A second time *unto the* work begun."

XXXIV.223
Of Thy choice to be a saint, whom all the earth

XXXIV.225
That Thou cam'st with the Virgin to guard us."

XXXIV.236
By an old Indian woman within *his gates,*

XXXIV.240
Having the fortunes of the withered branch,

XXXIV.242
Did *go about the country,* and, seeing

XXXIV.244
Being overwhelmed after so great a misfortune,

XXXIV.246
To be most skillful hunters and to come

XXXIV.249
From the great rock. And thus, *deceitfully,*

XXXIV.254
Not to err in the *matter,* for, once lost,

XXXIV.255
A great soldier might then be lost as well,

XXXIV.256
And so they were taken and, *having drawn*

XXXIV.257
A charge up and recorded it as well,

XXXIV.279
Our generous blood *which your boldness,*

XXXIV.280
Untiring yet, has taken pleasure in,

XXXIV.284
May here *sever our* throats for you,

XXXIV.289
As *those of yours,* which we despise."

XXXIV.300
And throwing these inside, they *then were seen*

XXXIV.327
Were tested for them, and, dragging

XXXIV.342
They show that they are testing the branches,

XXXIV.354
May you remain in joy for we now close

XXXIV.364
Sons more unfortunate than *yours shall be."*

XXXIV.373
And, as two vessels coming into port

XXXIV.374
Do turn their broad *gunwales* and bridle up

APPENDIX B

Voces Anotadas

abalorios—conjunto de cuentas de vidrio.
a barrisco—sin distinción.
abasto—abundante.
a bien librar—en el mejor de los casos.
abilitar—habilitar, proveer.
abrigo—defensa.
a bueltas de—a vueltas de, además de.
acabar con—conseguir de.
acaso—fortuitamente.
acicate—espuela.
(se) acogiessen—se acogiesen, se retiraran.
acuerdo—razón, juicio.
aderezaba—disponía.
aderezados—preparados, arreglados.
aplomo—aderece, enderezca, vuelva a la recta.
aderece—aderece, enderezca, vuelva a la recta.
a dos manos—con entusiasmo.
a dos puños—con ambas manos.
a escala vista—asaltar de día y a vista del enemigo.
aferró—agarró.
aforradas—cubiertas.
afrenillando—amarrando con frenillos.
agarrochado—herido de garrocha, vara con gancho en la punta.
agua de pie—agua de fuente.
aguado—diluido, rebajado.
aguage—aguaje, aguadero.
águilas caudales—águilas reales.
aguja—obelisco.
ahuchando—en la cetrería, llamando al pjaro desviado.
alárabes—árabes; todo enemigo no europeo.
a las vueltas andando—luchando.
albricias—recompensa al portador de noticias.
alcanza—se necesita/consigue.
alcanzase—llegase.
alcatraces—pelícanos.
al descubierto—al aire libre/abiertamente.
al descuido—inadvertidamente.
al desgaire—de mal talante.
alebrestados—acobardados.
alentar—tomar aliento.
alijar—aliviar, aligerar la carga.
al justo—justamente.
altenería—altanería, caza con pájaros de presa.
amainan—aflojan.
a más andar—muy de prisa.

anta—ante, piel de este mamífero o piel curtida de cualquier animal.
antigualla—noticia o relación de sucesos muy antiguos.
apañando—cogiendo.
apeñuscadas—apiñadas.
apercebidos—apercibidos, preparados, avisados.
a pique—hundiéndose/cerca.
a pique de—próximo a.
aplomo—a plomo, en vertical.
a porfía—porfiando entre sí.
aportaron—llegaron.
aprestara—aderezara, remediara.
arbolaban—encabritaban (caballos).
arfando—cabeceando, como los buques.
arriscado—atrevido, valiente.
arriscarse—arriesgarse.
(se) arriscó—se enojó.
assegurado—asegurado, confiado.
assentados—asentados, acordados.
(nos) assientan—nos asientan, nos sirven de base.
assiento—asiento, contrato.
assistencia—asistencia, presencia.
a su salvo—a su satisfacción.
atajado—parado.
atajos—grupos de ganado.
atentados—moderados, cuidadosos.
a todo trance—resueltamente.
atravesando—pasando, cruzando.
atreguado—loco con períodos de lucidez.
atriaca—triaca, contra—veneno.
atropellan—derriban, alcanzan.
atropellando—movimiento a tropel, raudo.
a una mano—con movimiento circular.
aurigas—conductores de caballerías.
autos en estrados—determinaciones de juzgado.
aventaban—ahuyentaban.
aventada—ahuyentada de ganado.
aventados—llenos de viento.
aventajarse—mejorarse.
aventura—riesgo.
avigados—entre o sobre vigas.
aviso—discreción.
a bueltas—a vueltas de, además.
azezando—acezando, jadeando.
azezidos—acezidos, jadeos.
aziones—aciones, correas del estribo.

bagaje—tren de bagaje.
bastos—albardas.
behetría—sin sujeción a señor/desorden, anarquía.

bejucos—nombre de varias plantas y maderas americanas.

bellas—verlas.

beneficia—extrae.

bezotes—adorno de labios de indios americanos.

blandón—receptáculo de antorcha.

boca—apertura entre montañas.

bofes—pulmones.

boga arrancada—remando con fuerza y hondura.

bogabante—bogavante, primer remero.

boga picada—remando con la pala muy en la superficie.

bogar sobre los cabos—remar puestos sobre los remos.

boiada—boyada, manada de bueyes.

boja—mide.

bolteado torno—volteado torno—torno girante.

borda—vela mayor.

bote—salto.

botos—desafilados.

bramadero—poste al que atan las bestias para herrarlas.

bravera—ventana o respiradero de horno.

brazas—medida de extensión de unas dos varas, metro y medio.

bridones—jinetes.

brinquiños—joyas pequeñas o juguetes.

brutos—animales.

buen despacho—eficiencia.

buzo—el que trabaja debajo del agua.

cabeza de processo—cabeza de proceso, oficio que provee el juez para investigar un delito.

cajas—tambores/piezas de madera en que se asegura el cañón de un arma.

cala y cata—inspección.

cálense—ciérrense.

cambrones—zarzas.

Cancro—Trópico de Cáncer.

cándidos—blancos.

cansada—de antecedentes hebraicos.

capitularon—concertaron.

cardume—banco de peces.

cargada—fuerte, dura.

carnestolendas—carnaval, fiesta.

cascajo—piedras pequeñas.

caudales—abundantes.

(se) ceba—se alimenta, se engorda.

cebado—prendado.

cebil—civil, vil, despreciable.

cegajoso—que hace lagrimear.

cercén—a cercén, enteramente.

cerco—círculo trazado para conjuros.

cerreras—yeguas mansas que andan sueltas.

cerro—espinazo.

cervatillas—ciervos pequeños, crías de rumiantes.

ciego—aplicado a nudo, difícil de desatar.

cierta—ciertamente.

cintas—maderas que van por fuera del costado del buque.

círculos—líneas de paralelo latitudinales.

clima—zona entre paralelos o líneas de latitud.

colocando—acomodando.

como—según, mientras.

cóncavo—concavidad.

con descuido—con menosprecio/sin atender.

con esto—a pesar de esto.

con pies de plomo—con cuidado y cautela.

contradicción de partes—contra otras opiniones.

contrastarle—combatirle.

copadas—de árboles de alto follaje.

copella—copela, crisol de huesos calcinados para fundición de metales preciosos.

copia—cantidad.

coz—culata.

cozida—cocida, proceso para teñir géneros.

criando—creando.

crianza de buena gorra—saludos

crudo—cruel.

crugía—paso entre remeros de la galera.

cuento—extremo, punta.

cuernos—alas de una agrupación militar.

cursados—entendidos.

chapada—corta.

chichimecas—indios mexicanos no apaciguados.

chueca—bolita pequeña con que juegan los campesinos.

chusma—tripulación.

dañados—condenados.

dar de mano—cesar.

dar de ojos—caer de pecho.

dar en qué entender—hostigar.

dar vado—dar paso, no molestar.

decrépita—decrepitud.

dechado—ejemplo, modelo.

del dicho—de lo dicho.

demediaron—recorrieron la mitad.

de parte de—en nombre de.

derezera—derecera, dirección.

derribada—arqueada, caída hacia atrás.

(se) derribó—se bajó.

derrota—camino.

(se) derrotase—se saliera del camino que llevara.

desabrida—áspera.

desabrido—disgustado.

desahuziados—desahuciados, sin remedio.

desapoderada—precipitada.

descubiertos—de caída.

descuidado—abandonado.

descuido—negligencia, incuplimiento.

desemboltura—desenvoltura, desvergüenza.

desengaño—verdad.

deservada—desyerbada.

desgalgada—precipitada desde lo alto.

desgarrada—licenciosa, rebelde.

desgracia—desagrado, aspereza.

deshecha—violenta.

desmandados—separados de sus compañeros.

desmandado—excesivo.

despacharse—ponerse en funciones.

despachos—cédulas, comisiones.

despojadas—desnudas.

destroncados—descoyuntados.

destroncasen—cortasen.

destrozado—aniquilado moralmente.

dexo—dejo, fin.

disgustosa—enfadosa.

dispensase—despensase, acumulase provisiones.

ditados—dictados, estados de los que toma nombre un
  señor.

donosos—graciosos.

doseles—cortinas.

echádoles por puertas—abandonádoles.

echaron bandos—anunciaron públicamente.

el alma entre los dientes—a punto de expirar.

embebiéndola—embutiéndola.

embijados—pintados.

embrazaban—abrazaban.

(se) empache—avergüence.

empacho—perturbación, vergüenza.

empedernido—endurecido.

en brama—en celo.

encendido—sonrojado.

encogida—tímida, miedosa.

encogido—reducido.

encogido tiempo—tiempo de frío.

en contorno—alrededor.

en cosso—en coso, acosado, lidiado.

encubertados—cubiertos.

endereza—adorna.

endrina—ciruela.

enjuta—seca.

enmienda—castigo.

en peso—sin inclinarse o volcarse.

en peso—enteramente.

en que—porque.

en raudal—en crecida.

en su fineza—en su punto más logrado.

en su tanto—en su favor.

(se) entablasen—se dispusiesen.

entena—mástil.

enternizada—enternecida.

en torno—por turno.

entricadas—intrincadas, enredadas, confusas.

en vanda—en banda, a un lado.

enzolbada—ensolvida, contraída.

escaramuza—batalla simulada.

escarcelas—armaduras desde la cintura al muslo.

esmeriles—piezas pequeñas de artillería.

espaciosos—lentos.

espadarte—pez espada.

esquilmenas—esquilmeñas, fructíferas.

estacada—desafío.

estados—medidas de la estatura de un hombre.

estalage—estalaje, estancia, puesto.

este siglo—esta vida.

estufa—kiva, lugar subterráneo para ritos religioso.

exsala—exhala, despide gases.

expuesto—preparado para la inspección.

extraño—inhumano.

fagina—leña menuda.

falta—fallo.

faroles—luz de lumbres.

ferrado—armado de hierro.

flameos—encendidos.

fortuna—hado/tiempo adverso.

forzados—galeotes.

franquezas y essenciones—franquicias y exenciones, derechos
  y libertades.

frasco—cajuela para la pólvora.

frasquillo—cajuela pequeña para la pólvora menuda.

frenesía—frenesí.

frenos—el bocado de hierro.

frisol—frijol, judía.

fuera de—adems.

fuerza—convence.

fuerza—fuerte, fortaleza.

fustes—armazones de silla de montar.

galga—peñasco despedido de lo alto.

gallardete—banderín rematado en puntas.

gallinas de la tierra—pavos, guajalotes.

ganado prieto—ganado moreno, de cerda.

gavias—cestos en lo alto de mástil.

generosa—noble.

genízaro—extranjero/miembro del cuerpo de choque turco.

gibado—corcovado.

gifa—jifa, restos de matanza.

gimio—simio.

gineta—lanza corta.

ginetas—jinetas, cinchas.

godo—noble.

gota coral—epilepsia.

goteras—alrededores.

gracioso—atractivo, airoso.

grato—agradecido.

grimossíssimos—grimosísimos, muy espantosos, amedrentadores.

guardando el punto—cuidando de respetar.

guarnición—defensa en las espadas para guardar la mano.

(se) guindase—se subiese con cuerda.

hacer despacho—mandar carta.

harta—mucha.

he dicho—he terminado.

herido—dividido.

hijadeando—ijadeando, moviendo los ijares por cansancio.

hircana—de Hircania, Caspio.

hierro—yerro.

hipando—resollando.

hipatos—hinchados.

hollándose—pisándose.

horca y cuchillo—jurisdicción para imponer la pena de muerte.

horrumbre—horrura, escoria de fundición.

hospicio—hospitalidad.

huiga—huya.

imputan—acusan.

incapazes—incapaces, indignos.

inficionar—infectar.

inter—entretanto.

(se) intimó—notificó oficialmente.

jalbegados—blanqueados.

jalbegue—arcilla blanca, cal.

jara—saeta de punta aguda y quemada.

jarretado—cortadas las piernas por el corvo.

jolito—calma.

jubón—prenda que viste desde los hombros a la cintura.

judiciaria—agorera.

jumentos—asnos.

justo—prenda que cubre hasta la cintura.

ladino—apto en varias lenguas.

la escarba—lo escarbado.

landre—tumor.

lanzeta—lanceta, instrumento para sangrar o abrir tumores.

largado—liberado.

largos—más de.

las manos puestas—humildemente.

lasos—cansados.

la vuelta de—camino de.

ledo—alegre, contento.

legos—sin órdenes religiosas.

lenguas—intérpretes.

levantados—rebeldes.

libertados—libres.

(se) libertaron—se escaparon

libreas—vestimentas distintivas.

libro de memorias—diario, crónica.

liga—materia viscosa.

ligítimas—legítimas, herencia de derecho.

lumbre—indicio.

lumbroso—alumbrado, miembro de esa secta.

llaves—mecanismos para disparar las armas.

llegado a razón—conforme a razón.

macanas—machetes de madera con filos de piedra.

máchina—máquina, cuerpo de partes señaladas.

machos—mazos grandes usados en las herrerías.

madejas—conjuntos de hilo aspado formado en círculos.

madrigado—malicioso.

maganta—triste.

majada—paraje nocturno del ganado.

manada—puñado.

manga—estrecho entre palos que conducen al corral.

maza—arma de palo con cabo grueso.

marina—costa.

mazas—cubos de la rueda.

medias lunas—fortificaciones delante de los baluartes.

mero mixto—mero y mixto, jurisdicción del soberano y sus jueces.

mesaban—arrancaban.

milano—flor seca del cardo.

millas—medida de mil pasos.

mojones—señales de límites o lindes.

molledo—parte carnosa del brazo.

monteros—cazadores.

nación—nacimiento.

negando—renegando, quejándose.

negar—decir, negando.

no me da más—me da igual.

notomía—esqueleto.

nudillo—material reforzado mediante nudos.

oficio—orden, mandato.

ogeo—ojeo, acción de espantar la caza con ruido.

olanda—holanda, lienzo fino.

(se) olvida—se descuida.

opuesto y blanco—modelo.

pagizos—pajizos, de paja.

pajas—polvo.

palamenta—conjunto de remos.

palenque—conjunto de tablas levantado para funciones
    públicas.

palio—paño que se daba al vencedor en las carreras.

palizada—lugar cercado de estacas.

palma—victoria.

palmo—medida vertical de la extensión de una mano.

pantasma—fantasma.

paradas—donde el ganado se para.

para mayor bagar—para mayor vagar, para tener ms
    tiempo.

parando—empinándose.

parbulito—niño.

parca—muerte.

pardo—leopardo.

parte—orden.

partidas—repartidas.

passadizos—pasadizos, pasos estrechos entre lugares.

passamán—pasamano, pasadizo.

passible—pasible, capaz de padecer.

passo—paso, efigie o grupo sacado en procesión/lugar de
    desafíos.

pausado espacio—despacio.

pavesas—restos ligeros de la combustión.

pedernales—piedras.

pellicos—zamarras de pastores, pieles que se le parecen.

peñol—peñón.

pértigos—lanzas del coche de caballos.

pertinaz—terco, obstinado.

peso—balanza.

pico—instrumento de trabajo.

pieza—rato.

pífanos—flautas.

pintan—construyen/untan.

piquemos—demolamos.

pítima—emplaste medicinal.

polvorín—pólvora.

por cabo—finalmente.

por crugía—entre personal mal dispuesto.

por el consiguiente—en virtud de lo precedente.

por extremo—por último.

por la posta—corriendo.

porque—por las que.

postas—puestos señalados al soldado/guardas.

pratica—platica, habla o comenta.

preces—ruegos, súplicas.

prefieran—excedan.

presago—agorero.

presta—aprovecha/dispuesta.

pretales—fajas de cuerdo puestas al caballo en el pecho.

pretina—correa.

prima—primer turno de vela.

primero—antes.

procuró—solicitó.

prohejando—proejando—remando contra corriente,
    luchando.

puerta—oportunidad.

pues que—puesto que.

pulgares—parte del sarmiento con yema.

punta—flecha.

puntas—extremos, alas.

puro—mero.

quadros—cuadros, la cuarta parte del círculo en la
    posición de los astros.

quál—cuál, de quién.

qual que—cual que, cualquier

quál o quál—cuál o cuál, qué pocos.

quanto—cuanto, como.

quarta—cuarta, medida, de extensión horizontal, de la
    mano abierta.

quarteles—cuarteles, divisiones, no necesariamente en
    cuartos.

quarto—cuarto, división del día.

quarto triste—cuarto triste, en cuadrúpedos, la cabeza.

quartos—cuartos, partes en que se divide una extensión.

quemazón—espuma de metal, señal de veta.

querencias—lugares a los que un animal está
    acostumbrado.

quintado—apartado para la corona.

ranchos—rancherías, viviendas de indios nomádicos.

raposo—zorro.

rastreros—rastreadores.

rayos—radios de la rueda.

real—campamento.

rebato—tocar a rebato, convocar al pueblo ante un
    peligro.

rebentaba—reventaba, descargaba sentimiento.

rebentando—reventando, trabajando duramente.

rebentando por—reventando por, deseoso de.

rebozado—disfrazado.

rebueltos—revueltos, dóciles.

recatado—cauto.

recordarnos—despertarnos.

redes—barreras.

reformada—retirada.

regalada—placentera/abundante, deleitosa.

regaladas—suaves, delicadas.

regalamos—derritimos.

regañando—mostrando los dientes con saña, como los perros.

regordida—abultada.

relajado—vicioso.

remolcadas—que se empujan o tiran las unas de las otras.

remendado—manchado.

remontadas—alejadas.

remota—apartada.

repara—detiene.

repara—arregla.

reparada—parada.

reparado—protegido.

reparando—remediando.

reparos—reparaciones.

repetición—reclamación.

repetir—reclamar.

reportado—comedido, controlado.

reposteros—paños con emblemas heráldicos.

repressas—represas, pasos retrocedentes.

requaje—recuaje, conjunto de bestias de carga.

requerir—intimar.

requirieron—examinaron.

rescates—dineros/prueba del valor de una muestra mineral.

reservado—encubierto.

respecto—causa o razón.

resto—apuesta constituyendo lo que le queda a un jugador.

restribando—apoyándose.

resuelto—decidido.

resurte—rebota.

resurtiendo—retrocediendo.

retorno—las gracias (materiales) por lo recibido.

riñan—disputen.

rizas—olas pequeñas.

rodelas—escudos pequeños.

romper—rasgar, cortar.

rompiendo—empezando.

rompiesse—rompiese, escapase.

sacre—tipo de halcón.

salas del juzgado—centros del juicio.

salieron—confrontaron.

salió de paso—actuó impertinentemente.

sambenito—saco, señal del penitente.

segur—hacha.

seguro—seguridad.

serpentín—pieza con que se mueve la llave en armas de fuego.

serrado—dentado.

sesgo—quieto.

signos—constelaciones.

simbolizan—concuerdan.

sobrada—innecesaria, impertinente.

sobrados—las partes más altas de las casas.

sobre aguando—sobreaguando, en la superficie.

socaire—abrigo, defensa.

solapas—disimulos.

sortija—competencia hípica, consiste en hacer pasar la lanza por un anillo.

sosta y carga—afloja y aprieta, en el manejo de los remos.

soterrando—penetrando, embutiendo.

soterrano—subterráneo.

sueltos—veloces.

suerte—tipo, clase.

sufridos—pacientes.

sufriendo—resistiendo.

suplicar—recurrir, apelar.

supuesto—autoridad.

surto—tranquilo.

suspenderse—colgarse, ahorcarse.

suspenso—admirado.

susto—crisis nerviosa.

tablas—partes llanas del río.

taco—vaqueta con que se aprieta la carga del arcabuz.

taimado—astuto.

tajón—tronco de madera en que corta el carnicero.

tardo—lento.

tascando—mordiendo.

tejones—mamíferos carniceros.

témpanos—sangre cuajada.

tendidas—extensas.

tendiendo—desplegando, mostrando.

tenido—considerado, respetado.

tentado los vados—comprobado las condiciones.

tentador—demonio.

teosas—inflamables.

tercios—miembros fuertes y robustos del hombre.

término—modo, trato.

términos vedados—terrenos desautorizados.

terná—tendrá.

tienden—extienden.

tiros de campaña—piezas de artillería.

tomó la mano—comenzó a hablar.

topes—extremos superiores de los mástiles.

tósigo—veneno.

trabadas—agarradas, de contacto físico.

tracendida—trascendida, perspicaz.

tracendiendo—trascendiendo, percibiendo perspicazmente.

tragada—aceptada.

trago—dificultad o peligro.

trasijados—los ijares encogidos de hambre o sed.

tratos de cuerda—latigazos.

traya—traía.

traza—plan.

trincheas—trincheras.

tristes—miserables.

trisulca—trisurca, tripartita.

tulliendo—hiriendo.

turando—durando.

turbado—alterado, conmovido.

turquescos—turcos.

vallenato—ballenato, ballena joven.

vagar—lentitud, pausa.

vago—vacío.

varato—barato, negocio, rendimiento.

vasa—basa, fundamento de una estructura.

vasos—naves.

vassa—basa, asiento de columna.

vasso—vaso, criatura.

vedegoso—vedijoso, lanudo, hirsuto.

vendido—traicionado.

vergüenza—honor, orgullo.

vilano—milano.

viniesse—viniese, conviniese.

visoño—bisoño, nuevo.

vista—propósito, intento.

vístose—viéndose.

vizarras—bizarras, gallardas.

zalomas—voces cadenciosas del trabajo de marineros.

zarco—de ojos azules.

Index

Barroso, Agustín, xl

Beltrán, Fray Bernardino, xxv

Bempol (Bampol)

[Eng] XXVI.31, 132, 194, 207, 249, 314; XXVIII.164;
XXIX.37, 53, 102, 140, 156, 160, 314; XXX.30;
XXXII.273, 390; XXX.28

[Sp] XXVI.31, 132, 194, 207, 249, 314; XXVIII.164;
XXIX.37, 53, 102, 240, 256, 260, 314; XXX.31;
XXXII.273, 390; XXXIII.28

Benítez, Juan. [Eng] XX.180. [Sp] XX.181

Bibero. [Eng] XXII.282, 316. [Sp] XXII.282, 316

Bison (wild cows)

[Eng] V.42–44; XVI.175; XVII.57, 72, 83, 338;
XXXI.105; (attempt at trapping) XVII.109–48;
(physical description) XVII.85–94

[Sp] V.42–44; XVI.176; XVII.57, 72, 84, 338;
XXXI.105; (attempt at trapping) XVII.109–48;
(physical description) XVII.85–94

Bocanegra, Juan Gutiérrez

[Eng] XXV.8; XXVII.243, 299

[Sp] XXV.8; XXVII.243, 299

Bocanegras. [Eng] X.244. [Sp] X.244

Bohorques, Martos [Eng] IV.417–18. [Sp] IV.418

Bolton, Herbert E. See Coronado, Knight of the Pueblo and
Plains; Spanish Exploration in the Southwest, 1542–1706

Bonilla. See Leyba Bonilla

Book of Memory (Libro de memoria)

[Eng] XVII.180, 183, n.4

[Sp] XVII.180, 183, n.17

Boreas. [Eng] I.122, n.27; XXXI.225. [Sp] I.122, n.30;
XXXI.225

Bove, xxxi

Braba, xxxi. See also Taos Pueblo

Brondate. [Eng] XXVII.263. [Sp] XXVII.263

Brutus and Cassius. [Eng] XXXII.275. [Sp] XXXII.275,
n.21

Buffalo, xxxv. See also Bison

Buzcoico

[Eng] XXVI.28, 51; XXX.31, 180, 230

[Sp] XXVI.28, 51; XXX.32, 181, 232

Caballero de Elvas, xviii

Cabanillas

[Eng] XVII.130; XXIII.124; XXIX.187; XXXI.12

[Sp] XVII.130; XXIII.125; XXIX.187; XXXI.12

Cabeza de Vaca

[Eng] III.30, (adventures) 41–108, (healing Indians) 43–
50, nn.4, 6

[Sp] III.30, (adventures) 41–108, (healing Indians) 42–
50, nn.5, 9

Cabrera (Cabero). [Eng] V.202. [Sp] V.203

Cadmus and Saturn. [Eng] IV.102, n.6. [Sp] IV.103, n.23

Caesar, Caius. [Eng] X.72, n.4. [Sp] X.72, n.10

Caesar, Julius. [Eng] VI.359; VIII.108. [Sp] VI.360;
VIII.107

Californio (Colorado River)

[Eng] I.72, n.19; VII.16, n.3

[Sp] I.72, n.21; VII.17, n.4

Calpo. [Eng] XXVI.51, 128; XXX.31. [Sp] XXVI.51,
128; XXX.32

Camacho. [Eng] XXII.371. [Sp] XXII.371

Camillus. [Eng] X.333, n.6. [Sp] X.333, n.36

Camino Real de Tierra Adentro, xli

Camp, of expedition

[Eng] Arms, I.186–98. Dress, I.161–67. Dress, animal
skins, I.170–81. Leadership, I.139–43. Organization
for march, X.11–46. Preparing for second inspection,
IX.130–214. Service with penitent whipping,
XI.313–14, 333–36, 343–46, n.11. Women, I.157–
59, XXVII.275–94, n.8

[Sp] Arms, I.186–98. Dress, I.161–68. Dress, animal
skins, I.170–80, n.44. Leadership, I.140–44.
Organization for march, X.11–46, n.8. Preparing for
second inspection, IX.131–215. Service with penitent
whipping, XI.313–14, 334–35, 341–51, n.27.
Women, I.158–60; XXVII.275–94, n.33

Campamigo. [Eng] XXVIII.119, n.5. [Sp] XXVIII.118,
n.9

Canadian River, xxxv

Cancer, Tropic of. [Eng] I.58, n.13. [Sp] I.58, n.14

Canciones lúgubres, xviii

Carabajal (Caravajal)

[Eng] XII.55; XIV.282; XVII.134; XXVII.300;
XXIX.213; XXX.224, 249

[Sp] XII.55; XIV.282; XVII.134; XXVII.300;
XXIX.213; XXX.226, 251

Carabajal, Esteban. [Eng] XXVII.238; XXXI.155. [Sp]
XXVII.238; XXXI.155

Cárdenas. [Eng] XIV.334. [Sp] XIV.334

Carlos V. [Eng] III.206; IX.303. [Sp] II.206; IX.306

Carnival battles. [Eng] XVIII.320–33, n.7. [Sp]
XVIII.322–35, n.21

Carrasco. [Eng] XXX.177. [Sp] XXX.178

Carrera. [Eng] XXIX.196. [Sp] XXIX.196

Carthage. [Eng] II.95, n.7; XXXIV.331, n.9. [Sp] II.97,
n.16; XXIV.333, n.28

Caso, Juan de. [Eng] XXVII.254. [Sp] XXVII.254

Castaño de Sosa, Gaspar, xxvi, xxviii, xxx, xxxi, xxxii

[Eng] V.168, n.12; XV.294

[Sp] V.169, n.20; XV.294

Castile, Kingdom of

[Eng] II.221; III.120; XIV pp.135, 137; (and Portugal)
XIV p.135; XV.347; XXV p.222

[Sp] II.222; III.120; XIV pp.135, 137; (and Portugal)
XIV p.135; XV.348; XXV p.222

Zutancalpo
  [Eng] XVIII.95, 158, 298; XXI.44, 82, 138, 183;
    XXVI.164, 207; XXVII.141; XXVIII.111, 163;
    XXIX.38, 109, 239, 256, 314; XXX.30, 180, 229;
    XXXI.334; XXXII.16, 57

  [Sp] XVIII.96, 160, 300; XXI.44, 82, 138, 183;
    XXVI.164, 207; XXVII.141; XXVIII.111, 163;
    XXIX.38, 109, 239, 256, 314; XXX.31, 181, 231;
    XXXI.334; XXXII.16, 57